FINANCIAL TIMES

Mastering **Finance**

The Complete Finance Companion

FINANCIAL TIMES

in association with

The University of Chicago
Graduate School of Business

Wharton

The Wharton School
University of Pennsylvania

The Complete Finance Companion

Mastering Finance

FTMastering**Series**

Mastering **Finance**

The University of Chicago Graduate School of Business has more Nobel Prize winners than all other business schools combined. Several of the most basic ideas governing corporate and academic finance originated at the school. A recent survey in *Business Week* magazine ranked Chicago number one in producing graduates with the best skills in finance.

Chicago has been at the forefront of bringing a discipline-based approach to the study of business, and its methods have been widely copied by other schools. In addition to its legendary strength in finance, the School is also known for its strength in accounting, economics, general management, decision making, international business, marketing, strategy and its innovative MBA program, which has campuses in Barcelona and Chicago. Through its Center for Decision Research, Chicago was the first business school to emphasize behavioral decision making in its MBA and PhD curriculum. Chicago offers six programs leading to an MBA degree, in addition to executive and corporate non-degree programs, and a PhD in business. Approximately 350 Chicago graduates hold key faculty posts at business schools and universities. More than 50 serve as deans.

Founded in 1965, London Business School has firmly established itself as a leading international business school – *Business Week* has stated that it believes LBS to offer one of the best MBA programs in Europe. The School has distinguished itself particularly in the area of finance, with a faculty whose reputation is unrivalled outside the United States.

London Business School has a predominantly international student body (75% non-domestic) representing over 60 countries world-wide. This contributes to the enormous success of School programs such as the one-year Masters in Finance and the 21-month MBA.

Wharton

The Wharton School
University of Pennsylvania

The Wharton School of the University of Pennslyvania, founded in 1881 as the first collegiate school of management in the United States, is recognized around the world for its innovative leadership and broad academic strengths across every major discipline and at every level of business education. With nearly 200 faculty members, 11 academic departments, 19 research centers, and leading programs at undergraduate, MBA, doctoral and executive education levels, the Wharton School is committed to creating the highest value and impact on the practice of business and management worldwide. Currently, Wharton has approximately 4,500 students enrolled in degree programs, more than 10,000 participants in its executive education programs each year, and a network of more than 70,000 alumni in more than 100 countries.

Mastering **Finance**

ROBERT S. HAMADA
Dean,
University of Chicago Graduate School of Business

In the next century, as barriers to global trade disappear and the international market explodes with opportunities, successful professionals around the world must keep abreast of developing trends in financial markets. Finely-tuned intellectual capital is now more valuable than ever. *FT Mastering Finance* sifts though the overwhelming amount of conflicting or inferior information to provide busy executives with the most important, useful and relevant knowledge available.

For more than a century, the University of Chicago Graduate School of Business has been a leader in providing research which supports the foundation of basic finance. In many cases, this research has changed the way business is conducted around the world. We recognize that the ability to understand global financial markets and investment management is now paramount to success in the next century. Rapid change is not only expected, it is encouraged. It is no longer impossible, but rather essential, to follow these new trends, and *FT Mastering Finance* is an invaluable tool to understanding the key principles underlying finance as it evolves. Within this book, prevailing theories are advanced, and also challenged, to create information which facilitiates sound decision making and provides practical business wisdom.

PROFESSOR GEORGE BAIN
Principal,
London Business School

The subject of finance was once little more than a mixture of financial accounting, law and unsupported opinion. It is now a well established discipline, embracing comprehensive and sometimes subtle theory backed by extensive statistical testing. It has also become a subject with which non-financial managers have to be familiar if their activities are to add shareholder value.

London Business School has a finance faculty with an international reputation that is unrivalled outside the United States. We are happy to join our American partners in this venture of bringing the modern subject of finance to a wide readership in Britain, the United States and elsewhere.

THOMAS P. GERRITY
Dean,
The Wharton School of the University of Pennsylvania

The field of finance is one in which today's academic discoveries are immediately translated into tomorrow's practice. The pressure to create value for shareholders has become the mantra for corporations around the world. These two facts together imply that every manager must be conversant with emerging developments in finance. This book presents some of the most recent thinking affecting the fields of corporate finance, investments and financial markets. From risk management to value enhancement to corporate restructuring, the articles constitute a roadmap to new ideas which every manager should know.

With a deep and rich history in finance, the Wharton School is delighted to join our colleagues to offer the intellectual leadership that will help managers, academics and students at all levels to advance their knowledge and practice of finance.

Executive Editor Tim Dickson
Editor George Bickerstaffe
School Co-ordinators Michael Baltes, University of Chicago Graduate School of Business
Emeritus Professor Harold Rose, London Business School
Allan Friedman, The Wharton School of the University of Pennsylvania

PITMAN PUBLISHING
128 Long Acre, London WC2E 9AN
Tel: +44(0)171 447 2000
Fax: +44(0)171 240 5771
http: //www.pitman.co.uk

A Division of Pearson Professional Limited

First published in Great Britain in 1998

ISBN 0 273 63091 1

British Library Cataloguing in Publication Data
A CIP catalogue record for this book can be obtained from the British Library

10 9 8 7 6 5 4 3 2 1

Typeset by Land and Unwin (Data Sciences) Limited, Bugbrooke
Charts and figures designed by Michaela Magas and Cleve Jones
Printed and bound in Great Britian by William Clowes Ltd

The Publishers' policy is to use paper manufactured from sustainable forests.

Contents

Introduction

The *Financial Times* Mastering Series has been the product of a unique collaboration between the FT and some of the world's leading international business schools. This is the third book to emerge from that partnership and like its predecessors *Mastering Management* and *Mastering Enterprise* (also FT Pitman Publishing) we believe it combines essential theory with both relevant and recent practice.

The book – a revised version of articles published in weekly instalments in the European editions of the *Financial Times* newspaper during the summer of 1997 – brings together more than 60 articles from contributing faculties at the Chicago Graduate School of Business, London Business School and the Wharton School of the University of Pennsylvania. This is a writing team which is virtually unbeatable in the field of finance and the result is a valuable compendium suitable for students and practitioners alike.

The book is structured into 13 modules: Value; Corporate finance; Accounting; Managing value; The nature of financial markets; Equity markets in action; Debt markets; Portfolio investment; Risk management; Derivatives; Financial institutions; Regulation and governance; and Finance and government.

Brief introductions to each module explain the significance of the different topics and the summaries at the end of each article are designed to help readers quickly identify subjects of special interest. Lists of further reading ideas will be helpful for those who want to delve deeper.

Mastering Finance is not a beginner's guide – many other books serve that purpose – and it therefore assumes a basic knowledge of such concepts as cash flow, working capital and dividend yield. The finance module of *Mastering Management* may be the best starting point for those in need of a basic grounding.

As with the other FT Mastering books there have been many people who made this project possible and without whom the challenge of bringing together such a diverse and distinguished group of contributors could not have been met. Inevitably, however, the burden fell most heavily on the academic and administrative co-ordinators at each school, namely Emeritus Professor Harold Rose (LBS), Professor Richard Leftwich and Allan Friedman (Chicago) and Professor Michael Gibbon and Michael Baltes (Wharton). For their tireless work and support we are extremely grateful.

Finally, if you have enjoyed this book you will be glad to know that there are more Mastering books on the way: the next two topics in the FT Mastering Series will be *Mastering Global Business* and *Mastering Marketing*.

Tim Dickson and George Bickerstaffe
November 1997

1 Value

Contributors

Jeremy J. Siegel is Professor of Finance at the Wharton School of the University of Pennsylvania. In addition, he is Academic Director of the US Securities Industry Institute and a member of the advisory board for the Asian Securities Industry Association.

Robert Z. Aliber is Professor of International Economics and Finance at the University of Chicago Graduate School of Business. He is director of the School's Center for International Finance.

Elroy Dimson is Professor of Finance at London Business School. With Paul Marsh he is editor of LBS's Risk Measurement Service.

Howard Kaufold is an adjunct Professor of Finance at the Wharton School of the University of Pennsylvania and Director of the Wharton Executive MBA Program.

Isik Inselbag is an adjunct Professor of Finance at the Wharton School of the University of Pennsylvania and former Vice Dean and Director of the Wharton Graduate Division.

Massoud Mussavian is Assistant Professor of Finance at London Business School. His research interests include continuous time finance, investment and fund management compensation.

Donald B. Keim is Professor of Finance at the Wharton School of the University of Pennsylvania.

Gabriel Hawawini is the Henry Grunfeld Professor of Investment Banking at INSEAD and the author of several books and research papers on various aspects of the financial services industry.

Luigi Zingales is Associate Professor of Finance at the University of Chicago Graduate School of Business. His research interests include capital structure and corporate control.

Contents

Introduction

Valuation lies at the heart of all stock market and business investment. This module introduces the concept of risk and return, examines different methods of capital budgeting (including the famous Capital Asset Pricing Model), offers advice on valuation to anyone contemplating a leveraged buy-out, and considers the benefits of being a controlling shareholder.

Risk and return: start with the building blocks

by Jeremy J. Siegel

Once risk and return are specified for a given asset or asset class, modern financial theory can identify the best portfolio allocations subject to the risk tolerance of the investor. Yet expected returns are not physical constants, like the speed of light, waiting to be discovered in the natural world. They must be deduced from historical data, tempered with an appreciation of how current economic, social and political factors may modify the parameters derived from the past.

There is certainly no lack of data in the field of finance. The breadth and scope of quantitative information available is unrivaled in the field of social science. Nevertheless, there is still widespread disagreement among professionals about the best estimates of the risk and return on the two largest classes of financial assets: stocks and bonds.

The plethora of data does not necessarily guarantee precision in estimating expected return because one can never be certain the underlying factors that generate asset prices will remain unchanged. As Nobel laureate Paul Samuelson is fond of saying: we have but one sample of history.

Historical estimates

Let us begin with the US and the UK shortly after the First World War. The virtue of this period is that it covers the major stock market cycle: the spectacular rise in stock prices in the late 1920s and the devastating decline which followed, as well as the Second World War and the great post-war expansion. However, using this period as a benchmark for estimating future returns has its drawbacks. In contrast to the 1930s, the greatest threat to economies today is from inflation, not deflation.

The reasons for the shift to an inflation-prone rather than deflation-threatened economy are well understood. The gold-based monetary standard, which had ruled in the industrialized world for more than two centuries, was abandoned in the 1930s following the Great Depression. Governments shifted to a paper-based standard, which is now universal in both developed and developing countries.

This shift dramatically changed the dynamics of the price level, leading to a decided bias towards inflation. In fact, in both the US and the UK, the whole of the accumulated rise in the prices of goods and services that has taken place in the past two centuries has occurred since the Second World War. From 1800 through 1945 the overall level of prices, although subject to substantial short-run volatility, was basically flat. The change in the monetary standard from gold to paper had its greatest effect on the returns to fixed income assets. It is clear in retrospect that the buyers of bonds in the 1940s, 1950s and early 1960s did not recognize the consequences of the change. How else can one explain why investors voluntarily purchased long-term bonds with three per cent and four per cent coupons despite the fact that government policy was geared to avoid deflation? Data from the post-war years will most certainly exhibit depressed returns on long bonds.

Popular benchmark

But what effect does the shift in the monetary standard have for the return on equities? In theory, stocks are claims on real assets: capital and land, which derive their value from the sale of real goods and services. Theory suggests that, at least in the long run, stock returns should not be influenced by fluctuations in the monetary standard. Yet in the short run equities have proved extremely poor hedges against inflation, as the 1970s dramatically demonstrated. Whether long-term equity returns are influenced by inflation can only be answered by comparing the returns of the past 50 years with those which came earlier.

Building on the work of Alfred Cowles and William Schwert, I derived the before and after-inflation returns on stocks and bonds in the US going back to the beginning of the 19th century. Figure 1 displays the growth in the total real returns from 1802 through 1996 (including capital gains, interest and dividends) on stocks, bonds, bills, gold and the value of the US dollar.

This two-century history is divided into three sub-periods. The first, from 1802 to 1871, represents the early stage of US economic development. During the second period, from 1871 to 1925, the US was transformed into one of the great industrial powers of the world. The third sub-period, from 1926 to the present, marks the mature phase of financial markets and has become the most popular benchmark for analyzing historical returns.

Equity returns

The growth of the purchasing power of a diversified equity portfolio not only dominates all other assets but is remarkable for the stability of its long-term after-inflation returns. Despite extraordinary changes in the economic, social and political environment over the past two centuries, US stocks have yielded between 6.5–7 per cent per year adjusted for inflation in all major sub-periods.

Fig.1 US stocks and bonds – a long view

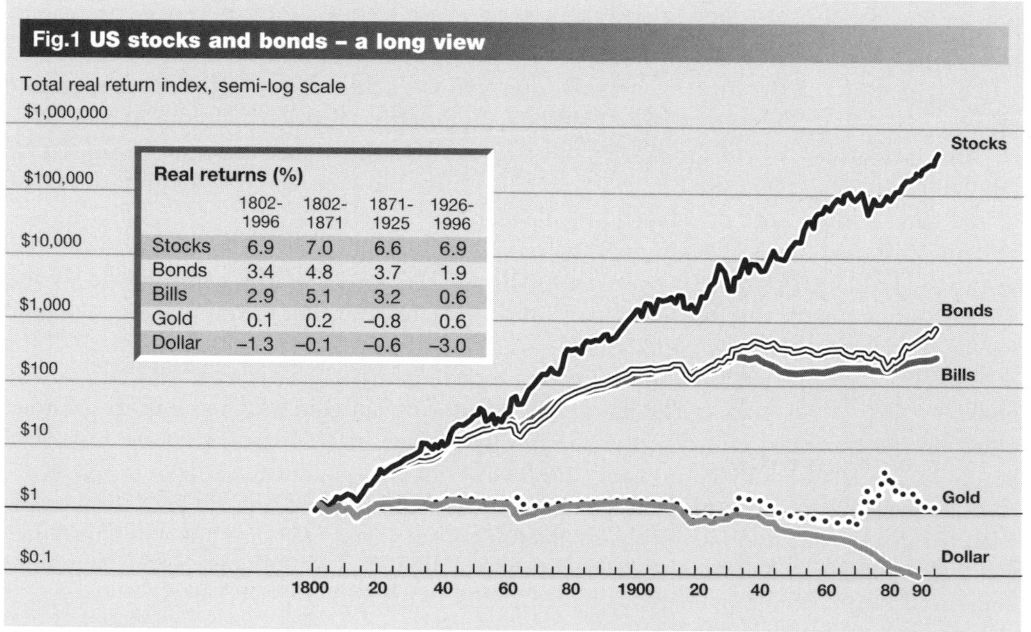

Real returns (%)

	1802-1996	1802-1871	1871-1925	1926-1996
Stocks	6.9	7.0	6.6	6.9
Bonds	3.4	4.8	3.7	1.9
Bills	2.9	5.1	3.2	0.6
Gold	0.1	0.2	–0.8	0.6
Dollar	–1.3	–0.1	–0.6	–3.0

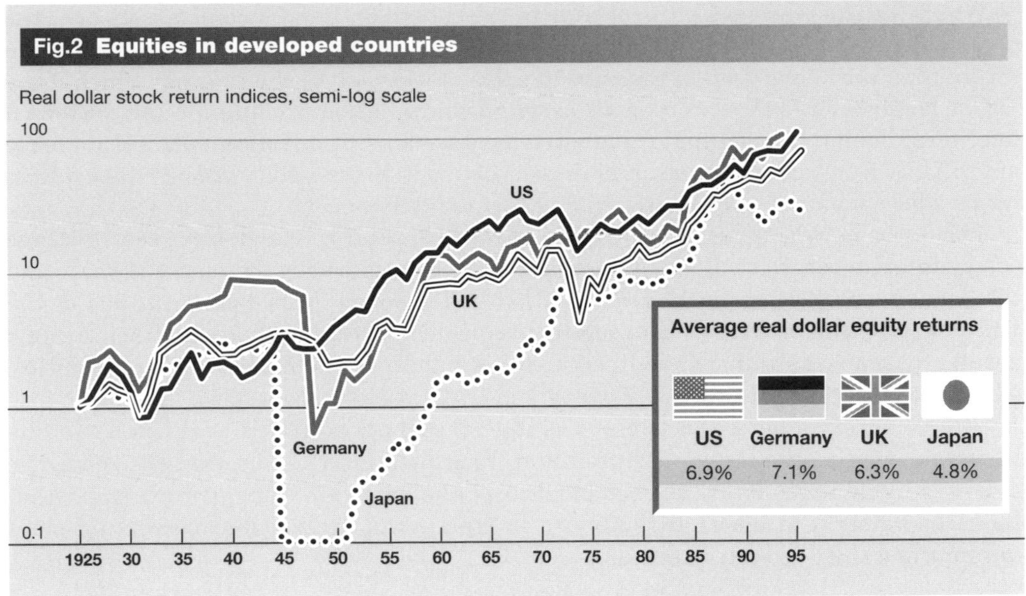

The consistency of the real return on equities is striking given the shift from a predominantly agricultural economy of the early 19th century to an industrialized economy and finally to a service and information-oriented, post-industrial economy as we head towards the next millennium. The long-term stability of the real return on equity also persisted whether the monetary system was based on gold or paper. Some economists have cast doubt on the use of US and even UK data to predict the future. They note that these countries have emerged victorious in all major wars and survived all the significant crises. They claim it is a grave mistake to take these countries as typical of equities worldwide.

Yet my examination of equity returns in foreign countries confirms, rather than casts doubt on the superior performance of equities. Figure 2 shows the real dollar returns on stocks in the US, the UK, Japan and Germany from 1926 to the present. Special attention is given to computing the returns on equities throughout the Second World War in order to maintain a continuous series.

The devastating defeat of the Axis powers did cause German and Japanese stocks to fall dramatically. But their recovery has been equally spectacular. The compound annual real dollar returns on stocks in the UK, Germany and the US fell within one percentage point of each other. Although real dollar Japanese equity returns lagged at 4.8 per cent a year, they easily exceeded the returns on fixed income assets in any country during this period. The ability of stocks in the developed nations to recover from wars, hyperinflations and depressions is remarkable and demonstrates that the superior long-term returns on equity are a worldwide phenomenon.

Fixed income returns

In contrast to the remarkable stability of real stock returns, real returns on fixed-income assets have declined markedly. In the first, and even second, sub-periods the returns on bonds and bills, although less than equities, were significantly positive. But since 1926, and especially since the Second World War, fixed income assets have returned little after inflation.

Whatever the reasons for the decline in the return on fixed income assets over the past century, it is almost certain that the real returns on bonds will be higher in the future than they have been in the past 70 years. As a result of the inflation shock of the 1970s, bondholders have incorporated a significant inflation premium in the coupon on long-term bonds. In most major industrialized nations, if inflation does not increase appreciably from current levels, real returns of about 3–4 per cent will be realized from bonds whose nominal rate is between 6 per cent and 8 per cent.

These projected real returns are remarkably similar to the 3.4 per cent average compound real return on US long-term government bonds over the past 194 years and the 3.4 per cent yield of the 10-year inflation-linked bonds floated early in 1997 by the US treasury. Despite the increased future projected real returns on fixed income assets, these assets will still be likely to fall far short of the real returns on equities, which have averaged between 6–7 per cent over the past two centuries.

The difference between the projected return on equities and fixed income investments is called the equity premium. Few question the fact that the return on stocks is likely to dominate that on bonds over the long run. The question is whether the risks inherent in stocks are sufficient to explain the three to four percentage point difference in their projected returns.

The risks and valuation

Explaining the equity premium

The difference between stock and bonds returns has traditionally been explained by the greater risk inherent in equity investments. This risk has been measured in several ways.

In the standard version of the Capital Asset Pricing Model (CAPM), the risk premium on an asset depends not on the standard deviation of its own return but on the correlation of its return with the 'market portfolio,' which comprises stocks, bonds, real estate and perhaps even human capital.

More recent formulations of CAPM replaced the market portfolio, which is always difficult to measure, with the variable that most directly affects an investor's welfare, the level of consumption. In this model, an investor's taste for taking risks in the market are critically linked to whether poor stock returns are correlated with other bad economic outcomes, such as economic recessions. But this approach (called the 'consumption CAPM') yielded bothersome results. Empirical tests revealed that the correlation of stock market returns with aggregate economic activity was very low. Therefore investors should not be very averse to taking risks in stocks, since a plunging stock market does not usually mean other forms of economic wealth are also sinking.

In order to explain the excess return of stocks over bonds in these models, one would have to postulate an extremely high level of risk aversion, a level which many regarded as an unrealistic description of individual behavior towards risk. But the difficulty of explaining the magnitude of the equity premium is not limited to the capital asset pricing model. The usual measure of risk that forms the basis of modern portfolio analysis is the standard deviation of one-year returns. Yet one can ask whether this measure is appropriate for an investor's portfolio whose holding period extends much longer than one year.

In the past, researchers have said the holding period does not matter. It can be proved mathematically that if returns follow random walks, that is, future returns are

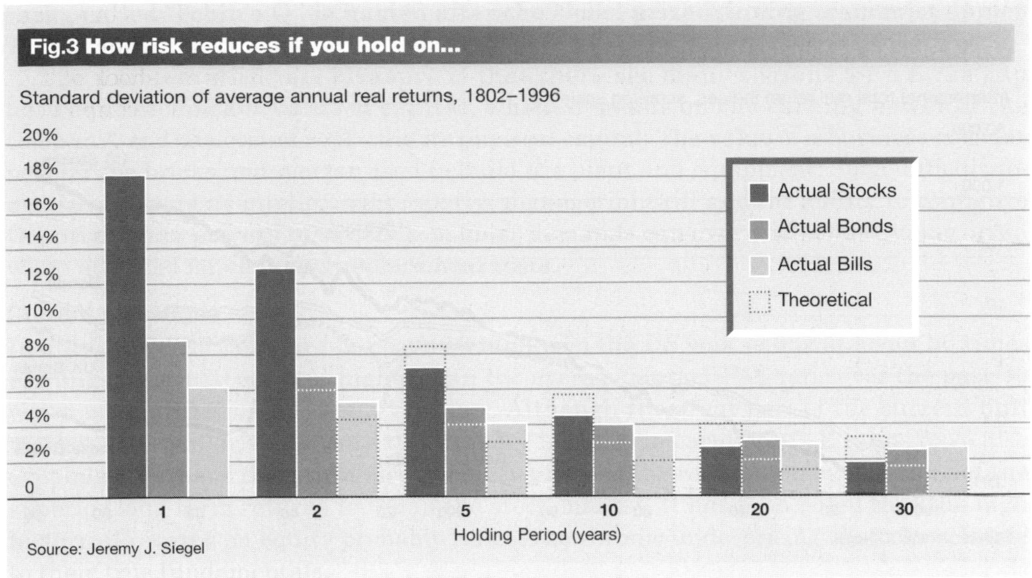

in no way dependent on past returns, then the period over which risk and return are measured is irrelevant. Specifically, both total risk and total return increase linearly in the time period, so the relative risks between assets remain unchanged and the length of the period chosen to measure risk is of no consequence.

But if asset returns do not follow a random walk, then the period chosen to measure risk matters substantially. The examination of longer-term return data show important deviations from random walk behavior. Figure 3 plots the standard deviation of average annual real returns over one, two, five, 10, 20 and 30 year periods for stocks, bonds and bills. Risk, defined as the standard deviation of average annual returns, declines almost twice as fast as the holding period increases for stocks compared with that predicted by the random walk theory (the 'theoretical risk'). There is clear evidence of mean reversion of real stock returns.

In sharp contrast to stocks, the standard deviation of the average annual real returns on fixed income assets declines more slowly than theory would predict as the holding period increases. This is called mean aversion, which describes the behavior of a variable that tends to wander from its mean value, rather than be drawn to it, as is the case for equities. Fixed income assets display mean aversion because their real return is critically influenced by inflation – and inflation cumulates over time.

The cumulative effects of inflation can be readily seen in Figure 4, which displays the total real return in stocks and fixed income assets of the US and the UK and fixed income assets in Germany, and Japan. It is not surprising that the worst bond returns come during periods of the most rapid inflation: the 1970s for the US and UK; the post-war period for Japan; and the German hyperinflation of the early 1920s.

Finance theory is thus presented with a conundrum. Stocks are riskier than bonds in the short-run but are actually less risky in the long-run. The optimal allocation of one's portfolio cannot be divorced from the holding period of the investor. Given the choice between stocks and bonds, the evidence is overwhelmingly in favor of the former for the long-term investor.

Summary

Risk and return are the building blocks of finance – but there is still sharp disagreement among professionals about the best way to value stocks and bonds. By looking at historical data and suggesting which are most relevant for judging the future, this article examines why equities, despite short-term fluctuations, are such a good inflation hedge not only in the Anglo-Saxon world but in most major developed countries and why the equity premium (the difference between stock and bond returns) has been justified. 'The optimal allocation of one's portfolio cannot be divorced from the holding period of the investor,' Siegel observes. The article continues with a brief overview of valuation yardsticks, including the Tobin's Q concept developed by the Nobel prize winning economist James Tobin and concludes with a discussion of current market levels. The author argues that if investors can overcome their aversion to short-term volatility, equities should support higher prices and lower earnings yields than the historical norm. Just this hypothesis, Siegel admits, was put forward by Irving Fisher months before the 1929 Stock Market Crash – 'but research has vindicated Fisher's long run enthusiasm for equities.'

Suggested further reading

Brown, S.J., Goetsmann, W.N. and Ross, S.A., (1995), 'Survival', *Journal of Finance,* 50, 853–873.

Cowles, Alfred and Associates, (1938), *Common Stock Indexes 1871–1937*, Bloomington Indiana Pricipia Press.

Schwert, G. W., (1990), 'Indexes of United States Stock Prices from 1802–1987', *Journal of Business* 63, 399–426.

Siegel, J.J., (1994), *Stocks for the Long Run*, Irwin Professional Publishing.

Siegel, J.J. and Thaler, R., (1997), 'The Equity Premium Puzzle', *The Journal of Economic Perspectives* 11 (1) Winter, 191–200.

Capital budgeting: will the project pay?

by Robert Z. Aliber

The key questions for any company contemplating a new investment or acquisition are: 'Will it pay?' and 'Will the stockholders be better off?' The corporate finance textbooks formalize the question as the capital budgeting algorithm – the company should undertake a new project only as long as its contribution to net revenues exceeds the costs of capital associated with the project. This is essentially a more formal version of 'Will it pay?' Managers need two basic types of information to employ the algorithm. One is an estimate of the cash flows associated with each project. The other is an interest rate to discount the future cash flows associated with each project. Because stockholders generally want to be compensated for holding risky assets, the riskier the project the higher the cost of capital.

Managers can then use this information to evaluate the contribution of each project to revenues and especially to the risks or variability of income in a portfolio context rather than in isolation from other projects. The implication of the algorithm is that managers act as intermediaries, or agents, between the anticipated cash flows associated with a range of projects and the minimum returns demanded by stockholders for portfolios with different risk levels.

If managers over-reach and overestimate the cash flows associated with a project then stockholders are made worse off because the project will not earn its cost of funds. Similarly, stockholders may be made worse off if managers use too low an interest rate to discount anticipated cash flows. In contrast if the managers are conservative in their estimates of cash flows then the growth of the company's earnings may be slowed because more aggressive concerns may acquire these projects; the sluggish growth of earnings may, for example, make the company the target of a buy-out.

Foreign projects

This article considers how managers of companies based in the US, UK or Japan as representative industrial countries should value the same projects in Korea or Mexico or another country with a faster income growth. The dual or twin problem is how managers of companies based in Korea or Mexico should value the same projects in an established industrial economy. Whether or not foreign investments pay is a more complex version of the domestic question.

Some managers may believe stockholders and the investing community are not especially knowledgeable about the currency composition of their cash flows; indeed a few managers may be less than fully confident that they are sufficiently knowledgeable. This question is central to the privatization of government-owned companies in industrial and emerging-market countries in recent years, which has involved airlines, banking and telecommunications. The preparation of the bid involves estimating future cash flows and selecting an interest rate to discount these cash flows. Three factors complicate the capital budgeting problem in cross-border deals.

While estimating cash flows for foreign projects is more or less an extension of domestic activity, the process may be more difficult because the cash might be more variable or even volatile. The choice of the interest rate to discount these foreign cash flows is a unique international problem. Should managers employ the interest rate used for domestic projects; an interest rate available in the country in which the project is located or should they employ some other interest rate or perhaps adopt another approach? Even after an interest rate has been selected, managers must determine the value for this rate and particularly whether at the time of the investment it is an 'average' of values over the business cycle.

Ad hoc approaches have been used to value a potential acquisition in a foreign country. One is to adjust the estimated cash flows downwards to reflect the assumption that foreign cash flows are riskier than domestic. Another is to increase 'the interest rate' used to discount the cash flows because they are risky. A more systematic approach is based on the projection of the 'parity conditions' that the difference in the interest rates on comparable securities denominated in different currencies corresponds with the anticipated rate of change in the exchange rate; the estimates of foreign income are converted into domestic income at estimates of future exchange rates and this income is discounted employing the same interest rate used to discount domestic income.

One of the shortcomings of *ad hoc* approaches is that the information content of the estimates of future cash flow data is lost when the data are adjusted; another is that there is no rationale for the size of the arbitrary adjustment. A criticism of the reliance on the parity conditions is that there is an implicit assumption that real interest rates are the same across countries. This is not consistent with the data; real interest rates are higher generally in capital-importing countries.

While changes in exchange rates may correspond with changes in the differential in national inflation rates in the long run, there are sharp deviations from the parity relationship for shorter intervals, which may often be as long as three or four years. Consider a company that is evaluating a new investment in a country subject to high and variable inflation rates. Because of inflation, the projection is likely to show rapid growth in cash flows. Discounting these cash flows by the interest rates of the country in which the company is headquartered would be inappropriate since the inflation premium in domestic interest rates would be much lower. The anticipated cash flows in the foreign country might be deflated by an adjustment for the inflation rate; in this case the estimates of future income and the interest rate would be those of the country in which the company is based and the 'foreignness' of the project would in essence disappear – the implicit assumption being that the risks of the foreign cash flows would not differ from those of domestic cash flows.

Alternatively, cash flow estimates connected with the foreign project might be discounted by an interest rate derived from that country, so there would be no currency mismatch. But this interest rate is probably too high. Take a US, UK or Japanese company considering an acquisition in Mexico. The variation in Mexican income is likely to be greater than that in domestic income, either because of the quality of economic management or because of variations in the peso price of the US dollar. Both macro policy and the foreign exchange value of the Mexican peso are especially sensitive to the presidential election cycle; the peso appears to appreciate in real terms in the years before presidential transitions in response to foreign capital inflows.

During the years of the presidential election and transition, the inflow of foreign capital diminishes sharply and the peso depreciates because Mexico no longer has the funds to finance a large trade deficit. The government then adopts contractive economic policies to limit inflation associated with depreciation of the peso. Thus the changes in the foreign exchange value of the peso in nominal and real or price-level adjusted terms are especially sensitive to changes in the pace of foreign capital inflows.

The conservative approach might be to use a peso interest rate to discount the project's anticipated peso cash flows. But should a company use the interest rate that it might pay if it borrowed funds from a Mexican bank or from a foreign bank in Mexico? Interest rates on peso securities will exceed those on dollar securities for several reasons. One is that Mexico has been subject to higher inflation rates and the peso has depreciated extensively in the foreign exchange market.

Moreover, the riskless interest rate in Mexico is significantly above that in the US even if the foreign exchange risk is fully hedged because of the default risk standing of the Mexican government. As a result the structure of interest rates in Mexico is higher. Hence a number of US and foreign companies are able to borrow dollars at interest rates below those that the governments in many emerging market countries would pay. One outstanding example of the currency mismatch involved the purchase of

Testing televisions at Samsung Electronics in Korea: how does it value new projects in more established economies?

Rockefeller Center, the Pebble Beach golf course, and other US properties by Japanese investors; discounting the dollar cash flows with low Japanese yen interest rates led to (excessively) high values for these properties.

The implication is that the interest rates these companies would pay if they borrowed in many foreign countries is excessively high for discounting the cash flows because they are based on the default risk standing of the foreign government.

Symmetry and asymmetry

So these companies might construct a peso interest rate based on two elements – the interest rate their own governments would pay if they were to borrow in these countries and then a premium that would reflect the amount they would pay when borrowing over the amount that their government would pay. (The interest rate used to discount these cash flows should be distinguished from the currency borrowed to finance these acquisitions.)

The projection of the revenues and cash flows in the foreign country is likely to be based on the estimates of the growth of national income there and the increase in market share, even if these forecasts are developed when the country is in recession. The implication is that the interest rate used to discount these cash flows should be based on the long-run view of real interest rates in the country rather than the real interest rates at the date of the forecast and the investment.

Increasingly, companies headquartered in one of the emerging market countries are undertaking investments in one of the mature industrial countries. How managers value these income streams should depend on how stockholders appraise the addition of the foreign income stream, and especially whether they believe the foreign income will reduce fluctuations in domestic income. Thus the shareholders may conclude that the acquisition of a plant in the US by a Mexican or Korean company might reduce the variability of its cash flows. These companies might discount these cash flows by a dollar interest rate.

Conclusion

The capital budgeting algorithm provides a framework to help managers determine whether a project will generate a rate of return higher than the cost of capital associated with the project. In a formal sense, this decision is identical in both the domestic and international contexts.

Estimating the income connected with a project in a foreign country is often more difficult than estimating that for a domestic project because the foreign income stream may be more variable; the growth rates of gross domestic product are more variable partly because of changes in exchange rates. But the exceptions to this statement are evident when the projects are in countries where rates of income growth are more stable than in the country where the company is based. The unique aspect of the capital budgeting decision involves the choice of the interest rate to use to discount the cash flow in a foreign country. The general principle is that this interest rate should be based on those in the country in which the cash flows will be generated.

Hence managers might develop an estimate of the interest rate to use to discount these cash flows based on projections of the interest rate their governments would pay if they borrowed in the foreign country, and a premium reflecting the difference between the interest rate they pay when at home over the interest rate the government pays. Just as the cash flows are estimated over the business cycle, so the interest rate used to discount these cash flows should be based on the 'average' of interest rates over the cycle. If host country interest rates are used to discount the cash flows it does not mean the acquisition should be financed with funds borrowed in the host country. The financing distinction should be distinguished from the valuation decision.

Summary

The articles 'Risk and return: start with the building blocks' (Module 1) and 'The many roles of financial markets' (Module 5) look at the broad concepts of risk and return and the role of financial markets. This article addresses the more specific topic of the valuation of projects. The key questions are: 'Will it pay?' and 'Will the stockholders be better off?'. Robert Aliber concentrates on how a manager in, say, the US, the UK or Japan should value projects in another country with a faster income growth such as Korea or Mexico. He suggests that what modern finance theory calls the capital budgeting algorithm provides the necessary framework both in a domestic and international context.

'The unique aspect of the capital budgeting decision involves the choice of the interest rate to use to discount the cash flow in another country. The general

principle is that this interest rate should be based on those in the country in which the cash flows will be generated', writes the author. Just as the cash flows are estimated over the business cycle, so the interest rate used to discount these cash flows should be based on the 'average' of interest rates over the cycle.

Suggested further reading

Copeland, T., Koller, T. and Murring, J., (1990), *Valuation: Measuring and Managing the Value of Companies*, John Wiley & Sons, New York.

Capital budgeting: a beta way to do it

by Elroy Dimson

An investment that is risk-free offers a known payoff over some period in the future; but, sadly, capital investments are not usually risk-free and this risk has to be properly assessed and accounted for.

The best known risk-free investments are government bonds. The government can be expected to honor its promises because it can always print sufficient money to meet its obligations, though of course there is then a risk of inflation. In some countries, such as the UK and the US, the government also issues index-linked bonds, which provide an income and capital repayment uplifted in line with inflation.

The promised return, or redemption yield, on government bonds is published daily in the *Financial Times* and *The Wall Street Journal*. These bonds provide a guaranteed return that is known today. For example, at the time of writing one can earn a gross yield to redemption of around 7.6 per cent on conventional UK government bonds with a five- to 15-year maturity. These gross yields equate to a yield after personal tax of a little under 6 per cent. Nominal yields vary over time and across currencies and issuers. Similarly, index-linked UK government bonds provide a gross redemption yield of around 3.6 per cent for maturities running as far into the future as the year 2030. Net of personal income tax, their yield is around 3 per cent. This yield is measured in real terms – over and above the level of retail price inflation.

If a capital project is risk-free, it should be required to earn a rate of return that is at least equal to the risk-free rate of interest. If the project is located in the UK, and cash flows are projected in real (inflation-adjusted) terms, then the cash flows should be discounted at the risk-free real rate of interest. Following the discounted cash flow method, the project should be accepted if its net present value is positive.

Risky investments

So what discount rate should we use if a project is risky? If we want to know the wholesale price for copper, cocoa or crude oil, we look at the Commodities Prices section of the *Financial Times*. By analogy, to learn about the wholesale price for capital, we must look to the Stock Exchange. For a capital investment project, such as building a new power station, we should find the required rate of return by reference to a similar investment on the stock market. To do this we need to examine what risk means in that market.

Figure 1 shows the range of returns (capital gain or loss plus reinvested dividends) on the US equity market since 1926. Although returns of 10–20 per cent are the most common, the equity market has often given returns of 30–40 per cent, and has frequently given negative returns. Within Figure 1, we identify the years in which particular levels of return were achieved. The US equity market fell by more than 40 per cent in 1931 and rose by more than 50 per cent in 1933 and 1954. These three extremes are shown in the left-hand and right-hand tails of the distribution.

Whereas equity investment is risky, treasury bills (essentially, government bonds with a maturity of under a year) are virtually risk-free. A histogram of the returns on treasury bills would show that in almost every year their return was between 0–10 per cent. The most extreme outliers were a few years at the beginning of the 1980s when treasury bills gave a return of a little above 10 per cent. Because we know the return over the life of a treasury bill when we buy it, we sometimes refer to the return on bills as the risk-free rate of interest.

Fig.1 Histogram of returns on US equities

1926–1996

Percentage return	Years (top to bottom)
−50 to −40	1931
−40 to −30	1937
−30 to −20	1974, 1930
−20 to −10	1973, 1966, 1957, 1941
−10 to 0	1990, 1981, 1977, 1969, 1962, 1953, 1946, 1940, 1939, 1934, 1932, 1929
0 to 10	1994, 1993, 1992, 1987, 1984, 1978, 1970, 1960, 1956, 1948, 1947
10 to 20	1988, 1986, 1979, 1972, 1971, 1968, 1965, 1964, 1959, 1952, 1949, 1944, 1926
20 to 30	1996, 1983, 1982, 1976, 1967, 1963, 1961, 1951, 1943, 1942
30 to 40	1995, 1991, 1989, 1985, 1980, 1975, 1955, 1950, 1945, 1938, 1936, 1927
40 to 50	1958, 1935, 1928
50 to 60	1954, 1933

Percentage return

Source: Used with permission. © 1997 Ibbotson Associates, Inc. All rights reserved.
(Certain portions of this work were derived from copyrighted works of Roger G. Ibbotson and Rex Sinquefield.)

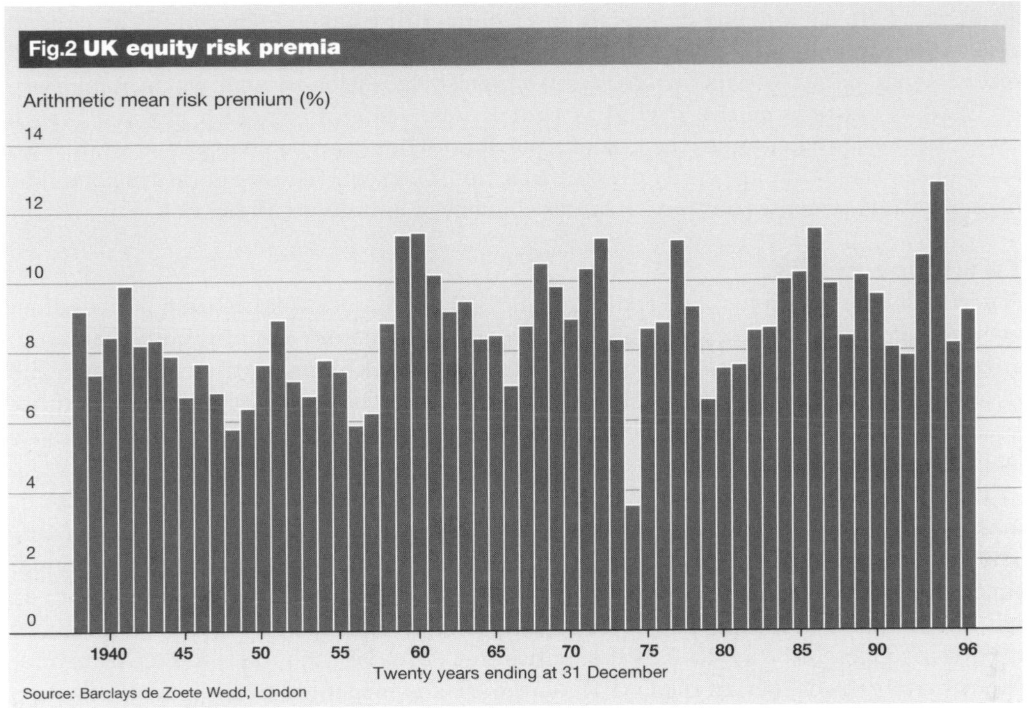

Investors do not like to be exposed to risk unless they can expect to receive compensation for their exposure. An interesting comparison, then, is between the risky return on equities and the risk-free interest rate. The difference between these two rates of return is called the excess return or equity risk premium. It measures the additional return received from investing in shares rather than in treasury bills. If the excess return is, on average, positive, then investors are receiving a premium for exposure to equity market risk.

Figure 2 shows the arithmetic average risk premium for the UK, measured in real terms, and estimated over rolling 20-year periods ending in 1938, 1939 and so on. Over the period from 1919 to date, the UK equity risk premium has averaged between 8–9 percentage points per year. Over the period since 1926, Ibbotson Associates estimate that US equities also provided an arithmetic average risk premium of between 8–9 percentage points. Similar figures are available for other countries. They may be used with caution as a guide to expectations for the future.

Projects that are riskless, therefore, should have their cash flows discounted at the risk-free rate of interest. If we expect the risk premium in the future to be similar to its average value in the past, then projects whose risk is the same as investing in the equity market should have their cash flows discounted at the risk-free rate plus, say, eight per cent. A project with intermediate risk merits an intermediate discount rate.

Capital asset pricing model

To implement this approach we need to agree on a method for estimating the riskiness of an investment. Until the 1960s, this would have been difficult. But in the early part of that decade there was an important breakthrough in the theory of finance. Building on work by Harry Markowitz and James Tobin, Bill Sharpe formulated the capital asset pricing model (CAPM), a simple yet elegant model that relates the expected return on an asset to its risk while giving a precise definition to what we mean by risk

The key insight of the CAPM is that investors can expect a reward for an investment's contribution to the risk of a portfolio. There can be no expected reward for exposure to risks that are easily diversified away. The required rate of return should be higher for investments that have a larger element of non-diversifiable risk.

Two types of risk

A portfolio invested in just one share is typically much more volatile than a diversified portfolio. By holding a large number of securities, investors can eliminate company-specific risk. However, there are limits to the power of diversification. Once the investor has holdings in every share in the market, the portfolio will still be quite risky. While diversification can eliminate company-specific risk, it cannot eliminate overall equity market risk.

Every share therefore fluctuates in value because of two elements of risk. The first is market risk – the tendency of the share to move with general stock market movements. The second is specific risk, which encapsulates all events that are specific to individual companies while having nothing to do with general market-wide factors. Investors do not like risk and need the prospect of higher returns before they will take it on. Since market risk cannot be avoided by diversification, investors require a higher return for exposure to market risk. In the CAPM, market risk is measured by beta. A stock with a beta of 1.0 tends to move broadly in line with the equity market; a share with a beta of 1.5 tends to move up or down by 1.5 per cent for each percentage point movement in the market.

The bar chart in Figure 3 lists recent estimates of beta for some well-known companies. Some companies have betas as high as 1.5 or even more and are an aggressive play on the equity market. If the market goes up, these shares can be

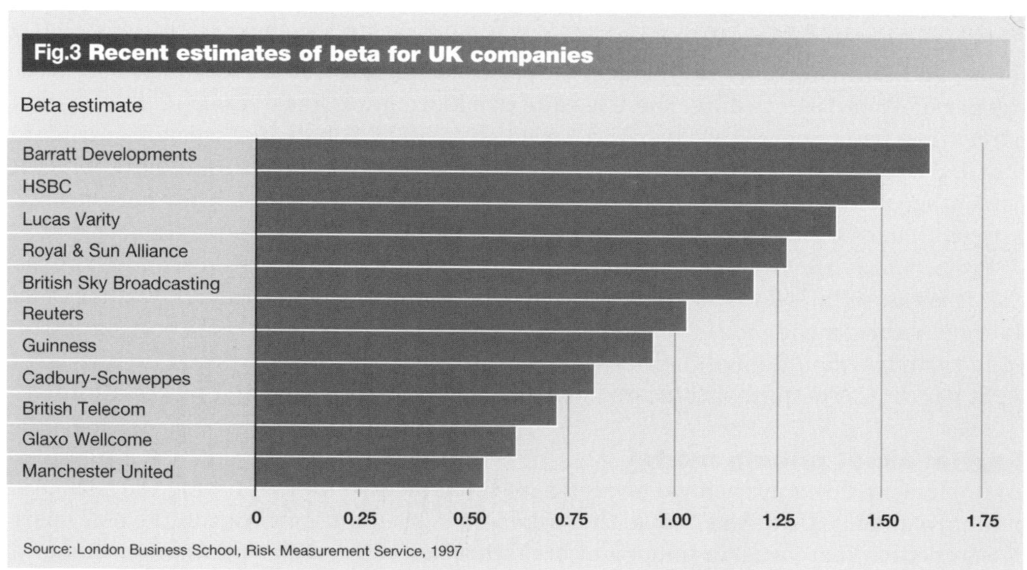

Source: London Business School, Risk Measurement Service, 1997

expected to outperform; in a bear market they can be expected to fall by more than average. Other shares have betas of 0.5 or less and these defensive companies are likely to be resistant to a bear market while being left behind when share prices surge ahead. Most companies, however, have a beta that is close to the average of 1.0.

Required rates of return

To estimate the required rate of return for an investment, we therefore need to estimate the beta for a capital project. This is easier to do if the project essentially replicates, probably on a smaller scale, the company's existing business. It is also easier if the project is typical of an industry sector for which betas are published.

A capital project with a beta of zero would be riskless, and its cash flows should be discounted at the risk-free rate of interest. An investment in an equity index fund would have the same risk as the market, namely a beta of 1.0. This investment would have a required rate of return equal to the riskless rate of interest plus the expected equity market risk premium.

Suppose we are considering building a power station, for which we have estimated a beta of 0.6. This is the same as the beta of a portfolio that is 40 per cent invested in treasury bills and 60 per cent invested in the equity market. The CAPM tells us that the required return should therefore be equal to the return on treasury bills plus 60 per cent of the expected market risk premium.

In general, the CAPM tells us that the required rate of return on an investment is equal to the risk-free rate of interest plus a premium for risk. The premium for risk is equal to beta multiplied by the equity market risk premium.

Most projects have a risk level that is different from the beta of their company's shares: using a single company-wide discount rate can therefore lead to inappropriate investment decisions.

The relationship between the required rate of return and beta is indicated in Figure 4 by the sloping line labeled 'risk-adjusted cost of capital.' The chart shows how the required rate of return increases as beta gets larger (*see* Box 1).

Fig.4 Estimating the cost of capital using the CAPM

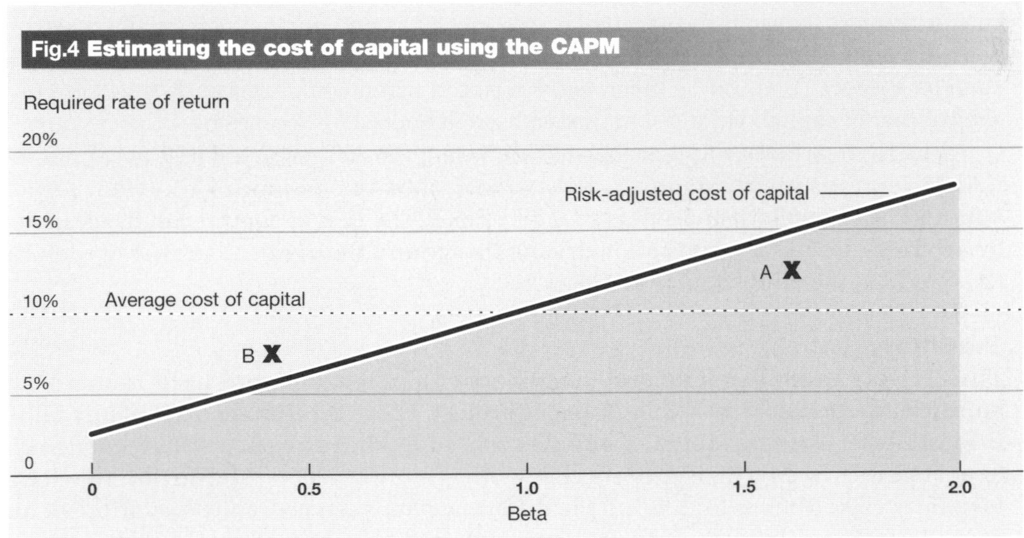

Box 1: Using the CAPM

To use the CAPM to calculate the required rate of return, we need three items of data:

- The risk-free interest rate, which may be obtained from the Currencies and Money page of the *Financial Times.*
- The beta of the investment, which may be derived from London Business School's *Risk Measurement Service.*
- The equity market risk premium, which has historically averaged around 8 per cent.

With a real interest rate of, say, 3 per cent and an investment with a beta of 0.6, we would have a required rate of return that is equal to 7.8 per cent (3 + 0.6 x 8 per cent). With a beta of 1.0, the required rate of return would be 11 per cent (3 + 1.0 x 8 per cent) in real terms.

Most projects have a risk level that is different from the beta of the company's shares. One reason for this is that many companies are financed partly with debt, which increases the riskiness of their shares. To estimate the riskiness of a capital investment project we therefore need to remove the effect of borrowing from the beta of the company's shares. The beta of the underlying business of the company is simply a weighted average of the beta of its equity and the beta of its debt. (The weights are the proportion of equity and the proportion of debt in the capital structure.) If we make the assumption that the company's debt is so safe as to make its beta virtually zero, then the beta of the company's underlying business is equal to the beta of its shares multiplied by the proportion of equity (at market value) in its capital structure.

Consider a company whose shares have a beta of 0.6. Assume the company is financed 83 per cent by equity and 17 per cent by debt. The beta of the underlying business would be equal to the beta of the shares multiplied by the proportion of equity. The company would have an 'asset beta' of 0.5 (0.6 x 0.83). To estimate the cost of equity capital for a company we should use the beta of its shares. But to estimate the cost of capital for the underlying business, we should use its asset beta.

Project risk

Some companies use only a single company-wide discount rate even though they operate in businesses that embrace a wide range of risks. However, this can lead to inappropriate investment decisions. Figure 4 shows why. The upward sloping risk-adjusted cost of capital line shows the required rate of return for projects with varying levels of beta. Projects with an expected return that plots above this security market line should be accepted while those beneath should be rejected. A high-risk proposal, such as Project A, would incorrectly be accepted by a company using a single, company-wide discount rate. On a risk-adjusted basis it should be rejected. A low-risk proposal, such as Project B, would be incorrectly rejected when compared with the company's overall cost of capital. On a risk-adjusted basis it should be accepted.

While there are other approaches to estimating the risk-adjusted cost of capital, the CAPM remains highly popular. It is widely used in company valuation, project appraisal and regulation. As illustrated in Box 2, the cost of capital can be estimated by arbitrage pricing theory, option pricing theory and the dividend growth model. But the CAPM is the most popular approach.

Summary

This article examines how stock markets can price risk and help identify the appropriate return for a new investment project. Elroy Dimson focuses mainly on the Capital Asset Pricing Model, a popular tool of modern finance which relates the expected return on an asset to its risk while giving a precise definition to what is meant by risk. Dimson highlights the difference between company-specific risk and overall equity market risk and goes on to explain the concept of beta, which measures

Box 2: Alternative approaches

The cost of capital is an opportunity cost. It is the return that could be obtained in the stock market from an investment of similar risk and maturity to the capital tied up in the project. Financial economics offers four approaches to estimating the cost of capital:

- The Capital Asset Pricing Model. Despite recent criticism, the CAPM remains the most popular approach to estimating the cost of capital.
- Arbitrage pricing theory, a competitor of the CAPM developed in the 1970s. As explained in 'An APT alternative to assessing risk' by Massoud Mussavian (Module 1), the APT can be seen as an extended version of CAPM, with multiple sources of risk and return.
- Option pricing theory also developed in the 1970s. The article 'How to put a price on options' by Anthony Neuberger (Module 10) explains how this approach is sometimes applied to valuing capital projects that have option-like characteristics.
- The dividend growth model, originated in the 1930s and popularized in the 1950s. Its drawback is that it assumes a dividend growth rate that can be sustained indefinitely. It also ignores the riskiness of an investment.

Some companies use accounting-based approaches for estimating the cost of capital. These seriously flawed methods include:

- The dividend yield. This tends to understate the cost of capital because it ignores the capital gains expected by investors.
- The p/e ratio or its reciprocal, the earnings yield. This ignores the expected growth in company earnings.
- Return on capital. Some companies use this as a guideline but it is absurd to estimate a low cost of capital just because a business earns a low accounting rate of return.
- Return on marginal project. Some companies rank projects from most to least attractive and accept those with the highest return. This is circular since projects cannot be ranked correctly unless one already knows the cost of capital.
- Funding cost. When projects are valued using the interest rate payable by the company, the discount rate fails to reflect the full risk of the investment.
- Past return on the company's shares. Use of the long-run return on a company's shares as a guide to the cost of capital implies that poorly performing companies have the lowest cost of capital. It is misleading.

Despite continued usage of inadequate methods for determining the cost of capital, more sophisticated businesses tend to use the CAPM. The APT tends to be used for utilities in the US, while option pricing theory is sometimes used for valuing natural resource investments such as mines.

market-related risk and allows investors to position portfolios in an aggressive or defensive way. In general the CAPM tells us that the required rate of return on an investment is equal to the risk-free rate of interest plus a premium for risk, where that premium is equal to beta multiplied by the equity market risk premium. The author warns that use of a single company-wide discount rate can lead to inappropriate investment decisions.

Suggested further reading

Brealey, R.A. and Myers S.C., (1995), *Principles of Corporate Finance*, 5th edn, The McGraw-Hill Companies, New York.

Dimson, E. and Marsh P. (eds) (1998), *Risk Management Service,* London Business School Vol 20.

Dimson, E., (1989), 'The discount rate for a power station', *Energy Economics*, Vol 11 No.3.

Ibbotson, R. (ed) (1997), *Stocks, Bonds, Bills and Inflation 1997 Yearbook*, Ibbotson Associates, Chicago.

Hughes, M. (ed) (1997), *The BZW Equity-Gilt Study*, Barclays de Zoete Wedd, London.

Valuation approaches to the LBO

by Howard Kaufold and Isik Inselbag

A large European multinational has as the result of a strategic review decided to move out of the personal computer business. The managers of the relevant subsidiary are interested in acquiring the business in a buy-out and have received proposals from banks and venture capitalists on methods of funding the deal.

The bankers are interested in providing senior debt funding to the new company while the venture capitalists are willing to provide subordinated financing if the loan terms include an equity stake in the new company. Management believes it can enhance the subsidiary's performance and eventually find a suitable buyer for it. Scenarios of this kind have occurred around the world as international competitiveness has forced companies to restructure in line with core competencies.

In Europe, the bulk of venture capital financing has been dedicated to funding such buy-out activity. In this article, we will explain the methods investors and companies should use to determine the appropriate values of such highly leveraged transactions. A leveraged buy-out (LBO) is the acquisition financed primarily with debt by a small group of equity investors of a public or private company. The equity holders service the heavy interest and principal payments of debt with cash from operations and/or asset sales. The shareholders generally hope to reverse the LBO within three to seven years through a public offering or company sale.

A buy-out is therefore likely to be successful only if the organization generates enough cash to service the debt in the early years and if it is attractive to other buyers as the buy-out matures. Determining the value of an LBO is critical to all parties to the transaction. Pre-buy-out owners, such as corporations evaluating the sale of a subsidiary, want to know the value of assets in order to decide whether or not to sell and to negotiate the highest possible price. Interested buyers must determine the transaction value in order to set their bidding limits and strategy. The valuation process affects lenders as well. Since debt levels are a significant part of the purchase price, creditors need to ensure operating cash flows and projected asset sales are sufficient to cover future debt obligations.

Most analysts determine buy-out prices by applying 'multiples' from comparable transactions to the target company's historical income or cash flow. Cash flow projections may be used in tandem with the multiples method but less for valuation than for structuring a financing package that meets lender coverage requirements. Another approach is to calculate the internal rate of return to equity investors as a function of different purchase prices. The maximum bid is then the price that just allows the required equity return to be satisfied.

From a valuation perspective, these practices have several shortcomings. A multiple can serve as a useful benchmark in the valuation process but rarely captures the unique future cash flow features underlying a company's true value. While it makes sense for equity investors to calculate the internal rate of return on a buy-out, these investors rarely compute their hurdle rate in a rational way. The required return depends on the riskiness of the target business's underlying cash flows and the repayment schedule for the debt financing. Most importantly, the required return changes dramatically over the life of an LBO as companies reduce debt and often sell assets.

Recognizing these drawbacks, experts in the field have begun using present value methods to appraise future cash flow prospects of highly leveraged transactions. The weighted average cost of capital (WACC) method is the best known of these approaches. It involves estimating a weighted average of the after-tax costs of debt and equity financing and using this average to discount the after-tax operating cash flows and terminal value. Although this method is appropriate for valuing transactions where capital structure is expected to remain stable, its use is questionable when the debt–equity mix is changing. Sophisticated users of this approach attempt to adjust the cost of capital over the life of an LBO to account for the effect of the changing capital structure. However, the discount rate correction is complicated and rarely done properly.

We have argued elsewhere that the adjusted present value (APV) method is an easier approach to valuing assets in an environment in which the capital structure is changing.[1] In this article, we will illustrate the use of this procedure in valuing the hypothetical management buy-out described above.

The formation of HighTech Inc

The management of Multinational Inc's personal computer business has put together a bid for the subsidiary of $97m. The newly formed company is to be called HighTech Inc.

Funding is to be provided by a combination of $70m of senior bank debt and $20m of junior venture capital lending. The venture capitalists have also been promised warrants that provide them with a share of the company in the likely event that the new organization is sold to the public or another company. The remaining $7m required to complete the purchase will be equity contributed by the subsidiary's management and private equity contributors. The buy-out will transfer both the plant and equipment and the working capital from Multinational to HighTech.

Projected sales for HighTech are expected to be $70m for the year ahead. The management believes it can increase sales by 10 per cent per year over the following two years with growth stabilizing at the three per cent expected rate of inflation indefinitely thereafter. Annual cash costs (materials, labor, selling and general and administrative expenses) are estimated to be 50 per cent of revenues.

Depreciation expense and annual investment in fixed assets are expected to be $9m in the first year of operation and then to grow in tandem with sales. Working capital levels are expected to be 10 per cent of sales in future years. The required rate of return on assets in the PC business is 18 per cent and the tax rate is 40 per cent.

We now illustrate a framework that can be used to analyze the value of HighTech under its operating projections and proposed financing package. Our approach will be to use a combination of APV and WACC. In the process, we show how the valuation methods reveal value-maximizing strategies for Multinational's shareholders.

---

1 See Inselbag, I. and Kaufold H. (1997), 'Two DCF Approaches for Valuing Companies under Alternative Financing Strategies (and How to Choose Between Them)', forthcoming in the *Journal of Applied Corporate Finance*, for the rationale of using APV method when capital structure changes, and Inselbag, I. and Kaufold, H. (1989), 'How to Value Recapitilizations and Leveraged Buy-outs', *Journal of Applied Corporate Finance*, Summer, pp 87–96, for an application of this method to a hypothetical LBO example.

Valuing the deal

The basis for the APV method is that the current value of a leveraged company (VL) is its value as an all-equity entity (VU), plus the discounted value of the interest tax shields from the debt its assets will support (PVTS).[2]

The principle of APV as presented in equation 1 is straightforward. The business's unleveraged value is determined by the operating income generated by its assets. The debt supported by these operating cash flows enhances value because interest on debt (but not dividends paid to shareholders) is deductible from the organization's income for corporate tax purposes. As a result, for given operating income, the after-tax amount available for bondholders and stockholders taken together increases as more of the payout is in the form of interest rather than dividends. We will illustrate how this APV approach is particularly well suited to valuing LBOs and other highly leveraged transactions.

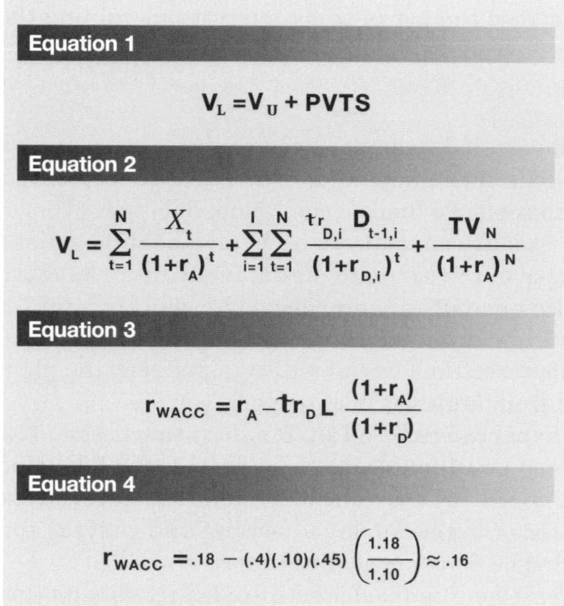

Equation 1
$$V_L = V_U + PVTS$$
Equation 2
$$V_L = \sum_{t=1}^{N} \frac{X_t}{(1+r_A)^t} + \sum_{i=1}^{I}\sum_{t=1}^{N} \frac{t r_{D,i} D_{t-1,i}}{(1+r_{D,i})^t} + \frac{TV_N}{(1+r_A)^N}$$
Equation 3
$$r_{WACC} = r_A - t r_D L \frac{(1+r_A)}{(1+r_D)}$$
Equation 4
$$r_{WACC} = .18 - (.4)(.10)(.45)\left(\frac{1.18}{1.10}\right) \approx .16$$

As we have indicated, in a typical LBO the purchasers plan to keep the company private for several years, during which time they enhance operations and pay down the significant debt burden. The owners reap the rewards of the transaction when the buy-out matures and the company is sold to another concern or to the public in a stock offering.

Letting N represent the number of years the company remains private under the LBO, we can rewrite equation 1 as equation 2. Equation 2 shows the transaction's value can be separated into three components. The first two terms equal the value

---

[2] One should also deduct from this value any costs of financial distress. For simplicity, we assume these are negligible in our example. In fact, well-planned LBOs have been carried out primarily in industries in which cash flows are relatively stable, where the probability of debt service difficulties is relatively low.

generated by the transaction during the LBO period. The final term is the present value of projected sale price of the company when it is sold or taken public. Practitioners refer to this sale as the 'reversal' of the LBO.

In the first term of equation 2, we estimate the value from operations over the life of the LBO by discounting the free cash flows from operations (X_t) by the required return on assets (^rA). In the second term, we calculate the present value of tax savings during the LBO due to deductibility of interest payments. In that term, $^rD_{,i}$ is the borrowing rate of debt type i; $D_{t,i}$ represents the debt balance remaining at the end of year t for debt type i and **t** is the corporate tax rate. Multiplying each year's interest payments by the tax rate and discounting by the appropriate borrowing rate yields the value of the tax shield associated with each source of debt financing. Adding values for each source of debt yields the total present value of interest tax savings. The third term is the present value of the price (TV_N) that the buy-out company will be worth when the LBO is reversed.

The WACC method is ideally suited for determining the terminal value in the typical circumstance in which the post-LBO owners fund the company with a stable debt equity blend. If a company intends to maintain a stable capital structure in market value terms, the weighted average cost of capital, appropriate for discounting an organization's operating cash flows is constant and can be represented as in equation 3[3] where **L** is the target debt-to-total value ratio and ^rD is the average cost of debt at target capital structure. The resulting terminal value is split between the LBO debt and equity investors according to their contractual claims.

The relation described in equation 2 reveals why the APV approach is ideally suited to valuing a leveraged buy-out. The distinguishing feature of an LBO, from a valuation perspective, is that the capital structure is not stable over time and the debt-to-equity ratio declines. As a result, the required return on equity and the weighted average cost of capital change as the lenders are paid.

The APV technique is especially useful in this context because ^rA, the discount rate needed to calculate the all-equity value of the company's LBO operating cash flows (first term in equation 2), is independent of its changing debt-equity mix. Furthermore, the value of the LBO debt interest tax shields (second term in equation 2) can be accurately estimated to the extent that the owners project a service schedule for debt outstanding over the life of the LBO.

Figure 1 presents operating projections for HighTech and includes management's projections as described above. The free cash flows are projected to be nearly \$15m over the year ahead, growing to around \$18.6m by the third year of operations. We will assume in our example that the LBO is reversed at the end of the third year. Thereafter, free cash flows are expected to grow at three per cent per year. The blend of these operating projections with HighTech's buy-out financing plan is presented in Figure 2.

Flows to debt and equity investors

The bank is willing to lend \$70m at a 14 per cent interest rate. HighTech will be required to repay \$7m of principal on this loan each year, with the expectation that the remaining balance on this debt will be retired when the LBO is reversed.

The venture capital group is willing to lend an additional \$20m at an interest rate of

---

3 For a derivation of this relationship, *see* Inselbag and Kaufold (1997).

HIGH TECH INC

Fig.1 Operating cash flows

	Year 1	Year 2	Year 3
Sales	70,000	77,000	84,700
Cash costs	35,000	38,500	42,350
Depreciation	9,000	9,000	10,890
Operating income	**26,000**	**28,600**	**31,460**
Tax on operating income	(10,400)	(11,440)	(12,584)
Earnings before interest after taxes	15,600	17,160	18,876
Add depreciation	9,000	9,900	10,890
Gross cash flow from operations	**24,600**	**27,060**	**29,766**
Less investment into:			
Fixed assets	(9,000)	(9,900)	(10,890)
Net working capital	(700)	(770)	(254)
Unlevered free cash flows	**14,900**	**16,390**	**18,622**

HIGH TECH INC

Fig.2 Flows to debt and equity investors

	Year 1	Year 2	Year 3
Operating income	26,000	28,600	31,460
Interest on senior debt (14%)	9,800	8,820	7,840
Interest on subordinated debt (9%)	1,800	1,800	1,800
Taxable income	**14,400**	**17,980**	**21,820**
Taxes	5,760	7,912	8,728
Earnings after taxes	**8,640**	**10,788**	**13,092**
Add depreciation	9,000	9,900	10,890
Gross cash flow	**17,640**	**20,688**	**23,982**
Less investments to:			
Fixed assets	9,000	9,900	10,890
Net working capital	700	770	254
Cash available for debt principal	**7,940**	**10,018**	**12,838**
Principal payments to senior debt	(7,000)	(7,000)	(7,000)
Flows to equity	**940**	**3,018**	**5,838**
Senior debt outstanding	63,000	56,000	49,000
Subordinated debt outstanding	20,000	20,000	20,000
Total debt outstanding	**83,000**	**76,000**	**69,000**

nine per cent with no reduction of principal prior to a balloon payment at the end of the fifth year. The venture capitalists are willing to lend at the lower rate, in spite of their junior status, because they will also receive warrants (with a $0 strike price assumed for simplicity) for 35 per cent of the equity value of the company.

These warrants are to be exercised at the lenders' discretion but the expectation is that this will occur at the time of LBO reversal. If this equity sweetener were not included, subordinated debt of this risk level would be priced to yield 15 per cent. Overall, market conditions are such that venture capitalists are likely to require a total rate of return on their investment of at least 30 per cent (*see* Figure 4).

Valuation of the management buy-out plan

The valuation of HighTech's buy-out plan shown in Figure 3 follows from the combination of APV and WACC approaches outlined in equation 2. The first component is the value of HighTech's operations during the LBO period. To calculate this, we discount the operating free cash flows during years 1 through 3 by the required asset return of 18 per cent, which yields a value of $35.7m (*see* Figure 3). To calculate the second term of equation 2 we must add the interest tax shields expected to be realized by senior and junior debt financing.

First, consider the tax savings generated by the interest paid on the senior debt during years 1–3. Every dollar of interest reduces taxes for HighTech by 40 cents. For example, the year 1 interest payment of $9.8m leads to tax savings of $3.9m. Discounting these three years of tax savings at the borrowing rate of 14 per cent yields a present value of interest tax shields from senior debt of $8.3m.

HIGH TECH INC

Fig.3 Valuation of the management buyout plan

	Year 0	Year 1	Year 2	Year 3
Unlevered free cash flow (UFCF)		14,900	16,390	18,622
Tax savings due to interest of senior debt		3,920	3,528	3,136
Tax savings due to interest of subordinated debt		720	720	720
Terminal value				146,763
Total debt outstanding				69,000
Terminal equity value				**77,763**
PV of UFCF at 18% (years 1–3)	35,732			
PV of interest tax shields of senior at 14% (years 1–3)	8,270			
PV of interest tax shields of subordinated at 15% (years 1–3)	1,644			
Total PV of interest tax shields	9,914			
PV of the terminal value of the firm at 18%	89,324			
Total highly levered value	**134,970**			

HIGH TECH INC

Fig.4 Flows to venture capital and initial equity

Percentage of company given to venture capital: 35%

	Year 0	Year 1	Year 2	Year 3	Year 4	Year 5
Flows to venture capital						
Flows to debt	(20,000)	1,800	1,800	1,800	1,800	21,800
Warrants	–	–	–	27,217	–	–
Total cash flows	**(20,000)**	**1,800**	**1,800**	**29,017**	**1,800**	**21,800**
IRR for venture capital	34%					
Initial equity (management)						
Flows to equity	(7,000)	940	3,018	5,838		
Share of terminal value	–	–	–	50,546		
Total	**(7,000)**	**940**	**3,018**	**56,384**		
IRR for initial equity	112%					

Second, consider the tax savings generated by interest paid on the subordinated debt during years 1–3. HighTech pays interest of nine per cent on the constant $20m balance, or $1.8m. These lead to tax savings (at the 40 per cent tax rate) of $0.7m. Discounting this annual savings at the market interest rate of 15 per cent implies a present value of tax savings of $1.6m. The total present value of interest tax shield of all debt capital used for the buy-out is $8.3m + $1.6m = $9.9m.

Finally, we must calculate the terminal value of the company at the end of year three, at which time the LBO is reversed. We will assume that HighTech will be financed using a 45–55 debt-equity blend after year three and the enterprise's borrowing rate at this capital structure will be 10 per cent. As explained earlier, under this assumption it is best to use the WACC method to calculate a terminal value for the organization. With this particular financing blend, the weighted average cost of capital is 16 per cent as shown in equation 4.

Since the post-LBO operating cash flows are expected to grow at a constant 3 per cent rate, this terminal value can be calculated as the discounted value of a growing perpetuity, 18.6(1.03) / (0.16-0.03) = $146.8m. This can be interpreted as fair market value for HighTech as of the end of year three. The present value of the $146.8m terminal value at 18 per cent is $89.3m.

Adding the three components together, the total value of HighTech under the buy-out proposal is $135m. Deducting the $97m of initial debt and equity used to fund the buy-out, the net present value to be shared among the equity investors (including warrant holders) is $38m. It is interesting to translate this present value into rates of return earned by equity investors. In Figure 4, we show the cash flows for both the venture capital investors and those providing the initial equity.

Flows to venture capital and initial equity

The venture capitalists provide $20m of the initial purchase price. This loan remains outstanding for the three years of the buy-out and for the two more years thereafter. They receive nine per cent interest for the entire five-year life of their loan. In addition, their warrants can be exercised at the end of year three for 35 per cent of the equity value at that time. As of the end of the year three, the equity investors' claim is equal to $77.8m, the terminal value of $146.8m less the $69m which HighTech's creditors are owed (*see* Figure 3). The venture capitalists' 35 per cent share of this equity value amounts to $27.2m. These cash flows generate an internal rate of return of 34 per cent.

The initial equity investors (management and their partners) commit $7m at the time of the buy-out and then earn, in each year, any cash flows in excess of debt service requirements. The bulk of their pay-off occurs when HighTech is re-sold at the end of year three, at which time these investors receive the remaining $50.5m, 65 per cent of the equity value. The resulting rate of return is 112 per cent.

Note that in our example Multinational is contemplating selling its PC business to management at a bargain price. If it seeks a buyer who would fund the buy-out of the business at the target 45–55 debt–equity blend from the outset, the inherent value of this division to the buyer would be around $130m.[4] To maximize the value for its shareholders of divesting the PC business, Multinational should regard this value as a minimum asking price for the division.

Summary

Determining the value of a leveraged buy-out (LBO) is critical to all parties involved in the transaction. Corporations considering the sale of a subsidiary need to know whether to sell and at what price. Interested buyers must set their bidding limits and strategy, and lenders need to ensure that operating cash flows and projected asset sales are sufficient to cover future debt obligations. As Isik Inselbag and Howard Kaufold explain, several different methodologies have been used, ranging from applying multiples to historic cash flows to calculating the equity investor's internal rate of return. Present value methods, of which the weighted average cost of capital is the best known, are increasingly popular but their use is questionable in a buy-out environment in which the company's capital structure is changing. Using this hypothetical case study the authors illustrate the advantages of the adjusted present value approach.

---

[4] This value is calculated by discounting High Tech's operating cash flows during years 1–3, and the terminal value, by the 16 per cent weighted average cost of capital at the target capital structure.

An APT alternative to assessing risk

by Massoud Mussavian

The core idea of the Capital Asset Pricing Model (CAPM) is that there is only one source of risk that affects the long-term average returns of capital investments and securities. The CAPM tells us that this risk is the market risk, which is the tendency of a stock to move relative to the equity market. In the CAPM this market risk is measured by beta. The CAPM and the importance of beta have not been without controversy. These range from arguments about the correct definition of the market index to lack of empirical evidence for beta.

The arbitrage pricing theory (APT) is an alternative theory that can potentially overcome the CAPM's problems while still keeping alive its underlying message. Although not the panacea that was first imagined, the APT remains a viable alternative to the CAPM for both academics and practitioners alike.

The core idea of the APT is that a small number of systematic influences affect the long-term average returns of securities. Even the most vocal adherents of the APT will not deny that there are a multitude of influences that determine stock and bond prices. However, the APT allows us to focus on a few significant factors that seem to determine returns of most assets – a problem that is difficult enough by itself – without having to look at a myriad of additional confounding issues. Furthermore, as in the CAPM, risks that are not due to the systematic influences are diversifiable and not rewarded.

Are two types of risk enough?

Asset returns show a strong pattern of co-movement. In particular, returns on equities and bonds tend to move up and down together. It is this observation that led Nobel prize laureate Bill Sharpe to develop the CAPM as a description of stock returns. One of the main conclusions of the CAPM is that there are two types of risk. The first is the risk associated with the stock market in general, as captured by beta, and the second is the risk that is specific to a company. By holding a sufficient number of stocks an investor can diversify-away company-specific risk. But even if the investor holds every stock in the market, he or she will still be exposed to market-wide risk. It is this market-wide risk – beta – that is rewarded in the long run, not company-specific risk.

Are these two types of risk enough? Consider, for example, a portfolio consisting of only utility stocks versus a portfolio of only financial stocks. Even if the two portfolios had the same beta and were reasonably well diversified, would we expect these two portfolios to react in the same manner to macroeconomic shocks? Not necessarily. For example, if the economy slows down or contracts then we may expect stocks of financial companies to do relatively worse than utilities. This is because utilities are regulated and can pass adverse economic shocks on to their customers, making their stock prices less sensitive to an economic downturn. Banks, on the other hand, may face an increase in the number of bad loans on their books, and their stock prices may be more sensitive to bad economic news. A similar effect can occur with other pervasive economic factors such as industrial production, inflation and long-term interest rates.

Box 1: Controversy over beta

The CAPM and the validity of beta has been hotly contested. Some of the criticisms of beta and CAPM are:

There is no risk-free asset. A risk-free asset is a short-dated asset whose pay-off over some period is known. The CAPM framework assumes that every investor can borrow and lend at the rate of interest of the risk-free asset. Clearly this is unrealistic since there is the possibility that some investors may default on their loans, thus making them no longer risk-free. However, even in this case a general version of the CAPM will still hold.

A possible explanation for this result was given by the late Fischer Black, whose arguments were based on considering the feasible investment strategies for different types of investors. Suppose that an investor wants to pursue a high-risk investment strategy. In a pure CAPM world he or she could achieve this by either buying high beta stocks or buying low beta stocks and leveraging this position (borrowing at the risk-free rate of interest).

If, however, investors cannot borrow unlimited amounts at the risk-free rate they must buy the high-risk stocks outright. This would imply that investors will bid up the price of high-risk stocks, and consequently the expected return on these assets should be lower than in the pure CAPM world. This result is known as the zero-beta CAPM and states that the reward for beta is lower than in a pure CAPM world.

There is no market portfolio. One of the severest deficiences of the CAPM was pointed out by Richard Roll of the University of California at Los Angeles in what has become known as the Roll Critique. He showed that the correct market index for the CAPM was not the stock market but an index of all the risky wealth in the world. The market therefore includes not just all the traded stocks and bonds but also property, human capital and anything else tangible or intangible that adds to the risky wealth of, not just the UK, say, but of all mankind. The Roll Critique has spawned a large number of novel statistical methods that avoid using the true market index. Although the resulting evidence for beta has been mixed, it is interesting to note that there is some evidence that the CAPM holds when indices that include property and other non-financial assets are used.

The theory does not stack up with reality. The CAPM predicts that a portfolio made up of high beta stocks will outperform a portfolio of low beta stocks. However, the reality seems to indicate investors who purchased high beta stocks have not achieved a higher rate of return than investors who purchased low beta stocks.

Fig.1 UK average monthly returns vs Beta

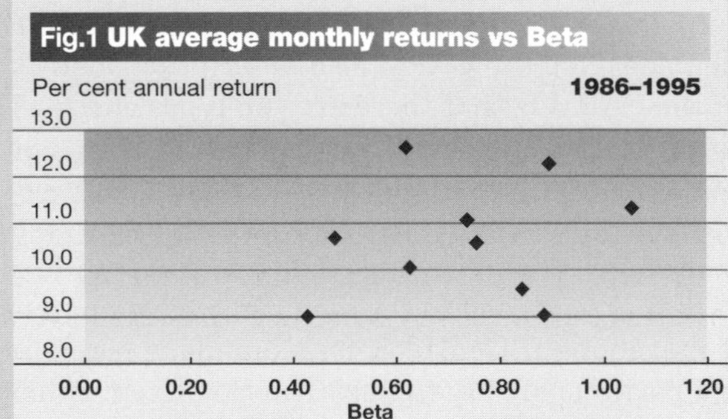

Figure 1 shows the evidence for UK stocks for the ten-year period ending December 1995. The figure shows the average return on ten portfolios grouped by their beta. It can be seen that the relationship between beta and return is essentially flat and that high beta stocks did not on average offer better returns than low beta stocks.
However, a number of authors have argued that ten years is not sufficient to come to any clear conclusion and that the longer-run evidence is much more favorable for beta. Other authors have argued that beta does actually work in times of large stock market moves – high beta stocks fall by more in stock market crashes than low beta stocks and vice versa.

Given that it is possible to hold two portfolios that have the same beta but different sensitivities to macroeconomic risk, investors may not expect the long-run average return on these portfolios to be the same. The APT captures these potential differences. Multiple sources of economic risk can be incorporated by having more than one beta. Each beta captures the sensitivity of the stock to the corresponding factor.

As with the CAPM, we can split the risk of an asset into several components. This can be seen for the case of Shell Transport in Figure 2. Under the CAPM, 55 per cent of the variation in Shell's return over the 10-year period was due to the FT All Share Index and 45 per cent of the variation in Shell's return was company-specific. But by considering five additional pervasive factors, only 39 per cent of the variation in the stock return is due to company-specific risk. Of the remaining 61 per cent of the pervasive risk in Shell, one per cent is due to both exchange rate risk and UK industrial production shocks, two per cent to inflation risk, five per cent to long-term interest rate risk, six per cent to oil price risk and 46 per cent to stock market risk.

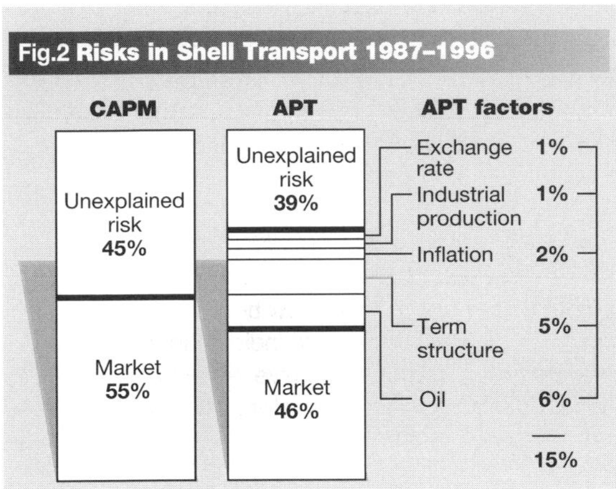

Fig.2 Risks in Shell Transport 1987–1996

The example has two interesting features. First, with six APT betas as opposed to one CAPM beta, the percentage of variation due to company-specific risk drops from 45 per cent to 39 per cent. This is because the APT betas can explain some of the risk that the CAPM beta could not. Second, by introducing additional pervasive factors the impact of the FT All Share Index drops. This is because the other five macroeconomic risks also affect the index itself and hence the APT betas can also further explain some of the risks previously captured by the CAPM beta.

The principle of arbitrage

The CAPM is based on the stringent assumption that all investors are effectively choosing investments by looking at the expected return (which they like) and volatility (which they dislike). The APT, however, is based on the law of one price, which says that in a well-functioning market, portfolios or assets that offer the same risks must trade for the same price. It does not make any assumptions about the investor's preferences.

Box 2: Using the APT to measure fund performance

The goal of performance measurement is to determine how well a given portfolio has performed when contrasted with some other comparable investment strategy.

What is a comparable investment strategy? One possibility is a portfolio with the same level of risk. However, risk-adjusted performance measurement clearly depends on what is the correct measure of risk. In a CAPM framework risk is measured by beta. This implies that the comparable investment strategy is a diversified portfolio with the same beta as the fund.

The APT on the other hand recognizes that there are additional systematic influences that determine the risk and return of a portfolio. Thus in an APT framework a comparable investment strategy is a diversified portfolio that has the same exposure to these multiple systematic influences. For example, consider the Schroders Smaller Companies Unit Trust. This is a UK unit trust (mutual fund) specializing in investments in small stocks. Over the ten-year period ending in December 1996 the average annual return on the fund was 12.8 per cent. The fund's beta, as measured against the FT All Share Index over the same period, was 0.80. The risk premium on the FT All Share index was 5.6 per cent and the return on UK Treasury Bills was 9.3 per cent over this period.

Therefore, according to the CAPM, the required rate of return on an investment with the same level of risk is 13.8 per cent (9.3 per cent + 0.80 x 5.6 per cent). That is, if an investor had held a diversified portfolio with the same beta over this ten-year period, then he or she would have achieved a return of 13.8 per cent as compared with an actual return of 12.8 per cent on the fund. Thus we might conclude that the Schroder Smaller Companies fund under-performed by one per cent per annum.

But this conclusion may be flawed. First, UK small stocks under-performed large companies – and the performance of the FT All Share index is dominated by large companies. Second, this fund is supposed to specialize in small stocks. Therefore, it is impossible to say whether the performance of the fund against the FT All Share index is due to the manager's selection skills or the overall performance of small stocks. Introducing another factor, corresponding to the risk in the Hoare Govett Smaller Companies index (not already inherent in the FT All Share) allows one to correct for this additional systematic influence. In actual fact, the risk premium on this factor was –4.3 per cent pa and the beta of the fund with respect to this second factor was 0.68.

Hence, according to a two factor APT with size as an additional risk factor, the return on an investment with the same level of systematic risk is 10.9 per cent (9.3 per cent + 0.80 x 5.6 per cent + 0.68 (–4.3 per cent)). Hence, after taking into account the relatively poor performance of small stocks the fund actually over-performed by 2.1 per cent pa.

An investor using a CAPM-style risk adjustment might have concluded that the managers of the fund were not particularly good. However, using the APT, which allows the possibility of multiple sources of systematic investment risk, leads to the conclusion that fund managers may have some ability to pick small stock winners!

What should the factors be?

Although the APT model assumes that every investor and trader knows which systematic influences affect stock and bond returns, it is silent on what these factors actually are. This is both a blessing and curse. For a practitioner it is a blessing, because it frees the investment manager, trader or analyst from the dogma of the CAPM and allows him or her to build a framework based on those influences that are believed to be important. In comparison, the CAPM gives a strict prescription of which (single) factor must be used to form expectations.

However, for academics the freedom to choose the appropriate factors has always presented a problem. Almost from the APT's inception the choice of factors, number of factors and their interpretation has been hotly debated in the academic literature. One popular approach is to develop an APT with macroeconomic factors. The choice of macroeconomic influences includes all the variables that can possibly affect current stock prices.

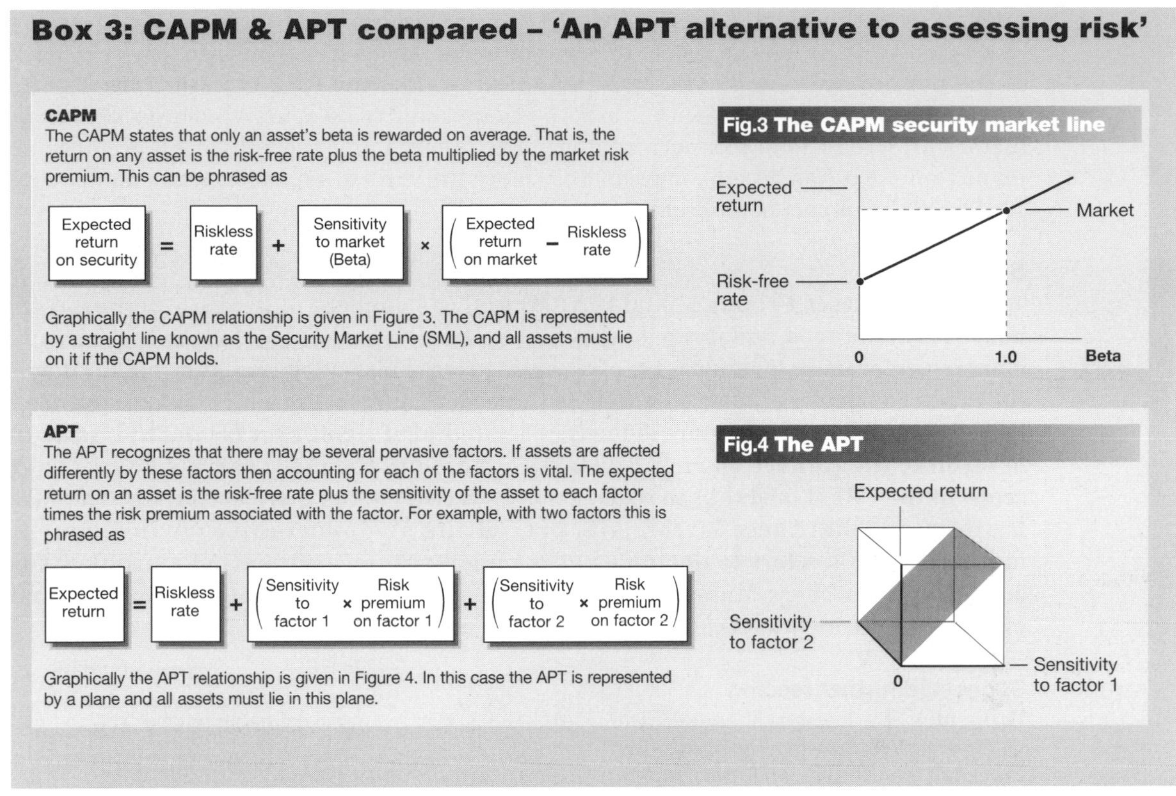

Box 3: CAPM & APT compared – 'An APT alternative to assessing risk'
CAPM
The CAPM states that only an asset's beta is rewarded on average. That is, the return on any asset is the risk-free rate plus the beta multiplied by the market risk premium. This can be phrased as
Expected return on security = Riskless rate + Sensitivity to market (Beta) × (Expected return on market − Riskless rate)
Graphically the CAPM relationship is given in Figure 3. The CAPM is represented by a straight line known as the Security Market Line (SML), and all assets must lie on it if the CAPM holds.
Fig.3 The CAPM security market line
Expected return
Market
Risk-free rate
0
1.0
Beta
APT
The APT recognizes that there may be several pervasive factors. If assets are affected differently by these factors then accounting for each of the factors is vital. The expected return on an asset is the risk-free rate plus the sensitivity of the asset to each factor times the risk premium associated with the factor. For example, with two factors this is phrased as
Expected return = Riskless rate + (Sensitivity to factor 1 × Risk premium on factor 1) + (Sensitivity to factor 2 × Risk premium on factor 2)
Graphically the APT relationship is given in Figure 4. In this case the APT is represented by a plane and all assets must lie in this plane.
Fig.4 The APT
Expected return
Sensitivity to factor 2
0
Sensitivity to factor 1

Stock prices should represent the fundamental value of a company, that is the discounted value of all expected future dividends. Therefore the choice of factors should include any systematic influences that affect future dividends, the way traders and investors form expectations of those dividends and the rate at which investors discount future cash flows. It is interesting to note that after accounting for these macroeconomic factors some researchers have found that the overall stock market index has no impact on stock returns. This indicates that the long-run average return of the US stock market is completely determined by macroeconomic risks.

APT models can also be derived from factor and principal component analysis, which are statistical techniques that extract the pervasive influences from the actual data. Several studies using these methods indicate that there are about four or five factors that affect US stock prices.

The advantage of factor and principal component analysis is that the derived factors will include all of the pervasive influences, whereas with specified factors it is quite possible that some factors are omitted. The drawback is that derived factors usually have no economic interpretation, so that these studies can really only indicate the number of pervasive influences affecting stock prices.

Using the APT

The APT can be used in many settings where the CAPM is used. For example, the APT can be used to determine the risk-adjusted rates of return in the appraisal of a capital project. In such a setting the APT would require a more precise view of the project's risks than the CAPM. The risk of the project is then measured by its sensitivity to each of the pertinent economic factors. A popular use of the APT is in measuring the performance of portfolios, since it allows the investor to measure which influences or factors affected the fund's performance. With increasing specialization of portfolio management it has become increasingly more difficult to separate performance and skill from the impact of different factors.

Summary

The Capital Asset Pricing Model (CAPM) and the concept of beta which lies at its heart is introduced and described by Elroy Dimson earlier in Module 1, with only glancing references to other ways of assessing risk. This article explains one of them – the arbitrage pricing theory – as well as the wider controversy which has surrounded beta. The APT allows investors to focus on a handful of significant factors that seem to determine the returns on most assets, as opposed to the more narrow and stricter scope of the CAPM, and thus to reach a more precise view of a project's risks. The APT is silent on what these factors are, presenting an opportunity for investment managers and traders to decide what is important, but presenting a problem for academic researchers. Mussavian's piece on fund performance should also please fund managers – it concludes that fund managers can pick small stock winners.

Suggested further reading

Berry, M.A., Burmeister, E. and McElroy, M.B., (1988), 'Sorting out risks using known APT factors' *Financial Analyst Journal,* March–April.

Elton, E.J. and Gruber, M.J., *Modern Portfolio Theory and Investment Analysis,* 5th edn, Wiley.

Beta, size and price/book: three risk measures or one?

by Gabriel Hawawini and Donald B. Keim

One of the fundamental tenets of modern finance has been that expected stock returns are determined by their corresponding level of systematic risk, or the beta factor. For more than 30 years, studies have found support for a positive and linear relation between return and risk known as the capital asset pricing model, or CAPM. Since the early 1980s, however, a growing number of studies have documented the presence of persistent patterns in stock returns that do not support CAPM.

The evidence suggests that betas of common stocks do not adequately explain cross-sectional differences in stock returns. Instead, other variables with no basis in current theoretical models seem to have a more significant predictive ability than beta. These other variables include: company size, as measured by market capitalization of common stock; the ratio of book-to-market value: the accounting value of a company's equity divided by its market capitalization; earnings yield: a company's reported accounting net profits divided by price per share; a company's prior return performance.

Many interpret the evidence as providing convincing support of market inefficiency: if stock returns can be predicted on the basis of historical factors such as market capitalization, book-to-market value and prior return performance, then it is difficult to characterize stock markets as informationally efficient. On the other hand, the rejection may be due to a test design based on an incorrect equilibrium model. The fact that so many of these regularities have persisted for more than 30 years suggests that our benchmark models may provide incomplete descriptions of equilibrium price formation.

An alternative explanation is that the failure of the evidence to provide unambiguous support for the CAPM is not necessarily proof of the model's invalidity but may simply reflect our inability to measure beta risk accurately. For example, one can argue that stocks with higher ratios of book-to-market value have higher average returns than stocks with lower ratios of book-to-market because they are riskier in a beta sense. If we could measure beta risk with less error, then the reported positive relation between book-to-market and size and beta-risk-adjusted returns may disappear.

There are additional empirical puzzles. Not only does the evidence indicate that future stock returns are related to factors such as size, book-to-market value and prior return performance, but these relations are usually more significant (and often only significant) during January than during the other 11 months of the year. The presence of this January effect raises a further challenge to current financial theory. Why would a return-generating factor (risk or any thing else) manifest itself during one month?

The central prominence of beta in the asset pricing paradigm came into question with the first tests of other alternatives to the CAPM in the late 1970s. The earliest of these tests found that the price-to-earnings ratio (P/E) and the market capitalization of common equity (company size) provided considerably more explanatory power than beta. Other studies have extended the list of predictive factors to include, among others, the ratio of book-to-market value, price per share and prior return performance. Combined, these studies have produced convincing evidence of cross-sectional return predictability that vitiates the marginal explanatory power of beta found in the earlier studies. Notably absent in these studies, however, is any supporting theory to justify the choice of factors. Nevertheless, the findings collectively represent a challenge for alternative asset pricing models.

The size effect

Much of the research on cross-sectional predictability of stock returns has focused on the relation between returns and the market value of common equity, commonly referred to as the size effect.

The first set of columns in Figure 1 reports the average monthly returns for ten value-weighted portfolios of New York Stock Exchange (NYSE) and American Stock Exchange (Amex) stocks for the period April 1962 to December 1994, along with corresponding values for portfolio beta and average market capitalization of the stocks

Fig.1 Monthly percentage returns

Porfolio*	Size (Market Capital)			Earnings-to-price ratio			Cash flow-to-price ratio**			Price-to-book ratio			Prior return		
	Size ($m)	Return (%)	Beta	E/P	Return (%)	Beta	CF/P	Return (%)	Beta	P/B	Return (%)	Beta	Prior return (%)	Return (%)	Beta
1	10	1.56 (0.37)	1.11	19.39	1.21 (0.27)	1.01	52.08	1.47 (0.33)	1.00	0.57	1.43 (0.28)	1.04	53.1	1.18 (0.29)	1.13
2	26	1.41 (0.34)	1.14	12.88	1.25 (0.23)	0.93	27.75	1.32 (0.29)	0.90	0.84	1.42 (0.25)	0.97	24.9	1.24 (0.26)	1.05
3	48	1.25 (0.31)	1.10	11.26	1.08 (0.23)	0.88	23.02	1.17 (0.29)	0.91	1.02	1.06 (0.23)	0.92	16.7	1.09 (0.24)	1.02
4	83	1.23 (0.31)	1.15	10.09	1.02 (0.23)	0.95	19.91	0.94 (0.31)	0.99	1.18	1.05 (0.21)	0.84	11.2	1.03 (0.23)	0.02
5	104	1.22 (0.28)	1.10	9.08	0.96 (0.23)	0.94	17.37	1.14 (0.31)	1.01	1.35	1.00 (0.22)	0.90	6.5	0.88 (0.22)	0.96
6	239	1.12 (0.26)	1.04	8.14	0.77 (0.23)	0.99	15.05	0.87 (0.30)	0.99	1.56	0.79 (0.22)	0.91	2.3	0.91 (0.22)	0.93
7	402	1.09 (0.25)	1.06	7.19	0.83 (0.22)	0.96	12.96	1.12 (0.30)	1.03	1.86	0.84 (0.23)	0.98	-1.9	0.85 (0.23)	0.95
8	715	1.09 (0.24)	1.05	6.13	0.89 (0.24)	1.04	10.85	1.05 (0.32)	1.08	2.30	0.91 (0.24)	1.03	-6.6	0.92 (0.24)	0.96
9	1,341	1.03 (0.23)	1.03	4.78	0.88 (0.25)	1.06	8.40	0.89 (0.31)	1.06	3.10	0.82 (0.25)	1.11	-13.1	0.62 (0.27)	1.05
10	5,820	0.83 (0.21)	0.95	2.49	0.82 (0.26)	1.08	4.77	0.80 (0.33)	1.07	10.00	0.90 (0.25)	10.00	-29.6	0.83 (0.28)	1.15

* Portfolio 1 (portfolio10) is the portfolio with the smallest (largest) market capitalization, highest (lowest) E/P and CF/P, lowest (highest) P/B, and largest (smallest) 6-month prior returns.
** All results for the cash flow-to-price portfolios are the period April 1972–December 1994.

in the portfolio. Note that the portfolio betas decline with increasing size though the differences are small.

The portfolio evidence from international equity markets is summarized in Figure 2 for the stock markets of Australia, New Zealand, Canada, Mexico, Japan, Korea, Singapore, Taiwan and eight European countries. The monthly size-premium is defined as the difference between the average monthly return on the portfolio of smallest stocks and the average monthly return on the portfolio of largest stocks.

In all countries, except Korea, the size premium is positive during the sample period. As expected, its magnitude varies significantly across markets. It is most pronounced in Australia and Mexico and least significant in Canada and the UK. As is the case for US data, differences in beta across size portfolios cannot explain differences in returns. (Note that the data in Figure 2 are likely to be sensitive to differences in sample dates and lengths).

There are, however, significant differences across the 15 markets in the spread between the size of the largest and smallest portfolios as indicated by the ratios of the average market capitalization of the largest portfolio to that of the smallest one, reported in Figure 2. There does not seem to be a relation between the magnitude of the size premium and the size ratio.

Earnings-related strategies have long been popular in the investment community. The most frequently used of these strategies, which calls for buying stocks that sell at low multiples of earnings, can be traced back at least to the pioneering work of Benjamin Graham and David Dodd.

In the second set of columns in Figure 1 we find that the portfolio returns confirm the E/P effect documented in previous studies. There is, however, less evidence of an

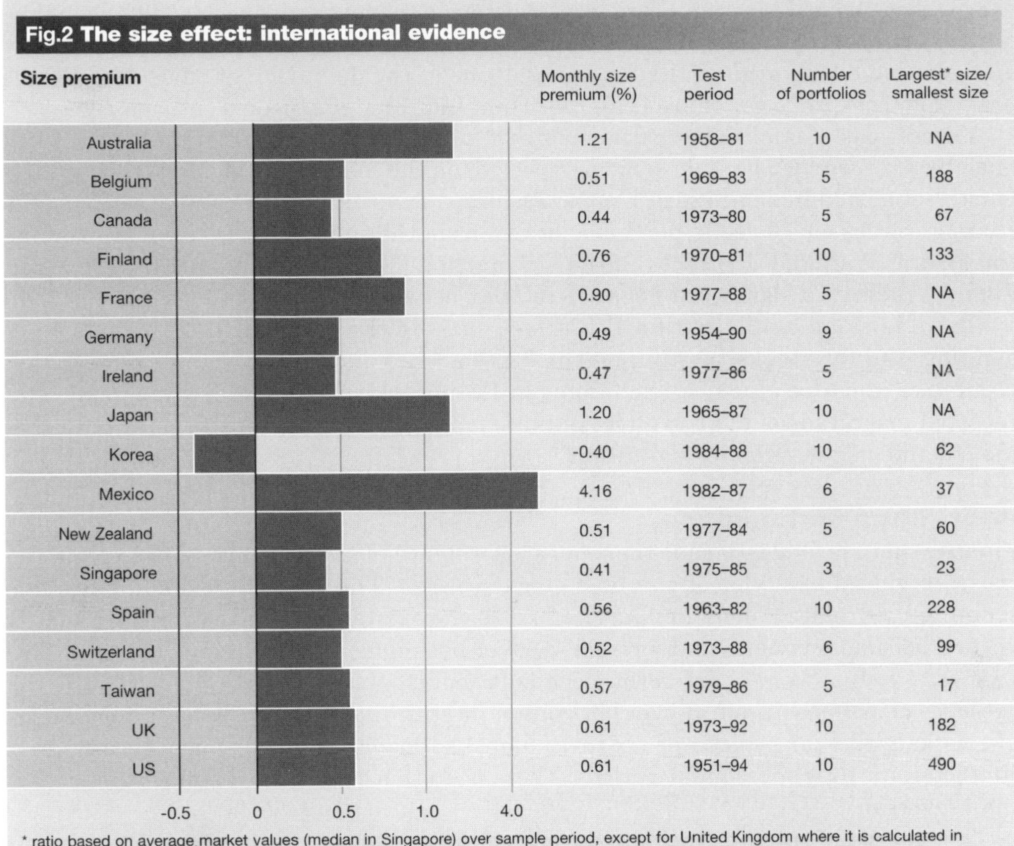

Fig.2 The size effect: international evidence

Size premium

Country	Monthly size premium (%)	Test period	Number of portfolios	Largest* size/ smallest size
Australia	1.21	1958–81	10	NA
Belgium	0.51	1969–83	5	188
Canada	0.44	1973–80	5	67
Finland	0.76	1970–81	10	133
France	0.90	1977–88	5	NA
Germany	0.49	1954–90	9	NA
Ireland	0.47	1977–86	5	NA
Japan	1.20	1965–87	10	NA
Korea	-0.40	1984–88	10	62
Mexico	4.16	1982–87	6	37
New Zealand	0.51	1977–84	5	60
Singapore	0.41	1975–85	3	23
Spain	0.56	1963–82	10	228
Switzerland	0.52	1973–88	6	99
Taiwan	0.57	1979–86	5	17
UK	0.61	1973–92	10	182
US	0.61	1951–94	10	490

* ratio based on average market values (median in Singapore) over sample period, except for United Kingdom where it is calculated in 1975 and Finland in 1970. NA = not available.

E/P effect in markets outside the US. This is partly due to a lack of computerized accounting databases available for academic research. The evidence is also more varied than that for the size effect. The evidence from six markets outside the US indicates that in the UK, Japan, Singapore and Taiwan there is a significant E/P effect similar to that found in the US market. There is no evidence, however, of a significant E/P effect in New Zealand and Korea. Given the small size and relatively short sample period for the cases of Taiwan, New Zealand and Korea, it is difficult to draw definitive conclusions from the evidence regarding these three markets.

One alternative to the E/P ratio is the ratio of cash flow to price (CF/P), where cash flow is defined as reported accounting earnings plus depreciation. Its appeal lies in the fact that accounting earnings may be a misleading and biased estimate of the economic earnings with which shareholders are concerned. There is evidence of a CF/P effect in the US and Japan. The US evidence is summarized in the third set of columns in Figure 1, which report average returns and other portfolio characteristics for 10 decile portfolios based on annual rankings of NYSE and Amex securities on the ratio of cash flow per share to price per share for the period 1972–94.

The ratio of price-per-share to book-value-per-share (P/B) has received considerable attention recently for its significant predictive power. As is the case for the other variables we have discussed, there is no theoretical model that says why P/B should be able to explain the cross-sectional behavior of stock returns. However, investment analysts have long argued that the magnitude of the deviation of current (market) price from book price per share is an important indicator of expected returns.

A succession of studies have documented a significant inverse relation between P/B and stock returns. To provide some perspective on the magnitude of the P/B effect, the fourth set of columns in Figure 1 reports average monthly returns and other portfolio characteristics for 10 decile portfolios drawn from the same data we used to examine the size, E/P and CF/P effects in the US market. The average monthly returns in Figure 1 indicate a significant negative relation between P/B and returns.

There is some evidence of a P/B effect outside the US. A P/B effect has been documented for stocks trading on the Tokyo Stock Exchange, the London Stock Exchange and also on stock exchanges in France, Germany and Switzerland. The reported magnitude of the P/B effect in these markets is smaller than that observed in the US and only marginally significant.

Prior return performance

Finally, there is evidence that the prior performance of stock returns can explain the cross-sectional behavior of common stock returns. The literature documents two seemingly unrelated phenomena. The first is the existence of return reversals (past 'losers' become 'winners' and vice versa) over both long-term horizons (three to five years) as well as very short-term periods (a month and shorter). The second is the presence of an opposite effect over horizons of intermediate lengths: when prior returns are measured over periods of six to 12 months, 'losers' and 'winners' retain their characteristic over subsequent periods. There is, in this case, return momentum rather than reversal.

The last set of columns in Figure 1 provides evidence of return momentum in our sample (we do not examine reversal strategies). We measure prior returns over the six months prior to the portfolio formation month, and then hold the portfolio over the next 12 months. Consistent with previous research, portfolios with the highest prior returns (the winners) earn, on average, higher subsequent returns. Also, portfolios with the lowest prior returns (the losers) earn, on average, the lowest subsequent returns.

One effect or many?

The difference in return between the extreme portfolios in Figure 1 can be loosely interpreted as risk premiums. Under the hypothesis that the variables we have dis-cussed are proxies for separate risk 'factors', then the premiums should be uncorrelated across variables. Figure 3 reports the pairwise correlations between the monthly premiums. Inconsistent with the hypothesis, all of the correlations are large (in absolute value) and are significantly different from zero.

Fig.3 Correlations between monthly premiums

April 1962 – December 1994

	Earnings/ Price	Cash flow/ Price	Price/ Book	Prior Return
Size	0.265	0.444	0.472	–0.017
Earnings/Price		0.727	0.590	–0.230
Cash Flow/Price			0.760	–0.212
Price/Book				–0.172

Interestingly, the prior return premiums are negatively correlated with the premiums associated with the other variables, suggesting that prior return captures a characteristic of stock returns that is quite different from the other variables. Otherwise, the significant correlations indicate a high degree of commonality among the effects. The significant correlation of the premiums partly reflects the fact that these effects are most pronounced in January. Specifically, the average premiums during January tend to be positive and are usually significantly larger than the average premiums measured during the rest of the year. Internationally, most of the evidence on January seasonality has been related to the size premiums. A significant January seasonal has been reported in Belgium, Finland, Taiwan and Japan. Countries in which the January size premium is insignificant include France, Germany and the UK. Studies in Japan report a significant January seasonal for E/P, P/B, and CF/P in Japan but no January seasonal for size.

The evidence above suggests a great deal of commonality among the various effects. The consensus from research is that the relation between market capitalization and average returns is robust. Variables such as E/P, P/B, and prior return seem to provide additional explanatory power for cross-sectional differences in average returns beyond the influence of size, although the evidence on E/P has recently been argued to be weak. Correspondingly, we compare the interaction between size, the P/B effect and the 6-month prior-return performance, using our sample of NYSE and Amex stocks to compute size-adjusted returns for portfolios created on the basis of both P/B and prior returns.

The 25 portfolios in Figure 4 are constructed as follows: first, for each stock in our sample we compute a size-adjusted return in which the influence of size is removed. Then we divide the sample into five groups of stocks based on P/B, and divide these groups further into five additional subgroups based on prior return. The stocks in each of the 25 groups are value-weighted to form a portfolio that is held for the following 12 months. Figure 4 reports average returns for the 25 portfolios separately for January and for the rest of the year.

First consider the P/B effect, which can be detected by reading down any column (within which

Fig.4 Size-adjusted monthly returns for 25 portfolios

NYSE and AMEX stocks ranked first by price-to-book ratio (P/B) and then by prior return

	Prior Return				
	Lowest	2	3	4	Highest
A. January					
Low P/B	3.71	3.13	2.13	2.15	1.34
	(1.32)	(0.69)	0.76	0.53	0.55
2	0.96	1.28	1.41	1.10	0.38
	(0.57)	(0.50)	(-0.53)	(0.54)	(0.52)
3	0.35	0.66	0.05	-0.16	-1.07
	(0.63)	(0.71)	(0.36)	(0.44)	(0.52)
4	0.92	-0.36	-0.03	-0.92	-0.83
	(0.53)	(0.56)	(0.40)	(0.47)	(0.74)
High P/B	-0.08	-0.06	-1.03	-1.02	-0.84
	(0.57)	(0.44)	(0.45)	(0.55)	(0.55)
B. February–December					
Low P/B	-0.16	0.10	0.10	0.33	0.36
	(0.20)	(0.15)	(0.15)	(0.13)	(0.16)
2	-0.21	-0.06	-0.11	0.04	0.39
	(0.15)	(0.15)	(0.13)	(0.12)	(0.15)
3	-0.16	-0.16	-0.09	0.10	0.27
	(0.15)	(0.13)	(0.11)	(0.11)	(0.14)
4	-0.36	-0.28	-0.08	0.03	0.42
	(0.14)	(-0.12)	(-0.10)	(0.12)	(0.15)
High P/B	-0.43	-0.09	0.21	0.40	0.10
	(0.15)	(0.12)	(0.11)	(0.13)	(0.17)

The size-adjusted monthly return for a security is defined as the return for that security minus the monthly portfolio return for the size docile in which the security is a member. P/B and prior return portfolios in the table are value-weighted combinations of these monthly size-adjusted returns. All portfolios are formed on March 31 of each year using year-end accounting values and March 31 market prices. Stocks with negative P/B values are excluded from the sample.

the influence of prior return is held constant). The relation between returns and P/B in January (Panel A) is significant in every column. In February-December, though, the relation between P/B and returns is flat. Thus, after controlling for size and momentum effects, the P/B effect is evident in the data primarily during the month of January.

The story is quite different for the momentum effect, which can be detected by reading across any row (within which the influence of P/B is held constant). After controlling for both size and P/B, the relation between prior and subsequent returns during February – December has the same significant positive relation as noted previously. In January, though, the 'momentum' effect has the appearance of a reversal effect in that subsequent returns increase as prior returns decrease. That is, stocks that have recently declined (and therefore more likely candidates for trading at the end of the year based on taxes or window dressing) have the largest returns in January, particularly if they are low price/book (or low price) stocks. Thus, in January, it appears that end-of-year trading patterns tend to offset the momentum effect. However, unlike the other effects, the momentum effect persists throughout the rest of the year.

Conclusion

Many have argued that a multidimensional model of risk and return is necessary to explain the cross section of stock returns. That is, beta by itself is insufficient to characterize the risks of common stocks. Prominent in this category are Eugene Fama and Kenneth French, who suggest a three-factor equity-pricing model to replace the CAPM. Their three-factor model adds two empirically-determined explanatory factors: size (market capitalization) and financial distress (B/M). Others propose an additional factor, prior return performance.

Our findings suggest that such conclusions may be premature. Aside from the absence of a theory that says why such variables have a place in the risk-return paradigm, the evidence strongly indicates that the statistical relation between returns and variables like size and B/M derives primarily from the month of January. It is difficult to tell an asset-pricing story where risk manifests itself only during one month. An exception is momentum, where the influence on returns is spread more evenly throughout the year. This latter finding is difficult to reconcile with current asset pricing models and/or an informationally efficient market.

These points notwithstanding, one of the most significant contributions of this entire line of research is that is has sharpened our focus on potential alternative sources of risk. On the other hand, there are good reasons that make it difficult to argue that the evidence constitutes proof that the CAPM is 'wrong.' For example, no one has yet conclusively shown that variables like size and P/B are not simply proxies for measurement error in betas. Are we certain that variation in ratios of P/B is not picking up variation in leverage that is not reflected in betas that are typically estimated with 60 months of prior – and arguably stale – prices? The book is not closed; more research is necessary to resolve these issues.

There is also the question of believability: is the evidence as robust as the sheer quantity of results would lead us to believe? First, there is the issue of data snooping – many of the papers we have cited were predicated on previous research that documented the same findings with the same data. Degrees of freedom are lost at each turn and several authors have warned about adjusting tests of significance for these.

Also, the existence of these patterns in our experiments does not necessarily imply that they exist in the returns of implementable portfolios – returns net of transactions costs – for example market illiquidity and transactions costs may render a small stock strategy infeasible.

Finally, the persistence of these effects for nearly 100 years does not guarantee their persistence in the future. How many years of data are necessary to construct powerful tests? Research over the next 100 years will, we hope, settle many of these issues.

Summary

The article 'An APT alternative to assessing risk' highlighted one alternative to the Capital Asset Pricing Model. But as Gabriel Hawawini and Donald Keim explain in this article there are many cross-sectional patterns in stock returns – variables such as company size, the ratio of book-to-market value and a company's prior return performance – that do not support the CAPM. The authors argue that the multidimensional model lacks a convincing theoretical underpinning and that the evidence which indicates a statistical relationship between certain variables and stock returns derives primarily – there is one important exception – from the month of January. It is difficult on this basis to argue that the CAPM is 'wrong' but at least the recent line of research has sharpened our focus on potential alternative sources of risk.

Why it's worth being in control

by Luigi Zingales

Hardly a day passes in the UK and the US without the news that a company is acquired for a hefty premium. The fact that in continental Europe such news is comparatively rare simply reflects a different structure of corporate ownership rather than a lack of interest in corporate control. In continental Europe, the voting majority of most companies is concentrated in a few hands, thanks to a complicated web of cross-shareholdings and voting trusts. As a result, control is generally transferred in classy negotiations at local country clubs rather than in noisy takeover battles under the media's spotlight. These differences in style notwithstanding, there is one common element throughout the world: investors care about control, which suggests it is valuable. But why is control valuable?

The value of control

This question, though perhaps a little naive, is not without merit. By their very nature, all common shares have equal rights. Thus a majority shareholder is not entitled to receive a penny more per share than all other shareholders. So why should any investor pay a premium to acquire control if he or she will receive no extra benefits from doing so?

The only possible answer is that, although all shares are created equal, some – like the pigs in George Orwell's *Animal Farm* – are more equal than others. What makes controlling shareholders more equal is that they have the right to shape corporate policy. The crucial question, then, becomes how this right translates into higher benefits for the controlling party that are not shared by other shareholders (the so-called private benefits of control). If private benefits of control exist, then it is easy to explain why control is valuable. But what exactly are these private benefits?

Private benefits of control

The academic literature often identifies private benefits of control as the 'psychic' value some shareholders attribute simply to being in control. For example, the Michelins probably would value being in control of the French tyre company founded by their ancestors even if they were not to receive a penny from it. Although this is certainly a factor in some cases, its practical importance is likely to be trivial. Can we really justify premia of multimillions of dollars with the pure pleasure of command?

A second, only slightly more convincing, explanation identifies private benefits of control in the perquisites enjoyed by top executives (and not by their fellow shareholders who pay the tab). There is no lack of examples, as masterfully illustrated in the book *Barbarians at the Gate*. Many executives enjoy golfing and partying with world celebrities at their company's expense and use corporate jets to fly friends and family around the country. Yet however outrageous some of these perquisites are, we have to admit that, if this is what private benefits are all about, we do not need to worry too much about the value of control.

In the context of companies worth billions of pounds or dollars, the value of these perquisites is simply too small to matter. Only in the presence of more significant sources of private benefits should the value of control play a prominent role in the theory and practice of finance. The use of a company's money to pay for perquisites may be the most visible but is not the most important way in which corporate resources can be used to the sole (or main) advantage of the controlling party. A few examples will help illustrate how widespread these opportunities are.

Some examples

Consider, for example, the value of the information a corporate executive acquires thanks to his or her role in the company. Some of this information pertains directly to the company's business while some reflects potential opportunities in other more or less related areas. It is fairly easy for a controlling shareholder to choose to exploit these opportunities through another company he or she owns or is associated with, with no advantage for the remaining shareholders. The net present value of these opportunities represents a private benefit of control.

Another source of private benefits is the possibility of internalizing, through other companies controlled by the same party, some of the externalities generated by corporate decisions. Consider, for example, a shareholder who controls 51 per cent of two companies, say A and B, operating in the same market. Suppose there is excess capacity in this market and, thus, some plants need to be closed. In this situation the closure of any plant will reduce over-capacity and so increase the value of all the other plants. If the controlling shareholder closes some plants in company B, he or she will experience an increase in value not only of the B shares but also of the A shares. This increase in A shares is a benefit enjoyed by the controlling party and not by B's minority shareholders (unless they own the same quantity of A's shares) and, thus, represents a private benefit of control. Note that in both previous examples the controlling shareholder receives a benefit denied to the remaining shareholders, even if he or she does not formally receive any larger payment from the company.

A third source of private benefits is associated with the controlling party's ability to fix transfer prices between a company and its customers and suppliers. A company controlled by its employees, for example, can pay higher wages and benefits to its workforce. Similarly, a bank controlled by one of its borrowers can make larger and cheaper loans to its parent company.

The ability to manipulate transfer prices can be used even in the absence of business dealings between the controlling company and its subsidiary. Imagine that company A owns 50 per cent of company B and 100 per cent of company C. In that case A would find it profitable to transfer B's assets to C at a below market price. For any pound that B's assets are underestimated, company A loses 50 pence through its B holdings but gains one pound through its C holdings. A net gain of 50 pence.

Is this legal?

I am sure the reader is now wondering whether most (if not all) of the sources of private benefits that I have described are *de facto* illegal and, as such, more in the realm of interest of criminal investigators than financial economists. In fact, there is no doubt that in their most extreme forms these strategies *are* illegal and extremely rare. Nevertheless, there are several reasons why we should expect more moderate versions of these strategies to be more pervasive.

First, in some countries some of these strategies are not illegal. In France, for example, corporate executives do not have a fiduciary obligation to exploit all corporate opportunities in the corporation's interest. As a result, a controlling party can exploit information acquired *qua* corporate executive to his or her own personal advantage without breaking the law.

Second, even when a law exists it might be impossible to enforce. Educated economists can legitimately disagree on what is the 'fair' transfer price of a certain asset or product. As a result, small deviations from the 'fair' transfer price might be difficult or impossible to prove in court. If these small deviations are applied to a large volume trade, however, they can easily generate sizeable private benefits.

Finally, even if these distortions can be proven in court, it is possible that nobody has the incentive to do so. For example, it might be prohibitively expensive for small shareholders to sue the management (especially in countries where contingent fees for lawyers are prohibited).

Unfortunately, it is very difficult to measure the private benefits directly. As argued above, a controlling party would find it possible to subtract corporate resources to his or her benefit only when it is difficult or impossible to prove that this is the case. In other words, if private benefits of control were easily quantifiable, then those benefits would not be private (accruing only to the control group) any longer because outside shareholders would claim them in court. Nevertheless, there are two indirect methods to try to assess empirically the magnitude of these private benefits of control.

Estimates of value of control

The first method, followed by Barclay and Holderness (1989), is simple. Whenever a control block changes hands, they measure the difference between the price per share paid by the acquirer and the price quoted in the market the day after the sale's announcement. The market price represents an unbiased estimate of the value of a share for minority shareholders. Any amount paid in excess of it by the acquirer of the control block represents a minimum estimate of the buyer's willingness to pay for the private benefits of control he or she expects to enjoy. Using a sample of control block transfers in the US, they found that the value of control is about four per cent of the total market value of a company. This method also makes clear why the takeover premium cannot be used by itself as a measure of the private benefits of control. When a takeover is announced the market price incorporates two pieces of information:

- that the company is likely to be run by a different management team
- that somebody is willing to pay a premium for control.

The takeover premium is a combination of these two elements and, in general, it is impossible to separate them. Only when there are two classes of common stock with differential voting rights can we try to disentangle these two components.

This leads to the second method of estimating the value of private benefits of control. By using the price difference between two classes of stock, with similar or identical dividend rights, but different voting rights, one can easily obtain an estimate of the value of a vote. If control is valuable, then corporate votes, which allocate control, should be valuable as well. How valuable?

It depends on how decisive some votes are in allocating control and how valuable control is. If one can find a reasonable proxy for the strategic value of votes in winning control – for example in forming a winning coalition block – then one can infer the value of control from the relationship between the market price of the votes and their strategic role. This is what I do in two articles (*see* Further Reading). I infer the value of control from the relationship between the value of corporate votes and a synthetic measure of the distribution of voting power called the Shapley value.

Country differences

Interestingly, when I applied this method to a sample of US companies I obtained the same value as Barclay and Holderness (four per cent). By contrast, when I applied it to a sample of Italian companies I estimated the value of control at 30 per cent of the market value of equity. In spite of the magnitude of this estimate, all the evidence I collected indicates that, if anything, it underestimates the true value of control in Italy. But why should the value of control be so much higher in Italy than in the US? And what should we expect it to be in other countries?

Since the value of control is simply the present value of the private benefits enjoyed by the controlling party, the answer is easy. The magnitude of the private benefits of control, and thus the value of control, depends on the degree of protection offered to minority investors in each country. Without proper disclosure, large investors can more easily hide their abuses and hence find it easier to take advantage of their controlling position. Similarly, lax law enforcement makes it more difficult to detect and punish these abuses, making them more attractive. That small investors are better protected in the US than in Continental Europe is not only consistent with casual empiricism, but has been documented in a systematic way by La Porta and others (1996).

Unfortunately, there is no systematic study of the value of control across countries. However, one can get a rough estimate by looking at the average premium paid to buy voting rather than non-voting stock in different countries. While this measure does not properly control for cross-country differences in the strategic value of votes, it is the only consistent measure available for a (small) cross-section of countries.

Figure 1 presents the level of the average voting premium for the countries for which this measure is available. This premium varies dramatically: in most countries it is between 10–20 per cent, with Israel and Italy being the main exceptions. While the number of observations is clearly too small to undertake any statistical study, it is interesting to see how this measure varies with characteristics within each country that are likely to influence the ability to extract private benefits of control. For example, better disclosure rules should reduce the ability to use some of the strategies described above. Consistent with this hypothesis, Figure 2 shows that the voting premium is inversely related to an index of the quality of accounting standards in each country.

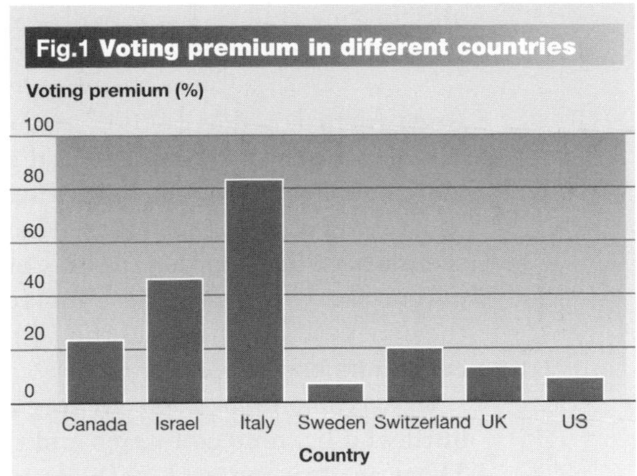

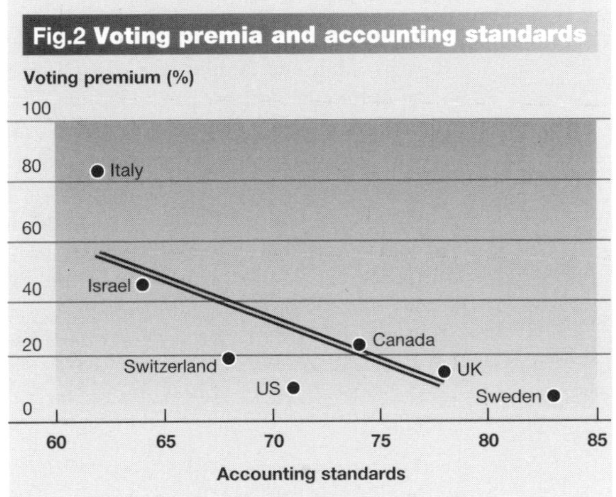

These results are suggestive but, of course, far from conclusive. Countries differ along many dimensions and with few observations it is difficult to identify which effect is driving the results. There is, however, another piece of evidence within the US that agrees with these findings. Even in the US, privately held companies carry large control premia (minority discounts). Interestingly, the reason appraisers adduce for this premium is the lack of protection of minority shareholders in privately held business. So it is not the good nature of Americans that refrains them from abusing their control position, but rather the rigid oversight by the Securities and Exchange Commission. It is not unusual, for example, for the SEC to investigate large personal expenses that a controlling shareholder bills to his or her company.

Why should we care?

Interestingly, once we admit the existence of sizeable private benefits of control, a lot of the standard finance results break down. For example, the value of a company cannot any longer be estimated simply by multiplying the market price of a share times the number of shares. If one shareholder controls a majority of votes, the market price will simply reflect the value of minority shares and will grossly underestimate the company's value. By contrast, when two large shareholders are fighting to reach a majority, the market price of a stock will be mainly influenced by the control value and will over-estimate the total value of a company.

More importantly, the efficient working of the financial market may be jeopardized. Large controlling shareholders will be more interested in maximizing the value of their private benefits than the total market value of their company. Consequently, investors, anticipating this behavior, will shy away from buying the stocks. This is an important lesson for developing countries.

Summary

All shares are in theory created equal – but what makes controlling shareholders more equal than others? Luigi Zingales looks at the private benefits of being the main controlling party in a company. Perks and the pure pleasure of command may provide the most visible answer in some cases – but as the author points out there are other potential advantages. These include using information gained from one company for the benefit of another, and the ability to fix transfer prices between a company and its customers and suppliers.

In extreme form these strategies are usually illegal but they are not necessarily outlawed in some countries and they may be pervasive in more moderate versions. There are two indirect methods of empirically assessing the value of private control benefits – measuring the takeover premium and using the price difference between two classes of stock with different voting rights.

Suggested further reading

Barclay, M.J. and Holderness, C.G., (1989), 'Private benefits of control of public corporations', *Journal of Financial Economics* 25, 371–95.

Burrough, B. and Helyar, J., (1991), *Barbarians at the gate*, Harper Collins, New York.

La Porta, R., Lopez de Silanes Shleifer, F., and Vishny, R., (1996), 'Law and finance', NBER Working paper 5661.

La Porta, R., Lopez de Silanes Shleifer, F., and Vishny, R., (1997), 'Legal determinanats of external finance', NBER Working paper 5879.

Zingales, L., (1994), 'The value of the voting right: a study of the Milan Stock Exchange', *Review of Financial Studies* 7, 125–148.

Zingales, L., (1995), 'What determines the value of corporate votes?', *Quarterly Journal of Economics,* 1047–1073.

2

Corporate finance

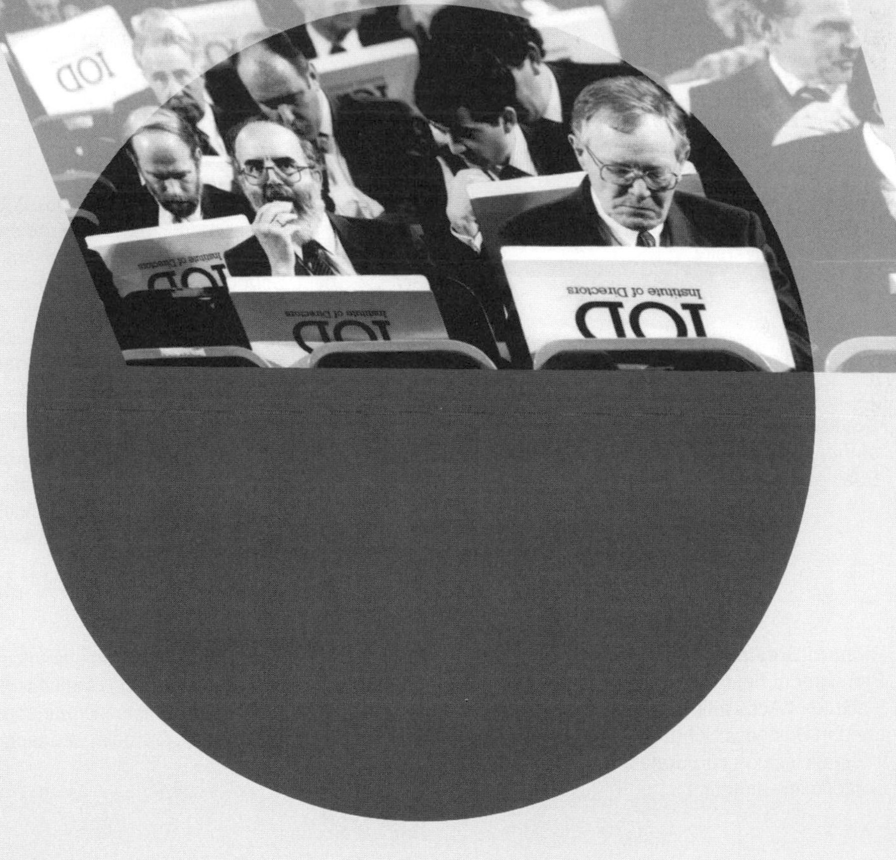

Contributors

Raghuram Rajan is Professor of Finance at the University of Chicago Graduate School of Business. His research interests include corporate finance and financial intermediation and regulation.

Luigi Zingales is Associate Professor of Finance at the University of Chicago Graduate School of Business. His research interests include capital structure and corporate control.

Philip G. Berger is an Assistant Professor of Accounting at the Wharton School of the University of Pennsylvania.

Eli Ofek is Assistant Professor of Finance at the Stern School of Business, New York University.

David Yermack is Assistant Professor of Finance at the Stern School of Business, New York University.

Richard Brealey is Tokai Bank Professor of Finance and Director of the Institute of Accounting and Finance at London Business School. His research interests include corporate finance and portfolio investment.

Kjell Nyborg is Associate Professor of Finance at the London Business School. His research interests include corporate finance and information economics.

Steven N. Kaplan is Professor of Finance at University of Chicago Graduate School of Business. His research interests include mergers and acquisitions, corporate governance and private equity.

Harold Rose is Emeritus Esmée Fairbairn Professor of Finance at London Business School. He was previously first director of LBS' Institute of Finance and was Group Economic Adviser at Barclays Bank.

Katherine Schipper is Eli B. and Harriet B. Williams Professor of Accounting at the University of Chicago Graduate School of Business. Her research interests include corporate governance, leveraged buyouts and acquisitions, and the effect of regulation on shareholder wealth.

Linda Vincent is Assistant Professor of Accounting at the University of Chicago Graduate School of Business. Her research interests include financial accounting and capital markets.

Michel Habib is Assistant Professor of Finance at London Business School. His research interests include corporate finance and financial intermediation.

Contents

Introduction

Corporate finance is concerned with the way companies handle their own financial affairs and the ways that the overall financial system, including the economy and government actions, affects companies.

As such, it covers such diverse areas as tax, debt, equities, demergers, acquisitions and ways of financing corporate activities. This module examines all of these issues in seven related articles.

Debt, folklore and financial structure

by Raghuram Rajan and Luigi Zingales

Germany and Japan are countries where, lore has it, companies enjoy much closer ties to banks than in countries such as the UK and US where relationships are more at arm's length. As a result, it is argued, Japanese and German companies can borrow more and are shielded from the tyrannical short-termism of the market. Gurus such as Michael Porter have suggested that organizations that do not have these relationships are at a competitive disadvantage that threatens the long-term growth of their economies. Are they? As companies increasingly compete in a global marketplace, questions such as these become important, and political efforts 'to do something' more urgent. What can academic research tell us? We start by describing why the ability to borrow more might be a source of advantage, go on to investigate whether enterprises in these countries do borrow more and end with evidence on whether this is a source of advantage.

The advantage of debt

Franco Modigliani of the Massachusetts Institute of Technology (MIT) and Merton Miller of the University of Chicago, in a Nobel Prize-winning work in the late 1950s, showed that if a company's investment policy is taken as given, then in a perfect world – a world with no taxes (of course!), perfect and credible disclosure of all information, and no transactions costs associated with raising money or going bankrupt – the extent of debt in a company's capital structure does not affect firm value.

Before the muttering about ivory tower economists gets too loud, let us explain why their work makes sense. When a company issues 'cheap' debt, say at six per cent, instead of 'costly' equity, say at 17 per cent, the cost of financing is not simply the coupon rate the company pays on the new debt. It is also the additional rate of return existing equity investors demand because their equity is now riskier. When you factor this additional cost in, the cost of financing is the same as if you issued 'costly' equity – the weighted average cost of capital, which is between the cost of debt and the cost of equity.

There are, however, warts in the real world that may make debt financing advantageous – though to a much lesser extent than suggested by the debt is 'cheap', equity is 'costly' argument. Modigliani and Miller's work helps us focus on what these are. First, changing capital structure (the mix of debt and equity) could affect the taxes a company and its claim holders pay and hence its value. Second, it will alter the probability of incurring the transactions costs of bankruptcy, or of raising equity. And third, it can affect investment policy.

Taxes

Think of the future cash flows from the investments the company has made as a pie. The taxes the organization pays on its income and the taxes that claim holders pay on their personal dividend and interest income are the slice of the pie that belongs to the government. Firm value is the rest.

The US government, in its wisdom, has declared that certain kinds of claims issued by the business are tax advantaged. For example, debt is tax advantaged at the corporate level in the US because interest is paid from before-tax earnings while dividends are paid from after-tax earnings. Even after accounting for the taxes that investors pay on their personal income, debt is typically tax advantaged with respect to equity in the G7 countries (with the possible exception of Germany). The ability to borrow more reduces the slice the government gets and acts, effectively, as a tax break. To the extent that tax breaks or subsidies work, this could be a source of competitive advantage.

Transactions costs

As a company loads up on debt, the tax benefits of additional debt decrease – since there is less and less additional income to shield from the government – while the costs increase. The costs are generally thought of as the costs of bankruptcy. Note that the event of bankruptcy itself does not affect firm value. In an ideal world, if a company cannot pay its debts the equity holders simply give up their claims and transfer the keys of the premises to the debt holders. This should not affect the value of the company's assets, and consequently, the sum of its debt and equity.

In practice, however, bankruptcy can hurt asset values. Lawyers take their cut; more importantly, customers stay away because of concerns that the enterprise might skimp on the quality of its products; assets are sold at fire-sale prices; and talented employees leave for more secure organizations. So, too much debt is bad for companies that rely on intangible or specialized assets such as customer confidence, ideas or people.

In addition, the ability to borrow is useful because there are transactions costs of raising equity at short notice. Since equity is the residual claim, it is much more sensitive to firm value than is debt. As a result, when organizations want to raise equity, the market is often not ready for it. Investors typically view equity issuances as bad news – regarding the announcement of an issue as a signal that the enterprise is not confident of servicing additional debt or that it intends to share impending losses with new investors.

Debt, being a fixed claim, is much less sensitive to impending bad news about company value and is thus much easier to issue without sending an adverse signal. This is another reason why companies do not borrow as much as warranted by the tax advantage of debt: they are preserving 'slack' – the ability to borrow so as to take advantage of unexpected investment opportunities or respond to unexpected competitive threats.

Investment policy

Modigliani and Miller take the investment policy of the company as given. Too much debt, can however, distort investments and reduce firm value. One need look no further than the savings and loan crisis in the US or Maxwell's travails in the UK to understand that when an organization is on the verge of defaulting, owners or managers may want to gamble through unprofitable but risky investments.

Managers have nothing to lose because if they do nothing they get fired anyway. Another possible distortion is that managers may simply stop investing when faced with too much debt since the revenues from investment will largely go to pay off the debt while the costs of raising the funding are borne by all claimants, especially equity. Too little debt can also be bad. In mature industries, managers who are not disciplined by the need to service debt can fritter away excess cash on unprofitable investments. The purpose of many of the leveraged buyouts in the US in the 1980s was to squeeze cash out of fat, complacent, mature companies.

Why the folklore?

Lore has it that enterprises in 'bank-oriented' economies, such as Germany and Japan, enjoy close ties with financial institutions. These institutions stand behind the companies when they are close to distress and they also exercise some control over investment policy to make sure it does not go awry.

As a result, the costs associated with debt – of bankruptcy and distorted investment – fall away while the benefits – the tax advantage and the lower sensitivity to firm value – remain. Companies in these countries can allegedly borrow more, and add more value by doing so, thus enjoying a competitive advantage over organizations in more market-oriented countries such as the UK and the US. Let us now look at the data and see how much of this lore is true.

What is debt in practice?

We face an immediate problem. All debt is not created the same. Short-term debt is much more onerous to service than long-term debt since both interest and principal have to be repaid in the short run (witness how the short-term Teso-bonos precipitated the Mexican 'Tequila' crisis in 1994). Secured lenders have much less incentive to bail out a business than unsecured lenders. Creditor rights are not the same in all countries, and this makes comparisons between countries extremely difficult.

Consider the balance sheet of a representative large German enterprise, Deutschland AG in 1991, and compare it with the balance sheet of a representative US company, USA Inc. (*see* Figure 1). If 'other liabilities' are forms of debt and leverage is the ratio of total book liabilities to total assets, then Deutschland appears much more highly leveraged than its US counterpart (73 per cent against 58 per cent). But if we measure leverage as the ratio of debt to total capital (capital is the sum of debt plus equity), the two companies are virtually at the same level (38 per cent versus 37 per cent). Finally, if the measure is coverage (the ratio of operating profits divided by interest expenses), then Deutschland appears much less leveraged than USA (6.8 versus 4.0).

Fig.1 US and German balance sheets compared (1991)

	USA INC	Deutschland AG
ASSETS		
Cash and short-term investment	11.2	8.8
Account receivable/debtors	17.8	26.9
Inventories	16.1	23.6
Current assets–other	2.9	0.1
Current assets–total	48.0	59.4
Fixed assets (tangible)	36.3	32.7
Investment and advances	4.5	4.8
Intangible assets	7.6	2.4
Assets–other	5.8	0.7
Assets–total	**100.0**	**100.0**
LIABILITIES		
Debt in current liabilities	7.4	9.9
Accounts payable/creditors	15.0	11.5
Current liabilities–other	11.0	8.7
Current liabilities–total	33.4	30.0
Deferred taxes	3.2	0.8
Long term debt	23.3	9.8
Minority interest	0.6	1.6
Reserves–untaxed	0.0	1.7
Liabilities–other	5.8	28.7
Liabilities–total	66.1	72.0
Shareholders equity	**34.1**	**28.0**
Total liabilities and shareholders equity	**100.0**	**100.0**

Source: Global Vantage Data Base, *What do we know about capital structure?* Rajan and Zingales.

So are German companies more or less leveraged than US organizations? The answer depends on why we are asking the question. If we want to know if the company is likely to go bankrupt at high cost, we should look at a modified version of coverage, probably adding short-term debt in the denominator and cash and liquid peripheral assets in the numerator. The number should be evaluated taking the country's bankruptcy laws and the out-of-court-settlement possibilities into account. This is also the right measure if we want to ask whether debt puts sufficient constraints on management's ability to over-invest. But if we want to know, as customers, whether we should have long-term confidence in a business, we should probably look at debt to capital.

And if we want to know a company's capacity to take advantage of sudden opportunities, we should look at its untapped lines of credit, the capital markets in which it has established a borrowing history, the relationships it has with its banks and suppliers, and even the debt capacity of the assets created by the opportunity. Here, the enterprise's potential leverage rather than its current leverage is of interest.

We also have to make accounting adjustments so as to compare organizations across countries. For example, both funded and unfunded pension liabilities are on the balance sheet in Germany, unlike in the US where only the latter are. Also, German accounting emphasizes conservatism rather than the Anglo-American ideal of presenting a 'true and fair' picture. So earnings are smoothed (the tax benefits of doing this are also not inconsiderable) and secret reserves are maintained. This may explain why 'other liabilities' for Deutschland account for a massive 29 per cent of liabilities and why Daimler Benz restated earnings by about $2bn when seeking a listing on the New York Stock Exchange.

Capital structure in the G7

Let us examine one indicator of leverage. Figure 2 compares debt to capital ratios obtained directly from the balance sheets of the big publicly traded companies in the G7 countries and the 'adjusted' debt to capital ratios, obtained after eliminating the significant differences in accounting practices. Note that correcting for accounting substantially changes leverage rankings. However, after correcting for accounting difference the ranking between countries is substantially unchanged no matter what measure of leverage we use and whether we measure assets at book or market value.

The rankings are surprising if we consider the remarkable institutional differences across these countries. Japanese businesses are no more highly leveraged than companies in the US despite the oft-heard complaint that Japanese organizations enjoy access to low-cost debt. In fact, studies of Japanese and US businesses show they tend to have similar costs of capital in the long run despite large temporary differences. One can speculate as to why institutional differences between countries as varied as those in the US and Japan do not seem to matter much for large companies. Perhaps they can finance cross-border in the most advantageous country. Alternatively, institutions may develop in a country to equalize advantages.

Why the differences?

One can, however, make too much of similarities. Contrary to the received wisdom, German companies are significantly less leveraged than those from all the other G7 countries, with the exception of the UK. Why are German and UK companies so different from the rest?

Fig.2 Debt to capital in 1991 (book values)

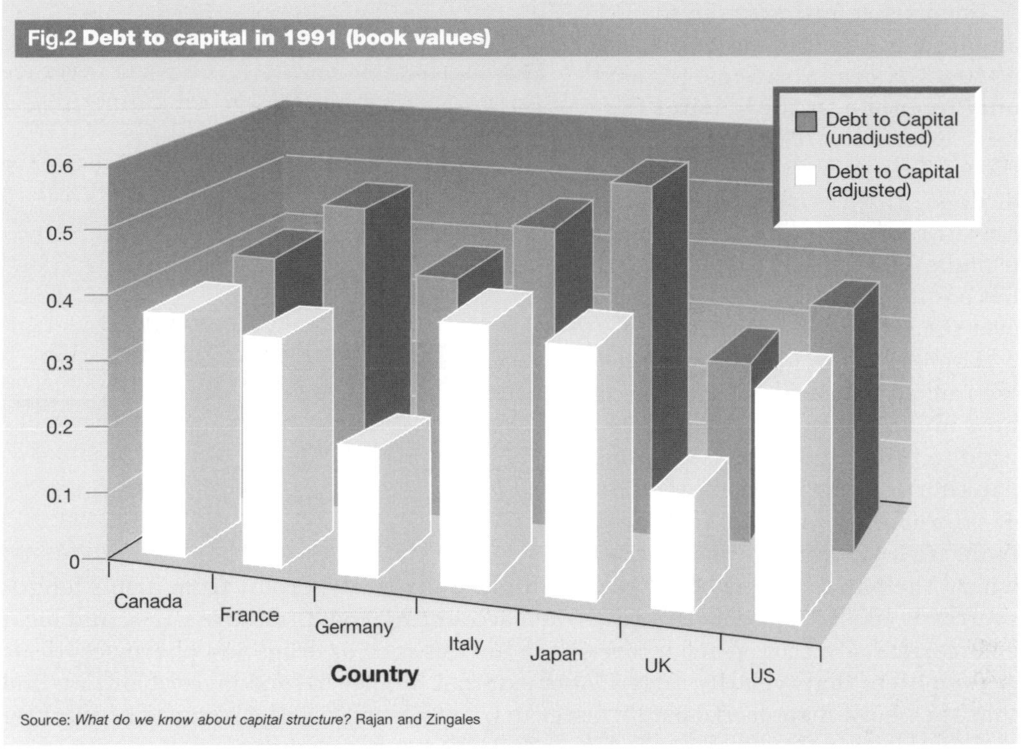

Source: *What do we know about capital structure?* Rajan and Zingales

Fig.3 Creditor rights in G7 countries

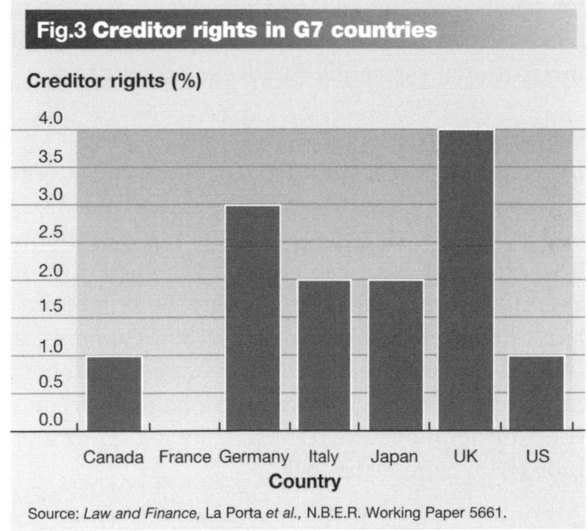

Source: *Law and Finance*, La Porta *et al.*, N.B.E.R. Working Paper 5661.

Tax codes in these countries do not offer debt a considerable advantage (if at all), so maybe enterprises do not want to gear up. More telling, perhaps, is Figure 3. This shows that the countries with the strongest creditor rights (the highest number on a scale of 0 to 4) are also the countries where large companies borrow the least. Is this a coincidence? Or do the managements of large enterprises prefer not to borrow when the law gives creditors such strong rights? Is this because they are fearful for their own skins or because the costs of bankruptcy are really high when creditors can easily liquidate businesses? More evidence is needed before we can draw strong conclusions. However, this raises an immediate question. Are UK companies worse off because they borrow less? The answer is probably no. The companies that one might expect to be worst hit by low borrowing are those dependent on external finance to fund investment. But large enterprises in the UK do not use disproportionately less external finance.

Comparing businesses in the US, Japan, UK and Canada during the 1980s, UK organizations are next only to Japan in the amount they raise externally (*see* Figure 4). Even though they do not issue a great deal of debt, they raise almost equal amounts from equity issuances (compared with, say, the US where net equity issuances were negative over the 1980s).

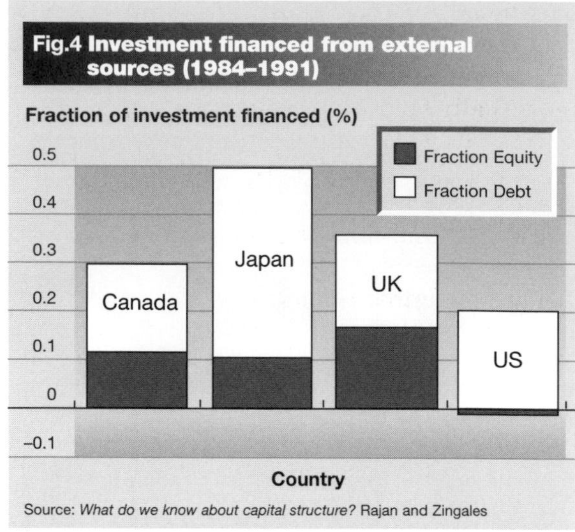

Fig.4 Investment financed from external sources (1984–1991)

Source: *What do we know about capital structure?* Rajan and Zingales

There is more telling evidence. We ranked industries on the basis of how much external finance they used to fund investment. If strong banking systems facilitate the flow of finance, we should see these industries grow faster in countries where the bank credit to GDP ratio is high. Conversely, credit from arm's length sources is likely to flow more easily when accounting and disclosure rules, and legal enforcement, are good. When it comes to industries such as drugs and pharmaceuticals or computers that typically raise a lot of external finance to fund investment, we find that they grow disproportionately faster in countries with well-developed accounting and disclosure rules (such as the UK or the US) compared with countries with more institution-based credit markets such as Japan and Germany. These results hold even for the G7 countries. In other words, well-regulated markets seem to be, at the very least, adequate substitutes for close relationships between companies and financial institutions, especially in developed countries.

Conclusion

First, as Modigliani and Miller's work suggests, it is more important for a large enterprise to worry about making the right investment than about which claim to issue and where to issue it. It is hard to make money on the Rockefeller Center, no matter how cheap it is to raise equity in Japan, if one pays $2bn more than it is sold for. Second, many of the popular myths do not stand up to scrutiny. Large businesses in bank-oriented economies do not borrow more, nor do industries dependent on external finance grow faster in these economies. In conclusion, while we believe that a poorly functioning financial system can be a source of competitive disadvantage, the nature of the financial system, whether based on banks or markets, seems to matter little for industrial competitiveness.

Summary

It is doubtless more important for a company to worry about making the right investment than about exactly how to finance it, as earlier owners of New York's Rockefeller Center can vouchsafe. But the question of finding the right mix of debt and equity has long been a preoccupation, especially since the Nobel Prize-winning work of Modigliani and Miller in the late 1950s. Raghuram Rajan and Luigi Zingales examine the argument that enterprises in 'bank oriented' economies such as Germany

and Japan are at a competitive advantage by being able to borrow more. They suggest that there are inherent, often tax driven, advantages of using debt but their evidence challenges the assumption that businesses in the so-called bank oriented economies do actually borrow more, or that industries that are dependent on external finance there grow more quickly.

A poorly functioning financial system can certainly be a source of competitive disadvantage but 'the nature of the financial system – whether based on banks or markets – seems to matter little for industrial competitiveness.'

Suggested further reading

Brealey R. and Myers S., *Principles of Corporate Finance,* 5th edn., McGraw Hill.

Jensen, M., (1994), 'The Modern Industrial Revolution, Exit, and the Failure of Internal Control Systems', Continental Bank *Journal of Applied Corporate Finance* 6 (4) 4–23.

Kester, W.C. and Luehrman, T., 'What Makes You Think US Capital is so Expensive?', *Journal of Applied Corporate Finance,* Summer 1992.

La Porta, R., Lopez-de-Silanes, F., Shleifer, A. and Vishny, R., (1996), 'Law and Finance', NBER working paper 5661.

Mayer, C., (1990) 'Financial Systems, Corporate Finance, and Economic Development' in R. Glenn Hubbard, ed: *Asymmetric Information, Corporate Finance and Investment,* University of Chicago Press, Chicago.

Miller, M.H, (1977), 'Debt and Taxes', *Journal of finance* 32, 261–275.

Myers, S.C., (1984), 'The Capital Structure Puzzle', *Journal of Finance* 39, 575–592.

Nobes, C. and Parker, R., (1991), *Comparative International Accounting,* Prentice Hall, New York.

Porter, M., (1992), 'Capital, Choices: Changing the Way America Invests in Industry', *Journal of Applied Corporate Finance.*

Rajan, R. and Zingales, L., (1995), 'What Do We Know about Capital Structure? Some Evidence from International Data', *Journal of Finance* 50, 1421–1460.

Rajan, R. and Zingales, L., (1996), 'Financial Dependence and Growth', NBER Working Paper 5788b.

Why CEOs use insufficient debt

by Philip Berger, Eli Ofek and David Yermack

Much of the theoretical research on capital structure in large businesses maintains that managers generally do not adopt capital structures with a value-maximizing level of debt. Anecdotal evidence supports the view that some managers entrench themselves against pressures from internal and external corporate governance mechanisms, which allow them to choose debt levels that benefit themselves more than the company's shareholders. We examined whether the degree of managerial entrenchment affects capital structure decisions and concluded that it does.

Entrenchment is the extent to which managers are not subject to any significant degree of discipline from corporate control mechanisms. These include monitoring by the board, the threat of dismissal or takeover, and stock or compensation-based performance incentives. Entrenched managers by definition have discretion over their companies' level of debt.

The arguments that managers prefer less leverage than is optimal rely on managers' desire to reduce risk to protect their own under-diversified financial and human capital. In other words, corporate risk is of greater concern to managers than to well-diversified shareholders. This is because managers generally have very large portions of both their financial wealth and their career reputations tied to their company's performance. Managers may also prefer a lower level of leverage because of their dislike of the performance pressures associated with having to make large, fixed-interest payments and repayments of principal.

A second set of theories suggests that entrenchment may result in managers increasing leverage beyond the optimal point in order to inflate the voting power of their equity stakes and reduce the possibility of takeover attempts.

A final set of theories contends that entrenched managers sometimes adopt excess leverage as a transitory device to signal a commitment to sell assets or otherwise restructure, thereby pre-empting takeover attempts by outsiders who might have different plans for increasing company value.

Our analysis of 434 US companies between 1984 and 1991 had two goals. First, we explored whether there are significant associations between patterns of corporate leverage and variables associated with managerial entrenchment. Second, we evaluated how closely our findings support each of the above three theories about how entrenchment might affect managers' leverage choices. We found significantly lower leverage in companies where the chief executive officer (CEO) has several characteristics of entrenchment, including a long tenure in office and compensation that is not directly tied to the company's performance. Leverage is also significantly lower when CEOs do not appear to face strong monitoring, as is the case when the board of directors is large or has a low percentage of outside directors, and when there are no significant stockholders.

We also explored the impact on corporate capital structures of large, discrete changes in corporate governance. We found that after CEO security had suffered a shock – for example attempts to acquire the organization, the involuntary departure of the previous CEO and the arrival of a large stockholder-director – a business's subsequent capital structure takes on significantly greater leverage. We also discovered that leverage increases after CEOs are subjected to greater performance incentives in the form of increased stock options.

Finally, we evaluated the three possible explanations of why managers might be motivated to change leverage when their security is threatened: to increase company value by moving toward a more beneficial, though less comfortable, capital structure; to increase their personal voting control; or to commit to a defensive restructuring that, while not necessarily optimal, creates sufficient value to keep raiders away. These three theories are not mutually exclusive and we found that each has some explanatory power. Since we found that special dividends and restructurings often occur after leverage rises, our results are superficially consistent with the theory that managers use leverage as a defensive device to commit to value-increasing changes.

However, we observe this pattern of events not just after failed attempts to acquire a business, but also after entrenchment-reducing events not necessarily related to takeover threats, including the dismissal of the previous CEO and the arrival of an important stockholder on the board of directors. Therefore, we think the results cannot be explained completely as temporary tactical moves to deter outside raiders. Rather, our findings also seem consistent with a conjecture that most businesses have less leverage in their capital structure than optimal and managers who sense threats to their security increase leverage permanently to enhance value.

Our parallel finding that leverage increases after managers receive large stock-option awards also seems to support this view. Stock options provide incentives to managers to increase the risk and expected value of the company's activities. We explored this possibility further by analyzing how leverage changes after entrenchment shocks as a function of a business's apparent leverage deficit or surplus at the start of each year.

Capital structure levels

If entrenched managers systematically make sub-optimal decisions about capital structure, we hypothesized that we should observe significant cross-sectional associations between leverage and variables that indicate greater entrenchment. Our results generally support the theory that entrenched CEOs seek to avoid leverage.

However, we hesitated to draw strong conclusions from our levels analysis alone since competing theories about corporate governance lead to similar predictions about how companies should design their capital structures in order to reduce agency costs (the difference between the actual and potential value of the company) and increase company value.

Our analysis shows a positive and generally significant association between business leverage and CEO direct stock ownership. These findings are consistent with an interpretation that managers whose financial incentives are more closely tied to stockholder wealth will adopt more levered capital structures to raise the company's value. Our findings also support the conjecture that managers might increase leverage as a means of consolidating their own voting control.

Regardless of the interpretation, the economic significance of these estimates appears low; the estimates imply only modest changes in leverage in relation to reasonable changes in the percentage of the equity held by a CEO. Estimates for executive compensation variables also point to an inverse association between leverage and managerial entrenchment.

Our results show a significant positive relation between leverage and CEO vested option holdings. This suggests that CEOs who are not entrenched, because they face financial pressure from compensation tied to company value, will take on greater debt. However, the option result is also consistent with arguments that stock options motivate managers to increase company risk. Interestingly, the option variable appears to have far greater economic significance than that for direct stock ownership.

Wall Street: companies that defeat takeover bids become heavy purchasers of their own stock

A CEO's tenure has a negative association with the level of leverage. The estimate is consistent with entrenched CEOs pursuing capital structures with lower leverage, perhaps to reduce the performance pressures that accompany high debt. However, as is the case for many of the variables in the levels model, the result supports alternative interpretations. For example, the CEO may have presided over many profitable years in which retained earnings accumulated at an above-average rate, resulting in a capital structure with high equity.

Variables associated with stronger monitoring also have positive connections with leverage. Our results indicate that leverage, for example, rises in the presence of a significant stockholder. Board size has a consistently negative estimated association with leverage. If CEOs with small boards are less entrenched due to superior monitoring by these bodies, the reverse is also true. We also found evidence that the presence of outside directors on the board is associated with greater leverage.

Analyzing the changes

Many variables related to capital structure, company performance and corporate governance are likely to be determined simultaneously, making any analysis of cross-sectional levels difficult to interpret. We feel that the theories relating leverage to corporate governance may be better studied by analyzing decisions to change leverage, rather than the cross-sectional variation in, say, debt/equity ratios. Our strategy was to study whether leverage changes significantly after apparent shocks to companies' governance structures. As mentioned above, we identified several corporate governance events that indicate a significant threat to managerial security: an outside offer to acquire the organization, the forced replacement of a company's CEO and a significant stockholder joining the board.

We expected managers to feel great pressure to raise the value of the organization following such events. We found there were significant increases in leverage in years that companies faced unsuccessful tender offers. Unsuccessful tender offers are followed the next year by increases in book leverage on the order of 13 per cent of total assets, after controlling for other reasons why book leverage might change.

Companies that defeat takeover bids become heavy purchasers of their own stock. These buybacks are apparently financed by new debt, which increases by about 12 per cent of total assets. Interestingly, some organizations experiencing unsuccessful tender offers also appear to issue equity.

Several explanations are possible. If managers had used a sub-optimal amount of debt because they disliked risk and performance pressure, the leverage increases may simply represent moves toward a value-increasing debt-to-equity mix that managers would otherwise prefer to avoid.

Alternatively, the heavy repurchases of stock after unsuccessful tender offers could represent 'greenmail' payments or attempts by managers to increase their own voting power. One could also regard higher leverage after unsuccessful tender offers as a type of 'scorched earth' tactic in which managers lever the business as a defensive measure to buy time to instigate a restructuring plan. However, direct evidence for the effectiveness of leverage as an entrenchment device is mixed. Moreover, even if defensive recapitalizations do increase the security of weak managers, they are of benefit because they force management to transfer a substantial portion of under-utilized resources to shareholders.

We also sought to verify that increases in leverage usually occurred after and not before takeover bids. We found that more than 98 per cent of the publicly disclosed dollar value of leverage increase during the fiscal year of the unsuccessful takeover occurs after the date of the offer.

In addition, we sought to assess whether a direct link exists between the takeover offer and the leverage increase, and, if so, to identify the purpose(s) of the leverage increase. The increase in net debt is generally used to finance large special dividends, equity repurchase or restructuring. Such uses of funds suggest the leverage increase generally helps companies remain independent by committing them to make the improvements that a potential acquirer would have made.

Another threat to managerial security – the forced replacement of a company's CEO – also leads to greater leverage. After controlling for other determinants, leverage rises on average by nine per cent of total assets after the forced departure of a CEO, with new debt issues accounting for most of this total, with some funds being devoted to stock repurchases as well. We found that 73 per cent of the publicly disclosed dollar value of the leverage increase during the fiscal year of the replacement occurs after the date the new CEO is appointed, with the debt increase generally being used to pay special dividends or to restructure operations.

Our third variable – an increase in the number of 5 per cent stockholder-directors – is also associated with greater leverage. After controlling for other determinants, leverage on average rises by seven per cent in the year after a stockholder joins the board, with this effect largely due to new debt issues.

Leverage changes

Our main results indicate that managers increase leverage in response to events that reduce their entrenchment. However, increased leverage may not always represent a value-increasing strategy and CEOs may over-lever companies beyond the value-maximizing level to protect their job security. We explored this issue by analyzing how leverage changed as a function of a company's apparent leverage deficit or surplus at the start of the year. We defined surplus as the difference between actual and predicted leverage.

In the absence of unusual shocks to managerial security, companies generally adjust leverage toward its expected level, closing about one-sixth of the surplus or deficit in a given year. We concluded that when businesses have been pursuing a low-debt capital structure, an outside event that threatens managerial security is an especially strong predictor of increased leverage.

This leverage generally takes companies beyond the expected debt/equity ratio for our sample. Interestingly, there was not a converse effect for businesses that had pursued a high-debt capital structure. These companies exhibit no significant change in leverage – and, in particular, do not reduce leverage in the direction of the expected level – in the aftermath of shocks to managerial entrenchment. This asymmetric pattern of leverage changes may suggest that most companies have less leverage than optimal in their capital structures.

Conclusions

Theories based on the premise that leverage reduces managerial discretion implicitly assume that managers will not issue the optimal amount of debt without pressure from a 'disciplining' force. Our results support such predictions. We find evidence that leverage is affected by the degree of managerial entrenchment and most of the results indicate that entrenched managers seek to avoid debt. We found that leverage is lower when the CEO has had a long tenure in office, has weak stock and compensation incentives, and does not face strong monitoring from the board or important stockholders.

But these results are also open to other interpretations. For example, the positive association between leverage and fractional CEO stock ownership is consistent with the theory that managers use leverage to inflate the voting power of their equity. The overall tenor of our results points to CEOs being hesitant to take on as much leverage as shareholders would like. Although we found evidence that this problem can be alleviated by extreme threats to the CEO's security, such as a takeover battle or the forced replacement of the CEO, shareholders and corporate governance experts are likely to prefer less extreme solutions.

Our evidence uncovered two less extreme mechanisms that are effective in reducing the problem. Providing compensation to the CEO through stock option grants encourages an increase in leverage because the value of these options is increased by raising the expected value and the risk level of the company. Alternatively, increasing the monitoring of the CEO by large stockholders and by adding representatives of such holders to the board of directors also results in the CEO increasing the business' leverage. Thus, more effective corporate governance can result in CEOs moving closer to the leverage levels desired by shareholders.

Summary

'Debt, folklore and financial structure' (Module 2) examines the impact of broad economic, fiscal and banking regimes on corporate capital structures worldwide. This fascinating article by Philip Berger, David Yermack and Eli Ofek – based on recent US research – turns the spotlight on chief executives and finds that many 'entrenched' managers seek to avoid levels of debt (and therefore risk) which are likely to be in shareholders' interest. Leverage levels, for instance, tend to be lower when CEOs do not face pressure from either ownership and compensation incentives or active monitoring. On the other hand, leverage increases in the aftermath of entrenchment reducing shocks to managerial security, such as unsuccessful tender offers, involuntary CEO replacements, and the addition to the board of major stockholders. More effective corporate governance, the authors argue, can result in managers moving closer to 'optimal' levels of gearing.

New equity issues and raising cash

by R.A. Brealey and K. Nyborg

Companies finance part of their investment programs from retained earnings, but retentions are generally insufficient to provide all the funds that are needed. Similarly, governments finance part of their expenditures from tax revenues but typically face a financial deficit that they make up by borrowing.

There is an almost endless variety of techniques for selling new debt or equity. These techniques differ by country, by type of security and from one period to another. There are, however, some broad choices to be made, which we describe below.

Private placements/public issues

Governments and firms can raise cash by placing their securities with a limited number of investors, by offering them to a broad *class* of investor such as a firm's existing shareholders, or by offering them to the public at large. Since there are relatively high fixed costs to a public issue, private placements tend to be more common for small issues. Moreover, the terms and conditions of public issues are generally standardized, and therefore firms needing to incorporate unusual features in their securities are more likely to make a private placement.

Usually there is little secondary market for securities that have been privately placed. For example, a bank that lends money to a company cannot easily sell that loan on to another investor, though sales of bank loans do occasionally take place. Lenders, such as banks, need to be compensated for the lack of a marketability, and therefore private placements generally carry a higher rate of interest. In some cases private placements can be bought and sold freely but only between a limited group of investors. For example, in the United States only 'qualified institutional buyers' (QIBs) are permitted to trade in so-called Rule 144a issues.

Those investments which are issued to the general public at large, are frequently listed on a Stock Exchange, or they may be freely traded 'over the counter' through investment dealers. However, there are also many investments which are publicly offered but cannot easily be resold. The common-or-garden time deposit with a building society is an obvious example for example.

Public issues: auctions and fixed-price offers for sale

Public issues can take many forms. Sometimes securities are auctioned off to the highest bidders; at other times securities are offered for sale at a fixed price. Within these two broad classifications there are many variations, some of which are listed in Figure 1 and which we discuss below.

Selling securities is not, in principle, very different from selling other goods, and the techniques used to sell securities have parallel in normal high street practice. When a supermarket offers cans of beans for sale, it states the price at which it is prepared to sell and customers then decide the quantity they wish to buy at that price. If the supermarket sets the price too low, then the quantity demanded may be greater than the supply on offer and a rule is needed to allocate the limited supply. In this case the rule is usually the simple one of 'First come, first served', but stores may sometimes use more complicated allocation rules – for example, they may hold back some stock to satisfy customers.

Not all goods are sold in this way. Sometimes the goods may be sold by auction, in which case would-be buyers submit orders that specify both quantity and price. For example, our imaginary supermarket could decide to auction off its stock of canned beans to the highest bidders, so that each customer would state the number of cans that he or she would be prepared to pay at a particular price.

Fig.1 New public issues methods

Method	Sellers decide	Buyers decide	Method used for
Offer for sale (fixed price offer)	Price	Quantity	Corporate securities
Discriminatory auction	Reservation price	Price and quantity (demand schedules)	Treasury securities
Uniform price auction	Reservation price	Price and quantity (demand schedules)	Corporate and treasury securities
Bookbuilding	Reservation price	Price and quantity (demand schedules)	Corporate securities

When firms and governments sell their securities, they need to decide between a fixed-price offer for sale and an auction, although the method of issue does not always fit so easily into the different categories that we described above.

Consider, for example, the decision by companies in the UK to offer stock to the public for the first time. These initial public offers (IPOs) generally take the form of a fixed-price offer for sale. In this case the firm advertises that it plans to sell so many shares at a fixed price, and investors then decide how many they wish to apply for. If the price is set low, then there may be applications for more shares than are on offer and the firm needs to establish an allocation rule. For example, it may simply scale down all applications by a constant proportion or it may ballot smaller applicants.

A smaller proportion of IPOs in the UK take the form of a 'tender offer.' In this case investors are invited to submit a sealed bid stating how many shares they wish to buy and the price. The firm then determines the maximum price at which the total issue can be sold and the successful bidders all receive stock at that uniform price. This method of selling new securities is often used in selling government securities, and is sometimes referred to as a uniform price auction, or even a Dutch auction. The US has experimented with this auction format for selling two- and five-year Treasury notes since September 1992.

What should determine the choice between the fixed price offer for sale and auction? One answer is the relative information advantage of investors on the one hand and of the firm and its advisors on the other. Sometimes the major uncertainty surrounds the environment in which the firm operates, and in these cases it may be desirable to pool the views of a large number of investors by auctioning the stock. On other occasions the technology and the market in which the firm operates may be relatively well known, the principal uncertainties surround the ability of the firm to operate successfully within its market. On these matters the firm and its advisors should be well-informed, and therefore best placed to assess the stock's value and determine the price at which it is offered for sale. Of course, investors are likely to be concerned as to whether they can trust the firm not to put too high a value on its stock and will be more inclined to take the firm's word if they know that the firm and its advisors will need their support in the future.

A drawback with auction procedures is that the selling price may be sensitive to collusive behavior among buyers. This is avoided with a fixed-price offer for sale since the selling price is determined by the seller rather than the bidders. Sellers can also protect themselves against collusive behavior in auctions by setting a reservation price. In auctions of Treasury securities, for example, it is common for sellers to reserve the right to withdraw some of the issue, if the bids are deemed too low.

Auction procedures

In organizing an auction, the seller has a number of decisions to make. Auctions often involved repeated bids, in which case participants can observe the bidding and change their offers correspondingly. For example, in an art auction the auctioneer usually calls out increasingly high prices until he has found the highest price at which the painting can be sold. In this case the winning bidder pays only a fraction more than the value placed on the painting by the second-highest bidder. Sometimes auctions are organized so that the auctioneer calls out a series of decreasing prices until sufficient bidders are revealed.

However, in auctions of securities, participants are often required to submit sealed bids and have no opportunity to revise these bids in the light of the bids submitted by others. Since bidders form different views of the item's value and submit different sealed bids, the auctioneer needs to decide pricing and allocation rules. The two most common auction mechanisms are known as the *discriminatory auction* and the *uniform price auction*. In both these formats bidders can typically submit multiple bids, each individual bid consisting of a price-quantity pair. In both auction formats, the securities go to the highest bidders. However, in uniform price auctions the winning bidders pay the same price, equal to the lowest winning bid, whereas in the discriminatory auction the winning bidders pay the price they bid. In other words, in the uniform auction, all bidders pay the same market-clearing price. In the discriminatory auction, the seller essentially acts as a price-discriminating monopolist by awarding securities to the highest winning bidders and working down through the aggregate demand schedule until the entire issue is sold.

A simple example may help to illustrate the difference between a discriminatory and uniform auction. Suppose that the seller wishes to sell four units of a good and that three would-be buyers submit bids. *A* bids \$10 for 1 unit, *B* bids \$8 for 3 units, and *C* bids \$7 for 2 units. The bids of the two highest bidders (*A* and *B*) absorb all the units on offer, so that *C* does not receive any allocation. If the auction is a discriminatory auction *A* and *B* pay their bid – that is, *A* pays \$10 and *B* pays \$8. In a uniform price auction both pay \$8, which is the price of the lowest winning bidder.

It might seem that the proceeds from a uniform price auction would be lower than from a discriminatory auction. However, this fails to recognize that bidders will act strategically when they submit their bids and are likely to bid at lower prices under the discriminatory format than under the uniform format. In a sense, it is cheaper for bidders to submit high bids in a uniform auction than in a discriminatory auction since most bidders end up paying a lower price than they bid. In fact, under some conditions, auction revenue might be expected to be higher under the uniform format than under the discriminatory format. To understand this, it is necessary to understand the concept of the *winner's curse* (*see* Box on p. 68).

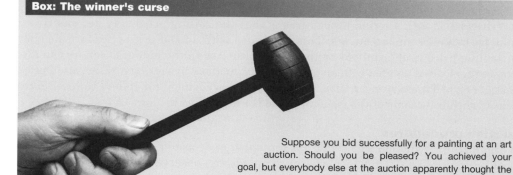

Box: The winner's curse

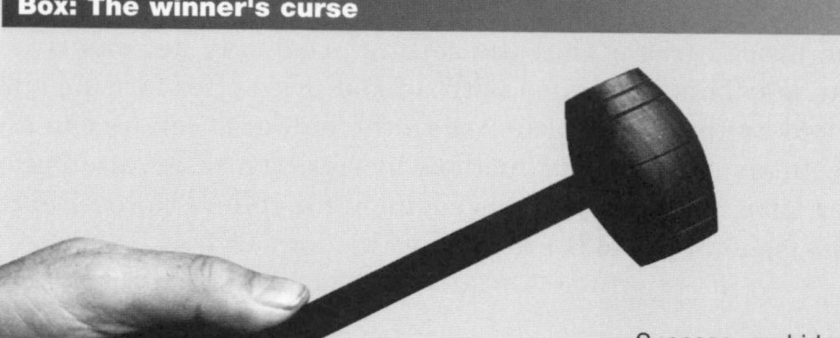

Suppose you bid successfully for a painting at an art auction. Should you be pleased? You achieved your goal, but everybody else at the auction apparently thought the painting was worth less than you did. Your success raises the specter of the winner's curse; you may have overpaid.

It may be that you have no intention of reselling the painting so you do not care about the value others place on it. But if you bought the painting with a view to reselling it, you are concerned about others' valuations.

The winner's curse arises when bidders have different information about the post-auction price. Although each bidder's individual estimate may be unbiased, the highest estimate is likely to overestimate value. In the case of securities the winner's curse is important, for whether the winning bidders get a good deal in the auction depends on what the secondary market price turns out to be.

As a result, the expected selling price is inversely related to uncertainty. In short, when uncertainty is higher, the winner's curse is higher. This should lead bidders to bid more cautiously, thus lowering expected revenue to the seller.

Rational bidders should take the winner's curse into account and submit bids at prices that are lower than their estimates – the less precise their information, the more they should shade down their bids.

Reducing uncertainty

The winner's curse suggests that anything done to decrease uncertainty will increase expected revenue to the seller. It is, therefore, in the seller's interest to disclose as much price-relevant information as possible. The seller can also encourage information production through the choice of auction mechanism. Surprisingly, auction theory suggests that the expected selling price is higher under the uniform-price auction because the price paid by winning bidders is linked to the private information of other bidders. By contrast, under the discriminatory format winning bidders do not learn much about the information of the other bidders. As a result, the uniform-price auction reduces the winner's curse. This conclusion obviously rests on several assumptions, one of which is that bidders are sophisticated and take the winner's curse into account. If bidders are naive and do not adjust their bids, the discriminatory price auction is likely to secure a higher price. Thus the best choice of auction procedure could depend on the sophistication of the bidders.

Another way in which the seller could encourage information production is through a when-issued or 'gray' market. This is a forward market where investors can buy or sell the to-be-auctioned securities before the auction is actually held. Such a market may reduce uncertainty by establishing a market price for the to-be auctioned security. The seller would like all private information held by potential bidders in the auction to be impounded in the when-issued price, thus eliminating the winner's curse. But this depends on how active the when-issued market is. Bidders may prefer to limit their trades in the when-issued market so as not to be informationally disadvantaged in the auction itself.

In a recent paper, Nyborg and Sundaresan (1996) use transactions data from the when-issued market for US Treasury securities to assess the US Treasury's recent experiment with uniform auctions. By studying volume in the when-issued market and the pattern of when-issued price volatility on the auction day, they find evidence that, under the discriminatory format, bidders tend to hold back their private information from the when-issued prices more informative. This pre-auction release of information augments the inherent advantage of the uniform auction in reduction the winner's curse. A study by Umlauf of the Mexican government auctions also supports the hypothesis that uniform auctions reduce the winner's curse and increase revenue.

Sometimes auctions make special arrangements for uninformed bidders by allowing them to enter non-competitive bids, whereby they submit a quantity but not a price. For example, in US Treasury auctions investors may submit non-competitive bids up to a maximum value and receive their full allocation at the average price paid by competitive bidders. Investors submitting non-competitive bids are free-riding on the information collected by other bidders. If collecting information is costly, allowing such bids may deter investors from doing their homework. In uniform price auctions sellers sometimes offer positive incentives to collect information. For example, initial public offers in France often take the form of a uniform price auction. However, bids at irrationally high prices are discarded and the price at which the stock is sold is correspondingly lower. You can think of the French arrangement as one that penalizes free-riders by ignoring their bids and offers rewards to other successful bidders for collecting information about the stock's value.

Bookbuilding

We have seen that one-shot, sealed-bid auctions are regularly used by governments to sell their bonds and sometimes by companies to make an initial public offering of stock. But often auctions of securities allow the bidders to revise their bids.

On the surface, the sale of new corporate securities in the US and the euromarkets is similar to a fixed-price offer for sale but often it has many of the features of an informal auction in which the bidders have an opportunity to revise their bids. For example, the underwriter to an initial public offering in the United States typically undertakes an analysis of the firm and then estimates a price range for the stock. The firm and the underwriter arrange a roadshow, which has the twin purpose of informing potential investors and discovering their attitude to the issue. The underwriter then accepts indications of interest which are non-binding orders for stock at different prices. These indications of interest are used to set the final offer price at which the underwriter allocates shares. Whilst investors are not bound by their indications and have the opportunity to revise their requirements, the continuing relationships between investors and underwriter ensure that investors cannot go back on their expressions of interest with impunity.

This process of solicitation is often formalized into a book-building procedure, so that by the sale date the underwriter has a more or less precise set of orders at different prices and is able to determine the (uniform) price at which the issue can be sold.

The interaction that takes place between a company and its advisors on the one hand and investors on the other may also provide information that allows the company or its advisors to change the amount of securities on offer. For example, new issues in the United States often include a 'greenshoe' option that allows the underwriters to increase the offering if demand is unexpectedly strong.

Underwriting and issue costs

If a company places its securities privately, it will generally negotiate directly with potential buyers. Sometimes firms also handle public sales of securities. For example, large firms may sell their commercial paper directly to investors on a regular basis. Usually, however, the company will employ one or more intermediaries to help with the issue.

The underwriters to an issue have several roles. By attaching their names to the issue, they provide certification. A company may issue new securities only rarely but underwriters do so repeatedly and are therefore particularly concerned to protect their reputation with possible buyers as well as with regulatory bodies and potential clients.

In addition to their advisory and certification roles, underwriters commonly buy the securities from the firm at a discount to the issue price and assume the risk that they can sell them on to investors. Thus in such cases underwriters guarantee the success of the issue. They have several advantages in providing this guarantee. First, they have specialist skills in pricing the new issue. Second, they have access to a network of investors to whom they can distribute the issue. And third, they have skills in managing and laying off the risk of providing the guarantee.

The risk to underwriters of providing a guarantee is greatest in the case of the fixed-price offer for sale. The more that the underwriters can pre-sell the issue, the less they are at risk. The need for underwriting is least in the case of a formal auction of securities, though even here the seller may specify a minimum bid price and the underwriters commit to buy any unsold securities at this reservation price.

In providing a guarantee the underwriters are effectively providing the firm with a put option. In other words, the firm acquires the option to sell the issue to the underwriters at the issue price and in compensation the firm pays the underwriter a spread or commission. An obvious question is whether the price that underwriters charge is commensurate with the risk that they run. A study by Paul Marsh of underwritten offers of stock in the UK used the Black-Scholes option pricing model to value the underwriting guarantee. Marsh's findings suggested that the average value of the put was about 0.2 per cent of the money raised, while the average price charged for the guarantee (the sub-underwriting commission) was 1.44 per cent. It remains possible that there are other hidden services for which the underwriting commission is compensation, but Marsh's findings raise some obvious questions about the competitiveness of parts of the underwriting market.

The costs of issuing new securities include both the cost of underwriting and a variety of administrative expenses. There is a substantial fixed element to these costs. Also the costs tend to be larger for a risky equity issue than for a relatively safe debt issue. Thus the costs for a large debt issue might amount to less than one per cent of the money raised while for the costs of a small initial public offer of stock could be as high as 20 per cent of the proceeds.

The price effects of new issues: the case of IPOs

In addition to the administrative and underwriting costs, there is the possible hidden cost of selling securities for less than their true value. For government securities this hidden cost is generally very low. For example, several studies of US Treasury issues have found that the yield in the auction is slightly higher than in the when-issued market, as predicted by auction theory, but only by a fraction of a basis point. By contrast, underpricing is important for initial public offers of equities, where it is likely to be difficult to assess the post-issue market price.

There are some dramatic examples of underpriced IPOs. For example, when the prospectus for the initial public offering of Netscape stock was first published, the underwriters indicated that the company would sell 3.5 million shares at a price between $12 and $14 each. However, by the day before the sale public enthusiasm was such that underwriters increased the shares available to 5 million and set an issue price of $28. The next morning the volume of orders was so large that trading was delayed by an hour and a half and, when it did begin, the shares were quoted at $71, over five times the underwriters' initial estimates.

Of course, the Netscape issue was unusual, but Figure 2 summarizes a number of studies of IPOs in different markets. In each case stock appears to be sold on average well below its market value. No-one knows precisely why this is the case. One possible explanation goes back to the problem of the winner's curse. Investors who apply for an equal amount of every issue will not realize the gains shown in Figure 2, for they will find that they receive only a small proportion of the shares that they apply for in the popular (i.e. underpriced) issues but a large proportion of shares applied for in the less popular (i.e. overpriced) ones. For example, Levis showed that in the UK an investor who applied for an equal amount of each IPO in the period 1985–88 would have just about broken even, even though the average underpricing was nine per cent. Thus, the firm will need to underprice on average to protect investors from the winner's curse. However, there are other possible explanations of IPO underpricing, such as a lack of competition among underwriters. It is also possible that some underpricing is required in order to compensate buyers for the costs associated with gathering information to value the new issue.

A more puzzling observation is the fact that after the initial euphoria there appears to be a prolonged decline in the price of IPOs. For example, Loughran and Ritter recorded a 20 per cent underperformance for US IPOs during the following three years. On the surface this appears inconsistent with the notion of efficient markets.

Price effects of seasoned issues

Studies in the United States by Asquith and Mullins, Masulis and Korwar, and Mikkelson and Partch have suggested that the announcement of a new 'seasoned' equity issue results in a fall in the stock price. Though this decline averages only about three per cent, it is substantial proportion of the money that is being raised.

A possible explanation is that investors are concerned that the additional supply of stock will cause temporary market indigestion, but there is little sign that the price fall increases with the size of the stock issue. It appears more likely that the cause of the price decline is that the issue is interpreted as an adverse signal. There are two ways in which this could come about. Just as an unexpected increase in the dividend suggests to investors that the company is generating more cash than they thought, the announcement of a new issue may have the reverse implication. Investors may worry

Fig.2 Average initial returns for 25 countries

Country	Source	Sample size	Time period	Average initial return (%)
Australia	Lee *et al.*	266	1976–89	11.9
Belgium	Rogiers *et al.*	28	1984–90	10.1
Brazil	Aggarwal *et al.*	62	1979–90	78.5
Canada	Jog and Riding; Jog and Srivastava	258	1971–92	5.4
Chile	Aggarwal *et al.*	19	1982–90	16.3
Finland	Keloharju	85	1984–92	9.6
France	Husson and Jacquillat; Leleux and Muzyka; Palliard and Belletante	187	1983–92	4.2
Germany	Ljungqvist	170	1978–92	10.9
Hong Kong	McGuinness	80	1980–90	17.6
Italy	Cherubini and Ratti	75	1985–91	27.1
Japan	Fukuda; Dawson and Hiraki; Hebner and Hiraki	472	1970–91	32.5
Korea	Dhatt *et al.*	347	1980–90	78.1
Malaysia	Isa	132	1980–91	80.3
Mexico	Aggarwal *et al.*	37	1987–90	33.0
Netherlands	Wessels; Eijgenhuijsen and Buijs	72	1982–91	7.2
New Zealand	Vos and Cheung	149	1979–91	28.8
Portugal	Alpalhao	62	1986–87	54.4
Singapore	Koh and Walter	66	1973–87	27.0
Spain	Rahnema *et al.*	71	1985–90	35.0
Sweden	Ridder; Rydqvist	213	1970–91	39.0
Switzerland	Kunz and Aggarwal	42	1983–89	35.8
Taiwan	Chen	168	1971–90	45.0
Thailand	Wethyavivorn and Koo-smith	32	1988–89	58.1
UK	Dimson; Levis	2,133	1959–90	12.0
USA	Ibbotson *et al.*	10,626	1960–92	15.3

Source: I. Lee, S. Lockhead, J. Ritter and Q. Zhao (1996)

that management is pessimistic about the future level of retentions or the cost of its capital projects.

This concern about future cash flows could be prompted by any sale of securities, but there is a somewhat different argument proposed by Myers and Majluf that suggests investors may be particularly concerned about issues of equity. This argument goes as follows. Managers are closer to the firm than investors and are often better placed to judge the value of their stock. If they wish to help their stockholders, they will not sell new stock when it is underpriced but will wish to do so when it is overpriced. Of course investors will recognize that managers are liable to behave in this way and will therefore mark down the price of the stock when an issue is announced. The result is that all firms are likely to have a pecking order for new funds. Optimistic managers will prefer to issue debt because they do not want to issue undervalued equity; pessimistic managers will prefer debt because they wish to avoid an issue of equity that would send a signal to investors and depress the stock price. If this is the case, equity issues are likely to be regarded as a last resort.

Fig.3 Share price announcement effects of US security issues

Type of security	Abnormal return[(a)] (over 2 days)
Straight bonds	–0.26*
Preferred stock	–0.19*
Convertible bonds	–2.07
Convertible preferred stock	–1.44
Common stock	–3.14

[(a)] i.e. adjusted for market movements
* denotes not statistically significant
Source: Reprinted from *Journal of Financial Economics* 15, Smith, 'Investment Banking and the Capital Acquisition Process', 3–29, © 1996, with permission from Elsevier Science, UK.

Myers and Majluf's theory predicts that the fall in the stock price should be greatest when the firm announces an equity issue and least for a debt issue. Figure 3 summarizes the US evidence on the matter. It confirms that the closer the security is to a straight equity, the greater the price impact.

General cash offers v rights issues

We point out that instead of offering their investments to the public at large, firms or governments may sometimes restrict the offering to a particular class of investor. For example, the British government initially restricted holdings of indexed bonds to the elderly, so that these bonds became known as 'granny bonds.'

The most common form of restriction is for companies to limit the offer of securities to their own shareholders who are then free to resell the securities to other investors. Indeed, a company's articles may often specify that shareholders have a pre-emptive right of first refusal of new issues of equity. Hence issues of equity made to existing shareholders are known as 'rights issues.' There are confusing international differences in terminology and procedures for rights issues, but an example based on UK practice should help to illustrate the basic principles.

Suppose that a company currently has in issue 8 million shares valued at £20 each. If the firm now wishes to raise an additional £80m, it can offer its shareholders the right to buy two new shares for each one that they currently hold at a price of £5. The first column of figures in Figure 4 summarizes the result. After the sale has been completed investors will own a total of 24 million shares and the assets will be worth the initial £160m plus the £80m of new cash. The 'ex rights' share price will therefore be £240 ÷ 24 = £10.

Consider a shareholder with an initial holding of 10 shares worth £200. Following the announcement of the issue, the firm sends the shareholder a document stating that she owns 10 shares plus 20 rights, which entitle her to buy 20 new shares for £5 each. These rights, and the shares without the rights can now be traded separately. The latter, we have seen, are worth £10 each. Since each right allows the share-holder to buy a share worth £10 for £5, it must be worth £5. Thus the total value of our shareholder's investment is unchanged at (£10 × £10) + (20 × £5) = £200.

Fig.4 New issues price in a right offer does not affect firm value

Before issue:	2 for 1 at £5	4 for 1 at £2.50
Total no. of shares	8 m	8 m
Cum-rights share price	£20	£20
Total value	£160 m	£160 m
After issue:		
No. of new shares issued	16 m	32 m
Issue price	£5	£2.50
Total money raised	£80 m	£80 m
Total no. of shares	24 m	40 m
Total firm value	160 + 80 = £240 m	160 + 80 = £240 m
Ex-rights share price	240/24 = £10	240/40 = £6
Price of right	10 – 5 = £5	6 – 2.50 = £3.50

Although the new stock is sold at a discount to its true value, the shareholder does not benefit from this. Nor is she damaged by the fact that the rights issue reduces the price per share of the initial holding. Indeed it should be clear that the price at which the company offers its shares in a rights issue is largely immaterial. As long as the total sum raised remains the same, the issue terms will not affect the assets that the company owns nor each shareholder's proportionate ownership.

To see this, consider one more example. Imagine now that the company changes the terms of the issue by offering 32 million new shares at £2.50 a share. Since it is selling twice as many shares at half the price, the total sum raised is the same as previously. The final column of Figure 4 shows that after the issue there will be 40 million shares in issue with an ex-rights price of six each. The value of each right will now be £3.50. It is simple to check that our shareholder with an initial holding of 10 shares will be entitled to 10 shares worth £60 and 40 rights worth £140, so that her wealth is unaffected by the change in issue terms.

While the price at which shareholders sell new stock to themselves is immaterial, the price at which stock is sold to outside investors is important. If a firm were to sell stock to outsiders at the large discounts envisaged in our example, the shareholders would be as badly damaged as if they had sold part of their own holdings for less than their fair value. Hence there is an argument for requiring that when firms issue new stock existing shareholders should have the right of first refusal. Since we have seen that the issue price is largely immaterial in a rights issue, we might suspect that the signals provided by a rights issue would be less marked. There is some indication that this may be the case, for a study by Paul Marsh of UK rights issues found a rather smaller decline in price than has been observed for the general cash offers in the United States. Nevertheless, in some countries, such as the USA and Japan, rights issues have become a rarity and general cash offers are the norm. Even in the UK or continental Europe, where equity is generally sold by rights, companies have increasingly argued that general cash offers are quicker and cheaper and have sought freedom to issue stock to the public at large.

Summary

What techniques can companies and governments use to sell new securities? Richard Brealey and Kjell Nyborg look at the range of available options and offer advice to issuers on when to choose them. They distinguish between private placements among a limited number of investors and issues to the public at large; they explain auction theory and emphasize the importance of information flow; they analyze the potential costs for issuers, not least the danger of selling securities for less than their true value (as happened in the initial public offering of Netscape); and they set out the principles behind rights issues, pointing out why the price at which shareholders sell new stock to themselves is largely immaterial. In some countries like the US and Japan rights issues have become a rarity and general cash offers are now the norm.

Suggested further reading

Lee, I., Lockhead, S., Ritter, J. and Zhao, Q., (1996), 'The Costs of Raising Capital', *The Journal of Financial Research,* 19(1), 59–74.

Marsh, P.R., (1994), 'Underwriting of Rights Issues: a Study of the Returns Earned by Sub-underwriters from the UK Rights Issues', Research Report 6, Office of Fair Trading, London.

Milgrom, P., (1989), 'Auctions and Bidding: A Primer', *Journal of Economic Perspectives,* 3: 3–22.

Nyborg, K.G. and Sundaresan, S., (1996), 'Discriminatory versus Uniform Treasury Auctions: Evidence from when Issued Transactions', *Journal of Financial Economics*, 42, 63–104.
Rock, K., (1986), 'Why New Issues are Underpriced', *Journal of Financial Economics*, 15: 187–212.
Smith, C., (1986), 'Investment Banking and the Capital Acquisition Process', *Journal of Financial Economics*, 15: 3–29.

Plenty of potential in private equity

by Steven N. Kaplan

Private equity investments have created a tremendous amount of wealth and, at times, controversy. These investments are made in the securities of companies that are not traded publicly on an organized exchange. As a result, they tend to be much less liquid than most other investments.

Partly for this reason, private equity investments are commonly referred to as alternative investments. Despite their staid titles, they are among the most interesting in finance because they consist largely of investments in venture capital and leveraged buy-outs (LBOs).

In recent years, the amount of private equity under management – by partnerships investing in venture capital, leveraged buy-outs, distressed companies, real estate and so on – has increased substantially. Figure 1 shows the amount of funds raised annually by private equity partnerships – both venture capital and non-venture capital – in the US from 1980 to 1996.

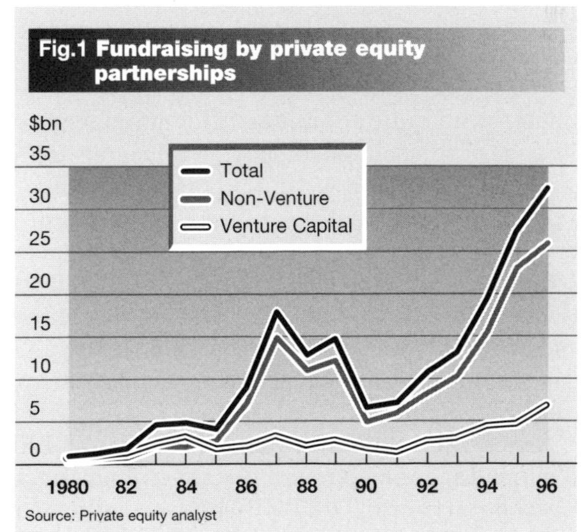

In 1996 alone, US venture capital funds obtained a record \$6.6bn in new commitments while US LBO funds obtained a record \$22.8bn. It is almost certain that these records will be broken again this year. Cumulatively, private equity funds under management have increased from under \$5bn in 1980 to more than \$130bn today.

This article describes the important characteristics of the private equity market and how these affect private equity market participants – users of private equity, private equity partnerships and the investors in/capital suppliers of the private equity partnerships. I conclude by discussing the state of the private equity market today and what to expect in future.

Issuers in the private equity market are of five broad types:

- start-ups or early-stage new ventures – typically start-up or young companies, sometimes no more than a concept, that have high growth potential
- later-stage new ventures – relatively new companies that have proved their technology, product and/or market and are in need of capital to grow
- existing private companies that require capital to finance growth or an ownership change
- private or public companies that require buy-out capital – often, but not always, companies operating in more mature businesses
- public or private companies in financial distress that require capital to restructure.

Private equity partnerships are typically characterized by the types of companies in which they invest. Venture capital partnerships – such as Kleiner Perkins or Greylock – typically provide equity capital to early and later-stage new companies with prospects for substantial growth. LBO partnerships – such as KKR or Forstmann Little in the US – provide equity capital to finance buy-outs of more mature companies. The two types of partnerships overlap sometimes, with some LBO partnerships investing in start-ups and some venture capital firms investing in later-stage companies or private companies needing capital to grow.

Fraught with uncertainty

There are four primary classes of investors in private equity partnerships. Roughly half of the money invested comes from pension funds – both public and corporate. Banks and insurance companies contribute 15–20 per cent. University endowments and foundations contribute another 10–15 per cent while wealthy families and individuals provide roughly 10 per cent.

What makes private equity investments unusual, and therefore unusually interesting, is the fact that they are illiquid investments in private companies. These investments – whether in start-ups or in mature companies – have the common characteristic of being fraught with uncertainty. This uncertainty is associated with at least two types of problems that are particularly severe in private equity situations.

First, outside investors typically know less about the company or technology than insiders (including founders and managers) at the time of the initial investment. Because of this, outsiders may be reluctant to invest. This problem is referred to as an adverse selection or sorting problem. Second, once financed, company managers will typically have incentives to take actions that benefit themselves but hurt outside investors. This is referred to as an incentive, moral hazard or agency problem.

The private equity business is organized to manage and mitigate the problems associated with this great degree of uncertainty.The primary investors in private equity are private equity partnerships (PEPs). ('Angels', typically wealthy individuals, also provide a great deal of private equity funding. Unfortunately, good data on angels are not available.)

Almost all well-known venture capital and LBO firms are organized as partnerships in which the managers are the general partners while institutional investors are the limited partners. The PEPs help to solve or manage the problems generated by uncertainty between outside investors and issuers. This uncertainty needs to be managed along two interfaces: that between the PEP and the companies it invests in; and that between the PEP and its investors/sources of capital.

Along the first interface, PEPs overcome selection problems by developing expertise in accessing and evaluating potential investments. This expertise may take many forms. Venture capitalists may benefit from an in-depth knowledge of a particular technology or industry while LBO partners put to use experience in operations and cost cutting. In most cases, the expertise includes a network of contacts and relationships that provide a stream of information and potential investments.

Once an attractive potential investment has been identified or sourced, the venture capital or LBO partner will expend a large amount of effort (using his or her expertise and relationships) to evaluate it. PEPs have also evolved structures that help solve incentive and agency problems.

Both venture capital and LBO partners have long understood the importance of providing equity incentives to their management teams, usually in the form of options. When managers have a meaningful stake in how well the company does, they will work harder to make it do well. It is common for the CEOs of companies funded by private equity to receive five per cent of the company, with the remaining management team receiving an additional 10–15 per cent.

PEPs commonly issue the options (or equity incentives) conditional on meeting certain hurdles. For example, the options may not vest (that is, be claimed by managers) unless they meet a performance benchmark. This gives management the incentive to meet the benchmark and protects the PEP against giving away equity to managers who have not performed.

It also is typical for options to vest over time to ensure that the management team does not go to another company. As I make clear in 'Riding on the benefits of the LBO wave' (Module 12) the success of these incentives has not been lost on public company boards. Public companies increasingly copy the incentive and compensation contracts used in private equity investments.

Private equity partners also typically receive representation on the boards of companies in which they invest. In most cases, the PEP effectively obtains majority control. Armed with such control, the private equity partners obviously have a substantial say in how the company is run.This might involve any or all of the following: helping to formulate strategy; providing advice on solving operational problems; finding members of the management team; and finding board members.

Bringing credibility

By helping to solve the problems associated with the huge uncertainty common to private equity investments, the PEPs also bring credibility to the companies in which they invest. This can be very valuable because it helps solve the information problems for others considering having relationships with those companies.

Particularly for venture capital-financed companies, an investment by a successful PEP signals three things. It tells outsiders that: a (presumably) sophisticated investor believes in the company and the accompanying technology/business concept; the company's management has incentives to make the business work; and a (presumably) sophisticated investor will provide some oversight to the company's management. These signals are potentially valuable in attracting additional members of a management team, board members, customers, suppliers and non-equity financing sources.

The second interface where a large amount of uncertainty needs to be managed is the one between the private equity partners and its institutional investors (that is, the limited partners). By their nature, private equity investments are illiquid. Investors in PEPs cannot get their money back quickly or on demand as investors in the stock market can. In fact, PEPs are typically structured to have life spans of 10 years or more. Limited partners, therefore, cannot be certain they will get their money back before that time. As a result, most investors in PEPs are large institutions that can tolerate a long period of illiquidity.

With funds available for 10 years or more, private equity partnerships have a huge amount of discretion and, potentially, ample opportunity to misuse the money. The primary response by investors/limited partners to provide incentives for the PEPs to do the right thing has been through compensation. This compensation virtually always has two components: an annual management fee and a carried interest.

The annual management fee, based on the percentage of capital committed to the PEP, is used to support salaries and the costs of investing. Venture capital funds typically have an annual fee of 2–2.5 per cent of capital committed while the larger LBO funds have smaller annual management fees of 1–1.5 per cent.

The second component is the carried interest, which is essentially an equity ownership in the profits of the fund. The general partners receive this carried interest – typically 20 per cent – only after they have returned the limited partners' investment. In other words, if a PEP invested $100m, the general partners typically would receive 20 per cent of any pay-out in excess of the original $100m. The positive aspect of this is that venture capital and LBO partners have significant incentives to make good investments.

The foregoing has described the important characteristics of the private equity market and how those characteristics affect private equity market participants. That discussion has left open where the private equity market is today and what is likely to happen in the future.

The future

As I mentioned earlier, PEP fund raising, or commitment levels, are at all-time highs. These investments are, no doubt, driven partially by the attractive returns PEPs have earned in the last several years (which have been buoyed by an extremely favorable overall stock market and market for initial public offerings). According to Venture Economics and Cambridge Associates, which track PEP returns, average returns to venture capital partnerships exceeded 40 per cent in 1995 and 1996. LBO partnerships have yielded handsome returns as well. It is unlikely that those returns will be repeated in the immediate future. First, the stock market is unlikely to match its performance of the last several years. And, as usual, unusually high returns tend to attract additional capital and competition.

Buyout specialist: Theodore Forstmann, dominant partner of Forstmann Little, helped invent the leverage buyout

The resulting influx of money into PEPs, according to anecdotal report, has led to higher prices for private equity investments. The size of the average fund raised by private equity partnerships also has increased, which may reveal the negative side of PEP compensation. It is possible for private equity partners to live quite nicely on their management fees even if they earn mediocre returns.

Successful PEPs will be those that can differentiate themselves in the sea of new capital. To do so, they must have a superior ability in solving selection problems – by having a better understanding of an industry or technology or by generating a stronger deal flow – or in solving incentive and management problems – by having a better understanding of an industry or operations.

On a positive note, the record amounts of funds committed to PEPs have also been driven by a secular shift in the assets large institutional investors allocate to private equity. This shift appears to be based partly on the assumption that private equity returns provide some diversification (vis-à-vis traditional stock market investments).

One might also speculate that it is based on the increased opportunities available to PEPs. The tremendous changes in technology today, particularly information technology, have probably created more opportunities for new businesses – and therefore venture capital funding – than at any time in the recent past. These technological changes have also changed the way existing businesses are managed, creating opportunities for LBO funding. Based on these factors, as well as recent returns, investments in PEPs are likely to continue to increase. This means that despite the almost unavoidable decline in returns, private equity will likely continue to be an important asset class in the foreseeable future.

This article relies heavily on 'The economics of the private equity market' by George Fenn, Nellie Liang and Stephen Prowse, published in 1995 by the Board of Governors of the US Federal Reserve System.

Summary

One of the largest and most interesting areas of modern finance is private equity investment – almost exclusively in venture capital and leveraged buy-out opportunities. In this article Steven Kaplan describes the main types of investments that attract private equity and also the main sources of such funding.

He outlines the main investment vehicles that are used (known as private equity partnerships, or PEPs, in the US) and how they are structured to overcome the problems of this type of investment (most notably the uncertainties and potential conflicts between a PEP and the companies it invests in and between a PEP and its sources of capital). Finally, Kaplan assesses the future direction of private equity investment. While the solid returns of recent years (largely due to a bouyant stock market) cannot be guaranteed to continue, he foresees no real slowdown, though PEPs themselves may have to work harder to differentiate themselves.

Building on the benefits of project financing

by Harold Rose

Both the private and public sectors have used project finance for large-scale undertakings such as the construction of power stations, tunnels, railways and roads. Such financing can provide considerable benefits for both sectors. In project financing an operation is financed and controlled separately from the operations of the 'sponsor,' who may be the main user of the product concerned, the main constructors or suppliers, a consortium or a government.

It is usually, but not necessarily, confined to large-scale capital-intensive projects and more often than not involves a high proportion of debt finance provided by a group of banks. In simple terms, lenders to an ordinary company have collectively a claim on its cash flows as a whole. It is also from the cash flows of the company or group that dividends are paid. By contrast, project finance lenders and equity investors (who may or may not be confined to the sponsor) can look only to a project's cash flows (this is called 'non-recourse' financing), except where the sponsor or some outside body such as a bank or insurance company provides lenders with some, usually temporary, credit reinforcement.

The advantages of project finance

The advantages of project finance derive from operating, financial and/or risk considerations.

The operating case for project financing may lie in the special knowledge needed to carry out the project or in its scale. Scale can make a project especially risky if the outcome is likely to be strongly correlated with other returns included in group operations, so that losses could coincide. This helps to explain, for example, the use of project finance for large-scale oil or mining exploration projects, which could otherwise be undertaken by the user of the mineral concerned. Furthermore, the performance of the project's managers is likely to be more visible and therefore more accurately assessable than if the project were simply part of an organization's wider operations. Managerial incentives are also likely to be more effective, except perhaps in the multi-activity group with a low correlation between the profitability of its divisions, where random factors cancel out.

If the project makes losses, the effect on the share price of the 'parent' may be less if it is separately identifiable. Otherwise the market might suspect that it was the profitability of the business' operations as a whole that had fallen. In this respect project financing provides clearer information to investors.

The financial advantages of project finance lie mainly in the use of debt finance to the sponsoring company holding the equity (or most of it). Where a project is spun-off by a company to which the debt holders in the project are given no recourse, the confinement of the debt liability to the project means that it falls outside the limit and conditions attached to debt financing set by the company's debt covenants.

Insofar as debt financing provides a net gain to the company's shareholders – in the form of tax saving, for example – this is a benefit to the company's shareholders that they might not be able to obtain if the company were already at its debt limit. (Note that the gain from debt financing does not lie in the fact that it raises equity earnings per share if the operating rate of return exceeds the cost of debt. This is merely a matter of arithmetic and ignores the additional risks which debt financing imposes on shareholders.)

Naturally, the inability to draw on the revenues of the 'parent' company is a disadvantage for lenders to the project, which could stiffen the terms on which they are prepared to lend. But the extent to which this will be the case might be small if the correlation between the profits of the project and those of the 'parent' were thought to be high. In such a case pooling would provide little reduction in the risks confronting debt holders. Moreover, the position of the latter is strengthened by the fact that project cash flows cannot be siphoned off by the 'parent' organization through dividends or other channels (fees to the 'parent' for any services it provides to the project will usually be subject to formal agreement).

The fact that the performance of the project's managers is readily identifiable also provides assurance to debt holders and shareholders that managers will not waste resources to their own private benefit; 'empire-building', in particular, is less likely in the case of a clearly defined project. As a result agency costs are reduced for both shareholders and lenders, and lenders may not require much, if any, of an extra default premium, compared with that required on loans to an operating group.

Furthermore, if the nature and boundaries of the project are clear and financial reports are adequate, lenders are less exposed to another form of agency cost. This is because a company suffering losses may be tempted to take on operating gambles, the gains from which go largely to shareholders, whereas if they fail shareholders have little more to lose, and it is the lenders who suffer most.

Indeed, an organization might take on a gamble with a very low or even negative expected return, for it is the possibility of the outcome being at the top of the range envisaged that is the attraction to shareholders in such a situation. (Shareholders are in the position of having a call option on the assets of a company with an exercise price equal to the cost of debt service, and the value of an option depends most of all on the range of possible outcomes.)

Project financing reduces all such agency costs. It should also be noted that some projects are financed with debt levels that would normally be considered unusually high. The reasons lie not only in the factors already outlined but also in the added incentive that high levels of debt give to project managers to be efficient – the threat of losing their jobs in the event of default is particularly powerful if the project is of the kind that calls for specialized skills that are not readily transferable to other businesses. The contrast with the much lower debt levels taken on by companies is explained not only by the higher degree of specialization required for most stand-alone projects but also by the fact that the actual degree of efficiency of their managers is more visible. Project managers, so to speak, can neither hide nor run!

To sum up, stand-alone project finance facilitates the undertaking of large projects and enlarges debt capacity without a commensurate increase in the risks to a 'parent' of distress or insolvency. It also ameliorates the various agency costs that arise from potential conflicts of interest and the asymmetry of information about efficiency and performance that could otherwise aggravate such conflicts.

Finally, there is one further and more subtle possible advantage to both potential lenders and shareholders. Separate project financing enlarges the range and precision of the choice open to both. By separating cash flows between companies it makes it unnecessary for investors to depend on all of them. But those investors who wish can still take a stake in the range of companies involved. In technical terms this amounts to making markets more 'complete,' which is usually a benefit to society.

Conditions for success

First, the project must be a stand-alone venture in terms of its operations. It will often have a definable terminable date and an agreed basis for returning interim and final surplus cash flows to investors. Costs and revenues must depend on the project alone; there must be no significant connection with those of any 'parent' company or sponsor. If the latter provides any services to the project they must be clearly definable, accounted and paid for in an agreed manner.

Second – and this is usually required to make the first condition apply – the success of the project must depend on clearly understood factors, such as the cost of and time taken to complete it or the market price of a mineral in the case of a mining project. Third, lenders and equity investors must be clear not only about the apportionment of surplus cash flows but about the risks involved in the project.

Note, however, that the alternatives to separate project financing are not confined to simply taking the project 'in-house' within an 'ordinary' company. If the specialized nature of the operations is the key issue, an organization that wants to undertake such a project can retain the asset but hire a specialist company to manage the project until it reaches fruition.

If shortage of finance is the problem, an 'ordinary' company may be able to lease the assets required for the life of the project; although leasing is not completely free from the constraints to which simple debt finance is subject. Whether it is economic to set up a separate project company, with its particular advantages, depends not only on the scale of the project but on whether synergy and risk-pooling advantages are lost and on the costs of setting up a separate business. These costs could include complex contractual arrangements and documentation involving the sponsor, the project manager, suppliers and customers. These are required to make clear the respective obligations and the distribution of risk between the parties involved.

Public sector projects

Since the early 1980s project finance companies have been increasingly used to carry out large infrastructure investments. In the US, for example, power stations have been built as private-sector utilities in this way, enabling the producers to raise large amounts of debt on the basis of long-term supply contracts with distributors. In other countries, power stations, tunnels, ports, transport and other infrastructure projects have been carried out for governments, government agencies or inter-

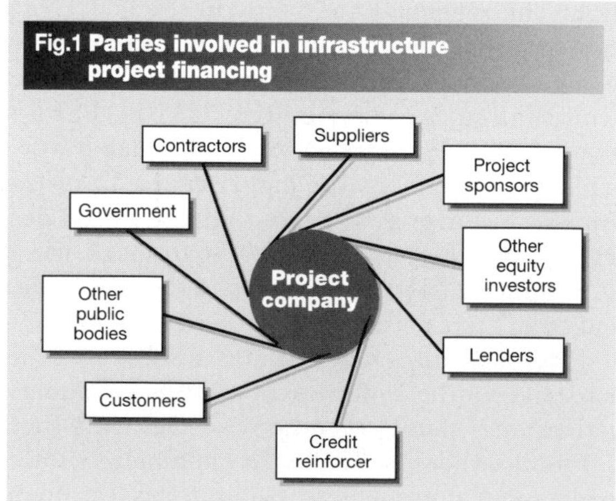

Fig.1 Parties involved in infrastructure project financing

national bodies such as the World Bank and its private-sector affiliate, the International Finance Corporation, mainly in developing countries in Latin America and Asia.

But project finance companies have also been used for infrastructure projects in mature economies. The Channel Tunnel, for example, was financed in this way, and other transport projects are in the pipeline in the UK, involving road and rail links and a new air traffic control system for Scotland. Under the Private Finance Initiative (PFI) introduced by the then UK government in 1992, contracts have been signed for an increasing variety of projects, including prisons, hospitals and a national health insurance computer system.

In most cases the project management company provides or raises the bulk of the equity, an efficiency incentive which to some degree is lacking in wholly public-sector projects. However, the new Labor government is to examine the working of the PFI. No doubt efficiency incentives could be provided for public-sector managers, but the question would then arise as to the incentives of their public-sector supervisors. Economic incentive contracts and the monitoring of managerial performance can be difficult to specify satisfactorily even in the private sector; market incentives and monitoring can be more effective. As in private-sector organizations the ownership of equity is likely to provide the most effective incentive for managers, especially as they then share in the risks of the project. It is the efficiency gain that tells against the argument that project finance is costly for governments and other public bodies.

There may be several parties involved in project financing. Usually a remarkably high proportion of the finance supplied is in the form of debt. Whereas in the 'ordinary' company, debt finance is on average less than one-third of the net total (excluding depreciation provisions) debt financing may represent two-thirds or more of project financing for infrastructure. The difference can be explained partly by the fact that the operating assets of most infrastructure projects survive heavy losses that would lead to a dissipation of assets in the case of many private-sector organizations. In some cases

Project financing is often used for infrastructure projects in mature economies such as the Channel Tunnel

lenders may also be influenced by the assumption that the state would provide support in the event of crippling losses.

In general, the particularly adverse consequences for management in the event of bankruptcy provide a sharp incentive to act efficiently, where care rather than enterprise is the crucial ingredient for success. Project financing in general, by making the monitoring of management an easier task than in a company with mixed activities, is particularly suitable for high levels of leverage.

Despite the long life of most infrastructure assets, debt financing is usually in the form of bank loans with a life of no more than 10–12 years. The alternative would be long-term open-market bond financing. But the syndicate of banks involved provides closer monitoring of performance and can more effectively enter into the renegotiation of financing terms should the project company fall short of the required debt servicing. Such a situation was illustrated by the renegotiation necessary for the Channel Tunnel.

Bank lending in general also overcomes the problems of duplication of monitoring and the temptation to be a 'free rider' that results when loans are made to a company by a large number of lenders. This is why market bond issues are usually made only by high-rated borrowers. Bond issues in project finance are confined to low-risk projects, such as road building, or to replace bank finance at the end of the construction phase. This is usually when, because of a possible cost overrun, risk is highest, as the case of the Channel Tunnel again demonstrates.

In some cases the concession agreement may require the government to provide supporting facilities, such as the high-speed rail link promised in the case of the Channel Tunnel, or guarantee the obligations of a state-owned utility that has entered into a purchasing agreement with a project company. Following completion, the project management company will either retain ownership of the assets or transfer them to the government or another public body that has granted the concession. Finally, governments may claim that project finance, by relieving them of the capital costs, reduces their spending and their deficits. But in many cases governments are left with longer-term residual obligations.

The true advantage of project finance lies in its potentially greater efficiency and more logical distribution of risk. Unlike the alternative of outright privatization, project finance has the merit of being simpler – as it involves only new assets – and of leaving a final role for government where, rightly or wrongly, full-scale private ownership is deemed to be inappropriate on social grounds.

Summary

Roads, power stations and tunnels (including the Channel Tunnel) have all been constructed recently with the aid of project finance. But what exactly is project finance, what are its advantages, and is it a viable alternative to privatization for the public sector? Harold Rose argues that such a method of financing facilitates the undertaking of large projects and enlarges a company's debt capacity without commensurately increasing the risk of distress or insolvency. It also reduces exposure to the agency costs that arise from potential conflicts of interest and helps remove the asymmetry of information about efficiency and performance that aggravates such conflicts.

Rose outlines what he sees as necessary conditions for a project's success – its stand-alone nature and a clear understanding of the success factors and risks – and

concludes with a look at the advantages of using project finance in the public sector. Efficiency and a more logical distribution of risk are its great merits.

Suggested further reading

Brealey, R.A., Cooper, I.A. and Habib, M.A., (1996), 'Using project Finance to fund Infrastructure Investments', *Journal of Applied Corporate Finance*, Fall.

Kensinger, J.W. and Martin, J.D., (1988),'Project finance: raising money the old-fashioned way', *Midland Corporate Finance Journal*, Fall.

Spin-offs: tax comparison with an asset sale

by Katherine Schipper and Linda Vincent

Spin-offs – or demergers as they are known in the UK – have been grabbing headlines in the financial press at an increasing rate. In the US, General Motors spun off EDS; AT&T spun off Lucent Technologies and NCR; and ITT divided itself into three companies via two spin-offs. In the UK, large demergers include Thorn-EMI, British Gas and the four-way split of Hanson. While rare, demergers are beginning to gain acceptance in continental Europe. In France, the demerger of Chargeurs's media and textile groups in 1996 was the first tax-free spin-off by a publicly traded company. Switzerland's first tax-free spin-off, Ciba Specialty Chemicals from Novartis, valued at $4.1bn, occurred in March 1997.

Are spin-offs just the latest financial fad or are they economically sound, long-term shareholder wealth-maximizing transactions? Why have they increased dramatically in volume during the past several years in the US in a trend that seems to be spreading to the UK and the rest of Europe? How do they compare with the alternative methods of divestiture?

Asset sales and spin-offs are the two most common means by which publicly traded US corporations divest unwanted lines of business. Spin-offs are tax-favored in the US and the UK as well as in France, Germany, Switzerland and many other European nations. Sales transactions, on the other hand, generally trigger large taxes at the corporate level. Although the first tax-free spin-off in the UK was Courtaulds' divestiture of its textile operations in 1990, several European countries have only recently changed their tax rules to accommodate tax-free spin-offs.

Why divest?

Once management decides to divest a subsidiary the next step is to consider the pros and cons of the ways to do so. What prompts the decision to divest? Management philosophies change and corporate focus is very much in fashion in the 1990s. Current management trends are based on downsizing, restructuring and returning to core competencies. Directors of conglomerates are pressured to improve shareholder returns, often by divesting under-performing lines of business that do not 'fit' with the core business. Recent academic studies report increased returns to investors in focused companies.

Managers, security analysts, management consultants, lawyers and investment bankers advocate divisive restructurings for several reasons:

- divestitures celebrate the corporate 'back to basics' movement;
- managements may believe that conglomerates trade at a discount to intrinsic value because investors and analysts, unable to decipher a complicated combination of businesses, assign the conglomerate a lower price multiple than the weighted average sum of its parts deserves. The desire to be a 'pure play' is based on the premise that investors can better understand and evaluate a single line of business, resulting in a more appropriate valuation of the organization. After all, investors can diversify their own portfolios – they don't necessarily want the companies they own to diversify on their behalf;
- competitive forces might dictate a divestiture; witness AT&T's spin-off of its equipment subsidiary Lucent Technologies, largely because AT&T's competitors chafed at buying equipment from its wholly owned subsidiary. Potential litigation can also spawn spin-offs, as illustrated by shareholders pressing RJR Nabisco and Philip Morris Kraft to separate its food subsidiaries from its tobacco businesses.

A taxing question

In a spin-off, a parent corporation distributes shares in a controlled subsidiary to its shareholders pro rata, as a dividend. The spun-off subsidiary thereby becomes a stand-alone public corporation. Pro rata distribution ensures no change in the shareholders' proportional ownership of the parent and the subsidiary. For example, when General Mills spun off its Darden Restaurants subsidiary in 1995, each General Mills shareholder received one share of Darden Restaurants stock for each share of General Mills stock owned. It was not an exchange offer; the Darden stock was in addition to the General Mills holdings.

To qualify as a non-taxable spin-off in the US, a transaction must meet stringent requirements of the Internal Revenue Code:

- the parent must have owned at least 80 per cent of the outstanding shares of the subsidiary for at least five years
- the parent must distribute at least 80 per cent of its stock in the subsidiary and relinquish all control of the subsidiary
- the transaction must have a valid corporate business purpose (other than minimizing taxes)
- there can be no pre-arranged plan for shareholders to sell the subsidiary stock following distribution
- both the parent and subsidiary must actively conduct the businesses previously owned and operated by the parent for at least five additional years.

Failure to satisfy these conditions generally results in capital gains taxes for the parent and either dividend income or capital gains taxes for the parent organization shareholders. The requirements for tax-free treatment in the UK and several other European countries are similar to those in the US and equally complex.

Tax-free treatment permits shareholders to defer gain (or loss) recognition until they sell the stock; parent shareholders allocate their tax basis in the pre-spin-off parent stock between the subsidiary stock and the post-spin-off parent stock based on the relative fair market values of the parent and subsidiary stock at the time of the spin-off.

Fig.1 Tax effects of sales and spin-offs

Sales	Spin-offs
• Parent firm recognizes gain or loss equal to difference between sales proceeds and tax basis in subsidiary	• Generally no gain or loss to parent firm or to its shareholders
• Buyer's tax basis in assets acquired is equal to amount paid	• Subsidiary retains its tax basis in underlying assets
• Parent firm shareholders recognize no income or loss unless proceeds are distributed as a dividend	• Shareholders allocate basis in pre-spin-off parent stock between subsidiary and post-spin-off parent based on relative fair market values

Importantly, the transaction is *non-taxable* to the parent corporation; any unrealized gain or loss of the parent in the subsidiary stock is *never* taxed – this feature makes the spin-off unique among divestiture transactions. The subsidiary's tax basis in its assets is not affected by the spin-off (there is no adjustment of basis to fair market value).

In a sale, all ties between the subsidiary and the parent (including ties to parent shareholders) are severed. Most sales are for cash, so most are taxable. In a taxable sale, the parent recognizes taxable gain or loss equal to the difference between the proceeds and its tax basis in the subsidiary. The acquiring organization takes a tax basis in the assets acquired equal to the amount paid by adjusting the assets to their fair market values. The divesting parent's shareholders face no tax consequences unless the parent pays out the cash proceeds in the form of a special dividend (a rare event). Figure 1 summarizes the tax differences between sales and spin-offs.

Visible value

The tax savings from choosing a non-taxable spin-off over a taxable sale can be considerable when the parent has a large unrealized taxable gain in the subsidiary and insufficient operating losses to shelter it.

Taxable sales are obviously more attractive for a parent with a tax loss on the sale and other taxable income to be sheltered. But there are also non-tax, and perhaps even non-economic, considerations. For example, a chief executive officer (CEO) may favor an asset sale, which alters the form but not the amount of total assets under his or her control, over a spin-off, which literally reduces the size of the 'empire.'

For a company in need of immediate cash, a sale can provide required funds; a spin-off gives the parent flexibility to allocate debt and cash between parent and subsidiary but generates no new cash from investors. Gains on sales increase reported earnings whereas spin-offs are accomplished using book values and treated as a dividend, with no boost to income.

A spin-off creates a new public company with a separately quoted stock price. The value of the subsidiary is thus readily apparent, a possibly unpleasant reminder to shareholders of previous poor acquisitions. And, of course, a sale requires a buyer at an 'acceptable' price; some spin-offs are simply the result of failed sales attempts. The

Fig.2 Advantages of spin-offs: an example

In the 1990 Annual Report to shareholders, Quaker Oats CEO William D. Smithburg described the impending spin-off of its toy subsidiary, Fisher-Price:

"The spin-off is good for our shareholders in several ways. It lets them decide whether they want to have a toy business in their portfolios. And, in the long term, the spin-off should allow Fisher-Price to operate more efficiently with faster decision-making and better flexibility. That should help it be more competitive and improve its ability to attract, retain and motivate employees. Fisher-Price remains one of the world's strongest and most trusted brand names. We fully expect Fisher-Price to have significantly improved performance over a two or three year recovery period. In addition, the spin-off lets Quaker concentrate on our core grocery business, where our future really lies."

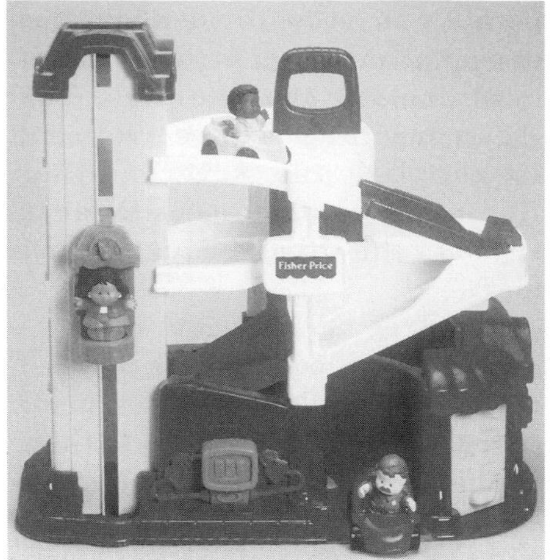

Taking a spin: Quaker Oats spin-off Fisher-Price was soon snapped up by Mattel

spun-off subsidiary, free of parent control, benefits from decentralized decision making, less bureaucracy and direct access to capital markets. (On the other hand, the subsidiary can no longer access its parent's capital).

Managers claim that spin-offs unlock otherwise hidden value by separating the subsidiary's operations and performance measures from those of the parent, thus allowing analysts and investors to value the subsidiary separately. Perhaps most importantly, a focused business makes it easier to link management actions to pay-off through stock ownership and stock options. Prior to its spin-off, Darden Restaurants' managers' compensation could not be tied to changes in shareholder value because the only traded shares were those of General Mills. Figure 2 contains a statement from the CEO of Quaker Oats describing the benefits of the spin-off of Fisher-Price toys.

US investors usually react positively to an announced spin-off, bidding shares up about three per cent (net of market effects). Both the parent and the spun-off business also outperform the overall securities market averages for several years following the divestiture. However, this favorable performance is largely due to an increased incidence of take-overs. For example, about a year after the double spin-off by ITT, the parent received a hostile bid, at a hefty premium, by Hilton Hotels. Likewise, less than 30 months after the spin-off, Mattel acquired Fisher-Price for about three times Fisher-Price's initial post-spin-off equity value. Investors also greet sales announcements favorably when the sales proceeds are to be paid out to either creditors or shareholders. However, the investor response is neutral when the funds are kept in the business.

Tax efficiency of divestitures

A 1995 study by J. P. Morgan reported that spin-offs increased from 10 per cent to 26 per cent of all US divestitures between 1988 and 1994. There were 23 spin-offs in 1992 valued at $5.7bn. By 1995, there were 31 spin-offs valued at $45.8bn and estimated volume for 1996 more than doubled to $100bn. The increase in non-taxable spin-offs presumably indicates an increase in tax efficient (that is, non-taxable) restructurings; however, most divisive restructurings remain tax inefficient (that is, taxable) sales. Thus it appears that divestitures, at least those in the US, are not structured to achieve maximum tax savings. To explore the reasons for this apparent anomaly, we analyzed 221 large subsidiary sales and 53 large spin-offs made by US public companies during 1987-1995 (all transactions exceeded $100m in market value).

We computed the tax costs or benefits for each of the 274 transactions under both the chosen divestiture method and the alternative method. We approximated the tax costs of sales using the taxable gains from the units that were sold and the tax benefits of spin-offs by estimating the 'as if' taxable gains assuming the units had been sold instead of being spun off. The taxable gain was multiplied by the divesting organization's estimated marginal tax rate to obtain the tax cost to the divesting unit in a sale transaction. The spin-offs were all non-taxable. The market value of a subsidiary may be higher in a sale than in a spin-off because of the tax benefits received by the buyer. A taxable sale provides for a basis step up (hence, increased tax depreciation deductions) while a non-taxable spin-off does not.

During negotiations, the seller attempts to capture these tax benefits from basis step up by increasing the sale price. Therefore, for spin-offs, we calculate the 'as if' sales proceeds incorporating this higher price due to the buyer's tax benefits. This adjustment assumes that a buyer would have had to pay this extra premium to close the sale, a reasonable assumption since a sale at the spin-off market value would make the parent worse off (relative to a non-taxable spin-off) by the taxes due on the gain.

We consider a transaction to be tax efficient or inefficient based on the sign of the 'net tax cost', which includes both the taxes due (or avoided) because of the choice of divestiture method and the higher price paid in a sale due to the buyer's tax benefit. A tax-inefficient sale results in avoidable tax payments, even after factoring in the increase in sales price enjoyed by the seller due to the buyer's tax benefits. Likewise, a tax-efficient spin-off avoids the payment of taxes, even after factoring in the increased sales price that could be obtained in excess of the spin-off market value, due to the buyer's tax benefits. Conversely, a tax-efficient sale generates a net tax loss (to be applied against other taxable income) and a tax-inefficient spin-off foregoes net tax benefits that would have been available to shelter other income had a taxable sale been undertaken with tax deductible losses.

Why so few spin-offs?

If a divestiture could qualify as either a spin-off or an asset sale, we would expect that, in the absence of non-tax factors, a company facing a positive tax rate would choose a non-taxable spin-off when the assets to be divested have an unrealized taxable gain and a taxable sale when these assets have an unrealized tax deductible loss. However, we find that non-tax considerations must play a considerable role in divestiture decisions. Of the 221 sales transactions in our sample, only 29 were tax efficient and 192 were tax inefficient. Of the 53 spin-offs, 47 were tax efficient and only six were tax inefficient.

The preponderance of tax-inefficient sales is not due to negligible tax costs. For our sample, the average net tax cost of the tax-inefficient sales is $38m or 2.4 per cent of the market value of equity of the parent. The tax-efficient spin-offs generate a mean $180m in tax savings (about 6.7 per cent of the parent's equity at market value). In more extreme cases, such as the 1996 non-taxable spin-off by Viacom of the US of its cable business, tax savings can be as much as $500m to $600m. The only way for managers to justify an avoidable tax cost of $38m is to point to at least $38m of non-tax benefits gained by the parent because the transaction was structured as a taxable sale rather than a non-taxable spin-off. (In our sample, we know the tax cost is avoidable because we included only divestitures that meet the criteria for a tax-free spin-off and thus could have been undertaken as either a non-taxable spin-off or a taxable sale.)

It is also possible that the real tax cost to the seller is immaterial because a buyer offers a premium (perhaps based on anticipated synergies) that exceeds the tax costs. In our sample, however, the acquisition premium paid by buyers, measured as the purchase price less the book value of the subsidiary, is not significantly different from the market premium afforded spun-off subsidiaries, measured as the initial traded share price less book value. Even if the tax costs are considerable, some companies may use tax dollars to buy accounting earnings. In its financial statements the parent recognizes gain (or loss) equal to the sale's proceeds minus the net asset book value of the subsidiary. In a spin-off there is no income effect since a spin-off is treated as a dividend and all accounting is done using book values.

By structuring divestitures as sales to increase accounting earnings, companies may end up paying higher taxes. While we find that financial reporting concerns are important to organizations in choosing a divestiture, we also find that managers do not maximize reported net income regardless of the cost. Not surprisingly, there is a limit to what they will pay for earnings.

Trade-off

We estimate that companies will trade off 15 cents in increased net tax costs in exchange for an additional $1 of financial reporting earnings. Figure 3 summarizes the financial reporting consequences of sales and spin-offs.

Regardless of income effects, managers may choose tax-inefficient sales simply because corporate financing needs dominate tax costs. For some businesses cash from taxable asset sales may be the least expensive source of outside capital. Cash-constrained firms are unable to borrow at acceptable terms and unable or unwilling to issue equity and so may be willing to incur tax costs to improve their liquidity. Funds provided by asset sales may also be attractive because they come with fewer restrictions than other external funds. We find that parents choosing sales have less financial flexibility than those choosing spin-offs and estimate that such companies are willing to trade 19 cents of increased net tax costs to obtain an additional $1 of cash flow from the sale.

In summary, we find that unrealized taxable gains for demerged/spun-off subsidiaries are about twice the gains for subsidiaries that are sold, measured as a percentage of the subsidiaries' market value. We find no significant difference in either the marginal tax rate or the ability to shelter taxable gains between the sales and spin-offs.

Therefore, managers appear willing to incur avoidable tax costs in order to obtain financial reporting benefits and cash – but only up to a point since such benefits ultimately become too expensive. Investors applaud divestitures – whether by sale or

Fig.3 Financial accounting effects of sales and spin-offs

Sales

- Parent firm recognizes gain or loss equal to difference between sales proceeds and book value
- Parent firm shareholders recognize no gain or loss

Spin-offs

- Generally no gain or loss to parent firm, subsidiary, or shareholders
- Parent firm accounts for the transaction on its books as a stock dividend
- Subsidiary keeps book values as reported on consolidated financial statements

spin-off – that result in more focused corporations but are generally more enthusiastic about spin-offs, perhaps because of their tax advantages.

Summary

Asset sales and spin-offs are the two most common means by which quoted US corporation divest unwanted lines of business. But should managers choose non-taxable spin-offs (involving the distribution of shares in a controlled subsidiary prorata to existing shareholders) or a straight sale? Katherine Schipper and Linda Vincent show that US managers appear willing to incur avoidable tax costs in order to obtain financial reporting benefits and cash. Investors are generally enthusiastic about divestments that result in more focus whether they are sales or spin-offs – but perhaps because of the tax advantages they seem to prefer the latter.

Suggested further reading

Comment, R. and Jarrell, G., (1995), 'Corporate Focus and Stock Returns', *Journal of Financial Economics,* January.

Cusatis, P., Miles, J. and Woolridge, J. R., (1994), 'Some New Evidence that Spinoffs Create Value', *Journal of Applied Corporate Finance,* Summer.

Schipper, K. and Smith, A., (1983), 'Effects of Recontracting on Shareholder Wealth: The Case of Voluntary Spinoffs', *Journal of Financial Economics* 12.

Spin-offs: why information flows better

by Michel Habib

Recent years have witnessed a large number of spin-offs, for example Sears and ITT in the US and Hanson in the UK. The announcement of these and other spin-offs has generally been accompanied by an increase in the value of the original business. In a spin-off one or more divisions of a quoted company have been detached from the original parent to become independent entities that are separately quoted on the stock market, yet remain owned, at least initially, by the shareholders of the original business.

Since a spin-off represents the division of a whole into parts, the increase in value that generally accompanies the announcement of a spin-off suggests that investors view the parts as being worth more separately than as part of the whole. Why this should be so is of particular interest at a time when many companies are busy restructuring, selling assets or divisions, buying others, merging with, acquiring, or being acquired by other organizations.

A number of explanations have been suggested for spin-offs. Many of these are reflected in comments made after the announcement of the split-up of Hanson. It was then said that 'head office was finding it increasingly difficult to assess the underlying performance of electricity and chemical companies in the group, making it harder to set them tough but realistic financial targets'. In addition 'people like the chairman of Quantum and SCM, two divisions that were spun off, would be much more motivated, with their personal wealth linked directly to the performance of their businesses through share options' and that 'separately listed, the chemical offshoot will be an inviting target for a big European or American chemical group'. The first comment illustrates the view that spin-offs serve to remedy the loss of focus inherent in large, diversified groups; the second that they make possible the provision of better incentives to managers; and the third that spin-offs facilitate the transfer of assets to those who value them most.

Conglomerate discount

The preceding explanations are examined in part in the accompanying article by Katherine Schipper and Linda Vincent (*see* page 85). This article looks in detail at a further explanation which centers on the role of spin-offs in improving the information available to investors and managers.

This is suggested by comments that appear to imply that companies comprising various divisions operating in different businesses with differing prospects are undervalued for informational reasons, and that spin-offs serve to remedy this undervaluation. For example, 'ITT's fast-growing leisure business' was said to be 'submerged by the more staid manufacturing and insurance businesses' before the group's decision to split itself into three parts. Similar remarks were directed at Chase Manhattan, the US bank, whose estimated break-up value, ranging from \$55–\$75 per share, was in sharp contrast to its market value of \$35 per share before its merger with Chemical Bank. It was said that 'the trouble for Chase is that the virtues of its best businesses ... have been shrouded in the lackluster performance of the group. As a result, the value of the whole has failed to keep pace with the sum of the parts'. In contrast, Sears Roebuck's spin-off of Dean Witter has been described as 'creating pieces that people will be able to understand so that the stock can fetch a fairer value'.

That investors appear to undervalue most diversified businesses is a well-known phenomenon, referred to as the 'conglomerate discount'. A reason often advanced for this is the 'opaqueness' of conglomerates, a term that is strongly suggestive of informational considerations. This article examines two ways in which informational considerations may lead to a conglomerate discount and thereby explain why spin-offs, which serve to transform the conglomerate's divisions into independent businesses, should lead to increases in value. Both are related to the role of share prices in transmitting information about a company's prospects or a division, or the value of their assets to investors and managers.

Consider the transmission of information to managers. Evidence of such communication is suggested by the near constant attention paid by managers to their company's share price, which reflects investors' views of the business, its strategy and its management. These are, eventually if not immediately, taken note of by the company's management or the board or by raiders who may attempt to acquire it. Thus, the poor share-price performance of those oil companies that maintained extensive exploration programs in the second part of the 1980s following the near collapse of the price of oil in 1986 eventually led their managers to reduce exploration programs and increase their reserves by buying other oil businesses rather than through exploration. These examples indicate that information transmitted by share prices is used by managers. This is true of both multiple-business conglomerates and single-business companies.

Better decisions

The share price of the former does, however, communicate information about the combined prospects of a multiplicity of generally unrelated businesses, whereas that of the latter provides information about the prospects of a single business. Managers of conglomerates therefore face the difficult task of inferring investors' views of the prospects of each of their multiple businesses from a single share price. They do so only very imperfectly.

The quality of their decisions is thus reduced by the imperfect information available to them. This lowers the value of conglomerates and results in the conglomerate discount. A spin-off of a division, or a complete split-up of a conglomerate, in which a single price pertaining to a multiplicity of businesses is replaced by multiple prices relating to single and separate businesses, creates value by making better decisions possible. But share prices also communicate information to investors. Indeed, their role in communicating information to investors may well be more important than in communicating data to managers. That is because the direct communication of information to managers is feasible but clearly impossible to literally millions of existing and potential investors.

As noted by Sanford Grossman in 1976, when each investor has only imperfect information about a company's prospects and the value of its assets, its share price will aggregate the information of all investors and communicate information of higher quality than initially possessed by each single investor. The higher quality information provided through the share price diminishes all investors' uncertainty about the company's prospects and the value of its assets and increases the price they are willing to pay for its shares.

Although the quality of the information every investor has is improved by trading in shares, it nonetheless remains lower in the case of multiple-business conglomerates than in that of single-business companies. Investors, as are managers, are confronted with the task of inferring the prospects of multiple businesses from a single share price. The lower quality of their information decreases the price they are willing to pay for the conglomerate's shares, again leading to the conglomerate discount. That a spin-off is viewed as serving to remedy the resulting undervaluation was true, for example, of New World Development, the Hong Kong conglomerate, which announced the spin-off of its hotel management and infrastructure divisions in summer of 1995. The *Financial Times* reported that 'New World believes the restructuring ... will make the group easier for investors to understand and release value in operations that has hitherto been masked by a complex and opaque corporate structure'.

Note this could refer to information communicated by accounting numbers and cash flows as well as by prices, to the extent that accounting figures and cash flows are aggregated at corporate rather than divisional level. But any undervaluation resulting from the possibly excessive aggregation of accounting numbers or cash flows can be remedied simply by reporting the relevant information at the divisional level and need not involve a spin-off. A spin-off is, by contrast, essential to achieving an increase in the quality of the information communicated through prices.

The above informational considerations suggest the conglomerate discount should be largest for those that are the most diversified. The difficulty of inferring the prospects of each of the multiple businesses of a conglomerate from the single share price is greatest when the conglomerate's businesses are least related. The value created by demergers and spin-offs should therefore be greatest for those spun-off divisions that most differ from the parent. Daley and others find this to be the case. Indeed, they find that same-industry spin-offs, in which both the spun-off division and the parent belong to the same industry, create no value, and that only cross-industry spin-offs do so.

Interestingly, Slovin and others find that the value of the competitors to a division of a group increases following the announcement of the division's spin-off, suggesting that the information released by a spin-off is of value not only to the company or the division involved but also to its competitors.

But spin-offs have costs as well as benefits, most clearly where there are significant synergies between a conglomerate's divisions. Such synergies would be foregone in a spin-off. Significant synergies appear to exist in the case of General Electric of the US, for example, which is essentially a highly profitable conglomerate with a large number of businesses, ranging from aero-engines to financial services.

No panacea

More importantly, spin-offs should not be viewed as panaceas. This is most clearly illustrated by the case of Hanson. Since most organizations have adopted strict financial controls after the takeover wave of the 1980s, the scope for value creation through take-overs and imposing such controls has dramatically decreased, in turn decreasing the growth prospects of acquisitive conglomerates such as Hanson.

An unmistakable signal of the decreased growth prospects was Hanson's announcement, concurrently with the disclosure of the demerger, that the demerged businesses would adopt dividend policies in line with those of their industries. This new policy implied a drastic cut in dividend, unmistakably a negative signal. Hanson's share price fell as a result, in spite of the spin-off.

To conclude, spin-offs are at least partly motivated by informational considerations related to the role of share prices in communicating information to investors and managers. They are most desirable when the divisions of a conglomerate are least related, because the improvement in the quality of the information communicated by prices is greatest in such cases. They are not, however, a cure-all, and certainly cannot offset the poor prospects of a division or a company.

Quotations are from the *Financial Times* and *The Economist.*

Summary

'Spin-offs: tax comparison with an asset sale' dwelt primarily on the tax implications of a spin-off. But what are the other advantages of this form of corporate restructuring? Michel Habib says that better focus and better management incentives are among the widely discussed benefits, but on this page he concentrates on the way spin-offs improve the information available to investors and managers. He argues that they are most desirable when the divisions of a conglomerate are least related, because the improvement in quality of the information communicated by prices is greatest in such cases.

Suggested further reading

Daley, I., Mehrotra, V. and Sivakumar, R., (1995), 'Corporate spin-offs: Trash or treasure' working paper 5–95, University of Alberta.

Grossman, S.J. 'On the efficiency of competitive stock markets where traders have diverse information' *Journal of Finance* 31, 573–585.

Habib, M.A., Johnsen, D.B. and Naik, N.Y., 'Spin-offs and Information' working paper, London Business School.

Nanda, V. and Narayanan, M.P. 'Dissentangling value: Misvaluation and the scope of the firm' working paper, University of Michigan.

Schipper, K. and Smith, A., (1983), 'Effects of recontracting on shareholder wealth: the case of voluntary spin-offs', *Journal of Financial Economics* 12, 437–487.

Slovin, M., Sushka, M. and Ferraro S., (1995), 'A comparison of the information conveyed by equity carve-outs, spin-offs, and asset sell-offs', *Journal of Financial Economics* 37, 89–104.

Suggested further reading

[illegible]

3

Accounting

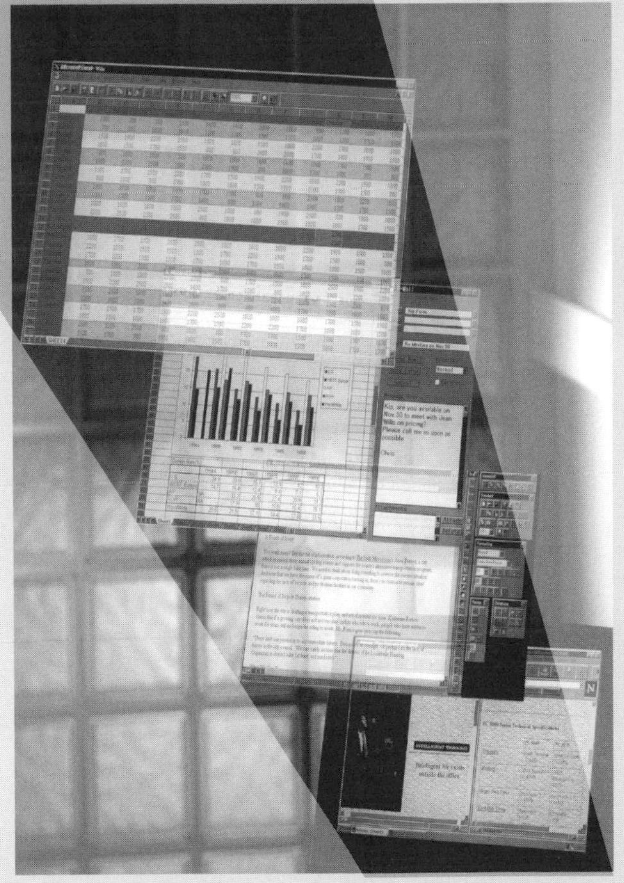

Contributors

Richard Leftwich is Fuji Bank and Hellor Professor of Accounting and Finance at the University of Chicago Graduate School of Business. His research interests include audit qualifications, bond ratings, corporate charter changes and block trades.

Alvin Carley is Practice Professor of Accounting at the Wharton School of the University of Pennsylvania.

Contents

Introduction

Accounting – the skill or practice of maintaining or auditing company accounts – is a vast topic in its own right. This module takes a global perspective, examining why national rules differ so markedly and considering what progress is being made to overcome them through the setting of international standards.

International accounting standards

by Richard Leftwich

Accounting rules governing external reporting to stockholders, creditors and other outside parties differ markedly across countries, and the differences persist despite the increased integration of the world's capital markets. This article discusses why accounting standards for external reports differ across countries, and why those differences persist. The United States' Securities and Exchange Commission (SEC) plays a key role in current attempts to develop a set of international accounting standards that could attain acceptance globally. Without the blessing of the SEC, firms seeking to raise capital in the US cannot use financial reports relying on international accounting standards to satisfy SEC disclosure requirements. To date, the SEC has taken the stance that they will endorse international accounting standards only if those standards comport closely with most features of US accounting standards. This is a serious threat to the viability of international accounting standards, because access to the US capital market is highly desired by many large non-US firms. It also presents a dilemma for the SEC because many of the constituents of the SEC, particularly US stock exchanges and institutional investors, stand to benefit considerably if access to US capital markets is made simpler for firms currently listed outside the US. It will require considerable political skill for the SEC to allow easier access to US capital markets for foreign firms by 'relaxing' reporting requirements while placating domestic firms who must produce reports based on what they perceive are more costly US accounting standards.

There are also international differences in accounting standards for internal accounting reports (reports prepared for managers within the firm), but those differences attract less attention for two reasons. First, ignorance is bliss – internal differences are less visible to the outside investment community and attract less scrutiny from external parties. Second, regulation has less influence on a firm's choice of internal accounting than on the firm's choice of external accounting standards. Firms are able to experiment more readily with internal accounting and can adopt practices and standards that they consider are superior (just as they can choose preferred manufacturing processes) without convincing accounting regulators of the wisdom of the choice. In contrast, the influence of regulators with difference economic and political agenda inhibits potential convergence of accounting standards for external reporting across countries.

Accounting differences across countries

The differences range from the trivial to the substantive. Consider some trivial differences that are revealed by even a brief perusal of financial statements from different countries. Even if two countries share the same language (e.g. English), different terminology is employed, for example: *sales* (US) and *turnover* (UK); *retained earnings* (US) and *undistributed profits* (UK); and *consolidated accounts* (US) and *group accounts* (UK). The form in which the accounts are presented differs even if the countries use similar standards. For example, in the US, assets appear on the left-hand side of the balance sheet, and assets are listed in order of liquidity with current assets listed first. In the UK, assets appear on the right-hand side of the balance sheet, and assets are listed in reverse order of liquidity with fixed assets listed first. In some countries (e.g. Belgium, France, Italy and Germany), stockholders receive only two financial statements (an income statement and a balance sheet). In some countries, where a third statement (a statement of changes in financial position) is provided, the statement traces only sources and uses of working capital, not sources and uses of cash.

If all the differences involved only terminology and the form of presentation, it would not be difficult to produce a set of universally accepted accounting standards. However, there are substantial differences in the treatment of many economic activities (such as mergers, pensions, leases and changes in the value of financial

Fig.1 Contrasts in accounting philosophy

	On the one hand	On the other
Primary purpose of external financing reporting	Provide information to stockholders (e.g. US and UK).	Protect creditors, guard against reporting information that will harm the company competitively (e.g. Japan and Germany).
Guidance provided by standards	Very specific operational and implementation details (e.g. US).	Broad principles only, allowing management considerable discretion for many transactions (e.g. Japan and Germany).
Topics covered by standards	Specific individual standards provide extensive coverage of major and minor business activities, including, for example, how to account for the costs of modifying computer software to cope with the year 2000 (US).	No specific individual standards for some major business activities (e.g. post-employment health benefits in Canada, Germany and Netherlands).
Relationship to income tax laws	External reporting and tax reporting based on such different rules that there are essentially two sets of books (e.g. Australia, Canada, US and Netherlands).	Income taxes based heavily on externally reported income (e.g. Germany, France and UK).
Reporting frequency	Quarterly (US, Canada, Mexico and Israel).	Semi-annually (UK, France, Netherlands, Germany and Japan).
Disclosure of accounting adjustments (transparency)	Extensive footnote and narrative discussion of: choices and applications of accounting methods, estimation techniques, transfers to and from reserves and provisions, and other accounting adjusting entries (e.g. Australia, New Zealand, US, Canada, and UK).	Considerable aggregation of asset and liability classes, few footnotes, and, at most, cryptic comments about: how accounting standards are applied, transfers to and from reserves, and the basis for various accounting adjustments (e.g. France, Japan, Germany and Switzerland).
Charges against owners' equity	Clean surplus – virtually all charges, including the cumulative effects of changes in accounting choices, must flow through the income statement (e.g. US and, with more exceptions, the UK).	No clean surplus – some charges, especially those associated with the prior-period effect of changes in accounting methods, can be made directly against retained earnings (e.g. Germany).

instruments) and those differences result from the very different philosophies and general principles that underlie accounting standards in different countries. Figures 1 and 3 provide some examples of contrasting philosophies and general principles. When the principles underlying one country's accounting standards are applied to a particular transaction, the result can be an accounting procedure that violates the principles underlying accounting standards in another country. The much maligned German *secret* or *hidden reserves* provide an excellent example. German accounting is heavily influenced by the desire to protect creditors, and income taxes in Germany are based primarily on externally reported accounting profit, so there are strong legal and economic pressures to report income and asset values conservatively. Consequently, German accounting standards require that allowances be made for all *possible* losses. Since virtually anything can be deemed possible, management has considerable flexibility when determining the appropriate allowance. In addition, the lack of supplementary disclosure about transfers to and from these reserves hinders attempts by external financial analysts to determine the extent to which income has been affected by these transfers to and from reserves, or more colorfully, to separate how much of the accounting income was generated in the factory and how much was created in the accounting department. Paradoxically, many of these apparently conservative techniques can be used subsequently to increase income by charging (and not disclosing) some expenses against reserves instead of against income. Such practices are expressly prohibited in other countries (such as the US and the UK) where reserves can be set aside for identifiable *probable* losses and where transfers to and from the reserves must be disclosed explicitly in the financial statements. Figure 2 uses information from the US filings of Daimler Benz to demonstrate the dramatic effects that can be achieved by transfer to and from reserves.

Fig.2 Dramatic differences from Daimler Benz

In DM (m)	Reported	Transfer	Before reserve transfer
1992	1,450	–770	2,220
1993	610	4,260	–3,650

Even though these philosophical differences are often expressed in language suggesting that one point of view is superior, the case is far from obvious. For example, how much discretion should managers have about the choice of accounting techniques for a particular transaction? Less discretion is preferred by those with an ingrained suspicion of management's motives, more is preferred by those who want to provide managers with the ability to convey private information to the capital market. Government and quasi-government regulators seem to have the former attitude; members of self-regulatory bodies (such as professional and management associations) are more likely to have the latter attitude.

Differences in philosophy are often exaggerated in debates about the relative merits of accounting standards in different countries, particularly since those debates occur primarily in the political arena. Consider the issue about how specific the accounting standards of a particular country are, or, put differently, how much discretion management is allowed in applying accounting standards to specific events or transactions. The standards in all countries allow management some latitude and the US is no exception. Some US companies with admired accounting policies, such as General Electric, have followed conservative accounting practices for so long that they

Fig.3 Accounting treatments across the globe

Event or transaction	Range of alternatives
Asset revaluation	Allowed (Australia, Hong Kong, India, UK) Allowed under some circumstances (France, Italy, Sweden) Not allowed (Canada, Germany, Japan, US)
Funds statement	Report sources and uses of cash (US, UK, Israel, Korea) Report sources and uses of working capital (Mexico, Sweden, Singapore) Not required (France, Germany, Netherlands, Switzerland)
Inflation accounting	Required (Argentina, Brazil, Israel, Mexico) Optional supplementary information (UK, Australia, Netherlands, US) Not required (Canada, Indonesia, Japan, Germany, Korea)
Goodwill	Capitalize and write-off against owners' equity (Italy, Singapore, South Africa and UK) Capitalize and write-off through income statement (Australia, Canada, France, US)
Research and development costs	Expense (US, Germany, Mexico) Capitalize (Argentina, Korea, Norway, Netherlands) Capitalize Development Costs, Expense Research (UK, Canada, Denmark, Israel, Nigeria) Not specified (China, Ireland)
Segment reporting	Sales, profits, and assets by industry and geographic segment (Canada, UK, Israel, Italy and Singapore) Sales by industry and geographic segment (France, Germany, Belgium, Netherlands) Sales and profits by industry (Korea) Not specified (India, Indonesia, Norway, Switzerland)
Non-operating leases	Capitalization required (Belgium, Hong Kong, Israel, US) Capitalization optional, or allowed under highly specific circumstances (Denmark, Sweden, France, Japan) Expense (India, Italy)
Other post-employment benefits	Accrue expenses (Indonesia, Nigeria, UK, US) Cash basis (Australia, Germany, Hong Kong, Japan)
Pension plans	Recognize unfunded liability (US, Mexico) Ignore unfunded liability (Canada, Germany, Netherlands, UK) Not specified (Hong Kong, New Zealand, Belgium)

have secret reserves in all but name. Moreover, despite US footnote and narrative disclosure policy, there are ample opportunities (for example with ubiquitous restructuring charges) to hide transfers to and from these ersatz reserves.

Why do the differences exist and persist?

External accounting reports are an important subset of the information and control devices designed to ameliorate some of the problems caused by the separation of ownership and control in large companies, or, in the rubric of economics, accounting is part of the corporate governance system designed to induce managers to act in the interests of the owners of the firm. Accounting standards for a particular country should be appreciated in the context of the other information and control systems employed in that country. Corporate governance systems differ dramatically from country to country, reflecting differences in: the legal system, the role of public capital markets, the role of the government in capital and other markets, and tradition and culture. Economically sound accounting in one environment need not be sensible accounting in another environment. For example, large banks are the dominant shareholders in large companies in Germany and have representatives on the boards of directors and access to internal accounting records. German managers are disciplined or rewarded primarily by representatives of these stockholders, not by the firm's fortunes as reflected in the stock market. In that environment, it is not surprising that external accounting reports disclose fewer details of the impact of accounting choices than would be found in an environment where suppliers of capital are not well represented on the board. Consider another example. In Japan, the *keiretsu* is a group of firms with significant cross-ownership of stock and very close working relationships as suppliers and customers. The relationships among these firms are not adequately captured by the organization structure akin to a controlling firm with subsidiaries that is so common in the UK and the US. In the Japanese economic environment it should not be surprising that domestic firms seldom produce consolidated reports, whereas those reports are the norm (for example, in the UK, US, Australia and New Zealand) where the parent-subsidiary relationship is common.

An additional level of complexity is added because, in every country, the choice of accounting standards is regulated. The accounting standards and corporate governance procedures in place in a particular country reflect the outcome of economic and political processes, not simply the result of a market-driven process. Moreover, there is no well-articulated economic rationale for the regulation of accounting standards. Accounting reports were prepared and used long before accounting standards were regulated and there is no compelling evidence that regulation improved the quality of accounting reports, even before taking into account the cost of the regulation, Since it is difficult to specify what economic problem accounting regulation was supposed to solve, it is difficult to understand why regulation took different forms in different countries.

There is also a deeper question of why corporate governance practices differ so dramatically across countries. It is simple to explain some differences away as the result of culture, tradition or historical accident. Economists prefer explanations based on exogenous factors such as the legal system and rules regarding property rights, although ultimately even those factors are endogenous. For the purposes of the debate about international accounting standards, the corporate governance system of a particular country is taken as given, but, to the extent that the debate about international standards is a debate about access to capital markets in other countries, differences in corporate governance systems are likely to attract attention also.

The previous discussion explains why accounting differences exist in an international setting, but not why those differences persist in a world where markets, especially capital markets, are becoming more closely integrated. Consider some other choices that are difficult in an international setting, for example, the decision about whether traffic keeps to the left or to the right. Even though the residents of Europe and the UK might agree that life would be easier if every country adopted the same rule, there would be sharp divisions about *which* rule. All citizens capture the benefits from the common rule but those who change incur the costs of changing the road system and the configuration of existing vehicles. The traffic rule decision is an order of magnitude different from the accounting rule decision because, at least from the perspective of an economist, there is no reason for citizens of any country to oppose the proposed new traffic rule other than the cost of changing the status quo. Presumably, whether vehicles stay (more accurately, are supposed to stay) to the left or right in a particular country is only a product of historical happenstance. In sharp contrast, accounting standards evolve because of existing economic and political forces within the environment, and it is not obvious that producers and consumers of accounting reports are made better off if a common set of standards is adopted for countries with vastly different economic and political environments. Since accounting is a product of those economic and political systems, accounting convergence is likely to follow, not lead, convergence in those systems. Moreover, since accounting standards are heavily influenced by laws and regulations, market forces alone are unlikely to bring about the convergence.

What are international accounting standards?

The International Accounting Standards Committee (IASC) was formed in 1973 by representatives of professional accounting associations of a number of countries and has issued 32 International Accounting Standards (IASs). For at least the first decade of its existence, the IASC toiled in relative obscurity (albeit at exotic locales) and the international accounting standard-setting process was regarded more as an intellectual exercise than as a means of achieving greater comparability of financial statements for companies from difference countries. Few of the world's major financial capital markets formally recognized international accounting standards and the IASC did not have any power to require companies to adopt their standards. Much of the early work of the IASC consisted of designing international standards that were consistent with widely varying standards. Consequently those international standards allowed numerous alternative treatments so that most countries' domestic standards were close to proper subsets of the international standards.

However, the IASC has a renewed lease on life. Some new terminology, harmonization, has crept into the debate about international standards, reflecting a subtle difference in the process, together with some marketing to make the proposed international standards more palatable to member countries. The driving force behind the resurgence of interest in international accounting standards has been the competition among national stock exchanges for new listings, coupled with very different regulatory regimes in the United States and the other global capital markets. The major stock exchanges are profit-oriented and their growth and profitability depend on attracting new listings, and the exchanges recognize that firms believe that accounting disclosure requirements represent a high implicit entry tax to many markets, particularly to the US market. A credible set of international accounting standards would strengthen the hand of the exchanges in their dealings with regulators and several exchanges (including the NYSE) have acted recently to enhance the budget, visibility and credibility of the IASC.

In 1987, the IASC embarked on a major project to reduce the range of choices available under international standards, culminating in the release of 10 new standards in 1993. More significantly, the IASC changed its attitude toward domestic standards. Previously, member countries were supposed to deep domestic standards compatible with international standards. Now the IASC seems committed to developing international standards that can be used as a substitute for domestic standards by a foreign issuer. In 1995, the International Organization of Securities Commissioners (IOSCO), an affiliation of regulators responsible for most of the world's capital markets, and the IASC agreed to produce a 'core' set of accounting standards by 1999 that could be adopted and required by all countries, at least for foreign issuers. The IASC has also announced plans to provide guidance for applying international standards to particular events or transactions to create additional uniformity across countries.

The IASC has achieved moderate success along other dimensions. Several countries, (e.g. Malaysia and Pakistan) have adopted the existing IASs as their domestic standards in their entirety and that option seems attractive for countries (such as those in Eastern Europe) with newly formed capital markets and no domestic accounting standards. Other countries have adopted specific portions of the international standards to replace existing domestic standards or to expand the range of topics covered by existing standards. Some national stock exchanges, most notably London, allow foreign issuers to rely on IASs and over 200 large companies (mainly domiciled in Canada, France and Switzerland) have provided supplementary statements consistent with international accounting standards. The US SEC has even allowed foreign firms to follow some international accounting standards, such as portions of the standards on cash flow statements (IAS 7), foreign currency (IAS 21), business combinations (IAS 22) and inflation accounting (IAS 29).

There have been some attempts to reduce the diversity of accounting standards within the European Union, primarily with the fourth and seventh directives. However, those directives have met the fate of many EU directives and have yet to produce discernible effects. Moreover, since the EU countries have adopted a policy of mutual recognition of each other's standards, the impetus for harmonization has diminished. Further narrowing of differences seems to have low priority since, although an EU harmonization task force was created in 1990, no proposals or pronouncements have been made since then.

Why is there so much focus on US GAAP?

It is common to benchmark the accounting standards of any country against those of the US. This is more than xenophobia on the part of US commentators, and does not imply that US standards are superior in every, or even any, respect. It is merely a reflection of basic economics and politics. Unless international accounting standards are accepted by the US SEC firms adopting them will not qualify for entry to US public capital markets. If a German company such as Daimler Benz wants to have its shares traded publicly in the United States, it must satisfy the rules and regulations (listing requirements) of the stock exchange on which its shares are to be traded and it must comply with the panoply of disclosure requirements imposed by the SEC, slightly modified as a concession to non-US issuers. In particular, the SEC requires that a company must either provide accounting reports that are prepared in accord with US Generally Accepted Accounting Principles (GAAP), or must reconcile accounting reports prepared in accord with the home country GAAP (Germany in the case of Daimler Benz) to accounting reports that are consistent with US GAAP. Few companies choose the former option, but even reconciliation is costly. The reported reconciliation statements (Form 20F) filed by non-US issuers reveal some large differences, according to an SEC study, even where the foreign standards are considered to be similar to US standards (e.g. for Canadian and UK firms). In addition, the direction of the differences is predictable – if there is a difference, there is a 70 per cent probability that the net income number reported for US purposes is lower. In contrast, listing a company's shares on most of the competing national exchanges (e.g. London, Hong Kong and Tokyo) requires only that the accounting reports provided to investors be prepared in accord with home country GAAP and translated into the official language of the country where the listing is sought.

If the US public capital market remains a major part of the world's capital market, international accounting standards that do not meet US regulatory standards will be damaged goods. Of course, there is some simultaneity here. If the US SEC persists in insisting that it is the only one in step, the US public capital market may lose its dominant position. This is precisely what concerns the profit-oriented participants in the US capital markets, particularly the New York Stock Exchange (NYSE). Members of the NYSE recognize that there is competition for new listings from non-US stock exchanges, and ultimately, there are competitive threats to existing listings. There are only a few billion dollar US companies not listed in the NYSE, but there are hundreds of billion dollar companies in other countries that would provide attractive NYSE listings. The profits of member firms, the prestige and visibility of the exchange, and the salaries and perquisites of NYSE management would be enhanced, or at least preserved, if those large foreign companies were to list on the NYSE. It seems clear that, if the NYSE were free to choose, it would allow foreign firms to list and provide reports that did not necessarily follow US accounting standards.

The task facing the IASC is formidable. The list of topics to be addressed by the core standards includes thorny accounting issues (such as goodwill, financial instruments, segment reporting, interim reporting, leases, non-cash compensation, and reserves and allowances) that are highly controversial even within domestic settings. Despite a heady rush of optimism leading to a promise of an earlier completion of the core program, current indications are that meeting the original schedule of 1999 will be difficult. There are no objective criteria for determining what the 'best' accounting treatment of any event or transaction is, and there is not even general agreement about basic philosophical issues among member countries. The simplest method of securing agreement about a proposed standard is to make the standard sufficiently flexible that all domestic standards are consistent with it. Such a task requires Delphic skills if the standards of some countries are virtually inconsistent. As would be expected, progress has been easiest where there is little conflict among extant domestic standards and where the promulgated international standard is sufficiently flexible to be compatible with many domestic standards.

Academic research

Accounting and finance researchers have studied various aspects of international accounting standards. This research is interesting in its own right, but it is unlikely to resolve the fundamental question about the appropriate choice of international accounting standards. That choice is ultimately a political issue, with the US SEC a major player. Policy makers may use economic arguments and research selectively to buttress their preferred positions, but their preferred positions will reflect political not economic trade-offs.

One stream of academic research compares the efficiency of various national stock markets to the efficiency of the US market. The SEC can prevent shares of firms that do not use US accounting standards from being sold in US public markets, but it cannot prevent US investors from buying those shares, with higher transactions costs, either through international mutual funds or through brokers who place orders in foreign capital markets. If other stock markets with allegedly inferior accounting standards are as efficient as the US market, some researchers argue, how can US investors be harmed by being able to purchase those efficiently priced shares in the US, especially if they can purchase them abroad? As interesting as that argument is, it is difficult to imagine the SEC placing much weight on it because the raison d'être of the SEC involves protecting the interests of uninformed investors and in making the capital market 'fair' to all participants. Regulators charged with that responsibility are unlikely to take much comfort in knowing that the market protects investors by pricing securities based on all available information.

Another stream of academic research attempts to rank the relative informativeness of different countries' accounting standards by measuring the relationship between stock prices and reported accounting numbers in various countries. Even though the rankings obtained from these studies comport with most observers' views of the relative strengths and weaknesses of different accounting standards (e.g. UK and US accounting numbers seem highly informative, German and Japanese standards appear markedly less informative), the relevance of this research to the policy debate is tenuous. Accounting information explains a relatively small amount of stock price variation, and researchers have been unable to document the strong stock-price effects of dramatically different accounting choices, even among firms using the same domestic accounting standards.

Is there a solution in sight?

The IASC has more than thorny accounting problems to solve. The IASC is between a rock and a hard place politically. The IASC now seems intent on developing accounting standards that could be adopted by foreign firms in lieu of domestic standards. Implicitly, this would create a two-tier reporting regime if domestic issuers used domestic standards, and two-tier reporting will produce considerable tension in countries like the US where domestic standards are considered to be costly. The SEC has sent strong signals that international accounting standards containing significant departure from the philosophy, coverage and specificity of US standards will not be acceptable. The SEC has strong support from the Financial Accounting Standards Board (FASB) on this score because widely accepted international accounting standards could undermine the credibility of standards promulgated by the FASB.

In opposing a two-tiered solution, the US SEC has come perilously close to admitting that the emperor has no clothes. The SEC argues that a race for the bottom would soon develop if foreign firms were allowed to rely on accounting standards that are perceived by US firms as lower cost or less stringent than US standards. If the SEC did not 'relax' US standards, the argument goes, US firms would reincorporate as foreign firms and enter the US capital markets with accounting reports prepared in accord with international accounting standards. The argument seems so simplistic as to be almost a straw man because it ignores the apparently obvious point that, if US standards are superior (after allowing for their higher cost) firms that switch to an allegedly inferior international standard should see their stock prices decline due to the higher cost of capital they then face. Anyone familiar with the economic, political and emotional turmoil associated with the proposal for a common currency in Europe, will recognize the obstacles to progress toward a set of widely accepted international accounting standards, particularly since there is not even consensus on what constitutes progress.

Summary

Despite the integration of world stock markets national differences in accounting rules governing external reporting persist. Some of these are trivial but as Richard Leftwich explains in this article many concern substantive issues such as mergers and pensions and stem from strongly held principles and philosophies, such as Germany's

overriding desire to protect creditors, and contrasting approaches to corporate governance.

Accounting, the author argues, is a product of economic and political systems and for this reason accounting convergence is likely to follow rather than lead any wider convergence. This said, competition among national stock exchanges for new listings, and the gulf between US and other regulatory regimes, have inspired a resurgence of interest in international standards and the work of the IASC (International Accounting Standards Committee). Formidable challenges remain and it looks as though progress is most likely where the promulgated international standard is sufficiently flexible to be compatible with many domestic standards. An implicit move towards two-tier reporting, though, and the temptation to reincorporate in more 'relaxed' accounting environments, would be fiercely resisted by the US Securities and Exchange Commission (SEC).

Suggested further reading

Afterman, A., (1996), *International Accounting, Financial Reporting and Analysis*, Warren, Gorham & Lamont.

Alford, A., Jones, J., Leftwich, R. and Zmijewski, M., (1993), 'The Relative Informativeness of Accounting Disclosures in Different Countries', *Journal of Accounting Research*.

Baumol, W. and Malkiel, B., (1993), 'Redundant Regulation of Foreign Security Trading and US Competitiveness', *Journal of Applied Corporate Finance*, Winter.

Bloomer, Carrie (ed), (1996), 'The IASC-US Comparison Project: A Report on the Similarities and Differences between IASC Standards and US GAAP', Financial Accounting Standards Board.

Coopers & Lybrand, (1993), *International Accounting Summaries: A Guide for Interpretation and Comparison*, 2nd ed, John Wiley.

Edwards, F., (1993), 'Listing of Foreign Securities on US Exchanges', *Journal of Applied Corporate Finance*, Winter.

Leftwich, R., (1980), 'Market Failure Fallacies and Accounting Information', *Journal of Accounting and Economics*, December.

United States Securities and Exchange Commission, (1993), 'Survey of Financial Statement Reconciliations by Foreign Registrants'.

Watts, Ross and Zimmerman, Jerold L., (1986), *Positive Accounting Theory,* Prentice-Hall US.

Creating a common accounting language

by Alvin Carley

You are a US executive contemplating an acquisition. A UK company is also interested in the potential target and has offered a price that will result in consolidation goodwill of $450m. Under UK generally accepted accounting principles (GAAP), the UK company has the option of charging goodwill directly to equity accounts, avoiding any effect on future net income. But your company will have to capitalize goodwill on the balance sheet and amortize it over a period not exceeding 40 years. That will depress future earnings – including, incidentally, the earnings amount used to determine executive compensation. It will also have an impact on ratios mentioned in the covenants and commitments section of loan agreements your company has with lenders. (By the way, the UK company can restore the depleted equity section of its balance sheet by assigning a value to the brand names of the company to be acquired and by crediting the equity section, a practice forbidden under US GAAP).

Let's take another example. You are a US mining company executive with significant operations in the Philippines. Your company and a Philippine mining company have debts denominated in US dollars and Japanese yen and both companies use the borrowed funds to increase productive capacity. The Philippine peso suddenly drops in value by 25 per cent. The resulting transaction loss must be charged against your earnings in the year of the devaluation. But the Philippine company, under Philippine GAAP, can capitalize all or a significant portion of its transaction loss to fixed assets and write it off against future earnings. The two companies are competitive – and that includes their ability to obtain capital through debt or equity offerings. There are many other such accounting differences that could result in significant differences in how companies report their net income and net worth in their financial statements.

Consider also the effect this has on international business: does the consolidation goodwill issue give the UK an advantage over US companies in the merger and acquisitions arena? Will the Philippine company be perceived as more valuable than its US competitor because of higher net income in the year of devaluation? Will its cost of capital be favorably affected? In addition there will be a considerable expenditure of time and money to restate financial statements to another GAAP in order to register securities outside a company's home country.

International organizations

The differences in GAAP world-wide are a serious issue and should be resolved by attaining a much higher level of commonality of GAAP and overall reporting practices. Some organizations are striving to achieve this objective. The International Accounting Standards Committee (IASC), an organization representing the accounting profession and financial analysts with members from more than 85 countries, is contributing significantly to a higher level of commonality in accounting principles. The

International Organization of Securities Commissions (IOSCO) plays a supportive role while keeping pressure on to assure a satisfactory set of core standards within a reasonable period. IASC has earned the respect and support of important professional entities, such as the US Financial Accounting Standards Board (FASB) and comparable standard-setting groups in other countries, governmental regulatory bodies and many multinational corporations.

Conforming countries

A good example of this co-operation is revision of the FASB statement on earnings per share and development of a standard on that matter by IASC. The groups pursued those projects concurrently, sharing research and discussing important issues. The Financial Executives Institute, also based in the US, has indicated that the International Association of Financial Executives Institutes will participate in IASC as a full board member, rather than simply as a member of the IASC Consultative Group. More than 200 companies state in their annual reports that their financial statements conform with international accounting standards. Further, many countries use the IASC standards as their own national requirements or as a basis against which to compare and measure their standards.

The early work of the IASC did not meet with wholehearted acceptance. Initially, standards included permissible alternative treatments that did not create an effective set of standards and which failed to achieve the objective of world-wide comparability of financial information. IASC addressed this problem in 1987 in its Comparability/ Improvements Project, which examined 29 alternative treatments covered in the 10 then existing standards and subsequently eliminated most of them, with a few held over for subsequent resolution. Efforts to eliminate permissible alternative treatments have, for the most part, been successful.

But let us examine the accepted alternative treatment issue with regard to other accounting standards. If we review the accounting principles of various countries, we find the same kind of practice. In the UK, for example, consolidation goodwill can either be written off to equity accounts immediately or capitalized and amortized. In addition, fixed assets may or may not be revalued on UK balance sheets and the values of brand names may or may not be recognized. In the US, on the other hand, it is permissible to use moving average, specific identification, last-in-first-out or first-in-first-out methods (one of the areas subject to benchmark treatment by IASC) as the inventory cost-flow assumption.

FASB has promulgated Financial Accounting Standard 123 on accounting for stock-based compensation which encourages, but does not require, employers to charge compensation expense to income based on the estimated fair value of employee stock options. This condition could clearly result in different treatment of the same condition in the financial statements of US companies. The conclusion? This alternative treatment condition is not an IASC creation; it has been with us for a long time and in many places. Therefore, the remaining alternative treatment conditions do not seem to be a sound reason to reject IASC standards for cross-registration purposes.

Another important participant in the standardization process is IOSCO, which is composed of regulatory authorities from more than 60 countries. It wants a higher level of commonality of accounting principles and financial reporting practices internationally because of the increasing use of cross-border registrations by multinational companies. Companies can achieve a much higher level of efficiency if they do not have to restate financial statements into another country's GAAP or provide elaborate reconciliations of net income and net worth.

Considerable progress

Since 1987, IOSCO has fostered the use of common standards for accounting and financial reporting internationally, working closely with IASC to achieve this. At the IOSCO's 1993 annual conference, attended by representatives from more than 65 countries, the organization's technical committee agreed a list of core standards to be included 'in the necessary components of a reasonably complete set of accounting standards'. In 1995, the committee agreed with the IASC board on a work plan that will create a comprehensive set of core international accounting standards.

Encouraged by IOSCO, IASC recently moved its target date from 1999 to early next year. IASC has made considerable progress, including acceptance by IOSCO of Standard 7 on cash flow statements and consideration of the acceptability of 24 of the IASC standards as core standards. IOSCO has declared 15 standards acceptable, including Standard 7. It considers four standards unacceptable and plans to review six others. IOSCO has yet to consider the remaining four issues.

However, 'acceptable' does not mean 'endorsed by' Of the 15 standards classified as acceptable, IOSCO has endorsed only Standard 7. As reported in the IASC's publication, *Insight*, of December 1994, IOSCO will not endorse any of the other standards until IASC has completed all the core standards to IOSCO's satisfaction. IASC regards this position as unsatisfactory, or least that was the belief of its most recent past chairman, Mr Ejicchi Shiratori. He believes it is time for IOSCO to adopt a different approach – to endorse the process of setting international accounting standards rather than conducting a detailed review of each standard.

Former IASC chairman Ejicchi Shiratori: time for IOSCO to adopt a different approach

But is this a reasonable request on IASC's part? IOSCO represents the regulatory authorities of many countries and, through them, the investing public in each of those countries. Is it reasonable to ask IOSCO simply to accept the result of the process? Should not a comprehensive set of IASC principles and universal international acceptance of the organization be necessary before IOSCO's acceptance of the process replaces its review of individual standards?

Once the core standards are complete, companies whose financial statements meet those standards presumably will be able to use them to cross-register securities in the US. Financial statements of various countries are, however, used by different parties for different reasons, such as loans, joint-venture relationships, acquisitions, or investing. Conversely, people in other countries familiar with IASC GAAP could use financial statements prepared according to US GAAP for similar purposes. It is important to be aware of the differences between IASC standards and US GAAP.

Two studies

Professor Trevor Harris of the Columbia Business School at Columbia University in New York recently studied this matter and produced a report called *International Accounting Standards vs US GAAP reporting: empirical evidence based on case studies.* His study involved eight non-US multinationals and identified 13 specific differences. However, he pointed out that 'while differences remain between revised IASC and US GAAP, the paucity of the specific measurement differences was surprising'. In May 1995 Price Waterhouse published *Financial Reporting – An International Survey*, part of which was devoted to differences in international accounting standards and the GAAP of various countries, including the US. Using the first 31 IASC standards as a basis for comparison, the report identifies 11 areas of differences.

The results of these two projects might lead one to think that US GAAP and the international accounting standards are not so far apart. But a number of the differences observed by Price Waterhouse are not the same as those cited by Professor Harris. When we eliminate the overlap, the total number is about 20, a significant number. Many of the areas US GAAP covers have not yet been incorporated into IASC standards, including accounting for creditors for impairment of a loan, accounting for the costs of computer software, accounting principles and reporting requirements of various specialized industries (regulated utilities, insurance companies, broadcasters, the motion picture industry and so on) and accounting for stock-based compensation.

US mining companies like this one can face problems abroad when local accounting rules may favor local companies

Many of these issues will be resolved. But in the meantime, those who try to compare financial statements prepared under international accounting standards with those prepared under US GAAP will need to know where the important differences in treatment may lie.

Overall, the differences between US GAAP and the IASC standards remain troublesome. Enough of those differences may be resolved to allow IOSCO to endorse the core standards by early-1998, setting the stage for far more convenient cross-border registrations. IOSCO, the US financial services industry and multinational corporations throughout the world are very interested in this goal.

But financial statements are not made for cross-border registrations alone. Reconciliations to US GAAP are likely to be necessary for some time. The organizations may never reach complete agreement on all issues but the remaining differences should become manageable. At some point, users of IASC-based financial statements will know that the differences between these statements and statements produced in accordance with US GAAP are few and they will be able to identify and quantify those differences with little difficulty.

The core standards goal, which aims at convenient cross-border registrations of securities, is certainly important and desirable. IASC can achieve this goal. Whether it can be achieved by March 1998 is not as important as the commitment to making progress, satisfying the interested parties and doing the work well.

There is no question about the need for comprehensive, effective accounting standards that will protect investors, lenders and others, including the securities regulators of IOSCO member countries. Interested parties must work together to achieve this goal and contribute to IASC's efforts by providing it time and other resources. With a concerted, co-operative effort, this important task can be completed.

Summary

The article 'International accounting standards' takes a broad look at national accounting standards, the cultural reasons for differences between them and the hurdles yet to be overcome in defining acceptable international standards. But exactly how much progress towards reconciliation is being made, who are the key players and what are the chances of success? This generally optimistic article by Alvin Carley provides some answers, starting with conflicting examples of generally accepted accounting principles (GAAP) around the globe, going on to review the sometimes strained relationship between the International Accounting Standards Committee and the international body of regulatory authorities, and concluding with an assessment of the areas of difference between US GAAP and the international standards agreed so far. He calls for 'a concerted, co-operative effort' towards a set of core standards.

4 Managing value

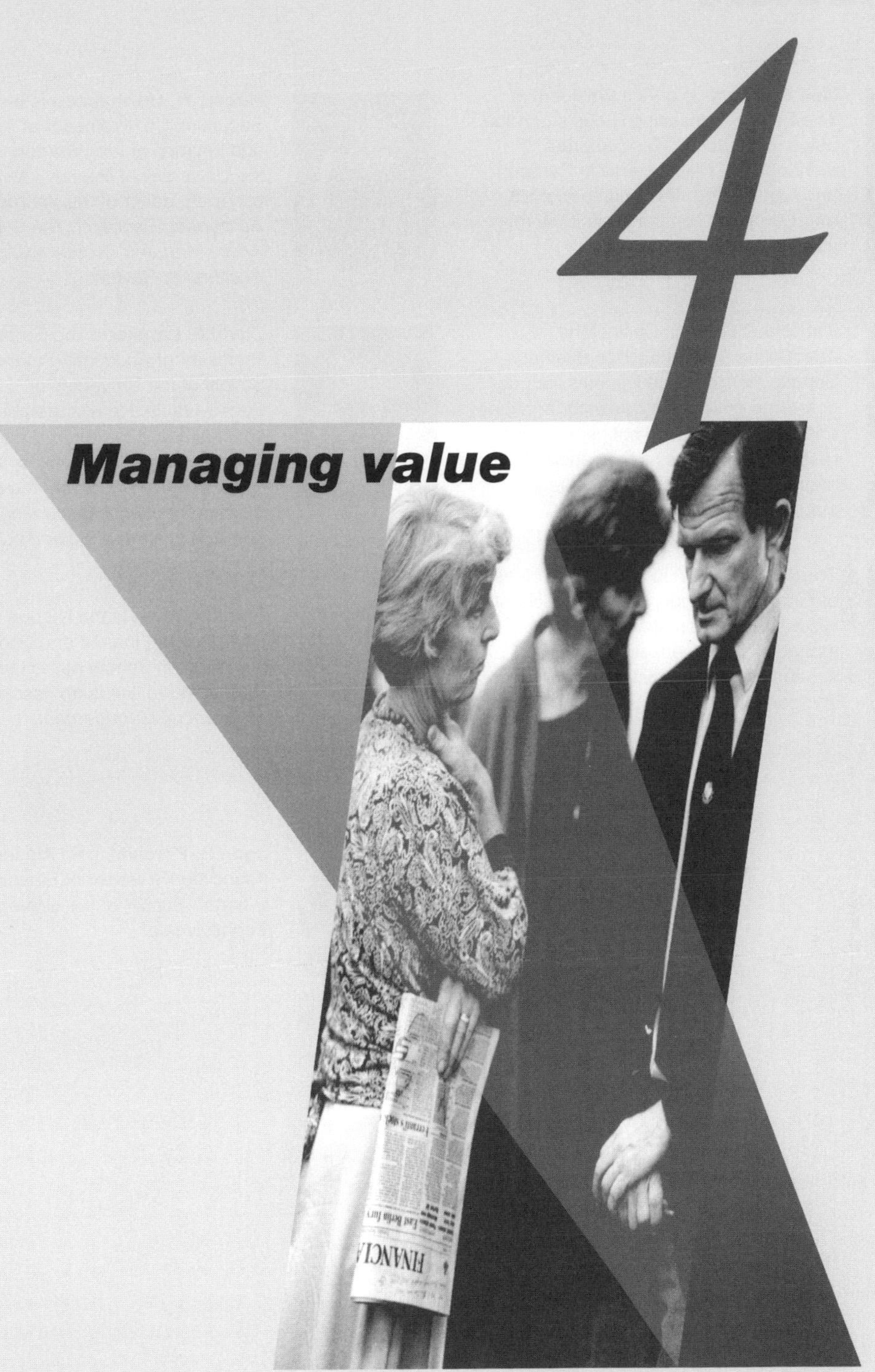

Contributors

Neil Monnery is a Vice President at The Boston Consulting Group's London office. He leads BCG's corporate development practice area in Europe, and has worked with a number of UK and European companies to implement value-based management.

Patricia O'Brien is Chair of the Accounting Area at London Business School. Her research interests include corporate governance, investor relations and capital regulation but her primary research focus has been financial analysts and the financial analysis industry.

Todd T. Milbourn is Assistant Professor of Finance at London Business School. His research interests include managerial compensation design, economics of asymmetric information and capital budgeting issues.

Robert W. Holthausen is the Nomura Securities Co. Professor of Accounting and Finance at the Wharton School of the University of Pennsylvania. He is associate editor of the *Journal of Accounting Research*, the *Journal of Accounting and Economics*, and *Accounting Review*.

David F. Larcker is the Ernst & Young Professor of Accounting at the Wharton School of the University of Pennsylvania. He is a member of the editorial board for the *Journal of Accounting and Economics*, the *Journal of Accounting Research*, the *Journal of Management and Accounting Research* and *Administrative Science Quarterly*.

Franklin Allen is the Nippon Life Professor of Finance and Economics at the Wharton School of the University of Pennsylvania. He is an associate editor of *Financial Management*.

John R. Percival is an Adjunct Associate Professor of Finance at the Wharton School of the University of Pennsylvania.

Contents

Introduction

The creation and management of value is the paramount activity of the modern corporation. Companies that effectively manage value are less prone to corporate raiders and to disillusioned investors.

Module 1 looked at the concept of value and here a collection of linked articles examines how value can be managed.

Motivations to manage value

by Neil Monnery

An increasing number of companies are adopting value creation as a key corporate goal. Behind this growing recognition of its importance are external pressures on executives. In the 1980s they came from corporate raiders, poised to bid for companies with under-performing shares, but they now come more from institutional investors – the activist shareholders who demand long-term value creation.

In the US and the UK, pressure has often centered on the subject of top managers' pay and its weak relationship to corporate performance. The National Association of Pension Funds/Association of British Insurers guidelines on remuneration, for example, propose a clearer link between performance and pay, and some companies now explicitly target value creation, neatly aligning managerial interests with those of shareholders.

Of course, improved compensation is not the only incentive motivating management. There is also the simple desire to improve your company and to enhance your professional reputation. Management success, prestige and visibility are increasingly driven by value achievements, which in parallel drive the success of companies over the longer term. In both the UK and the US, the lists of most admired companies are dominated by those that have created significant corporate value.

Value-creating companies have greater access to funds for growth and investment; they will also usually comprise businesses that both deliver customer value and enjoy competitive advantage. A long-term value focus is frequently a way to establish a virtuous circle of value creation, long-term competitive advantage and staff fulfilment. In practice, creating value is demanding. First managers need to know exactly what they are targeting; how specifically do you measure value creation? Second, they need to understand how to work towards that goal: what are the drivers of value creation? And third, they need to discover how to encourage people to do things differently; how do you align behavior throughout your organization?

Total shareholder return

It is essential to be able to measure value creation in a consistent and robust way, so that progress can be assessed, potential alternative courses compared, and appropriate behavior encouraged. Effective measures of value creation should be aligned with shareholders definition of value creation, and a measure that is rapidly becoming a standard is total shareholder return or TSR. This measure represents the internal rate of return of three cash flows associated with a share: its original purchase (cash out); the dividend stream received by the investor (cash in); and its sale at the end of the holding period (cash in).

It is usually helpful to compare company performances: of one share versus another, or against the market index or some other peer group. The difference between good performance and average or poor performance is often dramatic: for example over the years a top quartile performer makes over twice the return of an average performer and ten times the return of a bottom quartile company. Just as active fund managers aim to outperform the market, so corporate managers should aim to achieve returns superior to the average. Otherwise, investors will be better off buying the index.

This focus on relative performance insulates managers from macroeconomic factors which are beyond their control. It creates a high hurdle since, by definition, half the companies in a given market will under-perform the average. Beating the market consistently is difficult; industry factors, competitive pressures and investor expectations typically limit companies' ability to outdo the market repeatedly. Even those in attractive industries with strong competitive advantages are challenged.

Nevertheless, the overall goal must be value creation. But what does that mean in terms of corporate targets? Outperforming the market more frequently than you underperform it might be one objective. A more ambitious goal might be to appear consistently in the top quartile of your chosen peer group. Historical data provides some benchmarks: over the long term, to be an average performer in the FTSE 100 over a three-year period required a TSR of about 6–8 per cent (plus the inflation rate), while top quartile performance required an additional 5–8 per cent.

Corporate value creation

Many factors drive value creation, including good management, sound strategies, effective implementation and operating skills, and an appropriate skill base in the management and workforce. But, is it simply being good at everything, or are there some useful guides to help set priorities?

A first step in answering these questions is to build a picture of what drives value creation. Since TSR itself can be measured only for traded companies and only after the fact, a forward-looking model is needed to help managers make decisions today. In reality, managers have such a value model, either implicitly or explicitly, which they use to guide their decisions. The appropriate tests of such models are whether they fit (do they accurately predict how value is created?) and whether they are usable (normally a question of are they sufficiently simple and well understood by the users?). The right trade-off between these two somewhat contradictory objectives will vary from company to company. A good model will be sophisticated enough not to miss important value drivers within your business, but no more complicated than is really necessary to ensure appropriate decisions and actions.

One practical approach is to use an 'internal' total business return (TBR) to look at the past or potential value creation of individual businesses or even of individual products. Many managers are familiar with the discounting of future cash flows when considering incremental investments in the capital expenditure process. But this discipline also needs to be applied to the larger amount of assets tied up in the base businesses. An internal TBR does this by capturing both the changes in the value of a

Fig.1 Internal total business returns (TBR)

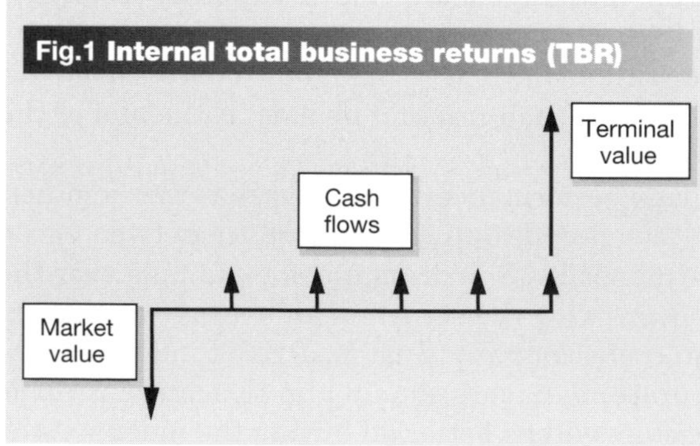

Fig.2 Value drivers

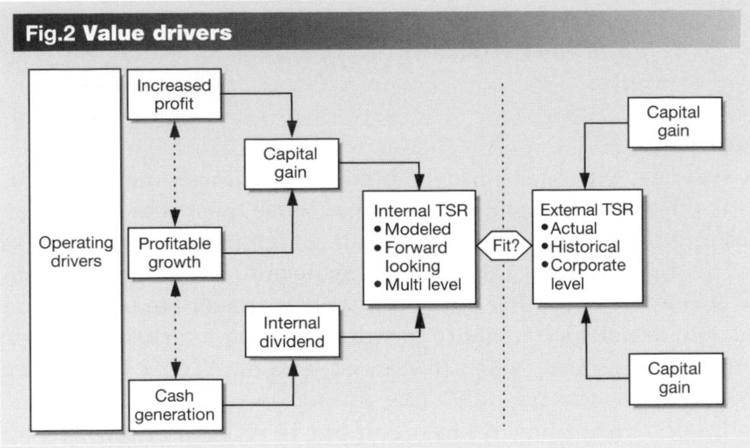

business (the difference between today's market value and the terminal value at the end of the planning period) and the associated cash flows or 'internal dividend' during that period (*see* Figure 1).

Behind the capital gains and internal dividends are the financial drivers of corporate value performance that are under management's control. These can be further peeled back layer-by-layer to the operating drivers in the business but at the financial level there are four: improving the returns on existing assets (raising profitability), beating expectations, investing in incremental projects that earn above the company's cost of capital (profitable growth) and delivering cash for investment (free cash flow) (*see* Figure 2).

These observations suggest first, the need to balance profit improvement and growth, and cash generation versus reinvestment; second, the value of a good measure of profitability that encourages focus on real profit enhancement rather than accounting adjustments; and thirdly the importance of an understanding of the cost of capital to indicate what growth is profitable.

Balancing the value of profit improvement, growth and cash generation is essential, and value managers understand that different businesses will place different emphasis on the different drivers. In general, poor-return businesses should focus more on profit improvement and cash. High-return businesses should tend to grow or throw off cash if their growth is constrained. Understanding how to craft strategies that will optimize these levers or value drivers, and then delivering the strategy, are at the heart of value management. This is illustrated by the performances of some of the most value-creating companies of the past few years. These are companies that have achieved comparable success despite starting from very different positions.

Value drivers are evidently not the same for all businesses and their management requires careful evaluation of the trade-offs. For example, if, you begin with high rates of return but little opportunity to grow, it will be value-creating to focus chiefly on cash generation. In contrast, with businesses earning below the cost of capital, the focus should be more on improving returns.

These companies pursued strategies that were appropriate to their starting positions and which drew on an appropriate mix of value drivers. Such strategies are entirely situational: not only do they vary across companies but since they depend on your starting position at any given moment they also vary over time. It is not where you start that matters; it is what you do from there in selecting and executing appropriate value-creating strategies.

Value-based management

Companies are complex systems, with skills, people, processes, histories and heritage, and differing opportunities. How does a company marshal those resources to look for value-creating strategies and then deliver them? In small companies, or for corporate restructuring decisions, a small group at the center may decide. But for most large companies, the key is to encourage operating units and their managers to understand clearly how their actions and decisions contribute to value creation via their strategic choices involving products and markets, when to expand, and managing day-to-day operations.

The method by which such value-based management is implemented will be different in each company but in general it should be based on adapting existing management processes and measures. These processes – strategic planning, target setting, annual budgeting, capital expenditure evaluation and incentive compensation – and the measures used within them can be employed to direct behavior in your organization. In seeking to change that behavior, the challenge is to translate the goal of value creation into practical tools that refocus and motivate behavior within different business and company cultures.

Fundamental to aligning processes and decision tools with value creation is the development of an appropriate set of internal measures that quantify, track and reward value-creating performance. Understanding existing measures will help determine whether the measures on which people make decisions are a good guide to future TSR performance. One way of assessing the starting position of your processes and measures is to draw a performance measurement map describing the key management processes, the measures used in them, and the strength or weakness of their effects on behavior (*see* Figure 3).

Value management in the strategic planning process should typically be conducted in the context of a value creation target set by the center. Business managers can then develop realistic alternatives which can be compared on their potential value creation. The planning process must be loose enough to encourage debate around different

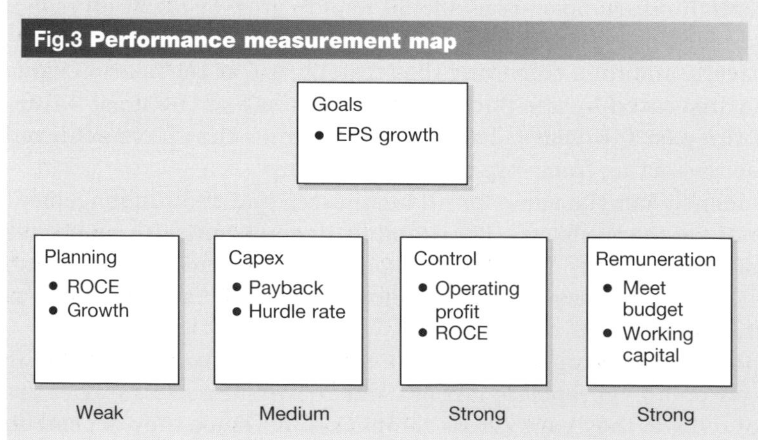

drivers and to allow room for management creativity but tight enough to ensure that all discussions rest on value creation.

Valuing strategic plans needs an appropriate value creation model, such as an internal TBR model. It should incorporate accurate measures of financial performance and cash flows, market expectations, and a means of calculating and comparing the current value of the business – its market value – with its expected value at the end of the planning period – its terminal value.

Once a value-creating business strategy is agreed, it must be implemented and delivered. In many companies the most important delivery contract is the annual budget, which should be a short-term reflection of the strategic plan. The problem is that budget accounting numbers can often be presented in ways that fail to deliver value. For example, many accounting measures will show improving performance as assets become older, and often fail to reflect the underlying cash performance of a business. There are complex economic measures of profit such as cash flow return on investment (CFROI), which avoid most of the shortcomings of traditional measures. CFROI is analogous to the internal rates of return (IRR) for a new project. It compares the cumulative cash invested in a business with the cash the business is producing while recognizing the importance of asset ages, asset lives and inflation.

CFROI is a useful benchmark measure against which to test a company's existing measures. Then a tailored set of new measures can be chosen which are simpler but which eliminate the biases that cause most distortions in your business. Again there is a trade-off between simplicity and accuracy; the challenge is to ensure that the measures and targets you use on a daily basis are aligned with value creation and simple enough to drive behavior. The ideal trade-off between accuracy and simplicity will vary by company and business. In general, simpler businesses will be able to use simpler measures.

It is essential that the measures used in different processes are aligned with one another. Managers and employees are frequently getting conflicting signals from the strategic planning budgeting, capex and incentive processes. While achieving alignment need not mean that the same measures are used everywhere, it is vital the measures are consistent with one another and with value creation.

Finally, the measurement system must be cascaded down through the organization. That need not mean pushing TSR all the way down the line: it is unlikely and undesirable that every single employee will be motivated by corporate value creation. But measures at lower levels in the company must be aligned with the relevant value drivers of the business. A properly designed and implemented value management program will create a common language between senior management and staff, providing appropriate tools for making complex choices throughout an organization and allowing greater latitude for informed decision-making.

The value of value creation

Launching a value-based management program generally requires transforming the organization at all levels. The most fundamental change will come at the top. There are many important corporate decisions which must be addressed from a value perspective, including issues of corporate shape, portfolio planning and resource allocation, mergers, demergers and acquisitions, and financial policies, such as leverage, rights issues and dividends. Equally importantly, especially given decentralization, empowerment and the move to smaller corporate centers, is the role the center plays in setting the framework, processes and measures which will encourage the whole company to deliver value.

One of the central messages of value-based management is that while the TSR goal should be identical for all companies, the means by which you achieve it can vary considerably. The same applies to where you choose to begin the implementation process. Some companies may start at the planning process, involving a fairly small group of senior managers; some may introduce value-oriented measures on a broader scale, perhaps through the budgeting process. Others may reorganize the remuneration system to encourage value-driven behavior. From each starting position, it is essential to push for wider awareness of the goal and the actions needed to achieve it, spreading the value message throughout the company.

Value-based management is much like implementing any program of change. For this reason, it is important to convey its analytical and behavioral objectives clearly. People's basic beliefs about what drives their businesses are challenged, so participation, training, buy-in and ultimate ownership are crucial to successful implementation.

It is important to be aware of these organizational issues and of traditional strategic management in relation to value creation. In reality, there should be little conflict in most companies. Superior TSR benefits not just shareholders but often also employees and customers. This is why a growing number of companies are successfully exploiting the power of explicit value-based management programs to rejuvenate their organizations, to improve their TSR performance and to build long-term competitive advantage.

Summary

In this article on shareholder value Neil Monnery takes a broad look at different models of value creation. Many factors drive it – from sound strategy to effective implementation skills – but are there useful guidelines when it comes to setting priorities?

The author argues that the appropriate tests are whether a model is accurate in predicting value, and whether it is simple enough to be understood by users. A good one will be sophisticated enough not to miss important value drivers but no more complicated than is really necessary to ensure that the appropriate actions are taken.

One practical approach is to use an 'internal' total business return which captures both the changes in the value of a business and the associated cash flows (or internal dividend).

Identifying the financial drivers which power profit improvement, growth and cash generation – and balancing them according to the type of company – is essential.

Cash flows versus earnings

by Patricia O'Brien

Capital budgeting analysis recognizes the time value of money, and so discounts future cash flows to account for their timing. Cash flows are indisputably the correct data input in the theoretical model. In most practical applications of capital budgeting or present value techniques, however, we do not know the future cash flows, but must estimate or predict them. Earnings may provide a better foundation for predicting future cash flows than the history of cash flows themselves. Earnings realign cash flows in a way that reflects replicable operating activity.

Cash flow predictions of cash flow

As a starting point, take a company in the ideal situation for predicting: mature, stable and successful. Successful and stable enterprises generate cash from their operations sufficient to maintain their fixed assets and provide a return to capital. For example, Maturity plc (*see* Figure 1) is profitable, is neither growing rapidly nor declining, can easily service its debts and pays a healthy 60 per cent dividend. If we examine Maturity's sources and uses of cash, we see that operations provide a net cash inflow of 300, which suffices to pay interest, dividends and taxes, and to finance the replacement of fixed assets.

Extrapolating from the past to predict the future is always perilous, but Maturity's stable situation is the best possible setting for doing so. If Maturity continues to operate in the same way, we can foresee cash flows in roughly the same amounts year after year. Free cash flow, or operating cash less debt service, taxes and investment, is 67 (= 300 – 57 – 36 – 140). Notice, however, that this is precisely the same as Maturity's reported earnings number. Though the example is contrived, its message is broadly true of stable, successful companies: earnings and free cash flows are similar in size, and are probably equally good for predicting the future.

Now consider another company, Growth Ltd (*see* Figure 2), which operates profitably while growing rapidly. Fixed assets nearly double in the year, and non-cash working capital more than quintuples. Like many growing companies, Growth Ltd does not pay dividends, as its operating cash needs are too great.

What happens to free cash flow in this period of rapid expansion? Because of the cash drain from expanding working capital, operating cash flows no longer cover debt service and taxes, so free cash flow is negative (–618 = 30 – 79 – 28 – 540). The company must raise cash to finance its expansion, and in this case it raises cash by borrowing. Nothing substantial would change in this example if the company issued new shares instead.

We should not expect the future to resemble the past in a case like this one, even if the company continues in exactly the same line of business. The rapid expansion of Growth Ltd cannot persist indefinitely. A company that triples in size annually would take over the world economy in a few decades. Obviously, countervailing forces such as competition and market saturation will constrain future growth. The cash flows themselves illustrate why this level of growth will not continue. The company cannot sustain itself on operating cash flows that do not cover taxes and debt service.

Fig.1 MATURITY PLC

Balance sheets	Year 1	Year 2
Cash	50	77
Other current assets	250	250
Fixed assets (net)	700	700
Total assets	**1,000**	**1,027**
Current liabilities	125	125
Borrowing	575	575
Paid-in-capital	50	50
Retained earnings	250	277
Total liabilities and ownership	**1,000**	**1,027**

P&L statement

Balance sheets	Year 2
Sales	1,000
COGS	(700)
Depreciation	(140)
Profit before interest and taxation	**160**
Interest	(58)
Taxation	(36)
Profit	**66**
Dividends	(40)
Profit retained for the year	**26**

Statement of cash flow

	Year 2	
Operations		
Profit before interest and taxation	160	
Add: Depreciation	140	
Subtract: Growth in non-cash working capital	0	
		300
Finance service		
Interest	(58)	
Dividends	(40)	
		(98)
Taxation	36	
		(36)
Investing		
Net (acquisitions)/disposals	140	
		(140)
Financing		
Net borrowing/(repayment)	0	
Net new stock Issues/(repurchases)	0	
		0
Change in cash		24
Free cash flow*		66

*Change in cash plus dividends and net borrrowing and net new stock issues

Fig.2 GROWTH LTD

Balance sheets	Year 1	Year 2
Cash	50	47
Other current assets	100	500
Fixed assets (net)	500	900
Total assets	**650**	**1,447**
Current liabilities	65	195
Borrowing	485	1,100
Paid-in-capital	50	50
Retained earnings	50	102
Total liabilities and ownership	**650**	**1,447**

P&L statement

Balance sheets	Year 2
Sales	1,000
COGS	(700)
Depreciation	(140)
Profit before interest and taxation	**160**
Interest	(79)
Taxation	(28)
Profit	**52**
Dividends	0
Profit retained for the year	**52**

Statement of cash flow

	Year 2	
Operations		
Profit before interest and taxation	160	
Add: Depreciation	140	
Subtract: Growth in non-cash working capital	(270)	
		30
Finance service		
Interest	79	
Dividends	0	
		(79)
Taxation	(28)	
		(28)
Investing		
Net (acquisitions)/disposals	(540)	
		(540)
Financing		
Net borrowing/(repayment)	615	
Net new stock Issues/(repurchases)	0	
		615
Change in cash		**(2)**
Free cash flow*		(617)

*Change in cash plus dividends and net borrrowing and net new stock issues

In the Growth case, current free cash flow is clearly not a good predictor of future cash flows. If we were to use Growth's free cash flow in a present value model, we would estimate a negative value for the company. The problem with the cash flow figure is that current investments in working capital and fixed assets drain cash now, but presumably will produce expanded inflows in future. Earnings, however, give a different picture. Earnings after depreciation, interest and taxation are positive. Might earnings be a better indicator of future cash flows in this case?

Earnings and operating cycles

Earnings and cash flows, though related, measure fundamentally different things. Cash flow is the net of cash inflows and outflows within a time period. Earnings, on the other hand, are the net of inflows and outflows from completed operating cycles.

The company's business defines its operating cycle. Manufacturers, retailers and service organizations, for example, acquire goods and services, combine them or present them, or display them in a way that increases their value, and find willing buyers for the resulting products. Along the way, they collect cash from buyers, and pay cash to providers of the goods and services. Conceptually, cash outlays and receipts drive the operating cycle, but they may in fact occur at any stage, depending on contracts or industry practice. For example, a company could collect cash from customers prior to delivering the good or service, as in the airline industry; or simultaneous with delivery, as is common in the retail sector; or after delivery, as wholesalers often do.

Most ongoing enterprises, of course, have many overlapping operating cycles at various stages of completion at any point in time. Earnings and cash flow give two different views of the ongoing cycles, by cutting them in different ways. Cash flow measures inflows and outflows within a time period, regardless of the state of the operating cycle. Earnings measure inflows and outflows from operating cycles that the company has completed within a time period, regardless of when the cash flows occur.

Earnings predictions of cash flows

The operating cycle is the key to understanding why earnings' value for predicting future cash flows. If it stays in the same line of business, the company will essentially replicate the operating cycle again and again. As long as each operating cycle generates positive net inflows, replications should have positive value. Earnings, then, measure the performance that the company will replicate in future.

Returning to the example of Growth Ltd, notice that earnings are positive. This means that on its completed sales, Growth's inflows from customers exceed the outflows associated with these sales. Cash flow is drained by investments in working capital and fixed assets, investments that will contribute to cycles that are not yet complete. Because the company is growing, the new investments are by definition disproportionately large in comparison with the cash inflows from completed operating cycles. Earnings, in contrast, contain cost of sales and depreciation in amounts more proportional to sales, because they measure operating cycles. This analysis suggests that, in cases where prediction is difficult, earnings may be more useful than current cash flows for predicting future cash flows.

To demonstrate that this is not unique to a growing company, consider a third case. Decline Inc. (*see* Figure 3) is shrinking rapidly, perhaps in response to a permanent contraction in demand. Lower profit margins characterize this situation. Decline is still barely profit-able, but omits its dividend. Anticipating lower future demand, the company reduces production, which shrinks working capital. Fixed assets are harder to reduce quickly, but these shrink somewhat as well, primarily because Decline chooses not to replace expired capacity.

The operating cash flows in this scenario are high, as Decline liquidates non-cash working capital, freeing up cash. These operating cash flows are more than sufficient to service debt and pay taxes. The company uses free cash flow to pay down debt. In this case, the operating cash flows and free cash flows are high because Decline has the foresight to manage its decline by shrinking operations. This is a rather more graceful decline than many we have seen, but it illustrates the point about predicting future operations using cash flows. The cash flows here do not represent results of business activities that the company will be able to replicate. Rather, to a large extent they represent one-time liquidations. Earnings, in contrast, reflect the reduced circumstances of the company and its limited potential for net inflows from future operating cycles.

As we mentioned above, predicting the future from the past is always a risky enterprise. The above examples illustrate that, by design, earnings give a better indicator of future cash flows by reflecting operating cycles rather than receipts and payments. In the case where the company is neither growing nor shrinking the scale of its operations, cash flows and earnings tell the same story. When the company is scaling up or down, earnings reflect the operating cycle that the company may replicate in future, while cash flows mix this operating information with information about investment and divestment.

Fig.3 DECLINE INC

Balance sheets	Year 1	Year 2
Cash	25	98
Other current assets	375	125
Fixed assets (net)	800	600
Total assets	**1,200**	**823**
Current liabilities	200	65
Borrowing	600	350
Paid-in-capital	50	50
Retained earnings	350	358
Total liabilities and ownership	**1,200**	**823**

P&L statement

Balance sheets	Year 2
Sales	900
COGS	(700)
Depreciation	(140)
Profit before interest and taxation	**60**
Interest	(48)
Taxation	(4)
Profit	**8**
Dividends	0
Profit retained for the year	**8**

Statement of cash flow

	Year 2	
Operations		
Profit before interest and taxation	60	
Add: Depreciation	140	
Subtract: Growth in non-cash working capital	115	
		315
Finance service		
Interest	(48)	
Dividends	0	
		(48)
Taxation	(4)	
		(4)
Investing		
Net (acquisitions)/disposals	60	
		60
Financing		
Net borrowing/(repayment)	(250)	
Net new stock Issues/(repurchases)	0	
		(250)
Change in cash		**73**
Free cash flow*		323

*Change in cash plus dividends and net borrrowing and net new stock issues

Some important caveats

Earnings are not a perfect solution, and it is important to understand the potential pitfalls of using earnings to predict future cash flows. First and most obviously, the company may not replicate its current business activity in the future. This could happen, for example, because the company changes strategic direction, pursuing new or different product markets. In this case the net inflows from operating cycles in the current business are irrelevant to the company's future cash flows. Notice, however, that cash flows from the old business are equally irrelevant.

A second, somewhat more serious concerns is that accounting numbers in most major economies are not adjusted for the effects of inflation. For short operating cycles in low-inflation economies, the time lags for most revenues and costs are not substantial, and therefore inflation creates only minor distortions. The depreciation charge on fixed assets is an important exception. In the examples used above, fixed assets depreciate at a rate of 20 per cent per year, corresponding to a 5-year useful life. This means that the depreciation cost in the P&L is, on average, 2½ years older than the current replacement cost of the asset. If inflation is three per cent per year, then the cost to replace fixed assets will on average be about eight per cent ($= 1.03^{2.5} - 1$) more than the amount reflected in the P&L. This understatement of cost will be more severe with higher inflation and longer asset lives.

The third and most serious concern is a well-known problem with earnings: that they involve a good deal of judgement. Judgement enters, for example, in defining when operating cycles are complete, and in identifying costs with sales. Two examples will illustrate these points. First, imagine a manufacturer that considers the operating cycle to be complete when it ships a product to a customer. This is a sensible end point for measuring performance, since the manufacturer usually completes its performance with shipment. The trouble is that some shipments will end in incomplete cycles: some customers may not pay, while others may return the product. Prudent managers will estimate and include the costs of defaults and returns in their profit figures, but imprudent or unskilled managers may not.

To illustrate the case of judgement involved in identifying costs with sales, suppose that the manufacturer advertises the product in hopes of increasing demand. Advertising is a nebulous thing: sometimes it works, and sometimes an ad campaign falls flat. One manager might assign all the advertising costs to sales in the year when the ads appear, assuming no longer-term benefit. Another might assume that the benefits from advertising will be realized over many years, and therefore spread the costs across many years' sales. Either could be correct, though analysts usually regard the first as more prudent.

Earnings and credibility

Analysts are justifiably wary of earnings numbers, because when judgement enters, selective or manipulative reporting can sidle in as well. Managers often feel pressure to produce an increasing stream of earnings, because investors demand it or because their pay depends on it. This pressure could, in the absence of real performance improvements, induce them to accelerate revenues and defer costs, leading to reported earnings that overstate true profits from completed operating cycles. No company can overstate indefinitely, but analysts are concerned with being misled in the short-run.

Compounding the credibility problem companies reporting rapid growth – where current cash flows are poor indicators of future cash flows – often have the least credible earnings. Young companies in relatively new industries have the greatest potential for explosive growth, and the least track record on which to judge credibility. In these circumstances, analysts often rely on other indicators, such as the aggressiveness or conservatism of the accounting choices the company makes. This brings the problem full-circle, since prudent or conservative accounting choices are typically closer to cash flows than are aggressive ones.

In the two examples of judgement cited above, for instance, the most conservative choice is the one closest to cash flow. If we are concerned about reported sales that later may not be realized in cash, then defining the end of the operating cycle to be the point of cash collection rather than the point of shipment would resolve the concern. If we are concerned that current advertising costs may yield no future benefit, then we can resolve the problem by expensing advertising costs when they are incurred, rather than deferring a portion to future years.

Cash flows are more credible than earnings because they involve less judgement. They are, on the other hand, less relevant than earnings to measuring replicable operating performance. This leaves us with the classic accounting conundrum: we want both relevance and reliability, but no single number provides both. The jumble of accounting rules within and across borders attests to the difficulty – or perhaps the impossibility – of devising an internally consistent system that trades off these crucial qualities.

The best number for forecasting future cash flows is one that credibly conveys the results of replicable operating cycles. Earnings measure the results of operating cycles, but involve judgement, which reduces their credibility. Cash flows involve less judgement, but do not measure the results of operating cycles. As a result, users of accounting numbers must be aware of the pitfalls and be informed enough to make their own trade-offs. Current best practice in financial analysis is to use reported earnings as the starting point for forecasting future cash flows, since earnings measure operating cycles. In each case, however, the analyst must judge where credibility is strained, and adjust accordingly.

Summary

Which number – earnings or cash flow – is better for predicting a company's future cash flows? It is often argued that only cash flow matters for present value analysis but as Patricia O'Brien argues in this article, earnings may be a better indicator in some cases. Emphasizing that there are different messages for mature and growing businesses, she explains that cash flow measures inflows and outflows within a period regardless of the state of the operating cycle, while earnings measure inflows and outflows from operating cycles that the business has completed within a period, regardless of when the cash flows occur. Cash flows are more credible since they involve less judgement but they are less relevant than earnings when it comes to measuring replicable operating performance. That is the classic accounting conundrum – no single number provides both. The jumble of national accounting rules – discussed in the articles 'International accounting standards' and 'Creating a common accounting language' (Module 3) – attests to the difficulty of devising a consistent system.

EVA's charm as a performance measure

by Todd Milbourn

A surge in shareholder activism has put increasing pressure on companies to consistently maximize shareholder value. However, this raises the important question of how senior executives should measure an organization's progress in meeting this goal. In particular, the question concerns defining measures of corporate financial performance that correlate highly with shareholder wealth. This issue is also concerned with motivating managers to do what is best for shareholders. The central idea in most organizations is to tie managerial compensation to measures of financial performance that are linked closely to changes in shareholder wealth. In theory, this should motivate managers to maximize shareholder value.

The most direct financial performance measurement is the business's stock price. However, stock prices can be limited in their usefulness. The litmus test for any performance measure is whether it accurately reflects the decisions taken by management. A good performance measure must, therefore, be responsive to a manager's actions and decisions. In this sense, stock prices (or, for that matter, stock returns) are often ineffective in assessing past performance because they reflect the expectations of all future decisions. In fact, stock prices are not necessarily that responsive to the actions of even the most senior-executive in a company. As one goes further down the organization, the problem becomes even more severe as lower-level employees have even less impact on the stock price.

Economic Value Added (EVA), like other performance measures, attempts to resolve the tension between the need for a performance measure that is both highly correlated with shareholder wealth and responsive to the actions of a company's managers. The number of companies that have adopted EVA (or one of its many close cousins, such as McKinsey's Economic Profit) is startling. Stern Stewart Management Services (the founders of EVA) claims that more than 200 companies globally have been in discussions with it about adopting EVA.

These companies are hoping to replicate the successes of other EVA users, including Lucas-Varity in the UK and Coca-Cola in the US. Why are so many organizations embarking on the EVA trail? This article attempts to answer this question and others, including: Why is EVA such a hot topic today? How is it defined and calculated? What are EVA's limitations and what is its future?

Why such a hot topic?

If an enterprise's objective is to maximize the value of the shareholders' claim to the assets, then this is quite easily done. A company will meet this objective if it does two things: invest only in new projects that are expected to create value and retain only projects that create value on an on-going basis.

To this end, finance theory offers managers a simple guide to choosing capital investments through the net present value (NPV) rule. That is, by investing in projects that have positive NPVs you will create value. However, when managers seek such a well-defined rule for evaluating their on-going investments, they are often met with frustration. In fact, most organizations are forced to rely on financial measures such as total sales, total earnings or even rates of return on their net assets as a means of differentiating between the 'peaches' and the 'lemons' in their businesses. However, assessing performance based on these measures can often distort the investment behavior of management away from that of their shareholders' wishes.

The misuse of assets is often the most critical among the many potential conflicts between a company's shareholders and its management. In fact, it is frequently argued that businesses are over-capitalized relative to the optimal investment level. This is typically caused by the flawed compensation schemes in companies which often force managers to focus on earnings and market share.

The most fundamental question, then, is why do companies still fail to choose the right projects even when the NPV tool is readily available? One reason for the misalignment between compensation and capital allocation systems is that NPV cannot be readily used for compensation. NPV is a summary measure based on projected cash flows and not realized performance. What is needed for compensation are measures that can be computed periodically as they are realized. Hence, it is easy to understand why companies reach for flow measures such as earnings and cash flow for determining compensation. Unfortunately, they can distort managerial behavior away from what is good for shareholders. A measure such as EVA can help since it theoretically produces the same recommendations as NPV, as will be shown below.

Defining and calculating

Investment distortions typically arise because a manager is not 'charged' for the capital he or she uses or even rewarded for the shareholder value created. This is the fundamental contribution of EVA. It rewards managers for the earnings they generate but is also conditional on the amount of capital employed to reap these earnings. In this vein, EVA is defined as:

$$\mathbf{EVA = NOPAT - (K_W \times Net\ Assets)}$$

where NOPAT = net operating profit after-tax
K_W = weighted average cost of capital and
Net Assets = adjusted book value of net capital

If managerial compensation is tied to EVA, then the manager's inclination to consume capital is now tempered by the fact that he or she must pay a capital charge evaluated at the weighted average cost of capital on the net capital he or she uses. Box 1 gives an example of the power of EVA-based compensation contracts on project selection. From the example above we can draw the following conclusions. Earnings-based compensation schemes can cause over-investment of capital, whereas return on net assets (RONA-based compensation) can result in under investment of capital. Therefore, EVA has evolved as the focal point in many organizations as a means of marrying their project selection and managerial compensation schemes.

Why does EVA offer the correct incentives in the example above? The answer is simply that EVA is fundamentally related to shareholder value. At a company level, the present value of EVAs equals a business's 'market value added' (MVA), which is defined as the difference between the market value of the organization and the

Box 1

Suppose that a manager at Jordan plc must choose one of three mutually exclusive projects. The company can invest £50m in project A, or £110m in project B or £240m in project C.

Project A generates incremental net operating profits after tax (NOPAT) of £50m one year from now and £20m two years from now, after which the project is terminated.

Project B generates incremental NOPATs of £45m the first year, £70m the second year and £70m the third year and then the project is terminated.

Project C is expected to generate incremental NOPATs of £55m the first year, £75m the second year, £80m the third year and again the project is terminated.

Which project will the manager select if: (i) his compensation is tied to the rate of return of the project, (ii) his compensation is tied to product earnings (NOPAT) and (iii) his compensation is tied to EVA? Assume a cost of capital of 10 per cent and that capital levels are maintained at their original levels throughout the life of each project. That is, new capital investment in any year equals depreciation in that year. Moreover, assume the capital is sold at its book value in the last year of each project's life. As a consequence, free cash flow will be equal to NOPAT in each year except for the last year, when the capital is recovered.

The internal rates of returns (IRRs), product earnings (NOPATs), free cash flows and NPVs are as follows:

Project	NOPAT (yearly)	Free cash flows (millions)	IRR	NPV=PV of FCFs
A	£50, £40	£50, £90	93%	£ 69.83
B	£45, £70, £70	£45, £70, £180	53%	£124
C	£55, £75, £80	£55, £75, £320	28%	£112.4

Clearly, project B is the best for Jordan's shareholders. However, a managerial compensation or capital allocation scheme based on IRR will lead the manager to propose project A. And if the manager is compensated based on product earnings, he will prefer introducing project C. But if EVA is used to compensate managers, the correct project will be chosen, as can be seen from the following table, where we define EVA = NOPAT – (Capital Employed at Beginning of Period multiplied by cost of capital):

Project	EVA	NPV=PV of EVAs
A	£45, £35	£ 69.83
B	£34, £59, £59	£124
C	£31, £51, £56	£112.4

(adjusted) book value of its assets. Moreover, at a project level, the present value of the future EVAs equals the NPV derived from the usual free cash flow forecasts. See Box 2 for a simple proof of this equivalence.

If EVA and free cash flow analyses give identical NPV estimates, why is it that EVA is useful for compensation and NPV is not? The reason is that one needs *flow* measures of performance for periodic compensation since compensation is designed to provide a flow of rewards. EVA is a *flow* measure, whereas NPV is a stock measure. Moreover, of the available flow measures, EVA is the only one that explicitly takes into account the cost of the capital and the amount of capital invested in the company. In this respect, EVA is superior to another flow measure, cash flow.

The goal of a good financial performance measure is to ask how well a company has performed in terms of generating operating profits over a period, given the amount of capital tied up to generate those profits. Eva is novel in that it provides an answer to this question. The idea is that the business's financiers could have liquidated their investment in the company and put the liberated capital to some other use. Thus, the financiers' opportunity cost of capital must be subtracted from operating profits to gauge the organization's financial performance. In this spirit, EVA views NOPAT as a representation of operating profit and subtracts a capital charge that views the economic book value of assets in place as a measure of the capital provided to the company by its financiers.

Estimating this capital base is the most cumbersome (yet necessary) aspect of calculating EVA. How do we arrive at this number? A company's balance sheet contains one measure of the value of the organization's assets in place. Consider the following accounting-based balance sheet in Box 2. Unfortunately, due to a plethora of accounting distortions, the total asset value on this balance sheet is not an accurate representation of either the liquidation value or the replacement-cost value of the business's assets, making it of limited use.

Stern Stewart is careful to adjust this accounting balance sheet before arriving at an estimate of the value of a company's assets in place. In fact, Stern Stewart considers more than 250 accounting adjustments in moving to EVA.

In practice, however, most organizations find that no more than 15 adjustments are truly significant. The adjustments include netting the non-interest bearing current liabilities (NIBCLs) against the current assets, adding back to equity the gross goodwill, restructuring and other write-offs, capitalized value of R&D (and possibly advertising), LIFO reserve and so on. (These accounting adjustments are referred to as 'Equity Equivalents' and their effects on capital and NOPAT are summarized in Box 3.) The debt balance is also increased by the capitalized value of operating lease payments. The goal of these adjustments is to produce a balance sheet that reflects the economic values of the organization's assets more accurately than the accounting balance sheet. After these adjustments are made, a typical company's 'economic book value' balance sheet would look as it does in Box 3.

Limitations and the future?

EVA is, therefore, a powerful concept. However, before all businesses rush to adopt it, they should note that EVA is not the holy grail since it has its limitations. A frequently-asked question is: what does EVA add to conventional valuation analysis? The answer is nothing. EVA-based financial analysis will not (and should not) change the conclusions reached on the basis of cash flow-based valuation analysis.

However, this equivalence is to EVA's credit. In fact, one limitation of EVA is that it is often touted as a new valuation tool, which is simply incorrect. EVA should be viewed primarily as a behavioral tool that alters the distortions prevalent in many companies. The most severe limitation of EVA is what it (as well as most other financial measures) fails to capture on an *ex post* basis.

Total company value can be derived as the sum of two fundamental components as shown in Figure 1. The most basic component is represented by its physical assets in place. If we assume that this is an economic value, then we can equate this part to EVA's estimated capital component. In addition to this component, however, is the present value of the business's growth opportunities. This latter component's value is certainly less tangible and can be large for many businesses. One can view this part of company value as being driven by what the market expects to happen.

Unfortunately, EVA is unable to capture changes in this value. In fact, attempts to capture this value bring us back to simply looking at changes in a organization's stock price. However, the limitations of stock price in judging corporate performance is what motivated our investigation of EVA in the first place.

Box 2

Using the subscript **t** to denote the end of the time period of occurrence, we have:

$$\mathbf{EVA_t = NOPAT_t - K_w \times NA_{t-1}}$$

where $\mathbf{NA_{t-1}}$ is the adjusted book value of the net asset base at the end of the period **t–1** (or equivalently the beginning of period **t**) and $\mathbf{K_w}$ is the firm's weighted average cost of capital. Summing present values over the life of the company, we have:

$$\sum_{t=1}^{\infty} \frac{EVA_t}{(1+k_w)^t} = \sum_{t=1}^{\infty} \frac{NOPAT_t}{(1+k_w)^t} - \sum_{t=1}^{\infty} k_w \times \frac{NA_{t=1}}{(1+k_w)^t}$$

For simplicity, suppose the net asset base remains unchanged over the life of the organisation. The proof goes through without this simplification but is more cumbersome. Then $\mathbf{NOPAT_t = Cash\ flow_t}$ and $\mathbf{NA_{t-1} = NA}$ (a constant) for all **t**.

Thus,

$$\textbf{PV of EVA} = \textbf{PV of Cash flows} - \textbf{NA} \times \sum_{t=1}^{\infty} \frac{k_w}{(1+k_w)^t}$$

or

PV of EVA = PV of Cash flows – NA

or

PV of EVA = Net Present value (NPV).

Box 3

Accounting-based balance sheet

Assets	**Liabilities and equity**
Current Assets	Non-interest bearing current liabilities (NIBCLs)
Net Goodwill	Interest-bearing current liabilities
Fixed Assets (net of depreciation)	Long-term interest bearing debt
	Equity (net of write-offs)
Total Assets	**Total liabilities and equity**

Economic (adjusted book value) balance sheet

Assets	**Liabilities and equity**
Current Assets (with inventory at FIFO) – NIBCLs	Interest-bearing current liabilities
Net Goodwill	Long-term interest bearing debt
Fixed Assets (net of depreciation)	Equity (net of write-offs)
Total economic value of the assets	**Total liabilities and equity**

Equity equivalents

Add to Capital	**Add to NOPAT**
Equity equivalents	Increases in equity equivalents
Deferred tax reserve	Increase in LIFO reserve
LIFO reserve	Increase in deferred tax reserve
Cumulative goodwill amortization	Goodwill amortization
Unrecorded goodwill	Increases in intangibles
Capitalized intangibles	Unusual gain (loss)
Cumulative unusual gain (loss)	Increase in other reserves
Other reserves (e.g., bad debt, warranty, etc.)	

Fig.1 The components of firm value

Present value of growth opportunities

Assets in place

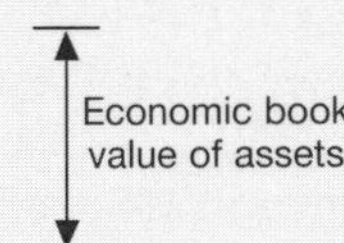

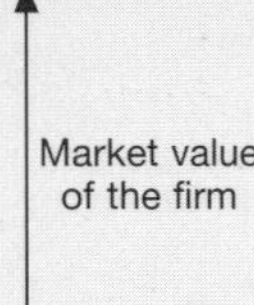

Conclusion

Be aware that measuring and assessing managerial and corporate performance is a very difficult task. While EVA is able to give us a better measure, it is not the panacea for corporate mismanagement. However, to the extent that it has increased managerial awareness of the capital costs in running a business, it has certainly emerged as an extremely useful concept in corporate finance.

Summary

Todd Milbourn looks at the highly topical subject of shareholder value with reference to Economic Value Added (EVA), a popular way of tying managerial compensation to financial performance measures which reflect changes in shareholder wealth. EVA, he argues, is not only correlated in this way but is responsive to executive actions. The author seeks to explain why so many companies are embarking on the EVA trail, how it is defined and calculated, and what is its future potential. Before all businesses rush to adopt it, he cautions, they should note that it has its limitations and it is not the holy grail.

EVA has increased managerial awareness of the capital costs of running a business, but it should be viewed primarily as a behavioral tool, not (as it is sometimes touted) as a new valuation tool.

Suggested further reading

Bacidore, J., Boquist, J., Milbourn, T. and Thakor, A.V., (1997), 'The Search for the Best Financial Performance Measure', *Financial Analysts Journal*, 11–20, May–June.

Bacidore, J., Boquist, J., Milbourn, T. and Thakor, A.V., (1997), 'EVA as an Incentive-Based Compensation Tool and its Relationship to TQM', *Journal of Applied Corporate Finance*.

Rogerson, W.P., (1997), 'Intertemporal Cost Allocation and Managerial Investment Incentives: A Theory Explaining the Use of Economic Value Added as a Performance Measure', *Journal of Political Economy*, 105–4, 770–795.

Performance and the reverse LBO

by Robert Holthausen and David Larcker

The performance of leveraged buyouts (LBOs) has received considerable attention in the financial literature. Research has argued that LBO-like organizations mitigate the incentive problems faced by more traditional corporate organizations, especially in sectors of the economy experiencing slow or no growth. One study has postulated that high-leverage, concentrated equity ownership by managers and monitoring by an LBO sponsor firm create an organizational form whose incentive structure leads to value maximization.

In particular, increasing the proportion of equity owned by managers can provide increased incentives for managers to create shareholder wealth. In addition, substantial debt service obligations can force managers to use particular care in seeking investment opportunities. Finally, non-management insiders (such as an LBO sponsor firm) typically own a significant proportion of the outstanding equity and exercise considerable control over managers through the board of directors. Thus they enhance monitoring within the organization.

Other studies have documented an improvement in the operating performance of companies that undergo an LBO. They suggest the explanation for the improved performance is the change in organizational incentives. While the operating performance and valuation implications of leveraged buyouts have been studied in numerous academic articles, the performance of *reverse* leveraged buyouts – companies that issue shares publicly after having gone private – has been a largely unanswered question.

Examination of reverse LBOs can provide additional evidence about the extent to which leverage and concentration of ownership provide desirable incentives within organizations. If the high leverage and concentrated equity ownership of LBOs motivate these companies to operate more efficiently while they are private, we might anticipate that the decline in leverage and the dispersion of equity ownership after an initial public offering would result in a decline in performance. However, to the extent that they continue to have higher leverage and more concentrated ownership than companies in their industries, these companies might continue to outperform their industries.

Despite the intuition of the incentive arguments presented by numerous studies, there are competing economic predictions about the effects of changes in leverage and managerial equity ownership. For example, increased managerial ownership of a company's common equity could increase financial performance because the key officers have a greater stake in any value-increasing actions taken. It is, however, possible that increased managerial ownership could decrease financial performance due to managerial risk aversion and the potential under-diversification of the managers' wealth.

Thus, managers with large equity stakes in highly leveraged companies could reject higher-risk, but more profitable, projects and accept lower-risk, but less profitable, projects. Indeed, it is plausible that managers in LBOs, faced with the pressure of servicing substantial debt, would not even consider all available projects, concentrating instead on those where the pay-offs are relatively assured and immediate.

Our study examined the performance and change in organizational structure (leverage and equity ownership) of a sample of LBOs. At the time of the initial public offering (IPO), there was a decline in the mean leverage ratio and the average equity ownership by insiders (all officers, directors and employees). However, equity ownership by managers and other insiders remained concentrated, and leverage remained high relative to typical public corporations. Thus, when these LBOs went public, they became hybrid organizations that retained some of the characteristics of the LBO organization.

We found that the operating performance of reverse LBOs is significantly better than that of the median company in their industries in the year before and in the year of the IPO. Moreover, the reverse-LBO companies continued to perform better than their industries for at least the four full fiscal years after the IPO (though the evidence in the third year is less strong). While these companies continued to outperform their industries, there was also evidence of a deterioration in the performance of the reverse-LBO companies after the IPO.

We also examined the capital expenditure and working-capital decisions of the reverse-LBO companies. We found evidence that before the IPO, reverse-LBO companies spent less on capital expenditures than the median companies in their industries and that after the IPO their capital expenditures returned to the median level of their industry counterparts.

As for working capital management, we found that reverse-LBO companies have significantly smaller amounts of working capital than their industry counterparts both before and after the reverse LBO. There was, however, evidence of an increase in working capital held by reverse-LBO companies after they went public. We also documented the extent to which changes in performance are associated with those in organizational incentives. The results indicated the change in operating performance (measured from one year before to up to four years after the reverse LBO) is unrelated to the change in leverage. It is, however, significantly related to the change in the percentage of equity owned by the operating management and other insiders that occurs at the time of the reverse LBO.

We found that as the equity owned by operating management and other insiders declined, so did operating performance. Moreover, as non-management insider ownership fell, working capital levels and capital expenditures increased. These results are consistent with changes in organizational incentives affecting performance.

Operating performance

To assess the relative performance of reverse LBOs, we measured operating performance using two widely used accounting ratios: operating income and operating cash flows. To avoid the mechanical effect of leverage on the results, both variables measure flows on a before-tax and before-interest basis. The first operating performance measure is the ratio of operating earnings before depreciation, interest and taxes deflated by total assets (denoted as OPINC/assets). The second measure is the ratio of operating cash flow before interest and taxes deflated by total assets (denoted as OCF/assets).

We assessed the performance of our sample companies using two different benchmarks. First, we examined an unadjusted measure which is simply the

Fig.1 Operating performance of reverse LBOs

Part A: Results on the levels of operating performance

Median level of OCF/assets (%)	**Year - 1***	**Year 0**	**Year + 1**	**Year + 2**	**Year + 3**	**Year + 4**	**Avg Years + 1 to + 4**
Firm	19.3†	14.6†	11.9†	14.3†	13.5†	15.4†	15.0†
Industry-adjusted	9.2†	4.7†	1.4	4.0†	2.3	2.9❖	4.1†
Number of observations	54	58	55	45	44	39	37
Median level of OPINC/assets (%)							
Firm	19.5†	19.8†	17.5†	17.1†	14.7†	15.3†	16.7†
Industry-adjusted	7.7†	7.9†	5.2†	5.4†	2.9✳	4.3†	4.7†
Number of observations	62	66	56	47	44	39	38

Part B: Results on the changes in accounting performance

Median change in OCF/assets (%)	**Year - 1 to Year 0**	**Year - 1 to Year + 1**	**Year - 1 to Year + 2**	**Year - 1 to Year + 3**	**Year - 1 to Year + 4**	**Year - 1 to Avg Years + 1 to + 4**
Firm	-4.7†	-6.2†	-4.4✳	-4.5✳	-2.1	-2.6
Industry-adjusted	-4.3❖	-6.5†	-4.5✳	-5.2❖	-3.1	-3.2
Number of observations	51	51	42	40	36	35
Median change in OPINC/assets (%)						
Firm	0.4	-1.3	-2.2	-4.1†	-3.4❖	-2.0
Industry-adjusted	0.2	-1.6	-1.9	-3.6❖	-2.0✳	-1.5
Number of observations	62	55	46	43	38	37

* Year -1 is the fiscal year ending prior to the IPO completion year (Year 0)

✳, ❖, †, - Significantly different from 0 at the 10%, 5% and 1% level (two-tailed test)

performance of the reverse-LBO company. Second, we considered an industry-adjusted performance measure which controls for time period and industry effects by examining the performance of the reverse-LBO company after subtracting the contemporaneous median performance of companies in the same two-digit SIC code as each reverse-LBO company.

Part A of Figure 1 presents median operating performance measures from one year before the IPO (year –1) to four years after the IPO. Year 0 is the fiscal year that includes the IPO.

Given that a large number of reverse-LBO companies are subsequently acquired or go bankrupt and that our tests required using accounting data that were not generally available for those concerns, the number of observations available varies across years. The performance of the reverse LBOs dominated that of their industries in the year before the IPO. OCF/assets and OPINC/assets of the reverse-LBO companies were about 92 per cent and 65 per cent higher than the comparative measure for the median business in their industries.

However, these results cannot be interpreted as evidence that companies completing an LBO outperform their industries. There is a potential selection bias associated with the subset of LBO companies that have a subsequent public offering. Results for the years subsequent to the IPO suggest these concerns continue to outperform their industries for the four years following the IPO (though the evidence at year +3 is weaker than at years +1, +2 or +4).

In Part B of Figure 1, we examine changes in operating performance for the reverse LBOs. The evidence suggests the accounting performance of companies that complete a reverse LBO exceeds the performance of their industries at the time of the IPO. Moreover, the evidence is reasonably consistent with the conclusion that this superior performance lasts for four fiscal years after the fiscal year of the IPO. There is also

Fig.2 Capital expentiture and working capital of reverse LBOs

Part A: Results on the level of capital expenditures and working capital

Median level of capital expenditures/assets (%)	**Year - 1***	**Year 0**	**Year + 1**	**Year + 2**	**Year + 3**	**Year + 4**	**+ 1 to + 4**
Firm	4.3†	4.8†	5.3†	4.7†	5.4†	4.4†	5.6†
Industry-adjusted	-1.3❖	-0.5	0.0	-0.5	0.0	-0.4	0.4
Number of observations	61	66	55	47	43	37	36
Median level of working/assets (%)							
Firm	14.4†	14.5†	15.0†	13.8†	13.1†	14.5†	13.4†
Industry-adjusted	-14.0†	-13.6†	-10.1†	-10.7†	-12.1†	-10.6†	-11.5†
Number of observations	54	53	55	45	43	38	37

Part B: Results on the changes in capital expenditures and working capital

Median change in capital expenditures/assets (%)	**Year - 1 to Year 0**	**Year - 1 to Year + 1**	**Year - 1 to Year + 2**	**Year - 1 to Year + 3**	**Year - 1 to Year + 4**	**Year - 1 to Avg Years + 1 to + 4**
Firm	0.8❖	0.6	0.0	0.7	-0.2	0.7
Industry-adjusted	1.2†	1.2✳	0.6	1.4	1.1	1.5
Number of observations	61	53	45	41	35	34
Median change in working capital/assets (%)						
Firm	0.0	1.5	0.8	0.5	1.3	0.8
Industry-adjusted	1.1	3.4❖	3.8❖	3.6❖	5.1❖	4.3❖
Number of observations	49	53	43	41	36	35

* Year -1 is the fiscal year ending prior to the IPO completion year (Year 0)
✳, ❖, †, - Significantly different from 0 at the 10%, 5% and 1% level (two-tailed test)

evidence of a decline in performance after the IPO, even though the companies continue to outperform their industry counterparts.

Capital expenditures

In addition to investigating accounting performance, we examined capital expenditures and working capital management. In particular, we wanted to determine whether the expenditure patterns and working capital management of reverse-LBO companies were significantly different from their industry counterparts and whether those patterns changed.

Part A of Figure 2 provides an analysis of the unadjusted and industry-adjusted level of capital expenditures and working capital, both relative to assets. Reverse-LBO companies spend significantly less than the industry norm on capital expenditures in the year before the IPO, but in the later years there is no difference in capital expenditures between the reverse-LBO companies and their industry medians. The industry-adjusted working capital/assets ratio is significantly negative in every year, indicating that reverse-LBO companies carry significantly less working capital than their industry counterparts. Moreover, the magnitude of the differences is large, indicating that the reverse-LBO concerns carry about half of the working capital carried by their industry counterparts.

Part B of Figure 2 provides an analysis of changes in capital expenditures and working capital. Unadjusted changes in capital expenditures show a significant increase from year –1 to year 0; none of the other differences is significant. Industry-adjusted changes in capital expenditures increase significantly between years –1 and 0 and year –1 and +1. While subsequent years generally have increases relative to year –1, no other observed changes are statistically significant. Changes in the level of capital expenditures in years 0 and +1 are probably expected given the infusion of cash from the public offering. Though there is no evidence of an increase in the level of unadjusted working capital for these concerns, industry-adjusted working capital increases.

Performance, ownership, leverage

We also examined the extent to which cross-sectional variation in the change in performance of the reverse-LBO companies can be explained by changes in leverage and ownership structure. Our analysis found no evidence that changes in leverage are associated with those in operating performance. However, the change in the percentage ownership by operating management and non-management insiders is generally significant and positively associated with changes in operating performance.

The positive coefficients on the percentage of equity owned by operating management and other insiders indicates the greater the decline in the percentage of outstanding equity owned by these groups, the greater the decline in subsequent accounting performance. To get a sense of the economic significance of the change in ownership, consider the following. Recall that the median OCF/assets in year –1 for this sample is 19.3 per cent. On average, the reverse LBO companies experience a drop of about 13 per cent in both the percentage of equity owned by operating management and in the percentage of equity owned by non-management insiders at the time of the IPO. A company experiencing the average decline in the percentage equity owned by management (13 per cent) loses an additional 5.7 per cent in OCF/assets relative to a company whose managers' percentage equity owned does not decline, other things being equal.

A business experiencing the average decline in the percentage equity owned by non-management insiders (13 per cent) loses an additional 4.55 per cent in OCF/assets, relative to a company whose non-management insiders' percentage equity owned does not decline, other things being equal. Given the median OCF/assets in year –1 of 19.3 per cent, these losses each represent about 25 per cent of the ratio's value in year –1.

In addition, we found no evidence that changes in leverage were associated with changes in working capital and only very weak evidence of a negative association between changes in leverage and changes in capital expenditures. Further, there is only very weak evidence of a negative association between changes in managerial ownership and changes in working capital and no evidence of an association between changes in managerial ownership and capital expenditures.

However, there is strong evidence of a negative association between changes in non-management insider ownership and both working capital and capital expenditures. This significantly negative coefficient implies that as non-management insiders' equity decreases, working capital and capital expenditures increase.

To get a sense of the economic magnitude of the effect of the change in non-management insider ownership on working capital and capital expenditures consider the following. A company experiencing the average decline in the percentage equity owned by non-management insiders (13 per cent), gains an additional three per cent in working capital/assets, relative to one whose non-managers' percentage equity owned did not decline, other things being equal. Given the median working capital/assets in year –1 of 14.4 per cent, this represents about a 20 per cent increase in working capital relative to the value in year –1.

A similar calculation to determine the effect of non-management insider ownership on capital expenditures implies an increase in capital expenditures/assets of 1.04 per cent, which approximates to a 25 per cent increase in the level of capital expenditures relative to year –1.

Overall, we find that changes in operating performance observed after the reverse LBO are related to changes in the concentration of ownership by operating management and non-management insiders. One interpretation is that reductions in the concentration of ownership lead to an inferior incentive structure and therefore performance deteriorates. But it could be that managers optimally choose the timing of the IPO transaction to take advantage of an information asymmetry between their private information and the information known to the market. However, examining the relation between changes in equity ownership and operating performance is only tangentially related to this timing explanation because it does not directly relate to changes in wealth.

We also examined the stock market performance of reverse LBOs to determine if there is any evidence that managers act opportunistically. If managers take advantage of an informational asymmetry to sell their shares at an inflated offering price, we would anticipate significantly negative returns after the IPO. Overall, we found the market performance of the reverse LBOs after their public offerings is either positive or insignificantly different from zero depending on the time period and performance metric chosen. Thus, there is no support for the conjecture that managers are able to take advantage of an information asymmetry to enrich themselves because reverse LBOs are fairly priced.

Interpreting the results

Our major findings are that companies outperform their industries for the four years following the IPO, though there is weak evidence of a decline in performance in that period. Further, reverse LBOs increase capital expenditures after the public offering while working capital levels increase. Most important, company performance decreases with declines in the concentration of equity ownership by operating management and other insiders and is unrelated to changes in leverage. Finally, both capital expenditures and working capital appear to increase with declines in the concentration of equity ownership by non-management insiders.

One interpretation of our findings is that there are positive incentive effects associated with more concentrated ownership by managers and active investors and that these organizational changes contribute to superior performance. However, we find no evidence of positive incentive effects associated with greater leverage, in that performance after the IPO is unrelated to changes in leverage at the time of the IPO.

These results leave us with a puzzle. If LBOs are value-increasing events, can reverse LBOs also be value-increasing? If reverse LBOs are not value increasing, why are they undertaken? One possibility is that as a company's value increases with improved performance after the LBO, the owners begin to place a higher value on holding more marketable and more diversified claims. Thus, even if performance declines after going public, owners prefer to hold claims that are marketable.

Another potential answer to the puzzle is that the change in organizational structure occurs because of significant changes in such things as the company's potential investments. For example, suppose there is an expansion in the size and number of profitable investments available to the company when it is private but its owners are reluctant to provide more funding because of their lack of diversification. Moreover, financing the new investment with debt is precluded by the high leverage levels. In this case, the shift to a public company is optimal and caused by the shift in the underlying change in the investment opportunities. Thus, the organizational structure of the reverse LBO company was optimal when it was private, as well as when it returned to being public. One possibility that we cannot rule out is that the association between ownership and performance is not created by incentive effects associated with ownership but that both are caused by the shift in a concern's investment opportunities.

Finally, since our tests provide at least evidence of a decline in performance after the reverse LBO and that this is related to the change in ownership structure, it is interesting to examine changes in organizational structure after the reverse LBO. If the change in organizational structure at the time of the reverse LBO is not optimal, we would expect companies to switch back to their LBO-like structure.

An analysis of these companies three years after the LBO indicated they were still hybrid organizations – they retained some of the ownership and board structure characteristics of the leverage buy-out. However, the ownership positions of these organizations are much less concentrated than immediately after the IPO. Moreover, the boards of these companies began to be represented by external members with no significant equity stake. Thus, these companies appeared to be evolving toward the board and ownership structure of a typical US corporation, as opposed to moving back toward an LBO-like structure.

Overall, the results in this paper add intriguing evidence on the link between performance and organizational incentives. In particular, there is strong evidence of a positive association between performance and managerial ownership and ownership by active investors (monitors).

Summary

The article 'Riding on the benefits of the LBO wave' (Module 12) describes how the LBO wave of the 1980s made a lasting impact on corporate culture in the US.

In this article Robert Holthausen and David Larcker put the spotlight on the performance of 'reverse' leveraged buyouts – companies that issue shares publicly after having gone private previously. Their recent research shows that at an operating level these businesses do significantly better than the median company in their industry sector in the year before, in the year of, and for at least four years after, the initial public offering. However, their own performance deteriorates after the IPO. There is also evidence that capital expenditures and working capital rise after the reverse LBO. Declines in performance are linked by the authors to changes in the percentage of equity owned by managers and other insiders at the time of the deal. The findings beg the question as to why reverse LBOs are undertaken.

Suggested further reading

Baker, G. and Wruck, K., (1989), 'Organizational changes and value creation in leveraged buyouts: the case of the O.M. Scott & Sons Company', *Journal of Financial Economics 25*, 163–190.

Byrd, J. W. and Hickman, K. A., (1992), 'Do outside directors monitor managers?', *Journal of Financial Economics* 32, 195–221.

Degeorge, F. and Zeckhauser, R., (1993), 'The reverse LBO decision and firm performance: Theory and evidence', *Journal of Finance 48*, 1323–1348.

Fama, E. and Jensen, M., (1985), 'Organizational forms and investment decisions', *Journal of Financial Economics* 14, 101–120.

Gore, J., Holthausen, R. and Larcker, D., (1997), 'Corporate governance, CEO compensation and firm performance', Working paper, Wharton School of the University of Pennsylvania.

Holthausen, R. and Larcker, D., (1997), 'Financial performance and organizational structure', Working paper, Wharton School of the University of Pennsylvania.

Riding on the crest of a wave can be easy but...

by Franklin Allen and John Percival

Corporations today face an increasingly challenging business environment. Competition in product markets has become both global in nature and more complex. Capital markets have also become global. Corporations in every country have been forced to become increasingly focused on the issue of creating value for their shareholders.

In order to compete successfully in this rapidly changing global economy, we argue that managers need more than a strategy that suggests possible directions in which to move; they need to have a clear idea of the financial implications of that strategy. They need the tools that will enable them to choose the specific plan that will allow them to use their organization's resources most effectively. Companies that earn a rate of return that consistently exceeds the opportunity cost of capital will create long-term shareholder value.

In order to understand the relationship between strategy and finance it is useful to draw a distinction between companies that 'ride a wave' and companies that create value. Riding a wave simply requires being in the right place at the right time with the right characteristics. Revenues grow, the company is profitable and the stock price rises. It is easy to fall into the trap of assuming that these financial outcomes are the direct result of strategy.

Profitability is, however, extraordinarily fragile. It emanates from special conditions in product markets involving customers, competition and the overall economic environment. If these conditions change and the company does not modify its strategy, the wave inevitably crashes. Only then do companies realize, with the benefit of painful hindsight, that profitability may have been due more to serendipity than to forward-looking management.

Companies that create value do so by consistently earning more than the opportunity cost of capital through several significant cycles of change in the business. Riding a wave is easy; creating value is exceedingly difficult. In order to create value, all managers must understand the relationship between strategy and financial results. It is tempting to believe that by doing good a company will do well. We all long to believe that if companies take care of their customers and if they care about the people who work for the organization then good financial results will automatically happen. Unfortunately, doing good is necessary, but not sufficient, for doing well.

We have developed a four-part management process designed to integrate strategy and finance with the aim of creating value:

Part 1: the objective

A company must have a passion for creating value for shareholders. If it is not the focus of strategies it will not happen by chance. Capital markets may be content with companies that ride waves. If investors can time their investment properly because they understand the financial implications of management actions they can earn acceptable rates of return. They get in early in the wave and get out before the crash. However, the implications for companies that fail actively to create value can be devastating. IBM, Apple and Kodak are examples of companies that had outstanding personnel and excellent products but suffered greatly from the cresting of their waves.

Part 2: the financial implications

Two methodologies are useful for understanding the relationship between strategy and value creation. The first is the Dupont System: margin x turnover = rate of return

This formula is useful because at some level most strategies involve a trade-off between margins and turnover. It allows simple insights into the effect of various possibilities on the rate of return. The Dupont System forces management to focus on how the rate of return comes from competitive conditions in a product market and customers' reactions to management's decisions. Rate of return does not come from margins or turnover but from margins and turnover. Actions that increase margins tend to reduce turnover and vice versa.

Among other things, pricing decisions, investing in technology, outsourcing and adjusting product mix can all be analysed using this tool. Find a company that has 'thought outside the box' and revolutionized a business, then analyse that business using the Dupont System and it is amazing how often you can see what management saw.

A good example is provided by the US retailer Walmart. The reason for its success can be seen using the Dupont System. Traditionally it has been manufacturers that have developed customer loyalty. This has enabled them to charge higher prices, and so reap higher margins. Retailers have focused more on higher turnover. Walmart, on the other hand, has been able to create a strong base of loyal customers and effectively combine high margins with high turnover. As a result, it has consistently earned higher returns than its competitors.

The Dupont system is most valuable when used prospectively. It provides a simple way for managers to gain insights about the return a strategy will generate.

The second methodology is discounted cash flow, which operates at a more detailed level. It provides a means of determining the relationship between the estimates of costs, future revenues and the risk of potential investments and a company's value. The starting point of any discounted cash flow exercise is the identification of the organization's opportunity cost of capital, *r*. This is the best expected return the company's owners could obtain with comparable risk in the capital markets (that is, including banks and other intermediaries as well as the stock market and other financial markets) if it did not invest funds in the strategy under consideration.

If the strategy has a higher expected return than the opportunity cost of capital, it creates value for shareholders. If it has a lower expected return it destroys value and should not be undertaken since investors would be better off investing their money in the capital markets.

A convenient way to measure the amount of wealth created for shareholders by particular strategies is to discount the projected cash flows from an investment, including both costs and revenues, at the opportunity cost of capital. To see why discounting gives a measure of wealth creation, consider the case where the shareholders' best available alternative is to put money in the bank at 10 per cent per year. As far as the shareholders are concerned this means that $100 now is equivalent to \$100 x (1+0.1) = \$110 one year from now. Turning this around, the present value of \$110 one year from now in terms of today's money is \$110 / (1+0.1) = \$100.

Suppose an investment project costs \$100 today, generates a net cash flow of \$115 one year from now and shareholders' opportunity cost of capital is 10 per cent. Since the project has a rate of return of 15 per cent it is clearly worth doing. How much wealth does the project create for shareholders? The present value of the \$115 revenue is \$115 / (1+0.1) = \$104.55. Since the project only costs \$100 the net present value – that is, the wealth created for shareholders – is \$104.55 – \$100 = \$4.55. If the business undertakes this investment project its value will increase by \$4.55.

If the project yielded only \$105 one year from now and was otherwise unchanged, it would not be worth doing. The rate of return on this project would be five per cent, below the opportunity cost of capital. It would be better to put the money in the bank at 10 per cent. If the managers decided to undertake the project the change in firm value would be –\$100 + \$105 / (1+0.1) = –\$4.54. Here \$4.54 of shareholder wealth would be destroyed.

The net present value (NPV) approach can readily be extended to more complex situations. Using the same logic as above concerning putting money in the bank, the present value of C, t years from now, is $C/(1+r)^t$. Hence, the general measure of how much value is created for shareholders by a project with a cost at the initial date 0 and net cash flows at subsequent dates from year 1 to year t is:

Equation 1:

$$\text{NPV} = -\text{Cost at initial date 0} + \frac{\text{Net cash flow date 1}}{(\text{L} + \text{r})} + \frac{\text{Net cash flow date 2}}{(\text{L} + \text{r})^2} + \ldots + \frac{\text{Net cash flow at date } t}{(\text{L} + \text{r})^t}$$

Net present value has the potential to be an extremely useful tool. Given the estimated costs and projected net cash flows an investment will generate, it provides a direct way of predicting the impact of managers' actions on stock price.

Finance academics have devoted a great deal of effort to finding methods to identify the appropriate discount rate. In our examples we simply used the rate shareholders could obtain at the bank as the opportunity cost of capital. To allow for risk, models such as the capital asset pricing model (CAPM) are used. In the CAPM model the opportunity cost of capital is found from the expected return on an investment in the stock market with equivalent risk. Significant attention has also been paid to the problem of adjusting for the choice between equity and debt finance using the Modigliani and Miller theorems and their extensions. The most popular formula, taking into account all these factors for the discount rate, called the weighted average cost of capital, is:

Equation 2:

$$r_{\text{WACC}} = \frac{\text{Equity}}{\text{Equity + Debt}}\ r_{\text{Equity}} + (1 - \text{Corporate tax rate}) \frac{\text{Debt}}{\text{Equity + Debt}}\ r_{\text{Debt}}$$

where 'Equity' and 'Debt' are the market values of the company's equity and debt, r_{Equity} is the cost of equity found using the CAPM, r_{Debt} is the cost of debt which can be found directly from bond yields or bank rates, and the corporate tax rate term adjusts for the tax deductibility of debt interest.

In contrast to the large amount of effort finance academics devote to identifying the discount rate, not much time has been devoted to understanding how future cash flows emanate from strategy. As typically implemented, finding costs and projecting revenues is the weakness of the NPV approach. The standard way of doing this is to extrapolate current accounting statements to forecast future cash flows. Little thought is put into the issue of where these cash flows come from and how likely it is that current levels will continue. This is where an understanding of customers, competitors and operations becomes crucial.

Part 3: integrating marketing, operations and finance

Value creation is a financial outcome but it emanates from marketing and operating strategies. It is necessary to understand the implications of these at the time strategy is formulated.

It is ironic that value creation is a financial outcome but the role of financial managers in creating value has been severely limited because financial choices, such as debt and dividend pay-out policies, can add only a limited amount of value.

The most that financial choices can do is to start with marketing and operating strategies that have the best revenue and cost trade-offs and obtain a little more value from them at the margin. Financial strategy, in the sense of capital structure, dividend policy and the like, can never overcome poorly developed or implemented marketing and operating strategies.

We believe that finance must have two separate roles. One continues to involve the things that finance staff have traditionally done, such as choosing capital structure and dividend policies and risk management. The other role, however, is not traditional. It is the development of the financial implications of non-financial strategies.

This second role for finance involves asking and answering questions about how a proposed strategy will provide future cash flows that will create value. How can we use the improved market position derived from a proposed strategy to earn more than the opportunity cost of capital?

A key to creating value is the financial awareness of non-financial people who use this thought process when formulating strategies involving competitive advantage, technology, investment, re-engineering and outsourcing.

Part 4: change

Strategy discussions ultimately come around to dealing with change. Strategies that earn more than the opportunity cost of capital under one set of circumstances may not earn those returns when customers, competitors, technologies and economic environment change. Integrating finance and strategy is crucial in dealing with what we call the change trilogy:

- knowing when to change;
- knowing how to change;
- changing.

For example, far too many companies have not moved on a timely basis to eliminate or change lower profitability businesses that take away sales from their core businesses. IBM is a good illustration of this. It did not pursue personal computers because it feared that PCs might erode its highly profitable mainframe business. Similarly, Bausch and Lomb failed to introduce disposable contact lenses, presumably because of concern about the impact they might have had on its existing contact lens and solutions business. This delay enabled Johnson & Johnson to enter the disposable lenses market and gain considerable market share at Bausch and Lomb's expense.

Understanding the financial implications of doing nothing, waiting or progressively changing is crucial to understanding which strategy creates the most shareholder value. Analyzing means of implementing change using the Dupont System and discounted cash flow integrates strategy and finance in determining how to change and motivate change. This is achieved through a clearer understanding of the reasons for, and the objectives of, the changes.

Conclusions

We believe that it is only when strategy and finance are integrated that managers can avoid the pitfalls of both and make effective decisions. The concepts of strategy need to be used to develop an understanding of how cash flows are generated. What is the competitive environment in which the business operates? How are the strategies or projects likely to affect revenues or costs? What actions will competitors take in response to changes in a company's products, pricing and other competitive decisions? How can it minimize its costs of production and maximize the quality of its products?

The usual objection to quantifying cash flows from the imprecise ideas that strategy focuses on is that there is a great deal of uncertainty associated with them. However, rather than being an argument against quantification, uncertainty is a good reason to undertake scenario and sensitivity analysis.

Although it is not possible to identify what will happen in the future, it is possible to rule out inconsistencies and contradictions in the analysis. For example, a manager may feel that costs will grow at six per cent per year and revenues at 15 per cent per year so net cash flows will rise at nine per cent per year. However, a careful analysis may show that tax effects and taking proper account of sunk costs means that net cash flows grow only by seven per cent per year.

In addition to ruling out inconsistencies, a quantification of the strategic analysis will usually help managers to understand better how strategies create value for shareholders. Such an exercise can indicate to what extent an increase in value is due to an increase in market share or a reduction in costs and how competitors' reactions are affecting value-creation. Only with quantification is it possible to understand the relative importance of each factor and how much managerial time and effort should be devoted to each one. Incorporating strategy thus corrects the weakness of finance by considering where projected cash flows come from with some degree of sophistication. This enables managers to understand how value is created and whether the current situation can be sustainable. Quantification also corrects strategy's weakness of not providing a way to choose between alternatives. By combining finance with strategy it is possible to gain an idea of which strategies are likely to create the most value for shareholders. The two methods are complementary in their approach, rather than substitutes.

A company that has been highly successful in creating shareholder value is Emerson Electric, a US-based manufacturer of industrial products which makes relatively low technology goods, such as electric motors and compressors. The key features of its products are performance, low cost and reliability. It has had 40 years of increased earnings and has earned at least its opportunity cost of capital for most of these years. The company has also created a large amount of wealth for its shareholders.

We believe Emerson's success has been achieved through the integration of the tools of strategy and finance. It is highly unlikely that any company would be consistently lucky for a period of 40 years, particularly in the cyclical, competitive, low-technology industries in which Emerson operates.

Emerson has a sophisticated planning process: each division has to prepare a detailed five-year plan that contains projections of financial results and a discussion of why they are sensible. Managers use the Dupont System to prepare their projections. The executives who prepare each division's plan are grilled by senior management. Managers are required to display an in-depth knowledge of how their plans will be implemented and why their financial projections are realistic in terms of the marketing and operating strategies involved. This has led to the company's long-term success over several business cycles. By understanding how integrated management and financial strategies create wealth, the company has been profitable in the long run.

Managers that ride waves bear significant risks. Even the most astute may not be able to predict when the wave will crest or crash. It is only through a thorough understanding of how the company creates value that executives will avoid crashes and assure consistent profitability. This can best be done through the intentional integration of strategy and finance.

Summary

This article focuses on the crucial relationship between strategy and finance – it is only when the two are integrated, argue Franklin Allen and John Percival, that managers can avoid the pitfalls inherent in both and make effective decisions.

The authors set out a four strand management process: first, develop a passion for creating shareholder value; use appropriate methodologies like the Dupont system (which focuses on the trade-off between margins and turnover) and discounted cash flow; integrate marketing and operations with finance so that the financial implications of non-financial strategies become clear; finally, remember that strategies which earn more than the opportunity cost of capital under one set of circumstances may not do so when customers, technologies and competitors change. A good model is provided by Emerson Electric of the US which has increased earnings for 40 years in cyclical, low technology industries.

5

The nature of financial markets

Contributors

Dr Narayan Naik is Assistant Professor of Finance and Citibank Research Fellow at London Business School. His current research interests include market microstructure, fund managers' contracts and herding in asset allocation.

Nicholas Barberis is Assistant Professor of Finance at the University of Chicago Graduate School of Business. His research interests include optimal asset allocation and the efficiency of markets.

Laurent Germain is EU Visiting Research Fellow at London Business School. His research interests include market microstructure.

Paul Marsh is Professor of Management and Finance at London Business School. His research interests include investment in smaller companies; investment management and short-termism.

Contents

Introduction

The goings-on in financial markets are daily front page news in most countries – but the underlying role of such markets is often overlooked or misunderstood. This module considers their various economic functions, discusses the so called efficient markets hypothesis, and concludes by examining critically the oft repeated refrain that markets are damagingly short-termist.

The many roles of financial markets

by Narayan Naik

The growth of financial markets has been one of the outstanding developments of the past 15 years or so. That period has seen a change in the composition of financial markets. The share of banks in total recorded financial assets has tended to fall while that of securities markets and even more that of financial derivatives – futures, options and swaps – has greatly increased. These developments have been most advanced in the US and UK but the removal of restrictions is leading to a similar expansion of financial market transactions in other countries, notably France, Germany and, most recently, Japan.

The role of banks in the economic system has long been understood but that of securities markets has been criticized on the grounds that they are driven by speculation – regarded as unproductive – and consume too many real resources. It is essential, however, to recognize the varied economic roles that financial markets play; it is clear, for example, that the absence of financial markets was one of the critical weaknesses of the Soviet bloc.

That financial markets, in the form of both banking and securities markets, are necessary for the effective allocation of real capital hardly needs saying, especially in the light of the Soviet experience and the failure by governments in other countries to plan production. But the economic functions of financial markets go beyond this and include: the provision of choice in the timing of consumption; the management of risk; the role of corporate management; and the provision of information.

Choice of consumption

Financial markets and instruments enable individuals to choose more effectively between current and future consumption. Borrowing enables them to consume more while lending, in the widest sense, enables them to exchange consumption today for more tomorrow. A market interest rate establishes the economic price of this exchange. For individuals as a whole, however, the provision of a higher level of consumption tomorrow, with given technology, can only come from the additional output generated by physical investment. So a choice of timing in consumption patterns is linked to the role of capital markets in providing producers with resources in excess of those generated out of their own income. In the process both borrowers and lenders are made better off.

Financial markets also allow efficient risk-sharing among investors. As we will see later in *Mastering Finance*, there are two types of risks: those which can be diversified away and those which cannot.

Diversifiable risk can be eliminated by holding assets on which the returns are not perfectly correlated with each other. Financial markets, therefore, enable investors to eliminate diversifiable risk. Furthermore, the operations of derivatives markets in particular enable individuals to choose which non-diversifiable risks they are willing to bear and which they lay off.

Non-diversifiable risk, by definition, cannot be eliminated merely by holding a spread of assets. But forward, futures and options markets allow the transfer of non-diversifiable risk from more risk-averse to less risk-averse individuals and from those who cannot manage risk to those who can. Thus, financial markets make efficient risk sharing among investors possible.

Financial markets offer an array of financial instruments with very different risk-return relationships. These make it easier for individuals and organizations to choose a degree of risk which corresponds more closely to their risk-tolerance levels.

For example, investors who are extremely risk-averse may invest a large part of their wealth in risk-free securities (such as government bonds), more risk-tolerant investors may select risky stocks while investors with intermediate risk preferences may choose a combination of bonds and stocks. In some cases risk-matching may take place in financial markets. For example, the user of copper loses if copper prices rise whereas the producer gains – and conversely. A forward purchase of copper by the former at an agreed price and a forward sale by the latter can enable them both to hedge their price risk.

However, if there is not an equal and opposite supply of hedging, the gap has to be filled by speculators. So, paradoxically, it is speculation that makes possible a wider range of risk reduction. Moreover, if speculators are more skilled at judging the right or, in the language of economics, the equilibrium, price than other traders, the effect of their transactions in moving prices towards this level enhances the role of markets in resource allocation.

The role of management

Financial markets enable the separation of ownership from day-to-day managerial control – a practical necessity for running large organizations. Many corporations have hundreds of thousands of shareholders with very different tastes, wealth, risk tolerances and personal investment opportunities. Yet, as the American economist Irving Fisher showed in 1930, they can all agree on one thing – managers should continue to invest in real assets until the marginal return on the investment equals the rate of return on investments of a similar degree of risk available in capital markets.

Since shareholders are unanimous about the investment criteria, they can safely delegate the operations of an enterprise to a professional manager. Managers do not need to know anything about the preferences of their shareholders nor do they need to consult their own tastes. They need to follow only one objective, to invest in projects that yield a higher return compared with that offered by investments of equal risk in capital markets (the opportunity cost of capital).

Put differently, the managers' objective becomes that of investing in projects that in present value terms cost less than the benefits they bring in, that is, investing in positive net present value projects. This objective maximizes the market value of each stockholder's stake in the company and is therefore in the best interest of all shareholders.The maximization of net present value incompetitive markets also implies the maximization of return over cost in terms of the use of real resources and, therefore achieves a social optimum in the widest sense.

Financial markets and information

The stock market aggregates the diverse opinions of market participants and conveys how much the equity of a company is worth under its current management. Suppose the shares of company A are trading at a given price and that company B can use the assets of company A more efficiently under its own management. Then company B may acquire company A. If there were no stock market to value performance it would have been very difficult for company B to discover that the assets of company A were not being put to the best use.

Thus, by providing information on performance a well-functioning stock market leads to the more efficient use of assets and enables poor management to be disciplined through a market for corporate control. When an organization announces a plan, such as a new project or a company takeover, the stock price may respond in a positive or a negative way. Thus the organization's management can see what market participants collectively think of its proposed plan.

If the stock price reaction is negative, management may decide to re-examine its own calculations and reconsider its plan. Thus the stock market helps management by providing a second opinion about its policy. Moreover, because stock prices reflect the value of the assets under current management, they give an indication of how well the management is performing and therefore help to evaluate its performance. There is considerable evidence to suggest financial markets act as efficient aggregators of information (*see* 'Market efficiency: a mirror for information' for the definition of different degrees of market efficiency) and help the efficient allocation of all resources via information conveyed through market prices.

Consider the case of a farmer who has land that can be used to grow wheat, corn or oatmeal. He is reasonably certain about how much it will cost him to grow any of these crops and how much output his land will yield. However, there is considerable uncertainty about the price his crop will fetch after harvesting. This uncertainty depends not only on the weather but also on the demand and supply conditions after harvesting. The farmer can look at the futures prices of wheat, corn and oatmeal and, knowing his cost structure, decide which is the most profitable crop for him. He can also use the futures markets to assure himself a guaranteed price for the crop. In this way financial markets provide signals as to the socially most desired and economically most efficient use of the farmer's land. Commercial banks clearly play important economic roles as well. In addition to bringing borrowers and lenders together, they also act as monitors of companies.

If finance is provided entirely through the diverse ownership of stockholders, no single investor has an incentive to incur the cost of monitoring management and ensure it is acting in stockholders' best interest. Such monitoring only needs to be done by one party; duplication might not result in better monitoring and would waste resources. Stockholders cannot profitably combine to hire a monitor because of a free rider problem; each would want others to bear the costs of monitoring. When a bank lends to a corporation, it has an incentive to be the single monitor. Further, by holding a large portfolio of loans to companies, the bank can guarantee it is undertaking the monitoring and thus overcome the free rider problem.

Summary

What role do financial markets play in the modern world? What is the response to critics who claim they are unproductive and driven by idle speculators? The economic

functions of markets go beyond mere allocation of capital – the need for which was vividly highlighted by the failure of Soviet and other experiments in central planning. They include choice in the timing of consumption, the management of risk, separation of ownership from day-to-day managerial control and aggregated information about company performance which can be useful to both outsiders and insiders alike.

In the next article, 'Market efficiency: a mirror for information', Laurent Germain develops this last point in his discussion of the efficient markets hypothesis (EMH), the controversial contention that all available information is reflected in prices. He argues that the extent to which this is true depends on the nature of the information: information contained in past prices; all public information, including that contained in past prices; or all public and private information.

Suggested further reading

Fama, E., (1970), 'Efficient Capital Markets: A Review of Theory and Empirical Work', *Journal of Finance.*

Fama, E., (1991), 'Efficient Capital Markets II', *Journal of Finance.*

Franklin, A. 'Stock Markets and Resource Allocation' in Mayer, C. and Vives, X. (eds), (1992), CEPR volume *Financial intermediation in the Construction of Europe.*

Martin, H. 'Banking, Financial Intermediation and Corporate Finance' in Giovannini, A. and Mayer C., (eds), (1990), *European Financial Integration,* Cambridge: Cambridge University Press.

Market efficiency: a mirror for information

by Laurent Germain

The efficient markets hypothesis (EMH) states that the price of a financial asset at a given point in time fully reflects all the available information relevant to the value of the asset at that time, where 'available' means the information that might recover the cost of obtaining it.

ICI's share price, for example, according to the EMH, should fully reflect at all times the prevailing general prospects for the UK and world economies and their effects on the chemical industry as well as the prospects specifically for ICI and its businesses. The share price of ICI should therefore equal its intrinsic value at all times, where intrinsic value is defined as the present value of all the cash flows shareholders expect to receive, with the expectation of these cash flows being formed on the basis of all available information.

The EMH has three important implications:

• First it should be impossible for an investor to profit from any information he or she might have regarding the prospects of a financial asset. So an investor should not be able to exploit any information as to ICI's prospects by selling its shares at a price that is higher than their intrinsic value or by buying the shares at a price lower than their intrinsic value. This is because the information the investor intends to exploit should, according to the EMH, already be reflected in ICI's share price.

- The second implication of the EMH, which is essentially the mirror image of the first, is that an investor should be able to infer the information relevant to the prospects of a financial asset from his observation of the share price. In other words, infer ICI's prospects by watching its share price.
- The third implication is that any change in the financial asset's price that differs from the normal appreciation required by investors for holding the asset should be due to new – that is, unexpected – information (news that has already been expected is not new information in this sense).

To what extent is the efficient market hypothesis true? In other words, to what extent is all information reflected in prices? The answer depends on the nature of the information that might be reflected in prices. Three types of information have been considered in financial theory: information contained in past prices; all public information, including that contained in past prices; and all public and private information.

An example of the first type is the series of price changes that have preceded the current price of a financial asset and, in particular, whether these were increases or decreases. An example of the second type of information is a company's earnings announcement or an interest rate statement made by a central bank. Finally, an example of the third type is information about an imminent takeover of one company by another, which is known only by the management of the acquiring organization.

These three types of information define the three forms of market efficiency: the weak form of the EMH, which states that current prices reflect all the information conveyed by past prices; the semi-strong form, that current prices reflect all public information; and the strong form, that current prices reflect all information, whether public or private.

Testing weak form efficiency is accomplished by examining whether current changes in security prices are related to past changes. If that were the case, investors would be able to infer future changes in price from past changes and profit from trading on the basis of such predictions. The evidence is that this is not the case. Instead, at least as a first approximation, changes in prices appear to follow what is called a random walk, with an upward drift.

The random walk concept, already studied in the early years of the century by the French mathematician Louis Bachelier, defines a series of movements, such as changes in prices, in which every movement is totally unrelated to preceding movements: in statistical terms, returns on the asset are independently and identically distributed. This is indeed the case with share prices, once the appreciation required by investors for holding an asset has been accounted for. This implies that chart or technical analysis should not be profitable, for such techniques rely on past changes in prices to predict future movements.

Testing semi-strong form efficiency is accomplished by examining whether the information revealed in a public announcement is incorporated in security prices instantaneously or only over a period of time. If the latter were the case, investors would be able to predict future prices from information that is already public and profit from trading on the basis of their predictions. This, again, turns out not to be the case. Studies focusing on price changes on the days announcements are made have revealed that information was incorporated in prices on the same day.

Box 1

In recent years, researchers have uncovered several anomalies which cast doubt about the extent of market efficiency. These are

- size and earnings related regularities in stock returns
- negative long run performance of initial public offerings
- calendar seasonalities (January effect, weekend effect etc.)
- Deviations of stock prices from random walk.

While some researchers have resorted to behavioral explanations to explain these anomalies, others have called for better models to capture expected returns and the variations in expected returns over time.

Testing strong-form efficiency is done by investigating whether company insiders, such as senior executives or directors, can profit from their private information regarding their company's prospects. Insiders do indeed appear to be able to do so, suggesting that strong-form efficiency does not hold, in marked contrast to the weak-form and semi strong-forms. Nevertheless, as soon as anyone starts trading on private information prices start reflecting this. Market participants infer from the price changes the presence of insiders and react accordingly.

These results should not be surprising, especially to those who are familiar with Oscar Wilde's *An Ideal Husband*, in which the main character makes the observation that all great fortunes were built on private information. Public information is by definition available to all and easily traded on in modern markets with their low transaction costs, such as the UK and US stock markets. Public information should, therefore, be easily and rapidly reflected in prices, thus precluding the possibility of profiting from such information. This is not the case with private information, to which by definition only a few are party.

Summary

This article introduces the efficient market hypothesis (EMH), stating that all relevant and available information is fully reflected in the current price of a financial asset. If this is the case, then firstly investors cannot profit from available information that they may have regarding a financial asset's prospects; secondly, those prospects can themselves be inferred from its price; and thirdly, that price will only change as a result of new, unexpected information. Laurent Germain examines the extent to which this hypothesis holds true in the financial markets in its strong, semi-strong and weak forms. The weak and semi-strong forms are supported by market evidence, while the strong form may not always hold in reality. The answer lies in the nature of the information, with only the existence of private information enabling those who possess it to profit.

Suggested further reading

Fama, E., (1970), 'Efficient Capital Markets: A Review of Theory and Empirical Work', *Journal of Finance.*

Fama, E., (1991), 'Efficient Capital Markets II', *Journal of Finance.*

Grossman, S.J. and Stiglitz, J.E., (1980), 'On the Impossibility of Informationally Efficient Markets', *American Economic Review.*

Markets: the price may not be right

by Nicholas Barberis

News and information hit the financial markets every hour of the day. A company might report earnings much higher than expected or announce a big acquisition. Traders and investors rush to digest the information and push the price to a level they think is consistent with what they have heard. But do they get it right? That is, do they react properly to the news they receive?

Michael Jensen: 'the efficient markets hypothesis is the best-established fact in all of social science'

Recent evidence suggests investors make systematic errors in processing new information that may be profitably exploited by others. These findings are therefore a direct affront to the so-called efficient markets hypothesis – the idea that prices are right and there is no 'free lunch' to be had. In 1978 Michael Jensen, a financial economist at Harvard Business School, wrote that 'the efficient markets hypothesis is the best-established fact in all of social science'. Twenty years later, in part because of the findings I will outline, the debate over the efficiency of markets is in turmoil once again.

Do investors over-react?

In 1985, Werner De Bondt of the University of Wisconsin and Richard Thaler of the University of Chicago Graduate School of Business caused a considerable stir by publishing an article presenting what they claimed was evidence that investors over-react to news. They found that stocks with very poor returns over a three-year period subsequently dramatically outperformed those with the highest returns over that three-year period. For example, a portfolio made up of the 35 biggest 'losers' earned a cumulative return 25 per cent higher than the portfolio of biggest 'winners' over the subsequent 36 months.

How might investor over-reaction explain these findings? Suppose that a company announces good news over the three years in question, such as earnings reports that are consistently above expectations. It is possible that investors over-react to such news and become excessively optimistic about the company's prospects, pushing its stock price to very high levels and making the stock a likely candidate for inclusion in the 'winners' portfolio.

In the subsequent months, however, investors realize they were unduly optimistic about the business and the stock price will correct itself downwards. This correction may well lie at the root of the poor performance of 'winner' stocks. In a similar way, 'loser' stocks may simply be stocks that investors have become excessively pessimistic about. As the misperception is corrected, these stocks earn high returns.

More recent studies have provided further evidence for this kind of over-reaction. Researchers have looked at stocks that are highly valued by the market – in the sense of having very high ratios of price to a measure of company fundamentals – and have found that such stocks may be too highly valued. For example, suppose you create a portfolio of stocks with very high ratios of price per share to earnings per share (often called 'growth' stocks) and a portfolio of stocks with very low values of this ratio (so-called 'value' stocks). Over a period of up to five years after the portfolios are formed, the 'value' stocks earn an average of almost eight per cent a year more than 'growth' stocks. For portfolios formed on other measures of price to fundamentals, the difference is even wider. Stocks with very low ratios of market value to book value, for example, earn an average of over 10 per cent a year more than stocks with very high market to book ratios.

Investor under-reaction

The evidence so far points to investors over-reacting to information. More recent studies, however, have shown that under-reaction to information may be just as prevalent. Perhaps the most remarkable of these findings appeared in 1989. The late Victor Bernard and Jacob Thomas of Columbia University in the US grouped stocks based on the size of the surprise in their most recent earnings announcement, where surprise was measured, among other ways, relative to analyst expectations. They placed the stocks with the largest positive surprises in their earnings into a portfolio – the 'good news' portfolio, say – and those with the biggest negative surprises into a 'bad news' portfolio. They then tracked the returns of these two portfolios over the next six months. Their astonishing finding was that the 'good news' portfolio earned an average six-month return six per cent higher than its 'bad news' counterpart. This result is surprising because one would expect the stock price to reflect the good or bad earnings news immediately after the announcement. The evidence however, suggests otherwise. It points to investors under-reacting to information in the following way.

Suppose a company announces earnings that are substantially higher than expected. Investors see this as good news and send the stock price higher but for some reason not high enough. This mistake is only gradually corrected; over the next six months the stock price slowly drifts upwards towards the level it should have attained at the time of the announcement. An investor buying the stock immediately after the announcement would capture this upward drift and enjoy higher returns.

Since the publication of this study, researchers have uncovered evidence that investors under-react not only to earnings announcements but also to many other kinds of company information such as changes in dividend policy or news about share repurchase programs. For example, suppose a company says it is cutting its dividend. This is normally interpreted as bad news by the market and the stock price falls on the announcement. Recent research has found, however, that it does not fall enough at the time of announcement and instead continues to drift downwards for several months. Once again, this suggests that investors initially under-react to the bad news and only gradually incorporate its full import into the stock price.

Another well-known phenomenon believed to be related to such under-reaction is the 'momentum' effect. This refers to the fact that companies that have performed particularly well over the previous year continue to perform well over the next, and those that have performed very badly continue to earn poor returns. One explanation for these results is that the companies performing well have announced good news but that investors have under-reacted to it. This mistake is only gradually corrected in the following months, leading to the continued upward drift in prices.

There are subtle differences between these studies that provide tantalizing clues about the way investors interpret information. Notice again that companies that have performed particularly badly over the previous three years subsequently reverse this trend and earn high returns. Companies that have performed badly over the previous year alone, however, do not reverse this trend but continue to do badly. Furthermore, it appears that while investors appear to under-react to isolated pieces of information, they over-react to a series of news which all points in the same direction, in other words is all good or all bad.

Can the evidence be reconciled?

The preceding evidence is puzzling for those who believe the stock market is efficient, for it appears to suggest quite profitable investment strategies that verge on being 'free lunches' even after taking transaction costs into account. Someone who bought De Bondt/Thaler 'loser' portfolios and sold or took a short position in 'winner portfolios' earned handsome returns using this strategy over the past 70 years, as did someone who bought 'good news' portfolios and sold 'bad news' portfolios or bought 'value' stocks and sold 'growth' stocks. If investors are systematically under-reacting or over-reacting to information, there may be opportunities for exploiting these errors.

The first reaction of efficient-market enthusiasts to this evidence is to claim that it has nothing to do with investors making mistakes but simply reflects risk. In the same way that we are not surprised that stocks earn higher returns than bonds on average – they are, after all, riskier and should therefore pay us something extra on average to bear this risk – we should not be surprised if 'loser' portfolios earn more than 'winner' portfolios. It must simply be that the stocks we have grouped into the 'loser' portfolio are fundamentally riskier than those in the 'winner' portfolio. The fact that they do better on average reflects their higher risk. Similarly, under this interpretation, the 'good news' stocks derive their superior performance from their higher risk.

This is a reasonable argument at first sight but comes up short on closer inspection. Take for example De Bondt and Thaler's 'loser' and 'winner' portfolios. The undeniable fact is that the average return on the 'loser' portfolio has been substantially higher in the historical data. What would we look for if we were trying to show that this superior performance is due to risk? We would hope to find that returns on 'loser' stocks, while higher on average, are also much more volatile and occasionally much worse than returns on 'winner' stocks.

Alternatively, we could calculate a more sophisticated measure of risk, the 'beta' of the strategy. Beta measures the extent to which the returns on the strategy move in line with movements in the overall market. Strategies with high betas are thought to be riskier because they offer poor opportunities for diversification.

Unfortunately, an advocate of the risk story would not have much success. It is true that 'loser' stocks are riskier than 'winner' stocks. Their returns are more volatile, they occasionally perform worse than winners and they have higher betas. However, their higher risk is not nearly sufficient to explain their higher returns. The conclusion is the same for all of the other strategies. 'Good news' stocks are a little riskier than 'bad news' stocks along the dimensions mentioned but this is not enough to explain the difference in their average returns.

The fact that measuring risk in the ways described fails to explain the findings does not mean an immediate victory for those who believe that some stocks may be mis-priced. For example, it is possible to argue that we have not measured risk properly. In a series of influential recent papers, Eugene Fama of the University of Chicago and Kenneth French of Yale University have argued that 'value' stocks may be subject to important sources of risk not captured by simpler measures, such as volatility and beta, and that this explains why they have a higher average return than 'growth' stocks. Debate is raging, however, on the significance of the risks identified by Fama and French. There is still no consensus among financial economists on the right way to think about the relationship between risk and return and this remains an area of active research.

Another line of attack by proponents of efficient markets is to ask why the effects have not disappeared. If they are really due to human misperceptions, why have they not been quickly exploited and whittled away by more canny investors? Why, for example, have investors not rushed to buy 'value' stocks and to sell 'growth' stocks?

There are a number of responses to this. First, it is possible that investors were not aware of the potential opportunities until recently. It is true that 'value' stocks were advocated as good investments as early as the 1930s but the statistical reliability of the evidence has only recently been proven. Furthermore, it may be difficult for money managers to justify buying 'loser' or 'value' stocks. Such stocks have often had poor recent performance and appear more vulnerable to falling into financial distress. It is much easier to justify buying 'winner' or 'growth' stocks.

'Data mining'

Beyond the controversy over the right way to measure risk, there is another interpretation of the findings, one that often goes by the name 'data-mining'. Advocates of this view point out that countless hours have been spent by innumerable hopeful investors trying to unearth strategies that have historically been profitable. A typical exercise is to group stocks into portfolios based on some characteristic, in much the same way that I described earlier, and to compare the relative performance of these portfolios over time.

The problem with this approach is that if you try enough different ways of grouping stocks, you are almost certain, as a matter of chance, to come upon a strategy that has yielded high returns historically. However, there is no reason to believe that such a strategy will continue to work. It may simply be a spurious statistical artefact. While the data-mining criticism is important, it can be addressed by seeing whether the various findings can be replicated using other data, perhaps covering other periods or different countries. The evidence has proved robust to such cross-testing. A recent study by Eugene Fama and Kenneth French has found that 'value' stocks outperform 'growth' stocks in many markets throughout the world.

Evidence from psychology

Even if the risk story and the data-mining critique have so far failed to explain the success of these investment strategies, the inefficient markets viewpoint faces a stiff challenge. Beyond merely presenting evidence that is consistent with investors under-reacting or over-reacting to information, it must show that this kind of investor behavior has firm foundations in human psychology. This challenge has been taken up by researchers in the new field of behavioral finance, which seeks to understand whether aspects of human behavior and psychology might influence the way prices are set in financial markets.

As an example, consider how we might explain why – and when – people over-react to information. One explanation relies on a widely documented bias in the way individuals interpret information, known as the 'representativeness heuristic'. This is a broad phenomenon but can be interpreted at one level as saying that people see regular patterns and order even in completely random data.

A well-known example of this comes from a study of scoring patterns in the US professional basketball league. A typical question posed is: 'Suppose we take two players of the same ability, one of whom has managed to score in the last three attempts, and the other who has failed in the last three attempts. Which of the two players is more likely to score on their next attempt?' Most people pick the player who has just scored three times in a row. Underlying their choice is the belief that this player is enjoying a 'hot streak' that is likely to continue. The remarkable fact is that an analysis of actual scoring patterns reveals that players who have scored many times in a row are in fact no more likely to score on their next attempt than players who have repeatedly failed. That is, people see patterns and trends such as 'hot streaks' where none exist.

A similar argument has been used in finance to explain why people may over-react to a sequence of positive earnings announcements. In reality, changes in company earnings follow a fairly random pattern. However, when people see a company's earnings go up several quarters in a row, they forget this means very little for the next quarter's earnings. They wrongly believe they have spotted a trend and extrapolate recent good performance too far out into the future. Such excessive optimism pushes prices too high and produces effects consistent with over-reaction.

There are also well-known biases in human information processing that would predict under-reaction to new pieces of information. Known variously as 'conservatism' or 'over-confidence', these biases document the fact that people cling too strongly to previously held beliefs and are slow to update their views in line with new information. Clearly this corresponds directly to under-reaction to news. Investors may have views about the earnings prospects of a company and may be reluctant to abandon these upon hearing news of surprisingly high earnings. While they do push up the stock price a little, they remain sceptical about the new information and only gradually update their views to the correct extent.

While such links between psychology and finance sound plausible to many, a substantial proportion of the academic finance community views them with considerable scepticism. They accuse behavioral finance theorists of going on a 'fishing' expedition, sifting through texts on human psychology until they find something that could be related to the effects they are trying to explain. The most convincing models to date are, therefore, those that rely on as small a number of psychological biases as possible.

The debate over the correct interpretation of the findings highlighted here is far from being resolved. Researchers in behavioral finance are trying to build more robust and convincing models of the interplay of psychology and finance. On another front, firm believers in efficient markets are trying to understand the relationship between risk and return better in the hope this might shed light on the evidence. Nearly 20 years after Michael Jensen's famous comment, the efficient markets hypothesis is far from being the best established fact in the social sciences.

Summary

Do investors react correctly to news? Or do they make systematic errors which can be profitably exploited by others? Module 6 gives a broad introduction to the controversial topic of behavioral finance, while in this article Nicholas Barberis explains how a whole batch of recent research has challenged the efficient markets hypothesis. He points to studies showing that investors both over-react and under-react to information, and that so-called 'value' stocks outperform 'growth' stocks. Efficient market theorists have fought back – suggesting, for example, that 'value' stocks may be subject to more risk than we realize and asking why the effects have not been whittled away by more canny investors. Links between psychology and finance sound plausible to many but a substantial proportion of the academic finance community views them with considerable scepticism. The debate is far from over.

Myths surrounding short-termism

by Paul Marsh

Short-termism has been a hot issue for many years. The belief is that Britain's and America's competitive edge has been blunted by a failure to emphasise long-term investment, and this is the fault of myopic financial markets.

Broadly, the short-termism argument runs as follows: financial markets, spurred by impatient investors, are short-term oriented, placing too much weight on current profits and dividends. This obliges companies to do the same, inhibiting long-term investment. For if companies invest in projects without an immediate pay-off, their profits and share price will fall, making them vulnerable to takeover.

According to this view, myopia by Wall Street and the City of London has been detrimental to growth and competitiveness in the US and UK, relative to Germany and Japan which have 'bank-based' financial systems. A worry for continental Europe and Asian countries is that, as their financial systems move towards the US model, they too will catch the Anglo-American disease.

These arguments, although widely believed, are unfortunately based on misunderstandings and a failure to examine the evidence. This article aims to set the record straight.

Are stock markets short-termist?

No reliable evidence has yet been presented to support the claim that stock markets are short-termist, or that share prices place too much weight on short-term profits and dividends. Instead, there is a large body of research which suggests precisely the opposite.

For example, if the stock market places too much weight on current dividends, then presumably low yielding stocks are undervalued, relative to their expected future cash flows. In such a short-sighted world, investors could earn superior returns from buying low yielders and holding them long-term, when true value must out.

But the US and UK evidence indicates that historically, low yielders have not been undervalued, and high yielders, far from being specially prized, have actually been the more lowly valued.

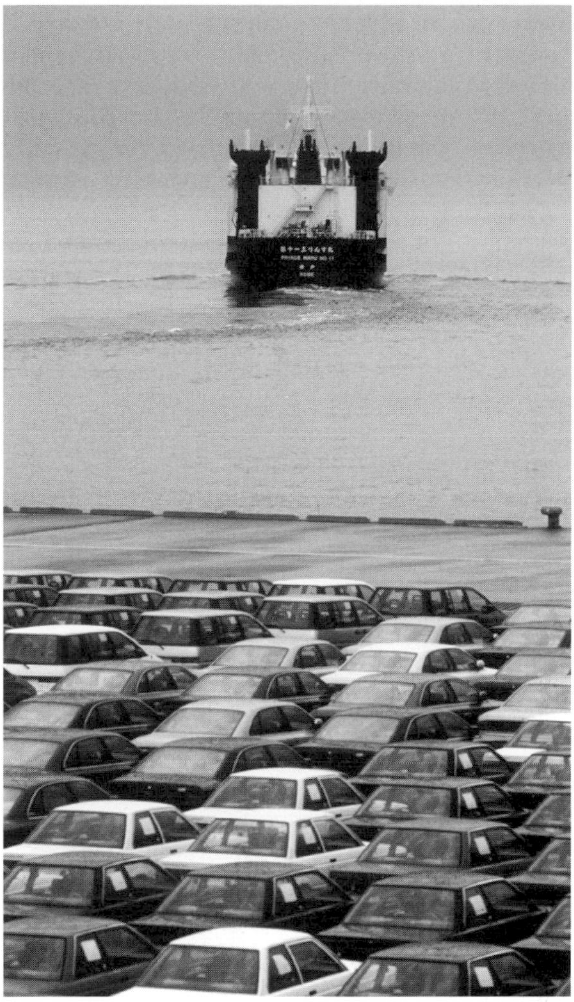

Famed for productivity but is Japan's 'bank-based' financial system really responsible?

Similarly, if the market undervalues prospects, investors could achieve superior returns by buying growth stocks (ie shares with high price/earnings ratios, but where the P/E ratios should presumably be even higher), and holding them long-term. However, research indicates precisely the opposite, namely that, if anything, long-term growth stocks may have been overvalued.

Finally, if the stock market dislikes companies which invest for the future, we should expect share prices to fall when companies announce increases in capital investment and research and development. But research indicates that such announcements are regarded as good news, and generally result in share price rises. Cuts in investment, on the other hand, coincide with share price falls.

These findings, combined with a wealth of other stock market research, provide no support for the proposition that the stock market is short-termist. To blame the stock market's pricing mechanism for the alleged ills of US and UK industry is thus to pick the wrong target.

Managerial short-termism

The accusations of short-termism are leveled mostly at the financial markets. Yet, ultimately, short-termism will be a problem only if companies fail to undertake profitable investments, ie, those with positive net present values (NPVs). By definition, therefore, the perpetrators of short-termism must be corporate managers, since they are the ones who are responsible for making long-term investments.

Managers may shun positive NPV investments because the costs (eg, R&D, product development, plant and equipment, strategic marketing, training, etc) show up immediately, depressing current profits, while the benefits may take years to show through. Their focus on current profits may be influenced by what they think the financial markets want, but it may also reflect 'managerial short-termism'. The latter can be defined as a tendency by managers to favor the short-term independently of any spur from the financial markets.

There are several aspects of managerial practice in the UK and US which can encourage managerial short-termism:

- Remuneration and reward systems. Traditionally, executive incentive systems have linked remuneration to short-term accounting profit, rather than to long-term value;
- Relatively high rates of executive mobility may shorten managers' time horizons within jobs, making them more concerned with short-term results, and less ready to invest long-term;
- The systems used to appraise new investments could encourage short-termism. Many companies still seem to over-emphasize payback, a notoriously short-termist measure. Others use discount rates which appear far too high.

Managers often argue, however, that any bias they have to short-termism results from pressures from the financial community. They claim that the real culprits for short-termism are the investment analysts, fund managers and institutional investors who encourage short-term orientation.

Investment analysts

Investment analysts often seem preoccupied with short-term profit and dividend announcements. However, their concern is entirely rational, since these are key news items, conveying significant information about the future. The way companies 'manage' their profits and decide on dividends ensures that these announcements provide important signals about management's own (inside) knowledge and judgements about the future.

Furthermore, research evidence on P/E ratios confirms that analysts and investors are not just focusing on current earnings. P/E ratios vary widely across stocks, and depend – as theory indicates they should – on long-term growth prospects, the retentions needed to finance these, the company's cost of capital and the accounting methods used.

There is, therefore, considerable evidence that analysts take a broad view when valuing shares, looking at far more than just current results. Nevertheless, some analysts may convey an unhelpful impression of short-termism through their behavior, and the questions they ask – and fail to ask.

Fund managers

Fund managers are also often viewed as short-termist. This is widely attributed to the pressures they themselves face from short-term, quarterly performance measurement. This is misleading, since in reality, the key performance measurers and those concerned with fund manager appraisal and selection all stress long- rather than short-run performance. Even if this were not so, any concern that quarterly performance measurement prevents fund managers from taking a long-term view would be misplaced.

Managers can improve their short-term performance only by identifying undervalued shares and buying them, and/or over-valued shares and selling them. This is difficult, given the competition they face (as borne out by the many studies which indicate that consistent out-performance is rare). Indeed, the only way they can succeed is through careful analysis of a company's short- and longer-term prospects – something widely held to be a good thing.

To maximize their own short-run performance, fund managers need to be concerned with companies' long-term prospects. Any insights the manager has about even the company's very long-term future are incorporated into the share price almost immediately, partly because of competition between investors, and partly because dealing activity itself alerts others that there may be information around, causing prices to adjust accordingly.

By spotting mispriced shares, fund managers thus help to keep the market efficient. Their short-term actions often reflect long-term views, and their own short-term performance will reflect changes in the capitalized value of the longer term prospects of the shares they hold.

Dividend pressures

It is often alleged that institutional investors place pressure on companies to pay high dividends, and this discourages investment and fosters short-termism. Indeed, the fact that dividend payouts have typically been higher in the UK and US is given as a reason why British and American companies have historically invested less than their German and Japanese counterparts.

In reality, the institutional pressures are greatly exaggerated. But more importantly, the concerns about high payout are based on a false assumption, namely that companies face a choice between dividends or investment. Well-managed concerns start from the premise that they should invest in all positive NPV projects.

If the cash required for this (plus dividends) exceeds internal resources, they should seek external funding, by borrowing or raising equity. Indeed, the existence of highly developed capital markets, such as those in the US and UK, makes this very straightforward.

One might still question the efficiency of paying out dividends with one hand, and seeking money back with the other via an equity issue. In the UK, the tax system provides a rationale for this, at least for tax-exempt investors. For them, high payouts, coupled with periodic equity issues, is tax efficient. At the same time, it may encourage efficient use and recycling of capital, and enhance the monitoring role of shareholders and the capital market. Changes to the tax system would undoubtedly alter these incentives, and would have unfortunate consequences for pension funds and other tax exempt investors.

Takeovers and short-termism

While the conduct of analysts, fund managers and institutional shareholders may sometimes give companies the wrong impression, the behavior outlined above hardly amounts to coercion into short-termism. However, one source of real duress is takeovers.

The concern here is that the threat of takeover may encourage managers to maximize short-term profits and dividends in the hope this will boost their share price and keep the predator from the door. This could cause them to cut back on long-term investment.

Such behavior would make no sense, however, since companies will not bolster their share prices by cutting back on positive NPV investments – in fact, quite the opposite. Moreover, there is no evidence that companies which invest heavily are more likely to be taken over – if anything, the reverse is true. Indeed, most of the research on takeovers suggests it is the worse performing companies which tend to be taken over by their better-performing counterparts. Nor is there any persuasive evidence that acquisitions herald cutbacks in investment or R&D.

Furthermore, most acquisitions involve no coercion, since they are agreed, not hostile. Even where coercion exists, takeovers are what one company does to another, rather than pressure imposed by fund managers. More importantly, most acquisitions are predicated on potentially sound industrial logic, and there is much evidence to suggest that shareholders have, on average, gained from mergers, and from the associated efficiency gains.

These findings need qualification. First, they relate to average behavior. On average, mergers have increased shareholders' wealth, but many have failed. Second, the published evidence does not take account of many hidden costs and benefits. For example, failed bids involve substantial costs – in terms of fees, time and motivation.

Moreover, the possibility of takeover may undermine contractual relationships between investors and employees and managers, making the latter reluctant to invest in company-specific assets and longer-term investments, if they may later be denied the benefits of such investment because of a change in ownership.

But balanced against these costs are the substantial benefits which can flow from the threat of takeovers and the value of 'keeping managements on their toes'. Indeed, in the UK and US, contested takeovers are one of the most effective disciplinary devices available.

This raises an obvious question, namely is there a better way of ensuring effective corporate control? In the past, two of the most successful industrialized nations, Japan and Germany, have managed without this disciplinary mechanism. If more effective corporate control and governance could yield shareholders the same gains they have achieved from takeover activity at a lower cost, this would be worth striving for.

Is short-termism really a problem?

Short-termism is a problem only if corporate managers are turning down positive NPV projects because of a concern about the short-run impact on reported earnings. This raises two fundamental questions. Do managers behave like this? And, if so, why?

Curiously, despite the extensive debate, there is very little systematic evidence that British and US managers are short-termist. The only direct evidence is anecdotal, and comes from business executives describing their own perceptions and behavior, but this provides a partial, and sometimes conflicting, account, which is hard to interpret.

Mostly, the existence of short-termism is simply inferred from the fact that British and American companies have invested less than their Japanese and German counterparts over the past 50 years. However, companies in different countries have faced different opportunities. In the earlier part of this period, Germany and Japan's higher investment reflected their greater scope for post-war reconstruction and catching-up. British and American managers may thus not have under-invested. Instead, they may have accepted every project with a positive NPV, but simply found fewer of these 'on offer'.

The UK, which has a worse record than the US, remained relatively unattractive for investment throughout the 1960s–70s. Macroeconomic management, including 'stop-go' policies, exchange rate instability, and higher inflation contributed to this. But supply-side factors were probably even more important, particularly those relating to the skills, working practices and productivity of the workforce; and to engineering, product design, marketing and management skills.

Indeed, conventional wisdom needs to be turned on its head. The popular belief is that the UK's lower economic growth rate resulted from too little investment. In reality, both lower growth and lower investment were the consequence of supply-side weaknesses. These depressed the profitability of existing activities, and made new investment less attractive.

A decade of convergence

From the 1980s onwards, the UK and US economies underwent considerable change. The UK experienced numerous supply-side reforms, coupled with deregulation and privatization. In the US, corporate America was restructured.

While on a 50-year view, the UK and US have invested less and enjoyed lower economic growth than Japan and Germany, during the 1980s and 1990s, the gap narrowed, and was sometimes reversed. For the past decade, the American and UK economies have performed as well as, or better than, those of Japan and Continental Europe.

Today, Germany and Japan are cited far less frequently as national exemplars. Partly, this is because both countries face new challenges, but it also reflects the fact that countries and companies have already learned much from each other. Meanwhile, ironically, many of the more successful and progressive companies in Japan, Germany and elsewhere in Continental Europe are busy switching their emphasis to shareholder value. At the same time, their financial systems are undergoing deregulation, and are slowly converging toward the Anglo-American model.

Remedies

In spite of these developments, there are still many who cling to the old arguments on short-termism, and to the notion that financial markets are malfunctioning or somehow to blame. While we have seen that this relates to perceptions which have no basis in reality, we cannot dismiss them, lest they become reality.

If industrialists believe the financial community is short-termist, the danger is that they may act accordingly, cutting back on long-term investment. Another danger lies in the implementation of inappropriate 'remedies' by governments in an attempt to cure a mis-diagnosed problem.

Many of the proposals put forward to 'cure short-termism' – such as higher rates of tax on short-term capital gains, turnover taxes, discouraging dividend distribution, or 'throwing sand in the takeover machine' – are predicated on the false premise that the financial markets are to blame. If implemented, such measures would yield perverse results, by lowering market liquidity, increasing the cost of capital, and reducing economic efficiency.

Measures aimed at closing the perceptional gap, however, seem worthy of serious pursuit. These include better financial education; improving relationships between companies and shareholders; better communications and greater disclosure; selective (and collective) direct interventions by shareholders; closer attention to managerial reward and incentive systems and their link to investment decisions; and more effective corporate governance.

It is important, however, to keep these measures in perspective, and be realistic about what they might achieve. In particular, it would be a great pity if the corporate sector – in any country – became sidetracked from the central issues which all companies share in common – international competitiveness, market orientation, innovation, quality and excellence – by further talk about short-termism from the financial markets.

Indeed, there is a real congruence of interests here. The very activities required to enhance business competitiveness, and to improve prospects for, and levels of, investment, are the self-same actions required to enhance share prices, create shareholder value, deter corporate raiders and improve investor relations. The way ahead for both the financial community and the corporate sector is to focus on managing as if tomorrow mattered.

Summary

The short-termism of financial markets – by which is generally meant a damaging focus on dividends and current profits – has become an article of faith for many in Britain and America. But according to Paul Marsh the arguments are based on misunderstandings and failure to look at the evidence.

He says research finds no support for the proposition that stock markets are short termist, and while investment analysts, fund managers and institutional shareholders sometimes behave in a way that invites criticism they generally take a broader view. Institutional pressures for high dividend payouts are greatly exaggerated, and in any case external funding for positive NPV projects should be available with well-developed capital markets. Takeover activity is an important feature of corporate control and governance, though there is a cost. If short-termism owes more to perception than reality, it should nevertheless not be dismissed: if industrialists believe the financial community is guilty of it managers may act accordingly, cutting back on long-term investment.

Suggested further reading

Bernstein, P., (1992), 'Are financial markets the problem or the solution?', *Journal of Applied Corporate Finance*, Summer.

Hutton, W., (1995), *The State We're In,* Jonathan Cape, London.

Marsh, P., (1990), *Short-termism on trial*, Institutional Fund Managers Association, London.

Porter, M., (1992), 'Capital choices: changing the way America invests in Industry', *Journal of Applied Corporate Finance*, Summer.

6

Equity markets in action

Contributors

Patricia M. Dechow is the Anheuser-Busch Term Assistant Professor of Accounting at the Wharton School of the University of Pennsylvania.

Richard Thaler is the Robert P. Gwinn Professor of Behavioral Science and Economics at the University of Chicago Graduate School of Business. He is also Director of the Center for Decision Research.

Amy P. Hutton is an Assistant Professor at Harvard Business School.

David K. Musto is Assistant Professor of Finance at the Wharton School of the University of Pennsylvania.

Richard G. Sloan is an Assistant Professor of Accounting at the Wharton School of the University of Pennsylvania.

Brad Barber is Associate Professor of Finance at the Graduate School of Management, University of California, Davis. His research interests include financial markets, the development of performance benchmarks, valuation, shareholder litigation, bankruptcy and cost of capital.

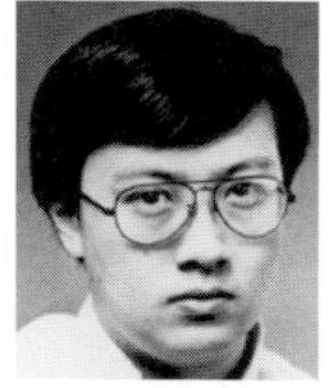

Andrew W. Lo is Harris & Harris Group Professor and Director of the Laboratory for Financial Engineering, MIT Sloan School.

Richard Leftwich is Fuji Bank and Heller Professor of Accounting and Finance at the University of Chicago Graduate School of Business. His research interests include audit qualifications, bond ratings, corporate charter changes and block trades.

Craig MacKinlay is Joseph P. Wargrove Professor of Finance at the Wharton School of the University of Pennsylvania.

Marshall E. Blume is the Howard Butcher III Professor of Financial Management at the Wharton School of the University of Pennsylvania, and Director of Wharton's Rodney L. White Center for Financial Research. He is a member of the editorial board of the *Journal of Pension Fund Management and Investment.*

Contents

Introduction

Module 5 looked at the nature of financial markets but here we are concerned with what rules, if any, govern the way markets behave. Most especially, does that Holy Grail – market predictability – exist?

Solving the new equity puzzle

by Patricia Dechow, Amy Hutton and Richard Sloan

When Yahoo!, a company that had developed a well-regarded Internet search-engine, went public last year, its stock at first seemed to live up to its name. The initial public offering (IPO), managed by Goldman Sachs, the US investment bank, did phenomenally well, and Yahoo!'s stock, priced at $13, increased to $43 on the first day

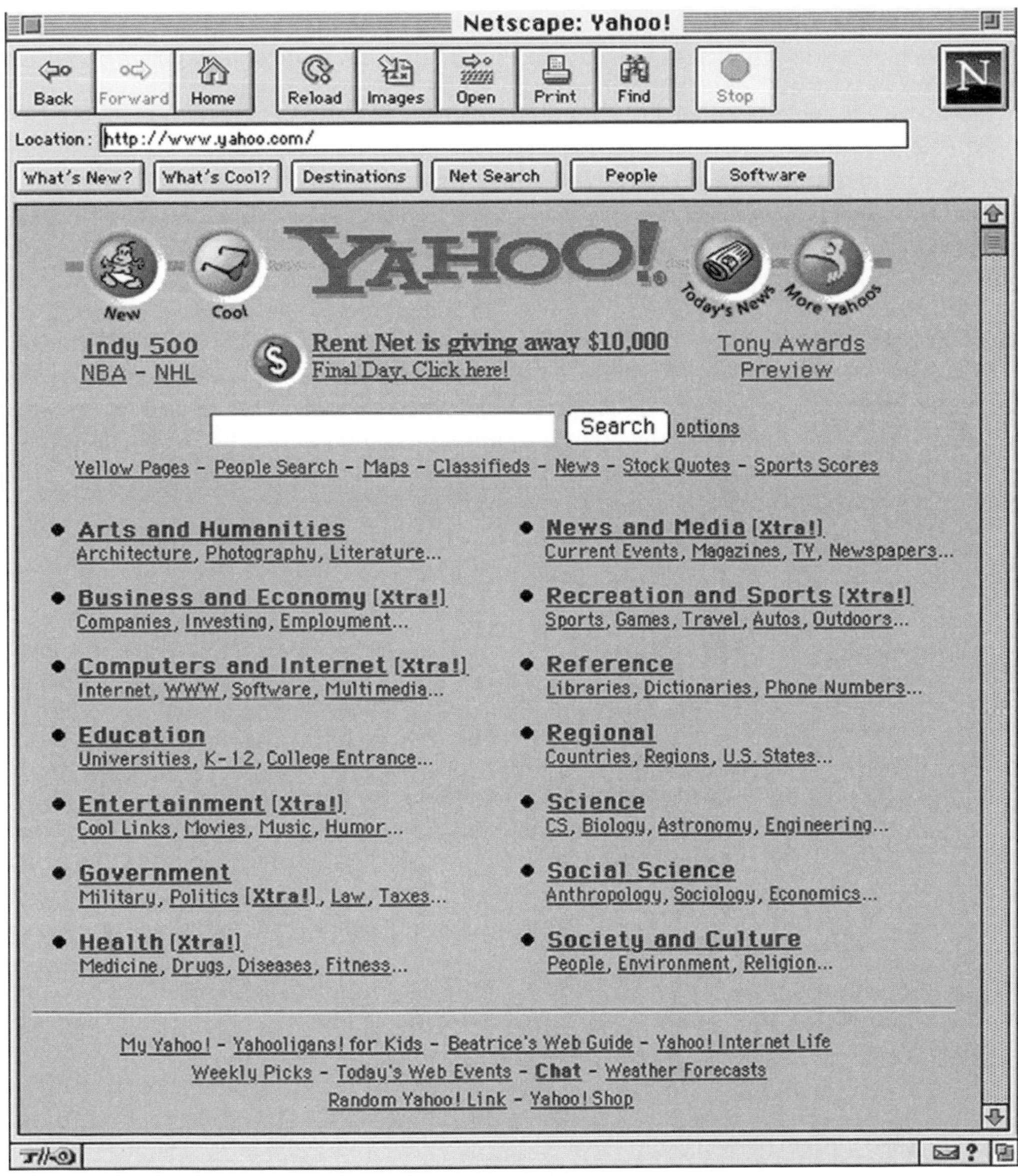

of trading. However by August the stock had declined to $18 and in mid-December it was trading in the low $20s and currently trades in the low $30s.

If this kind of stock price volatility for a new issue has a familiar ring, it is because Yahoo! is not the only company to show this kind of performance. Researchers have shown that many IPOs and seasoned equity offerings (SEOs) start out well. Their stock prices rise, but then over the following three to five years they perform far worse than the average stock. In fact they under-perform the rest of the market by around 30 per cent. In academic circles the phenomenon is known as the new equity puzzle. Our study examined the role of such analysts' long-term growth forecasts in the pricing of stock around the launch of new equity offerings.

Sell-side analysts act as valuation intermediaries, providing expertise in processing financial information. They act as investment advisors to their brokerage clients. However, top-rated analysts also play an important role in developing relationships with their employers' investment banking clients. As a result analysts have become instrumental in attracting underwriting business.

These two roles provide conflicting incentives for sell-side analysts. As investment advisors, sell-side analysts have incentives to act in the best interests of their brokerage clients and provide realistic (unbiased) growth forecasts. However, to attract lucrative underwriting business, these same analysts have incentives to provide overly optimistic growth prospects for their current or future investment banking clients.

Overly optimistic

Our research examines which of these two incentives dominates – do analysts make unbiased growth forecasts to serve their brokerage clients or do they make overly optimistic growth forecasts to assist their employers' investment banking clients? In particular, we look at whether analysts provide realistic or overly optimistic forecasts of earnings growth around the time of new equity offerings.

We investigate whether analysts employed by the investment bank acting as the lead underwriter of the offering provide more overly optimistic forecasts than other unaffiliated analysts. In addition, we look at whether investors naively rely on the growth forecasts made by analysts so that these growth forecasts are reflected in stock prices. That is, if analysts are overly optimistic and investors believe their forecasts, do companies with the highest growth forecasts at the time of the offering tend to have the poorest stock price performance after the new equity offering? Such a finding would suggest that investors initially believe analysts' growth forecasts and are subsequently disappointed when the less-than-expected earnings growth is realized.

To summarize, we found that analysts' growth forecasts are systematically overly optimistic around new equity offerings, and the most overly optimistic growth forecasts are issued by analysts employed by the lead underwriters of the offerings. We also found that analysts' overly optimistic growth forecasts are reflected in the stock prices of issuing firms, suggesting that investors naively rely on analysts' growth forecasts. Overall, our results suggest that sell-side analysts compromise their role as investment advisors to increase the stock prices of their investment banking clients and generate greater underwriting fees for their employers.

Other researchers found that, in general, analysts tend to be overly-optimistic in their forecasts of companies' earnings prospects (Abarbanell, 1991; Brown, Foster and Noreen, 1985). Some researchers have suggested that the over-optimism observed in analyst forecasts arises because they selectively report (Lin and McNichols, 1997).

That is, analysts only make forecasts when they have good news to report. The business press has reported that many analysts will no longer issue negative reports because of fear of retribution. In a survey of members of the 1989 All-American Research Team, *Institutional Investor* reported that 61 per cent of respondents said they had felt pressure to temper a negative opinion at least once in their careers.

Analysts indicated that corporate intimidation is an important force. They fear losing access to management of companies they follow after issuing negative reports. Analysts also indicated that they could not ignore the wishes of their firms' investment banking clients, even prospective ones, since fees from investment banking activities support their research.

Some have argued that as a result of the pressures to suppress negative reports financial resources are being diverted to companies with the most influence, and not those with the best investment opportunities. It has been argued that the objectivity and independence of the analyst community steadily eroded during the 1980s as analysts abandoned primary research because of declining commission fees to pursue investment banking fees.

Selling power

> 'When commissions on stock trading fell, investment research (which generated trading) no longer paid the freight. Today, analysts are supported partly by their corporate finance departments. And much of what they do – marketing and preparing IPOs, for instance – has little to do with pure research, and much to do with investment banking. In the US in particular, investment banks have persuaded clients to hire underwriters on the basis of their analysts' selling power. In turn, the analyst's worth is increasingly dependent on his or her ability to bring in deals. Of course, some money managers complain that the big emphasis on new-issue fees taints research results if the analysts try to avoid saying anything negative about their underwriting clients.' [1]

'It is little wonder that we are where we are. What do they expect for six cents a share?'[2] commented one Wall Streeter, who believes that self-censorship and watered-down research are the inevitable result of years of declining commission rates.

Recent evidence supports these views. For example, Michaely and Womack (1996) demonstrate that analysts affiliated with the underwriters of IPOs in 1990–91 issued 50 per cent more buy recommendations than did non-affiliated analysts. Lin and McNichols (1993) demonstrate that affiliated analysts provide significantly more optimistic annual earnings forecasts for their underwriting client companies than do unaffiliated analysts. However, as also documented in Dugar and Nathan (1995), Lin and McNichols do not find that affiliated analysts' forecasts are less accurate than unaffiliated analysts' forecasts.

Contrarian strategies

If investors are not fully aware of the bias in analysts' growth forecasts, then stock prices may reflect overly optimistic growth expectations. Recent research attempts to document whether anomalous stock return behavior is consistent with stock prices reflecting analysts' long-term growth forecasts, despite the bias in these forecasts.

---

1 From R. Lowenstein: 'Today's analyst often wears two hats', *Wall Street Journal*, May 2 1996.

2 From 'The hazards of negative research reports', *Institutional Investor*, July 30 1990.

Dechow and Sloan (1997) examine the extent to which the returns to the 'contrarian investment strategies' are consistent with security prices reflecting analysts' long-term earnings growth forecasts.

The 'contrarian investment strategies' or 'relative-value investing' involve buying and selling stocks that are priced low or high relative to various accounting measures of operating performance such as earnings, cash flows and book values.

The innovation in the Dechow and Sloan study is that they directly estimate the earnings growth rates embedded in stock prices and compare them with the expectations implied if investors recognize the bias in analysts' forecasts versus expectations implied if investors naively rely on analysts' forecasts. Stock return behavior is shown to be consistent with investors naively relying on overly optimistic analysts' forecasts. More than half of the returns to 'contrarian investment strategies' are explained by investors' naive reliance on analysts' long-term growth forecasts.

In this paper, we adopted a similar approach to help explain the new equity puzzle. The new equity puzzle is a well documented stock return anomaly – companies systematically experience low stock returns relative to various market indices in the three to five years following new equity offerings (Loughran and Ritter, 1995, and Spiess and Affleck-Graves, 1995).

We attempted to document whether the unusually low post-offering returns arise because analysts issue overly optimistic growth forecasts at the time of the offerings and investors rely on these forecasts. After documenting that analysts make overly optimistic growth forecasts for companies issuing new equity securities, we examined whether stock prices reflect these forecasts.

Pure and mixed deals

We directly estimated the earnings growth rates embedded in stock prices and compared them with the expectations implied if investors recognize the over optimism in analysts' forecasts versus the expectations implied if investors naively rely on analysts' growth forecasts.

We examined a sample of 1,179 new equity offerings, of these 86 are IPOs and the remaining 1,093 are seasoned equity offerings (SEOs). For these offerings there are 7,169 analysts' long-term earnings growth forecasts made in the 12 months (–9 to +3) surrounding the issue dates. We sort the individual analysts making the growth forecasts into two categories: affiliated and unaffiliated. If an analyst is employed by the lead manager or a related firm (a subsidiary or a parent of the lead manager), then he or she is classified as affiliated with the particular offering. Otherwise the analyst is classified as unaffiliated. We classified 622 analysts' growth forecasts as affiliated and 6,547 as unaffiliated.

We further classified the stock offerings as pure and mixed deals, depending on which analysts follow the deal and make long-term growth forecasts. Deals with only analysts from one category (affiliated or unaffiliated) making growth forecasts are classified as pure deals. Deals where both affiliated and unaffiliated analysts made forecasts are classified as mixed deals.

In Figure 1 we compare analysts' forecasts and five-year realized performance. The mean realised growth in earnings for the full sample over the five years following the offering is 5.7 per cent. The corresponding mean analysts' forecast of growth in earnings at the time of the offering is 16.2 per cent. Thus, on average, analysts over-estimate the five-year earnings growth of issuing firms by 10.6 per cent per year.

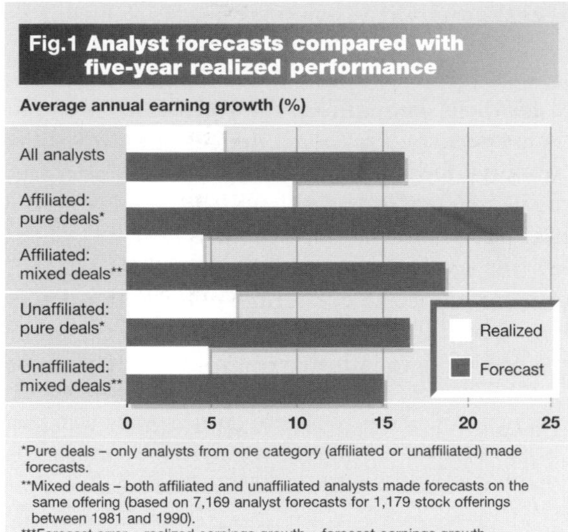

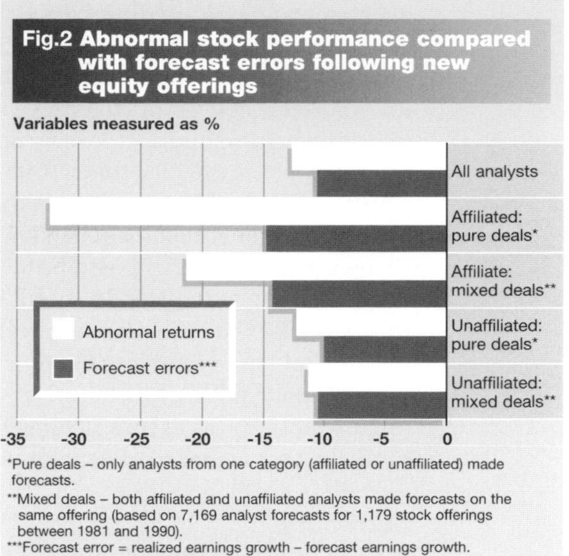

This indicates that less than half of the growth forecast by analysts is actually realized. Analysts' growth forecasts are overstated by about 65 per cent. This pattern holds for the various classifications of analysts – analysts' predicted growth is not realized. Note that affiliated analysts make the most aggressive predictions of growth for their clients. Realized growth is 9.7 per cent, while affiliated analysts predicted growth of 23.3 per cent per year. Thus, the affiliated analysts over-estimate the five-year earnings growth by 14.8 per cent per year for their investment banking clients.

Figure 2 summarizes analysts' forecast errors and the abnormal post-offering stock performance of issuing firms. It is useful to note the correlation between the magnitude of the forecast errors and the abnormal returns for these firms. The negative abnormal returns in the five years following the offering are consistent with investors expecting these companies to produce better performances. Measuring post-offering stock price performance using market-adjusted buy-hold stock returns, the mean abnormal stock return for the entire sample is –12.7 per cent for the five years following the offering. The mean abnormal return for affiliated: pure deals category is –32.3 per cent. This category has the largest forecast errors and the most negative stock price performance.

These results are consistent with the affiliated analysts issuing more overly optimistic earnings growth forecasts and with investors sharing these earnings expectations. The statistics show a similar pattern for the 491 forecasts in the affiliated: mixed deals category. The mean abnormal return is –21.3 per cent, which is more negative than the average for the entire sample, and the mean forecast error is –14.3 per cent, which is also more negative than the average for the entire sample.

Mistaken beliefs

Further, the deals followed by unaffiliated analysts have the least negative abnormal returns and the least overly optimistic forecasts. For the 2,938 forecasts in the unaffiliated, mixed deals category, the mean abnormal return is –12.3 per cent and the mean forecast error is –10.5 per cent. For the 3,609 deals in the unaffiliated, pure deals category, the mean abnormal return is –11.3 per cent and the mean forecast error is –10.0 per cent. This is consistent with the unaffiliated analysts issuing relatively less overly optimistic earnings growth forecasts and with investors sharing these less overly optimistic earnings expectations.

In the complete manuscript of this paper we provide formal tests that document the market's expectation of earnings growth for these companies. The results suggest that investors believe analysts' overly optimistic forecasts. Further it appears that investors are unaware of the fact that affiliated analysts' forecasts are the most optimistic. Our results indicate that the poor post-issuing return performance is at least in part driven by investors' mistaken beliefs. (The formal test results can be obtained from any of the three authors.) Our results have policy implications in that the analyst's primary responsibility is to provide sound investment advice to brokerage clients. It appears that the co-existence of brokerage services and underwriting services in the same institution leads analysts to compromise their responsibility to brokerage clients to attract underwriting business.

In practice, investment banks claim to have a 'Chinese Wall' to prevent such conflicts. Our evidence questions the depth of these 'Chinese Walls'.

Summary

It's the question, perhaps, you've always wanted to ask but never dared. Do stock market analysts make unbiased growth forecasts to serve their brokerage clients, or do they make overly optimistic forecasts to assist their employers' clients?

In this article based on recent US research Patricia Dechow, Amy Hutton and Richard Sloan found that analysts' growth forecasts are routinely over optimistic around new equity offerings, but that the most over optimistic are those analysts employed by the lead underwriters of the offerings. These forecasts are reflected in the stock prices of new issues, which suggests that investors believe them. According to the authors years of declining commission rates are to blame for self censorship and watered down research. In practice investment banks claim to have a Chinese Wall to prevent these conflicts but the evidence of this article seriously questions their depth.

Suggested further reading

Baker, M., 'Some analysts enter land of big bucks', *Wall Street Journal*, July 2 1996. 'The hazards of negative research reports', *Institutional Investor*, July 30 1990. 'Research, who is pulling the strings', *Euromoney*, April 30 1994.

Dechow, P., Hutton, A. and Sloan, R., (1997) 'The role of affiliated analysts' long-term earnings forecasts in the over-pricing of equity offerings', Working paper.

Lowenstein, R., (1996),'Today's analyst often wears two hats', *Wall Street Journal*, May 2.

Stumbling block for the random walk

by Andrew Lo and Craig MacKinlay

If, in January 1926, an individual had invested $1 in one-month US Treasury bills – one of the 'safest' assets in the world – and continued reinvesting the proceeds in Treasury bills month by month until December 1996 the $1 investment would have grown to $14. If, on the other hand, that individual had invested $1 in the S&P 500 and continued reinvesting the proceeds in this broad-based portfolio month by month over the same 71-year period, the $1 investment would have grown to $1,370, a considerably larger sum.

Now suppose that each month, an individual were able to divine which of these two investments would yield a higher return for that month and took advantage of this by switching the running total of his initial $1 investment into the higher-yielding asset, month by month. What would a $1 investment in such a 'perfect foresight' investment strategy have become by December 1996? The startling answer – $2,303,981,824 (yes, more than $2bn, this is no typographical error) – often comes as a shock to even the most seasoned professional investment manager. Despite the fact that few investors have perfect foresight, this extreme example suggests that even a modest ability to forecast financial asset returns may be handsomely rewarded: it does not take a large fraction of $2,303,981,824 to beat $1,370.

For this reason, whether or not stock prices contain predictable components has fascinated investors throughout the world. In this article, we describe some recent evidence regarding the predictability of the market, evidence that the celebrated 'random walk hypothesis' – the benchmark model of purely random and unpredictable behavior – does not hold for US stock market prices.

Although the random walk hypothesis dates back to the 16th century, modern statistical methods and computing power have shed new light on this important model of financial prices. In particular, we shall describe some empirical findings for aggregate US stock indices that suggest the presence of important short-term predictability in stock market movements.

Stocks and the random walk

One of the most enduring questions of financial economics is whether financial asset price changes are forecastable. Perhaps because of the obvious (and somewhat misleading) analogy between financial investments and games of chance, mathematical models of asset prices have an unusually rich history that pre-dates virtually every other aspect of economic analysis. The vast number of prominent mathematicians and scientists who have plied their considerable skills to forecasting stock and commodity prices is a testament to the fascination and the challenges that this problem poses. Indeed, the intellectual roots of modern financial economics are firmly planted in early attempts to 'beat the market', an endeavor that is still of interest and discussed and debated even in the most recent journals, conferences and cocktail parties.

Perhaps the earliest characterization of rationally determined stock prices is the random walk hypothesis, which says that future price changes cannot be predicted from past price changes. For example, under the hypothesis, if stock ABC fared poorly last month, this has no implications for how ABC will fare this month – or in any other month. In this respect, the random walk hypothesis is not unlike a sequence of coin tosses: the fact that one toss comes up heads, or that a sequence of five tosses is all heads, has nothing to say about what the next toss is likely to be. In short, past returns cannot be used to forecast future returns.

First developed from rudimentary economic considerations of 'fair games', the random walk hypothesis received broad support from the many early empirical studies in the 1960s and 1970s confirming the unpredictability of stock returns, generally using daily or monthly returns of individual securities. However, some of our own recent research sharply contradicts these findings. Using a statistical comparison of volatility across different investment horizons applied to the weekly returns of a portfolio of stocks from 1962–94, we find that the random walk hypothesis can be rejected with great statistical confidence (well in excess of 99.9 per cent). In fact, the weekly returns of a portfolio containing an equal dollar amount invested in each security traded on the New York and American Stock exchanges (called an equal-weighted portfolio) exhibit a striking relation from one week to the next: the correlation between one week's return and the next, or 'autocorrelation coefficient', is 20 per cent. A correlation coefficient is an index of association which lies between –100 per cent and 100 per cent, where –100 per cent represents a perfect negative correlation, 100 per cent a perfect positive correlation, and 0 per cent no relation).

An auto-correlation of 20 per cent implies that about four per cent of the variability of next week's return is explained by this week's return. An equally weighted portfolio containing only the stocks of 'smaller' companies, companies with market capitalization in the lowest quintile, has a autocorrelation coefficient of 35 per cent during the 1962–94 sample period. This implies that about 10 per cent of the variability in next week's return can be explained by this week's return. Although numbers such as four and 10 per cent may seem small, recall that 100 per cent predictability yields astronomically large investment returns; a very tiny fraction of such returns can still be economically meaningful.

These findings surprise many economists because a violation of the random walk hypothesis implies that price changes can be forecast to some degree. But since forecasts of price changes are also subject to random fluctuations, riskless profit opportunities are not an immediate consequence of forecastability. Nevertheless, economists still cannot completely explain why weekly returns are not a 'fair game'.

Two other facts add to this puzzle: first, weekly portfolio returns are strongly positively autocorrelated but the returns to individual securities generally are not; in fact, the average autocorrelation – averaged across individual securities – is negative (but insignificant). Second, the predictability of returns is quite sensitive to the holding period: serial dependence is strong and positive for daily and weekly returns, but is virtually zero for returns over a month, a quarter or a year.

Leads/lags and contrarian profits

Since the autocorrelation of portfolio returns is a weighted sum of the individual stocks' autocorrelations and their 'cross-autocorrelations' (for example, the correlation of this week's return on stock A with next week's return on stock B), we look to the cross-autocorrelations to explain the fact that portfolio returns are forecastable and individual stock returns are not.

In particular, we find that these cross-autocorrelations are strongly positive and exhibit a distinct 'lead/lag' pattern: the returns on 'larger' stocks, stocks with larger market capitalization, almost always lead those of 'smaller' stocks. That is, this week's returns of large stocks can forecast next week's returns of smaller stocks but not vice-versa. Since individual stocks are weakly negatively correlated on average, the positive correlation of weekly portfolio returns is completely attributable to these lead/lag effects.

Such effects are also an important source of the apparent profitability of contrarian investment strategies – strategies that buy 'losers' and sell 'winners'. For example, suppose the stock market consists of only two stocks, A and B, with returns that are uncorrelated individually but positively cross-autocorrelated. If A's return is higher than the market return this week (where, in this case, the 'market' return is simply the average of A and B's returns), the contrarian will sell it and buy B. But if A and B are positively cross-autocorrelated, a higher return for A this week implies a higher return for B next week (on average). Thus the contrarian investor profits (on average) from buying B. Although A's past returns cannot be used to forecast its own returns, they can be used to forecast B's returns and contrarian trading strategies inadvertently benefit from this cross-forecastability.

Our research shows that at least half of the expected profits from one particular contrarian strategy is the result of lead/lag effects. Economic models attempting to explain the 20 per cent autocorrelation in portfolio returns now must do so in a very specific way: they must provide a mechanism by which the returns of smaller companies lag those of larger ones.

But how these differences are manifested in the behavior of equity returns cannot be reliably determined through data analysis alone. We have demonstrated that when empirical facts motivate the search for additional empirical facts in the same data, this can lead to anomalous findings that are more apparent than real.

Moreover, the more we scrutinize a fixed collection of data, the more likely are we to find interesting (spurious) patterns. Since stock market prices are perhaps the most studied economic quantities to date, financial economists must be particularly vigilant about such 'data-snooping' biases.

The importance of size would be much more convincing if it were based on a model of economic equilibrium in which the relation between size and the behavior of asset returns is well-articulated.

Nonsynchronous trading

Perhaps the simplest explanation of the predictability in returns is a kind of measurement error to which financial data is particularly susceptible, often called the 'infrequent trading' or 'nonsynchronous trading' problem. This arises when prices recorded at different times are treated as if they were sampled simultaneously. For example, the daily prices of securities quoted in the financial press are usually 'closing' prices – prices at which the last transaction in each of those securities occurred on the previous business day.

If the last transaction in stock A occurs at 14:00 and the last in stock B occurs at 16:00, then included in B's closing price is information not available when A's closing price was set. This can create spurious predictability in asset returns since economy-wide shocks will be reflected first in the prices of the most frequently traded securities, with less frequently traded stocks responding with a lag. Even when there is no causal relation between stocks A and B, their measured returns will seem cross-autocorrelated simply because we have mistakenly assumed that they are measured simultaneously.

We have constructed an explicit model of this phenomenon that is capable of generating size-determined lead/lag patterns (since small stocks trade less frequently than large stocks) and positive portfolio correlation in weekly returns. Using this framework, we can estimate the degree of nonsynchronous trading implicit in the observed statistics of the data, for example, means, variances and autocorrelations. Using weekly portfolio returns, the infrequent trading necessary to produce an autocorrelation of 20 per cent is empirically implausible, requiring securities to go for several days without trading on average. Therefore, while nonsynchronous trading may be responsible for a portion of the observed autocorrelation, it cannot explain all of it.

Long-horizon stock returns

In contrast to the positive autocorrelation we have reported in short-horizon stock returns, other researchers have reported negative serial correlation in longer horizon (three- to five-year) returns using a longer sample period from 1926–94. For example, the autocorrelation coefficient of five-year returns for an equally-weighted portfolio over this sample period is –35 per cent.

This result has led many to conclude that there is 'mean-reversion' in stock prices, long-run predictable components that cause prices to temporarily swing away from but gradually return to 'fundamental' values. Recall that negative correlation implies an inverse relation, so that a large five-year return tends to be followed by a subsequent small five-year return on average, and vice versa.

A more troublesome inference that some have drawn from these numbers is that stocks are less risky in the long run and that all investors, young and old, ought to invest a larger proportion of their wealth in the stock market. There is, however, good reason to be wary of such inferences when they are based on long-horizon returns. Perhaps the most obvious concern is the extremely small sample size – from 1926 to 1994 there are only 13 non-overlapping five-year returns – and while overlapping returns do provide a modicum of additional information, a careful statistical analysis suggests this increment is modest at best.

This is reflected in the fact that autocorrelation coefficients for five-year returns tend to be extremely unstable and badly biased measures of true correlation. In particular, despite the impressive magnitude of –35 per cent for the five-year return autocorrelation, there is so much statistical 'noise' in this point estimate that it is statistically indistinguishable from an autocorrelation coefficient of 0 per cent. Moreover, slight changes in the starting date of the sample period, or value weighting instead of equal weighting the portfolios, can change both the sign and the magnitude of this autocorrelation. These limitations cast serious doubt on the importance of longer-horizon return autocorrelations for issues such as asset allocation and optimal portfolio rules.

Of course, the fact that the empirical results are so fragile may be merely evidence that our statistical tools are weak. After all, it may not be possible to say much about the behavior of five-year returns with only 60-some years of data, even if there is some form of predictability at the longer horizons. A more promising approach in distinguishing between genuine and spurious long-horizon effects is to construct a more specific model of short-horizon returns and derive its implications for longer holding periods. We turn to this approach next.

Maximizing predictability

In our recent investigations, we have developed a method for systematically maximizing the predictability in asset returns *explicitly* by constructing portfolios of assets that are the most predictable in a statistical sense. Such explicit maximization yields new insights to findings based on less formal methods. Perhaps the most obvious is that it yields an upper bound to what even the most industrious investigator will achieve in a search for predictability among portfolios. As such, it provides an informal yardstick against which other findings may be measured.

For example, we argued that about four per cent of the variation in the weekly returns of an equal-weighted portfolio of US stocks can be explained by the previous week's returns over the 1926–94 sample period – is this large or small? The answer will depend on whether the maximum predictability for weekly portfolio returns is five per cent or 75 per cent.

More importantly, the maximization of predictability can direct us towards more disaggregated sources of persistence and time-variation in asset returns, in the form of portfolio weights of the most predictable portfolio, and sensitivities of those weights to specific predictors, for example, industrial production, dividend yield and so on. A primitive example of this kind of disaggregation is the lead/lag relation among size-sorted portfolios described above. The more general framework we have developed includes lead/lag effects as a special case but captures predictability explicitly as a function of time-varying economic risk premia rather than as a function of past returns only.

When we apply our maximization procedure to monthly stock and bond returns from 1947–94, we find that predictability can be increased considerably both by portfolio selection and by horizon selection. For example, if we consider as our universe of assets the 11 portfolios formed by industry classification, 53 per cent of the variability in the annual returns of the maximally predictably portfolio can be explained by standard economic factors. Such findings suggest distinct forecasting horizons for the various sector assets and may signal important differences in how such groups of securities respond to economic events.

Practical implications

These recent research findings have several implications for both individual and institutional investors. The fact that the random walk hypothesis can be rejected for recent US equity returns suggests that the stock market is forecastable to some degree. This raises the possibility of superior investment returns through disciplined active investment management.

Such claims are often disputed by academics wedded to the efficient markets hypothesis – prices fully reflect all available information, therefore active investment management cannot add value because its information content has already been impounded into market prices. This fallacious argument is reminiscent of an old joke, widely told among economists, about an economist strolling down the street with a companion when they come upon a $100 bill lying on the ground. As the companion reaches down to pick it up, the economist says: 'Don't bother – if it were a real $100 bill, someone would have already picked it up'.

A less facetious counter-example to this extreme version of the efficient markets hypothesis can be constructed by applying the efficient markets argument to a non-financial market, say the market for biotechnology. Consider, for example, the goal of developing a vaccine for the AIDS virus. If the market for biotechnology is efficient in an informational sense, this suggests that such a vaccine can never be developed – if it could, someone would have already done it. This is clearly a ludicrous presumption since it ignores the difficulty and gestation lags of research and development in biotechnology. Moreover, if a pharmaceutical company does succeed in developing such a vaccine, the profits earned would be measured in the billions of dollars. Would this be considered 'excess' profits or economic rents that accrue to biotechnology patents?

Financial markets are no different in principle, only in degrees. Consequently, the profits that accrue to an active investment manager need not be a market *inefficiency* but may simply be the fair reward for breakthroughs in financial technology. After all, few analysts would regard the hefty profits of Amgen over the past few years as evidence of an inefficient market for pharmaceuticals – Amgen's recent profitability is readily identified with the development of several new drugs (Epogen, for example, a drug that stimulates the production of red blood cells), some of which are considered breakthroughs in biotechnology. Similarly, even in efficient financial markets there are very handsome returns to breakthroughs in financial technology.

Of course, barriers to entry are typically lower, the degree of competition is much higher and most financial technologies are not patentable (though this may soon change). Hence the 'half-life' of the profitability of financial innovation is considerably smaller.

These features imply that financial markets should be relatively more efficient, and indeed they are. The market for used securities is considerably more efficient than that for used cars. But to argue that financial markets must be perfectly efficient is tantamount to the claim that an AIDS vaccine cannot be found. In an efficient market, it is difficult to earn a good living but not impossible.

Nevertheless, several caveats must be kept in mind in assessing the vast array of active investment managers, each promising attractive returns at very low cost. First, the riskiness of active strategies can be very different from passive strategies, and such risks do not necessarily 'average out' over time. In particular, the investor's risk tolerance must be taken into account in selecting the long-term investment strategy that will best match the investor's goals.

Second, there are a plethora of active managers vying for the privilege of managing assets. But they cannot all outperform the market every year (nor should we necessarily expect them to). Though often judged against a common benchmark, for example, the S&P 500, active strategies can have very diverse risk characteristics and these must be weighed in assessing their performance. An active strategy involving high-risk venture-capital investments will tend to outperform the S&P 500 more often than a less aggressive 'enhanced indexing' strategy, yet one is not necessarily better than the other.

In particular, past performance should not be the *sole* criterion by which investment managers are judged. Unlike the experimental sciences, such as physics and biology, financial economics (and most other social sciences) relies primarily on statistical inference to test its theories. Therefore, we can never know with perfect certainty that a particular investment strategy is successful since even the most successful strategy can always be explained by pure luck. While statistical inference can be very helpful in tackling this question, in the final analysis the question is not about statistics but rather about economics and financial innovation.

So what are the sources of superior performance promised by an active manager and why have other competing managers not recognized these opportunities? Is it better mathematical models of financial markets? Or more accurate statistical methods for identifying investment opportunities? Or more timely data in a market where minute delays can mean the difference between profits and losses? By better understanding the sources of value-added of active managers, rather than focusing purely on past performance, the chances of obtaining consistently superior investment returns can be increased dramatically.

Summary

Perfect foresight could have turned a dollar bill invested in 1926 into more than $2bn today – but even a modest ability to forecast financial asset returns can be handsomely rewarded. The question of whether stock prices contain predictable components has been a dominant theme of *Mastering Finance*.

In this article Andrew Lo and Craig MacKinlay describe recent evidence that the celebrated random walk hypothesis does not hold for US stock prices. With the help of modern statistical methods and computing power they describe some empirical findings for aggregate US stock indices that suggest the presence of important short-term predictability in stock market movements. These represent a further challenge to those academics and others wedded to the efficient markets hypothesis.

Suggested further reading

Campbell, J.A., Lo, A. and MacKinlay, A.C., (1997), *The econometrics of financial markets*, Princeton University Press.

Lo, A. and MacKinlay, A.C., (1988), 'Stock market prices do not follow random walks: evidence from a simple specification test', *Review of Financial Studies* 1, 41–66.

Lo, A. and MacKinlay, A.C., (1990), 'When are contrarian profits due to stock market overreaction?' *Review of Financial Studies* 3, 175–208.

Lo, A. and MacKinlay, A.C., (1990), 'An econometric analysis of nonsynchronous trading', *Journal of Econometrics* 45, 203–238.

Lo, A. and MacKinlay, A.C., (1990), 'Data snooping biases in tests of financial asset pricing models', *Review of Financial Studies* 3, 431–488.

Lo, A. and MacKinlay, A.C., (1997), 'Maximizing predictability in the stock and bond markets', *Macroeconomic Dynamics* 1(1).

Giving markets a human dimension

by Richard Thaler

Ten years ago readers would have been surprised to see an article in *Mastering Finance* devoted to a topic called behavioral finance. They would be even more surprised to find that the author of the article was from the University of Chicago's Graduate School of Business, long considered the shrine of the rational economic agent and efficient markets. What is financial economics coming to? And, what is behavioral finance anyway?

Before turning to the topic at hand it is important to consider some history. What is often called modern finance is mostly an essentially post-Second World War phenomenon. The pioneers, including Markowitz, Miller, Modigliani, Samuelson and Sharpe (all Nobel laureates) helped take a field that was closer to accounting than to economics and introduce mathematical tools that had recently revolutionized economics. The process of making financial economics mathematically precise had an unintended by-product: finance became a field of inquiry that was devoid of human beings.

Finance professors are primarily concerned with the outcomes of financial markets: prices, volume, dividends, earnings and so on. Little attention is given to the agents who produce these outcomes: investors, traders, portfolio managers, pension fund managers and so on. Instead, these actors are modeled using the standard assumptions of modern economics: agents are assumed to make forecasts that are unbiased (they have rational expectations) and make decisions in the face of uncertainty according to the axioms of expected utility theory.

If only life were this simple. Unfortunately, over the past 20 years or so psychologists, especially Daniel Kahneman and the late Amos Tversky and their followers, have learned a lot about how real people make forecasts and decisions. The lessons of this research is that actual behavior is not well described by simple economic assumptions. Forecasts are predictably biased and choices are influenced by extraneous factors such as how the options are described.

Why then does modern finance remain the paradigm taught in every leading business school in the world, including Chicago? Financial economists have comforted themselves with two lines of defence against the attack that their models are based on flawed assumptions. First, there is the *as if* defence, first put forward by the Chicago economist Milton Friedman.

Friedman argued that theories should not be evaluated on the basis of the validity of their assumptions but rather on the accuracy of their predictions. He used the metaphor of an expert billiards player who could not pass a test in physics or trigonometry but played as if he could. A second defence, also suggested by Friedman (and others), is that markets drive out irrationality. Perhaps there are some traders who make bad decisions – but not for long! Personally, I am sensitive to both of these arguments. I am happy to judge theories on the basis of the predictions of the theory rather than the validity of the assumptions. And research in financial markets has to be especially sensitive to the obvious fact that there are armies of very smart, highly motivated and well-financed investors and arbitrageurs who are ready to pounce on any chance of making a quick profit.

So, in the spirit of Milton Friedman, let us evaluate modern finance based on the predictions the model makes (rather than on the validity of its assumptions) and see how it comes out. To do this exercise, I propose to use what I will call the man from Mars test. As you know, some scientists have recently claimed to have discovered life on Mars. Suppose this life is intelligent enough to have learned mathematics, statistics, economics and rational choice and that one such Martian has invented the concept of a financial market. What predictions would our Martian make about financial markets? And, what would he find were he to come down to earth and examine the real thing?

Prediction 1: price changes reflect news

In a rational efficient market, assets are priced at their true, intrinsic value. Therefore, prices only change when intrinsic values change, that is, when there is genuine news.

Fact 1: October 1987

Though we can all think of many instances of prices changing without any news, the most salient example of this is the week of October 19 1987, in which prices changed rapidly and drastically all around the world, although the only real financial news, or news of any sort, was that prices were rapidly changing. Does anyone think the present value of the US economy really fell more than 20 per cent on that Monday (after having fallen five per cent on Friday) and then rose over nine per cent on Wednesday?

Prediction 2: no trading

In economics this is sometimes called the Groucho Marx theorem. Groucho had a famous line that he would not want to belong to any club that would have him as a member. Similarly, if I know you are rational, and you know that I am rational and I know you know that I know, etc, then if you say you are willing to sell some shares in IBM I will wonder what you know that I don't know. I won't want to be part of any trade that will have anyone willing to take the other side!

Fact 2: lots of trading

We can see 400 million shares traded on a single boring day on the New York Stock Exchange and most professionally managed portfolios are still actively managed, with turnover rates of 50–100 per cent per year the norm. Why are all these people trading? Do they think that they are smarter than the person taking the other side? They may think so (roughly 90 per cent of the public think themselves above average on most dimensions – driving, getting along with people and so on) – but it isn't true.

A study of pension fund managers by Joseph Lakonishok, Andrei Shleifer and Robert Vishny finds that the stocks they sell perform better than the stocks they buy. And a study of the customers of a large US discount brokerage firm by Terrance Odean finds the same thing for individuals.

Indeed, I am thinking of starting a new mutual fund, modestly called the Thaler fund, which will simply buy all the shares the customers of this brokerage firm want to sell and sell them all the shares they want to buy. It appears that my fund will earn about 3 per cent a year above the S&P 500 index.

Prediction 3: prices are unpredictable

The first premise of the efficient market hypothesis is that it is impossible to predict future returns from past returns. If this were false, then investors could make money by investing on the basis of these predictions and, in so doing, eliminate them. The predictions would become self-denying.

Fact 3: prices are somewhat predictable

Prediction 3 was once called the best supported fact in social science but over the past 15 years or so researchers have uncovered numerous examples of classes of stocks that appear to do better (or worse) than they would be expected to (that is, compared to other stocks of similar risk). For example, in a study published in 1985 Werner De Bondt and I found that stocks that have done very badly over the past 3–5 years subsequently outperform the market while stocks that have done very well over the past subsequently underperform.

We concluded that stocks overreact. Subsequently, work by ourselves and others has shown that value stocks, stocks with low price/earnings ratios or low market value to book value ratios earn higher returns than so-called glamour stocks. (They are called glamour stocks by their detractors and growth stocks by their adherents.) According to behavioral finance, the value stocks do well because they are mispriced; investors have been too depressed about their performance over the past few years and have driven the prices down too low. When earnings come back (in part due to natural mean reversion) then prices will also rebound. In contrast, glamour stocks have been bid up too high by inflated expectations, and underperform when earnings fail to meet the irrationally exuberant expectations.

Even defenders of efficient markets, such as Eugene Fama and Kenneth French, agree value stocks earn high returns. However, they claim the high returns are produced by the high risk of value stocks. Behavioral researchers point out, however, that there is no evidence that the value stocks do worse in bear markets or recessions. Furthermore, it is difficult to explain the low returns on glamour stocks with a risk story since one has to believe that the low return to stocks with P/E ratios of 50 is because they are, collectively, very safe. Still, this is a debate that continues (though both sides are happy to declare victory).

Prediction 4: only non-diversifiable risk is priced

The Capital Asset Pricing Model (CAPM) tells us that if risk can be avoided through diversification then investors should not expect to be paid to bear it. However, if the returns on an asset are correlated with the return on the market (that is, beta is positive) then rational risk-averse investors will demand a higher return to bear this avoidable risk. Furthermore, assets with higher betas should earn higher returns.

Fact 4: Beta doesn't matter

In a series of studies, Fama and French have shown that beta has little ability to explain differences in returns across stocks. Rather, other variables such as firm size (market value of equity) and the ratio of book value to market value (B/M) do a better job of explaining returns. In fact, if size is held constant high beta firms actually earn lower returns than low beta firms.

Prediction 5: when dividends are taxed at a higher rate than capital gains, companies will repurchase shares rather than pay dividends

The famous Modigliani-Miller theorem proves that dividend policy is irrelevant in a world with efficient markets and no taxes. But when investors pay a higher tax rate on dividends than capital gains, a company can make some of its shareholders better off, and none worse off, by simply buying back shares instead of paying cash dividends.

Fact 5: most companies pay dividends

Economists have come up with theories to explain why companies pay dividends, including signaling models in which companies burn money (by forcing their stockholders to pay unnecessary taxes) to signal to the world that they have favorable earnings prospects. However, in a recent study Shlomo Benartzi, Roni Michaely and I have found that companies which increase dividends do not have higher earnings growth than those which leave their dividends unchanged. Why companies pay dividends remains a puzzle.

What would our Martian friend conclude at this point? I think he would conclude that the predictions of the theory do not hold up very well. Maybe it is time to rethink the theory. But how? Do we need a new way of thinking about financial markets? To get started, I would like you to consider the following little problem that was posed to readers of the *Financial Times*: Please write down a number between 0 and 100 such that your guess will be as close as possible to 2/3 of the average guess. For example, suppose five people enter and their guesses are 50, 40, 30, 20 and 10. Then the average guess would be 30, two thirds of which is 20, so the person guessing 20 would win. What would you guess? Please think about your answer before reading further. No cheating.

Let us consider how one might think about this game. One approach is not to think at all: 'This is complicated, I don't know what to do. I'll pick a number at random.' I'll call this zero-level thinking. The average guess for those engaging in zero-level thinking is 50. One step up in sophistication is first-level thinking. It works like this: 'The average participant in this game is not very thoughtful and can not really do much in the way of mathematics. He will pick several random numbers or something else equivalently foolish. This means the average guess will be 50, so I'll guess 33.' Second-level thinking is another step up: 'Most of the readers of the FT will understand the game but will think that others are not nearly so clever. They will therefore guess 33, so I should guess 22.' We come then to third-level thinking: 'Most readers of the FT will realize what this game is about and will judge that most readers will guess 33, so will themselves guess 22. I should therefore guess two-thirds of 22 or about 15'.

We see at this point that there is no convenient place to stop this analysis. Indeed, an economist would think about the game and look for an equilibrium, that is, a number which if everyone guessed it no one would have any incentive to change their guess. It is easy to confirm that the only equilibria in this game are zero and one! (We required people to submit whole numbers so both zero and one are equilibria. If fractions were permitted then only 0 would be an equilibrium.)

Does this game remind you of anything? Consider this passage from J. M. Keynes' General Theory: 'Professional investment may be likened to those newspaper competitions in which the competitors have to pick out the six prettiest faces from a hundred photographs, the prize being awarded to the competitor whose choice most nearly corresponds to the average preferences of the competitors as a whole: so that each competitor has to pick, not those faces which he himself finds prettiest, but those which he thinks likeliest to catch the fancy of the other competitors, all of whom are looking at the problem from the same point of view. It is not a case of choosing those which, to the best of one's judgment, are really the prettiest, nor even those which average opinion genuinely thinks the prettiest. We have reached the third degree where we devote our intelligences to anticipating what average opinion expects the average opinion to be. And there are some, I believe, who practice the fourth, fifth and higher degrees'.

Keynes' famous beauty contest is just like the number game and remains to this day a brilliant metaphor for thinking about financial markets. Consider that the only way to really play the number game, or the beauty contest, is to think exactly one level deeper than the average contestant. Most of readers of the FT that entered the contest were guilty of thinking either too little or too much. The average guess turned out to be 18.91, two thirds of which is 12.6 which rounds off to 13. However the numbers most frequently guessed were 0, 1, 22 and 33. Guessing 22 or 33 is evidence of giving others too little credit while guessing 0 or 1 is being much too clever. (The details of the contest are discussed in the box in this article.) Investing works the same way. It is not enough to figure out that some stock is undervalued (or overvalued). To make that stock a good investment (or potential short sale) it must be the case that other people will figure this out as well and soon enough to do some good.

Keynes once said that in the long run we are all dead. Portfolio managers may paraphrase Keynes thus: after three years of bad performance we are all fired. This means that good investing must combine good analysis (to determine when price is not equal to intrinsic value) and good psychology (to determine why the price has diverged from value and get a sense of when – if ever – it will move back).

What are the positive contributions of behavioral finance? I have already discussed the research linking the success of value investing to cognitive psychology; let me add to that with two other examples.

First, consider the case of closed-end mutual funds. These financial institutions have long been a puzzle to financial economists because they trade at prices that are different from the underlying value of the securities they own. Indeed, while it is common for these funds to trade at discounts of 10–20 per cent, there have been cases where the funds trade at substantial premia, most notably some so-called single country funds which at one point in the US traded at over 200 per cent of net asset value. (Clearer evidence of a bubble has rarely been seen; the premia disappeared within a few months and the funds now trade at small discounts.)

While large discrepancies between the price of the fund and the value of the securities it owns are embarrassing to efficient markets advocates, Charles Lee, Andrei Shleifer and I have also shown that the funds can be used to help understand more about financial markets. In a paper in the *Journal of Finance* we argued that the discounts on closed-end funds can be used as a measure of individual investor sentiment (since in the US, closed-end funds are owned primarily by individual investors). An implication of this view is that the discounts will be correlated with the returns on other assets held by individual investors. This is precisely what we find. When discounts on closed-end funds narrow (implying individual investors are more optimistic) small firms (held primarily by individual investors) do better than large firms (held primarily by institutions).

Equity premium puzzle

Another way in which psychology can help us understand the market is in explaining the so-called equity premium puzzle. The equity premium is the difference in the returns between stocks (equities) and bonds. The puzzle refers to the fact that this difference is so large. Over the past 70 years or so, real returns on stocks in the US and UK have averaged about six per cent to seven per cent per year while bond returns are closer to one per cent. Furthermore, this difference is true in nearly every country. Why do investors need to be compensated so much for holding stocks? Or, in other words, why are long-term investors willing to hold bonds? One answer offered by Shlomo Benartzi and me is what we call myopic loss aversion.

Research in psychology reveals that people display loss aversion, meaning they are much more sensitive to losing money than to gaining it. Roughly speaking, losing 100 hurts twice as much as gaining 100 yields pleasure. For investors, loss aversion makes investing in a risk asset such as equities unattractive if returns are evaluated frequently. (On a 20-year basis, stocks will almost certainly outperform bonds, but on a daily basis, stocks go down almost as often as they go up.) Benartzi and I estimated how often loss-averse investors have to be evaluating their portfolios in order to make them indifferent between stocks and bonds. Using US data we found that the answer was about 13 months – once a year. If our explanation is correct, then stock returns are high to compensate those who count their money too often. This implies that for those willing to be patient (or oblivious) stocks are an attractive investment.

Let me close with a passage from another Chicago economist of an earlier generation, John Maurice Clark. Writing in the Chicago house journal, the *Journal of Political Economy* in 1918, Clark said this: 'The economist may attempt to ignore psychology, but it is a sheer impossibility for him to ignore human nature. If the economist borrows his conception of man from the psychologist, his constructive work may have some chance of remaining purely economic in character. But if he does not, he will not thereby avoid psychology. Rather, he will force himself to make his own, and it will be bad psychology'. Behavioral finance is an attempt to follow Clark's advice, to borrow some good psychology rather than invent more bad psychology. In so doing, we hope to obtain a better understanding of how financial markets work.

Summary

This article is essentially a warning by Richard Thaler not to leave human beings out of the increasingly mathematical field of finance. Financial economists, he says, have two responses to accusations that their models are based on flawed assumptions – the 'as if' defence and the argument that markets drive out irrationality. Using 'the man from Mars' test, however, he challenges the conventional wisdom that prices only change in reaction to news, the 'Groucho Marx' theorem, the premise that future returns cannot be predicted from past data, the Capital Asset Pricing Model, and the belief that a regime which taxes dividends more highly than capital gains will force companies to repurchase their own shares.

The author explains how the success of value investing can be linked to cognitive psychology, and argues that behavioral finance enables us to understand the pricing of closed-end mutual funds and the so-called equity premium puzzle.

Suggested further reading

Benartzi, S. and Thaler, R. H., (1995), 'Myopic loss aversion and the equity premium puzzle', *Quarterly Journal of Economics*, February .

Haugen, R., (1995), *The new finance: the case against efficient markets*, Prentice Hall.

Shiller, R., (1989), *Market volatility*, MIT Press, Cambridge, MA.

Siegel, J., (1994), *Stocks for the long run*, Irwin.

Thaler, R. H., (1992), *The winner's curse: paradoxes and anomalies of economic life*, The Free Press, NY.

Thaler, R. H. (ed.) *Advances in behavioral finance*, Russell Sage Foundation, NY.

The end-of-the-year show

by David Musto

The turn of the year has an odd, but predictable, effect on US financial asset returns. Consider the commercial paper (CP) rates, as reported by the Federal Reserve Bank of New York, plotted in Figure 1 and notice the extra discount charged for paper due to be outstanding on December 31 1996. Before December 2, when new issues of seven, 15 and 30-day paper were all due to mature before the year end, the rates were similar and moved little. The same was true after December 31. But the rates in between shifted abruptly to impute a bonus yield for holding across the year end. For example, the seven-day rate jumped 90 basis points from December 24, when seven-day paper matured in 1996, to December 26, when it matured in 1997, and fell 110 basis points from December 31 to January 2. These rate shifts translate to a drop in price of about $200 per $1m face value or $160m on the $800bn face value of outstanding CP at the year end. The lower price for instruments maturing across the end of the year has been an annual feature of CP, negotiable time deposit (domestic as well as euro) and bankers acceptance rates for more than 25 years.

Why must corporations bear this extra cost for year-end funding? It appears to have something to do with their credit risk. For one thing, issuers with lower-rated programs pay a larger year-end bonus, about 15 basis points more for P2-rated (Moody's second-highest rating) paper than for P1-rated (Moody's highest) 30-day. But perhaps more tellingly, Treasury bills pay no year-end bonus at all.

From this perspective, the year-end rate shifts are consistent with a spike in either the level of credit risk or the price charged by investors for bearing it. That is, investors would pay less for paper maturing across the year-end if they perceived credit risk to be high at year-end or if they were less willing to bear a unit of credit risk at year end.

The first scenario is doubtful, given that no CP has defaulted at year end in recent memory, if ever. But the second scenario corresponds to the structural details of the money market. CP trades in such enormous blocks that almost all of it is purchased and held to maturity by large institutions which select, on behalf of their claimholders (shareholders, beneficiaries, policy holders and so on), instruments with more or less credit risk. The claimholders are presumably interested in these risk choices but can

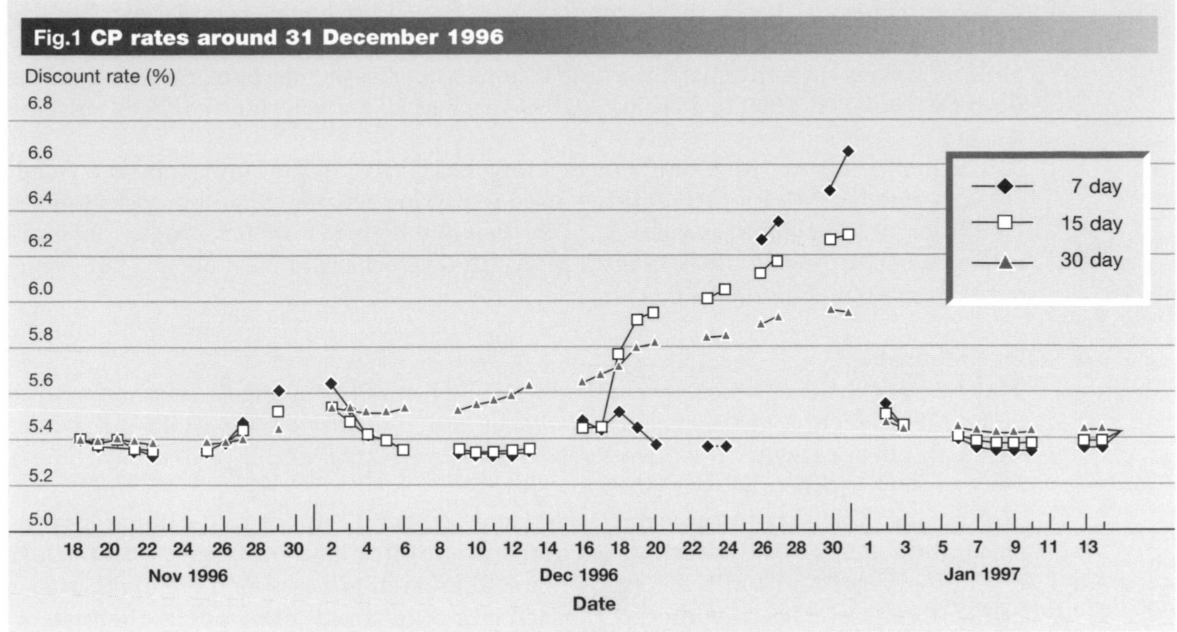

Fig.1 CP rates around 31 December 1996

observe them only at pre-arranged disclosure dates, of which the most popular by far is December 31.

Limited disclosure

Perhaps the most extreme case of this limited disclosure is the $2,000bn life insurance industry, where every company discloses every money market instrument held on December 31, but essentially nothing about money market instruments not held then. And in the $1,000bn money market mutual fund industry, the semi-annual disclosures correspond to fiscal years, not calendar years. December fiscal years, however, are most common.

If these and other institutions try to manage the opinions of claimholders and regulators by tilting their reported portfolios toward lower-risk instruments such as Treasury bills – a strategy that has become known as 'window dressing' – then the market price for bearing risk is likely to be higher on the main disclosure days. This is because non-disclosing investors are bearing more risk than they would otherwise choose to bear at the usual price. Observed patterns in price shifts would be the natural result. This is also consistent with the similar but smaller-scale CP price shifts around quarter ends. This 'window dressing' explanation fits well with money market history in that the onset of disclosure-time price shifts appears to coincide with the beginning of modern default-risk management.

Before the 1970 default of Penn Central's $82m of unrated paper, issuers rarely solicited CP ratings from the few agencies offering them. After the default the market abruptly shifted to demanding ratings as well as back-up lines of credit and has done so ever since. And while it is not possible to date the onset of next-year discounts with certainty, there is no evidence of them before 1970 and ample evidence in almost every year since. Window dressing can connect the dots: the incentive to avoid instruments with credit risk at disclosure dates to the event that alerted investors to money market credit risk.

Over the past 27 years, the discounts have tracked the business cycle, particularly in recessions. The combination of the Gulf War and the recent recession was especially hard on riskier corporations. According to some reports, the discount rate for funding from December 31 1990 to January 2 1991 reached 90 per cent (annualized) for some issuers.

The money market price shifts have a famous relative in the equity market. Small stocks – companies with little equity – used to pay big returns. Smaller stocks tend to be riskier by the popular measures, so the demand by investors for a higher average return is not surprising. But the extra return these stocks paid until about 1981 seems out of proportion with their extra risk.

Small-firm effect

This curious pattern, which became known as the 'small-firm effect', inspired a large body of research. Monthly returns isolated much of this excess in January (the 'January effect') and daily returns showed there were substantial returns over just a few days (the 'turn-of-the-year effect').

A series of papers in the early 1980s showed small stocks had almost always outperformed large-cap stocks in each of the five trading days beginning with the last one of the year. And while the small-firm effect itself appears to have dissipated – small stocks have actually underperformed large-cap stocks since 1982 – the turn-of-the-year effect persists. This is interesting not only as another puzzle but as a trading strategy that pays off consistently, albeit modestly.

One obvious way to cash in on the big returns is to buy a small-company index future and sell a large-company index future at the close of the year's penultimate trading day and then unwind the position at the close of the next year's fourth trading day. This pays you the relative price appreciation of smaller stocks over the five trading days. There are several contracts to choose from but two that have been around since 1982 are Kansas City's Value Line, whose weighting schemes have each made small stocks relatively influential, and the Chicago Merc's S&P 500, whose weighting by capitalization makes large stocks more influential.

Simulating this strategy with closing prices from the newspaper, I find a positive pay-off in 13 of 15 year-ends, including this last one (the losers were 1987 and 1995), with an average profit of about one per cent (that is, about $3, with $300 long and $300 short). As in the money market, the effect is strongest in recessions; investors following this strategy would have made seven per cent over the end of 1990.

The five-day small-stock rally is still largely a mystery to economists, but there are some theories about the price shifts on the first trading day of the year. Suspicion focuses on the tax code. The tax benefit from realizing investment losses sooner rather than later is particularly large when 'later' means next year because the realization would then reduce next year's taxes not this year's. Investors with losers in their portfolios in the last days of December should be better off selling them.

A disproportionate number of small stocks have recently been losers so the result could be widespread dumping of small stocks. By this theory, the turn-of-the-year effect is the recovery of small stocks when the tax-loss selling abates. Investors might know that the stocks they are selling are about to do well but they cannot buy them back for a month without 'wash-sale' rules reducing their write-offs. Of course, they would be much better off if they had realized their losses in November or earlier, because that would leave them free to buy the stocks before their annual rise. The effect is consistent with tax planning that is much worse than optimal but much better than no planning at all.

Another explanation brings the window dressing reasoning to bear on equities. Much of the equity market is held through institutional investors with year-end portfolio disclosures; Federal Reserve statistics trace over half of the $10,000bn in US equities to institutions rather than households.

Considering the higher risk of smaller stocks, a bias toward disclosing lower-risk portfolios would deliver the upward shift observed in small stock prices on the first trading day after December 31, because this would be the day when the disclosing intermediaries stop avoiding them. It is difficult to know how much of this is going on – that is, to know about the trades that the putative window dressers actively do not want us to know about – but it is an intriguing possibility.

Whatever the true cause or causes of these patterns in financial asset prices, they are both a strategic consideration for corporate treasurers and an opportunity for investors. Corporations must plan around the higher price that investors charge to hold their paper from one year to the next, especially during recessions. By the same token, money market investors briefly earn a much higher yield, with no apparent increase in risk, and equity investors continue to benefit from a trading strategy that has been well-known and exhaustively researched for years. It would seem that years of exposure would kill a reasonably good investing opportunity, but there it is.

Summary

The turn of the year has an odd, but predictable, effect on US financial assets which is both a strategic consideration for corporate treasurers and an opportunity for investors. In the case of commercial paper, says David Musto, the year-end patterns appear to have something to do with credit risk as institutions tilt their portfolios towards lower risk instruments such as Treasury Bills.

The resulting money market shifts – which require companies to bear an extra funding cost – have an interesting parallel in the equity markets: the five-day small stock rally. One explanation for this phenomenon, also around the turn of the year, may be that investors are selling losers in their portfolios for tax reasons (a disproportionate number of losers have recently been small stocks); another is CP-style 'window dressing' as institutions reduce the risks in their portfolios for disclosure purposes.

Suggested further reading

Haugen, R., and Lakonishok, J., (1988), *The Incredible January Effect,* Dow-Jones-Irwin, Homewood, Illinois.

Musto, D. K., (1997), 'Portfolio disclosures and year-end price shifts', *Journal of Finance,* 1(11), September.

Assessing the costs of security trading

by Brad Barber and Richard Leftwich

Security trading differs dramatically from country to country and from security to security within a country. For example, the hurly-burly of the open outcry system in the trading pits at the Chicago Mercantile Exchange (CME) and the Chicago Board of Trade (CBOT) stands in marked contrast to the tranquillity of the empty trading floor at the Sydney Stock Exchange, where all trades are conducted electronically off the floor of the exchange. The New York Stock Exchange (NYSE) relies on a specialist system to trade stocks whereas its chief US competitor, Nasdaq (the National Association of Securities Dealers Automated Quotation system), uses competing market-makers.

Should investors be concerned about the technology and organizational details of trading when making investment decisions? Should investors treat the trading process as a black box not worth scrutinizing for any reason other than intellectual curiosity? Or are there important lessons to be learned from studying the minutiae of the trading process?

Investors should be concerned about the returns they expect to realize in a market, net of the cost of trading. Various features of markets, such as their reliance on electronic technology, may be highly visible but ultimately the investor's real concern is with the economic cost of trading. These costs are more than the out-of-pocket costs associated with a trade. Some elements of the economic costs, however, are difficult to estimate.

Consequently, market features (such as low trading volume) are often used as indications of trading costs in lieu of precise measurements. Some short-term traders, especially those who buy and sell at least once during a day, base their strategies on institutional features of the market – which are not discussed in this article.

Designers of markets cannot treat the trading process as a black box because they need to understand how particular features of the trading process affect the cost of trading. Nevertheless, the cause and effect relationship is not well understood. In particular, why some markets are highly liquid and others are not remains a mystery. Academic inquiry into most aspects of the trading process is known as market microstructure (although our colleague Merton Miller argues that micromarket structure seems equally descriptive) and is in its relative infancy.

What constitutes a market?

An organized securities market or exchange is a network of potential buyers and sellers or their agents. Although the term 'market' originally connoted a central physical location, improvements in communication have allowed geographically dispersed individuals to form an organized market. Organized markets have rules about who is allowed to trade, what securities can be traded, the types of trades that can be made, how trades are consummated and how the integrity of trades is ensured.

Exchanges compete both domestically and internationally for trading volume and for new listings of securities. Even though most organized securities markets are privately owned and operated, virtually all securities markets that allow public participation are subject to government regulation. For example, in the US the Securities and Exchange Commission (SEC) regulates the behavior of stock exchanges.

Stocks can be bought and sold privately. For example, you may be able to convince your (soon to be ex) brother-in-law to pay $5 per share for your 10,000 Bre-X shares, even though those shares are no longer traded on a major stock exchange. However, private sales are typically not cost effective because of the costs of searching for potential buyers and sellers, negotiating a price and ensuring the trade will still be consummated if one of the parties reneges on the deal.

The potential volume of trading in some securities (such as corporate bonds, shares in limited partnerships and small firms) does not warrant the overheads associated with a public market. Markets for those securities closely resemble private transactions and these markets are labeled generically as over-the-counter (OTC) markets.

OTC trades are arranged between a would-be buyer or seller and a large institution, typically an investment bank such as Morgan Stanley. Those trades can be tailored to meet the specifications of the buyer or seller, whereas in a public market trades are relatively homogeneous in order to enhance liquidity.

The OTC markets are more active in derivative securities, such as options, where some buyers or sellers seek highly specific contracts (particularly in terms of the time to maturity). However, the foreign currency market involves homogeneous trades and is dominated by the interbank market, a principal-to-principal market akin to the OTC market.

Electronic technology has reduced search costs dramatically and electronic bulletin boards provide efficient ways to advertize willingness to buy or sell particular securities. However, the integrity of those trades is more difficult to guarantee.

Dealer and auction markets

Dealer markets are familiar to lay people. The dealer (or market-maker) is essentially a middle man who buys at one price (the bid) and sells at a slightly higher price (the ask, or offer).

Dealers buy stocks into inventory, sell stocks from that inventory and may even sell stocks short. Dealers attempt to make money from the spread (the difference between the bid and the ask) and bear the risk of adverse price moves in their inventory. They can manage their inventory by adjusting their quotes, by transacting with other dealers or by hedging in derivatives markets. Nasdaq and the London Stock Exchange (LSE) provide examples of important dealer markets for stocks; and most bond markets are dealer markets.

In an auction market, all orders to buy or sell are channeled to a central location (even if that location is an address in a computer) and a market-clearing price is determined by means of a set of rules (or an algorithm) that determines, among other things, the priority of different offers to buy and sell. These rules are more complex than those of auction houses such as Sotheby's because in securities markets the supply of the item is not known when potential buyers submit their bids. Moreover, auction markets for securities can be discrete or continuous.

In a discrete auction, orders to buy or sell a stock are accumulated and at a particular time a single price is set to clear the market, again according to a pre-specified set of rules. Opening prices on large markets such as the NYSE and Tokyo are set using this process. They are known as a call market. Some smaller markets, especially nascent emerging markets, operate a call market once or several times a day and in some a call market is operated for a sub-set of securities.

Call markets are seldom pure auction markets because a dealer (usually known as a specialist) is often introduced to supply liquidity. Occasionally, discrete auctions are designed to produce multiple prices, such as the auction for newly issued US government securities. In these auctions, the fixed supply is allocated first to the highest bidder at the bidder's price, then to the next highest bidder at that bidder's price and so on until the supply is exhausted.

A continuous auction market is a hybrid of an auction market and a dealer market because of the specialist's role. Customers submit market, or limit, orders to a retail or discount broker. Those orders are transmitted to the specialist either electronically or by a floor broker. The specialist for a particular stock matches (crosses) some customers' orders with each other where possible and provides additional liquidity by selling from inventory or buying into inventory to accommodate customers' orders.

Some continuous auction markets do not employ specialists although a subset of traders (variously known as 'locals', 'scalpers' or 'jobbers') assumes that de facto role by being prepared to take the opposite side of trades initiated by brokers on behalf of customers. During normal trading hours, the NYSE and the Tokyo Stock Exchange are continuous auction markets for stocks, and the CME and the CBOT for futures and options contracts.

One of the chief differences between auction and dealer markets (seen as an advantage by those who favor auction markets) is the greater extent to which customers trade with customers in an auction market with a limit order book. If there is a limit order book in an auction market, the current quote reflects either a limit order from a customer or the specialist's quote. Thus, an incoming market order can be executed at a price established by another investor.

In contrast, in many dealer markets (in particular Nasdaq) the current quote reflects the best quote (highest bid, lowest ask) by a dealer but not necessarily customers' limit orders. Consequently, in many dealer markets, customers market orders and limit orders are executed at dealers' quotes, not against each other. For example, if the best dealer quotes are bid $40 and ask $40.75, a limit order to buy at $40.50 will not execute even if a market order to sell arrives and is executed at the dealer's bid of $40. In fact, the limit order will not execute until the quoted ask falls to $40.50.

Recent rule changes by Nasdaq allow customer limit orders for some stocks to be executed against market orders so this distinction is not as sharp as it once was. Proponents of dealer markets point out that competition among dealers should provide more favorable trading conditions for investors than the auction market with its monopoly market-maker (the specialist). This issue is hotly debated and remains an open question.

Electronic trading

Many who witness the frenzy of trading floors are convinced electronic trading would be more efficient. This is a controversial topic, particularly in options and futures markets relying on trading pits with open outcry. Three points are crucial.

First, there is no unique electronic trading system. All of the protocols and rules necessary for trading must be programmed into the electronic market-clearing algorithm. Although those rules may be easier to monitor and enforce electronically, there is not a universally accepted set of protocols and rules.

Second, unless dealers monitor their posted quotes constantly, those quotes become stale when new information arrives and dealers risk being 'picked off' (taken advantage of by a trader with up-to-date information). It is not feasible to program electronic systems to replicate human judgment in revising or suspending quotes to accommodate flows of information.

For example, traders know that quotes and limit orders need to be revised dramatically when Intel warns of substantially lower earnings due to reduced demand for its products in Europe. But the algorithm or artificial intelligence that would produce the desired result is beyond the current capabilities of electronic systems. Manual revision of quotes on electronic systems is slower than human reaction time, especially if the electronic system becomes congested as traders try to exploit stale quotes.

Third, proponents of floor trading argue that the physical proximity of traders on the floor provides clues and strategic information to facilitate trading (especially to enhance liquidity) and those intangibles cannot be reproduced in an electronic system. No one has yet devised a scientific test of this proposition nor of a compelling alternative explanation, namely that those who have a comparative advantage at floor trading are reluctant to see it eroded. Some exchanges have converted to electronic trading (for example, London, Toronto, Paris and Sydney) without apparent harm; newly created exchanges are almost universally electronic; and some exchanges that have hard core 'eyeball-to-eyeball' trading systems during normal trading hours resort to electronic trading systems for after-hours trading.

Even exchanges with floor trading have made extensive use of electronics for transmitting or routing orders from customers to the trading floor. This creates interesting contrasts with orders being transcribed from computer screens to trade tickets by hand. One prominent US academic compared the process to the use of a telephone if it had been invented in the days of the Pony Express delivery system: the sender of the message could have used the telephone to warn the recipient that the rider had just left with an important message.

There are also electronic trading systems that are independent of any big exchange. Instinet, a continuous auction system now owned by Reuters, is the best known of these and is the only stand-alone electronic system with significant trading volume. The Arizona Stock Exchange, despite its name, is a computer (located in Arizona) and is a single-price auction system that, once a day, establishes a price that will produce the largest trading volume from a list of buy and sell orders.

Some systems (such as Posit) are little more than bulletin boards and are called crossing systems because they are simply a mechanism to match a buyer and seller at a price determined in another market, typically the closing price on a major exchange. Virtually all of the customers who trade on these electronic systems are institutions such as pension or mutual funds and market-makers.

Economic costs of trading

The economic cost of trading in a particular market comprises more than out-of-pocket transactions costs such as fees, commissions and transactions, or transfer taxes, that

Reuters' Instinet: a stand-alone continuous action system

are common outside the US. Investors' returns are reduced by the normal bid-ask spread and the price impact (if any) of the trade; counterparty risk can be prohibitive in some markets.

The bid-ask spread

The bid-ask spread represents a cost of trading because if an investor pays the ask (say $10⅛) and sells at the bid (say $10), the investor has lost the spread (12.5 cents, or 1.23 per cent). Equivalently, the stock price has to increase by the spread if the investor is to break even. For some stocks, the spread presents a considerable obstacle to earning returns. For example, in May 1997, Sharper Image (a catalog retailer of high-end electronic gadgets and 'toys') was quoted as $3⅛ (bid) and $3⅜ (ask). An investor who buys this stock requires a 25 cent price move to break even, a rate of return of 7.4 per cent. This is 7.4 per cent per transaction not 7.4 per cent per year, so if the investor is an active trader with a short holding period the spread looms large.

Consider an analogy. Instead of renting a car on your next three-day business trip you could buy a new car and sell it at the end of your trip. Car rental rates do not appear high compared with the cost of this round-trip transaction.

The bid-ask spread provides income to the dealer to compensate for the costs of carrying an inventory or of bearing the risks of short-selling if the dealer is willing to sell more than the inventory. Spreads are wider for more volatile stocks because the risk of holding inventory is greater and spreads widen when uncertainty about a particular stock increases. Actual transactions often occur at prices within the posted (quoted) spread (estimates range from 20 per cent to 40 per cent of the time), that is, at prices higher than the bid for sales and lower than the ask for purchases. Thus effective spreads are narrower than quoted or posted spreads. How this occurs depends on the trading system.

In a dealer market, trades can be negotiated within the spread, especially by institutions. In a continuous auction market, trades occur within the quoted spread when the specialist or a broker in 'the crowd' (essentially floor brokers who congregate at the trading post) fills an order at a better price than the quoted spread.

Transactions prices (and quotes) change by discrete amounts (the tick) and the smallest change is the minimum tick size, again set by exchange rules. In US markets, typical minimum tick sizes have been eighths of a dollar (12.5 cents) historically, although 32nds (3.25 cents), 16ths ('teenies', 6.25 cents) and quarters (25 cents) apply for some securities and for some markets. The bid-ask spread must be at least the minimum tick size.

In markets outside the US, prices are typically stated in decimals (for example, in London, £10.26). The NYSE has announced plans to move to decimals (for example $40.30) by the year 2000. Consequently, the minimum tick size will be 1 cent. There is considerable speculation about the effect of the proposed change on the size of the bid-ask spread. It is widely believed that the spread will be reduced. Unless there is a commensurate increase in volume, profits to those who post the spreads (specialists and dealers) must decline.

Liquidity

A market for a particular security is highly liquid (or very deep) if large quantities of that security can be bought or sold without affecting the price of the security. Price volatility is often taken as an indicator of illiquidity, but even a highly liquid security can have high volatility if there is considerable uncertainty about it. Similarly, large trades can move the price of even highly liquid securities if other traders believe that such a trade is a measure of the amount of information possessed by the trader.

Other common indicators of stock liquidity are the bid-ask spread, the float (the number of shares available for trading) and the typical trading volume of the stock. Liquidity is in great demand but its supply is something of a mystery. If a market is highly liquid, someone must be willing to take the opposite side of each trade. If that were not so, a buy order would languish until the arrival of a fortuitous sell order and a sell order would be in limbo until a buy order arrived.

Liquidity can be supplied in various ways. For example, a dealer or specialist might be prepared to buy into inventory any stock offered at the prevailing price and to sell from inventory (or sell short) at slightly above the prevailing price.

Additional liquidity can be provided by the limit order book. If there are offers to buy and sell large quantities of the stock at slightly below and above the current bid and ask, large quantities of the stock can be traded at close to prevailing market prices. Buying or selling large quantities of a stock relative to normal trading volume usually involves procedures that differ from those associated with a normal trade.

Quoted bids and asks apply to only a specific number of shares (ranging from 100 to several thousand) with the specific number set by the rules of the stock exchange. Larger trades must be negotiated with the dealer or the specialist and, if the trade is sufficiently large, the trade may occur outside the market in what is known as the third market or upstairs market.

Trades above a certain size (10,000 shares for the NYSE) are called 'blocks'. For actively traded, highly liquid stocks such as AT&T, GE or British Petroleum, 10,000-share trades may be accommodated readily in the normal trading process whereas for other companies, such as Sharper Image, such trades represent several days' normal trading volume. Would-be buyers and sellers of large blocks often rely on block houses (generally arms of investment banks) to trade the block off the exchange.

For a block sale, the block house can adopt one of two strategies: either 'shop the block' or buy the block and then attempt to resell it. To shop, or position, the block, the broker contacts large institutions to determine their interest in the block or in pieces of the block. Such a strategy exposes the customer to front running, that is, to the risk that when an institution is offered the block it will decline but then use its knowledge of the impending trade strategically in the market. Successful block houses mitigate front running by establishing working relationships with large institutional investors.

Alternatively, the block house can purchase the block outright and then attempt to resell it at a profit. For example, when the Kuwaiti government decided to sell its 170m shares in British Petroleum, it invited big investment banks to bid for the block. Goldman Sachs paid almost $2bn for the block when the closing price for BP in London was $12.25 per share. Goldman resold those shares to institutional clients around the world within 36 hours for a price of $11.75, a discount of four per cent from the closing price. It is estimated that Goldman's profit (before expenses) on the deal was $15m.

Similarly, in a $1.4bn transaction when Time Warner was trading at $48.875 per share, Merrill Lynch paid $46.33 per share for a block of 30 million Time Warner shares (formerly owned by Seagram), a discount of slightly over five per cent. Merrill resold the shares to institutional clients within a day for $46.75 per share, a profit (before expenses) of almost $13m. Time Warner then traded at $47.125, a discount of almost four per cent from its pre-block price.

Investors who want to buy or sell large quantities can accumulate or dispose of their position gradually but such a strategy has costs. First, it lacks immediacy so cash is not readily available if the investor is selling or cash sits idle if the investor is buying. Second, if the investor believes he or she is better informed than the market, delay makes it more likely others will become similarly informed or will detect the selling or buying activity and mimic it.

Professional investors attempt to measure the market impact of their trades and to adopt trading strategies to trade off market impact with their desire for immediacy. Market impact is measured by noting the price of the security when the buy or sell decision is made and comparing that with the price of the security after the trade has taken place.

Counterparty risk

Counterparty risk unambiguously increases the economic costs of trading but the magnitude of the increase is difficult to estimate. In some emerging markets, concern about counterparty risk may be sufficient to deter participation by rational investors. Every purchase and sale entails counterparty risk, that is, the risk that the other party to the transaction will not fulfil the terms of the agreed trade.

Stock exchanges establish clearing and settlement rules to eliminate or minimize counterparty risk. Essentially, the exchange (technically, the clearing house) becomes the counterparty to every trade. If either party defaults, the other party looks to the clearing house to fulfil the terms of the trade. The clearing house in turn protects itself by monitoring the creditworthiness and reputation of those who offer to buy and sell in the market. Although counterparty risk is negligible in well-established markets such as New York, London and Tokyo, it is a serious concern in some emerging markets.

Counterparty risk can manifest itself in various forms. For example, a buyer may not receive good title to the security or the seller may relinquish title to the security but may not be paid on time (or at all). Less obviously, the agreed-upon trade may not be honored under certain circumstances. If the stock price rises after the supposedly agreed trade, the seller experiences remorse and if the stock price falls the buyer experiences remorse. To prevent that remorse from being translated into action, there must be a mechanism (such as a well-capitalized clearing house) to ensure that the terms of the trade will be honoured by both parties regardless of any subsequent movement in the price of the security.

Some institutional investors claim that, even in some established markets, the incidence of 'misunderstandings' about the terms of the trade seems to be a function of the subsequent performance of the stock. In those markets, an offer to buy a stock is akin to giving the putative seller a free option to deliver the stock if its price declines and to retain the stock if its price rises.

Conclusions

The language and the picayune technical characteristics of securities markets can be daunting, even to an otherwise savvy investor. Ultimately, however the technical aspects of trading are relevant to an investor only to the extent that they affect the economic costs of trading.

Conceptually, the economic costs are easy to identify: the bid-ask spread, liquidity or depth, and counterparty risk. Precise measurement of these costs is not as simple but investors should recognize that these costs, not simply out-of-pocket costs, such as brokerage fees and commissions, potentially reduce the returns they can achieve in securities markets. Moreover, the costs of trading can differ substantially from market to market and from security to security within a market.

Summary

This article is about the minutiae of the security trading process, different types of international stock exchange (and over-the-counter markets), and the costs of dealing.

Brad Barber and Richard Leftwich note the fundamental distinction between 'dealer' markets in which middlemen stand ready to buy at one price and sell at another, making money from the spread, and 'auction' markets in which all orders are channeled to a central location and a market-clearing price determined.

The merits of electronic trading are often advanced, but this is a controversial topic and there are arguments in favor of human reaction time and the physical proximity of traders.

Conceptually, the economic costs of the bid-ask (offer) spread, liquidity and counterparty risk are easy to identify. Precise measurement is trickier and investors should realize that these as well as brokerage, fees and commission potentially reduce returns.

Suggested further reading

Christie, W.G. and Schultz, P., (1994), 'Why do NASDAQ market makers avoid Odd-Eighth Quotes?' *Journal of Finance* 49, 1813–1840.

Holthausen, R.W., Leftwich, R.W. and Mayers, D., (1990), 'Large-block transactions, the speed of response, and temporary and permanent stock-price effects', *Journal of Financial Economics* 26, July, 71–95.

Huang, R.D. and Stoll, H.R., (1996), 'Dealer versus auction markets: a paired comparison of execution costs on Nasdaq and the NYSE', *Journal of Financial Economics* 41, July, 313–357.

Keim, D.B. and Madhavan, A., (1996), 'Execution costs and investment performance: an empirical analysis of institutional equity trades', Working paper, The Wharton School of the University of Pennsylvania.

Peterson, M. and Fialkowski, D., (1994), *Posted versus effective spreads: good prices or bad quotes?* 35, 269–292.

Stoll, H.R., (1993), 'Equity trading costs in-the-large', *Journal of Portfolio Management,* Summer, 41–50.

Stock Exchanges: forces of change

by Marshall E. Blume

In the background of most equity trades is a stock market. In the US, the two major stock markets are the New York Stock Exchange (NYSE) and the National Association of Securities Dealers Automated Quotation system (Nasdaq). Traditionally, the NYSE has listed the larger stocks and Nasdaq the smaller. The NYSE still lists most of the larger, more active stocks but Nasdaq's listings now include a few of the largest companies in terms of market capitalization, such as Microsoft and Intel.

Stock markets are highly complex organizations that serve many constituencies. On the surface, the primary beneficiaries of a marketplace are its dealers and market-makers, who profit from its infrastructure and are closest to exercising control over its directors. With their diverse business interests, members often have conflicting goals.

There are also, of course, the customers who buy and sell stocks through the exchanges and the corporations that list their shares for trading. If the markets provide greater liquidity to their shares, corporations will be able to raise capital at lower cost and thereby benefit not only their stockholders but society as a whole. And there is also the management of the stock exchange.

There may be instances when the desires and goals of one group within an exchange conflict with those of others. To complicate matters further, a stock market is a semi-public entity and, at least in the US, has a statutory obligation to serve other stakeholders as well. In the US, the two major stock markets are self-regulatory organizations (SROs).

Under the law, these entities are responsible for regulating their members and trading processes to ensure that the public is well served. Defining the 'public' is problematic when there are various constituencies who may not all share the same goals and interests.

Seldom proactive

As a result of these often competing constituencies, both the NYSE and Nasdaq have seldom been proactive in making significant changes in their systems. Contemplated changes have in the past often caused concern that they would result in lower profits for their members or in some way harm other constituencies.

More genteel times: the New York Stock Exchange in 1853

When major changes have taken place, they have often occurred in response to an outside event. For example, a study by William Christie and Paul Schultz published in December 1996 in the *Journal of Finance* served as a fillip for a wide governmental review of the trading practices on Nasdaq. The study found that the bids and offers for stocks on Nasdaq clustered more often on even eighths than on odd eighths. The researchers intimated that the only logical explanation was collusion. The report was widely covered in the press and struck a popular chord with the investing public.

The immediate result was a series of lawsuits alleging all sorts of misconduct on the part of Nasdaq and its members. The more substantive result, however, was a thorough examination of its structure by the Department of Justice and the Securities and Exchange Commission (SEC). Despite the unfavorable publicity, Nasdaq and most of its members resisted initiating any significant changes.

Ultimately, the SEC imposed its own solutions. First, it ruled that investors using Nasdaq as well as other markets had the right to display their limit orders to all traders. Second, it required that broker-dealers not post better prices to one group of investors without posting identical prices for all investors. Retail investors were now able to compete directly with broker-dealers.

These two changes have had an immediate impact in lowering the spreads on Nasdaq. Like any major changes, they will require time for their full impact to be manifested. Without this outside prod for change, the trading of Nasdaq stocks would have continued to fragment as investors tried to find alternative ways to reduce their trading costs. Some dealers will undoubtedly make less money as a result of these rules, but others in this new, more competitive, environment will make more.

This seems to be the model for how changes in these semi-public entities have happened. There is a trigger that ultimately leads to public examination of the institution and then to change. When the change is significant, it will in all likelihood have been mandated. The interests of the different constituencies seem to lead to paralysis on the part of the stock markets, necessitating changes from the outside.

The elimination of fixed commissions on the NYSE in May 1975 has been the most prominent and significant change imposed on the exchanges since the creation of the SEC in 1934. The catalyst was the excessive commissions charged under a fixed-rate schedule, which did not provide larger customers with any direct quantity discount. A third market then developed for trading NYSE-listed stocks off the floor of the exchange and, as a result, the NYSE began to lose market share.

The exchange and its members resisted the imposition of competitive rates, but in fact their introduction benefited not only the customer but also the member firms that embraced a more competitive world. These firms built up new areas of business, including investment banking, real estate and financial consulting. The subsequent years saw a virtually endless stream of new investment vehicles: negotiable certificates of deposit, floating-rate bonds, puttable bonds, zero-coupon bonds, stripped bonds, options, financial futures, options on indexes, cash management accounts, income warrants, collateralized mortgages, home equity loans, currency swaps, floor-ceiling swaps and exchangeable bonds.

As these new offerings came to the marketplace, investors found themselves with a plethora of choice. Yet, at the same time, investors' need for the NYSE was declining. Increasingly, these new financial tools were traded virtually anywhere but the NYSE. The NYSE had failed to keep pace with changes in the financial marketplace. Investors found they did not even need to buy shares of companies listed on the NYSE; they could buy equity futures and options in markets centered in Chicago. By 1984, the value of futures contracts equaled the value of stocks traded in New York; from 1986 through the crash of October 1987, the value of futures contracts exceeded the value of stocks traded by about 50 per cent.

Index futures and options were only the beginning. The explosion in the market for financial derivatives over the past few years, virtually all of which has taken place outside the structure of the NYSE, has been another clear demonstration of its inability to maintain its competitiveness in a rapidly changing economy.

The NYSE successfully resisted the SECUs ill-conceived call for a national market system – a regulatory call that would have replaced one entrenched system with another. In 1971 the SEC declared as 'a major goal and ideal of the securities markets and the securities industry ... the creation of a strong central market system for securities of national importance, in which all buying and selling interest in these securities could participate and be represented under a competitive regime'.

Electronic umbrella

What the SEC had in mind was the creation of an electronic umbrella under which the New York and American Stock Exchanges, the regional exchanges, the third and fourth markets and anybody else would compete among themselves, providing all the benefits of a fully competitive market. If virtually all market-makers and traders competed under a single national umbrella, it was believed, orders would flow in a more orderly fashion and competitive forces would eliminate monopolistic practices and reduce the need for government regulation.

In effect, the theory of the national market system contended that if competition among marketplaces could be eliminated, competition among market-makers and traders would be enhanced. Under such conditions the monopolistic practices of the NYSE that existed at the time would wither away only to be replaced by another monopolistic entity. The NYSE itself was not likely to wither away, however. Its proud 200-year history combined with its base of electronic communications and processing knowledge has made it a formidable institution. By reducing the power of the NYSE, the SEC would have caused the scrapping of the exchange's electronic infrastructure and its replacement it with an entirely new one. Instead, the competitive marketplace has caused new products and services to develop outside the structure of the NYSE or Nasdaq.

Today, institutions are the chief traders and they are as difficult to regulate as the individual was easy in 1934. Institutions can bypass brokers and trade with each other; they can create their own internal markets; and they can trade anywhere in the world at virtually any hour. Can either the NYSE or the US government control this marketplace? More important, should it? Has the combination of global competition and technology rendered the need for control unnecessary?

Competition has replaced regulation as the primary determinant of the marketplace and will probably continue to do so for good reason: it serves the investor's needs better. To regulate the securities trading of US citizens effectively, the US government would have to regulate investors themselves – an impossible task. In addition, in today's global economy regulation is effective only if it is global. It is highly unlikely that we will see global regulations for the securities marketplace in the near future. How will competition work? As the securities markets become more competitive and global, we can expect to see the same exciting changes, for better or worse, that occurred when the telecommunications industry first encountered genuine competition.

In the past, the cost of technology prevented new trading systems from challenging established institutions such as the NYSE. But today's technology is so inexpensive that over the next decade many new trading systems will spring up to satisfy investors' needs. Institutional investors in particular, after decades of paying the bid-ask spread to dealers, may decide to develop a trading system among themselves. Or private entrepreneurs might develop such a system for institutions to use.

Every financial system does, however, require intermediaries who guarantee the transaction. But in the competitive world of the future, these intermediary services may be much less costly than they are today. A truly competitive world is driven by the customer – the supplier of services and products adapts to what the customer wants.

The successful trading system or systems will provide what investors want at the lowest cost consistent with available technology. Thus the key to envisioning the future of the securities industry lies in an analysis of the needs of the industry's ultimate customers: investors themselves.

Institutional investors are increasingly concerned with the costs of managing money. Trading is one of their biggest costs, so they will constantly demand less expensive ways to do their trading. Indeed, whatever an institutional investor's need may be in the future, some entrepreneur will be likely to respond to it. Specifically tailored products for specific institutions aimed at hedging specific risks will proliferate.

A fully competitive world will drive innovation to such an extent that it will blur the distinction between equities and derivative assets; and because derivative assets are so much less costly to trade, the costs of managing money are likely to shrink.

Even in the highly computerized future, not all trades will go through automated systems, nor should they. Large block trades will still be executed between the parties involved and crossed outside any central trading system, which, in effect, is what happens now. But brokers will still be needed to bring these buyers and sellers together.

The difference will be this: instead of limiting these brokers to a finite number of NYSE specialists or licensed dealers or members of a specific stock market, computerization will enable anyone to become, in effect, a dealer or a specialist in a given stock. And overall, this opening-up of the trading process could enhance the liquidity of the market.

Conclusion

The NYSE and Nasdaq have changed considerably over the past 25 years but too often those changes have been mandated and imposed by governmental agencies. In the future, global competition and technology will force the NYSE and Nasdaq to become far more proactive in implementing changes. But we still see the stock markets dragging their feet when it comes to change.

Recently, the SEC has been focusing on reducing spreads by moving toward decimalization. The NYSE has kept quotes in eighths, guaranteeing a spread of one-eighth on dealer-handled trades. Some non-NYSE firms concluded that these spreads were too high and found an attractive niche for themselves by undercutting NYSE prices through rebates to brokerage firms. Again the NYSE lost market share but this time it was the retail customer who was being channeled to other markets. Following the new SEC rules, Nasdaq voted to reduce its minimum tick to one sixteenth. Two of the regional markets have already followed. Finally, the Board of the NYSE bowed to the inevitable and agreed to move to decimals with their smaller spreads and possibly lower dealer profits.

Again, outside pressure has forced the NYSE to become more competitive to the benefit of its ultimate customer, the public. Just as in 1975, these new SEC rules have made markets adjust to the current needs of investors. Significant changes in primary quasi-public institutions such as the big stock exchanges appear to require outside force. There seems to be too many diverse and conflicting interests within institutions such as the NYSE and Nasdaq for them to change from within. Yet, these institutions must learn how to embrace change.

We need the NYSE and Nasdaq, as well as other markets. Within a given geographic area, securities trading operates most efficiently when it is concentrated in a single market. In the past, that meant a single stock market in each big city; in the future, it will mean a single global stock market.

Whatever the similar capabilities of exchanges in London and Tokyo may be, the US has the world's most open and best-monitored marketplaces for investors and traders. For a combination of size, openness and endurance, the NYSE and Nasdaq are unique. Together they can provide the best infrastructure for the most direct and least painful transition to a global market. If they fail to lead, they will find themselves left behind in the global marketplace of the 21st century.

Summary

In this article Marshall Blume homes in on the New York Stock Exchange and Nasdaq and the pressures which have faced these uniquely large, open and resilient 'semi-public' entities.

The author says that too often over the past 25 years change has been imposed and mandated by government agencies and argues that in future global competition and technology will force the exchanges to become more proactive. In particular there has been foot dragging when it comes to the reduction of spreads.

The article ends with a prediction that the world is moving towards a single global stock market, and with the assertion that the NYSE and Nasdaq can provide the best infrastructure for the most direct and least painful transition to this state.

7

Debt markets

Contributors

Robert Z. Aliber is Professor of International Economics and Finance at the University of Chicago Graduate School of Business. He is Director of the school's Center for International Finance.

Kjell Nyborg is Associate Professor of Finance at London Business School. His research interests include corporate finance and information economics.

Michael R. Gibbons is the I.W. Burnham II Professor of Investment Banking and Chairperson of the Finance Department at the Wharton School of the University of Pennsylvania.

Walter N. Torous is Corporation of London Professor of Finance at London Business School. His research interests include option pricing and volatility in stock, bond and futures markets.

Richard Leftwich is Fuji Bank and Heller Professor of Accounting and Finance at the University of Chicago Graduate School of Business. His research interests include audit qualifications, bond ratings, corporate charter changes and block trades.

Harold Rose is Emeritus Esmée Fairbairn Professor of Finance at London Business School. He was previously first director of LBS' Institute of Finance and was Group Economic Adviser at Barclays Bank.

Contents

Introduction

The world's capital markets are a major source of funds for companies and governments alike. This module looks at recent capital market trends and controversies, including the arguments surrounding securitization and globalization, methodologies for predicting long-term and short-term bonds, and interest rate forecasting. It also contains a valuable overview of the role and performance of bond rating agencies such as Moody's and Standard and Poor's.

Why markets are still worlds apart

by Robert Aliber

Globalization is a front-row business buzzword of the 1990s. The large commercial and investment banks have offices in London, New York and Tokyo and in many of the second-tier financial centers such as Frankfurt, Zurich, Hong Kong and Singapore. Information available in one center is almost immediately available in the others. The costs of large crossborder money and security transactions are small, only trivially larger than comparable domestic transactions.

Arbitrageurs seek to exploit any small discrepancy in the prices of the same comparable securities in different national centers. The rush by a thousand mutual funds and pension funds to the emerging markets in the early 1990s is an example of how institutional arrangements evolve to exploit differences in anticipated returns on somewhat similar securities available in different countries.

One inference often made from these developments is that national financial markets are integrated; in other words, the prices of comparable securities in different centers should not differ significantly and hence the returns on these securities should be similar as long as controls and taxes do not constrain investors from moving funds towards those areas where the anticipated returns are higher. Despite the closer institutional and technological links, however, investors remain concerned about the impacts of changes in national monetary policies on inflation and exchange rates. This might be one reason why national markets remain segmented.

One way of looking at whether national financial markets are in fact globally integrated is to examine whether the 'dispersion,' or differences, in returns on comparable securities available in different markets is similar to the dispersion of returns on each of these securities within a single market. Economic intuition tells us that arbitrageurs will limit the dispersion of returns on securities that are close substitutes for each other.

Figures are available on the returns on comparable bonds, stocks and money market instruments for seven industrial countries for the period since 1960. While there are gaps and other shortcomings in the data, it seems unlikely that the lack of full information would bias the conclusions. Later in the article these returns are compared over the extended period from 1960 to 1996 and then for each of the four decades 1960s, 1970s, 1980s and the truncated 1990s.

These decades include many varied economic and financial characteristics. Rates of economic growth were high in the 1960s and most foreign currencies were pegged to the US dollar, although there were periodic crises over the sustainability of currency parities in the last few years of the decade. The 1970s were marked by two oil price shocks and accelerating inflation rates; the Bretton Woods system of pegged exchange rates was abandoned in the early years of the decade. The 1980s began with sharp increases in nominal and real interest rates, which led to a severe worldwide recession and then losses of $200bn to $300bn on bank loans to developing countries. The hallmark of the early 1990s was the collapse in prices of commercial real estate in

The early 1990s were marked by falling property prices and low inflation – despite a surge after the Gulf War

virtually every industrial country and the return to low inflation rates – the lowest in 30 years – after the brief surge in oil prices triggered by the Iraqi invasion of Kuwait.

Three types of returns are noted for each of the three types of securities. The first is the nominal, or local currency, return, the second is the real return where the nominal return is adjusted to reflect the national inflation rate, and the third is the US dollar rate of return, which is obtained by adjusting the holding period return on the security denominated in the foreign currency for the change in the foreign currency price of the dollar during that holding period. The bonds and stocks in these seven countries account for about 75 per cent to 80 per cent of the world market value of these securities.

One reason that nominal returns on comparable bonds denominated in different currencies might differ is that current or anticipated inflation rates differ. However, in a perfect foresight world the real returns on these securities would be similar because the difference in nominal returns would reflect both differences in national inflation rates and the rate of change of the exchange rate. Nominal returns also might differ because the bonds in some countries are riskier than those available elsewhere, in much the same way that BBB bonds are riskier than AAA bonds; however, these rankings in terms of default risk are likely to change slowly and infrequently.

If the real returns on comparable instruments denominated in various currencies are not dissimilar the inference is that the national markets are not segmented. A similar inference can be made if the dollar returns on foreign securities are not significantly different from the dollar returns on comparable US securities. Differences in the riskiness of the securities available in different countries are not likely to lead to significant differences in the relationship among the returns from one period to another.

A key question is whether there is a trend towards a smaller dispersion of returns in the last decade that would be consistent with the globalization blather.

Conceivably, real returns on comparable instruments available in each country might be similar while dollar returns on these same instruments would differ; in this case the changes in the price of the dollar in terms of various foreign currencies would not be reflected or anticipated in the difference in real interest rates on bonds and bills denominated in the different currencies. In contrast, if the dollar returns on comparable instruments available in different currencies are similar while the real returns differ, then the apparent puzzle is why arbitrageurs fail to equalize the real returns across countries.

Return on bonds

The nominal returns, the real returns and the dollar returns on government bonds available in seven industrial countries for the period 1960 to 1996 and then for the four separate decades are summarized in Figure 1. Each country's share of the market is shown in the brackets in the first row. The differences in the local currency returns on these comparable securities might reflect differences in national inflation rates as well as differences in various structural factors such as the liquidity of national markets.

For the extended period 1960–96, the real returns are lower than the nominal returns. However, the dispersion in the real returns is about as large as the dispersion in nominal returns. During this period, the dispersion among the dollar returns on these seven different bonds is somewhat larger than the dispersion in nominal returns

Fig.1 Return on bonds

		US (40.7%)	Canada (2.2%)	Japan (21.5%)	Germany (12.3%)	France (3.8%)	Italy (4.6%)	UK (2.5%)
1960–96	LC	7.03	8.27	7.53	7.39	8.43	9.53	8.82
	R	2.27	3.08	3.61	3.95	2.48	1.10	1.52
	US$	7.03	7.22	12.31	10.29	8.25	6.71	7.05
1960–69	LC	2.46	3.59	6.51	6.21	4.32	4.86	2.38
	R	-3.03	0.96	1.18	3.74	0.36	1.32	-1.26
	US$	2.46	2.36	6.97	7.51	3.09	4.78	0.82
1970–79	LC	5.64	6.53	6.82	7.85	7.45	6.38	7.41
	R	-1.62	-0.96	-1.98	2.73	-1.58	-5.92	-4.99
	US$	5.64	5.63	11.18	16.33	10.98	3.74	6.59
1980–89	LC	12.15	12.58	7.94	7.59	12.62	16.19	14.82
	R	6.71	5.99	5.48	4.69	5.34	5.05	7.35
	US$	12.15	12.68	13.62	7.80	8.59	10.99	11.14
1990–96	LC	8.58	11.64	8.57	8.17	9.95	12.05	12.57
	R	5.08	8.89	6.99	4.98	7.56	6.54	8.20
	US$	8.58	8.99	14.76	9.53	11.54	7.99	11.92

LC = Local currency; R = Real; NA = Not available

because the appreciation of the German mark and Japanese yen led to an increase in the dollar returns on bonds denominated in those currencies.

During the 1960s and again in the 1970s the dispersion in the real returns and the dispersion in the dollar returns on bonds was larger than the dispersion in the local currency returns on these securities. In the 1980s, in contrast, the dispersion in the real returns on bonds was smaller than the dispersion in the nominal returns but the dispersion in dollar returns was larger. In the 1990s the dispersion of real and nominal returns was about the same but the dispersion of dollar returns was substantially larger.

As the length of the holding periods is reduced from ten years to five and then to three and two years, the dispersion among the nominal, real and dollar increases. Lengthening the period tends to reduce the variation in returns. Moreover, the dispersion of the real and dollar returns in the 1990s does not appear smaller in the 1990s than in the 1960s. The data do not permit the inference that the dispersion of returns has diminished over time as the increase in integration view suggests.

Return on equities

The local currency returns, the real returns and the dollar returns for equities in the same seven countries are shown in Figure 2. (This data is compiled from International Financial Statistics and covers the 1960–95 period but excludes dividends and other work, which includes dividends but only begins in 1970.) Each country's share of world market valuation is shown in the brackets. During the extended period there was a relative tight grouping of nominal returns on equities; the dispersion in real returns

Fig.2 Return on equities

		US (40.7%)	Canada (2.1%)	Japan (20.6%)	Germany (3.3%)	France (3.2%)	Italy (1.3%)	UK (7.6%)
1960–96	LC	9.44	9.22	9.88	6.99	8.23	6.81	11.75
	R	4.53	4.08	4.76	3.51	2.18	-1.41	4.25
	US$	9.44	8.13	13.76	10.21	8.25	4.07	9.93
1960–69	LC	4.66	6.28	7.18	4.99	0.32	0.00	4.10
	R	2.11	3.59	1.56	2.55	-3.49	-3.38	0.38
	US$	4.66	5.03	7.22	6.28	-0.85	-0.08	4.66
1970–79	LC	4.61	11.98	12.67	2.22	6.78	-3.01	9.11
	R	-2.58	4.08	3.39	-2.63	-2.20	-14.22	-3.49
	US$	4.61	11.01	17.27	10.25	10.28	-5.41	1.86
1980–89	LC	17.13	11.51	22.24	16.12	21.97	28.66	23.22
	R	11.45	4.98	19.46	12.99	14.08	16.33	15.21
	US$	17.13	11.61	28.68	16.35	17.60	22.91	12.67
1990–96	LC	13.53	5.92	-8.03	3.93	2.96	2.67	11.24
	R	9.87	3.41	-9.37	0.60	0.63	-2.37	6.92
	US$	13.54	3.05	-2.78	6.91	5.85	-1.04	11.81

LC = Local currency; R = Real; NA = Not available

Fig.3 Return on bills

		US	Canada	Japan	Germany	France	Italy	UK
1960–96	LC	6.06	7.45	6.65	5.79	8.56	NA	9.16
	R	1.34	2.46	1.85	2.26	2.32	NA	1.22
	US$	6.06	6.40	9.96	8.94	8.36	NA	7.11
1960–69	LC	3.88	4.37	8.23	3.77	5.45	NA	6.45
	R	1.39	1.72	2.55	1.37	1.42	NA	2.19
	US$	3.88	3.14	8.27	5.34	3.00	NA	3.29
1970–79	LC	6.19	6.87	7.25	6.20	8.32	NA	8.19
	R	-1.11	-0.65	-1.59	1.16	-0.79	NA	-3.86
	US$	6.19	5.96	11.63	14.55	11.88	NA	7.86
1980–89	LC	8.94	11.26	6.40	5.98	10.74	14.80	11.28
	R	3.68	4.74	3.98	3.13	3.58	3.80	4.05
	US$	8.94	11.36	12.00	6.19	6.77	9.67	7.71
1990–96	LC	4.97	7.39	3.96	6.37	8.10	11.74	8.72
	R	1.58	5.26	3.01	3.24	5.75	6.25	4.50
	US$	4.97	4.84	7.16	7.72	9.66	7.70	8.09

LC = Local currency; R = Real; NA = Not available

was modestly larger than the dispersion of nominal returns and the dispersion in dollar returns was even larger.

During the 1960s the dispersion in real return and in dollar returns was larger than the dispersion of local currency returns. The dispersion of nominal, real and dollar returns in the 1970s and 1980s was extremely large. (The real returns on equities were negative in the US and four other countries in the 1970s.) Similarly, the dispersion of real and dollar returns in the 1990s was large, substantially more so than in the 1960s.

These comparisons are inconsistent with the view that national equity markets are integrated. A substantial part of the movement in equity prices reflects the changes in interest rates in each country and changes in the price of the dollar in terms of these foreign currencies.

Money market instruments

Figure 3 shows the nominal, real and dollar returns on the money market instruments available in these seven countries. The dispersion in the real returns over the extended period is smaller than the dispersion in the local currency returns. However, the dispersion in the dollar returns is larger than the dispersion in the nominal returns.

The dispersion in real and dollar returns on these money market instruments is generally smaller than the dispersion in nominal returns.

Conclusion

The combination of the sharp decline in the costs of communication and the globalization of financial services groups suggests that national financial markets have become more fully integrated; the importance of distance in segmenting national markets has declined – and perhaps sharply.

While investors more readily move funds among different national markets in search of higher returns, these markets might remain segmented because of concern about the losses from unanticipated changes in exchange rates, which in turn would reflect differences in inflation rates and changes in monetary policy. Systematic differences in the real returns on comparable securities denominated in different currencies can be viewed as the return required by the marginal investor for incurring crossborder risks.

The test of whether national markets are integrated or segmented is whether the dispersion of real returns and the dollar returns on the comparable securities in these different countries is significantly smaller than the dispersion in nominal returns. The dispersion in local currency returns might reflect differences in national inflation rates or the fact that investors believe that the 'riskless' securities denominated in one or two currencies are less sensitive to default risk than those denominated in other currencies. The smaller the dispersion of the real returns and the dollar returns in intervals like one and two years, the stronger the case that these national markets are integrated.

The data on the dispersion of real returns and dollar returns over the last four decades does not lend support to the view that these national markets are integrated. Differences among countries in their inflation rates and in anticipated nominal returns on comparable securities in the anticipated changes in the foreign exchange values of national currencies induce substantial crossborder movements of funds in search of higher returns. These capital flows have not proven large enough to reduce the differences in real returns to the values anywhere near comparable to the values that would be observed within any of the national markets. The dispersion of real returns and dollar returns on bonds and equities is large within each of the four decades and is significantly larger for holding periods shorter than those summarized in Figures 1–3.

Summary

Are national financial markets really as integrated as the hype would suggest? Following the strong accounting focus of the articles 'International accounting standards' and 'Creating a common accounting language' in Module 3, Robert Aliber widens the lens to look at the trend towards 'globalization'. By analyzing real and dollar denominated returns on comparable securities in seven industrial countries between 1960 and 1996, the author challenges conventional wisdom and comes to the conclusion that segmentation still rules. Economic intuition tells us that arbitrageurs will limit the differences between returns on securities that are close substitutes for each other. Closer institutional and technological links notwithstanding, crossborder capital flows have not proven large enough to reduce the differences in real returns to the values anywhere near comparable to the values that would be observed within any of the national markets. 'The dispersion of real returns and dollar returns on bonds and equities is large within each of the four decades' he observes.

Suggested further reading

Goetezmann, W.N. and Jorion, P., (1997), 'A Century of Global Stock Markets', Working paper 5901, National Bureau of Economic Research, Cambridge, Mass, January.

International Monetary Fund, *International Financial Statistics,* Washington, various issues.

Salomon Brothers, (1996), *How Big is The World Bond Market*, New York, August.

Siegel, J. J., (1994), *Stocks for the Long Run,* Dow Jones, Burr Ridge.
Siegel, L. B., (1997),'The $40 Trillion Market: Global Stock and Bond Capitalizations and Returns' *Quantitative Investing for the Global Market,* Peter Carman, Glenlake Publishing Co., Chicago.

The long and the short of investing in bonds

by Michael R. Gibbons

'Man won't fly for a thousand years'. So said Wilbur Wright to his brother Orville after a disappointing flight experiment in 1901. Happily, the Wright brothers did not bandon their quest. We might also say that it will be another 1,000 years before investment professionals and economists accurately predict long-term and short-term interest rates. But, notwithstanding any difficulties in making accurate predictions, investors still find attractive returns in bonds.

Professional and novice alike ask the same fundamental questions before investing in any bond: what return should a bond investor anticipate for holding bonds? Should the investor buy short-term or long-term bonds? What are the rewards associated with forecasting interest rates? And, most controversial, do professional investors generate superior returns?

Historical returns

Figure 1 provides some evidence from international bond markets on the historical average returns from investing in both short-term and long-term bonds. Bond investors across countries experienced a wide range of average nominal returns – from a low of 6.26 per cent for Japanese short-term bonds to 12.02 per cent for short-term bonds in the UK. Yet, despite this wide range of average returns on short-term bonds, the striking feature in Figure 1 is the consistently small difference in average returns for short-term versus long-term bonds within the same country. For

Fig.1 Average cash and bond returns, 1978–93

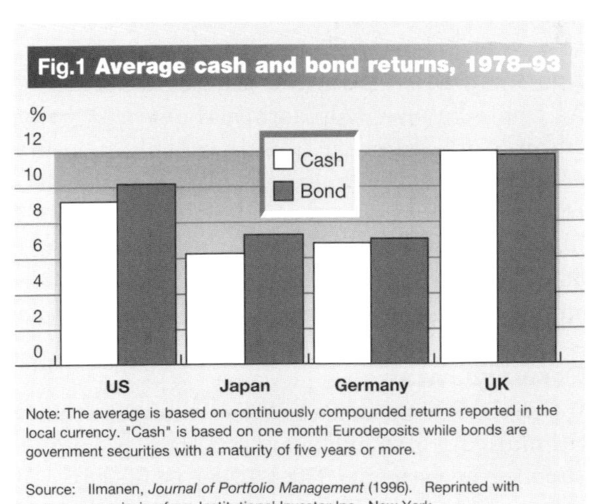

Note: The average is based on continuously compounded returns reported in the local currency. "Cash" is based on one month Eurodeposits while bonds are government securities with a maturity of five years or more.

Source: Ilmanen, *Journal of Portfolio Management* (1996). Reprinted with permission from Institutional Investor Inc., New York.

example, Japanese investors only earned 1.05 per cent more per year from investing in long-term bonds over short-term bonds, the largest difference among the five countries in Figure 1.

More surprising is the experience in the UK, where short-term bonds out-performed long-term bonds by 0.24 per cent per year. Despite the greater risk of holding long-term bonds relative to short-term bonds, the historical average returns suggest the compensation to bond investors who are willing to accept this risk is both economically and statistically insignificant.

Figure 1 is not very encouraging for long-term bond investors and the picture is not necessarily improved by calculating the average return for a longer historical time period. For example, the average return on long-term US government bonds is actually less than the average return on short-term US government bonds for much of the 1960s.

Whether or not the history of bond returns over the past 25 years is relevant for the future is not obvious for at least two reasons. First, investors did not expect interest rates to increase consistently, as they did from the mid-1960s until the early 1980s. Higher interest rates mean lower bond prices (and hence lower bond returns). Second, bond investors now anticipate more volatile returns on long-term bonds than they expected during the 1960s. Given such a belief, bond investors may demand higher returns than they received in the past to compensate this anticipated risk. Clearly, investors must think carefully before choosing long-term bonds over short-term bonds. The risk is obvious but the historical average return is low.

Are all short-term bonds the same?

If you decide to invest in short-term bonds, you still need to consider which maturity is best. Historically, there is a substantial difference between the average return on holding a 30-day bond versus the average return on holding, say, a three-month bond for 30 days.

If an investor is willing to hold a three-month bond or even a 12-month bond for 30 days, the historical evidence over the past 25 years suggests an added return of 80 to 160 basis points (on an annualized basis) relative to holding a 30-day bond until it matures. While the risk of a 12-month bond is greater than a 30-day bond, the added return is substantial.

Are long-term bonds a better bet?

As I noted above, the historical average return from buying long-term bonds is not significantly different from that of short-term bonds. While the average difference is small, there still may be situations where the long-term bond provides a significant return relative to the short-term bond. In fact, there is a substantial body of academic literature that suggests such situations can be identified where the forecasted return is economically and statistically significant relative to short-term bonds. Before summarizing the evidence, it will be helpful to digress and discuss forward rates.

Forward rates

If the yield to maturity on a two-year zero coupon bond is eight per cent while the yield till maturity on a one-year zero coupon bond is seven per cent, is the two-year bond a superior investment? The answer is, of course, it depends. It depends on what happens to interest rates. If the current yield curve persists (or, better yet, interest rates decrease), then the two-year bond is the superior investment. If future interest rates increase enough, then the current yield advantage of the two-year bond may not be sufficient to off-set future capital losses due to an increase in interest rates. Forward rates provide a tool for bond investors to calibrate the net benefit of current yields versus the risk of changes in future yields.

If one-year yields are seven per cent and two-year yields are eight per cent, then the forward rate F1, can be computed as:

$$(1 + F_1) = \frac{(1.08)^2}{1.07} \Rightarrow F_1 = 9.01\%$$

In general, the formula for computing a one-year forward rate on a $(T - 1)$ maturity, F_{T-1}, is to solve the following equation for F_{T-1}:

$$(1 + F_{T-1})^{T-1} = \frac{(1 + R_T)^T}{(1 + R_1)}$$

where R_T is the annually compounded rate on a T year zero coupon bond and R_1 is the annually compounded rate on a one-year zero coupon bond.

Forward rates computed in accordance with a specific formula provide answers to two 'what if' scenarios. For example, if current yields on one-year and two-year bonds are seven per cent and eight per cent, respectively, what if next year's yield on one-year bonds remain at seven per cent? Under this scenario the current forward rate we calculated to be 9.01 per cent is the rate of return an investor will realize from buying a two-year bond today and selling it as a one-year bond next year. Clearly, if interest rates remain constant, the two-year bond provides a substantial return (9.01 per cent) over the one-year bond (seven per cent). The forward rate measures this potential return.

What if a bond investor purchases the two-year bond and sells it as a one-year bond next year, assuming one-year interest rates increase from seven per cent to 9.01 per cent when the bond is sold? Under this scenario, the return from purchasing the two-year bond and selling it one year later is seven per cent, which is exactly the same return we would have received from a one-year bond and holding it until it matures. Thus, forward rates provide 'break-even rates', that is, they quantify the extent to which interest rates can increase before the capital loss on longer-term bonds dominates any yield advantage that they may offer.

In the prior example, if one-year rates increase less than 2.01 per cent (9.01 per cent – 7 per cent), than the one-year return on two-year bonds is superior to the one-year return on one-year bonds. Conversely, if one-year rates increase by more than 2.01 per cent, then the one-year bond turns out to provide a better return than the two-year bond.

These examples assume the two-year bond will be held for only one year and then sold. One could also analyze a situation in which the investor must decide between holding a two-year bond until it matures versus buying a one-year bond and then buying another one-year bond in one year. The break-even interpretation for forward rates is still applicable in such a setting.

What do forward rates forecast?

While forward rates provide a valuable tool to calibrate the relative desirability of holding short-term bonds versus long-term bonds, forward rates could also serve as a useful way to forecast future interest rates or bond returns.

Returning to our example, the current one-year yield is seven per cent and the two-year yield is eight per cent. If bond investors anticipated an increase in interest rates and if bond investors wanted bonds of all maturities to earn approximately the same as the one-year yield of seven per cent, then the current forward rate of 9.01 per cent could be a forecast of short-term interest rates to be observed in one year. We could think of this 9.01 per cent as a forecast that is implicit in current bond market yields (or prices) and which represents a consensus view among bond investors who are competing among one another in determining market prices for bonds.

Alternatively, bond investors may anticipate that the yield curve will not change over the next year and may desire that bonds of different maturities earn different expected rates of return. Under these assumptions the forward rate of 9.01 per cent is a forecast of the return on buying a two-year bond and selling it in one year when it has one year until it matures. Thus, the forward rate is not forecasting future interest rates but holding period returns.

Most evidence suggests that forward rates are not good predictors of interest rates to be observed in the near term. For example, forward rates are on average too high relative to future interest rates. This suggests that bond investors expect to earn on average a premium for holding long-term bonds relative to short-term bonds.

More surprising is the evidence suggesting that when forward rates are high (that is, the yield on long-term bonds is above the yield on short-term bonds), future yields on long-term bonds are more likely to go down, not up. While this evidence is based primarily on US data, there is some support in the data from other countries. Furthermore, the academic research that supports this conclusion has a long history, dating back more than 60 years.

Consider the implications of this empirical finding for investment strategies. When long-term bonds offer a yield advantage over short-term bonds, they are also likely to generate a capital gain from decreases in future interest rates. Such behavior could justify a bond investment strategy known as 'riding the yield curve' – an investment policy of lengthening the maturity of the bond portfolio whenever yields on long-term bonds exceed the yields on short-term bonds.

Table 1 provides a summary of the potential returns from buying long-term bonds when their yield is high relative to short-term bonds. While long-term bonds may not offer on average a return significantly more than short-term bonds, there are nevertheless periods when an investor could expect a substantial profit from investing in long-term bonds – namely when the yield curve is steeply upward-sloping.

Some caveats

Table 1 suggests that there is a useful and simple investment strategy that could provide superior returns to bond investors. Certainly, other strategies could be designed using similar information and more sophisticated approaches would be expected to enhance the performance. However, this empirical evidence is not without its weaknesses.

First, the usefulness of any

Table 1

Average return of the 20-year US treasury bond in months that begin with inverted, mildly upward-sloping, or steep yield curves, 1970–1994

Spread 20 year yield minus 1 month yield	Number of returns	Annualized returns
Less than 0 basis points	45	-2.57%
0 to 300 basis points	148	9.41%
Greater than 300 basis points	107	12.46%

Source: Ilmanen, *Journal of Fixed Income* (1996). Reprinted with permission from Institutional Investor, Inc., New York

empirical analysis always hinges on the extent to which history is a reliable guide to the future. Researchers have studied a number of strategies using past data. It would not be surprising to find something that worked in the past, but the key issue is, will it work in the future? For example, research suggests that forward rates seem to have some power to forecast interest rates in the more distant future (three to five years ahead), even though the forecasts are not very good in the near term. Furthermore, the forecasting power of forward rates, even for future interest rates in the near term, has improved recently.

Second, even if forward rates were useful in forecasting bond returns, the investment strategies that exploit these forecasts could prove very expensive. Table 1 does not incorporate the cost of trading when the yield curve changes and requires a switch to or from long-term bonds. Investors should calculate their returns net of all transactions costs.

Third, if the high average returns in Table 1 also occur when investors are required to accept high risks and vice versa, then the return may just be compensation for willingness to bear risk. Investors have a variety of ways to achieve high average returns if they are willing to bear risk and the results in Table 1 may not be significant after accounting for these opportunities. The academic research on the extent to which Table 1 reflects a premium for risk is still on-going. However, we do know that the shape of the term structure seems to be related to business cycles.

Other variables

While academic research has focused on forward rates (or the spread in yields between long-term and short-term bonds) as a useful variable to forecast future interest rates or bond returns, this is not the only variable that has been examined. For example, my colleague David Musto, in 'The end-of-the-year show' (Module 6), discusses the seasonal behavior of interest rates around the end of the year and to some extent even around the end of quarters. Professor Musto attributes some of this seasonal pattern to financial institutions which may be 'window dressing' their balance sheets around the time financial reports are produced.

Furthermore, bond and stock markets are reasonably well integrated. If certain variables are useful in forecasting stock returns, it is not surprising that these same variables may forecast bond returns. Gabriel Hawawini and Donald Keim summarized some of the relevant variables in forecasting stock returns in their article 'Beta, size and price/book: three measures or one?'.

Future stock returns seem to be associated with current information about the spread between the yield on low-grade and default-free debt, dividend yields on stocks and the level of interest rates (not just the spread between the yield on long-term and short-term bonds). There is evidence to suggest that these same variables may forecast future bond returns as well.

While all these variables show some promise of predicting future bond returns, the academic community continues to investigate the effectiveness of this information. Naturally, all the caveats of the prior section apply to this list of variables.

How good are forecasts?

The previous sections suggest simple approaches to forecasting interest rates on bond returns. Are professional economists better at forecasting than these simple approaches? The short answer is no. Based on a number of academic investigations of professional forecasts, it seems clear that professional economists find it difficult to beat a simple approach that always predicts that future interest rates are equal to current rates.

Professional economists make substantial errors in their forecasts and many times even fail to predict accurately the direction of the change from current rates. It would seem that professional economists could improve the accuracy of their forecasts by properly incorporating the variables discussed above.

Even if published forecasts of future interest rates are inaccurate, it may be that professional money managers are good at structuring their investment portfolios. Professional money managers do not necessarily publish their forecasts of future interest rates but they make investment decisions in the light of their forecasts. If their forecasts are good, then their investment performance should reveal substantial profits. Unhappily, the performance of bond mutual funds has not been very good relative to some simple alternative investments. After accounting for management fees, bond mutual funds tend to under-perform very simple passive investment strategies. For example, a mutual fund that attempts to mimic the performance of well-known and published bond indices will out-perform most bond mutual funds. The size of this under-performance is approximately equal to average management fees.

It appears that an increase in a percentage point of expenses leads to a percentage point drop in the performance. Thus investors should seek bond mutual funds with the lowest expenses since good performance seems to be correlated with the low expenses. Furthermore, current expenses of a mutual fund tend to predict future expenses, so future performance should be linked to the current expenses of a mutual fund. Looking at current expenses is probably a better predictor of future performance than looking at the past performance of a bond mutual fund. A successful bond mutual fund in the past is not a reliable indicator of successful performance in the future.

Conclusions

While there is evidence to suggest that bond returns can be predicted, the investor should be wary. Increasing the maturity of one's portfolio of bonds to take advantage of currently high yields and/or anticipate decreases in future yields is a risky strategy.

First, the historical average return on long-term bonds is not significantly higher than the historical average return on short-term bonds. Second, professional investors who manage bond mutual funds as well as economists have a lacklustre historical track record on average.

Nevertheless, there may be some worthwhile opportunities. For example, if an investor is holding very short-term bonds (say 30 days to maturity), it probably pays to extend the average maturity to three months or perhaps as long as one year.

Summary

In this article Michael Gibbons looks at returns from long-term and short-term bonds and weighs the evidence for the likelihood of being able to predict those returns. He also considers whether forward rates on bonds can be used to predict future interest rates.

Sadly, the evidence on both is mixed, though the author provides some simple approaches to forecasting interest rates. And, it is pointed out, these approaches are at least as good as the track record of professional economic forecasters.

Finally, although the historical average return on long-term bonds is not

significantly higher than that on short-term bonds, the author does suggest that an individual investor holding very short-term bonds (30 days) might like to consider extending their maturity to three months or even a year.

Suggested further reading

Blake, C.R., Elton, E.J., Gruber, M.J., (1993), 'The performance of bond mutual funds', *Journal of Business* 66, July 371–403.

Campbell, J.Y., (1995), 'Some lessons from the yield curve', *Journal of Economics Perspectives* 9, Summer, 129–152.

Ilmanen, A., (1996), 'Does duration extension enhance long-term expected returns?', *Journal of Fixed Income* 6, September, 23–36.

Ilmanen, A., (1996), 'When do bond markets reward investors for interest rate risk?', *Journal of Portfolio Management* 22, Winter, 52–64.

Evaluating the bond-rating agencies

by Richard Leftwich

Bond ratings now play an important role in most established capital markets and in many emerging markets. The bond rating industry originated in the US where public debt markets are well developed and has been expanding as those markets have grown in other countries and as non-US debt issuers have sought access to US capital markets.

A bond rating is an assessment of the default risk of a bond by an independent private agency. The ratings do not reflect other risks, such as interest rate risk, associated with investing in bonds nor are bond ratings recommendations to buy or sell particular bonds. They are specific to the quality of a particular debt issue. Companies in poor financial shape can issue highly-rated debt, for example by securing that debt against valuable assets or through third-party credit enhancement.

Ratings are a convenient label for the default risk of the bond, particularly for many regulatory and legal purposes. However, academic research demonstrates that they are more than a convenient label. Rating agency decisions convey information to the capital market, probably because the agencies have access to confidential data about an issuer's financial health and prospects.

Major players

Bond ratings were first published in the US by John Moody in 1909 and had their origins in the credit evaluation process developed by Dun and Bradstreet. Ironically, John Moody's company was acquired by Dun and Bradstreet in 1962.

There are now four big providers of bond ratings for publicly traded debt in the US: Standard and Poor's (S&P), Moody's Investors Service (Moody's), Fitch Investors Service (Fitch), and Duff and Phelps' Credit Rating Company (Duff and Phelps). S&P

John Moody first published bond ratings in 1909

and Moody's have the dominant share of the US market, split almost equally between them. Big players outside the US include: Australian Ratings (now owned by S&P), Canadian Bond Rating Service, Dominion Bond Rating Service (Canada), Japan Bond Research Institute (JBRI), Japan Credit Rating Agency (JCR), Nippon Investors Services (NIS), Agence d'Évaluation Financière (ADEF, a French agency now owned by S&P), Thai Rating and Information Service (TRIS) and Rating Agency Malaysia (RAM). Ratings for debt that is not publicly traded are provided to institutional clients by the larger players and by boutique organizations but are seldom disclosed publicly.

Other rating agencies specialize in the banking and insurance industries. For example, AM Best Company rates the claims-paying ability of insurance companies and Thomson Bankwatch and International Bank Credit Analysis (IBCA) in the UK rate the creditworthiness of a variety of obligations of banks and financial institutions. Although the bigger rating agencies have introduced similar bank and insurance rating products, the specialists dominate those industries.

Rating agencies assign debt issues to discrete risk categories and label those categories with letters. Table 1 lists the letter grades used by the big US agencies together with the summary interpretation given by S&P for each rating category or class. The industry has virtually standardized on the letter grade rating system employed by S&P. Fitch first used these symbols, a variant on John Moody's symbols, in 1922 and sold the rights to the symbols to S&P in 1960.

Debt rated BBB and above is classed as investment grade. Originally, debt below BBB was classed as speculative. Since the early 1980s that debt has been labeled 'junk', a marketing faux pas that rivals the most notorious consumer marketing gaffes. The term 'high yield' is slowly replacing the pejorative junk label.

The investment-grade label has considerable significance from a regulatory standpoint, especially in the US and Japan. For example, many US financial institutions are allowed to invest in investment-grade securities only. Table 2 lists some US regulations that rely on security ratings. In addition, state laws and legal precedents restrict the investments of trusts and fiduciaries to investment-grade securities.

Most of these laws and regulations require that the rating be given by a Nationally Recognized Statistical Rating Organization (NRSRO), a designation bestowed by the Securities and Exchange Commission (SEC). The NRSRO designation process is somewhat mysterious and considerably frustrating for non-US ratings agencies. There are no formal criteria for the designation and it is alleged that applications from several non-US rating agencies have been in limbo for several years. Each of the four major US players is an NRSRO; IBCA and Thomson Bankwatch are NRSROs for a restricted set of securities, essentially those issued by banks and financial institutions. Similar designations are made in other countries.

Table 1: Letter grades used by major US rating agencies: corporate bond ratings

AGENCY S&P	Moody's	Fitch	Duff & Phelps	EXPLANATION OF RATING (Standard & Poors)
Investment				
AAA	Aaa	AAA	AAA	Capacity to pay interest and repay principal is very strong.
AA	Aa	AA	AA	Strong capacity to pay interest and repay principal and differs from the highest rated debt only in small degree.
A	A	A	A	Strong capacity to pay interest and repay principal, although it is somewhat more susceptible to adverse effects of changes in circumstances and economic conditions than debt in higher-rated categories.
BBB	Baa	BBB	BBB	Adequate capacity to pay interest and repay principal. Normally exhibits adequate protection parameters, but adverse economic conditions or changing economic circumstances are more likely to lead to weakened capacity to pay. **(Debt below this rating is regarded as having predominantly speculative characteristics with respect to capacity to pay interest and repay principal).**
Speculative				
BB	Ba	BB	BB	**Less near-term vulnerability to default than other speculative grade debt. However, it faces major on-going uncertainties or exposure to adverse business, financial, or economic conditions that could lead to inadequate capacity to meet timely interest and principal payments.**
B	B	B	B	**Greater vulnerability to default but presently has the capacity to meet interest payments and principal payments. Adverse business, financial, or economic conditions would likely impair capacity or willingness to pay interest and repay principal.**
CCC	Caa	CCC	CCC	**Has a current identifiable vulnerability to default, and is dependent on favorable business, financial, or economic conditions to meet timely payment of interest and repayment of principal. In the event of adverse business, financial, or economic conditions, the obligor is not likey to have the capacity to meet its financial commitment on the obligation.**
CC		CC		**Highly vulnerable to nonpayment. (Fitch: Default seems probable).**
C	Ca	C		**A bankruptcy petition has been filed, but payments are continuing. (Fitch: Default is imminent).**
D	C	DDD/DD/D	DD	**The issue is in payment default or a bankruptcy petition has been filed. Rating is used when interest or principal payments are not made on the due date, even if the applicable grace period has not expired, unless S&P believes that such payments will be made during such grace period. (Fitch: DDD has highest recovery potential, D has lowest).**

S&P uses + and – qualifiers to create three sub-classes within rating grades AA to CCC. e.g. A+, A, A–. Moody's uses 1, 2, and 3 qualifiers to create three sub-classes Aa to B. e.g. Ba1, Ba2, Ba3. Fitch uses + and – qualifiers to create three sub-classes AA to C. Duff & Phelps uses + and – qualifiers to create three sub-classes AA to B.

Each of the rating agencies has extended its product range to provide ratings on a wide range of fixed-income products extending from short-term commercial paper to structured finance transactions. Although the rating scales often differ from the letter grades used for the standard bond ratings and, for some products (for example counterparty risk and claims-paying ability), the issuer, not the issue, is rated. Table 3 lists some of those products.

Table 2: US laws and regulations employing debt ratings

Focus of law or regulation

- Investment policy of money market funds, banks, pension funds, insurance companies.
- Haircuts for capital requirements of the broker-dealers, banks, and insurance companies.
- Listing of debt securities on the Amex and NYSE.
- Margin requirements set by stock exchanges.
- Shelf registration requirements.
- Securities underwritten by banks.
- Registration requirements for foreign insurers.

Promulgator of law or regulation

- SEC, Federal Reserve Board, Office of the Controller of the Currency, Federal Home Loan Bank, Department of Labor, National Association of Insurance Commissioners, NYSE, Amex, various state insurance company regulatory bodies.

Table 3: Rated securities and claims

Securities	***Institutions***
Corporate bonds	Sovereign credit
Municipal bonds	Counterparty risk
Commercial paper	Claims paying ability (insurance companies)
Certificates of deposit	Solvency (insurance companies)
Preferred stock	Exchange and clearing houses
Mutual bond funds	Special purpose derivative product subsidiaries
Money market funds	Sovereign issuers
Asset-backed securities:	Local government investment pools
Residential mortgages	International banks
Commercial mortgages	
Manufactured housing loans	
Trade receivables	
Equipment leasing trusts	
Tax liens	
Credit card receivables	
Mutual fund fees	
Small business loans	
Non-performing loans	

The rating process

The rating agencies provide an initial rating for a debt issue and monitor that issue during its life. Rating agencies base their decisions, in part, on publicly available data about the issue, the company, the industry and the economy. In addition, most agencies visit the business, interview key managers and obtain private information about performance, budgets, plans and forecasts. Some rating agencies employ statistical classification models, although ultimately, the rating is a judgment based on quantitative and qualitative data.

Most agencies give the organization advance notice of a proposed rating or proposed rating change and allow management an opportunity to respond. The ratings and rating changes are carried by financial newswires such as Reuters and PR Newswire, displayed on trading screens (such as Bloomberg and Telerate), reported in regular publications of the agencies and reviewed in the financial press.

Originally, rating services derived their revenue primarily from fees charged to subscribers to the rating bulletins. Now the revenues of US agencies come almost entirely from fees charged to the issuer of the security, although subscription fees are still important in some other markets outside the US. Typical issuer fees include an initial fee based on the size and complexity of the issue, together with monitoring fees. Both S&P and Moody's have a policy of publishing ratings for all large corporations with significant outstanding debt, even if the issuer does not solicit the rating. Presumably, these unsolicited ratings enhance the comparability of solicited ratings.

Some controversies

The 1970s were difficult for the rating agencies. Criticism came from politicians, issuers and investors and the rating agencies were threatened with government supervision. The agencies are always tempting political targets for politicians from cities and districts that face higher borrowing costs as a result of an 'unjustified' (in the politicians' view) bond rating downgrade. For example, the New York City financial crisis in the 1970s placed the agencies in a predicament. At one stage, S&P suspended the ratings on city debt and was vilified for causing, or at least exacerbating, the subsequent financial chaos. On the other hand, Moody's retained its A rating (perhaps attempting to counteract its 'me too' image). The bonds eventually defaulted and investors criticized the relatively safe rating assigned by Moody's. In another example, the Australian government forbade any contact with Moody's after losing its AAA rating in 1986.

Other spectacular financial collapses led to accusations that the agencies respond to bad news too slowly, perhaps out of concerns for the issuer who pays the rating fees. The most often cited examples of the alleged tardiness involve two instances where prominent companies (WT Grant and Penn Central) declared bankruptcy when their debt was highly rated and that of the real estate investment trusts and insurance companies in the 1970s. In the latter case their ratings were not changed until they experienced severe financial difficulties.

The corporate restructuring wave of the 1980s brought home a limitation of bond ratings that, although freely acknowledged by the agencies, had been ignored by many investors. Bond ratings do not reflect the vulnerability of the bond to what is known as 'event risk' – extraordinary changes in the financial or operating characteristics of a business. For example, some bonds are poorly protected by covenants. The default risk of those bonds changes dramatically if a company takes on massive quantities of additional debt or if it is acquired by a much riskier business. In several highly publicized instances, holders of highly rated debt experienced large losses when these events occurred. Despite disclaimers by the rating agencies, many critics attributed these losses to inadequate investigation by the agencies.

Similarly, the financial engineering innovations of the 1990s created securities with complex option-like features (such as mortgage-backed securities and their components) whose value could fluctuate dramatically even if their default risk was minimal. Currently, the antitrust division of the Justice Department is investigating the ratings industry for evidence of anti-competitive practices, apparently focusing on the issuing of unsolicited ratings.

Recent developments

In response to some of these criticisms, the rating agencies have greatly expanded their staffs, adopted new technology, worked at improving the timeliness of their ratings and stepped up their public relations efforts. In particular, in 1981 S&P introduced Credit Watch, which provides an early warning of a rating revision. Other major rating agencies quickly followed with similar services. All of the large agencies now have electronic services that notify subscribers of potential and actual ratings and revisions. The rating agencies have expanded not only the range of claims they rate but also, in response to criticisms discussed above, the types of ratings they issue. For example, S&P now issues supplementary ratings about event risk, designated E1–E5. These ratings are based on an analysis of the protection afforded by covenants, collateral and other contractual features of the issue (such as a put feature). They reflect judgment about an issue's susceptibility to loss if a deleterious event occurs but not the likelihood of such an event happening.

As public debt markets developed and expanded outside the US, S&P has grown internationally with an aggressive acquisition and affiliation strategy and both S&P and Moody's have opened local offices throughout the world. Foreign rating agencies have not penetrated the US market to any great extent, perhaps reflecting the barriers created by the NRSRO certification process.

Fig.1 Industrial yields, spreads and interest coverage

July 1988 – December 1994

	AAA	AA	A	BBB	BB	B	T-bond
Interest coverage	13.90	9.40	4.50	2.70	1.60	0.80	
Average yield (%)	8.49	8.81	9.26	9.74	10.96	12.86	7.96
Std dev yield (%)	0.88	0.87	0.84	0.94	1.21	2.34	0.94
Average spread (bp)	53.40	84.90	130.40	178.30	300.50	489.60	
Std dev spread (bp)	18.20	18.40	20.40	35.40	67.00	194.40	

January 1983 – December 1994

	AAA	AA	A	BBB	BB	B	T-bond
Interest coverage	13.80	9.20	5.10	3.00	2.00	1.20	
Average yield (%)	9.43	9.79	10.14	10.70			
Std dev yield (%)	1.53	1.53	1.47	1.58			
Average spread (bp)	49.00	85.00	120.50	176.80			
Std dev spread (bp)	25.40	28.00	29.80	35.40			

Source: Standard and Poor's *CreditWeek*

Performance evaluation

Evaluating the performance of rating agencies requires an appreciation of their economic purpose. In principle, the agencies have at least two roles: information processors and certifiers. The first role is primarily market driven; the second is primarily driven by regulation.

If there are economies of scale and special skills or training associated with information gathering and processing, rating agencies can reduce search costs by providing investors with information about the default risk of bonds, just as restaurant guides can provide value to discerning diners. Moreover, published debt ratings reduce the information costs of others who contract with an organization (such as suppliers, customers and employees) and are concerned about the company's financial health. In particular, ratings can reduce the costs associated with evaluating counterparty risk in over-the-counter derivatives transactions.

Certification demand is driven by laws and regulations that restrict the investment behavior of financial institutions, such as those described in Table 2. Certification demand is partly market driven because it reduces the cost of writing contracts by providing a convenient summary statistic (the bond rating, akin to a restaurant's rating in the Michelin guide.) For example, security ratings allow a corporation to restrict the behavior of someone in charge of short-term cash management to investing in securities with at least a given rating.

Academic research has emphasized the information content of bond ratings, the accuracy of bond ratings and the extent to which ratings can be predicted with publicly available information.

Timeliness of the information is more crucial with regard to information than for certification. Rating changes provide information to investors only if that information is not already incorporated in the price of the security. Research demonstrates that the announcement of a rating change for the debt of an organization affects the price of the

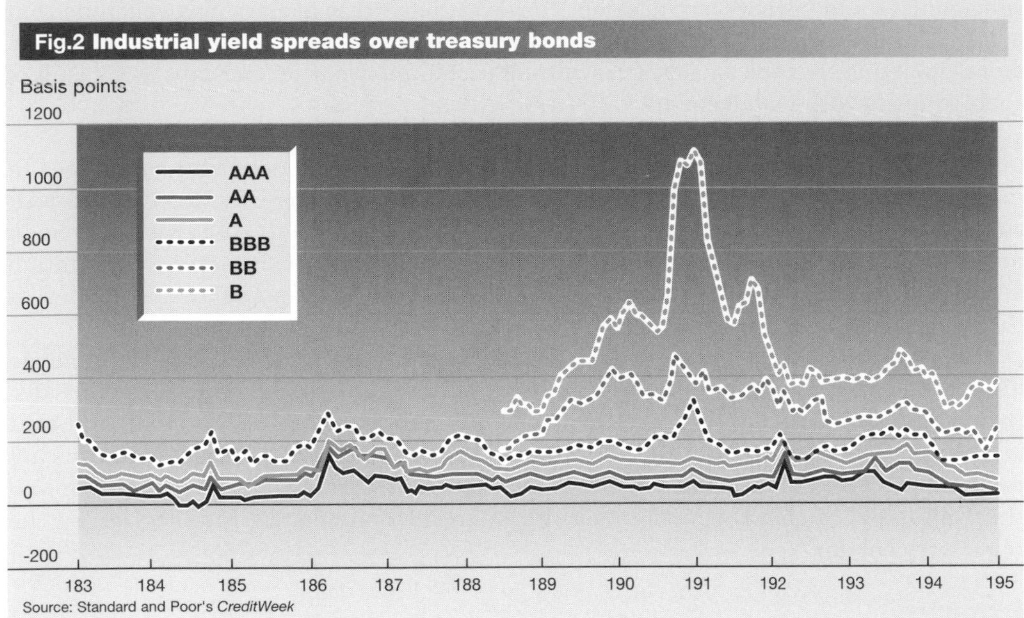

debt and the company's equity. The effects are stronger for downgrades than for upgrades, though the effect is relatively small (less than two per cent of the market value for the two-day period around the announcement). Furthermore, the rating changes follow much larger changes in the price of the security, suggesting that much of the information leading to the rating decision is incorporated in the security's price by the time the change is announced.

Of course, if it were not for the looming presence of the rating agencies, some of that earlier information might not be released as quickly. Does this mean that the agencies act too slowly? Research has yet to answer that question because the optimum speed of action depends on unknowns such as the costs and benefits of gathering and disseminating information more rapidly. However, competition among rating agencies should provide incentives for the agencies to provide more timely information if it is cost effective. Some of the innovations such as Credit Watch and the increased use of electronic dissemination of rating changes are examples of agencies reacting to their perception of market demand. The accuracy of bond ratings has been addressed by studies of bond yields and returns (*see* Figures 1 and 2). Yields on bonds are highly correlated with bond ratings. Yields vary within rating classes, providing evidence that investors do not accept ratings mindlessly, though there is not enough evidence to address the question thoroughly.

Conclusion

Actual returns on bonds strongly support the view that ratings provide reliable implicit assessments of the probability and magnitude of default. The track record for lower-rated investment-grade bonds, though, has been documented conclusively only recently and the rate of return earned by junk bonds remains an open question, primarily due to data limitations.

Academic research demonstrates that bond ratings can be predicted with a high degree of accuracy with publicly available data, leading some to question what value the agencies add beyond certification. However, most researchers now conclude that bond yields are associated more strongly with ratings than with publicly available data alone, implying that the agencies provide additional information, perhaps as a result of their contacts with management.

The alleged monopoly power of the rating agencies is difficult to substantiate. S&P and Moody's have dominant shares of the US market, as do successful businesses in many markets, especially if there are economies of scale. In the US, Moody's and S&P compete for new business and both Fitch and Duff and Phelps aggressively seek market share and introduce new products and services. The niche companies maintain large market shares in their areas of specialization, despite attempts by the big players to invade their turf.

Outside the US, there are strong independent competitors in some of the large markets such as Japan and the UK but S&P and Moody's have made some inroads. Ironically, there is a barrier to entry in the US market, the NRSRO label, and that barrier is created by regulators. No such barrier exists for organizations ranking mutual fund performance and a vigorous new entrant (Morningstar) has revolutionized that industry. Such a revolution is unlikely in the bond rating industry given the regulatory barrier.

Summary

Anyone even vaguely familiar with capital markets has heard of Moody's and Standard and Poor's (S&P). But just what role do bond ratings agencies play in helping assess risk? Richard Leftwich traces the history of the agencies both inside and outside the United States, describes how they actually go about their business, and recalls those occasions when they have run into controversy with issuers and investors. S&P, for example, was accused of exacerbating New York City's financial crisis in the 1970s, while there have been allegations (difficult to substantiate) of monopoly power.

Leftwich points out that ratings are more than just a convenient label for the default risk of a bond. 'Most researchers now conclude', he writes, 'that bond yields are associated more strongly with ratings than with publicly available data alone, implying that the agencies provide additional information, perhaps as a result of their contact with management'.

Suggested further reading

A.M. Best *http://www.ambest.com*
Brady bonds and debt of emerging markets *http://www.bradynet.com*
Duff and Phelps Credit Rating Co.*http://www.dcro.com*
Fitch Investors Services *http://www.fitchinv.com*
Japan Bond Rating Institute *http://www.jbri.com/jbri-eng.htm*
Moody *http://www.moodys.com*
Standard and Poor's *http://www.ratings.com*
Thomson Bankwatch *http://www.bankwatch.com*

Rationale for convertible bonds

by Kjell Nyborg

Convertible bonds are hybrid instruments which have both debt and equity characteristics. Like straight bonds, they are entitled to receive coupons and principal payments. However, the holders of convertible bonds can forego these cash flows by converting their bonds into a prespecified number of shares.

To price convertible bonds it is, therefore, essential to characterize this option. This article will show that, in their simplest form, convertible bonds can be divided into a straight bond and a warrant component. Pricing is then a matter of pricing individual components and adding up. The article will then address the delayed equity and sweetening debt rationales for issuing convertibles.

Pricing warrants

The first step in pricing convertible bonds is to understand how to price straight bonds and warrants. Pricing straight bonds is just a matter of discounting the coupons and the principal at an appropriate rate. Pricing warrants is a little more complicated. Warrants are corporate securities which give the holder the right to buy shares from the corporation at a specified price and at specified dates. Warrants are, therefore, call options. They are similar to standard exchange traded stock options. There are, however, three important differences:

- when warrants are issued the company receives the issue price (so that its assets increase)
- when warrants are exercised the company receives the exercise price
- when warrants are exercised the company issues new shares.

Here we will focus on how the last two items affect the pricing of warrants relative to standard call options. Consider an all-equity company that has N shares and M warrants outstanding. Assume each warrant can be converted into r shares at an exercise price of k per new share.

Suppose the maturity date of the warrants has been reached. The question to be addressed first is whether the warrants will be exercised if the value of the assets of the company, without warrants being exercised, equals V^*. This is a simple question of whether the value of the shares warrantholders receive by exercising is worth more than the exercise price they pay more for them.

On exercising, warrantholders will receive Mr newly created shares, for which they pay Mrk. Hence the company's number of shares will increase to $N+Mr$ and firm value will be V^*+Mrk. The fraction of all shares owned by warrantholders is therefore

$$\lambda = \frac{Mr}{N + Mr}$$

The Greek letter λ is the dilution factor of the warrants.

Value of shares received by warrantholders if they exercise = $\lambda(V^* + Mrk)$

Total exercise price = Mrk

Hence, the net value (or payoff) at maturity is: $\max[\lambda(V^* + Mrk) - Mrk, 0]$

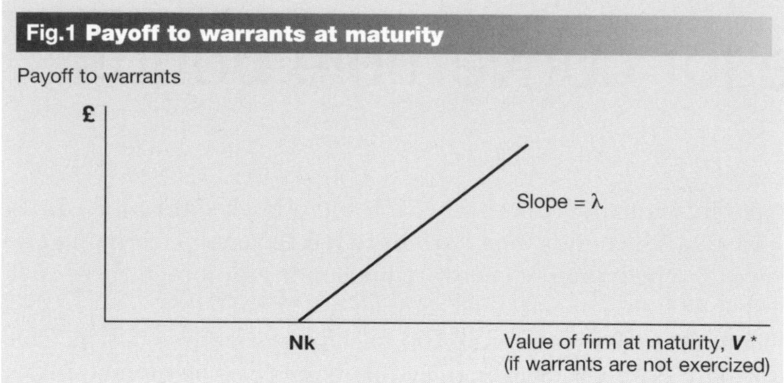

Fig.1 Payoff to warrants at maturity

This reflects the fact that warrantholders will only exercise if the net value from exercising is greater than zero. This can be rewritten as:

$$\lambda \max [V^* - Nk,0]$$

This equation is drawn in Figure 1. This looks a lot like the payoff diagram to a call option.

The main differences are as follows:

- The slope of the payoff line for a standard call option is 1. For the warrant the slope is $Mr/(N+Mr)$, which represents the dilution factor of the warrants. This is the fraction of all shares owned by the former warrantholders after exercise. It tells us that the warrants can be interpreted as a *fraction of a call option.*
- The payoff of a standard call option is a function of the stock price. Looking at Figure 1, however, we see that the payoff of a warrant can be written as a function of V^* the company's assets at maturity if the warrants are not exercized. So the warrants can be interpreted as a fraction of a call option on the concern's assets. If the firm were geared, the payoff to the warrants could be viewed as a fraction of a call option on the firm's equity.

Both these differences are a direct consequence of warrantholders receiving new shares when they exercise. After exercise, the former warrantholders hold a fraction of the company's equity. Hence, before exercise, the warrants can be viewed as a fraction of an option on the concern's equity. This option can be valued using the Black-Scholes option-pricing formula.

Pricing convertible bonds

The next step is to break up a convertible bond into a straight bond and a warrant component.

Dilution

Consider a convertible bond with a face value of F. A bondholder's right to convert into shares can be expressed in terms of the *conversion ratio, r*, which is the number of shares that each convertible can be converted into. The conversion privilege could also be represented by the *conversion price, k*, which is the price at which convertible bonds can be converted into new shares. The conversion price, the face value and the conversion ratio are related as follows:

conversion ratio = face value/conversion price.

If all the convertibles are converted, the total number of new shares is Mr, and the fraction of all the shares then owned by convertible bondholders is

$$\lambda = Mr/(N+Mr)$$

This represents the *dilution factor* of the convertible issue. Convertible bonds typically have anti-dilution clauses which protect them against reductions in their claim on equity, for example from rights issues.

Value at maturity

If convertible bondholders convert, they give up future coupons and principal repayments in exchange for a fraction of the shares of the company, equal to the dilution factor. Letting V^* denote the value of the company at maturity after the last coupon has been paid, convertible bondholders receive shares worth λV^* from converting at maturity. If they do not convert, they receive the principal, F, assuming the company is not insolvent. If V^* is less than F, convertible bonds collect V^*. As a result, the convertible bonds will be converted if, and only if, λV^* is greater than F. The value of the convertibles at maturity is, therefore, given by:

$$\text{Convertible value at maturity} = \begin{cases} V^* & \text{if } V^*<F \\ F & \text{if } F<V^*<F/\lambda \\ \lambda V^* & \text{if } V^*>F/\lambda \end{cases}$$

This is illustrated in Figure 2. Figure 3 depicts the payoffs of a straight bond and a warrant respectively. It can be seen that the convertible bond payoff can be constructed by adding the payoffs of the straight bond and the warrant.

This illustrates that a convertible bond can be broken into a package of a straight bond and a warrant. Knowing this, pricing the convertible is a simple matter of adding the price of the straight bond and the warrant components. The warrant component can be valued, as above by, using the Black-Scholes model.

Complicated convertible bonds

In practice, convertible bonds often have call features whereby the company can force convertible bondholders to decide whether or not to convert before maturity. Some convertible bonds also have put features whereby investors can sell the convertibles back to the company.

Fig.2 Payoff to convertibles at maturity

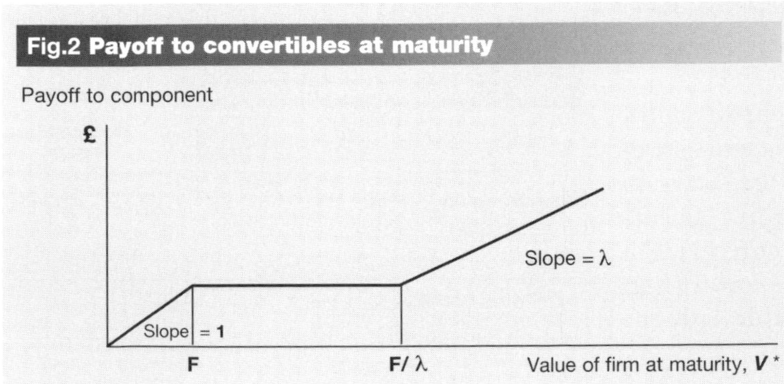

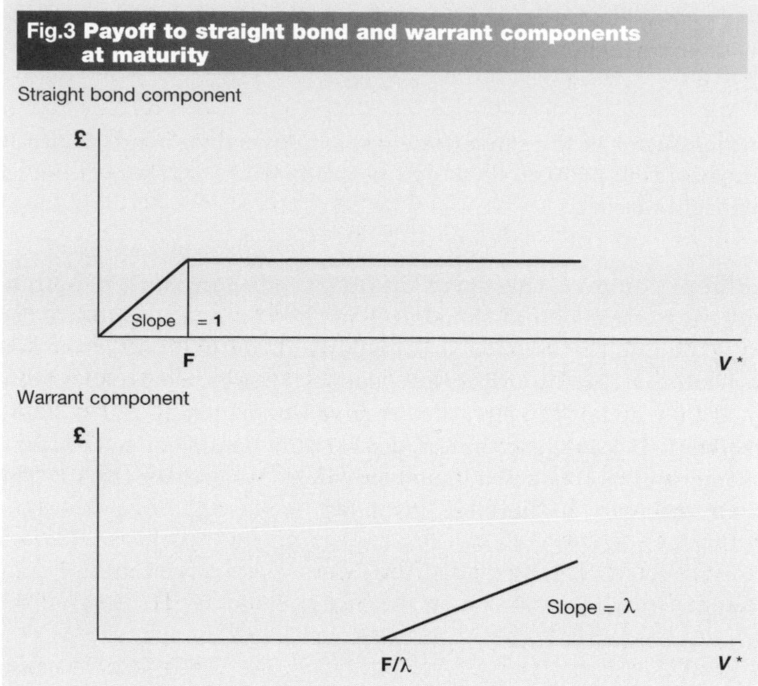

In these cases, simple pricing by the approach shown above is not sufficiently accurate in real market conditions. However, this does not affect the validity of the basic message that convertible bonds consist of a straight bond component and a warrant component.

Why issue convertible bonds?

The most direct way to find out why companies issue convertible bonds is to ask the managers who decided to issue them. Table 1 reports the findings of three such studies. It confirms the view that many companies issue convertible bonds as a form of delayed equity. Brigham (see below) reports that firms viewed issuing convertibles as preferable to outright equity issues because managers '...believed (their) stock's price would rise over time, and convertibles provide a way of selling common stock at a price above the existing market'. Essentially, if managers expect the convertibles to be converted, the advantage of convertibles to an outright equity issue is a lower dilution.

Table 1: Why do firms issue convertibles?

%	Pilcher (1955)	Brigham (1966)	Hoffmeister (1977)
Delayed equity	82	68	40
Sweeten debt	9	27	37
Other	9	5	23

Source: author interpretation of Brigham, E. (1966) 'An analysis of convertible debentures: theory and some empirical evidence', *Journal of Finance 21*, 35-54. Hoffmeister, J.R. (1977) 'Use of convertible debt in the early 1970s: a revaluation of corporate motives', *Quarterly Review of Economics and Business*. 17, 23-32. Pilcher, C. J. (1955) 'Raising capital with convertible securities', *Michigan Business Studies* no. 21/2 (University of Michigan, Ann Arbor, MI).

The sweeten debt reason shows that convertible bonds are sometimes viewed as an alternative to straight bonds. The equity 'sweetener' contained in a convertible allows the coupon to be lower than it would be on comparable straight bonds.

However, as we know from the Miller and Modigliani theorem, in perfect markets convertible bonds cannot be a cheaper source of financing than either straight bonds or equity. As shown above, convertible bonds can be viewed as a package of straight debt and warrants. The lower coupon on convertible bonds relative to straight bonds merely reflects the value of the warrant. Convertible bonds can also be viewed as a package of equity and a (limited liability) put (to sell the shares back to the company). The lower dilution created by convertible bonds if they are converted reflects the value of the put. The cited rationales for issuing convertibles are best understood in imperfect market settings, which will be explored next.

Sweetening debt

The sweetening debt rationale for convertible bonds relates to what is sometimes referred to as the moral hazard problem of debt. This is based on the observation that value can be shifted from debt to equity by increasing the riskiness of the company's projects, since limited liability protects equity if the company should perform poorly (equity can be viewed as a call option on the company's assets).

As a result, managers acting in shareholders interest have an incentive to increase risk after debt has been raised, even though total company value may fall. While such risk shifting may seem to benefit shareholders, the reality may be the opposite. When the company is trying to raise debt capital, rational investors will realize that risk may be increased and will demand compensation by way of higher coupons. The costs of the moral hazard problem of debt is, therefore, borne entirely by equityholders.

Shareholders would be better off if the company could commit not to increase risk. The problem is that promises not to do so are difficult to make credibly. Bond covenants go some way to limiting the company's ability to increase risk, but can hardly cover all contingencies. This is when convertibles become useful.

While the value of the straight debt component of a convertible decreases as risk is increased, the value of the warrant increases. Hence, by choosing the terms of the convertible bond judiciously, the total package can be made insensitive to risk. The cost of debt can be reduced and optimal investment restored.

A slightly different, but mathematically equivalent, argument goes as follows. Suppose managers and outside investors disagree about the riskiness of the company. If outside investors think the company's riskiness is higher than the managers believe it is, outside investors will demand a higher coupon on straight bonds than the managers consider is fair. By issuing convertibles, the two parties could come to an agreement, since the convertible could be constructed so that its value would be insensitive to the true risk of the company.

To summarize, in imperfect markets, convertible debt can be a cheaper source of financing than straight bonds because the 'equity sweetener' makes convertible bond values less sensitive to changes in risk. Compensation for increases in risk is, therefore, not required.

Delayed equity

The idea that there is an advantage to convertible debt as a form of delayed equity can be understood when managers have better information than outside investors about the company's prospects. If the market undervalues the company (relative to the value the market would place on it if the market had access to managers proprietary information) managers acting in shareholders interest would have a disincentive to issue equity. Shares would be sold too cheaply. This is sometimes referred to as the *lemons problem*. The idea is that the market does not know exactly how well the concern is performing, but places a positive probability on being a poor performer. The company is, therefore, considered to be a 'lemon'. If, in fact, it is not, it will be undervalued. In this case, debt might be a better alternative as a source of external financing since it's value is less sensitive to the company's true value (the lemons problem is less severe for debt than for equity).

A problem with straight debt, however, is that it increases the likelihood of financial distress, which typically involves large costs. In deciding which instrument to issue, the company faces a trade off between undervaluation (lemons) costs and expected bankruptcy costs. Undervalued companies would be tempted to issue debt, while overvalued ones would be tempted to issue equity. In terms of the undervaluation versus insurance against bankruptcy trade-off, convertible bonds fall in the middle between equity and straight bonds. Convertible bonds may, therefore, be chosen by companies which are undervalued, but not grossly so. In other words, the worst quality companies will issue equity, medium quality concerns issue convertibles, and the highest quality issue straight debt. In this sense, the company signals its quality by its choice of financing.

This view is consistent with the empirical evidence which shows that the market typically reacts negatively when companies announce equity issues. Convertible bonds are greeted with less negative reactions, while issues of straight debt seem to be neutral events.

The above argument does not explicitly address the notion that companies issue convertible debt as a form of delayed equity. For this, we need to discuss convertible bond call features. Most convertible bonds have a call feature. When a company calls its convertibles, investors must decide whether to convert their convertibles or take the call price. In principle, this is not a difficult decision. If the value of the shares that the convertibles can be converted into, the *conversion value*, is larger than the *call price*, investors will convert (but otherwise not). In this case, conversion is said to be forced. The possibility of forced conversion provides the company with additional insurance against financial distress.

It is particularly convertibles with call features which have been linked to the delayed equity argument. The idea is that undervalued companies that need external financing first issue convertibles. Later, when the market realizes the concern has been undervalued, the company's stock price goes up, and the company forces conversion, thus getting equity into its capital structure.

Forcing conversion is beneficial because it eliminates the convertible bondholders option not to take shares while reducing the likelihood of financial distress. However, a problem with this is that most companies tend to delay forcing conversion, perhaps because the market typically views calls forcing conversion as negative signals, leading to a drop in the share price.

Hence, a strategy of forcing conversion as soon as possible to implement convertible debt as delayed equity is not necessarily such a good idea. In practice it seems that companies would much rather achieve voluntary conversion of the convertibles. So while they may issue convertible bonds in the *hope* they will be converted, one should not view convertible bonds simply as delayed equity.

To summarize, for undervalued companies, issuing convertible bonds may be advantageous, compared with issuing equity outright, because the lemons problem is lower. However, the costs of financial distress are higher. These costs may be reduced by adding a call feature to the convertibles which allows the company to force convertible bondholders to convert into equity in some circumstances. Convertible bonds may be viewed as delayed equity in the sense that when convertibles are issued, the company may *hope* and *expect* that the convertibles will be converted into equity. But there is no guarantee that this will happen.

Summary

Convertible bonds, popular with many companies, are hybrid instruments which should be viewed as a package of straight debt and warrants.

Kjell Nyborg explains how to divide them into these separate components so that pricing becomes a simple matter of adding them up. Convertibles are often issued as a way of sweetening debt or delaying equity. In imperfect markets they can be a cheaper source of financing than straight bonds because the 'equity sweetener' makes convertible bond values less sensitive to changes in risk. Compensation for increased risk is, therefore, not required.

Equally, companies seen by the stock market as potentially poor performers, and unjustly valued as such, should gain advantages from issuing convertibles rather than outright equity. The costs of financial distress are potentially higher, though these can be reduced by adding a 'call' feature.

Suggested further reading

Brennan, M.J. and Schwartz, E.S., (1980), 'Analyzing convertible bonds', *Journal of Financial and Quantitative Analysis*, 15, 907–29.

Cox, J.C. and Rubinstein, M., (1985), *Options Markets*, Prentice-Hall Englewood Cliffs.

Nyborg, K.G., (1996), 'The use and pricing of convertible bonds', *Applied Mathematical Finance* 3, 167–190.

Forecasting short-term interest rates

by Walter N. Torous

A range of interest rates are offered in credit markets. For example, interest rates vary with the length of the loan (short-term rates versus long-term rates), with the credit worthiness of the borrower (default-free rates versus risky rates) and with the tax treatment of the payments (US municipal rates versus corporate rates).

In this article I discuss the behavior of short-term interest rates – rates quoted on credit instruments with terms to maturity of no more than one year. Comments are restricted to short-term rates that are default-free (US Treasury bills) or, at least, are regarded by market participants to be subject to minimal default risk (London inter-bank rates).

Fig.1 The time series behavior of short-term US interest rates

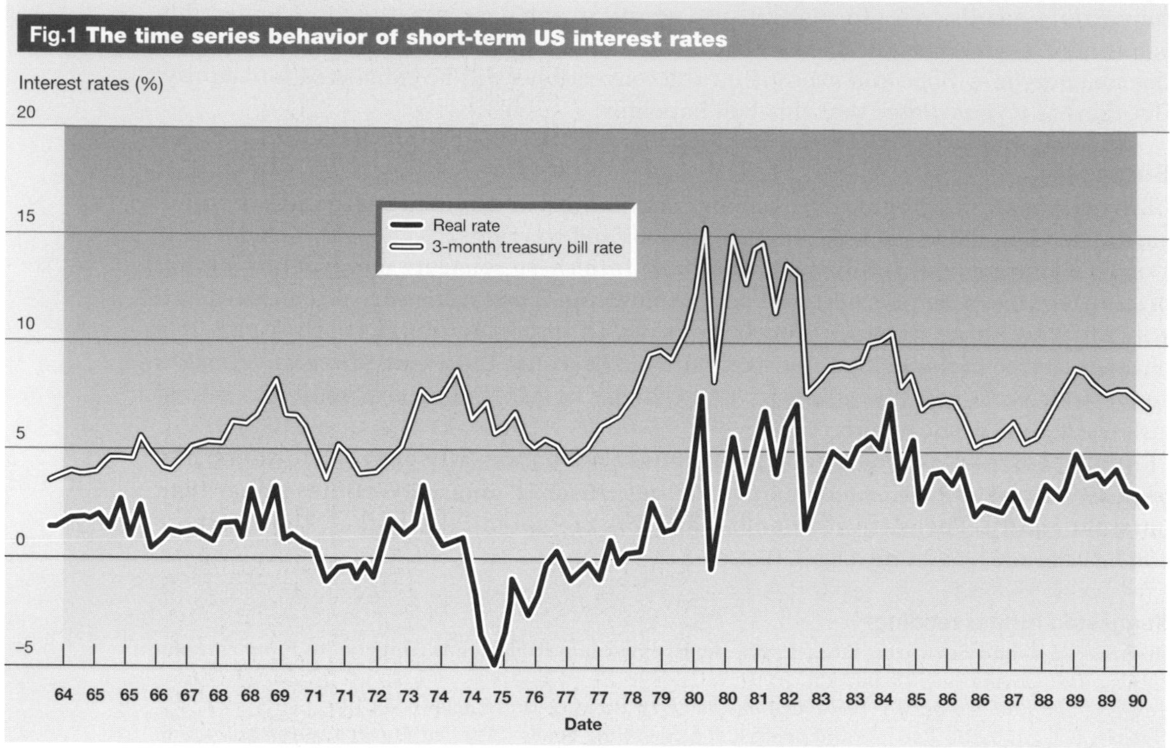

The white line in Figure 1 displays the times series behavior of quarterly observations on the three-month US Treasury bill rate over the sample period 1964–90.

Default-free short-term interest rates are important not only because the underlying credit instruments are themselves important securities but also because the pay-offs to many other securities, such as variable rate mortgages and interest rate derivatives, are contingent on their behavior.

The behavior of short-term interest rates, like many other economic variables, is characterized by mean reversion. That is, there is an average, or mean, level towards which short-term interest rates are pulled. When an unforeseen economic shock results in an interest rate being above this average, the resultant decrease in the demand for funds will push down the rate of interest.

As can be seen in Figure 1, the lofty short-term interest rates that characterized the credit markets of the early 1980s gave way to lower rates by the middle of the decade. Alternatively, when an interest rate finds itself below this average, it will subsequently be driven up by the resultant increase in the demand for funds. Without this mean reverting behavior, short-term interest rates would increase without bound and so be non-stationary. In this regard, it is important to determine the speed with which an interest rate reverts to its mean.

For example, faster mean-reverting behavior implies that, for a given shock, interest rates will return more quickly to their mean. So if one systematically mis-measures this speed of adjustment, one would systematically mis-estimate the future course of interest rates or significantly misprice interest rate derivatives. This is because the valuation of these derivative instruments will, in general, depend upon the speed with which interest rates are assumed to revert to their mean levels.

While this discussion assumes that the mean level remains constant, there is evidence that the mean itself varies over time, making forecasting the course of interest rates even more difficult. Forecasting the behavior of short-term interest rates is also made difficult by the fact that changes in interest rates are volatile. That is, there is uncertainty surrounding the magnitude of the change in interest rates from one period to the next.

The Bank of England's Eddie George now fixes interest rates

Short-term interest rates are far more volatile than long-term rates. The pricing of interest rate derivatives, like any other derivative security, critically depends upon correctly modeling interest rate volatility. NatWest Markets' loss of £50m in interest rate options in early 1997 was attributed in large part to its mis-measuring the volatility of short-term interest rates.

The uncertainty surrounding interest rate changes varies over time. The volatility of short-term interest rates also appears to vary with the level of interest rates themselves. For example, Figure 1 shows that the behavior of short-term interest rates in the early 1980s was not only characterized by their high levels but also by extreme volatility. However, by the end of the decade rates were again displaying volatility, even though the level of rates was itself rather low.

Needless to say, there is considerable evidence to suggest that the volatility of interest rates is itself volatile. Again this volatility appears to be mean reverting so that periods of excessively volatile interest rates, on average, revert to quieter periods, while periods of low volatility tend to be followed eventually by periods of high volatility. The volatility of interest rates is quite distinct from stock-price volatility. Changes in interest rate volatility do not appear to depend on changes in the level of interest rates since interest rate volatility is as likely to increase as a result of an unanticipated rise in rates, announced say, by a central bank, as by an unanticipated decline.

This is in contrast to stock returns, where there is a reliably negative relation between volatility changes and changes in the level of stock prices because increases in stock price volatility are on average associated with a decline in stock prices – witness the surge in stock price volatility after the October 1987 stock market crash. Macroeconomic events, such as the announcement of better-than-anticipated balance of payments statistics, also lead to increases in the volatility of short-term interest rates, though such volatility increases are transient and their effects dampen down quickly. This, again, is in contrast to stock returns where volatility tends to cluster or be more persistent over time.

The behavior of short-term interest rates is also affected by the inflation prospects. Changes in the value of money redistribute purchasing power between the borrower and the lender. For example, inflation decreases the purchasing power of money and so benefits the borrower who contracts to make nominally fixed-interest payments.

To the extent that inflation is expected, the borrower and lender can anticipate the resultant redistribution by altering the rate of interest charged. Hence, increases in the expected rate of inflation result in higher nominal interest rates, all else being equal. The higher nominal interest rate compensates the lender for the expected deterioration in the purchasing power of money caused by inflation.

That is, if r denotes the nominal short-term rate of interest, then

$$r = \rho + \pi$$

where ρ is the corresponding real rate of interest while π is the rate of inflation expected to prevail over the maturity of the loan.

According to the Fisher effect, named after the American economist Irving Fisher, the borrower and the lender can insulate the real rate of interest charged on a loan, that is the price that equates the supply and demand for capital, from perfectly foreseen inflation by making the nominal rate charged vary point for point with expected inflation.

Given the nominal three-month interest rates depicted by the white line in Figure 1, the solid line gives the corresponding real rates obtained by subtracting three-month inflation forecasts from these nominal rates. The inflation forecasts are based on a statistical time series model which uses only information available when the forecast is made. What is particularly noteworthy about the behavior of the estimated short-term real rates is that they were actually negative for extended periods in the 1970s.

The Fisher effect implies that movements in short-term nominal interest rates reflect fluctuations in expected inflation. As such, nominal interest rates should have predictive ability for future inflation. Empirical examination of the Fisher effect has involved testing for a significant correlation between the level of nominal interest rates and future inflation.

That is, testing for the statistical significance of the slope coefficient β in the following linear regression

$$\pi_t = \alpha + \beta r_t + \varepsilon_t$$

where π_t is, say, the three month future rate of inflation measured from the beginning of quarter t while r_t is the three month nominal interest rate set at the beginning of quarter t.

If we assume that individuals form expectations rationally – realized inflation differs from expected inflation only by random noise – then the regression also tests the correlation between nominal interest rates and expected inflation.

Measuring inflation by quarterly changes in the US Consumer Price Index and short-term nominal interest rates by the three-month Treasury bill rates depicted in Figure 1, the following regression results are obtained for our entire sample as well as two subsamples:

Sample period	β coefficient	t statistic	R^2
1960:I – 1990:IV	*0.506*	*4.02*	*23%*
1960:I – 1979:III	*1.572*	*16.02*	*78%*
1982:IV – 1990:IV	*– 0.053*	*0.82*	*1%*

The R^2 statistic in the table measures the percentage of variability in realized short-term inflation rates explained by the regression equation. What is particularly noteworthy about these results is their lack of robustness. The Fisher effect appears to characterize the US data until the Federal Reserve Board's change in operating policy in October 1979.

Notice that over this subsample the nominal short-term interest rates explain about 80 per cent of the variability in realized short-term inflation rates. However, the level of short-term interest rates has no ability to forecast short-term inflation in the US since the end of the Federal Reserve Board's experiment in 1982. Further, this short-run Fisher effect does not appear to empirically characterize data in other countries throughout the post-war period.

Why does the inflation-forecasting ability of short-term interest rates exhibit so little robustness? One argument is that this forecasting relation may simply be spurious and there is no short-run Fisher effect. Rather the empirical evidence appears to be consistent with a long-run Fisher effect in which inflation and interest rates trend together over the long-run.

Summary

In this article Walter Torous discusses the behavior of short-term interest rates – rates quoted on credit instruments with terms to maturity of no more than one year.

Default-free short-term interest rates, he observes, are important not only because of the significance of these underlying credit instruments but because many other securities, such as variable rate mortgages and interest rate derivatives, are contingent on their behavior.

Mean reversion is an important phenomenon here as with other economic variables: there is evidence that the mean itself varies over time, which along with volatility makes forecasting the course of short-term interest rates particularly difficult. Such volatility is quite different from stock price volatility.

The article concludes with an examination of the so called Fisher effect, which implies that movements in short-term nominal interest rates reflect fluctuations in expected inflation.

Suggested further reading

Ball, C. A. and Torous, W. N., 'The stochastic volatility of short-term interest rates: some international evidence', Working paper, The Institute for Finance and Accounting, London Business School.

Mishkin, F., (1992), 'Is the Fisher effect for real?: a re-examination of the relationship between inflation and interest rates', *Journal of Monetary Economics*, Vol. 30, 195–215.

Securitization: unbundling for value

by Harold Rose

Securitization has displayed rapid growth in the US while in most other countries its use has been restricted. In the UK, however, the relative freedom of the financial system has fostered its growth. Securitization is a relatively modern term and has come to have several meanings. Among these are:

- disintermediation (the replacement of financial intermediary lending functions by the direct issue of securities by businesses to investors)
- the sale to another institution of all or part of an institution's loan portfolio
- the transformation of all or part of a loan portfolio (or other assets such as property) into securities, which are then sold on the market
- the transformation of the cash flows from a loan security into two different securities. One provides interest (an interest-only 'strip' or I/O) and the other the original principal (a principal-only 'strip' or P/O).

There are also variants of the last of these. However, the different meanings all have one or both of two features: the increasing use of securities markets at the expense of traditional financial intermediation; and the 'unbundling' of the lending operation into different components.

Financial disintermediation is discussed later in *Mastering Finance* and I/O and P/O strips have special characteristics, which, with the main exception of certain mortgage obligations in the US, usually play no part in the sale of part or all of a loan book or its transformation into marketable securities. This article is, therefore, concerned only with the sale and transformation of institutional loans.

Loan book sales

The 'private placement' of part of a bank's loan portfolio with another bank is not new. US banks did this in the second half of the last century because of the geographically fragmented nature of the country's banking system. The aim was usually to obtain a higher degree of loan portfolio diversification or, more commonly, a closer match between the demand for funds by local borrowers and the local supply of deposits.

The same needs were being met in the UK even earlier. This was done not by interbank sales of loans but by purchases and sales of parcels of commercial bills issued by borrowers through a developing money market that was absent in other countries, including the US. Private placements of bank loan sales continue in the US, which, largely because of Federal and State legislation, still has a geographically fragmented banking system, although the legislative barriers have been lowered in recent years.

Sales of previous loans to developing countries, especially to South America after the oil price crisis which culminated in the Mexican debt moratorium of 1982, have also been carried out, particularly by US banks seeking to reduce this form of exposure.

In the UK the market in commercial bills has long given way to the overdraft system (technically illegal in some countries, including the US) and to the interbank market in short-term loans (common to most developed countries). In the US, on the other hand, the commercial paper market has grown more rapidly than bank lending over the past 20 years. This is largely because an increasing number of companies have a credit status higher than that of banks and because marketability is itself a feature that has value.

But US banks are involved in the issuing of commercial paper in that they provide stand-by credit facilities to commercial issuers of paper (thus further enhancing their credit status and insuring them against a possible disruption of the market) and play a part in distribution.

The involvement of US banks (like that of banks in other countries and in the euro commercial paper market) shows that disintermediation need not exclude a role for banks. It also has some of the features of bank loan sales and bank loan securitization in the form of the unbundling of lending function components.

Gains from unbundling

Unbundling goes farthest when part or all of an institution's loan portfolio are transformed into marketable securities. The components of the lending operation are: loan origination; borrower credit status investigation; the arrangement of loan terms; loan financing; loan servicing (the collection of interest and principal); borrower monitoring and distress and default management; 'warehousing'; and the bearing of risk.

In the case of traditional bank (or similar institutional) lending, all such component functions are carried out by the lending institution. In the case of loan sales they are divided between the selling and buying institutions; while in that of fully securitized loans they are usually divided between a number of institutions. In addition they are accompanied by market pricing and, therefore, market monitoring.

The originating institution will arrange the terms of the loans, usually continue to collect interest and principal and manage distressed and defaulting borrowers. Credit status assessment, however, will be shared with other institutions, such as the credit rating agencies. Risk-bearing is usually split between the buyers of securitized paper, outside institutions such as insurance companies, which for a fee will provide a partial guarantee or 'credit enhancement'; and the originating institution itself.

Finance is ultimately provided by the buyers of the securitized paper, except for whatever portion, if any, is retained by the originating institution as part of its own contribution to credit enhancement. The parties to full securitization are set out schematically in Figure 1. Together with marketability and the creation of new, relatively standardized securities, unbundling enables securitization to create value over and above that of traditional bank or other institutional lending.

It allows specialization of function, which reduces costs by enabling institutions to concentrate on those component functions, such as origination, in which they have a comparative advantage, and to carry that type or degree of risk that provides the best risk-return trade-off for their own portfolio. Unbundling, therefore, facilitates both cost and risk efficiency.

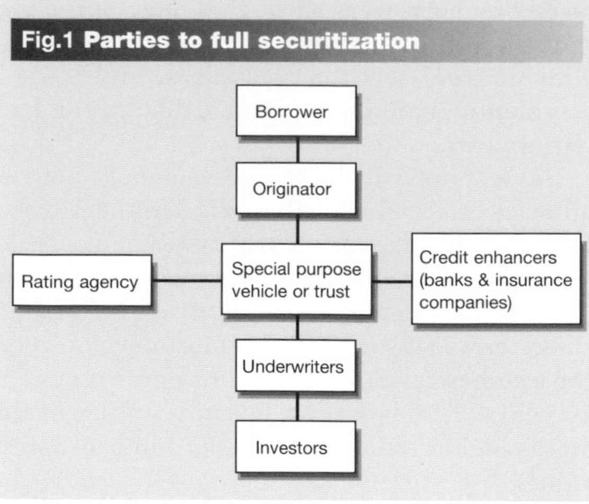

Fig.1 Parties to full securitization

Credit monitoring and credit enhancement also provide a transparency of loan quality that is partly denied to bank depositors and others. In addition, certain types of securitization, outlined below, provide different forms of interest rate risk that appeal to different investors (this is the essence of I/O and P/O strips). Securitization can, to some extent, be structured to meet the special needs of the selling institution or of investors with regard to possible tax, accounting or regulatory burdens.

Ultimately, however, the issuing institution hopes to earn a spread, in terms of interest and fees, over the cost of origination, servicing and credit enhancement. A partial exception, at least, may occur where the aim of securitization is primarily to lighten the issuer's balance sheet in order to improve liquidity, remove problem debts or lessen what, rightly or wrongly, is regarded as a costly capital ratio requirement.

Securitization in the US

Securitization in the US extends to many types of loan portfolios originated by different types of institution. Consumer durable loans are securitized mainly by non-banks, such as the finance subsidiaries of General Electric and General Motors and commercial loans by banks. Because commercial loans are of more uncertain and variable quality they are subject to the more complex forms of securitization, as are, for different reasons, the securitization of residential mortgages.

It is difficult to do justice to the many forms securitization now takes in the US, and the following summary is only a broad indication. The main form of asset-backed securities (ABS) is of the 'pass-through' type, in which a trust or other special-purpose vehicle acquires the loans from the bank or other institution in the first instance and issues the securities. The rights to the (specifically 'dedicated') loan cashflows pass to the investors buying the securities. The loans are removed from the bank's balance sheet, but it usually continues to collect the cash flows. Average maturities of ABS are commonly of 18–36 months, with a maximum of about six years.

Successful securitization usually requires at least an AA credit rating. The necessary credit enhancement may be provided in several ways, not only by an (AAA-rated) insurance company but also by the absorption of tranches of losses by the issuing bank, the issue by the bank of a subordinated loan stock or by some other form of over-collateralization.

In the case of the US asset-backed bond (ABB), a bank's loans are first sold to a subsidiary and, therefore, remain on the consolidated balance sheet. Unlike ABS, the cashflows from the loan pool are not specifically 'dedicated' to the securities issued but are usually supported by some form of credit enhancement. Pay-through bonds are similar to ABBs in that they remain on the originator's balance sheet, but the cashflows from the loan pool backing the bonds are dedicated to the bonds.

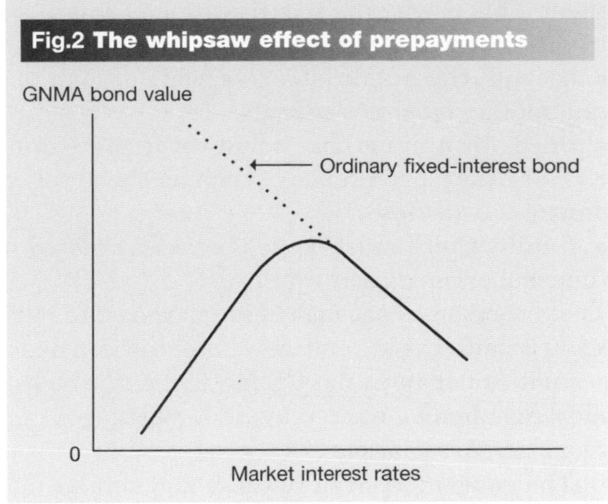

Fig.2 The whipsaw effect of prepayments

Securitization is predominant in the US mortgage market, where, for a fee, government or quasi-government agencies create or provide a measure of guarantee to mortgage-backed securities ('collateralized mortgage obligations' or CMOs) originated by savings and loan associations (S&Ls) and commercial and mortgage banks. Securitization undertaken by non-governmental institutions is backed by private insurance or some other form of credit enhancement. US mortgage pass-throughs are based on pools of fixed-rate, level-payment mortgages with similar coupon rates and a similar ratio of loan-to-house value.

Mortgage borrowers have the option of early repayment, which gives mortgage-backed securities an uncertain life. The degree of prepayment depends on a variety of economic factors and, most interestingly, on the contemporary level of mortgage interest rates. The typical US mortgage is a fixed-rate mortgage, so borrowers have an incentive to prepay and reborrow when market interest rates fall below the rate on existing mortgages by a margin sufficient to cover the legal and other costs of reborrowing.

Unexpected prepayments will reduce the value of mortgage-backed ABS, which means that the response of the value of CMOs to interest rate changes differs from that of ordinary fixed-interest rate securities. This is illustrated by the so-called 'whipsaw' effect shown in Figure 2. (In technical terms, CMOs may behave as though they had negative duration.) CMOs thus provide institutions with variable-rate liabilities, such as banks, with an additional instrument for hedging against interest rate risk.

CMOs may also be subject to 'double securitization', whereby an institution, such as an investment bank, will transform a CMO into I/O and P/O strips or into securities with differently timed rights to interest and principal. This, too, together with the prepayment option, means that the market price of such securities will respond to interest rate changes in a way different from that of ordinary fixed interest rate securities, thus enlarging the scope for interest rate hedging or risk bearing.

The growth of securitization

Successful securitization is dependent on several conditions:

- the loans to be securitized must be of an identifiable (but not necessarily low) degree of risk to overcome the problem of information asymmetry between the originator and the other parties involved, which would otherwise impose high monitoring costs on them. This is why the securitization of small business loans has not yet progressed far in the US.

- second, the administrative costs of loan quality assessment, loan servicing and unbundling must not be high.
- third, for unbundling to add value there must be differences in originating ability, risk or other 'preferences', such as those relating to marketability or to regulation, among the parties.
- finally, there must be no obstacles created by official restrictions or by cartelized financial organization.

These conditions are met in larger measure in the US than elsewhere and explain why securitization is of relatively recent origin even there. Regular issues of asset-backed securities began in the US in 1970 with the introduction of pass-through residential mortgage bonds, backed by S&L mortgages guaranteed by the Government National Mortgage Association.

The guarantee given to these and similar mortgages which meet certain conditions gives them a low-risk character absent in other countries. The development of securitization in consumer loans, credit card debts, car, truck and boat loans and trade debts (asset-backed commercial paper) has been facilitated by the revolution in accounting and information technology and the development of statistical approaches to risk management by rating agencies.

Just as the development of international trade in goods and services was fostered by the reduction in transport and communication costs, so securitization was helped in the 1980s by the reduction in information and administration costs brought by the development of the computer.

The securitization of bank loans in the US began in 1985 with lease receivables. It was fostered by the advent of high interest rates, paid on an increasing proportion of deposits, coinciding with capital ratio requirements which were regarded as costly by banks.

The difficulties experienced by the S&Ls and by many commercial banks in the late 1980s, a period of numerous failures, provided a further incentive to securitize. Traded bank loans have included distressed loans, sold at discounts to 'vulture' and other funds willing to accept the risk in the expectation of high returns.

Total amounts of securitized loans outstanding at the end of December 1996 (Federal Reserve Bulletin statistics) were approximately as follows:

Federal-related mortgage-backed securities	\$1,711bn
Other mortgage-backed securities	\$344bn
Consumer loan ABS	\$270bn
Other ABS	\$124bn
Total identified	\$2,449bn

Mortgage pools represent about 40 per cent of all outstanding residential mortgages and consumer loan pools a little more than one-fifth of total consumer non-mortgage credit outstanding. But other ABS outstanding are equivalent to only some six per cent of bank loans outside the consumer sector.

In other countries securitization has been much more restricted for several reasons, including the discouraging attitude of regulators or financial systems that are cartelized or otherwise disinclined to innovate. Residential mortgages lack the guarantee or insurance given by the state and quasi-state bodies of the US; and banking systems that are concentrated and fully 'universal' in character (that is embrace mortgage lending, investment banking and insurance) are also less likely to securitize. This also tends to be true where bank-customer relationships go deep. Securitization is usually 'without recourse' to the originating bank which may raise difficult questions of the management of borrower distress or default.

Notable variations on the securitization theme have occurred in the measures recently taken to deal with the problems of loss-making banks in Japan and France. It is not surprising, however, that outside the US securitization has gone farthest in the relatively free atmosphere of the UK financial system.

Issues of ABS were first made in the UK in 1985, since when they have been very erratic, with residential mortgage issues peaking in the temporary boom of 1988. Until 1996 total issues of all ABS averaged only some £2bn a year. Car and aircraft loans came second after mortgage loans, and a single large issuer, such as British Aerospace, has predominated in some years.

However, 1996 was notable in the UK for the large securitized issue of paper by NatWest Bank, backed by $5bn of loans to 300 large companies. Credit enhancement was provided by £100m of subordinated Notes taken up by NatWest to provide the first tranche or 'first-dollar-loss' cover. This operation involved the issue to investors, by the intermediary special purpose vehicle acquiring the loans, of both sterling and dollar floating rate notes (of a maximum term of five years). The demand for loan-backed securities, as in the US, comes partly from foreign banks wishing to diversify their loan portfolios.

Press comment concentrated on the lightening of capital ratio requirements, which, at least formally, are the same on low-risk, low-return non-mortgage loans as on riskier commercial loans, as the main motive for securitization. The general opinion was that NatWest would earn only a low net spread. But management of the securitized loans remains with the bank, which intends to continue to manage its relationship with its large corporate borrowers, and which presumably earn other forms of income.

Some questions

The NatWest operation, like the securitization of low-risk commercial and other loans in the US, raises the question of the reaction of regulators to any removal of relatively low-risk loans from an institution's portfolio. The response is likely to be a more formal differentiation of capital ratio requirements as between commercial and other loan portfolios of different degrees of risk. Regulatory problems would also arise if banks felt obliged to bear some of the burden of default, beyond that stipulated by their part in credit enhancement, in order to preserve their reputation for later securitization. In general, the complexities of securitization could be matched by a corresponding increase in the cost of regulation.

This, together with the problems of debt management in the event of default, could slow down the pace of securitization, even in the US. Despite this, and the fact that the securitization of commercial bank loans still plays only a relatively small part even in the US, some economists predict that unbundling is bound to provide growing opportunities. Countries where securities markets are awakening from a long history of restriction will benefit most.

The advent of European Monetary Union, by removing exchange rate risk, would almost certainly encourage securitization as a means of portfolio diversification; and perhaps it is within Europe that the potential scope is greatest.

Ultimately, there is the question of the potential effect of unbundling on the structure of financial systems. Origination advantages are not the monopoly of bank-type institutions, as the penetration of financial services by industrial companies and retail stores indicates. In addition credit assessment and credit enhancement can be further separated.

The ability to unbundle will no doubt add to the changes in institutional boundaries already taking place; unbundling has already been extended to insurance. Some economists go farther and foresee the day in which existing institutional definitions become increasingly meaningless.

Summary

The term securitization has a number of specialist meanings but in this article author Harold Rose concentrates on its use as a description of the 'unbundling' on institutional loans. In a conventional loan all components – loan origination, credit status investigation, loan terms, loan financing, collection of interest and principal and so on – are undertaken by a single lending institution. In securitization each elements is 'unbundled' and handled by a different institution. In addition, each element also bears a market price.

This form of securitization is most advanced in the US (and to a lesser extent in the UK), though even there it is relatively new. Rose provides guidance to how securitization works, the areas where it is most applicable and likely future developments. While there are some potential limits to the spread of securitization, many economists predict that it will continue to grow.

Suggested further reading

Chew, D., (ed.), (1991), *New developments in Commercial Banking*, Basil Blackwell.

Saunders, A., (1997), *Financial Institutions Management*, Irwin.

'Securitization: an international perspective', *Financial Market Trends*, OECD, June 1995.

Twinn, C.I., (1994), 'Asset-backed securitization in the United Kingdom', *Bank of England Quarterly Bulletin*, May.

8

Portfolio Investment

Contributors

Brad Barber is Associate Professor of Finance at the Graduate School of Management, University of California, Davis. His research interests include financial markets, the development of performance benchmarks, valuation, shareholder litigation, bankruptcy and cost of capital.

Richard Leftwich is Fuji Bank and Heller Professor of Accounting and Finance at the University of Chicago Graduate School of Business. His research interests include audit qualifications, bond ratings, corporate charter changes and block trades.

Nicholas Barberis is Assistant Professor of Finance at the University of Chicago Graduate School of Business. His research interests include optimal asset allocation and the efficiency of markets.

Karen K. Lewis is Professor of Finance at the Wharton School of the University of Pennsylvania.

Sanford J. Grossman is the Steinberg Trustee Professor of Finance at the Wharton School of the University of Pennsylvania and Director of Wharton's Center for Quantitative Finance. He was the 1987 recipient of the John Bates Clark Medal and was President of the American Finance Association in 1994. He is Director of an asset management firm, Quantitative Financial Strategies Inc.

Contents

Introduction

This module concentrates on investments in markets, both stocks and bonds. It begins with an assessment of the tricky problem of evaluating investment performance, and discusses how investors can decide their allocation between equities and government bonds. It then examines the phenomenon of investor bias towards domestic equities – a bias that has little rational basis – and ends with an analysis of the rise of passive equity investment, or simply 'holding the market'. While the importance of portfolio diversification to minimize risk is undoubted, this module examines whether diversifying purely on the basis of the equity markets not only fails to achieve a fully diversified portfolio but also raises the costs of the equities in which one is investing.

The elusive butterfly of superior returns

by Brad Barber and Richard Leftwich

Professional money managers rely on a variety of investment techniques to invest other people's money, either directly for wealthy individuals or indirectly via pension funds, trusts and life insurance companies. At first glance, identifying the best money managers or investment techniques seems straightforward – the best managers and techniques should, on average, achieve the highest returns.

However, focusing on average returns alone can be misleading – there must be some accounting for risk. Much of the debate on investment performance evaluation revolves around accounting for risk, or equivalently, the calculation of risk-adjusted returns. Even though that calculation involves difficult conceptual and practical issues, the Achilles heel of performance evaluation is the volatility of security returns. Separating good luck from superior insight is extremely difficult in the presence of high volatility.

A manager who can average even one per cent per year above otherwise comparable managers adds considerable economic value to a portfolio. But identifying that individual in a cohort of managers whose returns differ by as much as 20 per cent per year is a daunting task. Some inferior managers will inevitably outperform the superior manager simply by chance. Unless the performance history is long (and several decades of history might well be required), the superior manager will not be detected. Rather than chase the elusive butterfly of superior returns, those responsible for selecting money managers would be better served by placing greater emphasis on other dimensions of their performance, such as the ability to adhere to stated investment strategies and to economize on fees and expenses.

Performance measures

Even though economists' theories about the behavior of security returns often employ very different concepts of risk, those theories universally predict that higher-risk securities must offer higher expected returns to attract rational, risk-averse investors. But if securities are risky, higher *expected* returns do not always translate into higher *actual* returns.

The first step in calculating risk-adjusted performance is determining the expected return on the security that is required to compensate for its risk. The risk-adjusted return is then the actual return on the security minus the expected return. Clearly, measuring risk-adjusted returns depends heavily on the model used to adjust for risk. Two commonly used performance evaluation measures (the Sharpe Ratio and Jensen's Alpha) are based on the Capital Asset Pricing Model (CAPM). The central insight of the CAPM is that the expected return on a security is linearly related to its sensitivity to movements of a broad market index and to nothing else. This market sensitivity is measured by the ubiquitous and controversial beta.

Jensen's Alpha, named after Michael Jensen who pioneered its use, recognizes that, if a portfolio's expected return depends on its market sensitivity (beta), the portfolio's

Fig.1 Jensen's Alpha

Estimate regression:

$$R_{pt} - R_{ft} = \alpha_p + \beta_p (R_{mt} - R_{ft}) + \varepsilon_{pt}$$

where:

R_{pt} - the return on a portfolio
R_{mt} - the return on a market index
R_{ft} - the return on a risk-free instrument
ε_{pt} - a random error term

and the regression produces estimates of:

α_p - Jensen's alpha
β_p - the portfolio's beta

R-squared - the percentage variation in a portfolio's excess return explained by the excess return on the market

Fig.2 Sharpe's Ratio

$$S_P = \frac{\overline{R_{pt} - R_{ft}}}{\sigma(R_{pt} - R_{ft})}$$

where:

R_{pt} - the return on a portfolio
R_{ft} - the return on a risk-free instrument

and

$\overline{R_{pt} - R_{ft}}$ - the average excess return on the portfolio above the risk-free rate

$\sigma(R_{pt} - R_{ft})$ - the standard deviation of the excess return on the portfolio

risk-adjusted performance can be estimated by the intercept from a linear regression relating the portfolio's actual excess return to the actual excess return on a broadly based market index.

A large Jensen's Alpha indicates high returns after controlling for the market sensitivity (beta) of the portfolio. A less commonly used variation on Jensen's Alpha is the Treynor Index, which scales a portfolio's alpha by the beta of the portfolio. For example, if two portfolios each had alphas of two per cent, the Treynor Index would rank the lower beta portfolio as superior.

The eponymous Sharpe Ratio measures a portfolio's excess return per unit of risk, where risk is defined by the volatility (standard deviation) of the portfolio's excess return. The numerator of this ratio is the portfolio's average excess return – its actual return above an investment in a risk-free security. The denominator is the volatility of this excess return, reflecting how excess returns vary from one period (say a month) to another.

A high Sharpe Ratio for a portfolio indicates that the portfolio earned high returns per unit of risk. If a portfolio's Sharpe Ratio is higher than that of the market portfolio, the portfolio outperformed the market on a risk-adjusted basis. (The mathematical bases of Jensen's Alpha and the Sharpe Ratio are set out in Figures 1 and 2).

Jensen's Alpha and the Sharpe Ratio measure different attributes of a portfolio's performance; good or poor performance according to one measure does not ensure good or poor performance according to the other measure. The context of the performance evaluation determines which of the two measures is appropriate for a particular case.

For example, when measuring the performance of an investment vehicle for all or the bulk of an investor's wealth, excess returns relative to standard deviation (the Sharpe Ratio) is the appropriate measure because risk-averse investors are concerned about the volatility of their wealth. On the other hand, the return-beta trade-off (Jensen's Alpha) is the appropriate measure when we are evaluating the performance of an investment vehicle that an investor is considering as an addition to his or her portfolio.

Thus, if you are choosing one money manager to be responsible for your company's entire pension fund, the Sharpe Ratio (reflecting the expected return-volatility trade-off) is appropriate. In contrast, Jensen's Alpha (reflecting the expected return-beta trade-off) is appropriate if you are evaluating a manager who claims to be able to pick undervalued securities and who will manage only a small portion of a well-diversified portfolio.

The choice is not always as clear as in these examples but the appropriate choice depends on understanding the context of the evaluation and on recognizing that beta and volatility measure different aspects of risk.

Conceptual complications

Two conceptual issues severely complicate investment performance evaluation: choosing the appropriate risk-return model and incorporating tests of managers' market timing ability. Performance evaluation measures depend critically on the method used to reflect the risk-return trade-off. Statisticians would say that performance measures are joint tests of a manager's performance and of the validity of the risk-return model embedded in the performance tests.

Both the Sharpe Ratio and Jensen's Alpha assume that the CAPM captures the relation between expected returns and risk. However, academic research now casts some doubt on the empirical validity of the CAPM (although the interpretations of that research outnumber the researchers). For example, there is evidence that the returns on small companies are higher than the returns on large ones with the same beta. Thus, money managers can create portfolios with high alphas (indicating apparently successful performance) if they invest in small companies, even if those managers have no ability to discriminate among small companies. There is also evidence that companies with low market-to-book ratios have higher rates of return than are justified by their betas. Thus, money managers who concentrate their investments in those businesses are also likely to generate high alphas.

One interpretation of the empirical findings about risk and return is that small companies and organizations with low market-to-book ratios are risky and thus require higher expected rates of return to induce investment by rational, risk-averse investors. According to this interpretation, beta is not the only risk factor – size and market-to-book ratio are proxies for additional risk factors. If so, the CAPM should be augmented to allow for risk factors other than beta when estimating risk-adjusted returns.

Although there is no extant theory to support a model of risk and return incorporating these three factors (beta, size and market-to-book), some academics and practitioners advocate using such a model when calculating a portfolio's alpha. A more pragmatic approach is to compare performance measures of the portfolio under review with the measures for portfolios identified as similar using either style analysis or the self-reported styles of the portfolios.

However, self-reported styles (such as growth or value) are notoriously inaccurate, although some mutual fund reporting services, such as Morningstar, have expanded substantially the number of style categories they employ. Moreover, naive reliance on self-reported styles allows managers to 'game' performance measures. For example, if small companies are riskier than large, a portfolio manager can report a large company strategy, invest in small businesses, and produce a performance measure that is favorable but misleading.

Some (primarily the contrarians and their behavioral finance kin) dispute that size and market-to-book represent risk; they contend financial markets systematically undervalue small companies with low market-to-book ratios. Nonetheless, taking account of these empirical regularities when evaluating performance remains important. The contention is that, since the size and market-to-book effects are so well known, managers should not be rewarded for favorable performance statistics that result from investing in stocks with those attributes. Instead, performance should be judged superior only if it ranks highly in the class of managers following that strategy.

An intuitively appealing measure of performance that avoids much of the risk-return controversy can be constructed if the composition of the manager's portfolio at various points in time is known. If the manager has superior skills, the securities comprising the portfolio should earn higher returns when they are held as part of the portfolio than when they are not (either before the purchase or after the sale of the security).

In essence, this measure uses as the benchmark the returns on individual securities in the portfolio during a different period. Unfortunately, this evaluation relies on precise data regarding portfolio composition, which is often not widely available. Market timing ability presents another conceptual challenge to conventional performance measures.

A money manager who is able to forecast when stocks are likely to outperform bonds by a wide margin (but unable to identify individual stocks that are under- or overvalued) will increase the exposure of the portfolio when the market is expected to rise (for example, by investing in higher-beta securities) and reduce the exposure (for example, by investing in low-beta securities or even cash equivalents) when stocks are expected to perform poorly relative to bonds.

Though Sharpe's Ratio and Jensen's Alpha would capture this superior performance, one would not know whether the superior performance stemmed from market timing or superior stock selection. Complex performance measures can be constructed to detect market-timing ability but, typically, those measures are more sophisticated than is justified by the quality of most investment performance data.

Practical complications

There are also practical problems associated with measuring a portfolio's returns – identifying the appropriate index or benchmark for the performance measures and obtaining a track record for the manager that is sufficiently long. Performance measures are based on total returns (price appreciation plus dividends) whether the manager invests in stocks, bonds, commodities or real estate. For some investments (particularly real estate), the underlying security is not traded in a liquid market with publicly quoted prices. For those securities, measures of price appreciation included in the portfolio's returns and in the benchmark are unreliable. For similar reasons, scepticism is appropriate for returns allegedly earned by securities and indices in emerging markets.

The index selected as a benchmark must complement the stated objectives of the manager. For example, if a manager offers international diversification, the relevant benchmark is a global index. On the other hand, if a manager claims to be able to pick undervalued stocks in Lithuania, a Lithuanian stock index is the relevant benchmark. The availability of suitable benchmark indices is often a concern, particularly for more esoteric strategies (for example, a small-cap Lithuanian mutual fund).

A short track record for a manager severely limits inferences about performance. With a limited number of observations, it is impossible to identify superior or inferior performance simply because there is too much variability in the sample. Statisticians would say that the test lacks power.

Increasing the sample size (having a long history of returns for the same manager) would make discrimination easier. Unfortunately, with realistic assumptions about stock return volatility it would take more than three decades of monthly returns data to identify a manager who would be able to outperform the market on a risk-adjusted basis by an incredible 2.4 per cent per year.

There is a more subtle but pernicious effect of a short track record that is akin to the problem of measuring the profitability of selling earthquake insurance. If the underlying bad outcome has a very low probability of occurring but a very high cost when it does, managers can appear to be successful for some time (indeed most of the time). Of course, when the bad outcome occurs the performance record has an entirely different complexion, as is now well-known to many of Lloyds' Names who have experienced severe losses associated with low-probability events. Managers who include derivatives in their portfolios, particularly long-dated derivatives, can produce track records indicative of superior risk-adjusted performance until the unlikely, but catastrophic, outcome occurs.

A final caveat: professional money managers' published track records contain a 'survival' bias. Even if all managers are equally skilled, some will emerge at the top of the heap eventually, simply as a result of good fortune. If 12,000 people toss unbiased coins 12 times, approximately six people are likely to toss either all heads or all tails but those people would not possess superior (or inferior) coin-tossing skills. Money managers who perform poorly for long periods (due to lack of either luck or skill) leave the industry. Those who remain have above-average track records even if they have average skills.

Other dimensions of performance

The discussion to this point has focused on measuring risk-adjusted returns to evaluate investment performance. However, there are important dimensions of a money manager's performance other than achieving high rates of return, even after accounting for risk.

Most managers have stated investment styles and philosophies and managers should be held accountable for adhering to these because investors rely on them when selecting managers. For example, one of the authors knows from experience that a US citizen seeking international diversification by investing in a purported Japanese stock fund will find little comfort if that fund earns high returns by investing in US equities.

Style or attribution analysis investigates whether a portfolio's returns are correlated with indices representing the manager's professed philosophy. Similarly, if a manager claims to mimic an index (for example, the FTSE 100 or a more narrow industry index such as the healthcare industry), the association between the portfolio's returns and the index is a barometer of the manager's ability to adhere to his or her philosophy.

Performance summaries typically cite the R-squared statistic from a regression of a portfolio's return on index returns, especially for passive managers. If the portfolio tracks the index perfectly, the R-squared from this regression would be 100 per cent. Furthermore, the intercept from the regression will be zero, while the slope coefficient (or beta in the special case or a market index) will be 1. The R-squared statistic also measures the degree of diversification of the portfolio relative to the index, with a higher statistic representing a higher degree of diversification.

In addition to adherence to stated philosophies, investors should carefully scrutinize fund expenses. Professional money managers require compensation for their services, which is generally taken by charging expenses against the value of the managed fund.

Box 1: Performance evaluation – controlling for risk

Two of the largest US equity mutual funds, Fidelity Magellan and the Vanguard Index 500, provide an interesting contrast in investment philosophy. Fidelity Magellan relies heavily on research and 'stock-picking' in an attempt to beat the market. The Vanguard Index 500, with over $23bn now under the management of George Sauter, follows a passive 'index' strategy that attempts to mimic or 'track' the performance of the S&P 500. This index strategy requires no financial research or stock-picking skills.

The annual performance of these two funds for the five years ending in December 1995 is presented in Figure 3. Clearly, on the basis of mean return over this period, Magellan is the superior fund; it has bettered the S&P 500 by 4.14 per cent per year on average. In contrast, the Vanguard 500 has underperformed the S&P 500 by 0.17 per cent per year on average.

The slight underperformance of Vanguard can be attributed to transactions cost – the costs of executing stock trades and the costs of running the portfolio. The Vanguard Index has an annual expense ratio of 0.2 per cent. Though these costs are low for a well-managed index fund, they nonetheless represent a drag on investors' net returns. However, Vanguard tracks its benchmark portfolio quite well. In addition, it has annual turnover of only four per cent, yielding a relatively low cost of trading.

The picture is quite different for Magellan. Though the average annual return is higher than the return on the S&P 500, its performance in any one year can deviate substantially from the S&P 500. There are two reasons for this. First, Magellan emphasizes stock-picking – the identification of under- and over-valued securities. By its very nature, stock-picking engenders trading. Second, Magellan is not always fully invested in stocks. By not investing in stocks, Magellan attempts market timing. (This is in striking contrast to Vanguard, which is virtually 100 per cent invested in common stocks.) With its emphasis on financial research, stock picking and market timing Magellan has an annual turnover of 155 per cent. This turnover creates substantially higher costs of trading relative to the Vanguard Index approach. In addition, Magellan has an annual expense ratio of 0.92 per cent.

The stock-picking and market-timing performance enhancement of Magellan has to offset these costs if it is to exhibit superior performance. In some years this has been the case (for example 1993, when Magellan outperformed the S&P 500 by 14.6 per cent); in some years it has not (for example 1994, when it lagged the S&P by 3.13 per cent).

Has Fidelity Magellan outperformed the Vanguard Index 500 on a risk-adjusted basis? Here, the answer is not so obvious. Morningstar, a Chicago-based

Fig.3 Annual return

Fidelity Magellan and Vanguard 500 Index funds 1991–95 (% per year)

Year	Fidelity Magellan	Vanguard Index 500	S&P 500	Fidelity S&P 500	Vanguard S&P 500
1991	41.03	30.22	30.66	10.55	-0.26
1992	7.02	7.42	7.71	-0.60	-0.20
1993	24.66	9.89	9.87	14.60	-0.17
1994	-1.81	1.18	1.29	-3.13	-0.14
1995	36.82	37.45	37.71	-0.71	-0.08
Mean	**21.54**	**17.23**	**17.45**	**4.14**	**-0.17**

Fig.4 Summary of performance measures

1991–95 Portfolio	Jensen's Alpha*	Beta	R-squared %	Sharpe Ratio	Average return*	Standard deviation*
Vanguard Index 500	-0.01	1.00	100	0.334	1.32	2.91
Fidelity Magellen	0.21	1.08	76	0.357	1.62	3.57
S&P 500	0.00	1.00	100	0.339	1.33	2.91

* % per month

company that routinely rates the performance of mutual funds, characterizes Fidelity Magellan as a 'value' fund with average risk and above-average returns over the past 10 years. In contrast, Morningstar characterizes the Vanguard Index 500 as a 'blended' fund with below-average risk and above-average returns.

We calculate the Sharpe Ratio and Jensen's Alpha of Fidelity Magellan and the Vanguard Index 500 using monthly returns (Rpt) from January 1991 to December 1995. We use the return on the S&P 500 as the market index (Rmt) and the return on US treasury bills as the return on a risk-free investment (Rft). The results of this analysis are summarized in Figure 4.

During this five-year period, Magellan earned a mean monthly return that was 0.3 per cent higher than that earned by Vanguard. Magellan's superior monthly returns are also evident in the annual returns previously discussed; from 1991–95, it earned an annual return that was 4.31 per cent higher than that earned by Vanguard. Of course, these comparisons provide no accounting for differences in risk between the two funds. Consider first the Jensen's Alphas of Fidelity and Vanguard. Columns two to four of Figure 4 are derived from the regression of a portfolio's excess monthly return (Rit – Rft) on the excess return on the S&P 500 (Rmt – Rft).

Jensen's Alpha for Magellan (0.21 per cent) was indeed higher than that of Vanguard (–0.01 per cent). However, neither measure is reliably different from zero, which illustrates the volatility of security returns even for extremely large portfolios. In short, we are unable to reliably ascertain whether the higher returns of Magellan are due to superior ability or mere chance.

The analysis also reveals that Magellan (with a beta of 1.08) bore higher market risk than Vanguard (with a beta of 1.00). Furthermore, Vanguard had superior diversification (with an R-squared of 100 per cent) than Magellan (an R-squared of 76 per cent).

The Sharpe Ratios for the two funds and the S&P 500 are presented in the fifth column of the table. The Sharpe Ratios for all three funds are similar. Although Magellan earned higher mean monthly returns, these monthly returns were more volatile (with a standard deviation of 3.57 per cent) than those of either Vanguard or the S&P 500 (with standard deviations of 2.91 per cent).

In summary, Magellan earned higher mean monthly returns than both Vanguard and the S&P 500 during this five-year period but we are unable to conclude that its risk-adjusted performance was superior to either Vanguard or the S&P 500 using the traditional measures of Jensen's Alpha and the Sharpe Ratio.

This case highlights two important issues in investment performance evaluation.

First, focusing on mean returns is not sufficient; there must be some accounting for risk.

Second, disentangling superior risk-adjusted performance from luck is difficult; the volatility of security returns makes definitive conclusions in most contexts ambiguous at best and invalid at worst.

A dollar spent on security research, marketing or lavish corporate offices is a dollar not returned to fund investors. Though some of these expenses no doubt add value to investors, other expenses are likely not to. Not surprisingly, over time and across funds, funds with higher ratios of expenses to portfolio value have earned, on average, lower returns. Typical expense ratios for US equity mutual funds are 1.4 per cent.

Portfolio turnover can indicate other trading costs. When a fund manager replaces an existing security in a portfolio, the manager incurs costs that are seldom reflected in expense ratios. There are two components to those costs: the bid-ask spread (the difference between the buying and selling price of the stock at any point in time) and the market impact of the trade. If the fund engages in large trades, some of those trades may have an affect on price, such that the fund buys, on average, at a slightly higher price and sells, on average, at a slightly lower price.

This is of concern for a fund that trades actively, particularly if the stocks being bought or sold are not highly liquid. Although a fund that actively trades may have superior ability to select securities or time the market, this ability must be sufficiently high to compensate investors for the additional costs incurred from trading. Again, not surprisingly, the funds with higher turnover have fared no better than funds with low turnover. Typical annual turnover for US equity mutual funds is 89 per cent.

Summary

Evaluating investment performance is treacherous. Naive reliance on performance returns is clearly insufficient, since average performance does not reflect the risk borne by the strategy.

But as Brad Barber and Richard Leftwich explain, more sophisticated methods of performance evaluation (the Sharpe Ratio or Jensen's Alpha) provide sensible approaches to risk-adjustment and others are being developed. Unfortunately, all these methods are severely hampered by the Achilles heel of performance evaluation – the volatility of security returns. Knowing a portfolio's composition over time would allow a more reliable performance evaluation but these data are not yet widely available.

The good news, is that we can accurately measure and evaluate certain dimensions of performance. We can, for example evaluate whether a manager is meeting stated objectives or philosophies. Furthermore, investors would be well-advised to use managers who economize on expenses and minimize portfolio turnover. While some managers possess superior insights and skills, more often than not superior return performance is a result of serendipity.

Suggested further reading

Bodie, Z., Kane, A. and Marcus, A. J., (1993), *Investments*, Irwin.

Goetzmann, W. N. and Ibbotson, R., (1994), 'Do winners repeat? Patterns in mutual fund behavior', *Journal of Portfolio Management*, Winter, 9–18.

Lakonishok, J., Shleifer, A. and Vishny, R.W., (1994), 'Contrarian investment, extrapolation and risk', *Journal of Finance* 49, 1541–78.

Malkiel, B. G., (1995), 'Returns from investing in equity mutual funds 1971 to 1991', *Journal of Finance,* 50 (2), 549–572.

Sharpe, W. F., (1992), 'Asset allocation: management style and performance measurement', *Journal of Portfolio Management* 18 (2), 7–19.

Sharpe, W. F., Alexander, G.J. and Bailey J.V., (1995), *Investments*, Prentice Hall.

Asset allocation – have investors got it wrong?

by Nicholas Barberis

In the US alone, pension funds control more than $4,000bn in retirement assets. One of the basic questions facing these long-term investors is how to allocate this money between broad asset classes such as stocks and government bonds. This article examines what finance theory has to say about long-term allocation policies and why financial practice often differs from these recommendations.

Good news for stocks

The two most important factors to consider when weighing up different investment opportunities are risk and reward. The simplest way to quantify the reward from holding a security is to measure its average annual return. It will come as no surprise to most people that the reward from holding stocks has historically been higher than that for bonds. However, few realize just how much higher.

For example, the average annual real, or inflation-adjusted, return on the US stock market over the 1926–93 period was 6.6 per cent. This is considerably more than the average return on long-term government bonds over the same period, a mere 1.7 per cent. The difference between the two, 4.9 percentage points, is known as the 'equity premium'. The story is the same across many countries worldwide. The annual return on the UK stock market was 5.7 per cent over this period, 4.6 percentage points higher than the average bond return of 1.1 per cent.

The reward from holding stocks has, therefore, historically been substantially greater than that for bonds. This does not mean, of course, that we should automatically allocate all our money to stocks. It is possible that the superior performance of stocks is simply compensation for their higher risk. In other words, while stocks do earn more than bonds on average, over any one year stocks may significantly underperform bonds. Given the much higher reward from stocks, we might expect to find that they are also considerably riskier. In fact, looking at the data from a longer-term perspective, this does not appear to be the case.

Jeremy Siegel of the Wharton School of the University of Pennsylvania has used data on US stock and bond returns going back to 1802 and presented intriguing evidence about the risk of stocks. Over the 1802-1992 period, the highest real return on stocks in any one year was 66 per cent; the lowest was –39 per cent. The corresponding numbers for bonds are 35 per cent and –21 per cent. This is not very surprising. We typically think of stocks as being the riskier investment and these numbers are consistent with this view: the spread for stocks is wider than that for bonds.

For a long-term investor, though, this may not be the most relevant calculation. It may be more reasonable to use a 20-year rather than a one-year time-frame. The highest real return on stocks over any 20-year period was 12 per cent on an annualized basis and the lowest, one per cent. For bonds, the numbers are 9 per cent and –3 per cent. In other words, over any 20-year period, stocks have always earned a positive real return, something that cannot be said for bonds. Moreover, the spread between the highest and lowest 20-year return on stocks is smaller than that for bonds. The remarkable fact is that at long horizons, stocks appear less risky than bonds.

These results are confirmed by calculating a more direct measure of risk known as standard deviation, which measures the dispersion in returns. The standard deviation of annual stock returns has been 21 per cent historically, compared with 10 per cent on bonds, again confirming the usual notion that from a short-term perspective, stocks are riskier. Once again, though, our focus is on long-term investors with horizons much longer than one year. Therefore a more relevant statistic is the standard deviation of average returns over 20-year periods. For stocks, this is three per cent – lower than the corresponding figure for bonds of 3.4 per cent.

This is a remarkable reversal: from a short-term perspective, stocks are riskier than bonds. At long horizons, though, it is stocks that are less risky. Why do stocks offer a 4.9 percentage point average annual premium over bonds when they are not obviously more risky? It is worth thinking about these standard deviation figures a little more. Why is it that stocks appear riskier than bonds at short horizons but less risky at long horizons?

Some economists believe this is caused by mean-reversion in stock returns. Mean-reversion means that a particularly bad year for the stock market is slightly more likely to be followed by a good year, rather than by another bad year. Similarly, a good performance is more likely to lead to weak subsequent returns than to another good year. The effect of this is that bad years 'cancel' out good years, and vice-versa, so that over long periods of time, the risk of stocks is reduced. If there is more mean-reversion in stocks than bonds, stocks may eventually become less risky than bonds.

Can we believe the numbers?

The evidence so far casts stocks in a very favorable light. On the one hand, their average return is almost five percentage points a year higher than the average return on government bonds. Moreover, this higher reward does not appear to carry a substantial price in terms of increased riskiness. Over long horizons, stocks are not noticeably riskier than bonds. Taken at face value, the historical data seem to suggest that stocks are a far superior investment and that even quite risk-averse investors should weight them very highly in their portfolios.

Many prominent investment analysts disagree strongly with the preceding analysis of risk and reward. They claim, for example, that the 4.9 percentage point figure for the US equity premium, or indeed the 4.6 percentage points for the UK, greatly exaggerate the future rewards from holding stocks over bonds. They point out that the magnitude of the historical equity premia is largely explained by the very low returns on government bonds in both countries in the 1960s and early 1970s, which they in turn put down to the unexpectedly high inflation of the time.

Today, we have a much better understanding of the inflation process and it is unlikely that bondholders will be caught by surprise in the same way. Therefore, they say, we should not expect bond returns to be as low in the future as they were in the past century. There is undoubtedly some truth to this. But in fact it is not so clear why bonds suffered the way that they did. If inflation were the whole story, why did short-term government bonds perform just as poorly as the longer-maturity bonds? Would not short-term rates have quickly incorporated the rising inflation figures? If we do not fully understand the cause of the poor performance of bonds, it may be premature to argue that their historical performance is unlikely to be repeated.

The question of the long-run risk of stocks is even more controversial. The fact that the standard deviation of annual stock returns over 20-year periods is as low as three per cent suggests that mean-reversion in stock returns is making the risk of stocks fall faster than that of bonds. The problem is that our data only goes back a few decades and we do not have very many independent 20-year periods from which to draw reliable inferences. Formal statistical tests have been unable to establish convincingly that there is any mean-reversion in stock returns, even if the raw numbers do suggest it. If there is no mean-reversion in stock returns then there is no reason to believe that stocks become less risky than bonds at long horizons.

All the same, there are some good reasons for believing in mean-reversion. Here is one possible story. Suppose that investors become overly optimistic about the prospects of the economy and push the stock market to levels that are unreasonably high. A piece of sobering news will lead investors to correct their mistake, pushing the market back down. Any overreaction/correction story of this type automatically generates mean-reversion in returns.

Mean-reversion is often viewed with considerable scepticism because the predictability it implies appears to conflict with the idea that markets are 'efficient' and that prices are 'correct'. It is a common misconception that when prices reflect true fundamental value they should move randomly. In fact, mean-reversion can be completely consistent with a world where prices are set rationally. All that is required is that the risk of stocks changes over time. Suppose, for example, the market has plunged dramatically in the past few months. Such a move may lead to a shift in risk perceptions: investors may decide that stocks have become riskier. Basic finance theory tells us that risk must be compensated by a higher expected return. Therefore, following a stock market plunge, we would subsequently see higher returns on average, a phenomenon resembling mean-reversion.

The risk of a market collapse

Instead of arguing over how to interpret the standard deviation numbers, some analysts have claimed that standard deviation is an inadequate number to begin with. They say that simply looking at the dispersion of historical stock returns on existing stock markets misses a subtle but crucial form of risk: the risk of complete stock market collapse.

Proponents of this view point out that of the stock exchanges that existed at the turn of the century, as many as half subsequently experienced significant interruptions or were completely abolished. The Russian stock market, for example, was one of the world's largest in 1900, yet only a few years later investors had lost their entire holdings. Simply looking at the variability of US stock returns misses this kind of risk for the simple reason that the US market has never experienced such a collapse. This does not mean, however, that the risk of a future collapse is not present. Perhaps the observed high return on stocks relative to bonds is simply compensation for the unlikely but calamitous possibility of a complete stock market collapse.

The problem with this argument is that it is not clear why this kind of risk would confine itself to the stock market. Presumably something so devastating as to bring down the stock market should also affect the bond markets. Indeed, a more careful look at the historical facts shows that most of the time, it is in fact bond markets that suffer more. The Second World War, for example, reduced the value of the German stock exchange to a mere 10 per cent of its pre-war level. At the end of 1945, the Japanese stock market was worth only 35 per cent of its value just before the Japanese surrender. Political turmoil and labor unrest in the UK in 1973 and 1974 caused the British stock market to fall to a mere $50bn.

Striking as these events were, they had no lasting consequences. The Nikkei index's post-war performance is now legendary, rising as it did from 176 in 1949 to 20,000 in 1993. From 1948 to 1960, the German stock index provided real annual returns of more than 30 per cent. In spite of the effect of the war on the stock markets of these two countries, long-term investors eventually reaped rewards comparable to those of US investors. The same cannot be said, however, for the German and Japanese bond markets.

Japanese bondholders were devastated by the post-war inflation there while in Germany the hyperinflation of 1922–23 completely wiped out the value of German bonds. These facts make the 4.9 percentage point equity premium all the more surprising. Why is the average return on stocks so much higher than on bonds when the risk of catastrophic collapse actually seems higher for bonds than for stocks?

How much *is* held in stocks?

The numbers so far suggest the average return on stocks has been surprisingly high given that, over the long run, they appear not much riskier than bonds. What do these numbers imply for the portfolio holdings of long-term investors? Finance theory offers formal models for thinking about reasonable portfolio allocations across different classes of securities. The best known framework is mean-variance analysis, developed in the 1950s by Harry Markowitz, who later received a Nobel Prize for his work.

When historical numbers for bonds and stocks are fed into these quantitative models, the recommended long-term allocations to stocks are very high, often close to 100 per cent. Given the facts outlined earlier, this should not be surprising. The model sees that stocks have offered very high average returns historically and those returns have not been accompanied by a high level of risk over the long-run. Naturally, it recommends shifting most of one's wealth into the stock market.

How does this recommendation compare with actual portfolio holdings? By all accounts, both individuals and institutions hold rather less in stocks than it appears they should. In the US the typical asset allocation of a pension fund is 60 per cent to stocks and 40 per cent to bonds. Moreover, the asset allocation recommendations of leading brokerage houses published regularly in the financial press hover between 50 per cent and 60 per cent in stocks. These numbers raise a puzzle of their own. Given that historical data points to an allocation approaching 100 per cent in stocks, why do investors hold so much of their wealth in bonds?

One response is that even investors who, in principle, have a long-term outlook are forced for institutional or psychological reasons to take a short-term view, thus reducing their desired allocation to stocks. It is only when we cumulate returns over long time-periods that the risk of stocks falls below that of bonds. Annual returns on stocks are undeniably more variable than annual returns on bonds and a short-term investor will, therefore, limit his holdings of stocks.

Take pension funds, for example. Given the long-term nature of their liabilities, these funds should have a long-term investment outlook. However, behind every pension fund is a pension fund manager whose performance is frequently evaluated. To be sure of keeping their job, managers have to worry about short-term performance. This shortens their investment horizon and deters them from allocating too much to stocks. A different argument has been used to explain why individuals may act as if they have shorter horizons than would seem optimal.

Suppose you have an investment horizon of 20 years and are trying to decide on the right split between bonds and stocks. Would it matter that you are going to watch the year-by-year performance of your portfolio as opposed to going to sleep for 20 years and then awakening to see only the final outcome? At first sight, these distinctions may seem irrelevant. Why should it matter whether or not you are allowed to watch a blow-by-blow account of the performance of your portfolio? The remarkable fact is that psychologists who have simulated these types of experiments find that it does matter. Even if in principle you only care about the cumulative performance of your portfolio over a 20-year period, seeing poor performance over any one year may make you unhappy.

Given the regular updates from their investment managers and all the financial information at their fingertips, it is almost impossible for investors to avoid noticing occasional losses on their portfolios. Unwilling to watch these losses occur, investors may lean away from strategies that can produce poor short-term returns. Since stocks are more variable in the short-term, this reduces investors' desired allocation to stocks. The question of the right long-run mix of basic securities such as bonds and stocks is far from being resolved.

On the one hand, many investors are convinced by the historical data and are allocating larger and larger fractions of their portfolios to the stock market. In the US, for example, a government panel recently recommended that Social Security funds be invested in stocks, largely on the basis of their historical performance. On the other hand, even with two centuries of data, basic quantities such as the equity premium and risk, can only be measured very imprecisely, a problem known as 'estimation risk'.

This problem has led some investment managers to abandon the quantitative mean-variance models developed by academics precisely because these models appear to require accurate estimates of parameters that in practice we have little knowledge of. A better approach, though, may be to develop new models that explicitly incorporate our uncertainty about quantities such as the equity premium. It is models of this type that represent the current state of the art in practitioner and academic research on asset allocation.

Summary

An important challenge for long-term investors is how to allocate money between stocks and government bonds. So what does finance theory tell us and do practitioners take any notice?

Nicholas Barberis reminds us of the vastly superior returns achieved by equities over bonds, yet he suggests that equities are not noticeably risker.

One explanation for this is mean-reversion, whereby 'bad' years cancel out 'good' ones and vice versa. Others counter that the equity premium greatly exaggerates future rewards from holding equities over bonds – because of the distorting effect of high inflation on historical bond returns – and that looking at the dispersion of returns on existing stock markets ignores the risk from a complete stock market collapse. This said, equity weightings are lower than theoretical models would support, reflecting perhaps how even long-term investors are forced to take a short-term view.

Why financial investors like to stay at home

by Karen Lewis

Despite the apparent attractiveness of foreign investments, financial market investors display a puzzling 'bias' toward their own domestic stock. Research carried out over the past two decades suggests the foreign asset allocation of domestic investors is not consistent with what standard finance models would predict.

Basic investment theory highlights the diversification potential from holding assets that do not move in lock-step: if one security in a portfolio generates particularly bad returns in a given period, the other securities are unlikely to perform as poorly. Therefore, the lower the co-movement between the returns on securities in a portfolio, the better for diversification.

Equity and other financial markets across countries display just this type of pattern. Table 1 shows the correlation between returns on stock market indices converted into dollar terms. For instance, the correlation between the returns on the US index, measured by the S&P 500, and the returns on other stock markets range from 0.7 for Canada to 0.22 for Italy. These correlations suggest that holding foreign equities should reduce the variability on the overall equity portfolio of a US investor.

Risk and return trade-off

One way to demonstrate this is to examine the trade-off between risk and expected return for a US investor holding a portfolio of the S&P 500 and a successively higher portfolio weight in a mutual fund of G7 countries – Canada, Japan, the UK, France, Italy, and Germany. This trade-off is depicted in Figure 1 for a US investor.

The returns are converted into dollars and then adjusted for inflation with the US price level. At point A, the investor's portfolio is 100 per cent invested in the S&P 500. At point C, the investor's portfolio is about 15 per cent S&P 500 and 85 per cent foreign. At point D, the foreign share is even greater. Finally, at point Z, the portfolio is completely invested in the foreign mutual fund.

Table 1: International stock return correlations

Correlation with returns from:

	Canada	US	Japan	France	Germany	Italy	UK
Canada	1.00	0.70	0.27	0.43	0.31	0.29	0.52
US	0.70	1.00	0.26	0.44	0.36	0.22	0.52
Japan	0.27	0.26	1.00	0.39	0.38	0.37	0.37
France	0.43	0.44	0.39	1.00	0.60	0.42	0.55
Germany	0.31	0.36	0.38	0.60	1.00	0.38	0.43
Italy	0.29	0.22	0.37	0.42	0.38	1.00	0.35
UK	0.52	0.52	0.37	0.55	0.43	0.35	1.00

Source: author's estimates from Morgan Stanley equity data. Stock returns are in dollars with dividend reinvested.

As Figure 1 shows, placing a proportion of about 15 per cent of the portfolio into this foreign mutual fund will minimize the standard deviation of the overall portfolio. If the investor is willing to accept the same volatility as the US market, then he should place an even higher fraction of his wealth into foreign stocks as at point D and earn an expected real return of 5.75 per cent, instead of 4.40 per cent.

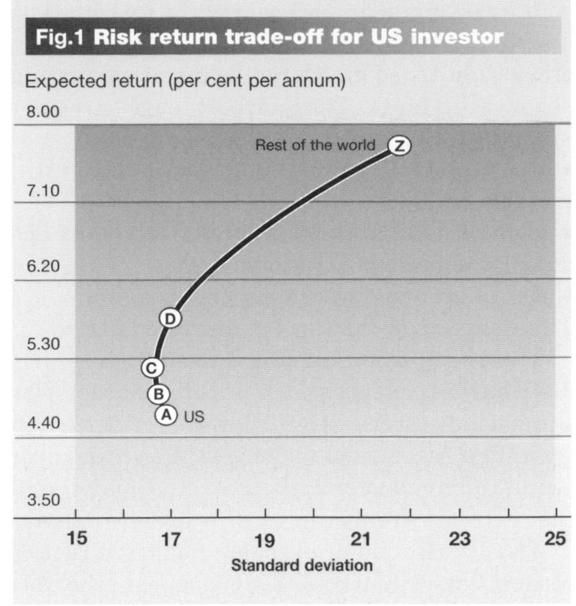

Foreign investments appear even more attractive when some of the assumptions behind this simple example are relaxed. For instance, the figure assumes that the US investor places all of his foreign assets into the particular foreign mutual fund of the G7 countries. If he allocates this portfolio efficiently among all possible combinations of domestic and foreign stock markets according to the so-called 'efficient frontier', then the gains from foreign investment are substantially higher. The benefits of foreign investment are greater still when the set of foreign assets is extended to include stocks from non-G7 countries such as the emerging markets, as well as bonds.

Despite the apparent attractiveness of foreign investments, financial market research has found that domestic investors hold a much smaller share of their portfolio wealth in foreign assets than investment theory would predict. Based upon aggregated equity data, French and Poterba (1991) found that US investors hold less than five per cent of their wealth in the equity of companies in Japan and in the UK.

This evidence would correspond to a point like B in Figure 1: a portfolio allocation that would imply a higher volatility and a lower return than even the most conservative efficient foreign investment allocation at point C. Furthermore, French and Poterba found this phenomenon was not unique to the US. Residents in Germany, Japan, the UK, France, and Canada all demonstrated a similar 'home bias' towards domestic stocks as well.

The apparent lack of international diversification is puzzling when global capital markets are integrating and governmental restrictions on international capital flows are being reduced. Financial researchers have examined explanations for this investor home bias, but have yet to provide a definitive answer to it. However, examining some of the plausible explanations helps to demonstrate both the strengths and the weaknesses of intuition based upon the simple methodology described thus far.

Extreme events

First, the risk on foreign assets perceived by investors may differ from that measured by the investment analysis. The investment analysis treats risk as the historical standard deviation of returns. The risk perceived by investors may differ from this for reasons ranging from irrational fears to rational, but alternative, characterizations of the risk.

If irrational fears are behind the investor home bias, then financial research will be unable to explain the bias. On the other hand, some of the perceptions of greater risk other than those measured by historical standard deviations may have some basis in observable facts. There are at least three reasons why these perceptions may be justifiable:

- the probability of adverse events occurring may be greater than the historical variance implies
- poor returns in the foreign portfolio may be correlated with each other, especially during the periods of adverse events
- risk of foreign government expropriation

These three possibilities are discussed below.

The assumption lurking behind the investment theory outlined above is that the distribution of returns can be fully characterized by their means and variances, as in the normal distribution. However, the distributions of both stock returns and the exchange rates used to convert the stock returns into domestic currency have been found to have fatter tails than a normal distribution. In other words, the likelihood that extreme events can occur is higher than a normal distribution would imply.

The likelihood of extreme negative returns is particularly high for emerging economy stock markets. For example, in the Mexican stock market decline of December 1994 through March 1995, the market declined by 30 per cent in Mexican peso terms. However, the return to dollar-based investors fell even more. On December 20 1994, the peso was devalued by 15 per cent. Two days later, it was allowed to float and the peso subsequently depreciated in value by about 50 per cent against the dollar through the end of March. Thus, a US investor holding Mexican stocks would have lost both because of the stock market collapse and the peso depreciation. The cumulative loss from both currency and equity from the beginning of December 1994 to the end of March 1995 was 65 per cent. Domestic investors thus have two components to their foreign asset risk: a stock market risk and a currency risk.

The events following Mexico point to another reason why domestic investors may consider the perceived risks to exceed the historical variances: bad news in one market can generate capital losses in other markets. Uncertainty about the wisdom of investing in Mexico following the crisis induced a re-balancing of portfolios by many US investors out of other emerging markets.

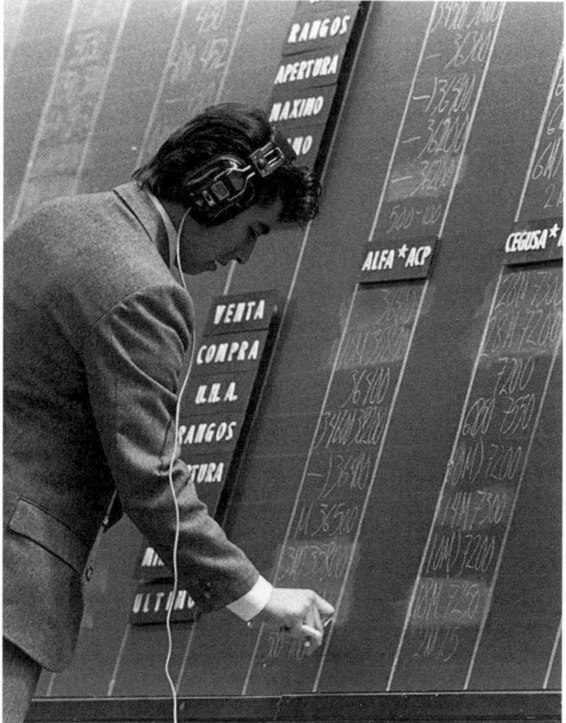

The Mexican stock exchange: uncertainty about Mexican investments created the 'tequila effect' felt in many other countries

This so-called 'tequila effect' was felt through stock market declines not only in Latin American countries such as Brazil, Chile, Argentina and Columbia, but also as far away as the Philippines, Thailand, Indonesia and Malaysia. Thus, a domestic US investor holding foreign equities in emerging markets following the crisis would not only have suffered losses in his Mexican investment, but also in his entire emerging market portfolio.

Domestic investors leery of foreign investments often cite concerns about rules and regulations in foreign countries. Variations in accounting rules, required disclosures, and reporting styles from country to country make analysis that much more problematic. These three justifications for perceived risk appear unlikely to explain entirely an investor's home bias. Even if the probability of a calamitous event, such as a market crash, exceeds the probability implied by the historical variance, these possibilities seem more likely to explain a bias against emerging market funds than foreign funds as a whole. If emerging market funds are correlated during crisis periods, then domestic investors would tend to treat these stocks as a group within their portfolios. But the home bias observation by domestic investors is that they skew their portfolio holdings away from foreign assets in general, including securities in industrialized countries such as Japan and the UK.

Moreover, even in the case of Mexico, the market decline was followed by a market rebound. Faster rebounds were experienced by the other emerging markets hit by the 'tequila effect'. Therefore, an investor with a 'buy and hold' strategy would have weathered even this rather severe storm. Finally, instances of foreign expropriation of investments are the exception rather than the rule, particularly as more governments relax restrictions on foreign investment. But is there still a way to understand the common perception that the risk is greater than the risk-return trade-off suggests? Yes, if the uncertainty surrounding this trade-off itself is considered. Indeed, the international risk-return trade-off itself varies over time and may be rather unpredictable. For instance, Figure 1 is drawn assuming that the expected returns are the historical means of the inflation-adjusted stock returns while the volatility is given by the historical standard deviation of these returns. However, both stock returns and exchange rates are notoriously variable. Therefore, re-estimating the same relationship over a different time period can give quite different results. Clearly, the set of shares of the foreign asset that would be optimal differs considerably depending upon what is the appropriate trade-off.

Efficient frontier

We must ask then, how much confidence domestic investors can have in the international 'efficient frontier?' One way to answer this question is to estimate the standard deviations around this trade-off itself. A recent study by Gorman and Jorgensen (1996) suggests the international efficient frontier has been extremely poorly estimated. In fact, there is so much uncertainty about the position of the efficient frontier that it may not be possible to know whether observations of the actual portfolio, such as point B, are actually on this efficient risk return trade-off. What this means is that investors who seek to find the truly optimal allocation of their portfolio into foreign stocks may have a hard time determining this allocation. Uncertainty about the position of the efficient frontier implies the position on this trade-off is difficult to pin down.

Table 2: Private capital flows to developing countries

($bn)	1990	1991	1992	1993	1994	1995
Total net portfolio investment of which to:	18.3	37.7	46.3	92.3	53.3	42.9
Western hemisphere	17.4	11.4	17.8	51.6	17.4	10.0
Countries in transition	–	0.8	–0.8	2.7	3.0	6.0
Asia	–0.9	2.9	9.8	23.8	16.0	18.5
Middle East and Europe	2.1	23.2	20.6	15.1	15.9	8.4

Source: International Monetary Fund, 'International Capital Markets', 1996

On the other hand, the large movements of capital into and out of emerging markets during the early 1990s suggests many investors do not follow 'buy and hold' strategies. Table 2 shows that over the 1990s portfolio investment in developing countries and countries in transition (such as the former Communist countries) has been quite volatile. During the period from 1990 to 1993, flows into these markets from developed countries grew from $18.3bn to $92.3bn. Following the increase in US interest rates beginning in early 1994, this pattern reversed, with a decline to a $42.9bn net increase in 1995. The pattern is even more pronounced when we focus on the Western hemisphere. Capital inflows grew from $17.4bn in 1990 to peak at $51.6bn in 1993, only to drop to $10bn in 1995. The table shows similar variability in portfolio investments in other parts of the world.

These movements are substantially more variable when viewed as net movements into US-based mutual funds invested in different parts of the world. In late 1994 and early 1995, some international funds experienced significant net outflows. These different flows – in response to such variables as changes in US interest rates and individual country events such as the Mexican peso crisis of December 1994 – suggest that domestic investors may be trying to follow market-timing strategies.

Market-timing

If domestic investors are following market-timing strategies, then the distribution of the stock returns themselves suggest complicated issues for optimal portfolio choice. For instance, the standard mean-variance analysis treats these means and variances of international stock returns as constant, as they are in the long run. However, over short-run periods, the distributions of stock returns and currencies are known to display time-varying variances and means. Therefore, investors considering re-balancing in response to changing events may face significantly greater risk than that implied by looking at long-run means and variances.

While these qualifications imply that it may not be possible to pinpoint where domestic investors should be on the efficient frontier, the relatively low correlation of international stock returns clearly suggests foreign stocks are important for diversification. As international capital markets become more integrated, this simple intuition would suggest that domestic investors should be holding more foreign assets. Transactions costs and perceptions of risk greater than measured risk may plausibly seem large to small individual investors, but these factors should be less important for institutional investors.

Indeed, if one examines the trend in foreign asset holdings instead of the level, domestic investors appear to be catching on to the benefits of international

Table 3: Institutional investors' holdings of foreign securities

Percentage of total assets

Pension funds	**1980**	**1988**	**1990**	**1991**	**1992**	**1993**
Canada	4.1	5.3	5.8	8.5	10.2	10.3
Germany	-	3.8	4.5	4.5	4.3	4.5
Japan	0.5	6.3	7.2	8.4	8.4	9.0
UK	10.1	16.5	18.0	20.8	22.0	19.7
US	0.7	2.7	4.2	4.1	4.6	5.7
Life insurance companies						
Canada	3.3	1.9	1.6	1.9	2.3	1.8
Germany	0.6	0.6	1.0	1.0	-	-
Japan	2.7	14.2	13.5	12.5	11.4	9.0
UK	5.5	9.5	10.8	12.4	12.7	11.6
US	4.1	3.6	3.6	3.6	3.7	-
Mutual funds						
Canada	19.9	19.5	17.5	16.2	16.7	17.1
Germany	-	-	56.3	53.5	47.6	45.2
Japan*	-	9.1	7.9	13.0	9.9	-
UK	-	-	37.1	39.2	37.9	36.0
US	-	-	-	6.6	-	10.1

* Investment trusts

Source: International Monetary Fund, 'International Capital Markets', 1995

diversification. This trend is particularly striking for some institutional investors. Table 3 and Figure 2 show the proportion of foreign securities held by these types of investors. In 1980, US pension fund managers held only 0.7 per cent of their portfolio in foreign securities. Just 13 years later, the fraction had increased to 5.7 per cent. This pattern is even more impressive for some of the other industrialized countries. The fractions of foreign securities held by these investors in the UK are large by comparison. In 1993, UK pension funds held almost 20 per cent, life insurance companies about 12 per cent, and mutual funds 36 per cent in foreign assets. Even the relatively conservative US mutual funds allocated 10 per cent to foreign securities.

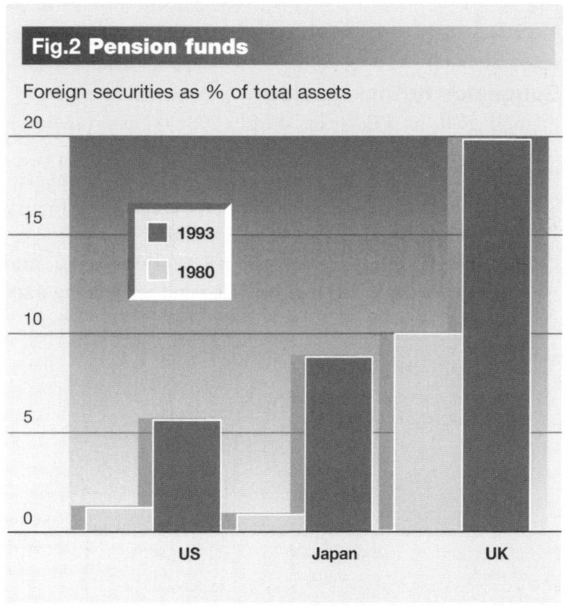

While domestic investors continue to hold only a small fraction of their portfolio wealth in foreign assets, the overall trends suggest that they are becoming more aware of these securities as investment opportunities. As many small investors have found domestic mutual funds to be relatively low-cost ways of diversifying their portfolio, these same investors have discovered the potential for investing in their foreign counterparts. Whether the vehicle is a 'country fund' comprised only of securities from an individual country or a 'global fund' that invests only a fraction of its portfolio in foreign securities, growth in the mutual fund industry in the international capital market has significantly reduced the costs of foreign investing.

These investment patterns suggest that perhaps the home bias will disappear over time. Domestic investors may not be biased towards home markets; they may just need time to learn about the costs and advantages of foreign asset allocation.

Summary

If you have already read the article 'Giving Markets a human dimension' (Module 6), you will be better prepared for Karen Lewis' focus on the phenomenon of investor bias towards domestic stocks – a good example of behavior inconsistent with what standard models would predict. She believes part of the explanation lies in a perception of foreign asset risk different to that derived from the historical standard deviation of returns.

The Mexican crisis of 1994 and 1995 is a good example of an event more adverse than the historical variance would imply; moreover, poor returns in a foreign portfolio may be correlated with each other, such as happened with the 'tequila effect' on emerging markets, and foreign rules and regulation can make analysis more problematic.

The author suggest that there is more to it than this, that the market-timing strategies pursued by many international investors complicate the issue of optimal portfolio choice and that those rebalancing their portfolios in response to changing events may face greater risk.

Suggested further reading

French, K.R. and Poterba, J.M., (1991), 'Investor diversification and international equity markets', *American Economic Review* 81: 222–226.

Gorman, L.R. and Jorgensen, B.N., (1996), 'Domestic versus international portfolio selections: A statistical examination of the home bias', Working paper, Kellogg Graduate School of Management, Northwestern University Evanston, IL.

Lewis, K.K., (1996), 'Consumption, stock returns, and the gains from international risk-sharing', National Bureau of Economic Research, Working paper, No. 5410.

Is passive investing optimal?

by Sanford Grossman

Modern portfolio theory has fundamentally altered individual and institutional approaches toward investment. The theory concludes that a well diversified portfolio is optimal and best acquired by passively holding the 'market'. The impact of this theory is readily apparent.

Before 1970 there were virtually no indexed funds, and the number of individual equities was far greater than that of mutual funds. Now a majority of investments are in indexed funds or are managed so that they closely track the returns of an index. There are as many mutual funds as there are individual stocks.

Many disciples of this theory interpret the 'market' as the portfolio of equities listed on the main stock exchanges. Paradoxically, this misinterpretation of the theory has caused investors to concentrate their savings in the very narrow asset class of listed equities. This is causing huge over-valuations as large amounts of money chase an ever smaller fraction of productive investments.

The optimality of passive indexing is based on the following argument. Consumption is acquired through the returns from productive but risky assets. The owner of such a risky asset can reduce his risk by selling rights to participation in the risky income stream (by 'equitizing' the income stream). He can then use the proceeds to buy rights to participate in other risky income streams whose returns may differ from those of his own assets – thereby diversifying the risks that his income stream is subject to and lowering overall consumption risk.

Risky assets

The principles of mean/variance efficient portfolio theory determine that there is one portfolio of risky assets which is optimal for everyone – i.e., which maximizes average return for a given level of risk. According to passive indexing theory, that one portfolio of risky assets that everyone holds will be the market portfolio. That is, it will be the portfolio containing all productive assets, because (a) all productive assets will be offered for equitization, and (b) the prices of all equities will adjust until all that is offered is sold. If all assets are offered for equitization, then all assets will be sold, and if everyone holds the same portfolio, then that must be the market portfolio.

Passive indexing – the idea of passively holding the 'market' – rests on the assumption of complete equitization of productive risks. Complete equitization of risks is where all individuals have sold claims to all their future income streams and use the proceeds to purchase claims to all of their present and future consumption and investment needs. Clearly, if there is complete equitization, then there is no active portfolio management; the optimal portfolio is the 'market' portfolio.

Unfortunately, this theory fails to describe a real world portfolio because there is no 'market' portfolio out there to buy and hold. The 'market' portfolio does not exist because all risky assets are not completely equitized. Some risky assets are not sold at all, and the risks of others are shared through mechanisms other than equitization, such as loans, forward contracts, swaps and insurance.

Passive equity indexing achieves the opposite of diversification, it concentrates savings in the small fraction of investments which have been equitized.

In the G7 countries, as elsewhere in the world, education, real estate and non-listed enterprises are financed almost exclusively in the debt market

There are numerous sources and uses of income which are not equitized. Investments in human capital and real estate are most often acknowledged in academic finance literature, because academics feel they understand the difficulties associated with selling shares tied to personal income or from listing individual homes on a stock exchange. However, there are whole countries with virtually no public equitization of income streams, such as China and, surprisingly, much of Continental Europe.

The fact that most income streams are not equitized does not mean that investors are unable to participate. Non-equitized projects are available as investments through the fixed-income market and its derivatives. Most investments that are externally financed are financed initially through debt. This is true not only of emerging markets such as Thailand, China and Poland but also of the G7 countries. For example, the rebuilding of East Germany which began in 1990, was financed by about $180bn of German debt issues. In the G7 countries, as elsewhere in the world, education, real estate, and non-listed enterprises raise capital exclusively from the debt markets. Contrary to theory, our students finance their education by borrowing rather than issuing equity, although Wharton would probably have done well to have accepted a claim to the income of its graduates instead of their debt.

Project finance

Passive investing is impossible in fixed-income markets. Entities borrow to finance projects, and pay back the loans as they receive income from projects. This dynamic pattern is quite regular, in regard to both business cycle time-frames, and the longer run time-frame of economic development. For example, as the expansion phase of a business cycle begins, companies borrow to finance inventories, and pay back the loans as the inventories are sold off. In the time frame of longer-run economic development, countries borrow to finance growth, and pay back the loans if and when such growth occurs.

If a project is financed by equities, then an investor can passively buy and hold the equity, and thereby buy and hold a share of the underlying risky project. This cannot occur with debt. A debt holder's 'investment' in a project is large at the beginning, and diminishes as the project is paid off. Equities can be bought and held for the long run, while a debt investment in a project is inherently temporary. However both debt and equity investing rely on the same type of risk reward calculus, which essentially involves active management at some level.

Contrary to academic theory, an investor in listed equities is not a passive investor in risky projects, he is only a passive participant in the active decisions of corporate management. The investor delegates to corporate management the active decisions as how, where, and when capital should be shifted from one project to another. All debt is not used to finance worthwhile investments. Someone has to evaluate risk and return from a debt investment. Further, it is impossible to create a passive index of debt investments which would be appropriate for all investors. People who are net borrowers obviously should not hold the same amount of debt as people who are net lenders.

A significant area of neglect by investors is global debt. Most of the capital inflows to countries are financed by debt issuance. The failure of investors to hold foreign debt is a big source of investment opportunity. Foreign debt has exchange rate risk. Many consultants to institutional investors regard exchange rate risk as inappropriate because, unlike investors in the fabled 'market' portfolio, all investors cannot symmetrically gain from bearing this risk (ie, if the dollar appreciates against the yen, then those people who borrow in yen and lend in dollars will make money, while those on the other side of the trade will lose money). Such consultants are wrong; the fact that some countries are lenders and others borrowers does not mean it is inappropriate to be either, and an investor who bears exchange rate risk is one or the other.

The Japanese experience in 1995 and 1996 provides an excellent example of the failure of the theory of passive equity investing and the success of global fixed-income investing. Japan had been in a severe recession, while the US had been enjoying strong economic growth. US companies and individuals had been borrowing to finance business expansion, investment in consumer durables and other activities. Japanese companies and individuals greatly reduced investment as the recession deepened. Yet there was a great deal of savings in Japan. With Japanese stocks and real estate offering no opportunities, where were the savings to go? Since Japanese savers hold primarily Japanese assets, most of the savings went into Japanese fixed-income instruments. The surplus of savings over investments caused Japanese interest rates to fall to extremely low levels, indeed the overnight rate fell to 50 basis points, and the 10-year yield fell to 250 basis points – about 500 basis points below comparable US rates. In the 1995–96 period, there was a net surplus of savings over investment in

Japan relative to what was available in the US. The interest rate differential between Japan and the US was a consequence of the failure of Japanese investors to globally diversify, and a consequence of incomplete equitization. If all investments in the US were equitized, then Japanese savers could have financed the US expansion by holding the listed equities issued by US entities.

Holding the global 'market' portfolio would give optimal diversification to investors, and finance all global projects. However since the 'market' portfolio is not available from listed equities, and Japanese investors did not even sufficiently diversify into US debt or listed equities, the net surplus of savings in Japan caused a deep interest rate differential between Japan and the US.

The failure of sufficient capital to flow from Japan to the US is typical of what happens when one country is in an expansionary phase of its business cycle while another is in recession. Insufficient capital flows from the long-term savers in the country suffering the recession to investments in the expanding country. If the expansion were financed by listed equities which appear in the portfolio of all savers, then this distortion would not occur.

What is the remedy

What is the remedy for this distortion? The global debt markets provide a remedy. It is easy to move capital from countries where it is in a surplus to those where it is relatively scarce. Conceptually, one borrows in the capital surplus country, and lends to the country where capital is relatively scarce. This movement of capital is easily accomplished in the foreign exchange forward swap market. A forward purchase of US dollars for yen with a settlement date three months in the future is equivalent to

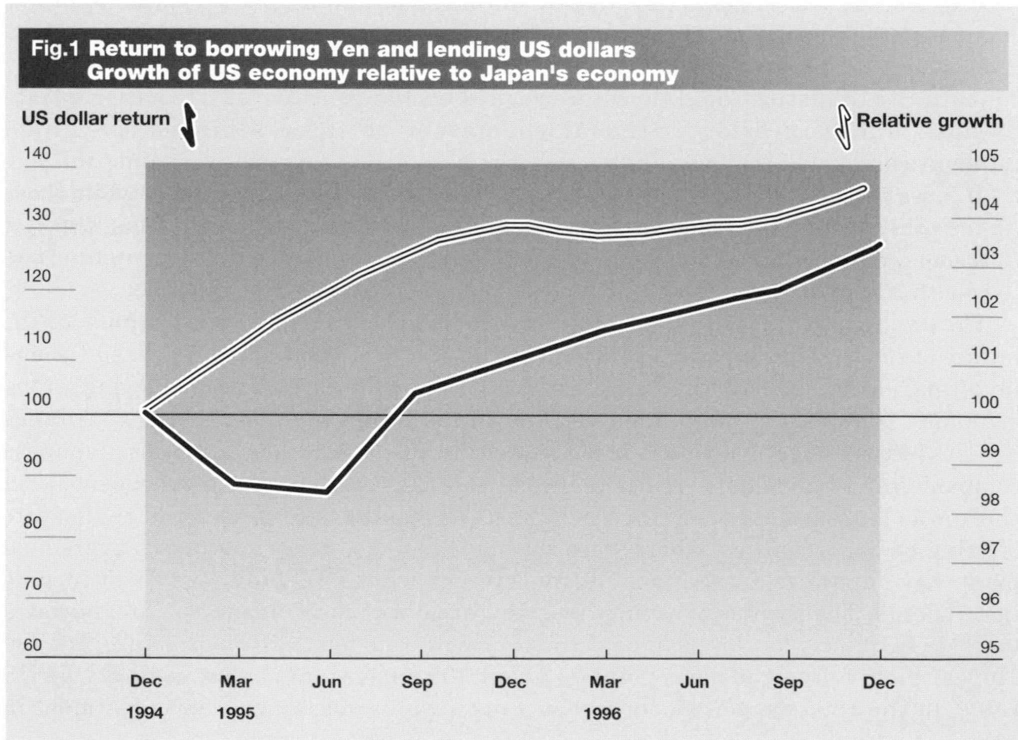

Fig.1 Return to borrowing Yen and lending US dollars Growth of US economy relative to Japan's economy

borrowing yen and lending dollars with three-month maturity loans. Figure 1 shows what the returns from such an activity were in 1995 and 1996, and juxtaposes the relative economic performances of Japan and the US (which is part of the driving force behind the returns).

Countries with substantial, productive investments have offered good real returns to holders of their short-term debt because most savers have ignored foreign currency debt as an investment. Countries with a lot of savings but poor domestic investment opportunities have been good places to borrow. Investors who understand these opportunities not only benefit from the positive returns generated by such an approach, but also enjoy significant diversification benefits from including asset classes in their portfolio which are totally uncorrelated with equities.

Lest the reader thinks this is academic fantasy, I have managed the investment of hundreds of millions of dollars since 1990 based upon this idea, earning well over 20 per cent per year with no investments in equities. The basic idea of financial theory is correct; investors should finance risky projects by holding well-diversified portfolios. Portfolio diversification and optimization are not achieved, however, by passively holding the small fraction of projects represented by listed equities. Indeed, this focus of savings on such a small fraction of global investments unreasonably raises the price of these investments.

The current global equity boom is similar to the bubble in Japan in the late 1980s, when savings in Japan were focused on buying Japanese assets, leading to an explosion of Japanese equity and land prices. Passive equity indexing may bring about its own downfall.

Summary

Modern portfolio theory – which concludes that a well-diversified portfolio is optimal and that this is best achieved by passively holding the 'market' – has dramatically gained in popularity since 1970.

But Sanford Grossman argues that the theory fails to describe a real world portfolio because not all risky assets are equitized (some are not sold at all, while the risk on others is shared via other mechanisms).

It is certainly right that investors should finance risky projects by holding well diversified portfolios; the trouble is that diversification is not achieved by passively holding the small fraction of projects represented by listed equities. Such a focus indeed unjustifiably raises the price of these investments. Diversification can be enhanced by holding actively managed foreign currency fixed income investments.

Suggested further reading

Grossman, S., (1995), 'Dynamic asset allocation and the informational efficiency of markets', *The Journal of Finance*, 1 (3), July, 773–87.

9

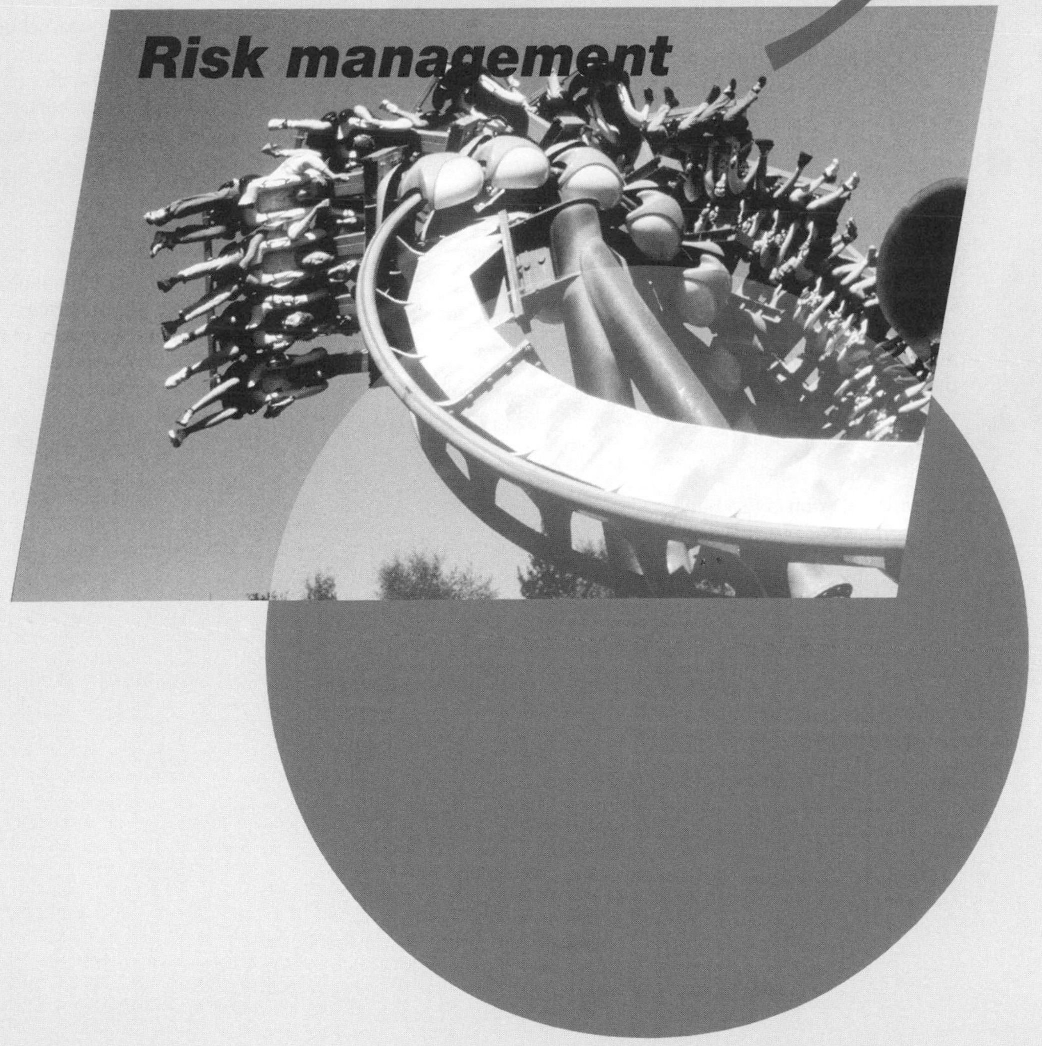

Contributors

John Holliwell is Managing Director of Smith & Williamson Consultancy Limited.

Anthony M. Santomero is the Richard King Mellon Professor of Finance at the Wharton School of the University of Pennsylvania and Director of Wharton's Financial Institutions Center.

Steven N. Kaplan is Professor of Finance at University of Chicago Graduate School of Business. His research interest include mergers and acquisitions, corporate governance and private equity.

Richard Leftwich is Fuji Bank and Heller Professor of Accounting and Finance at the University of Chicago Graduate School of Business. His research interests include audit qualifications, bond ratings, corporate charter changes and block trades.

Gordon M. Bodnar is Assistant Professor of Finance at the Wharton School of the University of Pennsylvania.

Ronnie Barnes is Teaching Fellow in Accounting at London Business School. His research interests include accounting for derivatives and the application of information economics and game theory to accounting issues.

Robert Z. Aliber is Professor of International Economics and Finance at the University of Chicago Graduate School of Business. He is Director of the School's Center for International Finance and is an authority on the international financial system, the multinational company and issues of public policy.

Contents

Introduction

Measuring and controlling risk are core themes of *Mastering Finance* – but how do you actually go about it? This module presents a variety of strategies for managing a variety of financial and non-financial risks, with particular reference to hedging and foreign exchange.

Risk: enough rope to hang the business?

by John Holliwell

There is nothing wrong with risk. It is the lifeblood of business and the test of entrepreneurs and managers. What matters is how you handle risk and the culture in which you operate.

Do you know the risks to which your business is exposed? Which exposures are big enough to worry about? If there is anything you could do to protect against them? What it would cost to reduce or to hedge your risks? Once you have the facts it is decision time. You can choose to do nothing or seek to reduce the exposures or to hedge them in whole or in part. The unforgivable sins are to fail to consider the risks or fail to act on any decisions.

The risk culture of your business is critical and must be established at the most senior level. Above all it calls for honesty. Too often individuals are criticized after the event for taking decisions that, at the time, were in tune with an organization's perceived appetite for risk.

But it is never easy to set down effective guidelines and the range of exposures for even a simple transaction can be extensive. For example, an exporter needing to borrow to finance a sale in foreign currency may have to consider counterparty credit risk, currency exchange rate risk, funding risk and interest rate risk. The permutations are endless and the costs of hedging transactions to reduce or eliminate every possible exposure could potentially swallow any profit from a deal.

While losses are likely to be quantitative, the potentially infinite number of risk combinations means that the skills needed to make good decisions are usually qualitative. Even a computer programmed to consider every conceivable permutation of risks needs to be told what level of exposure is acceptable. Any program is only as good as the parameters and data fed into it by people who have themselves been conditioned by experience.

But what of the improbable, the wholly unexpected or the never-seen-before? Effective risk management requires thinking the unthinkable. This does not in any way lessen the great value of the many sophisticated risk-management systems available. The problems come if people start to think of them, and the models they are based on, as infallible.

It is also common for the development of control systems to come after any new risk-related products. Be careful not to bet the business until the exposure is known. To be in business you must make decisions involving risk. However sophisticated the tools at your disposal you can never hope to provide for every contingency. But unpleasant surprises should be kept to a minimum.

Ask yourself:

- Can the risks to your business be identified, what forms do they take and are they clearly understood – particularly if you have a portfolio of activities?
- Do you grade the risks faced by your business in a structured way?
- Do you know the maximum potential liability of each exposure?

- Are decisions being made on the basis of reliable and timely information?
- Are the risks large in relation to the turnover of your business and what impact could they have on your profits and balance sheet?
- Are the exposures diversified or do you have too many eggs in one basket?
- Over what time periods do the risks exist?
- Are the exposures one-offs or are they recurring?
- Do you know enough about the ways in which your exposures can be reduced or hedged and what it would cost including the potential loss of any upside profit?
- Have trading and risk-management functions or decisions been adequately separated?
- Is there a clear differentiation between the actions taken to reduce potential loss by the hedging of exposures and those where you are speculating in the hope of profit?
- Do you have an effective risk-management policy with responsibility at senior executive officer level?
- Is this policy regularly reviewed to identify new and changing exposures? Even on single transactions the risk profile can change over time.
- Who decides whether or not to hedge any exposures?
- Are adequate risk monitoring procedures in place, including those for contingent liabilities? Exposures can change very quickly and you may need to be able to react without delay.
- Are your colleagues and staff risk conscious? They probably attend marketing and customer care meetings but what about risk management meetings? A single sale rarely changes a business's future but one mismanaged risk can destroy the hard work of years.
- Are the rewards matched to the risks?
- Are the owners of the business happy at the level of exposure or might they prefer a lower risk profile with a potentially reduced return? What is their 'appetite for risk'?
- What motivates individuals – is the pressure on management and staff, or the way they are remunerated, encouraging them to take unauthorized risks or to cover up their own or colleagues' mistakes?
- Do management and staff feel free to ask questions or admit they do not understand?
- Do you regularly update disaster-recovery plans?
- Are you proud of your business's culture and ethics?
- Do you learn from your mistakes?

The way in which staff are remunerated has become a hotly debated topic, doubtless fueled in part by envy at the large sums paid to some financial market dealers. Whatever the emotions generated, the skills of such people are in demand and they presumably receive what their employers hope they are worth. But it highlights an important risk-management concern, which is whether the interests of the employee and the business necessarily have much in common.

Unless prosecuted for fraud, the risks to any individual who makes a serious mistake are those of their employment, their reputation and any unpaid remuneration. This would be enough to make many people think twice but not necessarily those with whom you may be most concerned. By the very nature of their jobs the dealers and deal-doers in most industries are paid to take risks and to thrive in a fiercely competitive and often hostile environment.

When a business rewards any of its staff on the basis of volume or of risk-generated profits it encourages them to take excessive chances. And if they get it wrong the gambler's temptation is often to double up and try again. A 'rogue' dealer on a losing streak will need to keep increasing the volume or speculative nature of trades if he or she is to have any chance of wiping out an ever-mounting deficit. After all, it is not their money. Even when they derive no direct personal financial benefit from their actions a great deal of damage can be done by employees under pressure to produce results.

As with so much in risk management you may have to accept that a potential risk exists and then take steps to control it. This means ensuring that no single individual or any common-interest group is given enough rope to hang the business. The principles for achieving this are simple enough but are often not carried out in practice. Set limits, monitor exposures, have clear reporting lines, separate the trading 'front office' from the administrative and controling 'back office' and ensure that everything is subject to 'two pairs of eyes'.

How many people know and understand what is going on? If an individual is always too busy to take a day off the alarm bells should start ringing. Are they cracking up or covering up? When problems are suspected, colleagues often turn a blind eye because no-one loves a whistle-blower. This is where the culture of a business is so important; senior management should be judged in large measure by its ethical standards. The reputations of organizations without a high moral code are exposed risk. They often end up losing the customers they have let down and being cheated by their own employees.

In an increasingly complex world how do you monitor risks that you may not fully understand? Employing a poacher as gamekeeper may be a good idea, always assuming you can find one willing to give up their former life and rewards. But all too often the pay offered is inadequate and those you can attract are then buried up to their necks with paperwork and kept in the dark as to what is going on. The only thing to be said for this 'mushroom principle' is that it provides senior management with a convenient scapegoat when things go wrong.

Responsibility for risk management rests at the top and if the senior executives do not understand what is going on they must find out. It would be nonsense to suggest that they should know every detail of all that is happening in a business but their job is to ensure that adequate systems and controls are put in place.

Ask straightforward questions and if you do not get a straightforward answer then keep on asking until you understand. Replies couched in jargon or with apparent scorn for your ignorance should always arouse suspicion. Most honest people who are on top of their job are only too happy to explain what they do and why. The fear of looking foolish by asking simple questions or admitting you do not understand something is a considerable obstacle to effective risk management. Once again the culture of a business is all important.

Beware the self-deception endemic to bull markets. Just because it has not gone wrong does not mean it is right. Few organizations are immune from the collective mania of a booming economy and many fear being left behind in market share and profits if they do not keep pace with the competition. The voice of caution is then at best an embarrassment and often an obstruction to be removed. With the recession that so often follows the good years another generation learns the old lessons anew and strives to put in place the checks and balances to ensure 'it will never happen again'.

Box 1: A myriad of financial risks – how many does your business face?

Market risk – exposure to adverse change in the price or value of something in which you trade or are holding as an investment. Where market risk is a factor, and especially in volatile markets, the practice of 'marking to market' on a regular basis is an important discipline. This involves using current market prices to calculate any profit or loss that has arisen from price movements since the last time you calculated the value of your assets or the cost of meeting your liabilities.

Liquidity risk – where a market does not have the capacity to handle, at least without significant adverse impact on the price, the volume of whatever you are trying to buy or to sell at the time you want to deal. Also, an inability to meet debts when they fall due.

Counterparty (credit) risk – that a counterparty will not honour their obligations to you. If the default occurs before the date when settlement of the underlying transaction is due you may be exposed to the 'replacement risk' of having to bear any costs of replacing or canceling the deal, which are often less than the full amount of the transaction.

A potentially greater threat is 'settlement risk', which arises when you pay away cash or deliver assets before your counterparty is known to have performed their part of the deal. This exposure is normally for the full amount of the transaction and may exist during the course of a trading day, or last overnight or longer.

Political and country risks – never underestimate the potential impact on a business of decisions taken by national and supra-national governments, government agencies and regulatory bodies empowered to control trade or to set prices and industry standards. Their extensive armoury includes taxation, quotas, tariffs and other trade barriers, currency exchange controls and inconvertibility, restrictions on foreign ownership and the repatriation of profits or capital, availability of grants and subsidies, setting interest rates, granting licences and monopolies, nationalization, expropriation and restitution of assets to former owners.

When dealing with an overseas business or with a st'ate ('sovereign risk'), you may also need to consider the country's social and economic stability, its trading practices, customs and ethics, its commercial law – including insolvency – and the effectiveness of its legal system. Just as you normally set limits on your exposure to every business or individual with which you deal, so there may be a limit to the amount of exposure you will accept relating to any single country.

Currency exchange rate risk – even the major currencies may experience substantial exchange rate movements over relatively short periods of time. These can alter your balance sheet if you have assets or liabilities 'domiciled' in a currency other than that in which you prepare your accounts ('translation risk'). And they may affect your profit and loss account if the impact is on income or expenditure ('trading' or 'transaction risk'). There may also be longer-term strategic consequences for the value of your business if, for example, rates of exchange settle at levels that fundamentally alter your competitiveness in international markets.

Hedging risk – this occurs when you fail to achieve a satisfactory hedge for your exposure, either because it could not be arranged or as the result of an error. You may also be exposed to 'basis risk', where the available hedging instrument closely matches but does not exactly mirror or track the risk being hedged.

Funding risk – a business fails when it cannot pay its debts; how certain are your finances?

Interest rate risk – if you are a borrower or a lender there will be a direct impact from changes in the rates of interest you pay or receive; this may be compounded by exchange rate risk if the amounts are in foreign currency.

Operational risk – a potential 'catch-all' that includes human errors or defalcations, loss of documents and records, ineffective systems or controls and security breaches; how often do you consider the 'disaster scenario'?

Legal, jurisdiction, litigation and documentation risks – including netting agreements and cross-border insolvency. Are your contracts enforceable in the territories where you operate? Which country's laws regulate individual contracts and the arbitration of disputes? Could a plaintiff take action against you in an overseas court where they have better prospects of success or of higher awards? There is a growing and widespread belief that, whatever goes wrong, someone else must pay. This 'compensation culture', whatever its justification or causes, is becoming a big problem for many businesses.

Box 1 continued

Aggregation risk – where a transaction involves more than one market in which problems could be experienced.

Concentration risk – exposure to a high level of risk on any instrument or in any sector; an extension of concentration risk is that to a market dominated by only a small number of firms.

Systemic risk – the supervisor's nightmare, where problems in one financial institution or market may cross over to others and to other countries in a domino effect, potentially threatening chaos in the global financial markets.

Summary

Risk and the measurement of risk have been consistent themes of *Mastering Finance*. But how do you ensure it does not get out of control and threaten your business?

While a growing number of computer programs have been developed to aid in monitoring risk in the wake of recent financial scandals, John Holliwell urges managers to remember that these are not infallible. In asking themselves what can go wrong, managers should always consider the wholly unexpected, or 'never-seen-before', and think the unthinkable.

This article provides advice on monitoring risks but stresses that responsibility ultimately lies at the top. It concludes with a panel describing the main financial risks, such as political and country risks, hedging and currency risks, funding and interest rate risks and legal, jurisdictional, litigation and documentation risks.

The revolution in risk management

by Anthony Santomero

Economic thought has traditionally regarded the world as a place where agents maximize their gain, subject to a series of constraints. The typical consumer is assumed to be interested in consumption, with more being preferred to less. The key constraint is a budget limitation, which identifies the problem as essentially an economic one where choices have to be made.

At the same time, companies – organizations that are increasingly mere coalitions of individuals with investment opportunities – are viewed as providing profit opportunities for investors. These companies have been characterized as selecting investment opportunities with a single-minded emphasis on expected profit.

Investors can select which companies to invest in, in order to obtain their preferred risk–return trade-off. Therefore, companies have no reason to bundle projects to obtain a particular risk profile because their owners can diversify across businesses to achieve a specific bundle of risk and reward.

Recently, however, this view of the company's goals and operating mode has changed. Economists have begun to recognize firm-level risk issues as important considerations and have gone on to develop a way of thinking about risk and its place in the firm. In doing so, economic theory has developed positive theories of optimum volatility management. These ideas have developed under the title of financial risk management.

Why manage risk?

Why do managers of organizations, who are presumed to be working on behalf of the company's owners, concern themselves with both expected profit and the distribution of firm returns around their expected value? There are four reasons according to academic study:

- managerial self-interest
- the tax structure
- the cost of financial distress
- the existence of capital market imperfections.

In each case, management is shown to be in an environment in which expected profit does not provide sufficient information about a project or investment decision – managers must concern themselves with the variability of returns.

In the first case, the managers are risk averse, even though the shareholders are not. In the other three cases, a feature of the economic environment leads managers to maximize shareholder value by behaving in a risk-averse manner.

Managerial self-interest

The first reason given for risk aversion relates to managers' self-interest. It is argued that managers have limited ability to diversify their own personal wealth position, which is associated with their company-specific stock holdings and the value of their earnings in their current employment. They, therefore, prefer stability to volatility because, other things being equal, such stability improves their own position at little or no expense to other stakeholders.

Objections have been offered to this line of reasoning. Some find it unconvincing because it offers no reason for a manager to hedge his or her risk within the company rather than directly in the market. According to this view, managers could enter the financial market to off-set the effect of the close association of their wealth with company performance. By taking a short position in the market, managers could obtain any level of concentration in firm-specific profitability. However, this argument misses at least three important features of the employment relationship.

First, it is probably problematic for senior managers to be seen to divest, or to be systematically diversifying away, investments correlated with company performance. Such a public divestiture would be required to properly hedge management's personal investment profile.

Second, to the extent that some outcomes, defined as financial distress, lead to their employment contracts being terminated, it may be in the best interest of management to constrain firm-level outcomes, so that the future value of their employment earnings is not lost.

Thirdly, arguments in favor of simple expected-profit decisions neglect the fact that management's abilities are not directly observable. Therefore, observed outcomes may influence owners' perception of managerial talent. This would, in turn, favor reduced volatility or at least the protection of company profitability from large negative moves. For all, or any one of these reasons, there appears to be ample justification for the view that managers will and should worry about risk.

The tax structure

Beyond managerial motives, firm-level performance and market value may be directly associated with volatility for a number of other reasons.

The first is the nature of the tax code, which both historically and internationally, is not strictly proportional. With a progressive tax structure, income-smoothing reduces the effective tax rate and, therefore, the tax burden shouldered by a company. By reducing the effective long-term average tax rate, activities which reduce the volatility in reported earnings will enhance shareholder value. However, two points are worth mentioning in this context. First, with the advent of more proportional tax schedules, particularly in the US, the arguments here are somewhat mitigated. In fact, one should observe, other things being equal, a decline in the interest in risk management by American businesses over the past decade. No one, however, has suggested that such is the case.

Second, the tax argument rests on reported income not true economic profit. To the extent that generally accepted accounting principles permit tax planning, this argument may favor tax-motivated reporting and more careful management of the difference between the book and market value of profits. Since there is significant discretion in tax reporting, tax consideration may not motivate actual decision-making nearly as much as this theory suggests. However, the argument here is that real economic decisions are affected by the tax code not just their reporting.

The cost of financial distress

Companies may also be concerned about earnings volatility because of the consequences of profits differing greatly from expectations and the implications of such negative news for corporate viability. To the extent that a financial crisis or bankruptcy is associated with an increase in costs, a company will be forced to recognize this in its behavior. In such cases, it will behave in a risk-averse manner because it is in its best interest to do so.

Numerous studies offer evidence of the cost associated with financial crisis. The first paper dates back to 1977 and presents empirical evidence of very high bankruptcy costs. More recent studies continue to reinforce the importance of these additional burdens on the company.

Expenses associated with bankruptcy proceedings – legal costs and perhaps most importantly the diversion of management attention from creating real economic value – are large and management correctly seeks to avoid them.

As a result, standard corporate finance training frequently refers to the cost of bankruptcy in the analysis of investment decisions. It is also worth noting that this cost is, perhaps, even more important in regulated industries. In these cases, large losses may be associated with the withdrawal of a license or charter and the loss of a monopoly.

Capital market imperfections

The fourth explanation rests on the need for investment at the company level. According to this view, volatility disrupts investment because it forces a business to both reduce the amount of capital devoted to new projects and seek external resources at times of low profitability. However, external financing is more costly than internally generated funds due to capital market imperfections. These may include the transaction costs associated with obtaining external financing, imperfect information in the market about the risk of investment opportunities or the high cost of potential bankruptcy associated with a higher debt burden. These added costs result in under-investment in low profitability periods.

Put another way, the volatility of profitability causes the company to seek external finance to exploit investment opportunities when profits are low. The cost of such finance is higher than internal funds due to the market's higher cost structure associated with the factors enumerated above. This, in turn, reduces investment and expected profits.

The cost of volatility is the foregone investment or lowered earnings in each period that the company is forced to seek external funds. Recognizing this, the company embarks upon volatility-reducing strategies, which reduce earnings variability. Hence, risk management is optimal in that it allows the business to obtain the highest expected shareholder value.

Together, the stories work fairly well. Corporate managers are interested in both expected profitability and the risk, or the variability, of reported earnings. This concern is explained by the costs that vary across the range of possible profit figures associated with any given expected performance. Therefore, the company is led to treat the variability of earnings as a variable that it selects, subject to the usual constraints on management. How it proceeds to manage its risk position is dealt with next.

How are risks being managed?

The question is easy enough but the answer is not so easy. Risk management can quickly be divided into three sub-fields of research. While there are overlaps, the questions, answers and open issues vary by area of discussion. It is, therefore, useful to address each of the following questions:

- how should risks be managed?
- what have non-financial companies done by way of risk management?
- how have financial companies addressed the issue?

The three areas can be seen as two separate problems: theory and application. However, in as much as financial company risk management has developed separately, it is useful to treat the application of risk-management techniques in the financial sector as a separate issue.

How should risk be managed?

This first question is the easiest to answer but hard to implement. When a manager is making the decision to further advance his or her own best interests the problem becomes the usual one of portfolio choice.

Projects and/or activities are selected using the standard risk-return trade-off that finance has long promulgated. Projects are selected according to their expected profitability, their variance and the covariance of their returns with other projects within the firm.

On the other hand, if the manager's concern over risk is due to its effect on overall firm value, as discussed above, then managers must recognize the effect of volatility on market value. This will lead them to alter their decisions and encourage risk management and control. In either case, implementing such a risk-management procedure requires a strategy that includes both risk identification and risk reduction. The former involves an analysis of the drivers of firm performance and the reasons for the volatility in earnings and/or market value. The latter is accomplished through the standard procedures of risk reduction, such as standard diversification procedures, and rules that limit potential extreme downside results.

Non-financial companies

From theory to practice, we move from the neat realm of concept into the difficult area of implementation. Here, little information exists on the practices employed by non-financial companies. General management practices to dampen the variability of cash flow and/or profitability are not documented in any systematic way.

Nonetheless, it is generally accepted that risk management can be conducted in two ways. Either a business can engage in activities that together result in less volatility than they would exhibit individually or it can use financial transactions to similar effect.

The first approach is to embark upon a diversification strategy in the portfolio of businesses operated by the firm: in short, engage in diversification by conglomerate merger. However, conglomerate activity, while once a popular strategy, has fallen out of favor. Most companies have learned that they do not necessarily have value-added expertise in more than one area and have found it hard to prosper across industry lines. As a result, those concerned about the volatility of earnings have turned to the financial markets. This is because these markets have developed more direct approaches to risk management that transcend the need to invest directly in activities that reduce volatility.

Financial risk management, using financial products such as swaps, options and futures, can accomplish the same ends and has thereby experienced explosive growth. Such derivative products have proved to be an important means of risk trading. The result of such use on shareholder value, however, is still an open question. The popular

Lords White and Hanson: diversification through conglomerate activity, as at Hanson, has gone out of fashion

press has spotlighted the misuse and abuse of derivatives at Procter and Gamble, Metallgesellschaft and Gibson Greetings. Companies are, therefore, concerned that use of derivative products will hit their stock prices. At the very least, it is a public relations problem.

Financial companies

In many respects the story associated with risk management for industrial companies is transferable to their financial counterparts. However, the issue is more complicated for financial companies. These companies deal in financial markets, as principals and agents, and have a long history of both hedging capability and taking positive risk positions. In fact, it could be argued that their franchise involves taking the financial risk from the non-financial sector.

However, taking financial risk does not imply keeping it. As corporate entities, these organizations, like their non-financial counterparts, must deal with the same issues that motivate the rest of the private sector. They are run by managerial talent that must be concerned with risk for their own benefit. They face the same tax structure and are even more concerned by the cost of financial distress.

While it could be argued that regulatory oversight and its implicit guarantee makes them less risk averse, the existence of regulators that charter and sustain the institutions' franchise makes risk a real concern. Management, therefore, must find the correct place for risk management in a sector that has both a reason for taking financial risk and reasons for concern over doing so.

It is, therefore, useful to distinguish two ways of delivering financial services. These can be provided either as an agent or as a principal. In the former, risk is borne by the two sides of the transaction, with little remaining with the financial institution that facilitated it. In the latter, risk is absorbed by the financial institution itself because it places its balance sheet between the two sides of the transaction.

The choice between these two techniques seems to depend upon the institution's value-added or unique expertise in managing the associated risk. For some risks, the institution frequently finds itself absorbing risk associated with its asset services rather than transferring it, while for others the opposite is true.

The latter group, where financial transactions transfer risk to the buyer of assets, is growing more rapidly. As information and transaction costs have declined, the fraction of financial assets held by risk-transferring institutions, such as mutual funds, pension funds and unit trusts, has increased relative to those held in risk-absorbing institutions such as commercial banks and other depositories. This is due to the decline in the returns offered to these institutions to bear such risks.

Nonetheless, balance sheet risk management is still an important issue in the financial sector. Institutions that accept certain types of financial risk, because of their business strategy, require risk control and management procedures. These should involve the same steps and obtain the same results as indicated above. The drivers of uncertainty must be identified and risk-reduction strategies outlined. The distinction here is that the risks are different from those faced by the non-financial sector. Standard bank management texts, however, have long discussions on risk-identification and risk-management strategies. In a recent review of risk techniques and their application in the financial sector, Santomero and Babbel (1997) and Santomero (1997) catalog the procedures used, along with the compromises made along the way.

Where do we go from here?

The fact that risk matters is, perhaps, not news to senior managers. However, the news is that there is a better understanding of why risk matters and how it should be managed. Whether a company is in the manufacturing sector or financial services, it has risks that need to be managed. In today's business environment no organization is immune from risk and none can be without a risk-management and control process.

To do so, however, requires a risk-management system that measures, controls and monitors these risks. In addition, it must hold accountable all those that are responsible for controlling the complex set of risks that impact upon firm performance.

As a result of financial change and asset innovation, we have begun to develop a deep understanding of how to fashion an appropriate risk-management system. In fact, the implementation of broad risk-management systems has become big business – indeed a growth area of management interest and consulting.

What does such a system involve? As noted above, it begins with a careful identification of the causes of volatility – the factors that lead to variation in performance. Next, the risks that have been so identified must be actively managed. Recent research has shown how this is accomplished by standardized procedures that measure, monitor and limit the risk-taking activity in order to reduce the volatility of performance. Such systems usually include four parts:

- standards and reports, which identify, measure and monitor the factors that cause volatility
- limits and controls on each of the factors and on each member of the organization that adds risk to a company's performance profile
- guidelines and management recommendations concerning appropriate exposure to these same risks
- accountability and compensation programs that lead mid-level managers to take the process seriously.

While still in the formative stage, such systems have proved valuable to organizations that have implemented them and are rapidly becoming a standard part of the managerial tool kit. This should not be a surprise.

Shareholders care about risk, the stock market cares and, as has been said, so should senior management. The challenge for these managers is to adopt a risk-control system that reduces the volatility of profitability and engenders a risk-control mentality throughout the organization.

Summary

This article looks at the changing view of risk management within companies. In orthodox terms, says Anthony Santomero, managers ought not to be concerned with balancing risk within an organization since the owners of the business – the shareholders – will have balanced their own risk though holding a diversified portfolio of shares. However, managers are concerned to manage risk within their organizations. This can be attributed to a number of factors: managerial self-interest; the tax structure; the costs of financial distress; and imperfections in the capital market.

Santomero argues that managers are right to be concerned about risk since the effect of risk is to produce volatility in market value. The second part of his article deals with how risk should be managed and the steps that non-financial and financial companies have taken to manage risk. It concludes with a number of suggestions for a risk management policy.

Suggested further reading

Beaver, W.H. and Parker, G., (1995), *Risk management, problems and solutions*, McGraw Hill, Inc., New York.

Froot, K., Scharfstein, D. and Stein, J., (1994), 'A framework for risk management', *Harvard Business Review*, November.

Herring, R. and Santomero, A.M., (1990), 'The corporate structure of financial conglomerates', *Journal of Financial Services Research*, December.

Oldfield, G. and Santomero, A.M., (1997), 'The place of risk management in financial institutions', *Sloan Management Review*, Summer.

Santomero, A.M. and Babbel, D.F., (1997), *Financial markets, instruments, and institutions*, Irwin Publishing.

Santomero, A.M. and Babbel, D.F., (1997), 'Financial risk management by insurers: an analysis of the process', *Journal of Risk and Insurance*, June.

Santomero, A.M., (1997), 'Commercial bank risk management an analysis of the process', *Journal of Financial Services Research*, June.

Santomero, A.M., (1995), 'Financial risk management: the whys and hows', *Financial Markets, Institutions and Investments* 4.

Stulz, R., (1996), 'Rethinking risk management', *Journal of Applied Corporate Finance* 9, Fall.

Wharton School, (1994), 'Survey of derivatives usage among US Non-Financial Firms'.

Value at risk and hedging: pitfalls for the unwary

by Steven N. Kaplan and Richard Leftwich

Value At Risk (VAR) measures the maximum loss that a portfolio is likely to sustain over a particular period, given specific assumptions about the behavior of security prices. It was developed as an alternative to relying on position limits for monitoring and controlling risks associated with positions held by traders and trading desks. VAR is now applied widely in financial institutions for risk assessment, risk-based capital controls and risk-adjusted performance measurement. Although it is superior to the previous generation of risk management tools, it is far from a panacea even for those applications. Serious conceptual and implementation difficulties must be resolved before VAR can be applied other than perfunctorily. In addition, it relies on information about trades supposedly provided by an organization's control systems. But recent financial scandals suggest that control systems are the weakest link in the risk management process.

The disciples (and the vendors) of VAR are advocating its use in risk management systems for industrial corporations involved in hedging. Such applications are likely to produce risk measures that are simply inappropriate for corporate risk management.

VAR is not the first portfolio management tool to be applied out of context in the corporate arena. Diversification was, and is, an eminently sensible strategy for individual investors. However, as a corporate strategy, diversification generally does not add value for stockholders.

Risk management for portfolio managers

VAR measures the exposure of a portfolio to changes in market prices under a specific set of assumptions. For example, suppose that a portfolio manager holds a $100 million domestic government bond portfolio. If the rate of return on that portfolio is normally distributed with a daily standard deviation of one per cent, the loss experienced on any one day will exceed $1.6 million on five days out of every 100 days, so the VAR is $1.6m. VAR is not a unique number. The probability level and time interval (95 per cent and one day in this case) must be selected and assumptions made about the statistical properties of the rate of return on the under-lying portfolio (a normal distri-bution with a daily standard deviation of one per cent in this case). Table 1 lists VAR estimates for alternative probability levels and volatility assumptions for a normal distribution. The choice of the time horizon and the appropriate probability level are a function of the organization's ability and willingness to bear risk. For example, choosing a short time

Table 1: Value at risk ($m)

Value of portfolio = $100m

Standard deviation	Probability 90%	95%	99%
1%	1.28	1.64	2.33
2%	2.56	3.29	4.65
5%	6.41	8.22	11.63
10%	12.82	16.45	23.26
15%	19.22	24.67	34.90
20%	25.63	32.90	46.53

horizon, such as a day, implies that early warning signals are important, and choosing a high probability, say 99 per cent, implies that losses greater than the VAR can be tolerated only infrequently.

In the simple illustration given in Table 1, the portfolio consisted of only one security, domestic government bonds. Typical portfolios consist of more than one security or asset class. Moreover, when monitoring trading operations, the positions of different traders or trading desks must be aggregated. The portfolio volatility or the volatility of the aggregate trading position is not simply the sum of the volatilities of the component parts – interdependencies (as manifested by correlations) must also be accounted for. Proper risk management techniques recognize that some interdependencies can be risk reducing (as is the case with diversification). By taking advantage of diversification, the exposure of a portfolio of a particular size can be reduced or the size of a portfolio with a given exposure can be increased. Thus, correlations (or lack thereof) between and within asset classes are important components of VAR, but these correlations increase statistical estimation problems considerably. For example, if there are five components (asset classes or trading positions), there are 10 pairwise correlations to estimate; if there are 10 components, there are 45 pairwise correlations to estimate. In general, if there are N components there are N(N–1)/2 separate pairwise correlations. The extract from J.P. Morgan's disclosure about the VAR of its trading activities takes into account the interdependencies within and across asset classes.

Determining the appropriate statistical assumptions for modelling the volatility of the portfolio is the subject of much research and innovation. Estimation methods fall between two extremes – either the underlying statistical distribution can be represented by a theoretical distribution (typically a normal or lognormal distribution) or a distribution (called the empirical distribution) can be constructed from historical data. Neither method is necessarily superior (either in theory or in practice) and each has its advocates. Once a statistical distribution, either theoretical or empirical, has been selected, probabilities can be associated with potential outcomes. If an empirical distribution approach is employed, the probabilities of occurrences of given magnitudes are estimated directly from that distribution using Monte Carlo analysis or bootstrapping. On the other hand, if rates of return are assumed to follow a normal distribution, 99 per cent of outcomes are less than 2.33 units of standard deviation from the mean. If the mean is close to zero and the standard deviation is two per cent per day, this implies that there is only a one per cent chance that the portfolio will decline by more than 4.66 per cent on any day (or $4.66 million if the portfolio has a market value of $100m). By varying the parameters, various risk preferences or constraints can be accommodated (e.g. for a normal distribution, 90 per cent of the observations are less than 1.28 units of standard deviation from the mean, so if the mean is close to zero and the standard deviation is two per cent per day, there is a 10 per cent chance that the portfolio will decline by more than 2.56 per cent on any day, (or $2.56 million if the bond portfolio has a market value of $100 million).

Even in this, its most elementary form, VAR has severe limitations, resulting from extreme observations, non-stationarity, illiquidity, non-linearities and model risk. Extreme observations occur because many securities experience a higher frequency of extreme outcomes than is predicted by the commonly employed normal distribution, resulting in a VAR estimate that understates the risk of large losses. Some securities, particularly those with embedded options, have very low probabilities of extremely

Extract from J.P. Morgan 1996 Annual Report Discussion of Risk Management Using VAR

The estimation of potential losses that could arise from adverse changes in market conditions is a key element of managing market risk. J.P. Morgan generally employs a value at risk methodology to estimate such potential losses ... The firm's primary measure of value at risk is referred to as 'Daily Earnings at Risk' (DEaR). This measure takes into account numerous variables that may cause a change in the value of our portfolios, including interest rates, foreign exchange rates, securities and commodities prices, and their volatilities, as well as correlations among these variables. Option risks are measured using simulation analysis and other analytical techniques. These methods produce risk measures that are comparable to those generated for non-option positions in trading and investing activities assuming normal market conditions and market liquidity. These estimates also take into account the potential diversification effect of the different positions in each of our portfolios.

On a regular basis, the Corporate Risk Management Group, with support from the financial group, calculates, reviews and updates the historic volatilities and correlations that serve as the basis for these estimates. DEaR measures potential losses that are expected to occur within a 95 per cent confidence level, implying that a loss might exceed DEaR approximately 5 per cent of the time. In estimating DEaR, it is necessary to make assumptions about market behavior. The standard forecast used by J.P. Morgan assumes normal distributions and an adverse market movement of 1.65 standard deviations.

However, since no single measure can capture all the dimensions of market risk, we supplement DEaR with additional market risk information and tools such as stress testing. Stress tests measure the effect on portfolio values of unusual market movements and are performed on a portfolio and firm-wide basis to help identify potential sensitivities to abnormal events. Stress testing can take several forms, including: simulation analysis; sensitivity analysis, for moves in values of specific key variables such as volatilities and shifts in yield curves; and specific event analysis, for measuring the impact of abnormal market conditions associated with a specific market event. In selected cases, we supplement DEaR with 'tail risk' limits (i.e., risk of loss beyond the expected confidence level) for portfolios that are particularly susceptible to extreme market-related valuation losses.

DEaR for our aggregate trading and investing activities across all market risks averaged approximately $31 million and ranged from $24 million to $44 million in 1996. This compares with average DEaR of approximately $26 million and a range from $20 million to $38 million in 1995. Aggregate market risk levels increased in 1996, primarily as a result of higher risk levels in our proprietary investing activities.

	DEaR (Millions)	
	1995	*1996*
High	$31	$28
Low	$11	$13
Average	$19	$21
December 31	$27	$27

large losses. Those losses are difficult to capture with theoretical statistical distributions and require a long history to reveal the bad outcome in empirical distributions.

Non-stationarity is a statistical warning that the past is not necessarily a guide to the future. Historical data yield poor predictions about future outcomes if the process generating rates of returns changes due to alterations in the underlying economic situation. Under extreme economic conditions, such as the Gulf War or a currency crisis, historical relationships, especially correlations, may fall apart.

If securities do not trade in highly liquid markets, reliable prices are not available to calculate rates of return. More critically, if there are large adverse price moves, portfolio managers may not be able to sell large quantities of the security without further depressing the price, particularly if other portfolio managers are doing the same. VAR will underestimate the severity of bad outcomes unless markets are highly liquid.

Some classes of securities, such as exotic asset-backed securities, either trade in illiquid markets or are so new that an adequate historical record of prices does not exist. For these securities, VAR calculations rely on prices derived from models of the relationship between the security and a more fundamental economic variable such as the interest rate. Actual losses may then exceed the theoretical VAR maximum if the model is imprecise, thus introducing another source of risk dubbed 'model' risk or 'mark-to-model' risk.

Standard VAR calculations do not allow for non-linear relationships; but, for some portfolios, particularly those with embedded options, non-linear relationships are the norm. For example, a two per cent change in the price of a security may cause a portfolio to lose $1 million but a four per cent change may cause it to lose $10m. Non-linearities can be accommodated but only at the expense of additional estimation problems, typically due to model risk.

Despite these limitations, VAR is a useful risk-management tool for portfolio managers and trading desks. Instead of setting position limits for traders to limit the firm's exposure to unacceptably large losses, VAR allows each trader's exposure to losses to be restricted directly. Moreover, individual exposures can be aggregated to accurately reflect the exposure of a company by taking correlations into account. VAR is seldom used in isolation and its efficacy should not be judged on a stand-alone basis. For example, VAR is often accompanied by stress testing or scenario analysis – techniques with their own strengths and weaknesses. Even the process of collecting the requisite data for VAR calculations improves risk control in most organizations. A final VAR caveat: unless the internal control system records a firm's positions accurately, VAR is akin to whistling in the dark. Debacles such as Barings, Daiwa and Sumitomo provide politically expedient rallying calls for better risk management techniques. The use of VAR by those firms, however, would not have deprived us of the fascination associated with those catastrophic losses, because the 'rogue' traders allegedly did not disclose their positions to their employers.

Risk management for corporations

The stereotypical wheat farmer plays a prominent role in hedging examples used in finance textbooks and in marketing material distributed by futures and options exchanges. Rather than bear the price risk associated with this year's crop, risk-averse farmers rationally enter into forward or futures contracts to lock in a price and reduce the variability of the proceeds from the crop sale. The relevance of those examples for managing risk in a large publicly traded company is dubious. Public corporations are themselves risk-sharing vehicles; and it is difficult to see how risk reduction by the corporation adds value if stockholders can reduce risks on their own account at low cost by, for example, diversifying their investments. Investing in futures and options contracts is, at best, a zero-sum game unless a company's managers have superior information. And managers with superior information should be trading on that information (pejoratively called speculating), not hedging.

VAR applications in corporate risk management have two drawbacks: VAR does not measure the exposure that is relevant to value-maximizing corporate risk managers; and VAR is misleading in the presence of illiquid assets on corporate balance sheets, especially if accounting rules do not reflect economic reality.

It is well accepted that, in the classic Miller-Modigliani model of the firm, risk management *per se* does not add value to the firm. Departures from that model reveal that risk management can, under certain conditions, increase the company's cash flows. Those conditions involve the presence of either progressive corporate tax rates, high expected costs of financial distress or short-term financing constraints. Some would add investor clienteles and management performance systems as additional possibilities. Although these conditions justify corporate risk management they do not justify VAR as a risk management tool. VAR is based on the assumption that the volatility of changes in value is of paramount concern. The volatility of changes in value (of the firm or of the equity) is almost irrelevant in an economically justifiable corporate hedging policy.

Consider first how risk management can add value by smoothing taxable income when tax rates are progressive. Suppose that the first $5 million of profits are taxed at 20 per cent and profits above that level are taxed at 40 per cent. If a firm reports taxable profits of $1 million one year and $7 million the next year, its tax bill will be $2 million on profits of $8m. If adroit use of futures contracts allows managers to smooth taxable income so that $4 million is reported each year, the total tax bill for the two years will be reduced to $1.6m. Similar effects can be demonstrated if tax losses can be carried forward but not backward to earn a refund. Managers who engage in derivatives transactions to reduce income taxes follow strategies to lessen the volatility of reported taxable income and are not concerned about the volatility of changes in the value of the company or of the equity. VAR is uninformative about their strategy.

Alternatively, suppose that the corporate risk management program is designed to reduce the expected cost of financial distress, which depends on the probability of financial distress and the costs of financial distress if it occurs. Financial distress reduces a company's cash flows if suppliers, employees and customers are not willing to trade with it on the same terms if distress is likely. Apple Computer provides a classic example of distress costs now that its existence is in doubt. Customers are reluctant to buy a durable good, software developers are skittish about investing in products that are specific to Macintosh computers and employees are reluctant to invest in firm-specific skills. If there were financial instruments with pay-offs negatively correlated with Apple's fortunes, Apple's stockholders would benefit from lower costs of financial distress if management hedged using those instruments. Unfortunately, other than the stock of Intel and Microsoft, those instruments are not traded and it is difficult for a corporation to sell its own stock short.

Some short-term financing constraints create a role for risk management but, again, VAR has little relevance here, because profit-maximizing managers should focus on reducing the mis-match between cash required for short-term investments and cash available from financing, especially from internal financing. In contrast, for companies with ready access to capital markets (such as those with highly rated debt), it is difficult to see how risk management (particularly interest rate risk management) adds value for stockholders. The intuition behind risk management for financially constrained business is as follows: if cash available from internal and other financing sources falls short of cash required for potentially profitable investment projects in some states (e.g. when oil prices are high), managers can reduce or eliminate the costs of forgoing those projects by investing in financial contracts (for example, oil futures) that pay off when the undesirable states occur. Financial constraints are necessary but not sufficient to create value-maximizing demand for hedging of this kind. It must also

Check the oil: a 'pure play' approach allows investors in an airline, for example, to hedge the risks of fuel price fluctuations

be the case that, in bad times, a company's investment demands do not decline by as much as its available cash flows decline.

For example, consider two firms who face short-term financing constraints and whose fortunes depend heavily on the price of oil: an integrated exploration and production company and a natural resource group that pursues growth by acquisition. The oil producer's cash flows decline if the price of oil falls but its demand for investments in new oil exploration projects declines also since, at low oil prices, oil exploration is not as profitable. Hedging contracts that pay off if the price of oil falls will not add value since they will produce cash flows when investment demand declines. On the other hand, the natural resource company believes that, when times are bad, acquisitions are more profitable because companies can be bought at 'fire sale' prices. Such a company might add value by hedging to ensure that, in otherwise bad times, it has adequate funds to acquire distressed properties. When times are good, the hedging activities will restrict the availability of funds but lucrative acquisitions are then in scarce supply.

A 'pure play' argument in favor of hedging is sometimes given. It is argued that some stockholders would prefer to invest in a company's main line of business but avoid some of the ancillary price risks associated with some inputs or outputs. For example, a 'pure play' airline would allow investors to take only the risk of airline operating and marketing efficiencies by hedging oil price (fuel) risk. Even if there were such a class of investors, hedging to accommodate them would increase firm value only if the company could extract a premium from those investors. The logical and empirical validity of that possibility has not been demonstrated. Some theories of compensating management suggest that better performance measures could be obtained if the effects of some price changes were removed from the measured performance. Why that purging should be achieved with hedging instead of through the accounting system has not been demonstrated.

Of course, there may be managerial incentives to hedge if the ownership of the corporation represents a considerable part of management's wealth and if the corporate control system allows managers to focus on maximizing their utility rather than on maximizing the value of the stock. Hedging by these firms does not add value to stockholders, but VAR does not measure the costs imposed on stockholders by the unnecessary hedging behavior.

Even if the VAR concept corresponds with a company's hedging objectives in a corporate setting, VAR provides little relevant information because, for most non-financial companies, many assets and liabilities are not liquid and accounting rules do not mark even all liquid assets to market. Consequently, VAR tells investors about the exposure of its financial instruments to gain or loss, but not about potential gains or losses for the remainder of the firm's assets and liabilities. Nevertheless, in 1995, the US Securities and Exchange Commission (SEC) adopted VAR as an acceptable method of providing required information about a company's derivatives activity. Why information about a subset of a firm's assets (derivatives) warrants such attention reflects politics, not economics.

These limitations of VAR are mitigated for companies with highly liquid assets and liabilities, such as banks and insurance companies. They are close analogs of the trading companies and portfolios that were the origins of VAR and it is rational for them to reduce the volatility of their capital (assets less liabilities) so that the same capital can support a larger investment base or so that a given size of operations can be financed with less capital. However, even for financial institutions, the presence of illiquid assets or liabilities on balance sheets and accounting rules that do not mark even all liquid assets to market distort incentives if VAR becomes the focus of regulators.

Regulators of banks and financial institutions have embraced VAR as a regulatory tool. The Basle Committee of the Bank of International Settlements (BIS) has proposed that the capital requirement for commercial banks be based on VAR. VAR is defined as the maximum loss that will be incurred over a 10-day period with a 99 per cent probability and capital is then set at three times that VAR. Others who have followed suit in adopting VAR for capital adequacy standards, albeit with different parameters, include: the European Union Capital Adequacy Directive; the International Swaps and Derivatives Association; the Group of Thirty; the Derivatives Product Group; and, in the US, the National Association of Insurance Commissioners.

Conclusions

Like all tools, VAR has its limitations and it offers naive users false comfort. Nevertheless, it belongs in the risk management arsenal for monitoring and controlling the risk of trading positions and investment portfolios. Using VAR in a corporate setting is another matter entirely, especially for industrial corporations. They may have legitimate reasons to manage some of the risk they face but VAR is not likely to be an informative indicator of the efficacy of those risk management programs. VAR fails in a corporate setting because, for most non-financial companies, many of the assets and liabilities are not liquid. Consequently, VAR tells investors about the exposure of the financial instruments to gain or loss, but not about the gains or losses for the remainder of the company's assets and liabilities (such as a gold mine's reserves) or about the relationship between gains and losses on the hedging instruments and gains and losses on its other assets and liabilities.

Case study: American Barrick Resources

American Barrick Resources is a gold mining company that produces approximately two million ounces of gold per year and has reserves of 26 million ounces of gold. The market value of Barrick's equity is $4 billion (141 million shares at $28.00 per share) and its debt is negligible. Barrick uses a variety of esoteric financial instruments as hedges against gold price changes. Barrick believes that, when gold prices are low, gold properties can be purchased at distressed prices, so their policy is designed to shift some revenue from otherwise good times to otherwise bad times. To simplify, suppose that Barrick hedges by selling four years of production forward at $440 per ounce when the spot price of gold is $400 per ounce. (Forward prices for gold typically exceed spot prices, a relationship known as contango). That is, Barrick sells eight million ounces of gold in the forward market, a total dollar value of $3.52 billion (two million ounces per year for four years at $440 per ounce). What is Barrick's VAR and what does it tell you about Barrick's risk management program?

If the annual volatility of the percentage change in gold price is 15 per cent, the spot price of gold will increase by no more than 24.7 per cent with a probability of 95 per cent, assuming normality. If there is no relationship between interest rates and gold prices (an empirically justifiable assumption), the forward price of gold will increase by no more than 24.7 per cent per year ($108.68) with a probability of 95 per cent. Barrick's VAR is then $869 million because its forward contracts will lose no more than $869 million per year with a 95 per cent probability. The forward contracts lose money when the gold price rises, so those losses are offset by the gains on the long position (the reserves, 26 million ounces) which are not recorded by the accounting system. If the forward contracts lose $869 million, the value of the total reserves will increase by $2,824 million, and the value of the reserves net of the forward sales (18 million ounces) will increase by $1,955 million.

There is a simpler way of measuring Barrick's exposure to gold price risk, namely by calculating Barrick's gold beta, the percentage change in Barrick's stock price in response to a one percentage change in the price of gold. Barrick has reserves of 26 million ounces of which only eight million have been sold forward, leaving a net exposure of 18 million ounces. Thus a one per cent change in the spot price of gold ($4.00) changes the spot value of the unsold reserves by $72 million dollars or 1.8 per cent of the market value of the equity. Were it not to engage in hedging, a one per cent change in the spot price of gold would change the spot value of Barrick's reserves by $104 million, or 2.6 per cent of the market value of the equity.

Does this mean that Barrick has a well-run hedging program, that Barrick has hedged the appropriate amount, or that Barrick is trying to profit on what it views as a gold price that is temporarrily too high? Disclosures about VAR are not sufficient to answer those questions, and it is doubtful whether they are even necessary. For example, if Barrick had decided to *buy* not sell the same amount of gold in the forward market would it suggest that Barrick was not hedging?

Source: Tufano, P. and Serbin, J., 'American Barrick Resources Corporation: Managing Gold Price Risk', Harvard Business School Case no. 293–128, 1993.

Summary

This article deals with the technique of 'value at risk' (VAR) measurement. This is a way of assessing the maximum loss that a portfolio is likely to sustain over a particular time period. The approach has considerable benefits as a risk management tool but authors Richard Leftwich and Steven Kaplan are concerned about a growing trend to apply VAR in a corporate context. After explaining the basic VAR methodology, they point out some of its pitfalls. These include: extreme observations (the tendency of many securities to experience a higher frequency of extreme outcomes than predicted by a normal distribution); non-stationarity (the fact that the past is not a guide to the future); illiquidity (the problems of lack of price records); non-linearities (the lack of linear relationships in many portfolios); and model risk (problems with the model itself).

Suggested further reading

Beder, T.S., (1995), 'VAR: Seductive but Dangerous', *Financial Analysts Journal*, Sep–Oct.

Froot, K., Scharfstein, D. and Stein, J., (1994), 'A Framework for Risk Management', *Journal of Applied Corporate Finance*, Fall.

Jorion, P., (1996), 'Risk2: Measuring the Risk in Value at Risk', *Financial Analysts Journal*, Nov–Dec.

Litterman, R., (1996), 'Hot Spots and Heges', *Journal of Portfolio Management*.

Scott-Quinn, B., and Walmsley, J., (1996), 'Risk Management in International Securities Markets: Are Today's Standards Appropriate?', *The Financier*, Nov–Dec.

Tufano, P., (1996), 'Who Manages Risk? An Empirical Analysis of Risk Management Practices in the Gold Mining Industry', *Journal of Finance*.

Tufano, P., (1997), 'The Determinants of Stock Price Exposure: Financial Engineering and the Gold Mining Industry', Harvard Business School working paper.

Exchange rate exposure and market value

by Gordon M. Bodnar

Financial analysts and company managers frequently blame movements in exchange rates for changes in the performance of organizations with international activities. For example, many recent annual reports of US companies with international operations cite the strong US dollar for under-performance in foreign operations.

Exchange rates affect reported performance in several ways. The most visible is through their direct impact on financial statements. Under US and UK generally accepted accounting principles (GAAP), accountants adjust the value of foreign currency denominated monetary and non-monetary accounts in response to exchange rate changes, giving rise to both realized and unrealized exchange rate gains or losses on existing positions.

These gains/losses are recorded on the financial statement either implicitly or explicitly as an exchange rate gain or loss in the income statement or a change in the translation adjustment account in the equity section of the balance sheet. The nature of these impacts depends upon the accounting rules used to deal with foreign currency amounts on the consolidated financial statement.

In addition, exchange rate fluctuations affect companies with foreign operations by changing the reported home currency value of foreign income streams. The reported home currency value of the income from foreign operations increases when the home currency falls. Equally as important, but much less obvious, exchange rate changes also have an indirect impact on the reported financial performance by altering price and cost structures. This leads to changes in profit margins and/or quantities which in turn affect earnings streams for both foreign and domestic operations.

Exchange rate changes affect current reported financial performance, but the important issue for investors and managers interested in company value is how exchange rate changes influence the market value of an organization. This relation is a company's economic exchange rate exposure.

Nature of markets

Since the company's market value is related to the expected future cash flows, this exposure involves estimating the impact of exchange rate changes on current and expected future cash flows. Thus, in forward-looking capital markets, investors change the company's current market value by an estimate of the change in the present value of its cash flows resulting from the change in the exchange rate. The ratio of this change in the market value to the change in the economic exchange rate is the financial definition of the exchange rate exposure of a business.

To understand a company's exchange rate exposure it is necessary to consider how it generates its cash flows. The extent to which it exports or imports, the nature of the markets in which it acquires inputs, and the extent and structure of its foreign operations all affect exposure to exchange rate changes. In our study we consider how different types of international activities should affect companies' exchange-rate exposures.

To begin with, changes in the exchange rate can affect cash flows even in non-traded goods activities which have no apparent linkage with the international economy. Non-traded goods are goods for which high transportation costs prevent their international trade. Macroeconomic models predict that the relative price changes of an appreciation of the home currency will induce a shift of resources from traded to non-traded activities – as long as capital is more sector-specific than other inputs to production.

The reallocation of resources causes the market value of capital in non-traded goods activities in the short run to rise relative to the market value of capital in traded goods activities. This suggests that companies producing non-traded goods should see an increase in their market value in response to an appreciation of the home currency. The exchange rate is the relative price of domestic to foreign goods, so for a business producing traded goods exchange rate movements change relative input and output prices that affect its current and future operating cash flows and, thereby, its value.

Consider a country with companies in an imperfectly competitive export sector, an import sector (where companies generate cash flows from distributing imports) and an import-competing sector (local businesses that produce goods which compete with imported products). Initially, let all inputs to production be available from domestic markets that are insulated from international conditions. Now consider the response to a rise in the home currency across the three sectors.

Such an appreciation reduces the amount of home currency needed to purchase a unit of foreign currency, which, all other things being equal, results in a lower home currency price of foreign goods and a higher foreign currency price of home goods. In general, this increases the value of companies in the import sector and decreases the market value of those in the export and import-competing sectors.

More specifically, the appreciation reduces the cash flows (measured in the home currency) of exporters because it leads to a combination of a decrease in foreign demand and a lower price-cost margin, depending on the change in pricing policy. The appreciation lowers the home currency cost of goods for importers, leading to an increase in their cash flows through a combination of increased demand and higher price-cost margins (depending on the change in pricing policy). At the same time, the increased price competitiveness of foreign imports results in a loss of demand and squeezed margins for the import-competing sector. A depreciation of the home currency has the opposite effect on the cash flows of companies in each sector.

Changing the assumption of isolated domestic input markets to allow for internationally priced inputs highlights another possible effect of the exchange rate on cash flows of traded and non-traded industries.

Competitive environment

The term internationally priced input markets includes both inputs that are imported and inputs obtained domestically, but whose price is determined on world markets. Assuming input markets are competitive, an appreciation of the home currency lowers the home currency price of internationally priced inputs, so production costs fall and industry profitability rises. Similarly, a depreciation increases the home currency price of these inputs, increasing costs and decreasing profitability. Finally, exchange rate changes affect the home currency value of the cash flows from foreign operations. This occurs in two ways:

- Exchange rate changes can alter the competitive environment in which the foreign operations are active. These exchange rate induced changes in foreign currency prices and quantities sold can alter the foreign currency cash flows generated by foreign operations. The nature of this change generally depends on the exporting/importing activities of the foreign operations
- The movement in the exchange rate changes the measured home currency value of the foreign currency earnings stream when converting its value to its home currency either for measurement purposes or repatriation.

The combination of these two effects can make determining the exchange rate exposure from foreign operations more tricky than domestic operations. In most cases, for companies with foreign operations that sell primarily in the local foreign market, a depreciation of the home currency increases the company's value. However, if the majority of the sales of foreign operations are to other foreign markets or the parent's market, then this effect could be reversed.

Figure 1 summarizes the effects of exchange rate changes on different activities' values. Companies mainly in only one activity or in several with similar exposures have clear predictions as to their exchange rate exposure. However, the impact of exchange rate movements on an organization's value may be more difficult to predict if the company participates in activities with off-setting exposures.

Fig.1 The effects of an appreciation of the home currency

On the value of Industries involved in different activities

Activity	Sign of effect
Non-traded goods producer	(+)
Exporter	(−)
Importer	(+)
Import competitor	(−)
User of internationally-priced inputs	(+)
Foreign operations	(−)

Figure 2 displays estimates of residual exchange rate exposures for industry portfolios across the US, UK, Canada and Japan. Since companies in an industry are likely to share similar types of international activities, grouping organizations in this way can help to improve exposure estimates by reducing idiosyncratic effects. For each country, the exchange rate index is a weighted average price of the home currency against the currencies of the other six members of the G7, with the weights taken from the International Monetary Fund's exchange rate model.

Industries listed under the negative exposure heading display a statistically significant tendency to fall in market value by the reported percentage, on average, for each one per cent increase in the weighted average foreign currency value of the home currency. Similarly, industries listed under the positive exposures heading displayed a statistically significant tendency to rise in market value by the reported percentage, on average, for each one per cent increase in the weighted average foreign currency value of the home currency. Examining the industries with significant exposures in Figure 2 reveals interesting patterns that are consistent with the theoretical discussion above.

In general, the industries in the positive exposure column are either non-traded good producers, such as transportation services, or industries that are likely to import

Fig.2 Significant industry exchange rate exposures for the US, UK, Japan and Canada

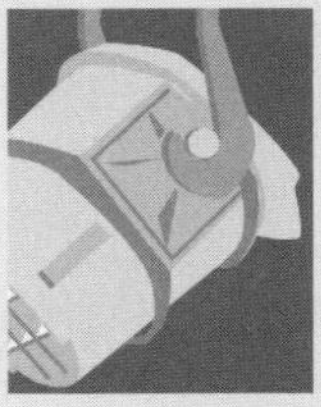

US Negative	%
Metal mining	–0.59
Heavy construction	–0.33
Petroleum refining	–0.30
Wholesale trade, durable goods	–0.14
Business services	–0.24

US Positive	%
Apparel and other clothes	0.30
Transport equipment	0.20
Motor freight transportation	0.45
Air transport	0.35
General merchandise stores	0.30
Miscellaneous retail	0.24

UK Negative	%
Chemicals	–0.29
Diversified industrial	–0.24
Media	–0.18
Healthcare	–0.19
Insurance	–0.31

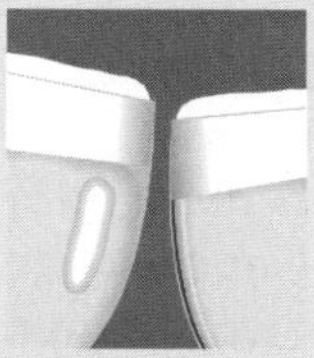

UK Positive	%
Alcoholic beverages	0.23
Retailers – food	0.17
Retailers – general	0.25
Telecoms	0.19

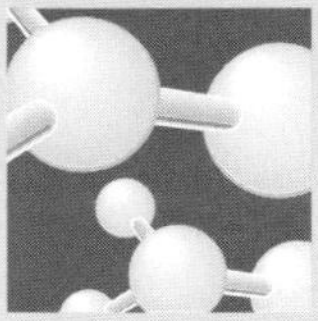

Japan Negative	%
Chemicals	–0.30
Electric machinery	–0.80
Precision instruments	–0.74

Japan Positive	%
Construction	0.70
Oil and coal products	0.85
Land transport	0.53
Services	0.56

Canada Negative	%
Metal mining	–0.97
Paper and forest products	–0.62

Canada Positive	%
Department stores	0.92
Transportation	1.30

US industries are based on equally weighted two digit primary SIC codes. Estimation uses monthly data over the period 1979:1 – 1988:12.
UK industries are defined by FTSE. Estimation was done using monthly data over the period 1986:1 – 1997:3.
Japanese industries are defined by Nikkei Securities. Estimation is done using monthly data over the period 1983:9 – 1988:12.
Canadian industries portfolios are defined by the TSE. Estimation is done using monthly data over the period 1979:1 – 1988:12.

Source for US, Canada and Japan estimates: Bodnar and Gentry (1993)
Source for UK estimates: author's calculations.

a significant amount of their inputs, such as retail industries. On the negative exposure side, the industries listed tend to be either big producers of exports for their country or industries with significant assets or revenues outside the home country. This suggests that companies' exchange rate exposures appear to be related to the types of activities in which they engage.

Trading up – or down: exchange rate movements can have positive or negative effects on firm value

These observations are in fact supported by statistical tests. One study, for example, looked across many industries in several countries and found that non-traded goods production and import intensity are positively associated with industry exchange rate exposures, while export-intensive and foreign operations were negatively associated with industry exchange rate exposures. This suggests that exchange rate exposures are related to the impact of exchange rate changes on current and future cash flows.

Despite the ability to explain to a large degree the sources of exchange rate exposure, one issue that has troubled academics is why more companies do not display significant exchange rate exposures. Traditionally, regression estimation of exchange rate exposures at the industry level, like those in Figure 2, tend to find that substantially less than half of the industries in a country display significant exchange rate exposures at even a 10 per cent significance level in either direction.

In Figure 2, the 11 significant US exposures come from a sample of 39 industries, the nine significant UK exposures from a sample of 25 industries, the seven Japanese from a sample of 20 industries, and the four Canadian from a sample of 19 industries. The low occurrence of significant exposures seems puzzling given the frequency with which exchange rates are mentioned as a factor in financial performance.

Frequency of exposure

There are several possible explanations for this. One is that industry portfolios aggregate companies too broadly. The businesses within these broad industry groupings may be sufficiently different for some to have positive and others negative exposures, making the aggregate exposure close to zero. While grouping companies can lead to problems, studies that have estimated company-specific exchange rate exposures tend to generate even lower proportions of significant exposure estimates. Another possible explanation is that the exchange rate index is inappropriate. This may be for several reasons:

- The index may not represent the relevant exchange rates for each company or industry. The solution would be to calculate industry- or company-specific exchange rate indices. However, while this would be helpful, it is not always feasible owing to availability of data.
- The use of a single index reduces econometric problems inherent in placing many highly correlated exchange rate changes in the exposure regression. Use of a single index, however, does not allow for the possibility that the sign of the exposure may vary across the currencies in the index. There is evidence that US companies have exposures with differing signs to the currencies commonly used in the dollar index.
- In addition, exchange rate exposures may not be constant over the estimation interval. If the true exposures vary by time, then a constant specification may not be able to identify a significant relation between exchange rate changes and changes in market value. There is evidence that the exposures of US industries vary over time with changes in export and import flows.
- A fourth possibility is that companies hedge their exposures, either by simultaneously taking part in activities with off-setting exposure implications or by using currency derivatives to reduce their exposures. While the use of currency derivatives can alter the exchange rate exposure, evidence from the 1995 Wharton Survey of Derivative Usage among US Non-Financial Firms suggests that only about 30 per cent of US companies use currency derivatives. Moreover, those that do participate mostly in short-term forward rate hedging (90 days or less) and typically hedge less than the full exposure over this horizon. Thus, while the survey suggests currency hedging is more pervasive among companies more involved in activities that give rise to currency exposures, the evidence also suggests that for the typical business using currency derivatives, hedging only partially stabilizes short-term cash flows, and future cash flows remain exposed.

A final possibility for the low level of observed exchange rate exposure may be that our methodology imposes too strong a requirement on the market to understand the nature of the exposure in order to reflect it instantaneously in market value. Determining the value impact on a particular company of a given change in the exchange rate can be a complex relation for investors to characterize. Such complexities include determining the possible impact of the exchange rate change on demand and supply conditions, predicting the possible strategic responses of the company and its competitors to the new competitive conditions, and incorporating the (until recently undisclosed) foreign currency hedging activities of the business.

Lag structure

It is possible that it may take some time for investors to incorporate fully the impact of an exchange rate change into the market value of a business. This may mean there is a lag structure involved in the response of firm value to an exchange rate change. In fact, evidence points to a significant lag structure in the relation between exchange rate changes and firm value.

A recent study looked at a sample of US companies with an observable negative impact of dollar appreciations on past reported performance. It showed that the change in value of the dollar in the current fiscal quarter was significantly related to the abnormal stock performance of the business in the subsequent quarter during the period 1978–89. A similar lagged reaction of firm value to exchange rate changes has been found by other studies on US data as well as large UK exporters. This suggests that an economically significant proportion of the impact of exchange rate changes on firm value is not immediately incorporated into value. Over the period 1978–90 there were significant excess returns to be had from recognizing the past impact exchange rates had on firm value and taking trading positions based on this information. Thus exchange rate changes do have an impact on firm value. This effect is likely to become larger and more extensive as economies become more open and companies become more globally oriented. Understanding the exchange rate exposures of companies will be an important issue for both investors and managers in the years to come.

Summary

The impact of exchange rates on company performance is often addressed in the business press and in company reports – but how do exchange rate changes affect a company's market value? This article examines the relationship between exchange rate changes and firm value, known as the company's exchange rate exposure. As Gordon Bodnar explains, currency movements will have varying influences on companies in the export sector, import distributors, and local businesses producing goods that compete with imported products. One puzzling feature of the research on economic exchange rate exposures is the low frequency with which significant exchange rate exposures are estimated.

The evidence also indicates that the market is slow to incorporate the full impact of exchange rate changes into firm value, which has implications for investors' trading strategies.

Suggested further reading

Adler, M. and Dumas, B., (1984), 'Exposure to Currency Risks: Definition and Management', *Financial Management.*

Bartov, Eli and Bodnar, Gordon M., (1994), 'Firm Valuation, Earnings Expectations and the Exchange Rate Exposure Effect', *Journal of Finance.*

Bodnar, Gordon M. and Gentry, William M., (1993), 'Exchange Rate Exposures and Industry Characteristics: Evidence for Canada, Japan and the USA', *Journal of International Money and Finance.*

Jorion, Phillipe, (1990), 'Exchange Rate Exposure of US Multinationals', *Journal of Business.*

Hedging – an obstacle or a blessing?

by Ronnie Barnes

One of the most striking developments in global financial markets over the past 25 years has been the ever-increasing use by non-financial corporations of derivative instruments. Futures, forwards, options, swaps and other, more complex, instruments are routinely used by companies to manage their exposures to interest rate, exchange rate and commodity price risk. Recently, however, some well-publicized derivatives

Taking a risk: but why do companies attempt to manage risk and who benefits?

disasters at leading household-name companies have led to increased scrutiny of the purposes for which these instruments are being used. Are corporations using derivatives to hedge risks arising from their underlying business or are they simply taking large speculative positions?

Much of the debate concerning these incidents has focused on the need for improved control, monitoring and reporting of derivatives usage. The consensus is that, if used properly, derivatives can be a valuable risk management tool but that measures are needed to prevent (as far as possible) their perceived 'misuse' for speculative purposes. Relatively little has been said about the more fundamental questions of why companies should choose to manage risk in the first place and who actually benefits from such risk management.

This article first argues that under certain (admittedly unrealistic) assumptions, risk management is at best irrelevant and at worst (because of transactions costs) expensive. It then shows how relaxing the various assumptions can lead to situations in which it makes sense for companies to hedge (at least some of) the risks to which they are exposed.

The aim is not to provide a checklist that companies can use to decide if, when and what they should hedge. What we are discussing is essentially a collection of competing theories. Hopefully, as the information provided by companies concerning their derivatives activity increases in response to new accounting requirements, it will be possible to extend the limited empirical work in this area. As a result we can refine and distinguish between these theories and better understand what actually motivates corporate hedging.

Is hedging irrelevant?

In 1958, Franco Modigliani and Merton Miller published a paper entitled 'The cost of capital, corporation finance and the theory of investment' in which they demonstrated that, assuming perfect capital markets, the value of any organization is determined solely by its operations and real investment decisions and is independent of how it finances those investments, i.e. its capital structure. Although published well before the advent of derivatives as a risk-management tool, the arguments in the paper can easily be adapted to the question of corporate hedging policies. The basic idea is as follows: investors will not be willing to pay a premium for the shares of a company that has simply undertaken some action that investors could themselves undertake. For example, consider an investor who is contemplating buying shares in one of two essentially identical companies, both of which are exposed to risks that the investor would prefer to hedge. The only difference between the companies is that one chooses to hedge the risks while the other remains un-hedged.

If the investor can hedge those risks by trading in the derivatives market on his or her own account, he or she will not pay a premium for the company that hedges. Equally, the investor will not demand a discount since he or she can easily trade on his or her own account to unwind the effect of company-level hedging.

Shareholder value

The above analysis depends on two critical assumptions. First, investors are fully aware both of the companies' underlying exposures and of their hedging decisions – there is no asymmetry of information. Second, there must be no transaction costs of trading in the derivatives markets. Both of these assumptions are subsumed under the perfect markets heading. Broadly speaking, corporate risk management has a potentially valuable role to play, and the irrelevancy result breaks down when one or other of the perfect market assumptions is invalidated. In what follows, I consider four of these assumptions and show how hedging can increase shareholder value when the assumptions are inappropriate.

Taxes

One of the key features of a perfect capital market is that there are no taxes. The importance of this assumption is illustrated by the fact that when, in a subsequent article, Modigliani and Miller considered a world with corporate (but no personal) taxes, the irrelevancy result was overturned.

To illustrate the impact of taxes on hedging, consider a company that has in any year a pre-corporate tax result that is (with equal probability) either a 100 million loss or a 200 million profit. That is, its expected pre-tax profit is (50 per cent x –100m) + (50 per cent x 200m) = 50m. Suppose the company operates under an onerous tax system whereby any profits are taxed at 40 per cent but relief for losses is only given at 20 per cent. The expected corporate tax bill is thus (50 per cent x 20 per cent x –100m) + (50 per cent x 40 per cent x 200m) = 30m and the expected post-tax profit is 50m – 30m = 20m.

Suppose we allow the organization to hedge in such a way that it 'locks in' its expected pre-tax profit; that is, after hedging, the company's pre-tax result will be a 500 million profit with certainty. In this case, the corporate tax bill will be 40 per cent x 50m = 20m and the post-tax profit will be 50m – 20m = 30m, both with certainty. In other words, hedging has increased expected cash flows (and therefore shareholder value) by reducing the expected tax bill.

At this point, we discuss a question arising out of the previous example: even in the absence of taxes, hedging is beneficial since it reduces risk. An expected cash flow of 500m is replaced with a guaranteed cash flow of the same level. Risk-averse investors will, therefore, discount the 500m at a lower rate, thereby increasing value. It is certainly true that a company's value is essentially its expected cash flows discounted at a rate that reflects the risk of those cash flows, and that to increase value either the expected cash flows need to be increased or the discount rate lowered (or both). However, the key point is that the risks that are important in determining the discount rate to be used are market-wide or systematic. Much of modern financial theory is based on the idea of well-diversified investors who, through their diversification, can eliminate risks that are specific to a particular business or industry.

Investors only apply a lower discount rate to a company's cash flows if the risks that are reduced are systematic. Even if this is the case, is it reasonable to assume that the hedge will be costless? In other words, can we assume that the counterparty to the hedge transaction will not demand compensation for taking on the systematic risk that the company is eliminating. In general, any reduction in the discount rate that results from eliminating certain systematic risks is likely to be offset by a reduction in expected cash flows that are 'paid out' as compensation to the party assuming these risks. Risk reduction *per se* is therefore likely to be a spurious reason for hedging. Likewise, hedging in order to smooth reported earnings on the grounds that the market will pay a premium for companies with a smoother earnings stream is equally invalid.

Bankruptcy costs

Bankruptcy costs refer to the direct (such as legal and accountancy fees) and indirect (such as diversion of management time and loss of competitiveness) costs that arise when the cash flows of a company that is partially financed by debt are (or appear to be about to be) insufficient to meet its debt obligations.

In this case, hedging can create value by reducing the probability of such so-called financial distress. A hedging strategy that leaves expected operating cash flows unchanged but reduces the spread of possible cash flows will lower the probability that some of these cash flows are diverted to meet the dead-weight costs of financial distress. In other words, the expected costs of financial distress are reduced and the expected payout to shareholders increased. As in the case of taxes, it is not the reduced risk that leads to the increase in value but rather the increase in the expected level of operating cash flows available to investors. Additionally, reducing the probability of financial distress may enable a company to move to a higher debt-to-equity ratio. This can create value by virtue of the fact that debt financing has tax advantages when compared with equity.

Financing costs

In general, raising external financing to fund new investment is costly in the sense that the proceeds raised are lower than the value of the securities (equity, debt and so on) that are issued. These costs may take the form of direct costs such as underwriting fees. Alternatively (and probably more significant), the costs may be indirect – such as the underpricing of an equity issue.

The intuition here is that managers typically have information about their organization's prospects that is superior to that possessed by investors. On the announcement of an equity issue, investors will assume on average that if managers are acting in the best interests of their existing shareholders, the issue indicates that the business is overvalued.

Consequently, in order to be induced to take up the issue, investors will demand a discount to the current share price. If the company is correctly valued at the present time, this discount represents a loss to existing shareholders. If their share of the value added by the new investment is insufficient to outweigh this loss, the shareholders' best interests are served by management foregoing the investment.

Obviously, this problem would not arise if the company were able to finance the investment from retained earnings. Hence, a hedging strategy that reduces the probability that cash flows will be insufficient to meet the business's investment needs can increase value by helping to prevent valuable opportunities being foregone (or at least by reducing the likelihood that security issue costs will be incurred).

Asymmetric information

The final perfect market assumption that we consider is that of symmetric information. In the real world, asymmetric information – particularly between managers and investors – is one of the key features of most financial markets and has been used to explain a number of initially puzzling phenomena in corporate finance. In terms of its impact on corporate hedging behavior, it has been suggested that if companies have private information concerning their exposure to various risks, hedging may benefit investors. This is because it reduces the 'noise' in reported profits, thereby enabling investors to make better portfolio choices.

Similarly, asymmetric information has also been proposed as a reason why companies speculate using derivatives. A company with a relatively unprofitable underlying business may attempt to mask this by speculating and hoping the speculation pays off. Even with symmetric information, speculation may be valuable to the shareholders of a geared company that is close to financial distress. If the speculation does pay off, the rewards accrue to shareholders while if it is unsuccessful, the costs are borne by the organization's debtholders. This is an example of the so-called 'risk-shifting' problem.

Managerial motives for hedging

So far, we have made the implicit assumption that managers will always act in the best interests of their company's existing shareholders. We now relax that assumption and consider how corporate hedging policies might actually be motivated by managerial self-interest. As noted above, managers will typically have superior information to investors, including shareholders.

One of the most difficult challenges facing shareholders is to design a compensation scheme that aligns managerial incentives with those of the shareholders, namely the maximization of the company's share price. The result is that compensation packages will typically include 'performance-related' elements such as a bonus linked to earnings, share options and so on. Unlike shareholders who are well-diversified and can therefore be treated as if they are effectively indifferent to risk, managers have a large amount of human capital tied up in their company. Consequently, managerial risk aversion is a real issue in determining the effectiveness of incentive schemes and creates a natural role for hedging at the corporate level.

By hedging against risks that are outside a manager's control, he or she is effectively being compensated based on factors over which he or she is able to exert an influence. A manager is more likely to work hard to secure a big sales contract that adds considerable value to the company if he knows his compensation is effectively insulated against a fall in the stock price due to a sudden unexpected increase in interest rates.

A second potential, managerially-driven, motive for corporate risk management is that of communicating ability. Suppose that there are two types of manager, 'good' and 'bad'. The level of profits generated by the good is either £320m or £340m with equal probability while the bad generates either £310m or £320m, again with equal probability. If managers are attempting to develop a reputation in the labor market, the good manager certainly has the incentive to hedge and lock-in an expected profit level of £330m. In this way, there is no danger of his being mistaken for a bad manager.

Conclusion

The question of why companies use derivatives to manage risk is one that has gained increasing attention in recent years as a result of corporate crises linked to this activity.

As the information concerning what companies actually do continues to improve both in volume and in quality, this is likely to remain a topical issue for some time. This article has attempted to outline some of the theories of corporate risk management, distinguishing between those that add shareholder value and those that are driven by managerial self-interest. In practice, it seems likely that risk management policies are actually motivated by a combination of these factors – only further empirical work can identify those that are truly important.

Summary

In this discussion of corporate risk management theory, Ronnie Barnes shows that hedging is irrelevant if you make certain assumptions about the perfect functioning of capital markets. These assumptions, however, are unrealistic. The author goes on to show that where hedging reduces an expected tax bill, the probability of financial distress, the danger that a company may not be able to finance its investments from retained earnings and the 'noise' in reported profits, it can at the same time increase shareholder value. Corporate hedging policies can also be motivated by managerial self-interest, but in practice it seems likely that risk management policies are motivated by a combination of factors.

Suggested further reading

Fite, D. and Fleiderer, P., 'Should Firms Use Derivatives to Manage Risk?' in Beaver, W. and Parker, G. (ed.), *Risk Management Problems and Solutions.*

Mian, S.L., (1996), 'Evidence on Corporate Hedging Policy', *The Journal of Finance and Quantitative Analysis,* September.

A strategy for managing foreign exchange

by Robert Z. Aliber

In the first half of 1997 Japanese motor and electronics companies enjoyed exceptional profits as the yen slid to below Y125 to the US dollar. At the same time, some US businesses reported that profits had been hit by the strength of the US dollar. Impacts such as these suggest that managers had more or less 'bet the company' – or at least a non-trivial part of their earnings – that exchange rate changes would not have unfavorable effects on their companies' incomes.

Consider the impact of a five per cent appreciation of the Japanese yen on the profits of a company based in Tokyo or Osaka that sells 30–40 per cent of its products in North America. Most of this organization's costs are in Japanese yen while a substantial part of its revenues are in US and Canadian dollars. Each one percentage point increase in the price of the yen in the foreign exchange market would lead to a one percentage point decline in the yen receipts from US and Canadian sales. If the profit rate on these sales is 10 per cent, then an appreciation of the yen by more than 10 per cent would mean that losses would be suffered on these export sales – a 15 per cent appreciation of the yen would result in a loss of five per cent on each unit sold in North America.

If the Japanese organization were to raise its selling prices in the US dollar and in the Canadian dollar to minimize the reduction in profits per unit of export sales, then unit sales would decline and profits fall. But if the Japanese yen should depreciate, then yen revenues would increase for each unit sold in North America. The effective selling prices in both US and Canadian dollars, therefore, could be reduced to increase unit sales. The depreciation of the Japanese yen by nearly 50 per cent over the past two years has moved Japanese auto companies as close to financial heaven as they are ever likely to be.

Managers, however, might feel that in the long run the appreciation and depreciation of the yen and the mark are more or less off-setting, and the same applies to the profit implications. But over the past 25 years this has proven an expensive proposition for companies headquartered in Japan, Germany, Switzerland and the Netherlands, all of whose currencies have appreciated significantly relative to the US dollar. Alternatively, the managers of these businesses might hedge their foreign exchange exposures.

First they would need to measure these exposures, particularly the sensitivity of revenues and costs and hence operating profits to changes in the foreign exchange value of their domestic currency. They would then have to identify a low-cost approach to hedging these exposures. Finally, they would have to decide when hedging foreign exchange exposures is likely to be cost-effective.

Some managers appear to believe that their companies' incomes can be enhanced by maintaining and even increasing the foreign exchange exposure – the treasurer's office has become a profit center. The increase in income from an exposed position in foreign exchange might result from reduced net interest payments (for example, the foregone cost of hedging) or from periodic gains from holding assets denominated in currencies that appreciate.

Measuring exchange exposure

Most countries have standardized how national companies should translate assets and liabilities denominated in foreign currencies into their domestic currency when drawing up consolidated quarterly or yearly balance sheets. Increasingly, foreign exchange gains and losses go to a separate shareholder's equity account and hence directly to retained earnings so that these gains and losses do not directly impact the income statement. This approach is also applied to the assets and liabilities of foreign subsidiaries. But such an accounting approach provides few clues as to how an organization's revenues and costs would be affected by changes in exchange rates. If a company's managers want to manage its foreign exchange exposure they need to forecast how its operating cash flows would be affected by exchange rate changes.

A company is usually regarded as having a foreign exchange exposure if the currency denomination of its receipts and the currency denomination of its payments differ. A substantial part of Porsche's sales are in dollars in the US and Canada while most of its costs are in the D-Mark. The German group has a long operating foreign exchange exposure in the US dollar.

Many companies might have a foreign exchange exposure, even though all their revenues and costs are in the same currency; the foreign exchange exposure arises because changes in exchange rates lead to changes in the revenue-cost relationship. Thus the sales of most of Porsche's suppliers in Germany will decline if the appreciation of the D-Mark reduces its sales in North America.

Take Hydro Quebec, which sells a small part of its output of electricity to electric companies in New York and Vermont at US dollar prices and for payment in US dollars. Some of these sales are under long-term contracts and provide for fixed US dollar payments for periods up to 20 years. Some of these sales are under short-term or non-firm contracts; the US buyers are committed to pay if Hydro has the electricity to sell. (Hydro's production of electricity might be handicapped by lack of rainfall, for example.)

A substantial part of Porsche's sales are in US dollars but its costs are in D-marks

Increasingly, as the structure of the electrical industry changes, more of Hydro's electricity sales to these US buyers will be in the spot market. Hydro's operating exposure in the US dollar under these long-term contracts can be measured as the present value of the US dollar receipts. Similarly, its exposure on its short-term contracts can be measured as the present value of US dollar receipts. Since the company is uncertain how much electricity will be sold, the US dollar receipts are, accordingly, also uncertain.

The exports of German, Swedish and Japanese automobile companies to the US are similar to Hydro's exports of electricity under short-term contracts. The US dollar prices of the units sold are firm (or at least known within a somewhat narrow range), even though sales volume is rather uncertain.

These automobile companies will make errors in estimating their future US dollar revenues and these errors are likely to be larger, the more distant the year of the forecast. Because actual sales will differ from the estimate, these organizations will have foreign exchange exposures even if they fully hedged their first estimates of their US dollar sales. However, the size of unhedged foreign exchange exposures due to errors of estimation are likely to be much smaller than if the companies forego hedging because of inherent difficulties in forecasting.

Most companies would hesitate to estimate sales in foreign countries for periods beyond a year or two. Nevertheless, when these businesses are planning investments in plant and equipment they almost certainly include projected foreign sales, along with the projections of domestic sales. It is inconsistent to include foreign sales when the expenditures for new plant and equipment are being justified and then to ignore these estimates when dealing with the foreign exchange exposure. Traditionally, US companies have not been concerned about the exposure problem because most of their exports and imports are denominated in the US dollar. If the volume of their exports and imports is sensitive to changes in the foreign exchange value of the US dollar, then their net revenues will be affected by changes in the foreign exchange value of the US dollar. Thus they have an operating foreign exchange exposure. One of the great clichés of foreign exchange management is that 'we don't speculate' in foreign exchange. The sensitivity of reported earnings to changes in the exchange rate is remarkable proof of the emptiness of this adage.

Cost of hedging

One reason why managers of many companies are reluctant to hedge their foreign exchange exposure is that they believe the cost of hedging is high. Hedging is viewed as a form of insurance and the reasoning is that because insurance is costly hedging must be. The key question is whether hedging the measured foreign exchange exposure is cost-effective. If it were free, most managers probably would choose to hedge an organization's foreign exchange exposure and reduce variations in reported income that might result from unanticipated changes in the exchange rate.

If markets were 'perfect', in an elementary finance textbook sense, then the cost of hedging by one approach would not differ significantly from the cost of hedging in another. But if markets were perfect, executive vice-presidents of finance would and should earn far less; they are paid well for exploiting deviations from the textbook arbitrage relationships. Many managers would prefer to hedge using forward exchange contracts, partly because they do not want to clutter the balance sheet with a lot of debt solely to reduce their foreign exchange exposure.

If the interest rate parity theorem held continuously – that is if the percentage difference between the forward exchange rate and the spot exchange rate was equal to the difference between the domestic interest rate and the foreign interest rate at which the company might borrow or invest – then in financial terms the managers should be indifferent when choosing between these two hedging techniques. Often, though, there will be deviations of 10–20 per cent from this arbitrage relationship (the deviations can be much larger if one currency is subject to exchange controls) so that one approach will prove significantly less costly than the other. The product of 10 basis points and a $100m exposure pays quite a few salaries.

If a German company with a long operating exposure in the US dollar finds it less costly to hedge this exposure by buying German marks in the forward exchange market, then the US company with a mirror image exposure in the German mark will find it less costly to hedge its exposure by borrowing marks and using the funds to pay down US dollar debt. Hydro has hedged its US dollar operating foreign exchange exposure by issuing long-term bonds denominated in the US dollar and paying down its Canadian dollar debt. Because interest rates on long-term US dollar securities have generally been below the interest rates on comparable Canadian dollar securities, Hydro has reduced its foreign exchange exposure and its net interest costs at the same time. So there is a 'free lunch' after all – hedging has been profitable rather than costly for Hydro. The inference from the Hydro example is that organizations based in countries with interest rates higher than those in which they have long operating foreign exchange exposures could cut both their interest costs and reduce their foreign exchange exposures.

To hedge or not to hedge

Once a company has measured its foreign exchange exposure and chosen a low-cost hedge, it then has to decide whether hedging is cost-effective. The answer takes in the cost of hedging, the importance of exchange losses to the income of the business and the risk associated with an exposure in different foreign currencies.

The availability of a free lunch to companies headquartered in Canada with long operating exposures in the US dollar should not automatically lead to the conclusion that these businesses should seek to minimize their total foreign exchange exposure. Hedging may still be costly, even if the move to a non-exposed position would also reduce net interest costs. By definition, the cost of hedging is the return for not hedging. Over the past 100 years interest rates on Canadian dollar bonds have exceeded interest rates on comparable US dollar bonds by about 125 basis points.

The traditional inference from the interest rate differential on comparable bonds is that investors anticipate that the Canadian dollar will depreciate by 1.25 per cent a year. Assume Hydro had fully hedged its US dollar operating exposure and that on average the Canadian dollar had depreciated by 1.25 per cent a year; in this case there would be no cost to hedging – the free lunch metaphor is appropriate.

In fact, over this extended period the interest rate differential has exceeded the average annual rate of depreciation by about 70 basis points. Hydro would have reduced its net financing costs by increasing its short financial exposure in the US dollar by more than its long operating exposure in the US dollar. In the few years when the Canadian dollar depreciated sharply, then Hydro would have had to report a translation loss because of the increase in the Canadian dollar equivalent of its short financial exposure in the US dollar. In most years, however, the savings in net interest costs would exceed the revaluation losses from the depreciation of the Canadian dollar.

The force of this example is that the cost of hedging can and should be estimated using forecasts of the spot exchange rate for various future dates. The actual cost of hedging will only be determined at the conclusion of the investment period, when the observed spot exchange rate can be compared with the forecast rate. Thus, some managers might be reluctant to hedge because they have concluded that the cost is too high – that the anticipated return from maintaining a foreign exchange exposure is positive and sufficiently so to justify carrying the risky position. The positive

Hydro-Quebec: selling hydroelectricity across borders evades managing foreign exchange exposure

anticipated return would usually reflect the fact that in the long run the difference in interest rates on comparable securities denominated in different currencies would differ from the realized changes in exchange rates.

This difference reflects the fact that investors want to be compensated for incurring cross-border risks and for shifting funds from countries identified with low interest rates to those with higher interest rates. At times the positive real return from not hedging would be associated with the appreciation of the currency in which a company has a long exposure.

Managers of companies based in Canada who can reduce their net financing costs by developing a short financial exposure in the US dollar might be said to be involved in foreign exchange speculation. One might add: 'If they wouldn't do it with their own money then why should they do it with the shareholders' money?'

Playing the yield curve

The response is that managers receive compensation for doing smart finance. Most managers would feel comfortable 'playing the yield curve' – altering the share of short-term borrowing relative to long-term borrowing in anticipation of changes in the relation between short-term and long-term interest rates.

Changing the amount of debt denominated in various foreign currencies in response to persistent differences between the domestic and foreign interest rates and the average annual rate of change of the exchange rate is actually less risky than playing the yield curve.

If Hydro chooses to reduce its net interest costs further by substituting US dollar debt for Canadian dollar debt, then how much of a foreign exchange exposure should it take on? The general answer is that the company should not take on such a large exposure that a big depreciation of the US dollar would lead to a sharp decline in Hydro's income.

The size of the exposure almost certainly should differ by currency because the relationship between the cross-border differences in interest rates and the variability of exchange rates differs significantly by currency. Thus the cross-country comparison of interest rate differentials and the variability of exchange rates suggests that organizations might acquire a much larger exposure in the Canadian dollar than in the German mark.

Moreover, to the extent that changes in the foreign exchange values of national currencies are not fully correlated in terms of domestic currency, then a company might acquire a portfolio of exposures. This is because the increase in interest income or the reduction in borrowing costs across a range of currencies would probably more than offset the losses associated with the changes in currency values.

Summary

The article 'Exchange rate exposure and market value' looks at the relationship between currency changes and a firm's market value. But how can managers develop a systematic approach to analyzing the impact of exchange rates on their company's profits and deciding whether hedging is worth it? Robert Aliber points out that a traditional accounting approach to consolidating foreign assets and liabilities provides little clue to the effect on revenues and costs of future exchange rate changes.

Once a company has measured its operating exposure in each currency – which means among other things anticipating future foreign sales – it ought to be able to use different financial instruments to reduce the risks. Effective hedging will depend on the costs involved, the importance of exchange losses to the income of the business and the risks associated with an exposure in different currencies.

10

Derivatives

Contributors

Ian Cooper is BZW Professor of Finance at London Business School. His research interests include corporate finance, derivative products and international finance.

Gregory S. Hayt is Director, CIBC Wood Gundy.

Anthony Neuberger is Assistant Professor of Finance and Director of the full-time Masters in Finance program at London Business School. His research interests include option theory and the structure of securities markets.

Gordon M. Bodnar is Assistant Professor of Finance at the Wharton School of the University of Pennsylvania.

Richard Marston is the James R. F. Guy Professor of Finance, Professor of Economics at the Wharton School of the University of Pennsylvania, and Director of Wharton's Weiss Center for International Financial Research.

Contents

Introduction

Derivatives – forward contracts, futures, options and swaps – are at the center of modern financial theory and practice. Much of the development of financial markets since the 1980s has been directly attributable to the expansion of the derivatives industry. This module explores the use of derivatives in risk management, and provides details of one spectacular derivatives disaster.

The world of futures, forwards and swaps

by Ian Cooper

In the past 20 years the fastest-growing global financial markets have been futures and swaps. Apart from currency markets, these are now the largest markets in the world. This explosion signifies the fundamental role of these markets: they are the backbone of most financial innovation. On the other hand, they have been vilified for financial scandals, such as the Barings affair, and are regarded by some as a threat to the stability of the global banking system.

These aspects of futures and swaps are two sides of the same coin: the enhanced ability to manage and trade risk. These instruments make it possible to control the risk of interest rates, bond prices, currencies, equity prices, commodity prices, credit risk, inflation and real estate prices. The markets operate in every country with a significant capital market.

Underlying and derivative markets

Futures, forward contracts and swaps are derivative products, a category that also includes options. The first three are variants of each other and represent the unconditional buying and selling of risks. Options are structurally different in that they allow the conditional trading of risks. The key idea in futures, forwards and swaps is that you can buy and sell all the risk of an underlying asset without trading the asset itself. For example, an investor who holds a portfolio of UK shares can reduce the risk of the portfolio by selling UK equity index futures.

Suppose the FTSE 100 index level is 400 and an investor has a well-diversified portfolio of UK shares worth 4 million pounds. The investor is concerned that the UK equity market will fall over the next month but does not want permanently to sell his or her shares. Figure 1 shows how the investor can protect the portfolio against this risk by selling index futures. The first row shows possible values of the index level, about which the investor is uncertain. If the index falls to 350 at the end of the month the gain on the futures exactly offsets the loss on the portfolio, so the portfolio is hedged against the risk of the market decline. The last row of the table gives a value that is independent of what the market does because the risk of the portfolio is fully hedged.

The benefit of being able to control risks in this way can be seen through a comparison with the alternative of selling the shares in the portfolio and then buying them back once the expected market fall had occurred (if it did). Such a strategy would protect against a decline in the market but would involve the large transactions costs incurred in trading individual shares. The futures contract, by comparison, can

Fig.1 Hedging an equity portfolio with stock index futures

Index level after 1 month	350	375	400	425	450
Portfolio value (£m)	3.5	3.75	4.0	4.25	4.5
Gain or loss to futures position (£m)	0.5	0.25	0.0	-0.25	-0.5
Combined value (£m)	4.0	4.0	4.0	4.0	4.0

be traded with very low transactions costs and represents a much more efficient vehicle to achieve this temporary risk adjustment. The power of the futures contract in this case lies in the fact that it mimics the behavior of the underlying market and so allows trading of the risk of the underlying asset with low costs.

Futures strategies

Because the futures contract mimics the underlying asset it can be used in a variety of ways as a substitute for that asset. Figure 2 shows two strategies where this is the case. In the first, the investor is simply selling futures and waiting for one month. At the end of the month the investor will have made money if the index level has fallen and lost money if the index level has risen. Thus the investor who expects the market to decline can effectively hold a short position in the market (selling the portfolio of shares represented by the FTSE 100 index without owning it). Because of restrictions on short selling this transaction would be very hard to achieve in the absence of the futures market.

Fig.2 Pay-offs to two strategies using futures

Index level after 1 month	350	375	400	425	450
Set futures (£m)	0.5	0.25	0.0	-0.25	-0.5
Buy futures and hold bank deposits (£m)	3.5	3.75	4.0	4.25	4.5

Another common strategy employing index futures is to buy the futures contract and also hold bank deposits. The last row of Figure 2 shows the result of doing this. In this case the result is the same as the first row of Figure 1, the result of simply holding the portfolio of shares itself. The investor in this case has achieved a 'synthetic' equity portfolio by using a combination of the futures contract and a bank deposit. Such a strategy is used by international equity funds that want to achieve temporary exposure to the UK market without going to the trouble of buying and selling a portfolio of shares. In other cases it might be more tax efficient for an investor to effectively hold an investment in the UK stock market through the synthetic trade using futures rather than directly by buying shares.

Pricing and arbitrage

The examples given above assume that the futures price mimics precisely the price in the underlying market. Though this may seem a rather arbitrary assumption there is a powerful force that guarantees that it is always close to being true: arbitrage. If the futures price were to deviate significantly from its correct theoretical relationship with the price of the underlying asset, then arbitrageurs would take advantage of the discrepancy and restore the relationship.

The theoretical relationship between the futures price and the underlying asset that avoids arbitrage is given by:

Theoretical futures price = underlying asset price – future value of yield on underlying asset up to futures maturity + future value of interest on underlying asset price up to futures maturity.

This pricing condition is based on the equivalence of the futures contract to a combination of the underlying asset and borrowing:

Buying the futures contract = buying the underlying asset, lending the present value of the yield on the underlying asset and borrowing the underlying asset price.

Looking at it this way a futures contract is the same as a leveraged position in the underlying asset. Arbitrageurs use the equivalence of the futures contract and a leveraged trade in the underlying asset to take advantage of any divergence in the relative pricing of the futures and the underlying asset.

For example, if the futures price is higher than its theoretical value the arbitrageur will buy the underlying asset using borrowed money and sell the futures. As long as the futures contract and the underlying asset are matched exactly and the mispricing exceeds the transactions cost of setting up the position, this transaction is riskless, costs nothing and is guaranteed to make money. Unfortunately such wonderful opportunities are rare and short-lived, so the effect of arbitrageurs is usually to guarantee that deviations from the theoretical futures price are small.

Speculation

The leverage inherent in futures is also the basis of their attraction to speculators. As shown in Figure 3, a strategy of buying futures on their own (naked futures) gives a net pay-off that is equal to the gain or loss from holding £4m of the index portfolio (the underlying asset). If the investor bought that portfolio he or she would have to pay the £4m purchase price. If, on the other hand, the investor buys futures contract on 4m of the index he or she pays initially nothing. Even the margin that must be posted to enter the contract still belongs to the investor. So the futures contract is equivalent to a fully leveraged position in the underlying asset.

This power of the futures contract – to allow the trading of risks with limited capital – is what makes it such a useful tool in hedging risks. As Figure 3 illustrates, it also gives opportunities to hold highly speculative positions. The only difference between hedging and speculation is that hedging involves an existing risk that is being off-set by the futures contract, whereas speculation does not. The identification and measurement of risk is, therefore, a key part of using futures and other derivative products. Failure to do so lies behind many of the recent financial scandals involving derivative products.

Fig.3 Pay-offs to a naked futures position

Index level after 1 month	350	375	400	425	450
Buy futures (£m)	-0.5	-0.25	0.0	0.25	0.5

Forward contracts

Another way of looking at a futures contract is that it is a contract to make a deferred purchase or sale. If such a contract is entered into privately it is called a forward contract. If it is traded on an organized exchange subject to rules about margin and settling gains and losses as they occur it is called a futures contract.

For some underlying assets, futures contracts are the most common type. The benefit of futures contracts in these cases is that the margining arrangements limit credit risk and the concentration of trading into a few contract maturities increases liquidity. In other cases, such as currencies, where these considerations are not so important, forward contracts predominate.

An example of a forward contract would be an agreement to buy one year from now 1m at a price of $1.60 per £. As with the futures contract, no money changes hands at the time that the contract is initiated. The demand for such a contract might come from a US company that is due to receive 1m in one year and wishes to hedge the risk of sterling depreciating against the dollar. If a bank were to sell this contract to the company and do nothing else it would make or lose money of an amount that depends on the way the exchange rate moves over the next year. This is shown in Figure 4.

Fig.4 A currency forward contract

Exchange rate after 1 year ($/£)	1.50	1.60	1.70
Cash flow to bank after 1 year	+$1.6-£1.0	+$1.60-£1.0	+$1.60-£1.0
Net value cash flow	+$0.1	$0.0	-$0.1

If, for example, the exchange rate is $1.7 per pound after a year then the bank that has agreed to sell £1m for $1.6m will lose $100,000 when it buys for $1.7m the sterling it has committed to sell. If it does nothing else, the bank would be in the position of selling a naked forward contract on sterling. The effect would be essentially identical to the second row of Figure 2, where the investor sold the naked futures contract. It is not, however, the business of banks to take bets on currency moves simply because their customers want to buy a particular forward contract, so the bank would eliminate the risk of being exposed to the currency rate. It can do so by buying sterling (the underlying asset) of a present value amount equal to the amount that it has agreed to sell in the forward contract. In doing so it is effectively performing the role of the arbitrageur described above.

Swaps

In another situation, the customer of the bank might be an American investor who is due to receive a stream of payments in sterling from a UK bond. To hedge the currency risk of these payments the investor could enter into a separate forward contract for each payment (a strip of forward contracts). It is usually more convenient to buy the contracts as a pre-packaged bundle, in which case the transaction is called a currency swap. So swaps are nothing more than bundles of forward contracts and the logic of their pricing and use mirrors exactly that of futures and forward contracts.

Complications and opportunities

All the examples above relate to cases where the underlying asset is financial, the risk being hedged is exactly the same as the underlying asset and the contract is to buy or sell the underlying asset at a fixed price. The same basic ideas apply, however, for a much broader set of contracts and uses. There are futures, forwards and swaps where the underlying asset is a commodity, such as oil, or an economic indicator, such as inflation.

For these derivatives there are additional complications that must be taken into account when pricing or using them. In the case of commodity futures, the holders of the underlying asset derive a value from having the commodity available for use (the convenience yield of the commodity). This influences the pricing of the derivative product and can make the price of the derivative deviate from its simple theoretical value so that additional risks appear in the behavior of the commodity futures price.

The uses need not be restricted to situations where the derivative is hedging its own underlying asset. It is possible, for example, to use a futures contract on a stock market index to hedge the risk of an individual share. This is called cross-hedging, and widens considerably the scope for the use of futures, forwards and swaps. An example would be where an investor thinks that the prospects for a particular share are good but is worried that a general market decline might overwhelm the specific success of the share. In this case the investor could buy the share and sell index futures, giving an investment in the performance of the share relative to the market. Such uses must, however, be analyzed with great care because the derivative is hedging only part of the risk, so an accurate measurement of the remaining residual risk is essential.

Another dimension to these products is to get away from the notion that the contracts must simply involve the exchange of an underlying asset for money. The basic structure of a swap can be used to exchange anything, for example a stream of payments linked to an inflation index for a stream of payments linked to a commodity price. Such a transaction might be attractive to an investor holding an inflation-linked bond who wishes to change the exposure of his portfolio cheaply. Finally, a whole range of possibilities is opened up by strategies of trading futures dynamically through time.

It is possible, for example, to create an exposure to the underlying asset with characteristics similar to an option by trading the futures contract in varying amounts as the price of the underlying asset moves up and down. This is the basis of the pricing of options and also strategies such as portfolio insurance that some believe to have contributed to the crash of 1987.

Summary

The three types of outright derivative products – forwards, futures and swaps – are variants of a single idea.

As Ian Cooper explains they are all basically agreements to buy or sell the risk of an underlying asset without trading the asset itself. The opportunities they offer for hedging risks and enhanced trading opportunities have placed them at the heart of financial innovation and ensured their explosive growth in recent years. The author examines various strategies for investors, looks at the role of arbitrageurs in guaranteeing that the futures price mimics precisely the price in the underlying market, and considers the attractions for speculators.

Besides financial assets, the assets underlying futures, forwards and swaps can be a commodity, such as oil, or an economic indicator such as inflation. But these assets involve additional complications which must be taken into account when pricing or using them.

Suggested further reading

Brealey, R.A. and Myers, S.C., (1996), *Principles of Corporate Finance*, 5th edn, McGraw-Hill, New York, NY.

Figlewski, S., John, K. and Merrick, J., (1986), *Hedging with Financial Futures for Institutional Investors: from Theory to Practice*, Ballinger Publishing Company, Cambridge, Mass.

Hull, J.C., (1993), *Options, Futures and Other Derivative Securities*, 2nd edn, Prentice-Hall, Inc, Englewood Cliffs, N.J.

How to put a price on options

by Anthony Neuberger

Financial markets have become very much more sophisticated over the past 25 years. The range of products available to the corporate treasurer and to the ordinary household has widened greatly. It is now routine for companies to limit the impact of interest rate changes and foreign exchange fluctuations on their financial position through strategies involving interest rate options, caps, floors, options, swaps and so on.

The retail sector too has seen the growth of guaranteed investment products through which investors can participate in the stock market with capital protection and mortgages with embedded options which combine some degree of certainty over the level of payments with flexibility to respond to changes in interest rates.

What has made this flood of innovation possible? In this article I will argue that the key factor has been a radical improvement in our understanding of how to measure and manage risk. Much of this has stemmed from the seminal article by two American economists, Fischer Black and Myron Scholes, which was published in 1973. They developed a methodology for valuing and hedging call options on equities. But their

Leaning on options: even the humdrum mortgage market is now closely involved with sophisticated financial instruments

insights go far beyond simple options, which give the investor the right to buy a share at a fixed price at some future point. The methodology is used widely for valuing all kinds of derivative instrument.

The importance of pricing models

Companies and individuals will be interested in buying risk-management products from financial institutions if the price is right. But the risks which they thus off-load do not disappear; they are transferred onto the books of the institutions selling the products. If the institutions have not sufficiently sophisticated technology for analyzing, pricing and managing the risks they are taking on, they will have to set aside a lot of capital to absorb potential losses. As a result the products will be expensive, few people will buy them and the market in the products will be illiquid, with low volumes of activity. Banks need good pricing models which will not only come up with a theoretical fair price for the product, but will include a methodology for hedging the risks of writing the product.

Given certain key assumptions, the model will say that if the bank writes the product at a certain 'fair' price and then hedges it in a certain way it will break even whatever happens. Of course no model is perfect. There are risks which the model does not capture. But these risks are generally far smaller than the risks of the original product. As risk management becomes more sophisticated, it is the analysis of these residual risks which is posing the most difficult questions for financial engineers, managers of financial institutions and regulators alike.

A simple example

To illustrate some of the thinking behind the Black and Scholes model consider the case of a UK company which is due to receive a sum of DM10m in four months time. It has therefore a foreign exchange exposure which it needs to manage. It could enter into a forward agreement with the bank; under this agreement, the bank would promise to buy, and the customer would promise to sell, the DM10m at a rate of 0.35/DM in four months. So the company could lock in 3.5m for certain.

But the company thinks the D-Mark could well appreciate over the period and is not prepared to forego the upside. So it decides to buy a put option, which enables it to sell its D-Marks at a rate of 0.35/DM in four months should it choose to do so. That will lock in a minimum of 3.5m but if the D-Mark does appreciate the company can allow the option to lapse and sell the foreign currency on the spot market.

Of course the bank will demand a price for offering this option. It will also want to handle the risk it is taking on in writing the put option. In the boxed example I describe the way in which the bank might choose to model the risk, price the option and manage the risk all at the same time. The basic concept is that the bank wants to neutralize the risk of writing the option. The bank is at risk because if the D-Mark falls the option will be exercized and the bank has to pay out. The bank is therefore long D-Marks – it does better if the D-Mark goes up and worse if it goes down.

To get rid of this risk it needs to go short D-Marks. It can do this by borrowing in D-Marks, using the D-Marks to buy pounds and putting the pounds on deposit. If the D-Mark falls, the chance of the bank having to pay up under the option contract increases but the sterling value of its D-Mark debt falls. If it can determine the right amount of D-Marks to borrow it can make itself completely indifferent about whether the rate goes up or down.

But the bank cannot then just sit back. For as the D-Mark falls, the chance of the option being exercized rises. The bank must increase the size of the borrowing if it is to remain hedged. It has to borrow more D-Marks and use them to buy pounds. Conversely if the D-Mark rises, the option is less likely to be exercized and the hedge can be reduced.

If the bank gets this process right and remains perfectly hedged throughout the life of the option it takes no risk. If it bears no risk, its profit must be the same whatever happens – in this case zero. In the very simple world we have described, banks could freely write or buy these options at the fair price, hedge them and be sure of exactly breaking even every time.

The trick behind option pricing

The method of risk reduction that involves buying and selling the foreign currency to stay perfectly hedged is called delta hedging. If the D-Mark moves up the bank buys D-Marks. If it moves down the bank sells them. If it moves up then down, the bank will buy D-Marks at a high price and sell them at a low price. This sounds like a recipe for losing money.

The bank was paid £75,000 for the option. This exactly compensates it for the money it loses to keep itself hedged. We assumed that the exchange rate would move up or down by 1p per D-Mark four times over the life of the option. If the exchange rate had been more volatile, and made more than four 1p moves, the bank would have had to buy and sell more frequently. It would then have lost money. So the bank's profit will depend on whether volatility is higher or lower than forecast – the lower the volatility the better it is for the bank. The crucial assumption underlying option pricing models is that one can forecast volatility. The Black-Scholes model is just a more sophisticated version of the model set out in the boxed example. Using the Black-Scholes model, the user has to forecast just one variable – the future level of volatility.

Volatility is a measure of the uncertainty in the level of the future price. For a typical currency pair, the annual volatility may be around 10 per cent, meaning that the rate is likely to move by 10 per cent up or down on average. Equities tend to be more volatile than currencies, typically in the range 25–60 per cent per annum. The importance of volatility in option pricing should not be surprising. If you know what is going to happen you can decide to buy or sell the asset outright. Options give you the right to delay the decision. The more the asset could move up or down, the greater the value of the right to delay.

Behavior of volatility in practice

In practice, volatility is very hard to predict. In the market, practitioners often make use of recent experience to help guide their forecasts for the future. But volatility is very changeable. Much effort is expended on improving volatility models because better forecasts translate into better pricing of options and hence into higher profits for options traders.

Another area of growing importance is making better forecasts of the way volatility will itself behave. For example, we assumed that the exchange rate was just as likely to move up or down 1p in three months time whether the rate was still at its current level or whether it had gone up or declined sharply in the interim. But in general the higher the price, the higher the size of move that is likely. It would have been more usual in the DM option example to have assumed four three per cent moves rather than four 1p moves in the exchange rate. The logic would have remained the same, though the arithmetic would have been a bit messier.

Pricing a German D-Mark put option

In this example we ignore financing costs in the interests of simplicity

Step 1:
The bank estimates how much the exchange rate is likely to move. The current rate of exchange is £0.35/DM. Based on past history, it appears that the rate changes by some £0.01/DM (up or down) in a month. The bank feels that this estimate is a plausible assumption for the next four months.

Step 2:
The bank puts this assumption (which is really an assumption about the future *volatility* of the exchange rate) into its model. The model comes up with two related outputs. First, it says that the fair price of the option is £75,000. Second, it comes up with a tree which looks like this:

Rate	Period: 1	2	3	4
£0.38/DM				0
£0.37/DM			0	
£0.36/DM		**DM2.5m**		0
£0.35/DM	**DM5.0m**		**DM5.0m**	
£0.34/DM		DM7.5m		**DM10m**
£0.33/DM			DM10m	
£0.32/DM				DM10m

Step 3:
Assume the bank chooses to write the option for zero profit. The customer pays £75,000 for the option. We are in period 1. The exchange rate is £0.35/DM. The tree says the bank should borrow DM5m to hedge itself. So it borrows DM5m and exchanges them for sterling at the rate of £0.35/DM, giving it £1.75m. The bank has now written a put option, and has hedged itself by having a debt of DM5m and holding a total of £1.825m in sterling.

Step 4:
The bank now waits for the exchange rate to move from £0.35/DM either up to £0.36 or down to £0.34/DM. When that happens the model says that the bank should revise its hedge. The bank forecasts that it might take a month for this to happen. Suppose for example the rate goes to £0.36. The following month it goes back to £0.35 and then on down to £0.34. The bank does the following trades:

Position:	£('000)	DM('000)
Sell option	+75	
Borrow DM5m and sell at £0.35/DM	+1750	–5000
Period 2: buy DM2.5m at £0.36/DM to reduce debt to DM2.5m:	–900	+2500
Period 3: borrow DM2.5m to increase debt to DM5m and exchange at £0.35/DM:	+875	–2500
Period 4: borrow DM5m to increase debt to DM10m and exchange at £0.34/DM:	+1700	–5000
Net position after four months	**+3500**	**–10000**

Step 5:
At the end of four months, the option expires. In this case the exchange rate is £0.34/DM, the customer will certainly want to take the opportunity of selling the D-Marks to the bank at £0.35/DM. The bank will receive DM10m and pay £3.5m; this exactly matches its borrowing of DM10m and cash of £3.5m.

Note: any other path through the tree would have had the same outcome; either the option is exercized and the bank's D-Mark debt and sterling cash are canceled, or the option ends up out of the money, with the bank having neither D-Mark debts nor sterling cash.

The basic model of Black and Scholes has been subjected to numerous refinements which try to capture the complex behavior of volatility. As the simpler models become universally accepted, prices become tighter, margins become smaller and there is an increasing incentive to develop better models. No-one can forecast volatility with any great accuracy but the bank with a slightly better model can make money at the expense of its less-sophisticated competitors.

Where does all this lead?

If the bank writing the exchange rate option had simply pocketed the premium and hoped for the best, it would have been very exposed to a fall in the D-Mark. This is a large risk – the bank could easily lose an amount equal to several times the premium it was paid. It is also a risk which is simple to understand. By delta hedging it removed the directional risk and greatly reduced the size of possible losses.

At the same time the residual risk becomes much more complex. In the model the bank breaks even exactly. The calculations could go wrong because the exchange rate proves more volatile than assumed. There could be a sudden realignment of exchange rates which made it impossible to rebalance the portfolio as the model assumes. Large changes in sterling and D-Mark interest rates could impose substantial unforeseen financing costs on the bank.

As banks become more proficient at hedging and managing the big risks, they are left with risks which are smaller but also more complex and harder to control. This in turn creates a demand for more complex models. These take account of the way volatility may vary in future, which can capture the joint behavior of exchange and interest rates and which help the bank hedge itself against changes in volatility.

Another related phenomenon is a growing sophistication in the products offered by financial institutions. Straightforward put and call options have become virtual commodity products, traded on relatively narrow spreads. There is a growing demand for more complex products tailored to the specific needs of clients. As well as options on interest rates, there are options on interest rate differentials between currencies and options on changes in the shape of the yield. As well as ordinary call options, there are options which are knocked out if the price goes very low or very high. In addition to options on financial assets, companies are turning increasingly to the derivatives market to handle commodity price risk and credit risk.

While the same broad approach which underlies the Black-Scholes model can be used, these problems require more sophisticated implementation. This places heavy demand on the modeling ability of the specialists who produce them and on the power of their computers as well as heavy demands on data to validate and test models.

The overall trend is towards ever more sophisticated risk management by financial institutions allowing greater economy in the use of risk capital, finer pricing and cheaper and more elaborate risk management services for their customers. These developments create a significant challenge for the control, incentive and information systems within both financial and non-financial organizations.

Summary

Financial innovation has enabled companies to limit the impact of interest rate changes and currency fluctuations through a wide range of instruments – but what has made this possible?

Anthony Neuberger argues that our understanding of how to measure and manage risk has radically improved, notably after publication of the Black and Scholes model in 1973. Using the example of a German D-Mark put option the author explains how a bank can reduce its risk through 'delta hedging' – the method of buying and selling the foreign currency to stay perfectly hedged.

More complex models take account of the way volatility may vary in future, capturing the joint behavior of interest rates and exchange rates. With put and call products virtually commodity items, there is a growing demand for more complex products tailored to the specific needs of clients.

Suggested further reading

Black, F. and Scholes, M., (1973), 'The pricing of corporate liabilities', *Journal of Political Economy* 81, 637–59.

Black, F., (1988), 'How to use the holes in Black-Scholes', *Risk*, March.

Hull, J., (1997), *Options, Futures and Other Derivatives*, 3rd edn, Prentice-Hall.

Macbeth, J.D. and Merville, L.J., (1979), 'An empirical examination of the Black-Scholes call option pricing model', *Journal of Finance* 34, December, 1173–86.

Rubinstein, M., (1994), 'Implied binomial trees', *Journal of Finance* 49, July, 771–818.

Derivatives as a way of reducing risk

by Richard Marston, Gregory S. Hayt and Gordon M. Bodnar

The Weiss Center for International Financial Research of the Wharton School undertook a survey of derivatives usage and practice by non-financial corporations in the US in November 1994. In late 1995, with the support of CIBC Wood Gundy, a more detailed survey was conducted, with a broader range of questions about valuation and risk measurement and with more specific questions about the use of derivatives. This article reports some of the findings of the second survey.

For the survey, derivatives are defined narrowly as forwards, futures, options and swaps plus broader contracts that contained one or more of these instruments in their structure. The primary objectives of this survey, as with the original 1994 survey, were to sample derivatives activity from a broad cross-section of US firms to better understand current practice as well as to develop a database on risk-management practices suitable for academic research.

Derivatives by size and industry

The survey was sent to a sampling of more than 2,000 US businesses. A total of 350 companies responded: 176 from the manufacturing sector; 77 from the primary products sector, which includes agriculture, mining, energy and utilities; and 97 from the service sector.

The first question asked whether companies use derivatives. Of the respondents, 142 (41 per cent) said they used derivatives. Figure 1 presents the responses broken down by company size and industry sector. Fifty nine per cent of large companies (market value greater than $250m) use derivatives. The percentage drops to 48 per cent for medium-sized businesses (between $50m and $250m market value) and to only 13 per cent for small organizations (less than $50m).

By industry, derivatives use is greatest among primary product producers, which is not surprising given that futures exchanges were originally established to help such companies manage their commodity risks. Not quite so many manufacturing companies use derivatives. The use of derivatives is smallest in the service sector. We found that notwithstanding several widely publicized financial debacles related to the improper use of derivatives, our sample results suggested that the number of businesses using derivatives increased in 1995 over 1994. The increase, however, was very small.

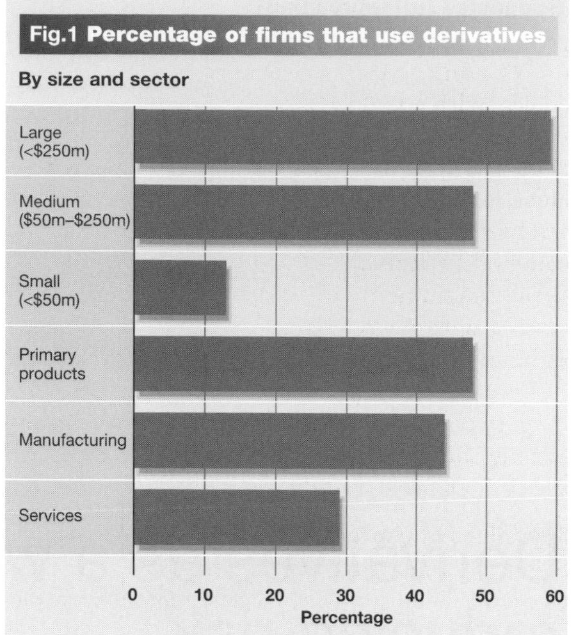

Risk management

Types of risk hedged and choices of instruments

The survey asked companies to indicate how they used particular types of derivatives instruments to manage exposure across four broad classes of financial price risk: foreign currency, interest rate, commodity and equity.

For each source of risk, we asked if they managed their exposure, and if so, to rank their usage of seven types of derivative instruments: forwards, futures, swaps, over-the-counter (OTC) options, exchange-traded options, structured derivatives (combinations of forwards, swaps and options) and hybrid debt (straight debt with embedded derivative instruments) in terms of importance to their company for managing that exposure.

Seventy six per cent of all derivatives users in our survey manage foreign exchange risk using foreign currency derivatives. Among the foreign currency derivatives the companies use, the forward contract is the most popular choice. More than 75 per cent of businesses rank the forward contract as one of their top three choices among foreign currency derivative instruments with more than 50 per cent ranking it as their first choice. OTC options are also a popular foreign currency derivative instrument, with about 50 per cent of the organizations choosing this as one of their top choices. Among the remaining instruments, swaps and futures are the most popular.

Among derivatives users in the survey, 73 per cent indicate they manage interest rate risk. Not surprisingly, the overwhelmingly popular choice among instruments in this area is the swap; 78 per cent of companies list swaps as their first choice among interest rate derivative instruments, with 95 per cent ranking it as one of their three top choices. Structured derivatives, OTC options and futures are the next most popular.

Commodity price risk is managed using derivatives by just 37 per cent of the derivatives users in our survey. Among instruments in this risk class, futures contracts

Table 1: Primary risk management goal of using derivatives	
To manage the cash flows of the firm	49 per cent
To manage accounting earnings of the firm	42 per cent
To manage the market value of the firm	8 per cent
To manage the balance sheet accounts of the firms	1 per cent

are the most popular derivative; 42 per cent of all commodity derivatives users rank futures as their first choice, with an additional 23 per cent ranking them as a second or third choice. Swaps and forwards come in close behind futures in popularity, with more than 50 per cent of commodity derivatives users putting these instruments among their top three choices. Both OTC options and exchange-traded options are listed as the first-choice instrument by eight per cent of users, although OTC options are far more popular as second or third choices.

Finally, equity risk is the risk class least likely to be managed with derivatives: just 12 per cent of all derivatives users in the sample indicate usage of equity derivatives. Among the instruments used in this class, OTC options are the most popular. They are the first choice of nearly 50 per cent of users.

Objectives of use in risk management

Since the most common use of derivative instruments is for risk management, we wanted to identify what risk-management objectives companies were trying to achieve. We asked those that use derivatives for hedging to rank the importance of four different goals of their hedging strategies: managing volatility in accounting earnings; managing volatility in cash flows; managing balance sheet accounts or ratios; and managing the market value of the company.

The responses for the 'most important' are summarized in Table 1. Managing cash flows is the top choice, with 49 per cent of respondents indicating that this is the most important objective of their hedging strategy.

Managing the fluctuations in accounting earnings is a close second with 42 per cent of businesses indicating this is the 'most important' objective of their hedging strategy. While in many cases the impact of hedging on reported earnings and cash flows may be similar, the popularity of the former objective may suggest that some companies focus hedging strategy more on stabilizing the reported numbers presented to investors than stabilizing the actual internal cash flows.

A distant third among the objectives is managing the total market value of the company, which is the 'most important' objective of just eight per cent of the respondents. Since firm value is theoretically equal to the present value of expected future cash flows, the difference between the importance of this objective and the cash flow objective may be more a matter of the time frame of hedging than its intent. Finally, only one per cent of the companies indicated that they hedge to manage balance sheet ratios.

Concerns about derivatives usage

The use of derivatives in today's market involves many issues. Respondents were asked to indicate their degree of concern about a series of issues regarding the use of derivatives. These include: credit risk, uncertainty about hedge accounting treatment, tax and legal issues, disclosure requirements, transaction costs, liquidity risk, lack of knowledge about derivatives within the organization, difficulty quantifying the business's underlying exposure, perceptions about derivatives use by outsiders, pricing and valuing derivatives, monitoring and evaluating hedge results and evaluating risks of proposed derivative transactions. For each issue, businesses were asked to indicate a high, moderate, or low level of concern or indicate that the issue was not a concern.

Credit risk is the issue that most seriously concerns derivatives users. Thirty-three per cent express a high degree of concern, with an additional 35 per cent indicating a moderate degree of concern about credit risk. Whether this concern is due to systemic risk (wide-spread market collapse due to an initial set of defaults) or non-delivery on individual contracts is not clear. However, the issue of timely and complete payment of derivative transactions is of significant concern among derivatives users.

Perhaps in light of the large losses that occurred in well-known derivatives disasters in 1994, companies expressed considerable concern about their ability to evaluate the risk involved in proposed derivatives transactions. Thirty-one per cent of responding companies indicated a high degree of concern and 36 per cent a moderate degree.

The next most important issue among derivatives users is uncertainty about the accounting treatment for hedges. This is not surprising given the lack of well-specified rules and the importance of such rules to reported results of derivative use. Thirty per cent of organizations expressed a high degree of concern over this issue, with another 30 per cent indicating a moderate degree of concern. In addition to accounting issues, tax and legal issues also generated significant concern.

Finally, the fifth and sixth issues most concerning derivatives users were transaction costs and the liquidity risk of using derivatives. Transaction costs (dealer fees) associated with derivatives generated a high degree of concern for 20 per cent of responding companies while risks concerning liquidity in the derivative markets caused a high degree of concern for 19 per cent of the companies.

Foreign exchange exposure

Foreign currency derivative markets

Given the popularity of currency derivatives, the survey asked detailed questions about the use of currency derivatives. Businesses were asked to indicate how often they transacted in the derivatives market for six commonly cited rationales for foreign currency risk management: contractual commitments, anticipated transactions of one year or less, anticipated transactions beyond one year, competitive economic exposure, foreign repatriations and translation of foreign accounting statements.

The most frequently cited motivations for transacting in the foreign currency derivatives markets were for hedging contractual commitments (91 per cent hedge frequently or sometimes) and anticipated transactions expected within the year (91 per cent hedge frequently or sometimes).

Anticipated transactions beyond one year were frequently hedged by only 11 per cent of the companies but sometimes hedged by 43 per cent, suggesting that a majority of companies at least sometimes hedge over a longer horizon. Economic and translation exposures were cited by a minority of companies as a reason for using foreign currency derivatives.

Foreign currency hedging is also used frequently to protect foreign repatriations (dividends, royalties/fees, internal interest payments and so on). Thirty four per cent of businesses frequently hedge these flows while another 38 per cent do so sometimes.

Given that not all companies using currency derivatives have foreign operations, this suggests that an even larger proportion of the set of multinational businesses use currency derivatives at least sometimes to hedge the dollar value of foreign repatriations.

Options are widely thought to be better suited than forwards and futures for hedging anticipated transactions, particularly those with longer maturities, as well as competitive/economic exposure. Consistent with this, more than half of the firms hedging longer term anticipated transactions used options.

Table 2: Frequency with which a market view impacts foreign currency derivative use

A market view on the exchange rates causes the company to...	Frequently	Sometimes
alter the timing of a hedge	11 per cent	61 per cent
alter the size of a hedge	12 per cent	48 per cent
actively take a position	6 per cent	33 per cent

Market view on foreign currency derivatives

One area of risk management that has been hard to measure is the degree to which companies alter their strategy based on their view of the direction or level of foreign exchange rates. To gauge the impact of market views on companies' derivatives activity, the survey asked them to indicate the frequency with which their market view caused them to alter the timing or size of hedges or to actively take a position in the market using derivatives. The responses are presented in Table 2.

Only about 11–12 per cent of organizations reported 'frequently' altering the size or timing of hedges based on a market view on the exchange rate. A relatively large number would 'sometimes' incorporate their market views into their foreign currency hedging decision, with 61 per cent of firms sometimes altering the timing of their hedges and 48 per cent sometimes altering the size.

Without entering the debate about what constitutes a hedge and what constitutes speculation, it is apparent that a large percentage of companies sometimes take into account their view of future market movements before choosing a strategy. What may be more surprising is the large percentage that 'actively take positions' based on a market view of the exchange rate. While only six per cent of firms 'frequently' take positions, another 33 per cent do so at least 'sometimes'.

Interest rate exposure

The survey also asked detailed questions about interest rate derivative usage. A total of 83 per cent of the organizations using interest rate derivatives used these to swap floating rate for fixed rate debt. Nearly 70 per cent of the companies reported doing the opposite. Fifty eight per cent said they used derivatives to fix the spread on new debt issues.

These three motivations are typical of companies that use swaps to tailor their financing needs. Another motivation for using swaps is locking-in borrowing rates (spread) in advance of a debit issue based on a business's view of the market. About 60 per cent indicated this motivation as being at least sometimes important. The majority indicated that they undertake interest rate derivative transactions occasionally. This is consistent with these transactions being carried out primarily when businesses undertake financing activities.

Table 3: Frequency with which a market view impacts interest rate derivative use

A market view on interest rates causes the company to...	Frequently	Sometimes
alter the timing of a hedge	8 per cent	64 per cent
alter the size of a hedge	4 per cent	53 per cent
actively take a position	3 per cent	36 per cent

We also asked an analogous

question about the impact of a market view of interest rates on the use of interest rate derivatives. According to Table 3, market views seem to have the same effect on the use of interest rates derivatives as those reported for foreign currency derivatives. The impact of taking a market view on interest rates causes a majority of companies to alter the size or timing of hedges and nearly 40 per cent of them to take a position at least sometimes.

Control and reporting procedures

Counterparty risk

Companies obtain derivatives from counterparties ranging from commercial and investment banks to futures and options exchanges. The survey asked companies to rank derivative counterparties based on whether they are a 'primary' source, a 'secondary' source or not used at all. Commercial banks were rated as a primary source 89 per cent of the time with investment banks second at 44 per cent. Insurance companies were the most common secondary source, mentioned by 30 per cent of the companies. Exchanges were least important to end users; fewer than 10 per cent of businesses listed them as either a primary or secondary source.

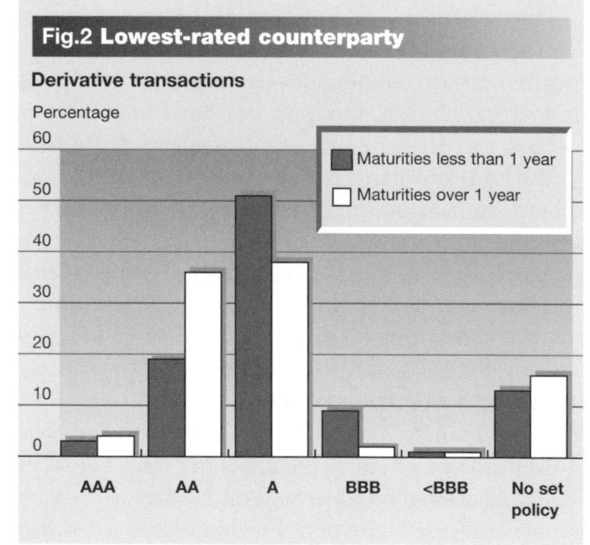

To investigate policies with respect to counterparty risk, the survey asked what was the lowest-rated counterparty with which the organizations would enter a derivatives transaction? As shown in Figure 2, for derivatives with maturities equal to 12 months or less 22 per cent of the companies insisted on a rating of AA or above for the counterparty and 73 per cent on A or above.

Policies were even stricter for derivatives with maturities greater than 12 months: 40 per cent of companies insisted on a rating of AA or above.

It is evident that a rating of A or below significantly handicaps a bank in offering derivatives, especially those with longer maturities. Despite this high level of concern about counterparty risk, only one of the 142 companies using derivatives reports ever having experienced a default by a counterparty.

Internal control and reporting

The survey asked two questions about internal procedures regarding derivatives: whether the organization had a documented policy covering the use of derivatives (76 per cent reported having such a policy) and how frequently derivatives activity was reported to the board of directors. Figure 3 shows that 51 per cent of companies had no pre-set schedule while 29 per cent reported to the board either monthly or quarterly.

By cross-checking the answers to these two questions, we found that 23 companies, or 16 per cent, indicated having neither a documented policy nor regular reporting of derivative activity to the board.

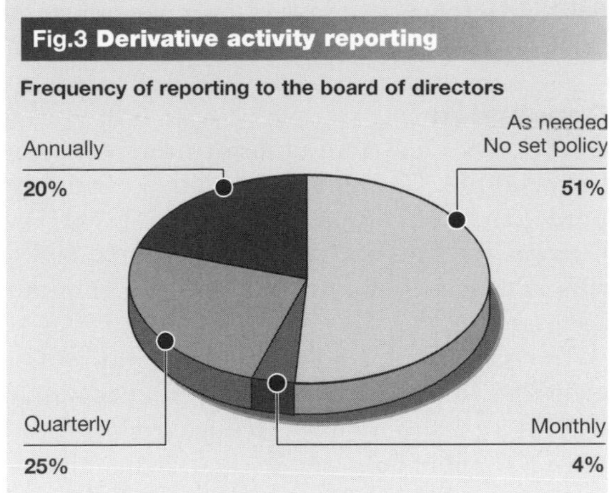

Fig.3 Derivative activity reporting

Market risk assessment

We were also interested in the organizations' philosophy for managing derivatives positions. The survey asked whether they viewed their derivatives positions in terms of transactions linked to specific corporate exposures or as a portfolio of derivatives to be managed separately or jointly with the company's exposure. Just 18 per cent of the firms viewed their derivatives as a portfolio linked to an aggregate corporate exposure while another 15 per cent regarded them as a stand-alone portfolio for at least some purposes.

Non-use of derivatives

We also asked organizations that did not use derivatives to provide information on why they chose not to do so. We asked non-users to rank the three primary factors from a list of eight possible factors (including an 'other' category).

The most important reason, not surprisingly, is because their exposures did not warrant using derivatives. Nearly 45 per cent of all non-derivatives users ranked this as the most important reason for not using derivatives with an additional 21 per cent citing this as the second or third most important reason.

Another 13 per cent listed the fact that exposures could be managed by other means as a primary reason for not using derivatives while another 21 per cent listed this as the second or third most important reason. Presumably this means the companies could manage their exposure through operating hedges (for example, producing in export markets) or by contractual arrangements which shift or share risk with other parties (for example, pricing in dollars). Other companies, however, refrained from using derivatives even though they were exposed to financial price risk.

The second most popular reason for not using derivatives was a simple cost-benefit explanation – the costs of using derivatives exceeded the benefit. This was cited as one of the top three reasons by 47 per cent of non-users with 12 per cent citing this as the primary reason.

Another interesting finding from this question was that many non-users appeared to refrain from using derivatives simply because of a lack of knowledge. This reason was the second most frequently chosen 'most important' factor for not using derivatives, offered by 17 per cent of non-users. This is not just a concern of small companies. While 22 per cent of small companies ranked this as the most important factor, it was regarded as most important by almost as many large-firm non-users at 17 per cent.

Finally, non-users also expressed significant concerns about the perceptions of derivatives. Thirteen per cent ranked concerns about the perceptions of derivative use by investors, regulators and the public as the most important factor in their decision not to use them. In addition, over one-quarter of the other companies put this as one of their top three concerns.

Conclusion

Derivatives use among non-financial companies appears to be a fact of modern financial life. Despite the derivatives 'train wrecks' of 1994, the evidence suggests the percentage of companies using derivatives has not fallen off from 1994 levels. Currently less than half of all non-financial organizations use derivatives, although this is tilted heavily towards larger companies in commodity and manufacturing sectors.

Derivatives are powerful financial tools that can either help or harm. Despite concerns to the contrary, the evidence suggests that the primary reason for using derivatives is to manage (reduce) risk rather than add it. Some companies appear to have a flexible policy on derivative use that allows them to incorporate views on the markets into their risk-management decision. Most businesses, however, said they had documented corporate policies for derivative use as well as established reporting and measurement procedures to prevent abuses and avoid financial disasters in case of large market movements.

Will derivative use increase? Some of the companies not using derivatives may begin to use them as knowledge of these instruments increases and public perception of derivatives improves. In addition, because price volatility appears to be here to stay, companies are likely to make increasing use of derivatives as a tool to manage this risk.

The 1995 survey was sponsored by CIBC Wood Gundy and carried out under the auspices of the Weiss Center for International Financial Research at the Wharton School. The authors would like to thank Charles Smithson for his guidance and support.

Summary

The use of derivatives among non-financial companies appears to be a fact of modern financial life, according to the findings of a survey of US businesses conducted in 1995 and discussed in this article by Gordon Bodnar, Richard Marston and Gregory Hayt. Well-publicized debacles in 1994 do not appear to have discouraged respondents.

Despite fears to the contrary the evidence seems to be that the primary use of derivatives (defined here as forwards, futures, options and swaps plus broader contracts that contained one or more of these) is to reduce risk rather than add to it. Most businesses said they had documented corporate policies for derivative use as well as established reporting and measurement procedures. Use of derivatives may increase because of price volatility and as companies' knowledge of them and public perceptions improve.

Metallgesellschaft: a hedge too far

by Anthony Neuberger

Of all the large losses involving the use of derivatives – Barings, Orange County, Showa Oil, Procter and Gamble – few have attracted as much interest as the Metallgesellschaft (MG) case. The problems at MG first surfaced publicly with a report on December 6 1993 in the *Frankfurter Allgemeine Zeitung* alleging that the company was experiencing liquidity problems due to speculation in US oil futures. By the end of the month, the MG board decided to get rid of its chairman and some senior executives; to liquidate \$4bn worth of oil supply contracts with customers and in the process to crystallize losses amounting to some \$1.3bn.

The company

MG is a large diversified metals, mining and industrial conglomerate. In 1993 it had a turnover of DM26bn (\$15bn). Its US subsidiary, MG Refining & Marketing (MGRM), built up a substantial business during the 1980s and early 1990s supplying oil and oil-related products such as diesel, gasoline and heating oil to some 500 large customers including retail gasoline suppliers, manufacturing companies and government departments.

In November 1991, MGRM recruited a new president. Arthur Benson brought with him a 50-person team. Benson had worked for MG's US operations in the 1980s, marketing oil product contracts until being made redundant in 1988. He had moved to Louis Dreyfus Energy where, in the summer of 1990, a seemingly disastrous position in jet fuel was turned into a rumored \$500m profit by the Iraqi invasion of Kuwait.

The customer contracts

During the 1980s, worries about the security of oil supplies gradually receded as the price of crude oil dropped from \$35 to \$12/barrel. Then in 1990, with the Iraqi invasion of Kuwait, prices doubled from US\$18 to US\$36 per barrel within days (*see* Figure 1). Many oil consumers found they were in a vicious squeeze – supplies disappeared, prices soared and in many cases they were unable to pass on the increased costs in full to their customers.

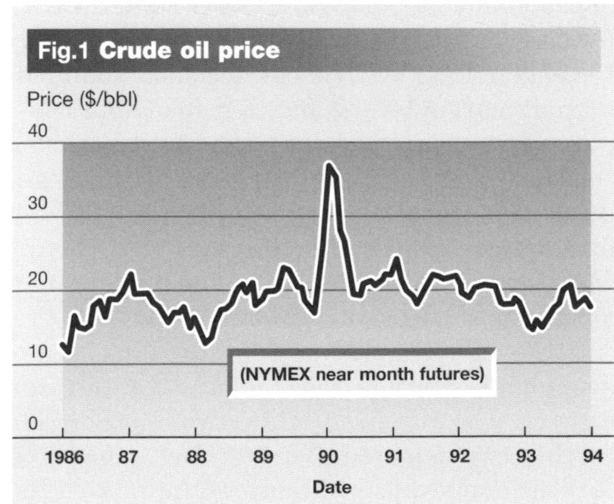

The Gulf War gave oil distributors and consumers a reminder of the volatility of oil prices and of the pain caused by a sharp rise in prices. Benson spotted an opening for his salesmen. MGRM would supply agreed monthly quantities of oil products on fixed-price long-term contracts (between five and 10 years). By covering a fraction (typically no more than 20 per cent of their demand) in this way customers could protect themselves in a simple and effective fashion from a sudden spike in the oil price. They could not insulate themselves permanently from a rise in oil prices but they could buy time until they could pass it on to their customers.

MGRM also offered customers the option of liquidating the contracts early if the futures price rose above the fixed supply price. In such a case customers could require MGRM to pay them one half of the difference between the two prices on the remaining volume to be delivered under the contract. This opened up the attractive prospect of being able to turn another oil price spike into a huge cash windfall. At the same time customers could be reassured that a long-term fall in oil prices would not threaten their viability. Since the obligation to buy oil from MGRM at fixed prices would only cover some 20 per cent of their requirements, they would be able to exploit any fall in oil prices on the remaining 80 per cent.

Hedging the contracts

MGRM could not buy the oil and store it to deliver to customers later; financing and storage costs would make the transaction quite uneconomic. Nor could MGRM simply hope that it would be able to buy the oil cheaply when the time came to deliver; oil prices could easily rise by 50 per cent, leading to huge losses. It would have to hedge itself in the financial markets. The obvious instruments to use were the oil futures contracts traded on the New York Mercantile Exchange (Nymex).

By December 1993, MGRM had signed contracts with customers that committed it to delivering some 160m barrels of gasoline and heating oil over a 10-year period (a total value of around $4bn). One third of this (55m barrels) was hedged using Nymex contracts. The rest (110m barrels) was hedged on the over-the-counter (OTC) market through oil swaps. These swaps resembled the Nymex contracts.

The hedging strategy goes wrong

Spot oil prices fell from $21.65 per barrel on September 30 1992 to US$13.91 per barrel on December 17 1993. As a direct result, MGRM had to pay out more than $1.2bn on its hedge. The financial problems caused by margin calls were exacerbated in December 1993 by Nymex's decisions to impose 'supermargin' (more than twice the normal margin levels) and to revoke MGRM's 'hedger exemption', thus obliging it to put up more cash as security and to reduce substantially its open positions. This was the source of the rumors reported by the *Frankfurter Allgemeine Zeitung*. A special meeting of the MG supervisory board was convened on December 17 to consider the preliminary results of investigations by Deutsche Bank and Dresdner Bank (which were large shareholders as well as lenders) into the group's liquidity. They did not accept the strategy pursued by MGRM.

MG's chairman, Hans Schimmelbusch, was removed after being accused of not keeping the board properly informed of the problems in the US operation. His finance director was also fired, while two other directors were forced into retirement and a further two demoted. Between December 20 and 31, MGRM liquidated most of its futures and swaps positions. It liquidated its forward physical delivery contracts, waiving the amounts potentially receivable under its customer contracts.

MG chairman Hans Schimmelbusch: ousted following the oil futures debate

Assessment of the strategy

The losses at MGRM prompted a fierce debate about whether the strategy was fundamentally flawed or whether it was a good strategy that was prematurely and unnecessarily aborted. To assess the strategy, it is necessary to understand the risks faced by MGRM even after hedging the oil price risk:

- The contracts extended five or 10 years; futures contracts do go out to 36 months but the longer-dated contracts are too illiquid to be of much use. Most of MGRM's trading was in the near months. This made MGRM vulnerable to variations in the relative price of short- and longer-term contracts.
- The strategy required MGRM to do a lot of trading. At its peak, MGRM's oil purchase requirements equaled about 20 per cent of the total open interest in the Nymex crude oil futures contract. MGRM was heavily dependent on the continuing depth and liquidity of the market to enable it to roll its positions at reasonable cost.
- The oil products it was contracted to deliver were not identical to the products traded on the exchange. The company was at risk from variations in the prices of different oil products.
- Losses and gains on the futures markets appear as cash immediately; losses and gains on delivery contracts appear at the time of delivery. MGRM was vulnerable to fluctuations in funding costs.
- If oil prices fell (as they did) MGRM would be vulnerable to customers defaulting on their purchase commitments. In the face of all these risks (and with the benefit of hindsight about the size of losses) it is tempting to assert that the strategy was always a gamble. That is not fair.

The strategic concept was quite defensible. There was clearly a demand among customers for long-term fixed-price oil contracts. There was apparently little competition and consumers were not well placed to provide the service themselves. So there was potentially a profitable opportunity to be exploited by someone who could manage the risks effectively.

The question to be asked is not whether the transaction was risky but whether the expected profits were large enough to compensate for the risks and whether the strategy was implemented in a sensible way.

Potential profitability

The single most important source of risk (and of profit) for MGRM was the mismatch between the long-term maturity of its liabilities and the short-term maturity of its hedge. To understand the nature of this, consider the following simplified example: MGRM contracts to sell one barrel of oil in five years time. It hedges by buying one barrel of oil six months forward. In six months time, it closes out the position in what is now a maturing contract and buys a new six-month contract. Assume zero interest rates and ignore financing issues – we will come back to these later.

The accountant who keeps the profit and loss account needs to put a value on MGRM's liability to supply the barrel of oil. He uses the price of the futures contract that MGRM is using for hedging as a proxy for the five-year price. This is not the cleverest or most prudent accounting system. But we are only concerned with the total profit, and that will not be affected by the rule used for valuing the supply contract.

Suppose that MGRM signs the contract at $22/barrel when the six-month futures contract is $20/barrel. The accountant records an immediate profit of $2/barrel. After six months, the price on the contract, which is now near maturity, has gone to, say, $25/barrel. MGRM will have made $5 profit on the rise in the price of the futures. But the accountant will say that this is exactly offset by an increase of $5 in the cost of meeting its commitment to supply. So the hedge appears to be perfect.

But now MGRM has to liquidate its futures position and buy one of the new six-month contracts. Suppose that the six-month contract is trading at $24/barrel – $1 less than the spot. As MGRM switches contracts, the accountant will reduce the valuation on MGRM's liability to supply from $25 to $24 – so creating a profit of $1/barrel. A revaluation will occur every time the hedge is rolled forward. By the end of five years, the total profit made by MGRM will therefore be the sum of two components: the difference between the contract price and the spot price; and the difference between the spot price and the six-month futures price each time the contract is rolled over.

MGRM's profits depend on whether the market is in 'backwardation' over the life of the supply contracts. Backwardation is when the price for long-term delivery falls below the price for immediate delivery.

Backwardation in the oil market

Over the period 1986 to 1992 the degree of backwardation averaged some $0.14/barrel/month (*see* Figure 2). Had MGRM written a contract to supply oil in five years time at a price equal to the current spot price and had it hedged by rolling short-maturity futures contracts, it would have generated a profit of $8.40/barrel.

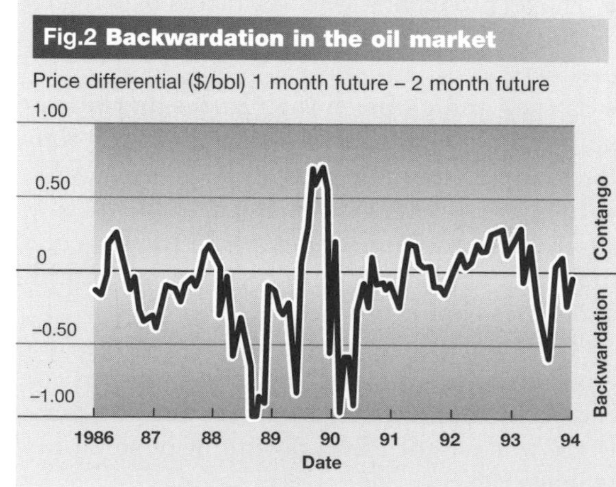

Fig.2 Backwardation in the oil market

This may exaggerate the potential gain since it includes the Gulf War when backwardation was enormous. If that period is ignored, the average level of backwardation is halved. But even profits of $4 per barrel are substantial.

Backwardation has been quite persistent but its causes are not well understood and it might not persist at historic levels. The very fact that customers were prepared to buy oil long-term at or above the spot price when the term structure of futures prices is downward sloping suggests a degree of disequilibrium that would attract other traders to follow MGRM. This could well lead to a decline in backwardation.

MGRM's strategy meant that it had to be in the market on a permanent basis, rolling out of its position in maturing contracts into slightly longer-dated contracts. Such a strategy was likely to affect the prices it faced given the large amounts with which it was operating and this too would tend to reduce profitability. Historical evidence gives grounds for believing in continuing backwardation and hence in the profitability of writing long-term contracts at or above current prices. But there was never any certainty that MGRM's strategy would be profitable.

Financing the strategy

There were substantial risks in a strategy of hedging long commitments using short-dated futures. My calculations suggest that on the most favorable assumptions, the risk was likely to be around $3/barrel. That is to say, if MGRM hedged as closely as possible, hedging changes in the slope of the term structure as well as in its level, it could easily end up making $3 more or less per barrel than expected. Thus, even if the future broadly resembles the past, it is likely that the strategy will fail to make money. The fact that the best hedge is not very good affects the financing of the position. If the hedge is demonstrably a good one, there is likely to be little problem in getting a bank or other institution to finance it. They are lending against an asset whose value is known to exceed the debt. But if the hedge is risky, a bank will not finance it because it would bear the loss if things turn out badly without sharing the profits if they go well. The strategy needs to be financed with equity.

MG itself needed to set aside enough capital to absorb potential losses; otherwise it faces the risk of having to liquidate its position prematurely. It requires that the strategy be understood throughout the company and by its investors, and this understanding appears to have been lacking.

Implementation

MGRM seems to have bought one barrel of futures for every barrel of oil to be sold. This would lead to overhedging for two important reasons.

First, a $1 increase in the spot price of oil is unlikely to imply a $1 increase in the price of delivery in five years. Many factors might affect the short-term supply/demand balance that have little significance for long-term prices. Over 1993, the spot and near-term futures moved down far more sharply than longer-term futures (*see* Figure 3). The losses on the hedge were far larger than the expected profits on the supply contracts.

The second reason is that a $1 fall in the oil price at all maturities costs the company $1 today on the futures market; the corresponding $1 gain in the supply contract only occurs when the oil is supplied.

The overhedging means that MGRM was net long oil; as the oil price fell it was actually losing money. If the minimum risk hedge was 0.5 to 1 rather than 1 to 1, then roughly half the loss that MGRM incurred was due to the fact that, intentionally or not, it had a huge exposure to the oil market when the oil price was falling very sharply.

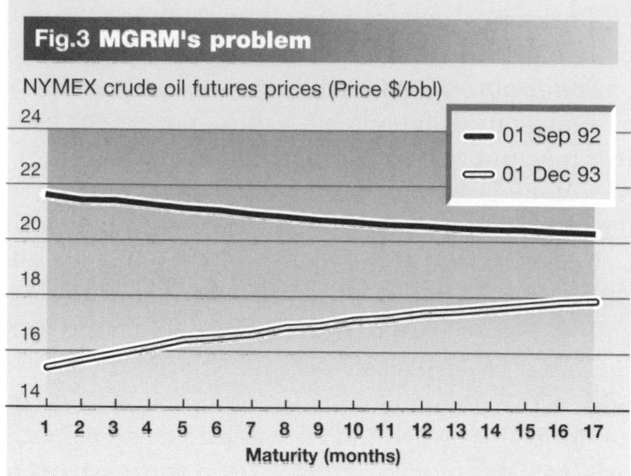

The most difficult question to resolve is how much of the loss can be attributed to the decision to unwind the contracts at the end of 1993. Customers were committed to buying large volumes of oil from MGRM at what was by then a huge premium to the spot price. These contracts seem to have been terminated without MGRM extracting any value from them. Yet in theory they were valuable to MGRM – worth many hundreds of millions of dollars.

Realizing this value required a continued hedging program, with the associated financing; it would not have been riskless – there was always a fear of customer defaults. Yet it is hard to believe that the best solution was to tear them up.

Lessons

MGRM's role was similar to that of a financial intermediary. It recognized that clients were prepared to pay a premium for a service above its fair market value. It designed a product to meet that need and a hedging strategy that passed most of the risks to the market. It kept some risks that it managed in house.

The problems appear to have been of two kinds. First, MGRM took on, intentionally or not, a huge amount of oil price risk that it need not have done. It is not clear that it had any particular expertise in guessing the level of the oil price. Second, MGRM did not ensure it had enough capital to hold to its strategy as the market moved away from it. It was trying to exploit a deviation between the price at which customers were prepared to buy oil and its estimate of the equilibrium price.

Large and persistent deviations can only be exploited with some risk. If deviations exist, they can get worse. An institution seeking to exploit them needs to have the financial strength to see the transaction through to the end; a forced exit is almost bound to be costly. In MGRM's case that meant having the commitment and understanding of both its parent and its bankers. The parent needed to understand and accept the risks it was taking and the bankers needed to be convinced they were lending no more than could be confidently recovered from customers. Clearly this was lacking.

Summary

Few derivatives disasters have inspired as much interest as the case of Metallgesellschaft – the metals, mining and industrial conglomerate which lost $1.3bn in 1993. In this article Anthony Neuberger explains the background to the story and draws some important lessons.

He argues that given clear customer demand for long-term fixed-price oil contracts the strategic concept was perfectly defensible – the question is not, therefore, whether

the transaction was risky but whether the expected profits were large enough to compensate for the risks and whether the strategy was sensibly implemented.

The problems, he believes, were of two kinds: intentionally or not the US subsidiary took on a huge amount of oil price risk which it need not have done; second, in trying to exploit a deviation between the price at which customers were prepared to buy oil and its estimate of the equilibrium price, the company did not ensure that it had enough capital to hold to the strategy as the market moved against it.

Suggested further reading

Canter, M.S. and Edwards, F.R., (1995), 'The collapse of Metallgesellschaft: unbridgeable risks, poor hedging strategy or just bad luck?', *Journal of Futures Markets*, May, 15(3).

Culp, C.L. and Miller, M.M., (1994), 'Hedging a flow of commodities with futures: lessons from Metallgesellschaft', *Derivatives Quarterly*, Fall, 1, 7–15.

Culp, C.L. and Miller, M.M., (1995), 'Metallgesellschaft and the economics of synthetic storage', *Journal of Applied Corporate Finance*, Winter, 7(4).

11

Financial institutions

Contributors

Harold Rose is Emeritus Esmée Fairbairn Professor of Finance at London Business School. He was previously first director of LBS' Institute of Finance and was group economic advisor at Barclays Bank.

Gary B. Gorton is a Professor of Finance at the Wharton School of the University of Pennsylvania.

Raghuram Rajan is the Joseph Gidwidz Professor of Finance at the University of Chicago Graduate School of Business. His research interests focus on corporate finance, financial intermediation and regulation.

Richard J. Herring is the Julian Aresty Professor of Finance at the Wharton School of the University of Pennsylvania and Vice Dean and Director of Wharton's undergraduate division. He is also a member of the Shadow Financial Regulatory Committee.

Contents

Introduction

Banks and other financial service industries such as insurance companies and pension funds are at the center of the financial sector – or are they? Most are under intense pressure from traditional and non-traditional competitors. This module considers the current role and future prospects of this part of the finance industry.

The key role of the financial 'middle men'

by Harold Rose

Until two US economists, John Gurley and Edward Shaw, published *Money in a Theory of Finance* in 1960, banks, insurance companies and other types of financial institution were studied in terms that implied that they had almost nothing in common. Although important differences between financial institutions are still recognized, they are now regarded by academics, at any rate, as all being species of the genus of financial intermediary. The roles financial institutions play are seen as reflecting the advantages of financial intermediation; and the changes in their role, most notably in the case of banks, are to a great extent regarded as reflecting a rise or fall in these advantages.

Financial intermediaries are so-called because they transfer funds from agents in the economy with free cash flows or financial surpluses – an excess of current saving over physical investment – to those with financial deficits. On balance this usually results in funds shifting from the personal to the business sector. Banks, insurance companies, pension funds and so on all possess this intermediation function, although financial flows also involve flows between intermediaries themselves and between businesses in general (in the form of trade credit). Some financial institutions, such as mutual funds, are not intermediaries as defined above. Three main questions arise: why does intermediation, rather than 'direct' financing, occur; what are the results of financial intermediation; and what changes in the economics of intermediation help to explain the changing weight of different types of institution in the economy?

Why financial intermediation?

Intermediaries may originate or develop either on the liabilities or assets side of their business. The conventional history of banks, for example, places their origin mainly in their role as deposit liability takers, and similarly with the liabilities of insurance companies. However, leasing companies, for example, have developed on the assets side. Whatever the case, the development of all financial intermediaries is tied up with two main factors: the insurance principle and cost saving.

The insurance principle

This is involved in the creation of diversified loan or other portfolios, which reduces the risks of financial institutions and their creditors and, by minimizing the influence of random events, also makes it possible for their creditors, such as bank depositors, to judge their performance more accurately. Moreover, it is the insurance principle, in the form of a low correlation between withdrawals by individual depositors or policyholders, that makes it possible for a bank to offer demand deposits and a life insurance company surrender facilities. All financial institutions can be described as selling the law of large numbers.

Cost savings

As with many forms of organization, financial intermediaries may have an advantage over 'direct' financing through economies of scale, standardization or specialization. Second, financial intermediaries save costs through the mathematics of the 'dating' agency. If there are, say, four prospective lenders and four would-be borrowers, there are 16 possible pairings; but if they all transact through a single intermediary acting as an allocating agent only eight links are needed. With 10 borrowers and 10 lenders a single intermediary has to put through only 20 transactions rather than a possible 100. In general, there are n^2 possible links between n pairs, whereas a single intermediary requires only 2n; and the larger the number of lenders and borrowers the greater the cost saving afforded by intermediaries. This aspect underlies the important role of intermediaries in reducing search and investigation costs.

Financial intermediation avoids the costs that would otherwise result from the duplication of monitoring of borrowers and the management of financial distress and defaults. Without banks, or some equivalent agent appointed collectively, we would individually have to monitor loans to a number of borrowers and individually have to bear the duplicated costs of default management. Other types of financial institution, such as insurance companies, also relieve us of transaction costs in this way. This is why some economists have stressed the role of financial intermediaries, particularly banks, as being 'delegated monitors'. Financial intermediaries also solve what would otherwise be the 'free rider' problem, in which we might individually assume that we could leave it to others to bear the costs of monitoring and default management.

Finally, in addition to reducing search and monitoring costs, financial intermediaries reduce information costs not only by interpreting information about borrower quality, for example, but also by receiving information that borrowers, or life insurance policyholders, would not wish to see published. Moreover, banks obtain a unique form of information about borrower behavior by virtue of their knowledge of bank account transactions. These factors help to explain why, according to the US evidence, the share prices of companies tend to rise on the announcement of a large increase in bank borrowing facilities.

Some results of intermediation

By reducing risk and costs, financial intermediation results in a higher level of saving and investment. This is possibly at the cost of a greater degree of financial interdependence and the transmission of shocks within the financial system. As a result, regulation has become a common feature of financial intermediation. Financial intermediation has also had the greatly beneficial effect of asset-liability transformation. A bank, for example, is able to make its deposit liabilities more liquid, less risky and individually smaller than its loans. In the development of intermediation a variety of financial instruments has been created, producing more efficient and lower-cost payments services than would otherwise be the case and creating a wider range of choices about risk and the time path of consumption.

Monetary policy difficulties

Modern banking has also created two areas of controversy, besides that of regulation. One is that of monetary policy, most of all as a result of the development of interest-bearing instruments with flexible withdrawal facilities and especially in the form of interest-bearing demand deposits.

The boundary between non-interest bearing 'money' and 'bonds', which was crucial to early forms of monetary theory, has become increasingly blurred. Post-war monetary theories that did not make so clear a distinction, but which nevertheless rested on the assumption of a predictable relationship between the level of money incomes and the demand for a particular measure of the quantity of money, have also proved to be unreliable in many countries.

As a result monetarist policies in which firm 'money' supply targets have been set and adhered to have proved problematical, involving disputes as to exactly what measure of money is critical and how current money supply behavior should be interpreted.

The dictum that inflation everywhere is and has been a monetary phenomenon probably commands widespread acceptance, at least as a long-term proposition. The consequence, however, has been the development of policies in which short-term interest rates (or the exchange rate) have become the focus of anti-inflationary policy. Money supply statistics are now only one guide among several.

Continued change in the development of instruments, payments technology and institutions is likely to prolong this more tentative approach. Furthermore, differences between national financial systems and national money-holding habits might make the task of any future European central bank even more difficult if, as might well be the case, a change in interest rates had a different effect nationally. For example, variable rate mortgages play a larger part in the UK than in other European countries, so a change in money rates might have a speedier effect on the British economy.

Financial systems and growth

It is generally accepted that financial intermediation brings economic benefits. Some economists and politicians, however, have gone further and have argued that so-called bank-dominated economic systems are more effective in promoting economic growth than those in which stock markets form a significant part of the capital-raising process. A contrast has therefore been drawn between France, Germany and Japan on the one hand and the US and UK on the other. It has been contended that systems in which long-term relationships exist between banks and borrowers enable the latter to take a longer view of investment, whereas stock markets are said to be afflicted by a 'short-termism' that forces companies in the US and UK to follow suit.

Several economists, however, who have examined the German financial system in particular, contend that the contrast drawn between the role of banks in that country and the UK is not valid. The charge of stock-market short-termism remains unproven; and, largely because of international competition, most countries are dismantling various restrictions, a process which is leading their financial systems to become more like that of the UK and US.

The dangers of the banking systems having too great an influence can be seen in Japan's current problems. And the special part stock markets can play in promoting industrial innovation is evident in the unparalleled development of information technology companies in the US. Stock markets not only play a part in raising finance but also have an information-diffusion function that is missing from so-called bank-dominated systems.

Changes in intermediation

In primitive economies local moneylenders were the chief form of financial 'institution'. The process of economic development, however, has everywhere been associated with

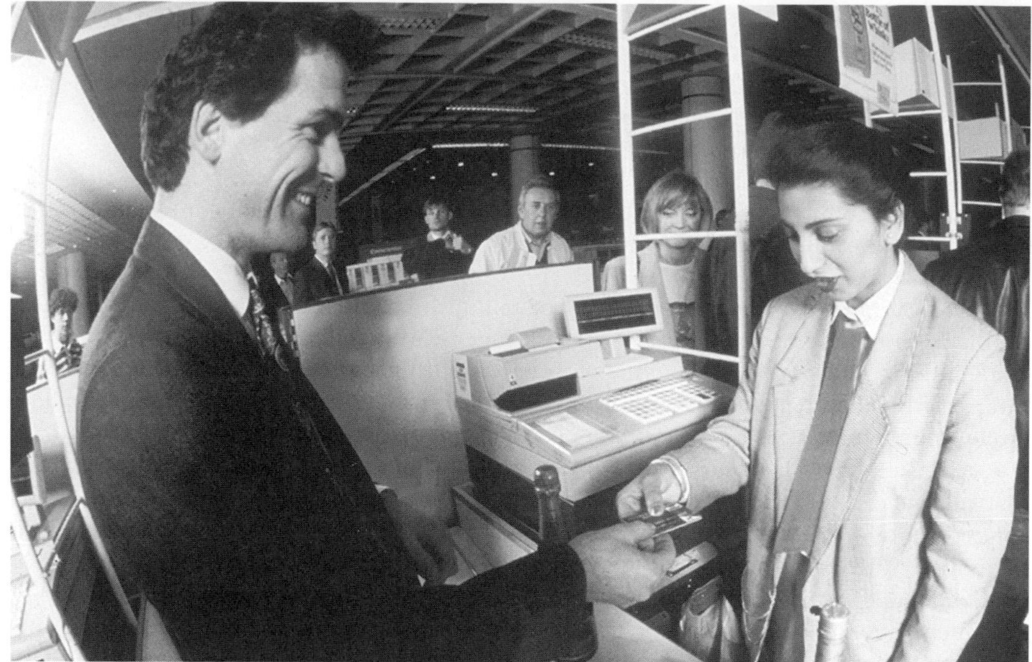

'Take my card': card technology, and especially its exploitation by retailers, has had a dramatic effect on intermediation

that of intermediation, with intermediaries' assets rising faster than physical assets: in this phase banks clearly predominate.

In the UK it looked as if the ratio of intermediary liabilities to gross domestic product was leveling out before the liberalization of banks and building societies in the 1980s and the strong rise in the prices of shares held by institutions in the 1990s interrupted this phase.

Against a long perspective the share of bank deposits in intermediary liabilities has been found to decline in many mature economies. Certainly, over the past 20 years or so improvements in security market practices, bringing lower transaction costs and new risk-reducing instruments, together with a tougher company law, fuller accounting disclosure and the growth of credit rating agencies, have combined to reduce the relative advantages of banks as corporate credit monitors, at least of quoted company borrowers. Interest margins on loans to the latter have fallen in the UK and US, where corporate borrowers have turned to securities markets, including eurobonds, and, in the US and elsewhere, commercial paper markets.

Banks have turned increasingly to personal lending; but other financial institutions and a growing number of large retail stores have used their customer information and modern card technology to enter this field. Card technology in general has reduced the demand for working balances; and this, together with telephone banking and postal accounts, has diminished the need for bank branches. Rising real incomes and, in some countries, tax advantages have favored the growth of non-bank financial intermediaries such as insurance companies and pension funds. The result is that, measured in terms of the ratio of deposits to total intermediary liabilities, the relative weight of banks and similar institutions has fallen in both the UK and the US (*see* Tables 1 and 2).

Table 1: Shares of assets of financial institutions in the US 1860–1993

%	1860	1880	1900	1910	1929	1939	1948	1960	1970	1980	1993
Commercial banks	71.4	60.6	62.9	64.5	53.7	51.2	55.9	38.2	37.9	34.8	25.4
Thrift institutions	17.8	22.8	18.2	14.8	14.0	13.6	12.3	19.7	20.4	21.4	9.4
Insurance companies	10.7	13.9	13.8	16.6	18.6	27.2	24.3	23.8	18.9	16.1	17.4
Investment companies	NA	NA	NA	NA	2.4	1.9	1.3	2.9	3.5	3.6	14.9
Pension funds	NA	NA	0.0	0.0	0.7	2.1	3.1	9.7	13.0	17.4	24.4
Finance companies	NA	0.0	0.0	0.0	2.0	2.2	2.0	4.6	4.8	5.1	4.7
Securities brokers & dealers	0.0	0.0	3.8	3.0	8.1	1.5	1.0	1.1	1.2	1.1	3.3
Mortgage companies	0.0	2.7	1.3	1.2	0.6	0.3	0.1	NA	NA	0.4	0.2
Real estate investment trusts	NA	NA	NA	NA	NA	NA	NA	0.0	0.3	0.1	0.1
Total (per cent)	100	100	100	100	100	100	100	100	100	100	100

Source: 'Is banking a declining industry? A historical perspective', George G. Kaufman and Larry R. Mote (*Economic Perspectives*, Federal Reserve Bank of Chicago, May/June 1994).

Table 2: Intermediary shares in the UK 1913–1995

	1913	1930	1939	1950	1960	1970	1980	1990	1995
Banks	64	60	55	65	40	30	31	33	28
Building societies	4	8	12	9	12	18	22	17	11
Insurance companies	32	31	32	26	30	28	23	23	30
Pension funds	NA	NA	NA	NA	14	16	18	25	27
Investment trusts	NA	NA	NA	NA	NA	7	4	3	3
Finance companies	NA	NA	NA	NA	NA	1	1	1	1
Total as % of GDP	71	99	109	112	106	131	129	251	310

Source: Various, financial statistics from 1960

Note: Approximate figures only, with differences in definition and changing over time. For example, those for banks and building societies are deposit liabilities (sterling only from 1970 for banks) whereas those for insurance companies and pension funds are assets. The figures for banks from 1990 include former building societies.

But the question of whether commercial banks as changing businesses, as distinct from banking in the traditional sense, have lost ground in terms of their share of income or value-added in the growing financial services industry is more questionable. Banks retain an information advantage in lending to small firms, which could well represent a growing share of some economies. They have also been able to replace lending to large companies by other services and more profitable personal lending.

It is clear that there has been a widespread tendency for the boundaries between different types of financial institution to become blurred. Deregulation and the abandonment of traditional and cartelized dividing lines have been taking place in many countries of differing political complexions. This suggests that the causes are rooted in common economic forces, of which the most evident have been the pressures of competition brought about by the internationalization of finance and the development of electronic information and payments technology. So today we see banks offering insurance and retail investment products; and insurance companies, retail stores and, especially in the US, mutual funds offering banking and other financial services.

Whether retail banks choose to undertake investment banking on any scale has become a question of perceived profitability rather than one of any deep structural principle. Some of the most profitable banks are those which have chosen not to become heavily involved in investment banking. Securities firms and other financial institutions lack the means as well as the incentive to become retail banks, which still dominate the payments system and whose branch network, although shrinking, remains a formidable barrier to entry.

But even retail banks combine traditional corporate lending with transactions in marketable instruments for their corporate customers. The so-called demographic time-bomb will clearly lead to the replacement or supplementation of state pensions by funded market schemes, offered by institutions, thus enhancing the role of securities markets.

Modern technology, by reducing transaction and distance costs, is commonly expected to have an extensive influence over a growing range of transactions throughout the world. The conclusion usually drawn is that the boundaries between financial intermediaries and between these and non-financial firms will become even more blurred. This may well prove to be the case, but the balance of advantage between relatively specialized firms and conglomerates does not depend on technology alone; and outside the world of finance, at any rate, the pendulum seems to be swinging back towards specialization.

Summary

Harold Rose considers the historic and the contemporary role of financial intermediaries – those banks, insurance companies, and pension funds which transfer funds from economic agents with surpluses to those with deficits. Two broad factors are at work: the reduction of risk which lies behind the creation of diversified loan or other portfolios and the saving of search, investigation and monitoring costs.

Financial intermediation has had a number of macro effects, including the development of regulation to control the transmission of financial shocks which it has set off, more efficient payments systems, and complications for the control of monetary policy. The author concludes with a discussion of the changing patterns of

intermediation, the blurring of boundaries between different types of financial intermediary and between these and non-financial firms.

Suggested further reading

Edwards, J. and Fischer, K., (1994), *Banks, finance and investment in Germany*, Cambridge University Press.
Goldsmith, R. W., (1969), *Financial structure and development*, Yale University Press.
Greenbaum, S. I. and Thakor, A. V., (1995), *Contemporary financial intermediation*, The Dryden Press.
Gurley, J. C. and Shaw, E. S., (1960), *Money in a theory of finance*, The Brookings Institution.

The bank is dead! Long live the bank!

by Raghuram Rajan

The commercial bank – the institution that accepts deposits payable on demand and originates loans – has outlived its usefulness and is in terminal decline, according to many observers. Commercial banks' share of total assets in financial institutions in the US has fallen dramatically, from over 70 per cent around the turn of the century to just around 30 per cent today (*see* Figure 1). Bank share of corporate debt in the US has declined from 19.6 per cent in 1979 to 14.5 per cent in 1994.

Competition on both sides of the bank's balance sheet has increased. On the asset side, the growth of the commercial paper and junk bond markets has given large companies an alternative to borrowing from the bank. On the liability side, new technologies and deregulation have given customers choice. Instead of being forced to deposit at the local bank branch or make payments through a bank cheque account, a mutual fund which offers much the same services is just a telephone call away.

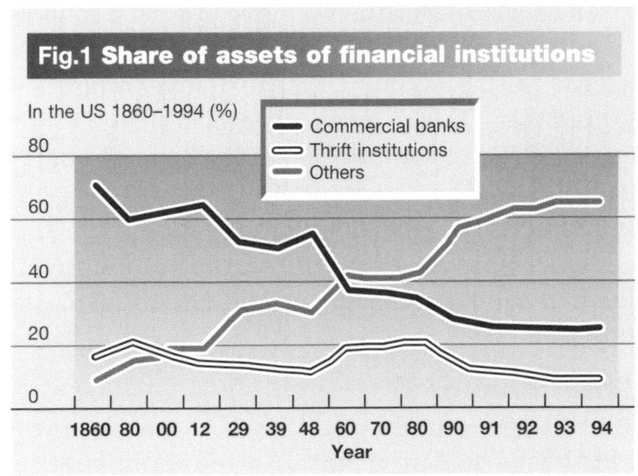

As competition has increased, there has been tremendous consolidation in the banking industry – often, though not always, a sign of overcapacity. The share of bank assets in megabanks (banks with assets over $100bn in 1994 dollars) in the US has gone up from nine per cent in 1979 to 19 per cent in 1994. Over the same period, the share of bank assets in small banks (banks with assets less than $100m in 1994 dollars) has fallen from 14 per cent to seven per cent.

Given these changes, it is, therefore, legitimate to ask: are commercial banks dead? I will argue that the traditional commercial bank, which offers the twin products of loans and demandable deposits, is indeed withering away. But if one defines banks more broadly, not in terms of the products they offer but in terms of their functions, then banks continue to flourish. Deregulation and technological change have forced them to rethink the form in which they deliver these functions. But the functions themselves continue to be important and it is premature to declare banks dead. Instead, we may be seeing the emergence of a new kind of bank, hence the title of this article.

Banks' traditional functions

A commercial bank has traditionally offered borrowers short-term loans such as lines of credit or overdraft facilities. It offers depositors the ability to withdraw or pay money on demand at a fixed return, independent of the vagaries of financial markets. Why have both lines of credit and demand deposits been typically offered by the same institution? The answer is simple. Strip away the product labels and you find a common underlying function: the guarantee of money at short notice.

A bank can achieve scale economies by using the same underlying reserve of liquid assets and the same institutional arrangements (lines to the central bank and to other banks) to meet the unexpected demands of both borrowers and depositors. Also, the demands may off-set each other (borrowers draw down lines of credit at different times from depositors), reducing the funds the bank has to keep in reserve.

In addition to the bank's access to liquidity, there are other competencies that both products draw on. Customers will pay for guarantees of funding only if they know the guarantor will deliver. Thus the reputation for probity of the commercial bank matters to both depositors and borrowers.

There are also synergies between products. The bank has to keep itself up-to-date on the health of borrowers. The products complement each other here: every self-respecting loan officer goes through the checking and deposit activity of large clients for early warning signals on payment difficulty. Individual depositors also build up credit histories with their bank through steady deposits. Thus multiple products enhance the bank's ability to produce timely information about the client and the client's ability to keep tabs on the bank.

Of course, governments have offered a helping hand to commercial banks. Typically, they have offered banks protection from competition in raising deposits and privileged access to the payment system. Governments have also provided implicit or explicit guarantees to the banks, which in turn enabled the banks to offer guarantees to customers far sounder than that of any their competitors. Thus, in countries with untrustworthy stock markets, banks have been the main avenue through which individuals have been able to invest safely. Of course, in some countries the other half of this Faustian bargain is that banks have been a creature of the governments, lending to those who enjoy government favor and withholding credit from those who do not.

What changed?

What upset this equilibrium? First, the information technology revolution. New databases and information-producing agencies, such as rating agencies and news services, reduced the advantage banks had in being more informed about clients than anyone else. Companies became sufficiently well-known and analyzed to tap markets directly. Faster data processing made the markets themselves more liquid, enabling companies to raise large pools of money. The revolution affected individual customers too. They now had credit histories which they could take to any potential lender and automatic teller machines that further reduced their dependence on the local branch.

The information technology revolution gave traditional bank clients a choice of service provider. In many countries, however, archaic regulations protected bank monopolies. Some large clients (and service providers) simply by-passed the regulations, eventually forcing them to be repealed. For example, Japanese companies' access to domestic bond markets was severely restricted until the early 1980s. As a result, large firms started tapping the Eurobond markets. Faced with the risk of losing their best clients to foreign underwriters, banks relented and the domestic bond markets were freed up.

Banks themselves have been split in their opposition to the deregulation of their monopolies, with the forward-looking seeing more opportunities than threats. Consequently, the banking sector in country after country has been deregulated. Deregulation had two immediate adverse effects.

As the information revolution unleashed competition, deregulation eliminated many of the economic rents that had traditionally bolstered bank capital. From being the soundest risks in the economy because of their huge franchise value, bank balance sheets have typically become far less sound than those of their best clients.

Deregulation also had a more subtle, though perhaps equally important, effect. Banks could roam further afield in search of new business, which led to increased uncertainty about what was actually on bank balance sheets. Many were surprised when Continental Illinois Bank got into trouble in 1984 because the source of its problems were billions of dollars of energy loans bought from a small bank in Oklahoma City. So the twin effects of loss of franchise value or rents and the increased opacity of bank balance sheets substantially increased the banks' costs of funding.

How banks have responded

The industry as a whole has responded by rethinking where its comparative advantage lies. There are three aspects to guaranteeing funding at short notice. The first is credit evaluation; the second is providing the guarantee; and the third is coming up with the funding.

Since banks have little advantage in evaluating high-quality credits, they have attempted to move down-market – away from the high-quality credits to more information-intensive borrowers such as the medium-sized companies in the so-called middle-market. Banks have also realized that providing the guarantee does not necessarily require coming up with the funding since, often, the funding is not required or can be arranged easily through non-bank sources. It is enough to have the ability to come up with the funding quickly. Thus banks can use their advantage of having large balance sheets to write off-balance sheet guarantees.

Finally, instead of tying up their precious funds in long-term inactive loans, banks have realized that all they need to do to meet a guarantee is to provide bridge financing – between when the borrower demands money and when the loan is sold or securitized to lenders with cheaper access to funding.

The move towards guarantees is best seen in the development of the commercial

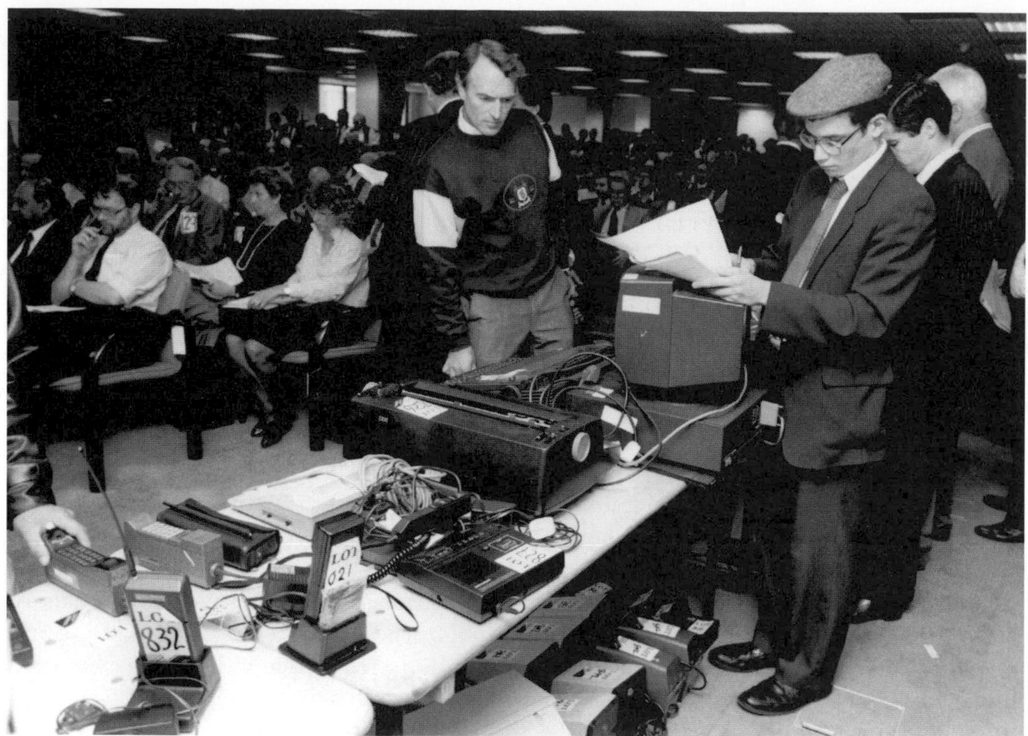

Evidence of refocusing: looking for bargains at bankrupt Drexel Burnham Lambert's auction

paper market in the US. Since 1972, this market has increased in size from 23 per cent of commercial and industrial bank loans to 92 per cent in 1993. It would appear that banks are losing short-term lending business to the commercial paper market. But if one looks closer, one sees that the commercial paper issued by a company is typically backed with a line of credit from a bank. If the company finds it difficult to roll over the commercial paper, the back-up line kicks in, enabling it to refund the paper.

Therefore, instead of funding the business directly, banks let investors in commercial paper fund it, except in the worst case scenarios where the bank guarantee kicks in. However, the bank still makes fees from the guarantee on the commercial paper. Some have suggested these fees are not much smaller than the margins from making the loan itself.

Evidence of the refocusing of commercial banks comes, of all places, from that scourge of Wall Street, Drexel Burnham Lambert. When Drexel filed for bankruptcy in 1990, the share prices of large money-center banks went up by an astonishing seven per cent. By contrast, the share prices of comparable investment banks rose by only 1.6 per cent. Clearly, Drexel was more of a competitor to commercial banks than to investment banks. But what exactly did it do?

Essentially, Michael Milken set up a network of junk bond buyers who accepted almost any deal he sponsored. In return, he exercized control over the borrower to make sure the buyers did not lose out. Furthermore, if a particular issue underperformed, he made it up to the buyer in future transactions. With placement power assured, he could guarantee borrowers short-notice finance – exactly what I argue a

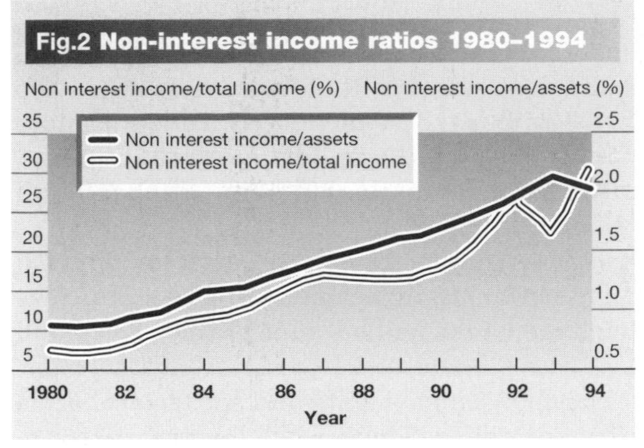

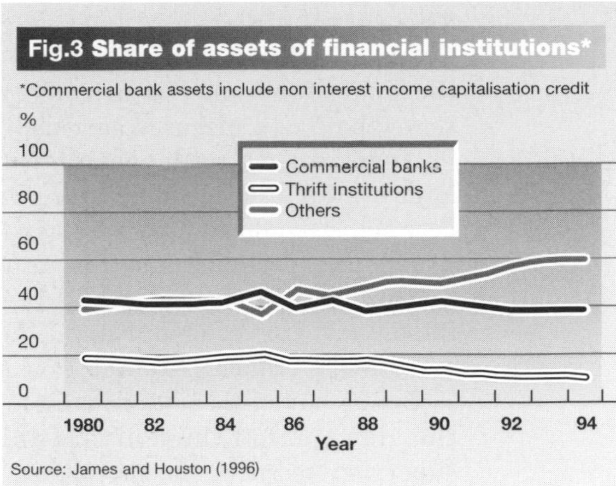

bank does. In fact, Drexel's letter assuring a company board under hostile attack that Drexel was 'highly confident' of raising finance for the takeover became virtually a loan commitment, albeit for a very large sum of money. No wonder bank stockholders rejoiced at Drexel's demise.

More evidence for re-focusing comes from Figures 2 and 3. Non-interest income has increased steadily for US banks from 11 per cent in 1980 to over 25 per cent in 1994. When capitalized and added to bank assets (*see* Figure 3), bank assets as a fraction of financial institution assets have remained steady, and this is at a time when financial assets are growing as a percentage of gross domestic product. Reports of the demise of commercial banking are indeed highly exaggerated in the US.

The wholesale side

If bank products are increasingly off-balance sheet rather than on-balance sheet, it makes sense not to classify their businesses on the asset- or liability-side basis. I find it most useful to classify businesses on the basis of the intended client. On the wholesale side, where the clients are companies, large banks no longer have better information than other service providers about their most creditworthy clients. Yet even here, banks provide value, especially when they enjoy strong relationships. Even though information about credit quality is widely available, knowledge of the preferences of client managers and more importantly, mutual trust, are scarcer.

Banks are not in the narrowly defined business of providing funding, or even of providing guarantees, but of providing customized solutions to strategic problems, in which their ability to use their balance sheets is part of the solution. In the light of this the assets of client knowledge and trust that come from banking relationships become very important.

A strong relationship with a client enables a bank to go the extra mile to find customized innovative solutions, using the latest financial engineering techniques, to the client's problems. Conversely, the client is confident that if innovations do not work out, or if the entire, increasingly interconnected, financial market turns against it, it will enjoy the bank's support. Thus relationships and innovation help banks differentiate themselves in an otherwise extremely competitive, commodity-like, market.

The retail side

On the retail side, competition has again forced banks to reconsider how they perform their core function. Historically, time and demand deposits offered by banks have served both as a means to save as well as a way to make payments. With other avenues for investment – such as money market funds and stock and bond mutual funds – opening up and with investors becoming more sophisticated about the trade-off between risk and return, banks are becoming less important for savers.

This is especially so because communications technology has rendered the physical distance between savers and institutions offering investment alternatives less important. It is commonly said the advantage banks had because of their brick and mortar (the branch system) is now gone.

Banks have also enjoyed a historical monopoly on payments and settlement. From the viewpoint of the central bank this made sense. There were fewer entities to supervise, reducing the risk that a rogue institution would receive payments and then default, leading to the possible collapse of the payment system.

With the advent of real-time collateralized settlement systems, however, institutions have to put up collateral to back payments. They can no longer put the system at risk, so the need to restrict access to only those who are supervised diminishes. It is no longer clear that this last bastion of bank privilege will continue to hold out. Some banks have been rethinking their retail businesses. Customers do not really want the product – demand deposits or time deposits. Instead they want a convenient way to invest and make payments. Traditionally, they have seen the local branch as the only place to do this. But with the customer having new alternatives, banks have to either join the hordes attempting to engage customers in electronic commerce or change what they offer in the branch.

To see the threat posed by electronic commerce consider the services offered by Charles Schwab, a discount brokerage in the US. Schwab was one of the first brokerages to allow customers to trade electronically. It also enabled the company to invest in a wide range of stock and bond mutual funds (not just those that Schwab managed) as well as maintain cheque accounts. Schwab also offers customers information and price services. But most important of all, it provides one consolidated statement for all the customer's transactions and describes the performance of his or her investments.

In an electronic world where the costs for a customer to switch to an alternative provider are low, Schwab has achieved the impossible; it has locked the customer in. It does so in two ways. First, the customer who invests in a family of funds not offered by Schwab has to incur the substantial costs of consolidating the statements the fund issues with Schwab's statements. Few funds are attractive enough, compared with those offered by Schwab, to be worthwhile. Second, the customer finds it hard to abandon Schwab because he or she will have to recontract with all the funds he or she has access to through Schwab. And unless a Schwab competitor provides access to much the same range of funds, the competitor will not be attractive. So Schwab ultimately has locked-in customers whom it can deliver, at a substantial cost, to eager providers of financial services. It is a measure of its clout in the market that even the mighty Fidelity backed down in a recent spat between the two.

Banks, however, have two important advantages, relative to other financial institutions, in the search for the captive customer. The number of people willing to try electronic media for their financial transactions is still small. The local branch is still the most trusted financial service provider and it offers the comfort of an immediate paper receipt. Perhaps more important, most people do not know how to manage their financial affairs and look for a trusted source of financial advice.

Savvy banks capitalize on these two advantages. They offer the same access that a discounter like Schwab does but also providing a human face in trustworthy surroundings to guide customers through financial mazes. In this way banks can attract many more customers. Eventually, these customers will feel confident enough to go electronic but by then the bank may be their obvious access point.

This suggests that the brick and mortar branch system may still have substantial life in it. The number of bank branches in the US increased by 27 per cent between 1985 and 1994. Of course, some of the increase is accounted for by mini-branches at supermarkets, malls and the like. The point, however, is that personal relationships may still be important. One bank that emphasizes its branches is Norwest of Minneapolis. As its CEO asks: 'If we sell comparable products, who has the competitive advantage: Our guy who knows you or someone calling from Dallas who interrupts your dinner?' Norwest sells its customers an average of 3.8 bank products against 1.25 to 2.75 for large banks.

More generally ...

So banks offer guarantees to companies without necessarily providing funding. And they offer an access point to services without necessarily providing all the financial services themselves. What banks do provide in both cases is an overlay of financial expertise in customizing the transaction.

It seems that the most successful banks of the future will be those that use technology and financial capital to back the creative solutions its human capital develops and who have client relationships that permit these solutions to be implemented in an atmosphere of trust.

All this points to the increasing importance of expert human capital in the industry. The evidence is consistent with this. The percentage of employees who were low-skilled (tellers, records processors, administrative support staff and so on) in the US banking industry went down from 60.6 per cent in 1983–85 to 52.5 per cent in 1993–95. Over the same period, the fraction of high-skilled financial managers nearly doubled from 5.5 per cent to 10.1 per cent. This does not just reflect a redesignation of low-skilled jobs. The percentage of those employed with just a high school degree or lower declined substantially at the same time.

The future

In this new world, bank managers face substantial challenges. With technology and deregulation creating new opportunities, there is a temptation to enter every business that opens up. It seems that every bank wants to become a universal bank and that not many heed the costs that a new business could impose on existing ones – and these could be substantial.

First, a new business creates a different culture and compensation structure. The culture may clash with that of existing businesses (the stereotypical conservative loan officer against the brash investment banker) and its compensation structure may attract jealousy. Often, the solution seems to be to escalate compensation to keep everyone happy, with attendant adverse consequences to the bottom line.

Second, top management must understand the new business and have ways of controlling it. Existing audit systems and incentive structures can prove totally inadequate for new businesses. Until these can be modified, a bank can take on considerable risk by entering a new area.

The bank's reputation is crucial to the guarantee function it performs and this can be destroyed by one rogue operation. Salomon Brothers, the US investment bank, experienced this soon after the controversy over its involvement in the treasury auction surfaced in 1991. It saw a dramatic drop in even unrelated business. It lost key personnel, paid fines, liquidated about one-third of its assets and suffered a loss in market capitalization of $1.5bn because companies were worried about the adverse publicity from doing business with, and the reliability of, a 'tainted' investment bank. This in a bank where management understood the business perfectly. It may require humility for top management to admit it does not understand a business or cannot control it but in this increasingly complex world, staying away from such businesses may be the best strategy.

Thirdly, customers themselves may be wary of banks that do too many things. Banks are increasingly in the financial advisory business, and should be concerned that their image for impartial advice may be compromised by products they want to sell. A number of banks have responded by building strict firewalls between advisory activities and sales. Often, though, firewalls may be inadequate.

Finally, the more varied the businesses the bank is involved in, the more difficult it is for investors to understand. In the same way as conglomerates trade at a discount relative to their pure play value, analysts suggest that a bank's cost of funding can increase if it enters new, exotic, areas. In fact, some analysts argue that the market appears to discount the value of banks that are excessively focused on proprietary trading.

The wild card

Will banks continue to be regulated? Even if real-time settlement systems mean the risk of bank failure poses no risk to the payment system and if there are safe investment opportunities for small investors (so that the government can stop insuring bank deposits), there might still be a rationale for bank regulation, at least of large banks.

Banks are repositories of information and relationships, all of which may be lost when a bank fails. Failures are also political dynamite. If a bank is large enough, governments may have no option but to rescue it. Anticipating this, governments must ensure that banks do not misuse the fact that they are too big to fail.

But while regulation should sensibly be focused on large banks, and those that are more in retail businesses, the activities of banks are becoming hard to value and faster moving. Regulators have little idea of what prudent behavior is. This suggests that regulation should focus on improving a bank's incentives to regulate itself, with direct bank supervision and capital requirements aimed only at keeping out truly malevolent or incompetent managements.

Incentives for self-regulation may take the form of putting bank directors on notice that they will bear civil or criminal responsibility if negligence can be established after the fact. Regulators may also want to use the market to keep tabs on banks. Ideas such as requiring large banks to issue credit derivatives regularly (these pay nothing if the bank has to be rescued) and using the price of the derivatives to judge what the market thinks is going on in the bank may be implemented.

The danger, of course, is that regulators may continue to treat banks as special, issue blanket guarantees and end up bearing risks they do not understand. In such a situation, every bank failure may be treated as a failure of regulation, instead of a cost of doing business, and draw forth fresh regulations. If there is a nightmare vision of the future of commercial banking, this is it.

Summary

This article focuses on the role of commercial banks, and whether their future is threatened by growing competition, changing technology and deregulation.

Raghuram Rajan argues that looked at in terms of functions rather than products, banks continue to flourish and are reinventing themselves. They have responded by moving from high quality credits to more information sensitive medium-sized borrowers and making fees from the guarantee of commercial paper.

Banks can also use their strong relationships with clients to provide customized, innovative solutions. On the retail side they have two advantages relative to other financial institutions – the number of people willing to try electronic media for their transactions is still small and most people still seek a trusted source of advice. New business opportunities are opening up but banks should be wary of the dangers of entering new, exotic areas.

Suggested further reading

Ackley, D, et al. *Bank one at the cross-roads* New York University Case, http://www.stem.nyu.edu/MET/Case/Case.html.

Benveniste, L. Singh, M. and Wilhelm, W., (1993), 'The failure of Drexel Burnham Lambert: evidence on the implications for commercial banks', *Journal of Financial Intermediation*, 3, 104–137.

Berger, A. Kashyap, A. and Scalise, J., (1965), 'The transformation of the U.S. Banking industry: what a long strange trip it's been', Brookings Papers on Economic Activity, 2, 55–217.

Boyd, J. and Gertler, M., (1994), 'Are banks dead? Or are the reports greatly exaggerated?', *Quarterly Review of the Federal Reserve Bank of Minneapolis*, Summer, 2–23.

James, C. and Houston, J., (1996), 'Evolution or extinction: where are banks headed?', *Bank of America Journal of Applied Corporate Finance*, Summer.

Merton, R., (1995), 'Financial innovation and the management and regulation of financial institutions' *Journal of Banking and Finance* 19, 461–482.

Rajan, R., (1996), 'Why banks have a future: towards a new theory of commercial banks', *Bank of America Journal of Applied Corporate Finance*, Summer.

Tufano, P., (1996), 'How financial engineering can advance corporate strategy', *Harvard Business Review*, January–February.

Banks respond to a changing world

by Gary B. Gorton

The world of commercial banking is undergoing a transformation as a result of marketable instruments competing with bank loans and demand deposits. This raises important questions for bankers and bank regulators. At the same time many economies, such as those of Eastern Europe, must decide on the shape of their capital markets. Essentially, their choice is between a bank-based economy, such as Germany (where banks engage in a wide range of activities, including investment banking) or a stock market-based economy. This article reviews some of the history of banking with an eye towards understanding the future of banks and banking. A good place to begin is by asking what do banks do that markets cannot do.

In the US in 1845 the answer would have been that banks made loans and issued mortgages but their most important role was to provide a medium of exchange by issuing private money. By the late 19th century US capital markets were more developed and large banks resembled German universal banks. The passage of the Glass-Steagal Act by the US Congress in 1934 changed that by barring banks from investment banking activities such as the underwriting of corporate securities.

In 1997 banks in most developed countries face competition for business from non-bank institutions. US banks have to compete with money market mutual funds for deposit business and from junk bonds, commercial paper and medium-term notes for bank loans. While smaller companies continue to rely heavily on banks, banks are now engaged in many new activities such as interest rate and currency swaps. Whatever it is that defines banks as unique institutions, the pattern of bank activities has changed over the past 150 years as banking has interacted with the development of security markets.

It is not an exaggeration to say that it is now very hard to define what constitutes 'banking'. The challenge is to explain the persistence of banking in the face of the developing securities markets. Part of the problem in understanding what banks do is the fact that the function of securities markets is not well understood.

Research addressing the issue of the connection between stock market price 'efficiency' and economic efficiency has found that companies are operated by managers who must be compensated in such a way as to induce them to find desirable investment projects. But managers are not always successful in receiving information, in which case they may be induced by their compensation contracts to rely on inferences drawn from a change in their company's stock market price.

In a stock market-based economy two types of information must be produced and transmitted in order to achieve the most efficient allocation of resources. First, the stock market provides forward-looking, or prospective, information when informed traders find it optimal to produce information about a company's investment opportunities, which managers then act on. Second, the stock market provides backward-looking or retrospective information when stock prices reflect informed traders' production of information about the outcome of investment decisions. Managerial

DEUTSCHE BANK
SPAREINLAGEN
So ist's richtig!
DENN . . .

A 1920s German advert: Germany was a bank-based economy up to the 1980s

compensation based on stock prices can then induce managerial effort. This model of the stock market seems to be what most economists have in mind when they speak of 'market efficiency'. Stock prices allocate resources by influencing investment decisions and by providing a way of monitoring corporate managers.

Now consider the same economy without the stock market but with banks instead. Banks design contracts to hire information-producing loan analysts who write prospective and retrospective reports about investment opportunities and managerial performance. Research with which I was involved has shown that the banks can implement the same allocation as the efficient equilibrium of the stock market economy. Efficient security prices are neither necessary nor sufficient for economic efficiency.

That the savings/investment process might be equally well-organized around banks as security markets suggests investigating empirically the role of banks in economies where securities markets are less important than they are in the US. In Germany, for example, for much of its recent history, the stock market has been small and illiquid. German banks, though, can own stock. The question is whether bank block-share holding is, in some sense, a substitute for a liquid stock market.

An examination of the role of banks in Germany had shown that in the 1970s corporate performance was better when a bank was a large shareholder. The evidence is consistent with the proposition that when banks obtain a block of stock (via a family selling out or because of financial distress) the bank has an incentive to improve firm performance by monitoring. That is, it oversees the management decisions because, effectively, the block cannot be sold since the stock market is so thinly traded. By the 1980s, however, capital markets had developed further in Germany. At the same time German bank shareholding has declined and banks have apparently become less active in corporate governance.

Bank uniqueness

Banks and securities markets may be substitute institutions but, even in economies with highly developed capital markets, banking persists as an important institution. This suggests that banks perform tasks that markets cannot accomplish, even when they are highly developed.

On the asset side of the balance sheet, banks originate loans. To the extent that bank loans are held by the bank, which puts bank equity at risk, there is an incentive to oversee the activities of borrowers to maintain the loan's value.

Because of free-riding, it is difficult for a large number of debt holders to interact with borrowers when they need to be motivated, for example, when they are distressed. A bank, by concentrating the debt, eliminates this problem. Beyond this the details of what 'monitoring' really means are fuzzy. Moreover, the argument about concentration would seem to apply to all debt and so cannot explain the role of bank loans as distinct from corporate bonds.

The ability to renegotiate bank loans emanates from a contract provision that gives banks the right to seize collateral and from the fact that a single agent is in a position to renegotiate. The optimality of this contract provision can be examined by analyzing the interaction between a bank and a borrower when the borrower may have an incentive to (at a cost) increase the risk of a project if it goes badly while the bank may have an incentive to threaten its early termination. When the borrower seeks to add risk the bank may respond by forgiving some debt to eliminate the borrower's incentive to add risk, liquidating the loan by seizing the collateral, raising the interest rate or doing nothing.

Interestingly, the volatility of firm value depends on whether the company is distressed or not and on the outcome of the negotiations between a borrower and lender. Contract provision allowing the bank the right to initiate renegotiation by threatening to seize the collateral actually makes the company more valuable when the contract is first signed.

Banks not only provide unique services on the asset side of the balance sheet, they also produce a medium of exchange on the liability side. If companies or consumers need cash they will often have to sell securities. When they sell securities they may do so in a market where better-informed traders take advantage of this liquidity need. Imagine you had to sell a painting by an old master quickly to pay a sudden medical bill. You would not have time to research the value of the painting and so you might sell it for less than it was worth. Similarly, companies or consumers lose money, on average, when they are less informed about the value of the risky securities they are selling.

Therefore, a low-variance security or, in particular, a riskless security with a known value, would minimize or avoid such losses. Banks produce such a riskless trading security by issuing debt, which is a claim on a diversified portfolio (of loans). If the debt is not riskless, the government can improve matters with deposit insurance.

Bank panics

In the US large numbers of relatively undiversified banks issuing demand deposits faced repeated banking panics. There is nothing mysterious about banking panics. Gorton (1988) shows that in the US they occurred at the peak of the business cycle when consumers were told there would be a recession.

At the peak consumers know that they will want to dis-save in the coming recession. Their savings are in banks, some of which will fail during the recession. Because of asymmetric information about the value of the non-traded bank loans, depositors cannot distinguish which banks will fail. As a result, rational, risk-averse depositors withdraw from all banks, resulting in a banking panic.

During the 19th century, banks formed coalitions – clearing houses – partly to address the problem of banking panics. Clearing houses monitored member banks by restricting their activities, conducted strict bank examinations and enforced sanctions against members to enforce compliance. During panics clearing houses organized suspensions of the payment of cash to honor demand deposits. Instead of paying out cash they provided a form of deposit insurance by issuing their own private money (claims on the clearing house) to honor deposit contracts.

Demand deposits are a medium of exchange that clears internally in the banking system, not externally through trade in a market. Internal clearing closed the external market in which bank claims were traded – the bank note market of the pre-civil war era. But this created an information asymmetry since there was no longer any information revealing market about the value of banks. So, how are depositors to monitor banks?

Banking panics can be regarded as a monitoring mechanism and, in this sense, were desirable. The information asymmetry created the necessary condition for panics but also the incentives for the private provision of bank regulation, examination and insurance. Ultimately, government bank regulation and insurance took over the clearing house functions.

Regulatory issues

In the 1980s while new debt markets opened or grew significantly (including junk bonds and commercial paper), commercial banks failed at increasing rates as they became unprofitable. One widespread explanation for their high failure rate concerns the moral hazard due to underpriced deposit insurance. In this view, bank shareholders have an incentive to take on risk when the value of the bank charter falls sufficiently. This view is inconsistent with banks being run by managers and, it turns out, without empirical evidence on which types of banks want to take on inefficient risk.

If managers have different objectives to those of outside shareholders, and disciplining managers is costly, then managerial decisions may be at odds with decisions outside shareholders would like them to take.

I found that, contrary to the moral hazard view, excessive risk-taking by banks occurred at those controlled by managers with stockholdings of well below 50 per cent but which were large enough to be important. This result suggests that a failure in the market for corporate control in banking can explain the persistence of unprofitability of banking in the 1980s.

Another explanation for the persistence of bank failures during the 1980s concerns 'regulatory forbearance', that is, the unwillingness of regulators to close insolvent banks. This view raises more general welfare questions concerning bank regulation. What is the objective function of regulators? What should they do when banks become riskier?

In research I conducted in 1996 with Andrew Winton, I considered the question of bank capital requirements. We found that there are unique costs associated with bank capital and that regulators optimally will not, indeed cannot, force banks to raise costly capital. The basic argument is that consumers need a riskless transactions medium supplied by banks. Holding bank equity exposes consumers to possible losses should they need to sell the equity. To the extent that they must hold bank equity, and not demand deposits, they face losses if they have unanticipated needs requiring them to sell their bank equity. But this risk is priced and so imposes a cost on equity that is unique to the banking industry.

We showed that capital requirements can never be binding. If they are too onerous they can be avoided by getting out of the banking industry. But then banks do not supply the socially valuable services that markets cannot supply. To avoid such socially undesirable exits, the regulators may take actions that resemble forbearance. This, however, is socially optimal.

Recent developments

Banking has changed considerably over the past 15 years. One big change has been the opening and growth of the market for loans. According to theory, bank loans are not liquid: no one should buy a loan because banks then lack incentives to monitor.

Moreover, if loans and bonds are substitutes, a direct contract with the company is better than purchasing a loan since in bankruptcy the buyer of a loan must rely on the bank to represent them. Yet the bank, having sold the loan, would appear to have little incentive to perform.

Despite this, the market for such loans is enormous. Researchers have searched for implicit contract features that make loan sales incentive-compatible. This research found evidence that banks selling loans keep a portion of the loan and that the price of the loan being sold reflects this.

Related to the development of a market for bank loans is the recent advent of a related market: credit derivatives. Credit derivatives allow the credit risk of particular companies to be traded without the transfer of the underlying bond or loan.

The marketability of bank loans and credit risk *per se* blur the distinction between banks and other companies involved in the capital markets. Banks must now compete in a way that is unfamiliar to them.

Securitization of bank products puts banks in competition with a new set of sophisticated rivals. To the extent that capital requirements are costly to banks these trends are likely to continue. More and more traditional bank products will be securitized, creating enormous headaches for regulators who face the difficult task of trying to define a 'bank' in a global environment so that they can regulate it.

Summary

The previous article looked at how banks are responding to competition and change; in this article Gary Gorton also considers the industry's future, with particular reference to securities markets. The author argues that while the latter can be a substitute for the former, the continuing presence of banks even in highly developed economies suggests they perform certain tasks on both sides of the balance sheet which markets cannot accomplish.

Banking panics, he points out, could be seen as a desirable part of the monitoring mechanism, information asymmetry creating the necessary incentives for the private provision of bank regulation, examination and insurance. Finally, the reasons why commercial banks failed in increasing numbers in the 1980s – and the relationship between managers and shareholders – are considered. Research suggests 'that a failure in the market for corporate control in banking can explain the persistence of the unprofitablity of banking in the 1980s'.

This article was adapted from a National Bureau of Economic Research publication.

Banking disasters: causes and prevention

by Richard J. Herring

As recently as 1990 it was reasonable to ask why the US, alone among advanced industrial economies, had been plagued by banking disasters. The 1980s was indeed a troubled era for depository institutions in the US. Over the decade more of them failed in the US than at any time since the Depression. By 1995, however, banks and Saving and Loan institutions (S&Ls) were earning record profits and had greatly strengthened their capital positions. Moreover, by then it was clear that banking disasters were not confined to the US. Serious banking problems had swept over most of Scandinavia, France and Japan.

Disasters in the banking system are often preceded by a lengthy period of relative calm. In the US during the first 20 years following the Second World War, for example,

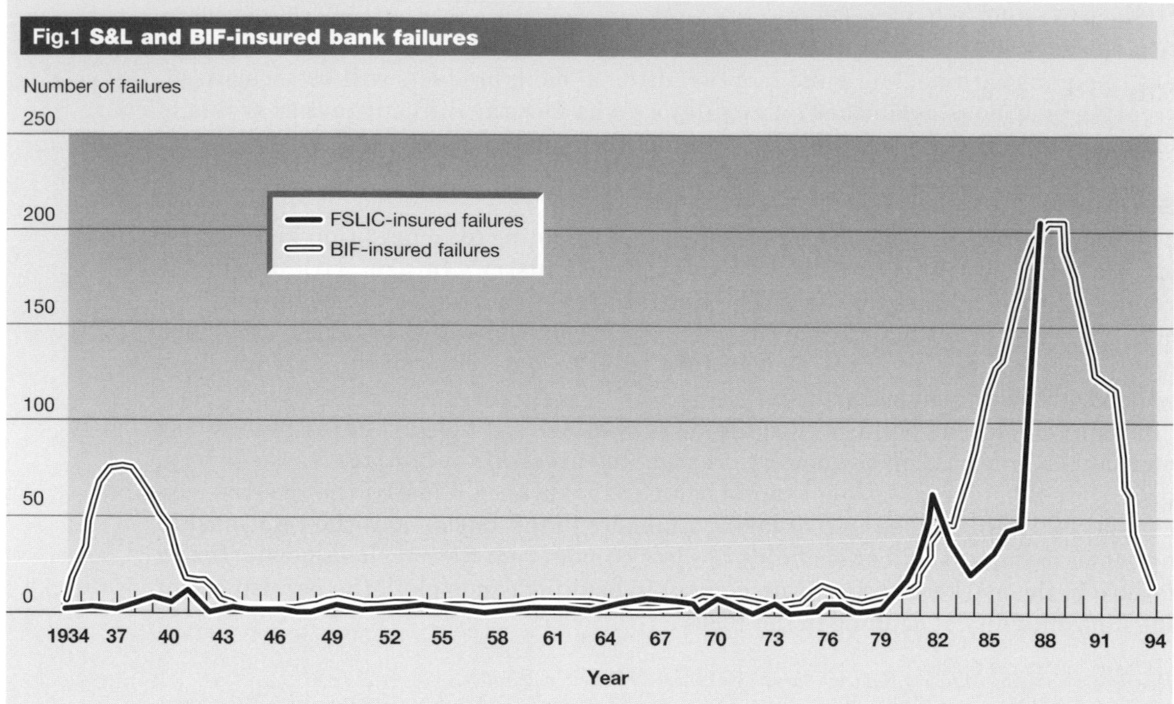

bank failures were extremely rare and usually the result of idiosyncratic circumstances, often involving fraud. (See Figure 1 showing bank and S&L failures since 1934.)

After a shock to the banking system, it becomes clear that the banks damaged by the shock had assumed excessive insolvency exposure. It is important, however, to focus on the period before the shock occurs and pose the question: why do banks become increasingly vulnerable to shock?

Consider two possible answers. First, managers may underestimate the probability that a shock will occur. Second, they may perceive the probability of a shock correctly but willingly assume greater insolvency exposure because they expect it to be profitable. In earlier work with Jack Guttentag, I argued that underestimation of such shocks may be a plausible consequence of the way in which decisions are made within an environment of uncertainty.

Our ability to estimate the probability of a shock depends on two key factors. First is the frequency with which the shock occurs relative to the frequency of changes in the underlying causal structure. If the structure changes every time a shock occurs, then events do not generate useful evidence regarding probabilities. On the other hand, if the shock occurs many times while the structure is stable, probabilities may be estimated with considerable confidence, such as default rates on portfolios of car loans and credit card receivables.

In general, high-frequency shocks are not a source of insolvency exposure for banks. Banks have both the knowledge and incentive to price high-frequency shocks properly and to make adequate provisions to serve as a buffer against loss.

Second, our ability to predict the probability of a shock depends on our understanding of the causal structure. Banks often lack the knowledge to price low-frequency shocks with uncertain probabilities and are likely to rely on subjective probability estimates.

'Disaster myopia' hypothesis

Researchers in cognitive psychology have found that decision-makers tend to formulate subjective probabilities on the basis of the 'availability heuristic', that is, the ease with which the decision maker can imagine that the event will occur. Since the ease of imagining an event is highly correlated with the frequency that the event occurs, this rule of thumb provides a reasonably accurate, although imperfect, estimate of high-frequency events.

At some point, the tendency to underestimate shock probabilities is exacerbated by the 'threshold heuristic'. This is the rule of thumb by which busy decision makers allocate their scarcest resource: managerial attention. The availability and threshold heuristics together cause 'disaster myopia', the tendency over time to underestimate the probability of low-frequency shocks.

Disaster myopia can lead banks to become more vulnerable to a disaster without anyone having made a decision to increase insolvency exposure. It is likely to be shared by a large number of banks because uncertainty may also be conducive to 'herding', in which banks take on largely similar exposures to some shock.

Being part of a group provides an apparent vindication of the individual banker's judgment and some defence against recriminations if the shock occurs. John Maynard Keynes perceived this clearly, writing in 1931:

> A 'sound' banker, alas, is not one who foresees danger and avoids it, but one who, when he is ruined, is ruined in a conventional way along with his fellows so that no one can really blame him.

Perhaps even more important, the banker knows that the supervisory authorities cannot terminate all the banks or discipline them harshly. Indeed the authorities may be obliged to soften the impact of the shock on individual banks in order to protect the banking system.

Disaster myopia may also afflict the regulators and supervisors who should constrain the increasing vulnerability of banks. Regulators and supervisors, after all, are likely to be subject to the same perceptual biases as bankers.

Institutional factors

The tendency toward disaster myopia may be reinforced by several institutional factors. Managerial accounting systems, for example, may inadvertently favor activities subject to low-frequency shocks. Although generally accepted accounting principles are extremely helpful in monitoring, pricing and provisioning for high-frequency shocks, they are not very useful in controlling exposure to a low-frequency hazard because the shock occurs so infrequently that it will not be captured in the usual reporting period.

Moreover, in the absence of appropriate provisions for potential losses, an activity subject to low-probability shocks will appear misleadingly profitable. The illusion of high profitability creates additional problems. To the extent that salaries and bonuses are based on reported short-term profits without adjustment for reserves against shocks, the line officers who are in the best position to assess such dangers will be rewarded for disregarding them. The *appearance* of high profitability may also impede the effectiveness of the supervisory authorities, which find it very difficult to discipline banks that appear to be highly profitable.

In addition, competition may interact with disaster myopia in two related ways to increase vulnerability. First, competitive markets make it impossible for banks that are not disaster myopic to price transactions as if there were a finite probability of a big shock when banks and other competitors that are disaster myopic price them as if that probability were zero. Second, if banks are apparently earning returns above the competitive level, equally myopic banks will be encouraged to enter the market, thereby eroding returns. Banks may respond by increasing their leverage to protect their returns on equity, accelerating the process through which banks make themselves more vulnerable to a major shock.

Disaster myopia in the US

Trends that are consistent with, and conditions that are conducive to, disaster myopia are apparent in the evolution of the S&L industry over the 1970s. The sector prospered in the post-Second World War era by making fixed-rate, long-term, residential mortgages backed by short-term savings deposits.

The S&Ls' charter gave them a structural asset/liability mismatch, with the duration of their assets greatly exceeding that of their liabilities. For more than 20 years following the war, their exposure to interest rate risk generated substantial profits. The yield curve was generally upward sloping so that interest rates on 30-year residential mortgages exceeded short-term rates on deposits.

A series of increasingly severe interest-rate spikes beginning in 1966, however, led to temporary yield curve inversions and an erosion of the net worth of S&Ls. More important, this erosion was greatly exacerbated by the upward trend in interest rates. This forced S&Ls to reprice their liabilities at higher interest rates more rapidly than they could reprice their assets. During the 1970s interest rates became more volatile and the upward trend accelerated. Instead of reducing their vulnerability to an interest rate shock or reinforcing their capacity to withstand it by increasing their capital, S&Ls let the book value of their capital positions decline steadily throughout the 1970s. Of course, the economic value of their capital positions declined even more sharply since the book value measures did not reflect the decline in the market values of mortgage portfolios.

The tendency to disaster myopia was undoubtedly reinforced by the accounting system. It took no account of the impact on balance sheets of changing market values in response to rising interest rates and created no reserves to deal with an interest rate shock. This obscured the erosion of economic net worth from owners, managers, creditors and regulators. It led to an overstatement of profits that sustained the salaries and bonuses of managers who might otherwise have reduced exposures.

Increasing competition from other financial institutions may have hastened the process of increasing vulnerability. S&Ls were subject to disintermediation as depositors shifted to money market mutual funds in search of higher returns and as banks and insurance companies became more active in the mortgage market.

In the face of shrinking margins, it may have seemed tempting to increase leverage in order to maintain returns on equity. Any residual doubts about the prudence of such a policy may have been eased by herding.

Because commercial banks were better diversified and had a much more balanced asset/liability mix, they were less exposed to the interest rate shock and generally weathered it with less difficulty than the S&Ls. This was not true, however, of some important bank borrowers. When borrowers found that they could not meet sharply higher interest payment obligations, banks were confronted with higher credit and transfer risks.

Financial institutions differ substantially from most other companies because they are regulated and protected by a safety net. This fact makes disaster myopia in banks a public policy concern. In addition, regulation and the safety net may lead to increased vulnerability to disaster. US depository institutions are subject to relatively tight restrictions on what they may do and where they may do it. In general, these restrictions constrain their ability to diversify and make them more accident prone than less-constrained counterparts. The vulnerability of S&Ls to an interest rate shock was implicit in their charter. Moreover, their enforced specialization in residential mortgage lending left them vulnerable to the vicissitudes of just one industry. Banks were also subject to activity restrictions such as prohibitions on underwriting corporate securities and selling insurance, which impeded their ability to evolve as the needs of their customers changed.

In addition, both banks and S&Ls were subject to geographic restrictions that limited their ability to diversify deposits and loan portfolios and made them more vulnerable to local economic conditions. These restrictions are implicated in a large proportion of bank failures.

Although rigid constraints on the activity and branching powers of depository institutions undoubtedly made them more vulnerable to shocks, this need not have resulted in the enormous costs borne by US taxpayers and prudently managed institutions. The magnitude of the losses is directly attributable to the design and implementation of the safety net.

Virtually every industrial country has erected a safety net for depository institutions to guard against a banking disaster that might ignite a financial crisis. The safety net includes the chartering function, prudential supervision, authority to terminate a failing institution, deposit insurance, lender of last resort and policy control over bank reserves.

Moral hazard and the safety net

In most industrialized countries, the safety net has been successful in preventing a disaster at one bank from escalating into a financial crisis that damages the nation's economy. In an important sense, however, the safety net has been too successful in protecting depositors. Because depositors are confident they will be protected against loss, they have little or no incentive to monitor and discipline risk-taking by their banks. This is the classic moral hazard problem in which insurance may undermine the incentive for depositors to be concerned with preventing the insured risk – in this case, the risk of insolvency – from occurring.

In addition, depositors at larger banks in the US have benefited from implicit deposit insurance that arose from the way in which the other two components of the safety net were deployed. First, the Federal Reserve, as lender of last resort, lent routinely to banks long after they became insolvent rather than lending solely to solvent, but illiquid, banks. This gave anxious creditors who were not covered by explicit deposit insurance the opportunity to withdraw their deposits before a bank was terminated.

Second, the termination authorities generally did not intervene to terminate a bank promptly, that is before it became insolvent. Instead they usually delayed until the bank was deeply insolvent. Then, rather than liquidating the bank and imposing loss on uninsured depositors and creditors, the authorities provided assistance. They kept the bank open or arranged a purchase and assumption transaction in which all commitments to uninsured depositors and other creditors were honored by the acquiring bank. This policy applied to all banks with more than $500m in assets and gave credibility to the notion that such banks were too big to fail.

In sum, the safety net increased incentives for bank and S&L executives to take excessive risks, which then put greater pressure on the supervisory function to constrain risk-taking. But at the same time, it reduced incentives for regulators and supervisors to take prompt corrective measures. Without the market pressure of a bank run, the supervisory authorities were free to engage in forbearance, which often exacerbated bank disasters.

Go-for-broke behavior

Managers, who may exercise a constraining influence while an institution has positive net worth, find that when capital is exhausted their main hope for survival is in very high-risk ventures. Although some institutions in the 1980s rode out the interest rate cycle and were restored to healthy condition, many others played go-for-broke. At mid-year 1983 almost all insolvencies were attributable to the interest rate shock and could have been resolved for about $25bn. But authorities chose to forbear. S&Ls played go-for-broke and many of the gambles failed. The result was an increase in losses due to asset quality problems that totaled about $140bn.

The rolling regional recessions that caused losses at S&Ls damaged smaller banks as well. Banks regulators practised forbearance just as their S&L counterparts did. The number of failures and losses increased sharply and, by 1990, led to concerns that insurance reserves were inadequate to pay off insured deposits at all banks expected to fail. The prospect of yet another taxpayer bail-out of financial institutions led to the adoption of fundamental reforms in the Federal Deposit Insurance Improvement Act (FDICIA).

Just as the act was being implemented, banks benefited from favorable macroeconomic developments. The overall level of interest rates fell and the yield curve took on a much steeper positive slope, giving most banks a more favorable interest rate spread. The economy began to recover from recession and commercial and residential real estate markets rebounded. By the mid-1990s US banks had fully recovered and are now generally in stronger financial condition that at any time since the 1960s.

Lessons from the US

What can we learn from the US experience about preventing future disasters? The remedy depends on the diagnosis – and as we have seen several pathogens are suspected. The traditional bank-supervisory process is not well-designed to deal with disaster myopia and exposure to large shocks of unknown probability. While the identification of weak banks is useful for managing crises, it is inadequate for their prevention. To prevent crises, the central concern of prudential supervision should be to identify banks that are becoming heavily exposed to a major shock.

The identification of emerging sources of systemic vulnerability involves a continuing interplay between assessing the exposure of banks to particular shocks, and assessing the probability that a particular shock may occur. Once exposure data measuring vulnerability are collected, the supervisory authorities have three basic policy options.

First, they can return the information to the individual banks, perhaps accompanied by supervisory commentary, but permit each bank to determine whether its exposure is prudent. This is a 'measure and confront' approach. It has the merit of forcing the bank to face the issue of whether its exposure is prudent. To the extent that excessive exposure is inadvertent – the result of inattention or poor communications among operating officers, senior management and directors – this approach may be sufficient to prevent excessive vulnerability.

But the bank may already be aware of its exposure to the shock, having made a deliberate choice to accept a larger exposure in the belief that shock probabilities are low and in anticipation of higher expected profits. Indeed, the bank may take comfort in the knowledge that its peers are equally exposed. Under such conditions, the policy of measure and confront may prove wholly inadequate to prevent systemic vulnerability to a major shock and may actually facilitate herding behavior.

Second, the supervisory agency may release exposure data to the public in the hope that markets will discipline banks regarded as excessively exposed. The disclosure of exposure data, however, may reveal proprietary information, abrogate confidential relationships and, if disclosure occurs only after the shock, undermine confidence. Moreover, it may not be sufficient to constrain exposures because creditors may also suffer from disaster myopia or because they anticipate being protected by the safety net in the event of trouble.

Third, the supervisor can specify stress tests that banks should be prepared to meet. This would constitute specifying the minimum shock magnitude that a bank should be able to sustain. Banks using the internal models approach to market risk sanctioned by the Basle Committee, for example, must conduct regular stress tests to gauge their vulnerability to low-probability events in several types of risks.

The basic problem with this approach is that judgments about whether vulnerability to a particular shock is excessive and what minimum shock magnitudes should be are inherently subjective. Moreover, if the supervisory authorities suffer from disaster myopia to the same degree as bankers, they may not identify the appropriate shocks to stress test.

From a regulatory perspective, perhaps the most important reform to counter vulnerability to disaster myopia is to reduce regulatory restrictions on diversification. Liberalization of powers for solvent, well-capitalized banks should help reduce vulnerability to future shocks. The greater the degree of diversification across activities and geographic regions, the lower the vulnerability to any particular shock, even if disaster myopia cannot be corrected.

In addition to these direct supervisory measures to counter disaster myopia, it is also important to deal with factors that encourage it. Accounting practices that mask deterioration in the market value of exposures to hazards are a fundamental source of vulnerability. They impede the ability of managers, owners, creditors and supervisors to monitor insolvency exposure and they may also make a risky activity appear misleadingly profitable.

In contrast to the measures for countering disaster myopia, the measures for countering moral hazard are quite straightforward. The first principle is to refrain from providing full protection for all creditors – especially large creditors such as corporations, other banks and institutional investors. This is largely a matter of ending implicit deposit insurance. A policy of 'too big to fail' places the entire burden of monitoring risk-taking on the supervisory authorities.

The other channel through which implicit insurance is extended is lender-of-last-resort assistance to insolvent banks. FDICIA attempts to deter such practices by depriving the Federal Reserve Bank of the protection of collateral for extended advances to banks near insolvency, except when such advances are necessary to prevent 'a severe adverse effect on ... the national economy'. The second principle to counter moral hazard is to prevent banks from operating without substantial amounts of shareholders' funds at risk.

One clear lesson from the S&L debacle is that losses surge as institutions find their capital depleted and shareholders and managers are tempted to play go-for-broke. FDICIA tries to reduce the scope for forbearance by replacing supervisory discretion with rules designed to stimulate prompt corrective action as soon as a bank's capital position deteriorates.

Although FDICIA calls for accounting reforms that would move regulatory measures of capital closer to market values, little progress has been made. This is a crucial omission. The rules for prompt corrective action will be effective only to the extent they capture the deterioration in the economic value of capital. Without more transparent accounting practices, it will be difficult for supervisors to monitor the moral hazard incentives of banks and difficult for taxpayers to monitor the performance of their agents, the supervisors.

Although this article has focused on illustrations of disaster myopia, moral hazard and go-for-broke behavior drawn from the S&L disaster in the US, examples could have been readily based on Scandinavian and Spanish banking crises, banking problems in France and Italy, and the ongoing financial debacle in Japan. Looking beyond the rich industrial nations, indications of disaster myopia and go-for-broke behavior can be discerned in many of the developing countries that have sustained banking crises over the past 20 years.

History may not repeat itself, but with regard to banking disasters, as Mark Twain once observed, it almost certainly rhymes. Failure to learn from these painful experiences can be costly. At least a dozen countries over the past 20 years have sustained banking losses or government bailouts of the banking sector amounting to 10 per cent or more of gross domestic product.

Summary

This article deals with banking disasters. Author Richard Herring starts by wondering why the US banking and finance scene was so prone to disasters during the 1980s. He suggests that one of the main reasons was 'disaster myopia' – a tendency to underestimate the probability of infrequent shocks (such as bank failure). This was coupled with institutional factors such as accounting practices, managerial bonuses, the tendency of bankers to 'herd' (all follow the same policy) and inactivity by regulators.

Herring also points out that the very safety nets designed to cushion bank failures can actually help bring them about by increasing the incentives for banking executives to take excessive risk, especially in 'go-for-broke' behavior.

He concludes that the lessons to be drawn from the US banking disasters of the 1980s is that US banks should be allowed greater diversity and that banks and other institutions should not be allowed to operate without risking large amounts of shareholder funds.

Suggested further reading

Guttentag, J.M. and Herring, R.J., (1984), 'Credit rationing and financial disorder', *Journal of Finance*, December.

Guttentag, J.M. and Herring, R.J., (1996), 'Disaster myopia in international banking', *Princeton Essays in International Finance* 164, September.

Herring, R.J. and Litan, R.E., (1995), *Financial regulation in the global economy*, The Brookings Institution.

Suggested further reading

12

Regulation and governance

Contributors

Randall S. Kroszner is Associate Professor of Business Economics at the University of Chicago Graduate School of Business. His research interests focus on the economics and politics of banking and financial regulation, corporate governance and organization design.

Kjell Nyborg is Associate Professor of Finance at London Business School. His research interests include corporate finance and information economics.

Steven N. Kaplan is Professor of Finance at University of Chicago Graduate School of Business. His research interests include mergers and acquisitions, corporate governance and private equity.

Julian R. Franks is Professor of Finance and has been Director of the Institute of Finance and Accounting at London Business School.

Walter N. Torous is Corporation of London Professor of Finance at London Business School. His research interests include derivatives and corporate bankruptcy and reorganization.

Contents

Introduction

Regulators are a burgeoning breed in modern financial markets as previously state-dominated industries are opened to the private sector and self regulation comes under fire. But are more of these public sector 'policemen' the solution? This module takes a contrary view with articles arguing that effective private regulation primarily accounts for the success of international financial markets, and that the red-blooded leveraged buy out wave of the 1980s had a lasting impact on standards of corporate governance.

One area, however, where public intervention is essential is in the highly charged atmosphere of insolvency. The module concludes with a useful comparison of the codes of the United States, the United Kingdom and Germany.

The market as international regulator

by Randall S. Kroszner

International financial transactions are carried out in a realm that is close to anarchy. Numerous committees and organizations attempt to co-ordinate domestic regulatory policies and negotiate international standards but they have no enforcement powers. The Cayman Islands and Bermuda offer not only beautiful beaches but also harbors that are safe from most financial regulation and international agreements. In international financial transactions, where private contractual disputes are litigated and what laws would apply are often highly ambiguous.

Even when the wheels of international justice do turn, they do so slowly, as creditors of BCCI, many of whom have been waiting more than five years to receive their first whiff of compensation, can attest. Fraudsters can hide from judgment in countries that will not extradite them. The chief of Bre-X, who recently 'discovered' the world's largest – if non-existent – gold deposit in Indonesia, has applied to become a permanent resident of the Caymans (only those with at least $250,000 to invest need apply) where his extradition could be delayed for years.

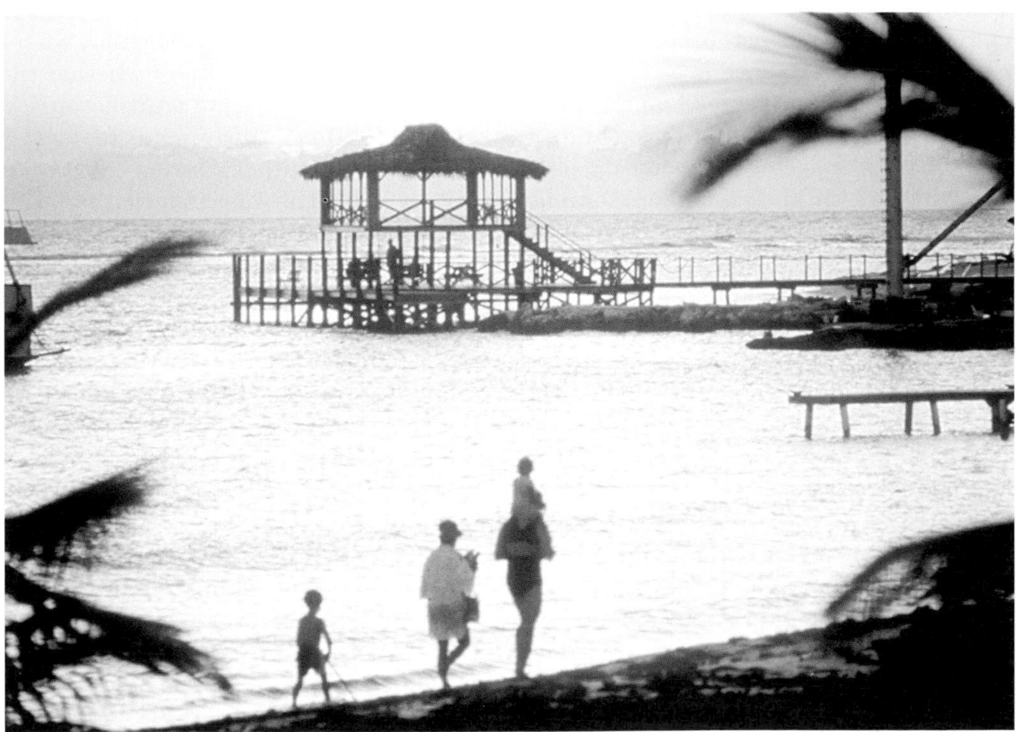

No rules: the Cayman Islands and Bermuda offer financial innovation as well as beautiful beaches

Yet, international financial markets and institutions have grown rapidly and have performed remarkably well. The unregulated euro market, in which securities issuers go to avoid domestic securities regulation has grown from nothing 30 years ago to a multi-trillion dollar market without a major incident. In fact, the growth of many of the largest and most active international financial markets has been spurred by the avoidance of traditional government regulation. While frauds, mismanagement and bankruptcies do occur – sometimes on a spectacular scale, as with the collapses of BCCI and Barings – market forces have been highly effective regulators that have created order out of the apparent chaos of the international financial markets.

This article analyzes how striving for competitive advantage in these markets tends to generate the private regulation that then accounts for the success of international financial markets. The overall stability and integrity of these markets is due primarily to the role of private regulators, not public ones.

To be successful in this anarchic, but orderly, realm companies and markets must develop strategies that promote credibility and induce contractual performance, largely without recourse to traditional government-supplied legal devices. I argue that innovations in strategic organizational design and governance for financial institutions can handle international regulatory challenges more effectively than traditional public regulation. This analysis will then have implications for global reform of government financial regulation.

Challenges of stability and integrity

The potential for fraud is present in all types of transactions but is particularly acute in financial deals. When buying simple items, such as pencils, it is easy to verify the quality of the goods before the purchase. For other types of transactions, this process is more subtle and the potential for duplicity greater. In long-term relationships, where payment or performance is promised in the future, it is difficult to know whether the other party will make good on the promise. Also, in many types of transactions, a purchaser relies on the advice of an expert who is also selling what he or she recommends. A doctor may advise a particular treatment to improve your health but how will you ever know whether the treatment really helped or was irrelevant?

An underwriter may say the prospects for a particular company's stock are quite rosy. You buy the new issue but the business goes bankrupt. Did the underwriter dissemble or did he or she make an honest error of judgment? Both the company and the underwriter may have a conflict of interest in which they have an incentive to overstate the prospects for the company in order to boost the price artificially and thereby gain at your expense. Given these problems, how do the financial markets operate at all? Why isn't fraud omnipresent?

When anti-fraud laws are easy to enforce, of course, legal penalties can reduce such bad behavior. In international financial dealings, however, legal action may be prohibitively expensive and the punishments highly uncertain. In these cases, transactors must rely upon private remedies. Market pressures clearly have not eliminated duplicitous and destabilizing practices; rewards for developing and enforcing credible strategies for reputable behavior, however, are important substitutes for traditional legal enforcement. Repeated dealings, a common feature of the international financial markets, permit the development of reputations for honest dealing (*see* Darby and Karni, 1973; and Klein, 1997) and strategic choices by institutions can enhance their credibility.

Private strategic responses

Private strategic responses to concerns about stability and integrity take many forms. A traditional solution had been to create a members-only club with high standards for membership. Clearing houses and organized exchanges are classic examples of this approach. Long before regulators were setting minimum capital and liquidity standards, bankers were policing each others' private note issuance through privately developed clearing systems. This was so during the free-banking eras in 18th and 19th century Scotland and in the early 19th century, through the Suffolk System in New England, in the US.

Since the 19th century, the clearing house associations of the Chicago Board of Trade and Chicago Mercantile Exchanges have been monitoring the financial health of their members and provide a form of insurance against failure of the clearing members. Most recent growth in the international markets has been outside traditional members-only institutions. Over-the-counter (OTC) derivatives trading, for example, has grown sharply during the past decade and, since 1994, has shown explosive growth. Much of the movement toward OTC markets is driven by the desire to avoid the domestic regulation imposed on organized exchanges. Since OTC markets have no physical location, sovereign regulators have great difficulty in claiming that such activity falls within their jurisdictions.

In these effectively unregulated OTC markets, the strategic responses to the challenges of stability and integrity have taken various forms. Independent credit-rating agencies play a key role in certifying the quality of potential counterparties to a transaction. These third-party monitors publicly grade the health of the big players.

Contracts that involve long-term relationships often include clauses that permit early termination if a counterparty falls below a specified rating threshold. Some participants simply will not deal with those that do not meet a minimum rating. Private regulators have thus fulfilled the auditing, screening and monitoring functions of the public regulators and have been quite effective, even though they do not have the same legal powers as public regulators to obtain information.

The emphasis on top ratings is a market-generated response to concerns about the risks of entering long-term contracts in the OTC derivatives market. Many institutions saw their ratings slip by the early 1990s. They began to face increasing costs of participating in these markets and were excluded entirely from some transactions. These companies then decided to create new organizational forms to address the concerns about credit risk.

The innovation is a special purpose vehicle, called a derivative product company (DPC), that is structured to garner a top rating. Institutions without high ratings incorporated DPC subsidiaries that have capital and governance structure distinct from their parent. A DPC can win an AAA rating because its capital cannot be tapped by creditors of the parent company if the parent becomes bankrupt. Also, it may have credit enhancements that do not rely upon the parent's health.

Moody's and Standard & Poor's, the US credit-rating agencies, provide flexible definitions of DPC structure to allow businesses to achieve AAA status in a variety of ways. The strategic restructuring of a company, thereby, improved the long-term stability and integrity of these derivative markets. The innovation was driven by market forces.

In addition to the rapid growth in derivatives, cross-border lending and international securities issues are also at record highs. The role of banks in these activities raises another challenge for stability and integrity in the international markets; namely, the conflict of interest that can arise when underwriting and lending are combined. Consider a company that suddenly experiences a shock that is likely to reduce its future profitability. A bank with a lending relationship with that company may know before the market does that its prospects have dimmed.

The bank's superior knowledge, however, is a double-edged sword. If the bank were free from conflicts, it would make an objective analysis of the business's future and, if new securities were to be issued, reveal the information to the public. Alternatively, a rogue bank may try to take advantage of its superior knowledge by underwriting and distributing securities to an unsuspecting public and using the proceeds to repay the outstanding bank loan.

This concern was a key factor driving the passage of the 1933 Glass-Steagall Act in the US, which forbids commercial banks from underwriting and dealing in corporate securities. The fear that such conflicts can lead to a destabilizing loss of confidence in public securities markets continues to be a significant obstacle to universal banking in the US and plays an important role in the debate over financial reform in transition and emerging economies. The public regulatory solution generally involves mandating complete separation or strict 'Chinese Walls' between lending and underwriting operations.

Market forces, however, have been able to provide the incentives for banks to reduce the potential for conflicts voluntarily, through the strategic reorganization of the company. Banks that lack credibility are penalized in the marketplace because purchasers will pay lower prices and demand higher yields from securities underwritten by institutions they cannot trust.

Before the Glass-Steagall Act in the US, banks organized their investment banking operations either as an internal securities department within the bank or as a separately incorporated and capitalized affiliate with its own board of directors. In a study with Raghuram Rajan (1997), we found that the internal departments obtained lower prices than did the separate affiliates for the otherwise similar issues they underwrote. The pricing penalty suffered by the internal department is consistent with investors' discounting for the greater likelihood of conflicts problems when lending and underwriting are done within the same structure.

We found that the pricing benefit for the separate affiliates increased with the number of affiliate board members who were independent of the parent bank. Banks thus can enhance their underwriting credibility and performance through a strategic reorganization that separates the lending and underwriting and uses independent board members as internal monitors. Consequently, we also found that US banks increasingly adopted the separate affiliate structure in the decade before the passage of the Glass-Steagall Act.

German universal banks, which had traditionally underwritten through internal departments, have been moving these operations to separate affiliates in London. Until recently, the German securities markets had been relatively uncompetitive and dominated by the banks themselves, with relatively low participation by individuals or outsiders. In these circumstances, the chief players would be equally well-informed, so there would be little value in setting up a separate structure.

To achieve credibility in an internationally competitive market, however, they have found it in their interest to separate these functions. Market competition thus propels banks voluntarily to adopt Chinese Wall structures without any regulatory requirements.

Public regulatory responses

Having examined the private strategic responses to promote stability and integrity in the anarchy of the international markets, let us consider the roles and incentives of public regulators. Public regulators can, and often do, perform the same functions as the credit-rating agencies by evaluating and rating the soundness of financial institutions. But the incentives of the private and public regulators differ.

The private rating agencies are rewarded for being the most effective and accurate monitor, particularly for being the first to spot a problem and warn the public about it. In contrast, distress that would trigger a downgrade is perceived as trouble not only for the institution but for the regulators as well. No one holds S&P responsible when a company experiences a shock that lowers its credit quality. To avoid taking the blame, public regulators have an incentive to delay recognizing and publicly announcing problems since a positive shock could resolve the distress. Waiting also could allow them to place the burden on future regulators or politicians.

The poor record of US regulators during the 1980s of giving high grades to institutions whose failures were imminent and the consistent official under-reporting of the bad loan problem in Japan during the 1990s illustrate this tendency. In the US Savings and Loan crisis, for example, the desire to put off the day of reckoning led regulators to undertake perverse policies that obscured problems in the short run – such as permitting economically insolvent institutions to pay dividends – but were extremely costly to taxpayers in the long run (*see* Kroszner and Strahan, 1996).

In addition, public regulators cannot be insulated from political and interest group pressures. In Chicago, the police cars are emblazoned with the phrase 'we serve and protect' and often that phrase can be applied to public regulators. Rather than promote the supposed public interest, the regulators may largely serve the private interest of the industry that they are regulating and protect it from competition (*see* Stigler, 1988). Co-operative public regulators may be rewarded with lucrative employment opportunities in the industry after leaving the government, a practice the Japanese call amakudari, or 'the descent from heaven'. While certainly not all or even most public regulators may make regulatory policy with this 'descent' in mind, it provides a background incentive very different than that for the private regulators.

Finally, the public regulators have much greater difficulty accommodating the dynamic change of the market than do private regulators. Moody's and S&P can provide general guidelines for good practice and then exercise their judgment as innovations occur. Giving public regulators wide discretion is an invitation to political and interest group pressure and to arbitrariness in application of their powers.

The key lesson for regulatory reform is that public regulation should not be permitted to crowd out dynamic private regulation. One of the proposals from the G7 summit in Denver this past spring was to increase information sharing and co-ordination among public regulators. If that information is also shared with the public, applying to themselves the regulators' advice to the markets for greater transparency, then this effort is to be applauded. Some have gone further, suggesting that an international super-regulator be created to set common standards worldwide. However, a unified international regulator is likely to slow the engine that generates the innovations that have driven the spectacular growth of the international financial markets.

Strategic organizational choices by financial institutions and third-party monitors, such as credit-rating agencies, have been quite successful in providing stability and integrity for the international financial markets. While the market is not a perfect regulator – the Caymans can still provide a haven for rogues – the alternative is likely to be a much less efficient and innovative international financial sector in which public regulation crowds out the creative experimentation that the lovely beaches of the Caymans foster.

Summary

This article looks at the regulation of international finance. In fact, international financial transactions, according to author Randall Kroszner, are carried out 'in a realm that is close to anarchy'.

But, Kroszner argues, the lack of government-supported regulation may be no bad thing. In fact, the absence of formal regulation has spurred private solutions to the need for stability and integrity that have proved highly effective.

In other words, he says, 'striving for competitive advantage in these markets tends to generate the private regulation that then accounts for the success of international financial markets'. The article goes on to compare and contrast both formal and private regulation and concludes that while the market may not be a perfect self-regulator the alternative of public regulation – with its threat to creative experimentation – would be much less efficient.

Suggested further reading

Darby, M. and Kami, E., (1973), 'Free competition and the optimal amount of fraud', *Journal of Law and Economics* August, 67–88.

Klein, D., (ed.) (1997), 'Reputation: studies in the voluntary elicitation of good conduct', Ann Arbor, University of Michigan Press.

Kroszner, R.S., (1997), 'Free banking: lessons from the Scottish experience for emerging market economies' in Caprio, G. and Vittas D., (eds). *Reforming financial systems: historical implications for policy*, Cambridge University Press, New York.

Kroszner, R.S. and Rajan, R.G., (1997), 'Organization structure and credibility: evidence from commercial bank securities activities before the Glass-Steagall Act', *Journal of Monetary Economics*, June.

Kroszner, R.S. and Strahan, P., (1988),'Regulatory incentives and the thrift crisis: dividends, mutual-to-stock conversions, and financial distress', *Journal of Finance* 51 September, 1285–1320.

Stigler, G., (ed.) (1988), 'Chicago Studies in the Political Economy', University of Chicago Press, Chicago.

Riding on the benefits of the LBO wave

by Steven Kaplan

Corporate governance has changed substantially in the past 15 years, particularly in the US. But how has it altered and how can it be expected to evolve both in the US and the rest of the industrialized world? Many recent changes, as well as those likely in the future, are rooted in the 1980s takeover and leveraged buy-out (LBO) wave in the US, which was driven by several important corporate governance insights. In the 1990s, executives, boards of directors and shareholders in the US and elsewhere have increasingly applied those LBO insights. In that sense we are all becoming Henry Kravis of KKR fame.

Before 1980, the status of corporate governance in the US and elsewhere was very different from that of today. Executives then held modest amounts of stock and options in their companies. Top executives and their incentives were more focused on traditional performance measures such as sales or earnings growth. Boards of directors were not particularly active and shareholders were relatively passive.

In the 1980s this began to change. The catalyst was an unprecedented amount of takeover and restructuring activity. Figure 1 makes this clear. It shows acquisition activity in the US from 1968 to 1996 measured as a fraction of total stock market capitalization. During that period, seven of the nine years with the greatest amount of takeover activity occurred in the 1980s. The annual measures in the figure understate the true extent of takeovers and restructuring in the 1980s because many companies restructured without being taken over.

Despite media reports of record takeover activity today, the current volume of activity is much less than that in the 1980s. The value of the stock market has increased by more than the value of acquisitions. Takeovers and restructuring in the 1980s were distinguished by the use of leverage. Leveraged buy-outs (LBOs), Kohlberg Kravis & Roberts (KKR), and Michael Milken became houschold names. The extent of this activity was so great that from 1984 to 1990 net new issues of equity were negative and corporate America became more leveraged.

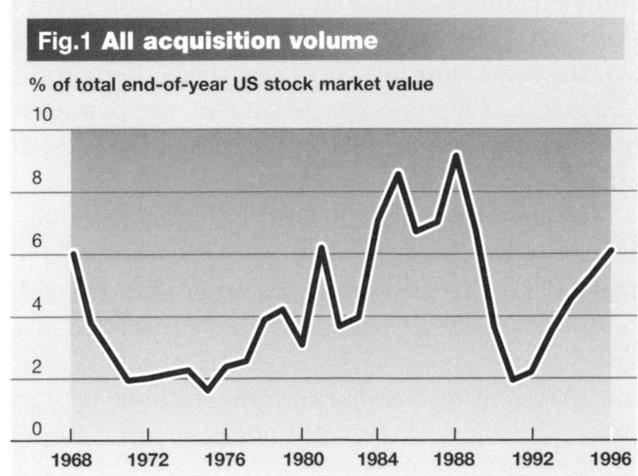

The insights of LBOs

The LBOs of the early 1980s were driven by three basic insights:

- The large amount of debt incurred in LBOs imposed a strong discipline on buy-out company management. With that debt, it was no longer possible for managers to treat capital, particularly equity capital, as costless. On the contrary, failure to generate a sufficient return on capital meant default and, possibly, bankruptcy.

- LBOs provided managers with substantial equity stakes in the buy-out company. These stakes gave managers the incentives to undertake the buy-out, to work hard to pay off the debt and to increase shareholder value. If successful, buy-out company managers could expect to make a great deal of money. In my early work, I found that the chief executive officers of the typical LBO increased their ownership stake from 1.4 per cent pre-LBO to 6.4 per cent post-LBO. Management teams, overall, experienced similar increases in equity ownership. In the early 1980s, this approach to executive compensation was fundamentally different from common practice.
- LBO sponsors or associations closely monitored and governed the companies they leveraged. Unlike public company boards that were large and dominated by distant outsiders with small ownership stakes, LBO company boards were small and dominated by LBO sponsors with substantial equity stakes in the companies (and the companies' successes).

What did these insights lead to? In the first half of the 1980s, they were highly successful. LBO companies saw improved operating profits and few defaults. Even after accounting for the returns on the overall stock market or companies in the same industry, these early buy-outs generated positive returns. In other words, LBO investors earned more than a leveraged investment in the stock market. Because the overall stock market increased over this period, buy-out sponsors earned substantial returns.

The LBO experience was substantially different in the latter half of the 1980s. Roughly one-third of those completed after 1985 defaulted on their debt, sometimes spectacularly – witness Campeau and Federated Department Stores, Macy's and Gateway. Such defaults led many to criticize LBOs and, in fact, the entire 1980s. But did this mean the LBO insights were wrong? Not at all. The evidence, even for the late 1980s, indicates that the LBO strategies hold. Overall, the larger LBOs of the later 1980s also generated improvements in operating profits despite the relatively large number of defaults. In a recent paper, Gregor Andrade and I found that even companies that defaulted maintained or increased their value.

The case of Federated Department Stores in the US illustrates this effect. Campeau's 1988 acquisition of Federated is still widely considered the nadir of LBOs and the 1980s. Yet the facts say otherwise. At the start of 1988, Federated's debt and equity traded at $4.25bn. From that point until Federated emerged from bankruptcy in February 1992, it returned roughly $5.85bn in value (adjusted for changes in the overall stock market). In other words, Federated was worth $1.6bn more because of the LBO than it would have been if its performance had matched that of the overall stock market. Unfortunately for Campeau, he paid $7.67bn, almost $2bn more than he got out of it.

The question is if the LBOs increased value, why did so many default? The answer seems to be that the success of the early 1980s LBOs attracted new investors and capital to the LBO market who understood the basic LBO insights. Increased competition then pushed purchase prices to levels that reflected the expected benefits and improvements. As a result, much of the benefits of the improved discipline, incentives and governance went to those who sold out to the LBO investors – in many cases, the old public shareholders – rather than to the LBO investors themselves.

The key point is that even in the worst deals, when the post-buy-out investors lost, the pre-buy-out shareholders gained more so that the combined returns to pre- and post-buy-out investors were positive overall. In the deals that did not default, the combined gains were larger. In other words, the LBO benefits were real.

What caused the wave?

More generally, the takeover wave of the 1980s in the US appears to have been a capital market response to corporate governance deficiencies. The rise of institutional shareholders and greater availability of information to the capital markets placed more pressure on corporate management to maximize shareholder value in the US. As Gordon Donaldson, among others, has argued, the governance and ownership structures of the 1960s and early 1970s were not sufficiently efficient for the financial markets of the 1980s.

Before 1980, top executives were as loyal to employees and other stakeholders as they were to shareholders. This loyalty led to under-utilized resources. The 1980s brought a shareholder correction. In other words, the takeover and restructuring wave of the 1980s is best explained by an ascendancy of the capital markets over corporate managers. In some cases, the capital markets reversed ill-advised diversification; in others, the capital markets helped to eliminate excess capacity; in still others, the capital markets disciplined managers who had ignored shareholders to benefit other stakeholders. LBOs and the insights behind them are particularly representative of the changes that the capital markets imposed.

At the end of the 1980s, the takeover and LBO wave ended in the US. Anti-takeover legislation and jurisprudence, overt political pressure against leverage and a credit crunch were among the explanations offered for the decline. Since then, takeover volume – sometimes hostile – has revived, but LBOs and raiders have not. Because the political pressure against leverage and the credit crunch have both abated, the explanations given for the end of the takeover and LBO wave do not explain the continued absence of LBOs and raiders.

Applying LBO insights

A more likely reason for the decline of LBOs and raiders is that shareholders and corporations increasingly obtain the benefits of LBOs and raiders without actually doing an LBO.

Remember that the first LBO insight was to impose a cost of capital on management so that management did not view (equity) capital as costless. Corporations (and consulting firms) now implement this insight through innovative performance measurement and compensation programs. The best-known of these are marketed by consulting firms. For example, Stern Stewart markets Economic Value Added (EVA) and other consulting firms market similar concepts. EVA and its analogs compare the after-tax profit earned by a company or division to the after-tax profit that is required by the capital invested.

There is also anecdotal evidence that companies increasingly approach decisions with the goal of maximizing shareholder value. For example, consulting firms, such as McKinsey & Co, routinely measure the effects of their consulting assignments on shareholder value.

Compensation committees and consultants increasingly apply the second LBO insight – providing more high-powered equity-based incentives to top executives. The use of stock options, restricted stock grants and other forms of equity-based compensation have increased substantially. A recent paper by Hall and Liebman of Harvard finds a remarkable increase in equity-based compensation for US CEOs. From 1980 to 1994, the average annual CEO option grant (valued at issuance) increased more than seven-fold from $145,000 to just under $1.2m. As a result, equity-based compensation made up almost 50 per cent of total CEO compensation in 1994, compared with less than 20 per cent in 1980. This increase, combined with the strong performance of the stock market, is partially responsible for the even larger realized increases in top executive compensation.

Again, the increased emphasis on equity-based compensation among corporations in general has as its direct antecedent the emphasis by LBO sponsors on such compensation. Ironically, the large pay-offs earned by LBO sponsors and, more importantly, by the top executives of LBO companies probably made it more acceptable for top executives of public companies to become wealthy through equity-based compensation. Disney's $190m-plus option grant to Michael Eisner and Scott Paper's compensation contract for Al Dunlap are two of the more prominent examples.

Finally, public companies appear to have increasingly applied the third LBO insight – closer and more active monitoring by boards and shareholders. There is increasing pressure on boards to become more active and more shareholder-oriented. For example, the National Association of Corporate Directors in the US called for a substantial increase in equity-based compensation for directors. In a survey of institutional investors, McKinsey found that many will pay a premium of about 10 per cent for companies with good corporate governance. Based on these developments, I would expect boards to continue to evolve to be more like those of LBOs – more active with more equity ownership.

US shareholders also have increased the pressure they place on corporate boards and corporate management. Prominent institutional investors have mounted active and public campaigns against a selected group of under-performing and under-governed public companies. Other investors target under-performing, under-governed companies one at a time and attempt to change their governance (and performance). In other words, today's institutional shareholders are the raiders and LBO sponsors of the 1990s.

As corporations impose a cost on internal capital, provide more equity-based incentive and have more active boards and shareholders, they begin to look increasingly like companies that undertook LBOs. In that sense, we are all becoming Henry Kravis now.

Why has this happened?

While it is clear that public companies increasingly apply the insights emphasized by the LBOs of the early 1980s, it may be less clear whether this will continue. To answer that question, it is important to understand why all this is happening now in the US. There are at least three interrelated reasons.

First, the shareholdings of professional institutional investors continue to increase. For example, individual ownership of corporations in the US declined from 70 per cent in 1970, to 60 per cent in 1980, to 48 cent in 1994. Those figures include the ownership of private companies. Individual ownership of public companies is even lower. This means that more sophisticated shareholders own an increasingly large percentage of US corporations.

Second, in 1992, the US Securities and Exchange Commission (SEC) substantially reduced the costs to shareholders of co-ordinating challenges against under-performing management teams by relaxing the proxy rules regarding shareholder communications. Under the old rules, if a shareholder wanted to talk to ten other shareholders he or she had to file a detailed proxy statement with the SEC. Under the new rules, shareholders can communicate at any time in any way as long as they send a copy of the substance of the communication to the SEC afterwards. By reducing the role of the SEC, this rule change has made it substantially less expensive for several large shareholders to confront managers and boards of under-performing companies.

A third reason for the corporate governance changes we see today was a result of the SEC's requirement, also in 1992, that public companies provide more detailed disclosure of top executive compensation and its relation to company performance, particularly stock performance. This requirement focused boards of directors on stock performance. Companies now routinely report corporate, industry and market stock performance in their proxy statements.

This represents a substantial shift from the pre-1980s. The requirement also makes large equity-based compensation packages defensible, if not desirable. Boards of directors are less likely to be criticized by shareholders (and, even, the media) if company executives are compensated based on stock performance. Executive compensation will be high only if the company has performed well. Given these three developments, it seems likely that institutional investors and boards will work at least as aggressively for shareholder value in the US in the future.

What about the rest of the world?

The discussion so far has focused on the US corporate governance system and its evolution. This leaves two important questions unanswered: how well does the US system work; and what does it mean for the rest of the world? The short answers are that the US system works well and the rest of the world has been moving and will continue to move closer to the US system.

In the 1980s, the German and Japanese capital markets and governance system were lauded by some as being superior to the US system because of their ability to ignore short-term distractions and manage for the long term. Academic work and subsequent events have discredited this position.

On several important dimensions, corporate governance generates virtually similar outcomes in very different countries and systems. In particular, top executives face broadly similar incentives in most industrialized countries. For example, systematic studies of top executives in Germany, Italy, Japan, Spain, the UK and the US find that executives are all more likely to lose their jobs when their companies have poor earnings and poor stock returns. What this means is that corporate governance in all these countries is similarly unforgiving of poor current performance. The German and Japanese systems are not more patient.

The primary way in which US corporate governance differs from others is that the US provides much stronger incentives to executives to work for shareholders when performance is not obviously poor. US companies provide greater equity stakes to top executives, face a more active takeover market and confront increasingly more co-ordinated and aggressive shareholders. By contrast, Japanese companies are severely restricted in their ability to provide stock options to executives and employees.

In addition, the US legal and tax system makes it relatively easy for US companies to pay cash out to shareholders, either as dividends or by repurchasing shares. In contrast, historically, it has been expensive if not illegal in many other countries for companies to repurchase their shares.

The importance of this difference becomes clear when one considers what some companies did with the cash they did not pay out. The ill-fated diversification attempts at Germany's Daimler-Benz and the unsuccessful acquisitions of US entertainment companies – Universal Studios and Columbia Pictures – by Matsushita and Sony of Japan are good examples.

If the US system works so well, one might expect that corporate governance in other countries would copy that of the US. This already appears to be happening. European and Japanese companies are beginning to realize that internal capital is not costless. The use of stock options for executives and boards seems to be increasing in Europe – Glaxo-Wellcome's announcement that it was paying board members in stock is a recent example.

Many countries, including Japan and Germany, have made it, or are trying to make it, easier for companies to repurchase their shares. Finally, boards and shareholders are putting more pressure on companies to manage in shareholders' interests. It is likely that the rest of the world will continue to copy the LBO insights and move closer to the US corporate governance system.

There are (at least) two reasons for this. First, companies and countries that do not adjust will be at a decided disadvantage in raising capital from a global capital market. Second, and more important, companies and countries with better corporate governance make better decisions. In the long run, better decisions create stronger competitors and more valuable companies.

Summary

Leveraged buy-outs were a largely 1980s phenomenon – but as Steven Kaplan explains, the raiders left behind a legacy which is still with us today. LBOs were representative of restructuring changes which capital markets imposed on corporate managers, notably in the way they demonstrated that equity capital is not costless, provided high-powered equity incentives for top executives, and actively monitored and governed the companies they leveraged. Companies now absorb these insights themselves and will most likely continue to do so in the US under the influence of more professional institutional investors and new regulatory requirements. The US system with its legitimacy of strong incentives works well and seems set to be copied by other countries. Those that do not adjust will be at a decided disadvantage when it comes to raising capital in a global capital market.

The tale of three insolvency codes

by Walter N. Torous, Kjell Nyborg and Julian Franks

The costs of bankruptcy can be significantly altered by a country's insolvency code. The code will potentially affect creditors' rights to repossess assets, the priority of their claims and the timing of repayment. The resulting costs will affect the interest rate paid and the amount that can be borrowed. The code will also alter the incentives to restructure outside the insolvency process as well as inside. This article provides a comparative study of the costs and benefits of three insolvency codes, those of the UK, the US and Germany.

UK insolvency code

Before the 1986 Insolvency Act there were three possible routes to formal reorganization: liquidation; receivership; and company voluntary arrangements. An additional procedure, administration, was introduced in 1986. The most widely used route is the liquidation code. In 1990 this accounted for about three-quarters of all formal reorganizations and receivership accounted for a further 22 per cent.

The aim of the liquidator is to sell sufficient of the company's assets to repay creditors. The liquidator can sell the company as a going concern or in a non-operating state but cannot, at the risk of dismissal or legal action, use funds belonging to creditors to delay the sale. A lack of positive cash flow will most likely lead to the immediate closure of the enterprise.

Receivership can only take place when one or more of the company's creditors has a particular kind of lien on its assets, known as a floating charge. This is a claim on moveable assets such as stocks and work in progress. The receiver is appointed by the creditor with the floating charge and represents the interests of that creditor alone.

The powers of the receiver are significant. He has complete control of the company and does not require permission from the court or from other creditors for his actions. However, the receiver does not have the power to stay the claims of the company (that is, to postpone interest and capital repayments) or to raise funds that are (equally) senior to existing claims. In the absence of a creditor with a floating charge, a receiver cannot be appointed and the only alternative available pre-1986 was liquidation. The position of administrator was established in the 1986 Insolvency Act to fill that gap.

An important difference between the two is that the receiver represents just one creditor and the administrator represents all. The number of administrations has been limited, in part because a creditor with a floating charge can always pre-empt the appointment of the administrator by appointing a receiver instead. Under receivership such a creditor has greater control rights than in administration.

There are also a considerable number of reorganizations of distressed companies outside the formal process. In a recent survey by the Society of Practitioners in Insolvency more than 1,800 companies in 1995–96, including 130 listed companies, called in 'company doctors' to restructure their operations and financial liabilities.

End of the sales line: 'The costs of bankruptcy can be significantly altered by a country's insolvency code'

US bankruptcy code

There are two main bankruptcy procedures for corporations in the US: Chapter 7 and Chapter 11. Chapter 7 is the liquidation code and provides for the appointment of a trustee by the court to oversee the liquidation of the company. Invariably, the business is closed down before sale and the assets auctioned. Chapter 11 allows a firm to remain in operation while a plan of reorganization is worked out with creditors. The directors are permitted to remain in charge and substantial rights are given to the company, often referred to as the debtor-in-possession.

The rationale is that existing management, representing equityholders, will have incentives to maintain the company as a going concern in order to preserve some value for the equity's claim. Most companies enter Chapter 11 only after attempting an informal reorganization, or workout, outside the bankruptcy process. A workout can take the form of an exchange offer for outstanding debt, renegotiation of bond covenants, or the negotiation of a reduction in interest payments and an extension of loan maturities. In a workout the court does not supervize the affairs of the distressed company whereas in Chapter 11, the day-to-day affairs of the company are under the scrutiny of its creditors and the court.

Some businesses attempt to combine the lower administrative costs of a workout with the non-unanimity requirements and the tax benefits of Chapter 11 by filing a 'pre-packaged' bankruptcy petition. This involves arranging a reorganization plan with the main creditors outside formal bankruptcy, entering Chapter 11 and immediately submitting the plan to the judge and then to creditors for approval so as to take advantage of the code's non-unanimity provisions. Court approval also has the advantage of forestalling future litigation. 'Pre-packs' constitute an important trend in recent filings for Chapter 11 and accounted for 43 per cent of filings in the first six months of 1993 for companies with assets greater than $100m.

The majority of bankruptcies are processed through Chapter 7. For example, in the Central District of the California Bankruptcy Court there were 57,752 Chapter 7 cases pending, compared with only 6,739 Chapter 11 cases in December 1993.

The German code

Current German bankruptcy law consists of two codes: compulsory liquidation and composition proceedings. In July 1994 new bankruptcy legislation was passed and is scheduled to come into force in 1999. Currently, the most common procedure is compulsory liquidation, in which control of the assets of the company is transferred from management to an insolvency practitioner, or administrator, typically appointed by the court and supervised by a creditors' committee.

Although the practitioner's directive is to sell the business for cash, there is no rush to sell off its assets. There is in effect an unlimited stay against unsecured creditors and the administrator can raise new senior financing. Thus he can keep a company alive if he deems economic conditions to be unfavorable for a sale. As a result the average time spent in compulsory liquidation is 27.5 months.

The composition proceeding is a relatively recent addition to the statutes and is an alternative to compulsory liquidation. However, it is seldom used. In 1992 only 0.3 per cent of all insolvencies were composition proceedings. Composition proceedings may fail if, in the court's opinion, the company is not viable as a going concern or because of stringent requirements for the repayment of creditors' claims.

The new code bears some similarity to the compulsory liquidation code. The main differences are that there is an automatic stay of secured claims for three months; there are no preferred creditors; and in the liquidation code the practitioner has considerable control rights whereas under the reform these rights are much reduced.

The reform provides a fairly flexible framework in which to reorganize or sell the business in part or in whole. The three-month automatic stay is designed to give the practitioner and all interested parties an opportunity to share information so that efficient solutions can be achieved.

On entering formal bankruptcy, the court appoints a creditors' committee and an insolvency administrator. Both of these appointments can be overturned at a creditors' assembly held within three months. Secured and unsecured creditors vote in separate groups. Simple majority by number and by claim in each group is required for a favorable vote. Confirmation by the court is also necessary.

As with Chapter 11 in the US, such confirmation will not be given if the plan would put a creditor opposing the plan in a worse position than the creditor would be in the next best alternative. This provides a guarantee that a large group of creditors cannot disadvantage other creditors. Below we discuss six factors that influence the costs and benefits of these different codes.

Control rights

Control rights provide creditors and the debtor with pre-specified rights over a company's assets should it enter the insolvency process. Frequently, these control rights create a tension between different creditors. For example, in UK receivership only secured creditors have significant control rights. This may encourage them to liquidate or keep the firm as a going concern at the expense of unsecured creditors.

In Germany, although the insolvency administrator in a liquidation can stay unsecured claims, raise new senior financing and in theory has the rights necessary to maintain the company as a going concern, these rights are in practice often nullified by the secured creditors' right to take possession of their assets. In the majority of insolvencies, after secured creditors have grabbed their assets there are insufficient funds in the company to open formal insolvency procedures.

In contrast, in the US in Chapter 11 the debtor-in-possession frequently remains in control of the business throughout the entire reorganization process. As a consequence, the equity usually has some value even when the business is technically insolvent. However, the company's management is subject to detailed supervision by the court, which potentially limits its discretion to raise financing, sell assets and even fix the size of the salaries of the board of directors. About 50 per cent of financially distressed companies' top management remains in place throughout the formal reorganization process.

Automatic stay

There are no automatic stay provisions in the UK's receivership code. Indeed, secured creditors often precipitate liquidation by repossessing their assets, which are often essential to keep the business running. The administrator has strong powers to delay or stay creditors' claims, including interest and repayment on loans. However, administration can be terminated by creditors after three months. In Chapter 11 there are strong automatic stay provisions. Perhaps most importantly, all payments of interest and principal on much of the company's debt is stayed while the company is in Chapter 11. Interest continues to accrue on fully secured debt but not on unsecured debt.

Furthermore, in contrast to the UK's receivership code, the filing of a bankruptcy petition automatically restrains almost all creditors from enforcing their claims. Nor is there any statutory time limit on the length of proceedings in Chapter 11. In the new German code there is a three-month automatic stay against all claims.

Management of liabilities

In the UK, since the receiver represents the interests of only one creditor, he has very little discretion in renegotiating the distressed business's liabilities. For example, the issuance of further debt cannot be made without the agreement of other creditors unless the new debt is junior to all existing claims.

This may be a particular disadvantage if the receiver wishes to maintain the company as a going concern and it requires an injection of funds. Typically this leads to under-investment in the distressed company. In comparison, the court-appointed administrator has greater flexibility in managing liabilities since there is a court-administered process for obtaining the agreement of creditors to new financing arrangements. Both the US and new German bankruptcy codes allow for the renegotiation of all claims against the distressed company. While court approval is necessary, only a majority of creditors (and two-thirds by value) within each class need approve.

Bankruptcy financing

Financing of the distressed company's continued operations during bankruptcy may be required to maintain it as a going concern. In the UK the receiver can raise these additional funds but, as described above, any new borrowings will be junior to all existing loans. The difficulties of arranging new financing, as well as the lack of automatic stay provisions, may explain why large companies will go to great lengths to remain outside the court-administered process.

Eurotunnel, the financially distressed company that operates the Channel Tunnel, has recently carried out a major restructuring of its debts that saw its total debt of £9.1bn reduced to £7.1bn. The restructuring involved a £1bn debt-for-equity swap, the issuance of convertibles and warrants, a reduction in the interest rate on remaining debt and further facilities for raising new financing should there be shortfalls in revenues. This agreement was made outside the formal bankruptcy process and was negotiated by the company and a small group of banks with large loans outstanding to it. The agreement has been approved by most of the 225 banks affected and by the company's shareholders.

This position is in contrast to the US's Chapter 11, which explicitly recognizes the importance of new financing during reorganization by providing for debtor-in-possession financing. Such financing takes priority over many outstanding obligations. New senior financing can be raised under the current German code. This will be maintained in the new code.

Deviations from absolute priority

The UK code of receivership results in a speedy settlement of claims and adherence to the priority of claims. This is achieved because creditors obtain control of the company when it enters the formal insolvency process.

Olsen's (1996) empirical analysis of financially distressed UK public companies over the period 1987 to 1995 (*see* Suggested further reading) confirms a complete absence of deviations from absolute priority in receivership. However, he finds substantial deviations from absolute priority in workouts, with bank creditors giving up, on average, approximately 12 per cent of their entitlements.

The majority of Chapter 11 reorganizations in the US allow for deviations from absolute priority in favor of shareholders and some creditors. In addition, equity deviations occur in voluntary reorganizations or workouts and they are substantially greater than those in Chapter 11.

Table 1 summarizes the results for deviations in the UK and US data. Deviations in favor of equity are comparable for the sample of UK and US workouts. While a systematic analysis of relevant German data does not exist, the recent financial distress of Germany's Klöckner-Werke, the steelmaker, illustrates that deviations may occur under the German

Table 1

Deviations from absolute priority for a sample of UK firms which successfully completed a workout and US firms which were reorganized in Chapter 11 or successfully completed a distressed exchange.

Creditor class	UK Workouts	Chapter 11	US Distressed exchanges
Secured	–12%	–4%	–7%
Unsecured	6%	1%	–1%
Equity	6%	3%	8%

The UK sample consists of 35 firms that successfully restructured their secured bank debt between 1987 and 1995. The US sample consists of 82 firms from the period 1983-1988. The definitions of the creditor include secured debt, bank debt and senior debt.

Sources: author adaptation of Olsen (1996) and Franks and Torous (1994).

code. The company filed for composition in December 1992 with a total debt of DM2.7bn and the plan of composition was approved in June 1993. The plan provided for payments to creditors to be made at the end of 1994.

Unsecured creditors incurred writedowns of 60 per cent (the maximum allowed by law) while secured creditors incurred writedowns of 40 per cent. Creditors with debts of less than DM10,000 were paid in full to secure approval of the plan since a majority of creditors by number was required. In addition, equityholders retained an interest.

Direct costs of each system

In the UK, there is little communication between the receiver and creditors other than the former's appointer. This absence of on-going consultation makes the receivership process relatively fast, frequently weeks rather than months.

The need for speed and existing management's knowledge of the business often provides them with an advantage in the purchase of the assets from the receiver. Administration in the UK takes longer because of the need to obtain the agreement of the court and creditors to any reorganization plan.

In Germany, the existing liquidation code can be very lengthy and costly because unsecured creditors cannot easily terminate the proceedings. It is widely believed that the practitioner often does not act in the interest of creditors. The new code, like the UK administration code, provides creditors with the ability to liquidate after the compulsory stay of three months has been exhausted. Another means of comparing the costs of reorganization is to examine writedowns of creditor claims. Writedowns may reflect the costs of financial distress and the reorganization process or the decline in the value of the firm prior to financial distress.

A comparison of data from the UK and the US gives some clue as to whether there are differences in costs of distress and reorganization, as shown in Table 2. For the UK data we see, on average, substantially larger writedowns of creditors' claims in receiverships than in workouts. In particular, unsecured creditors in receiverships experience an almost total elimination of their claims; this may reflect their lack of control over the proceedings as well as the financial state of the company. Table 2 also suggests that writedowns are always larger in receivership than in Chapter 11. For example, for secured creditors the writedowns are 47 per cent in receiverships and only 29 per cent in Chapter 11s. This pattern is repeated for all creditors with writedowns of 66 per cent in receiverships and 49 per cent for Chapter 11s.

The pattern is not the same for reorganizations outside the court-administered process. For example, for unsecured creditors the write-downs are only five per cent in the UK sample, compared with 20 per cent in US distressed exchanges. Comparisons are complicated because of different definitions for particular claims and because of different incentives to reorganize

Table 2

Average writedowns for a sample of UK and US firms which completed a reorganization outside the court administered process or within it.

Creditor class	Receivership	Workouts	Chapter 11	US Distressed exchanges
Secured	74%	19%	29%	17%
Preferential	59%	0%		
Unsecured	97%	5%	71%	20%
All creditors	66%	15%	49%	20%

The UK sample consists of 61 firms from the period 1987 and 1995. The US sample consists of 82 firms from the period 1983–1988. The definitions of the creditor class may not match in the two jurisdictions. In the US, secured creditors include secured debt, bank debt and senior debt.

Sources: author adaptation of Olsen (1996) and Franks and Torous (1994).

both within and outside the court-administered process. However, the comparison of all creditors' claims suggests that taking both forms of reorganizations together the writedowns are not dissimilar between the two codes. This suggests that costs may not be very different. A different picture emerges from a comparison of the administrative costs of insolvency in the two countries.

Olsen (1996) finds that costs in receivership are more than 20 per cent of the proceeds, though if the costs are measured on the pre-receivership book value the ratio falls to six per cent. In contrast, in UK workouts the costs are considerably lower, at three per cent of firm value. Cost in US bankruptcies are estimated by Warner (1977) at about 5.3 per cent for a sample of US railroads. In a later study, Altman (1984) estimated the administrative costs of bankruptcy at 6.2 per cent. Cross-country comparisons are especially difficult because of size and industry effects between the samples, and because more solvent companies enter Chapter 11 compared with receivership. However, there is little evidence that the direct costs are higher in Chapter 11 compared with those in receivership.

Conclusions

It should be clear that all three codes have potentially significant defects. The US code is lengthy, expensive and encourages complex bargaining that leads to changes in the priority of claims and, therefore, a lack of adherence to the original terms of the debt contract. Furthermore there are strong incentives for management to over-invest in order to increase the possibility of their company remaining a going concern. However, commercial arrangements have evolved to reduce those costs through workouts and pre-packaged Chapter 11s.

The UK process of receivership, on the other hand, is usually speedy. Creditors obtain control of the business and, therefore, there is greater adherence to the debt contract. However, this may be achieved at the costs of premature or inefficient liquidations and under-investment. Nor does it appear that the appointment of an administrator has significantly rectified these faults, if for no better reason than that the number of appointments has been relatively few and an appointment can be blocked by other secured creditors.

The new German code is simpler and should shorten the reorganization process. It will also reduce the incidence of inefficient liquidations by curtailing the rights of secured creditors. The fact that control rights are in the hands of all creditors rather than the debtor company makes it closer to the UK's administration than to Chapter 11.

The article draws heavily on material published in a paper entitled, 'A Comparison of US, UK and German insolvency codes', *Financial Management*, Autumn 1996, by Julian R. Franks, Kjell Nyborg and Walter N. Torous.

Summary

This article compares and contrasts the insolvency codes of the United States, the United Kingdom and Germany. As Julian Franks, Kjell Nyborg and Walter Torous point out, all three have defects.

The US code is lengthy, expensive and encourages complex bargaining, though work-outs and pre-packaged Chapter 11s have evolved to offset some of the costs.

The UK process of receivership is usually speedy but this may be achieved at the costs of premature or inefficient liquidations and under-investment. Nor does it appear that the appointment of an administrator has significantly rectified these faults.

The new German code is simpler than its predecessor and should shorten the reorganization process. Closer to the UK's administration than to Chapter 11, it will also reduce the incidence of inefficient liquidations by curtailing the rights of secured creditors.

Suggested further reading

Bhandari, Jagdeep, S., and Weiss, Lawrence A., (1996), *Corporate bankruptcy: economic and legal perspectives*, Cambridge University Press.

Franks, J. and Torous, W., (1994), 'How shareholders and creditors fare in workouts and Chapter 11 reorganizations', *Journal of Financial Economics*, May.

Olsen, J.P., (1996), 'A restructuring of distressed bank debt: some empirical evidence from the UK' unpublished manuscript, London Business School.

13

Finance and government

Contributors

Jeremy C. Stein is J. C. Penney Professor of Management at the MIT Sloan School of Management. His research interests focus on corporate finance and monetary policy.

Harold Rose is Emeritus Esmée Fairbairn Professor of Finance at London Business School. He was previously first director of LBS' Institute of Finance and was Group Economic Adviser at Barclays Bank.

Anil K. Kashyap is Professor of Economics at the University of Chicago Graduate School of Business. He teaches, researches and consults on issues related to money and banking.

Robert P. Inman is Professor of Finance and Economics at the Wharton School of the University of Pennsylvania and Research Associate, National Bureau of Economic Research.

Contents

Introduction

Financial markets may epitomize the raw edge of the capitalist system – but no one working in this sector can ignore the pronouncements and policies of Governments. This module deals mainly with US and UK monetary policy, how it works and the ways banks and companies respond to it. It also offers advice on the good management of government finances, notably with regard to choosing the correct accounting and investment rules and incentive setting.

Unraveling the workings of monetary policy

by Jeremy C. Stein and Anil K. Kashyap

The man on the street typically assumes that central banks set interest rates. This is a fairly accurate description of the day-to-day behavior of most major central banks. However, to both the man on the street and most professional economists the link between the very short-term actions of the monetary authorities and the spending decisions of businesses and individuals is more murky.

The goal of this article is to review some recent work on the way in which monetary policy operates and to discuss policy implications, particularly for the impending European Monetary Union (Emu).

Conventional monetary economics

In the classic textbook treatment of monetary policy students are encouraged to think about how a central bank's actions affect portfolios. The simplification commonly adopted is that people's portfolios are allocated between 'bonds' – a shorthand for all types of financial assets that are not used for transactions purposes – and money, the asset used in transactions. Importantly, money is always viewed as more than just currency, with bank accounts being the obvious substitute to include in narrow measures of money. Finally, it is assumed that central banks can control the quantity of money.

If it is reasonable to split a portfolio into these two pieces and the central bank can control one of them, then by adjusting the relative supply of the two types of assets, a central bank can control the relative prices. Since most transactions–facilitating assets do not pay interest, the relative price of money and bonds is the 'interest rate'. In this sense the common view and the textbook view of the central bank coincide.

This coincidence depends on both of the assumptions discussed above: that there is a clean distinction between assets used in transactions and those used for savings and that the central bank can control the supply of money. Against this backdrop it is not surprising economists have worked for decades trying to confirm these assumptions.

The work on controlling the money supply highlights two further regularities. First, a central bank is the only entity that can create currency, so one part of the control problem is relatively simple. Second, a central bank can usually indirectly control banks' ability to create accounts and other close substitutes for currency.

Control over the transactions products offered by banks is needed because banks are required to hold 'reserves' (which can be thought of as vault cash) against these accounts. These reserves ensure that money will be available to people who want the money they have deposited.

Banks have long recognized that most people will not want access to all the money they have deposited so banks can make profits by lending some of the deposits they receive. The more that can safely be recycled and lent out, the greater the profits banks can make from collecting a given deposit. Thus, they have a strong incentive to lend out as much of their deposits as possible. Central banks gain leverage over the banks because they typically set the rules for how much of the deposits can be lent out and determine which assets can be used as reserves.

It is relatively straightforward to see how a central bank can manipulate the money supply. When a central bank wants more money in the economy it simply provides the banks with more currency that can be used as reserves (say by trading reserves for other bank securities). Banks then lever up the reserves through lending and crediting the bank accounts of borrowers who receive the funds. Thus, the willingness of banks to lend matters only to the extent to which this influences the creation of transaction-facilitating assets – that is, deposits.

The textbook model maintains that once the supply of transactions accounts has been adjusted following a central bank's reserve injection, interest rates respond in a predictable manner. When more transactions balances become available to households, the households' valuation of these balances falls and money becomes cheaper to hold than before; in other words interest rates fall. With falling interest rates certain investment options may become more attractive and if this happens the monetary injection can affect the actual spending throughout the rest of the economy.

New view of monetary transmission

The research reviewed in this article diverges from the conventional model by assuming that there are three important assets: money, bonds and bank loans. In essence, the research refines the standard story by emphasizing that when a central bank adds reserves both the increase in lending and the expansion of the transactions accounts are important.

The importance of bank loans is justified because some spending can only be financed through borrowing and this spending can only occur with bank lendings. The theory makes strong predictions about which type of spending is most dependent on bank lending. The most dependent is assumed to involve companies and individuals whose repayment abilities are most difficult to gauge. These borrowers tend to be smaller and engaged in more opaque activities. In other words, there is little reliable public information about the quality of the investments made by the borrowers.

In such circumstances lenders who are not already acquainted with the borrowers are reluctant to lend; even those people who might be willing to lend will need to monitor the activities of the borrower to make sure their funds are not misused. Banks have a particular advantage in lending to such borrowers because they can specialize in information gathering to determine creditworthiness. Moreover, by developing repeat business banks can remain informed about their customers. By careful monitoring of borrowers the banks can make prudent lending decisions that an unfamiliar lender could not make.

Unfortunately, because banks will tend to pile up lots of loans to these very special customers the banks themselves might find it difficult to raise money. Without huge compensation for risk, who will deposit their money in a bank that lends to these kinds of customers? Worse still, it is possible that banks paying the highest rate on deposits are doing so only because the loans they have made are especially risky.

Of course, checking up on the quality of the banks' customers directly is very costly, otherwise the borrowers presumably would have obtained their funding elsewhere. One way to overcome this problem is through deposit insurance. If banks can issue insured deposits then depositors need not worry about the lending decisions. So banks offering insured deposits will be able to raise money from depositors even if their lending is concentrated on these difficult-to-monitor customers.

The banks usually have to agree to several restrictions in order to be allowed to fund themselves with insured deposits. First, they normally have to allow the entity providing the deposit guarantee to oversee their lending decisions. The conventional view of the US Savings and Loan losses is that the regulators failed miserably in this respect. So it is certainly possible that there can be costs to running a deposit insurance system that outweigh the benefits of getting cheaper financing.

Second, banks offering insured deposits are usually required to put aside reserves against these deposits. For precisely the control reasons mentioned above, the banks are generally forced by the central banks to hold currency as the reserves. This link between deposits that are insured and those requiring reserves gives the monetary authorities a powerful lever. The reserves can be thought of as permits, issued by the central bank, that allow banks to raise funds without having to take actions to generate lots of information about the quality of their own assets.

In this setting a reduction in the supply of reserves has an additional impact beyond those emphasized in the textbook description. For the banks, it pushes them towards a more costly form of financing. Because of the extra premium banks will have to pay to bring in non-insured deposits, they will make fewer loans after the reserve outflow. For the borrowers who lose their loans, they may need to adjust their spending. If they cannot obtain new funds quickly their spending may fall.

Because these consequences can be anticipated, both banks and companies will take steps to hedge the risk. Banks will find it advantageous not to fully lend all their deposits. By holding some securities as a buffer-stock, a reserve outflow can be mitigated without changing lending. Similarly, companies will want to hold some liquid assets on their books. If a loan is withdrawn they can then use internal funds to finance their activities.

To sum up, this new theory of monetary policy suggests that one must move beyond traditional macro stories that emphasize households' relative preferences across 'money' and other less liquid assets. The theory instead asserts that the role of the commercial banking sector is central to the transmission of monetary policy.

More specifically, two key factors shape the way in which monetary policy works: the extent to which banks are reliant on reservable deposit financing and hence are led to adjust their loan supply schedules in the wake of changes in bank reserves; and the extent to which certain borrowers are 'bank dependent' and, therefore, cannot easily off-set these monetary policy induced shifts in bank loan supply.

Lending and monetary transmission

There has been an explosion of research designed to test the predictions of this bank-centric theory of monetary transmission. While most of the work at this point has been done using US data, there is no reason to think that the same factors do not operate (perhaps even more powerfully) in Europe and other developed countries.

The findings can be summarized by saying that smaller and more illiquid companies, as well as less well-known and illiquid banks, are especially sensitive to monetary policy. When a monetary authority tightens policy, aggregate lending by banks gradually slows down and there is a surge in non-bank financing (for example commercial paper). This change in the mix of financing is exactly as would be predicted if banks had reduced their lending and some companies were scurrying to find other sources of financing.

When this substitution of financing is taking place, aggregate investment is cut back (by more than would be predicted solely on the basis of rising interest rates). The additional decline in investment is consistent with the presumption that not all the borrowers who lost their loans were able to find alternative financing.

Cross-sectionally, small companies that do not have significant buffer-stock cash holdings are most likely to trim investment (particularly inventory investment) around the periods of tight money. Importantly, the differences in the investment rates are not pronounced during other episodes. This finding corroborates the prediction that by holding some liquid assets companies can smooth through normal fluctuations in credit availability. However, in periods where large reductions occur it appears that the self-insurance is incomplete.

The same type of pattern holds for banks. When monetary policy contracts, smaller banks seem more prone than large to reduce their lending. This is to be expected if one assumes that smaller banks will find it more difficult to secure uninsured financing.

Presumably, in anticipation of this problem, it is also true that small banks are much more likely than large to hold extra securities as a buffer-stock on their balance sheets. Nevertheless, even confining the analysis to small banks, the liquid banks are much less prone to reduce their lending following a tightening of monetary policy. Overall, the results suggest that monetary policy may have important real consequences but not because of the standard interest rate effects emphasized by textbook models.

Policy implications

This work has shown that a single simple story can explain a number of facts about the ways companies and banks respond to monetary policy. One unresolved and important issue is determining how much of the impact of monetary policy on the economy comes through this non-standard channel, as opposed to the usual interest rate channel. Although this final step is yet to be completed, existing findings already imply a number of things about how to conduct monetary policy. We close with a brief rundown of these policy implications.

One conclusion from this work is that standard indicators of monetary policy are likely to be incomplete. Conventional summary measures, such as the quantity of money or the level of short-term interest rates, will not capture the bank lending component of policy. Because the research shows that banks do use buffer-stocks to partially insulate their lending, we suspect that the potency of these lending effects may vary considerably.

A potential recent example was the so-called 1991–92 'credit crunch' in the US. While the Federal Reserve was trying to ease monetary conditions once the recession had become apparent, it is possible that its actions were initially ineffective since bank balance sheets were so impaired. This could explain why the recovery in the US was so slow in starting. Similar arguments can be made today about monetary policy in Japan.

Put differently, the textbook model, which ignores the financial conditions of the banks, has a hard time explaining why the monetary stimulus in these cases was so slow in taking hold. This research also suggests that banking regulation can have significant macroeconomic implications.

Consider the role of banks in a European Monetary Union. Banking regulations have officially been harmonized for several years in the European Union. Yet, the health of banks across EU countries varies considerably. Without intervention by the central governments in most of these countries, it also seems likely that these differences in bank profitability and capital levels will continue to persist for the next few years. If so, the response of banks in member countries to common monetary policy may prove to be quite different.

The flip side of the lending differences is distributional impact on companies and consumers in different countries. In countries with weaker banking systems, a bank credit crunch caused by a monetary tightening can be expected. Because the non-bank sources of financing also vary across the EU the spending responses to bank lending reductions will be likely to differ. Finally, there has been little discussion over the importance of opening and deepening capital markets in all regions that might be covered by monetary union. The research suggests that this is an area of considerable importance.

Similarly, the usual description of how monetary policy may be politicized focuses on differences in inflation tolerance across countries. This research suggests that countries' policy preferences may also depend on the strength of their banking systems. Ironically, some of the debate of the potency of the bank lending channel may be resolved if Emu goes ahead. Economists are rarely able to study controlled experiments. For gauging the importance of this mechanism one would like to find a situation where there is wide heterogeneity in bank health that is accompanied by a sudden shift in monetary conditions. If a European central bank is forced to quickly establish its credibility by raising interest rates this may be exactly the kind of experiment that is conducted.

Summary

This article deals with the role of commercial banks in the transmission of monetary policy. In traditional terms, say authors Anil Kashyap and Jeremy Stein, central banks pursue policy through acting on the supply of 'money' – defined as both cash and near-money such as deposit accounts – through the reserves required of commercial banks. In theory, this manipulation by a central bank will have an impact on interest rates – the difference between the price of money and the price of 'bonds'. However, the authors suggest that this may be an oversimplification and that a third element – bank loans – needs to be introduced. This is because when a central bank acts to influence the money supply, by, for example, increasing the reserves held by commercial banks, this is then leveraged into extra lending. The authors conclude that more research is required to ascertain how much of the impact of monetary policy is the result of this effect compared with the standard interest rate channel.

Unraveling the workings of monetary policy – a UK postscript

by Harold Rose

The article by Stein and Kashyap mirrors the operations and some possible effects of monetary policy in the US and other countries. However, two sets of modifications are required for any discussion of policy in the UK.

The first concerns the techniques used by the monetary authorities. In the US, as in France, Germany and Italy, banks (and in the US comparable depositary institutions) are subject to compulsory minimum reserve requirements in the form of non-interest-bearing balances with the central bank. In the UK this has not been the case since 1980, apart from an insignificant balance intended to meet some of the operating costs of the Bank of England.

This means that the discussion of policy operations in the US embraces the role of 'required' reserves and the possible behavior of bank 'excess' reserves, those held above the minimum, in a way that is not today relevant to operations of both the central bank and the banks themselves in the UK. In the US it is possible to talk of monetary policy as operating, via the bank reserve mechanism, on both short-term interest rates and the supply of bank credit. (In most countries bank capital ratios may also constrain lending on occasions.)

Central bank control over money market rates in all countries derives from the fact that, whether or not compulsory reserve ratios exist, banks need balances with the central bank to meet their clearing and currency obligations. In the UK Bank of England operations affect economic activity through interest rates alone; here these influence the demand for, rather than the supply of, bank loans.

The main reason is that it is clear that the Bank of England has always been prepared to supply whatever level of primary reserves is required to support the level of bank deposits that results from the pattern of interest rates, the level of economic activity and the public's asset-holding preferences. It is, of course, the Bank of England's ability to define the *terms* on which it is prepared to supply these reserves that gives it its power to determine short-term rates.

Even in countries with compulsory reserve requirements the situation is fundamentally the same in this respect; for failure to supply reserves – or, in some countries, to allow banks to obtain them through the foreign exchange market – would lead to intolerable fluctuations in short-term rates and possibly to bank collapse. But the enforcement of compulsory minimum reserve ratios does lead central banks to have an additional 'intermediate' target – for bank reserves – which, in turn, leads commercial banks to take this into account in framing their lending policies. This is not the case in the UK.

The second possible difference between conditions in the US and UK concerns the effects of monetary policy, its so-called 'transmission mechanism'. Stein and Kashyap (but not all US economists) emphasize the liquidity effect on (particularly small) firms, which may find it more difficult to obtain bank loans in a period of 'tight' monetary policy (as distinct from having to react to an increase in their price).

As it happens, until the 1970s, when UK bank lending could be constrained by the supply of required 'secondary' liquid assets, British monetary policy placed even more emphasis on credit supply effects. Indeed policy was always described officially as a 'credit' rather than a 'money' supply policy; and in the post-war period direct controls over bank lending were also in force from time to time. But over the years the rationale of policy has shifted to 'money' supply behavior, in which interest rates play a vital if not always predictable part, and finally more or less to interest rates alone as the most reliable determinant of economic activity and the level of inflation, at least in the short-run.

Business surveys have revealed little evidence of bank credit availability effects on the corporate sector in the UK, which is perhaps unsurprising in view of the increasing access even of relatively small firms to non-bank finance in domestic and euro markets.

It also needs to be said that monetary policy operates powerfully on the personal sector in the UK and perhaps more so than in the US. In Britain, where almost 70 per cent of households own their own homes, variable interest rate mortgages are overwhelmingly the rule, unlike the case in the US. Interest rate changes can thus have a powerful net effect on the finances of the household sector, even allowing for the opposite effect on savers, as well as on the wealth of both sets of households through the repercussions for house prices. In the US, where personal holdings of securities are relatively much larger, it is the wealth effect via the stock market that is more significant than in the UK. In addition, because foreign trade represents a much larger proportion of economic activity in the UK – exports of goods and services form 29 per cent of GDP at market prices in the UK but only 11 per cent in the US – the exchange rate effects of interest rate changes are also stronger than in the US.

Finally, when considering the possible differences in the transmission mechanism between countries, the question arises as to whether a unified monetary policy of a European Central Bank would have differential effects as between the member countries of the European Monetary Union. Their financial structures are still sufficiently diverse to make this a likelihood.

Summary

In this second article examining the links between the actions of monetary authorities and the spending decisions of individuals and businesses, Harold Rose highlights the particular factors that need to be taken into account when looking at the United Kingdom.

The first set of modifications result from differences in the *techniques* used by monetary authorities. In the UK, the Bank of England's operations affect economic activity largely via interest rates, with less emphasis on reserve requirements. Its operations work on the demand for bank loans rather than the supply. The second possible modification concerns the *effects* of monetary policy; its 'transmission mechanism'. In the UK, changes in interest rates are shown to have a more powerful effect on both the personal financial sector and the prevailing exchange rates.

Suggested further reading

Boris, C.E.V., (1997), 'The Implementation of Monetary Policy in Industrial Countries: A Survey', Board for International Settlements, July.

Dale, S. and Haldane, A., (1993), 'Bank behaviour and the monetary transmission mechanism', *Bank of England Quarterly Bulletin*, November.

Managing government finances

by Robert P. Inman

The economic prosperity of nations has long been linked with the size and capacities of government. Governments provide essential infrastructures, educate workers and set and enforce the rules for private market transactions. They can do these things well and economies can grow; or they can do them poorly and economies decline. The new empirical literature explaining economic growth is reaching a consensus: an educated and healthy labor force, well-maintained public and private capital stocks, and the protection of private property from external attack and domestic corruption are the three necessary components for sustained economic growth (Barro, 1996). Governments play an essential role in the provision of all three.

Not only do governments help define the size of a nation's economic pie, they also help to allocate it, both across people and across goods and services. The overall distribution of income can be significantly altered through government tax and transfer policies while the allocation of national income to defence, education, health care, environmental protection, basic research or promotion of the arts is largely determined by government.

National resources controlled by government exceed that of any single industry in any economy, and in many developed economies can be greater than all resources controlled by the private sector. The share of government in gross domestic product is never less than 10 per cent and is over 50 per cent in many of the industrialized nations of Europe. There are good reasons to expect – even in this age of 'privatization' – government to remain an important, if not dominant, player in the world's economies (*see* Rosen and Weinberg, 1997).

In this article I outline what is needed to manage well the finances of government. There are three requirements:

- the correct investment rule
- the correct accounting
- wise managers to implement the rule and the accounting.

Below I outline the rule and the accounting and then discuss what we know about setting the right incentives for the efficient allocation of the public budget.

Principles of public finance

What economic activities are good candidates for government investment? While markets determine the potential for good private-sector investments, market failures determine the best opportunities for public-sector investments.

The starting point of modern public finance theory is that government should do no harm. If the market economy is working well – satisfying consumer demands at the lowest cost – then there is no need for direct government investments. It is when markets fail to work well – when demands go unmet or costs are high – that we should consider government intervention.

Markets work well when self-interested consumers and companies internalize all the benefits and costs of their economic activities – that is, when an individual's demand curve measures all the benefits of the goods being purchased and a company's

Fig.1 Is the public budget efficient?

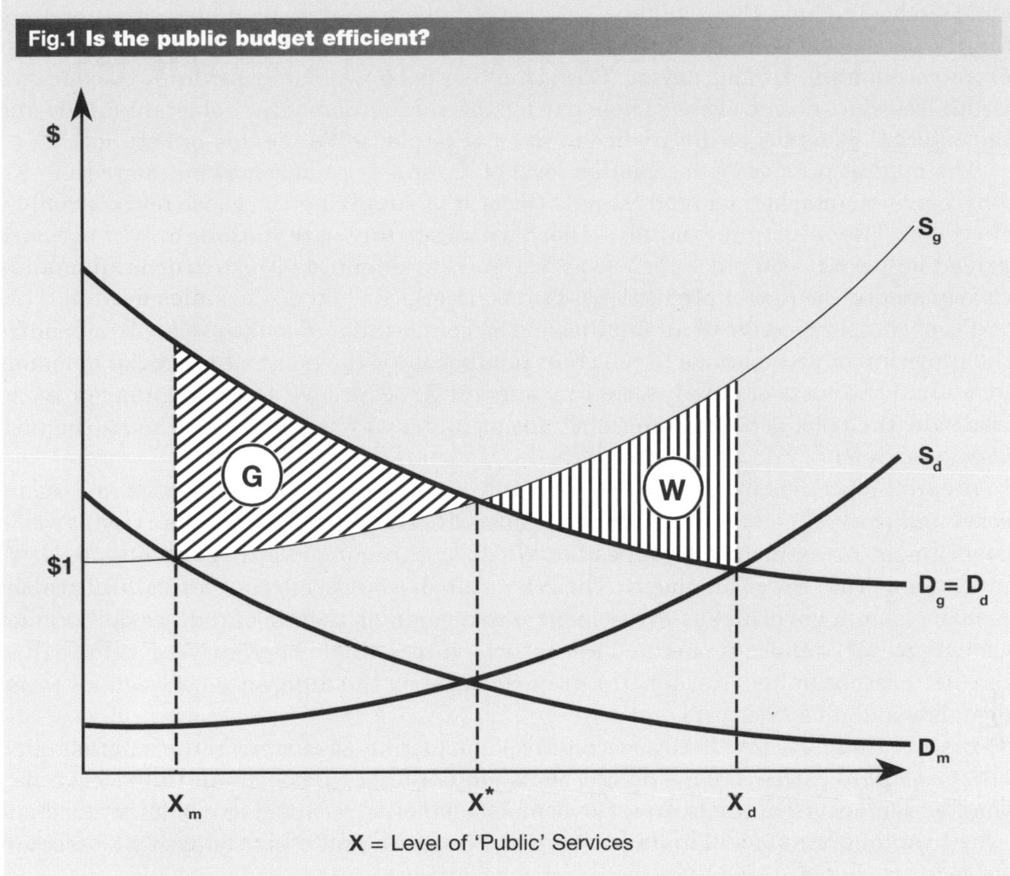

cost curve captures all the costs of goods being produced. When some benefits and costs are ignored by market participants, however, markets fail to provide an efficient allocation. In this case an extra-market institution will be needed to bring those additional costs and benefits – called 'externalities' – into play. Here is the potential role for government.

Figure 1 illustrates how markets fail and when governments might succeed. The curve represented by the downward sloping line Dm is the demand for good X, say children's vaccinations, that occurs in the marketplace. Dm represents what parents would pay in dollars (measured along the vertical axis) when different levels of vaccinations (measured along the horizontal axis) are sold in the market. In addition to the direct benefits that good X provides to the consuming families, there also may be important 'external' – benefits accruing to people outside the immediate family. As every nursery school parent knows, children benefit when their playmates are vaccinated. These extra benefits to other families from the consumption of good X are measured by the upward shift in aggregate demand from the private demands measured in Dm to a 'social' demand measured by Dg. This aggregate social demand includes private demands as well as the extra 'external' demands.

Markets, however, only respond to private demands. External demands, and thus total social demands, are likely to go unmet when markets alone provide the good or service. It is true that I might offer some money to a poor or reluctant family in my child's school to have their children vaccinated but why not wait and hope that another family in the school makes the same offer? If they do, I will get the benefits of that extra vaccination without paying. Such thinking is known as 'free-riding'. Of course, if we all free-ride, no one offers to help pay for the vaccination of the reluctant family and the external demands go unsatisfied in the marketplace. We see this in Figure 1.

The market provides a vaccination level of X_m at a price of somewhat more than $1, where private market demands equals the cost of supplying the good (represented by curve S_g). The reluctant families – those willing to buy vaccinations only if they are priced below $1 – do not buy. Yet at X_m, market demands plus external demands clearly exceed the cost of production – that is, $D_g > S_g$.

From the perspective of all families in the community, it makes sense to subsidize the provision of vaccinations to reluctant families until the point where social demands just equal the costs of supply – that is, to point X*. Since we all have an incentive to free-ride, the trick is to find the right subsidy and a way to pay for it. That is the task of government.

As public finance practitioners, we need to give content to social demand, social costs and that efficient point X* where the additional social benefits and costs from a government investment are just equal. We do so through a Net Present Value (NPV) investment rule for government. The NPV rule discounts current and all future net returns from a government investment into a common metric of today's dollars and then aggregates those discounted net returns into a single current-year value called the 'net present value'. Net returns are measured by the difference between all social demands and all social costs.

Discounting puts future returns on the same footing as current returns, presuming citizens would rather have a dollar, or its equivalent in government services, today than at some time in the future. Government benefits received or costs incurred one year from now can be evaluated in terms of benefits and costs today if we discount those future benefits and costs by the citizens' discount rate (r).

For example, if the citizens' discount rate is 10 per cent and the future benefits of government spending equals $1.10, then a citizen will consider benefits today of $1 just as good as $1.10 tomorrow. Most government investments incur costs and provide benefits for many years. It is necessary, therefore, to first convert all those future costs and benefits into present dollar values via discounting and then to add them up.

If benefits, costs and the discount rate are appropriately measured, then all projects where the NPV is equal to or greater than zero should be adopted. The last project adopted has an NPV just equal to 0, that is, where the discounted stream of social benefits just equals the discounted stream of social costs. This is point X* in Figure 1, where we gain the added net economic benefits of area G. Successful implementation of the NPV rule for government finance requires correct measurement. We have to get the accounting right. There is a set of basic guidelines which should be followed.

Measuring benefits

Measuring the benefits received by consumers from a good they have purchased in the marketplace is easy; it is the price they pay for the last unit purchased. Matters are a good deal more complicated for goods provided by government, however, for those goods are often not bought in the market. How should we evaluate the benefits of national defence, a new interstate highway, space exploration or the vaccination of a neighbour's child?

There are a few simple rules. First, when the government provides a small increase in the provision of a good bought in the marketplace (for example, library services), use the market price of the last unit purchased in the market. Second, when the government provides a large increase in a good provided in the marketplace (for example, police protection), approximate the benefits using the market-revealed demand curve. Third, when government provides a good not provided by the marketplace (for example, vaccination of other people's children), use the market price or demand curve of a substitute good (for example, your own children's vaccinations) but allow for the fact that the two goods are probably not perfect substitutes. Finally, when government provides a good not provided by the marketplace and with no obvious market substitutes (for example, protection from foreign invasion or clean air), then survey all potential beneficiaries to see what they would be willing to pay to have government provide the good.

Measuring costs

The provision of a good or service by government involves two costs: the direct production cost of the good and the efficiency cost of the taxes needed to pay for those production costs. There is a simple and general rule for measuring direct production costs: use the opportunity cost of the resources employed, where opportunity cost equals the value of the lost private-sector output because an input is used by the government.

If an input used by government is purchased in a market, then the market price provides a measure of this opportunity cost. If an input is conscripted from the private sector, market prices are still the relevant measure; only in this case use the price the conscripted input might have earned in its most likely private-sector activity.

The only time that market prices are not the appropriate measure of the cost of a government input is when the input is unemployed – for example, labor in rural developing economies. Even here, however, opportunity costs are relevant, measured now as the value of the leisure and home care services foregone when government hires the worker.

More difficult to measure, but just as important to good fiscal management, are the efficiency costs associated with the taxes needed to pay for government inputs. With few exceptions taxes distort private-sector behavior. When the government taxes my consumption of housing, I buy a smaller house. In addition to paying the direct burden of the tax – say $4,000 per year – I also pay an 'excess burden' through lost housing services as my study becomes the family room.

Excess burdens are particularly large – perhaps as high as $0.50 for each additional dollar of revenue raised – when tax rates are high and when consumers and companies change their economic behaviors in response to taxation. A consensus is growing that the most efficient tax from the point of view of a low excess burden is a broad-based, equal-rate consumption tax. A broad-based tax allows lower rates and a uniform rate across all commodities minimizes tax-induced reallocations of household spending. More important, savings and investment are not taxed.

In addition to the choice of taxes, government debt can also play a positive role in minimizing the excess burdens of taxation. When government spending spikes upward, say because of a war or a particularly large government project (for example, China's Three Gorges Dam), government taxes will have to spike upward too to pay for it. This means a potentially large increase in tax rates in the years of new spending. It is better to smooth this temporary increase in taxation over many years rather than pay in one

Construction work at China's Three Gorges Dam: borrowing helps prevent the tax spikes that such large projects would otherwise require

large, but potentially crippling, payment. Government borrowing is one way to achieve tax smoothing. What the country pays in future interest payments is more than compensated for by the economic damage that is prevented by avoiding the large, one-time increase in taxation.

In summary, the costs of government activities should include both the production costs of inputs and the efficiency costs, or excess burdens, of the taxation required to buy those inputs. In Figure 1 the economic cost of government activity, shown as curve S_g, includes both costs; it rises as X rises because of the increasing excess burdens of government taxation. The excess burdens of taxation can be minimized through the wise selection of tax and debt policies.

Selecting the discount rate

Perhaps no aspect of government finance is less understood or more widely abused than the selection of the appropriate discount rate for government investments. Discount rates used by US government agencies for similarly financed projects range from 0 per cent (no discounting) to 12 per cent. Like accounting for benefits and costs, the principle is clear; the devil is in the details.

The appropriate discount rate is that rate, r, at which the project's beneficiaries (for benefits) or taxpayers (for costs) equate the economic value of \$1 today to \$(1+r) next year. If a beneficiary or taxpayer sees \$1.10 next year as just as valuable as \$1 today, then r=0.10. As defined here, this discount rate can clearly vary both over time and from group to group. Logically, there is no reason why governments should not use the different rates – if only we knew them.

How might we actually measure r? If beneficiaries and taxpayers are participating in the capital market, either as savers or as borrowers, then using the interest rates at which they are willing to invest or borrow money is appropriate. This approach works, but only if all citizens affected by the government's project are participating in the capital markets, if the maturities of their investments and loans match the horizon of the public project and if the benefits of public projects can be converted into income and thus future private-sector investments (if that is what beneficiaries want).

If these assumptions are not met, then adjustments to the households' market rates are necessary. In each case, the appropriate adjustment will be to increase the discount rate above a typical household's market rate of interest. A rule of thumb might be to use the pre-tax rate of return on the marginal private-sector investment in developed economies and the rate available for investment in international capital markets for developing economies.

Preference for the poor?

One of the central tasks of government investment is to ensure all citizens have access to primary education, healthcare, clean water, personal safety and essential infrastructures. The benefits of such investments, particularly in developing economies, accrue primarily to low-income families. An important question – one debated extensively by academics and practitioners alike – is whether the benefits to poor families ought to receive an extra weight when doing the NPV analysis. There are compelling arguments to think they should.

Receiving \$100 in benefits surely means more to a family making \$1,000 per year than to one making \$100,000 per year. Societies act on this fact every time they choose to redistribute income from rich to poor households. The issue is not whether extra weights should be given to the benefits received by the poor – most societies already do so – but specifying what those weights should be. In setting these weights, the public finance analyst has no special expertise, but we can help clarify the discussion and focus the debate.

When doing the NPV analysis, separate NPV calculations can be made for each project using alternative weightings. Calculating the NPV using the unweighted stream of benefits provides an estimate of the aggregate economic potential of a project. Choosing projects by this criterion will maximize the size of the economic pie, though perhaps the biggest slice of that pie goes to rich landowners. If so, we could tax those landowners, give the proceeds to the poor, and so have the best of both worlds: a fast-growing economy and an appropriate distribution of income.

Unfortunately, it may not always be possible to tax the rich and redistribute to the poor, or when we do, the taxes on the rich have very large efficiency costs (excess burdens) of their own. In cases where tax and transfers are not possible or economically inefficient, the NPV rule for project investments should use a weighted stream of benefits.

Projects that have large NPVs for all plausible weightings should clearly be adopted. Those whose rankings depend on the exact weightings chosen – for example, an inefficient project that only helps the poor – should be singled out for more detailed discussion. They should only be adopted if it is agreed that the extra weights are compelling and no other feasible policy (including direct transfers) is available to help the favored group. Simply put, the poor can and should be favored, but only in the most efficient manner possible.

Implementing the NPV rule

In a paper for the World Bank's 1990 Annual Conference on Development Economics, Professor I.M.D. Little and Nobel Laureate James Mirrlees (1991) evaluated the success of the NPV investment rule for selecting government projects in developed and developing economies. They show that the rule has not had a great impact on the quality of government decision-making; economically inefficient, low-return projects are still adopted with regularity. The problem, they conclude, is not the rule but its implementation.

It is easy to understand why implementation might be a problem. The NPV rule leaves much room for discretion. Though there are sound economic principles for measuring benefits, costs and the discount rate, judgment calls are inevitable. Benefit weights for services received by low-income households is also a free card. It is not hard to make a marginally rejected project (NPV<0) a marginally acceptable project (NPV>0) with a small adjustment in the accounting. The NPV rule alone is not enough for sound fiscal management.

Unfortunately, democratic governments face a fundamental problem when it comes to selecting efficient policies. In his Nobel Prize research on democracy and the economy, Kenneth Arrow (1966) proves that any policy chosen by a majority – even an efficient policy – can be undone by a side-deal between a portion of the majority and the excluded minority.

The new policy can even be inefficient – less resources for everyone – as long as members of the new majority do better under the new policy than under the old. In democracies, the majority-rule outcome 'cycles' from one policy to another. We call this gridlock. Of course, legislatures do overcome gridlock and select projects for public investment. They create political parties with outside resources to hold members in the coalition. They give power to leaders – presidents and prime ministers – to set agendas and to veto policies. And they agree not to disagree through 'norms of deference'.

Each of these institutional strategies, however, creates incentives to abuse the NPV rule. To break gridlock, power over project choice must be allocated to someone to make the final choice. What is best for the decision-makers, however, is frequently to select those projects that concentrate benefits on their constituents and that allocate the costs to others. The incentive then is to overspend, choosing point Xd in Figure 1 where the decision-makers' marginal benefits (D_d) equal their marginal costs (S_d).

The incentive problem for decision-makers in a democracy is analogous to the problem faced by friends agreeing to share the bill for lunch. Since everyone shares the costs of lunch, the effective price to each of buying the expensive entree and dessert is only a fraction of the true costs. We all eat too much. The size of this economic waste is the difference between the true economic costs and the true economic benefits of the overspending (area W in Figure 1).

The trick to controlling overspending is to align the incentives of our elected officials with the true social benefits and costs of government activities. As Nobel Laureate Ronald Coase (1960) points out in his research on social costs, when there are economic inefficiencies, even in governments, there are also strong incentives to search for alternative institutions to remove those inefficiencies.

Governmental institutions that might improve upon the inefficiencies of crude majority-rule politics include strong political parties or presidents with the ability to negotiate with the legislature for a cut in excessive government spending in return for sharing the tax savings that those cutbacks yield.

Competition between government and private providers or between governments themselves might also work to control inefficiencies. Here is the case for privatization or decentralized federal fiscal systems. Economists and political scientists are finding that political and economic competition joined with strong executive or party powers does make a significant difference in fiscal performance. Government spending is less, government taxes are less and government borrowing is less. Further, more efficient government means higher economic growth. Robert Barro estimates that reducing the share of government spending and associated taxation (other than for education and defence) in GDP by five percentage points – say, from 40 to 35 per cent – will increase the rate of growth of the economy by about 0.5 per cent per year.

My own research with Michael Fitts (1990) on US budgeting suggests such a reduction in the size of government is quite possible when strong presidents or strong political parties control the legislature. Alberto Alesina (1997) reaches the same conclusion in a cross-national comparison of economic growth and political institutions: strong, stable and honest political institutions foster growth.

If shrinking government by a small amount is good, then is shrinking government by a lot even better? Not necessarily. When the gaps in the economy left by market failures are large, even inefficient governments have a role to play. Though government financing is inefficient, it still may be better than the alternative of no government at all. (In Figure 1, the gains from government (G) exceed the waste (W).) In any case, good financial management should seek to establish a system of incentives that minimizes government's inefficiencies. This is most likely to occur when our elected officials are held accountable through political and economic competition for the social costs their decisions impose upon the economy.

Conclusion

When markets fail to satisfy all demands for valued services, governments through their collective powers to tax and spend can fill the gap. While the principles of sound public finance provide the guidelines needed to efficiently set the public budget, the incentives in most democratic governments is to ignore or misuse the guidelines and to overspend.

More than clear thinking is needed for efficient government. Effective leadership with the political ability to say no to special interests, even within one's own party, is required. The incentive to say no comes from the threat of a more efficient competitor, be it another political party, government or a private company. Just as participants in competitive markets gain from good government, so too can the citizens of government benefit from a healthy dose of competition.

Summary

This article deals with the question of the provision of government-financed services. Modern public finance theory starts from the basis that when markets are functioning efficiently – satisfying consumer demands at the lowest cost – there is no need for government intervention.

The role of government is to intervene when private markets are inefficient, especially when additional costs and benefits – 'externalities' – are ignored by the market. Such externalities might include, for example, the costs and benefits of vaccinating schoolchildren against disease. Robert Inman outlines a simple but effective model for determining cases that are suitable for intervention and also argues through some of the more 'moral' issues involved – for example, should government policy favor the poor?

Suggested further reading

Alesina, A., (1997), 'The political economy of high and low growth', paper completed for the 1997 World Bank annual conference on development economics, May.

Arrow, K., (1996) 'Social choice and individual values', John Wiley and Sons, New York.

Barro, R., (1996), 'Democracy and growth', *Journal of Economic Growth,* March, pp. 1–27.

Coase, R. (1960), 'The problem of social cost', *Journal of Law and Economics*, Fall, 1–44.

Dreze, J. and Stern N., (1987), 'The theory of benefit-cost analysis' in Auerbach, A., and Feldstein, M. (eds), *Handbook of public economics*, Amsterdam, North-Holland.

Inman, R. and Fitts, M. (1990), 'Political institutions and fiscal policy: evidence from the US historical record', *Journal of Law Economics and Organization*, December, 79–132.

Little, I.M.D. and Mirrlees, K., (1991), 'Project appraisal and planning twenty years on' in Fischer, S. and Pleskovic, B. (eds), *Procedings of the World Bank annual conference on development economics*, Washington, DC., World Bank.

Rosen, H., (1995), *Public finance*, New York, Irwin.

Rosen, S. and Weinberg, B., (1997), 'Incentives, efficiency and government provision of public services', paper completed for the 1997 World Bank annual conference on development economics, May.

Squire, L., 'Project evaluation in theory and practice' in Chenery, H., and Srnivasan, T.N. (eds). *Handbook of development economics*, Amsterdam, North-Holland.

Viscuysi, Kip, (1993), 'The value of risks to life and health', *Journal of Economic Literature*, December 1912–1946.

Glossary

A

Administrators
Accountants appointed to run insolvent companies.

Agency costs
Potential costs in the role of an agent. An agent works on behalf of someone else, the 'principal'. Managers are agents for shareholders, stockbrokers are agents for their clients, and so forth. These agency relationships can be fraught if the agent puts his interests in front of the principal, as often happens, particularly if the principal's interests are not carefully defined.

Alpha
1. As in Alpha stock, the most traded shares on the UK stock market.
2. As in Alpha factor, the difference between the expected risk-adjusted yield of a portfolio and the return actually achieved.

Alternative Investment Market (AIM)
The London Stock Exchange's market for young, small and growing companies. Companies admitted to AIM must comply with the stringent rules of the Stock Exchange, but investors should take into account that these securities are higher-risk and less liquid than companies on the main exchange.

Amortization
The amount deducted each year from the book value of an intangible or paper asset. Similar to depreciation, except that the latter applies to tangible fixed assets.

Arbitrage
1. Technically, the process whereby someone exploits differences in prices between two similar instruments or markets to make a virtually riskless profit.
2. Used imprecisely to indicate any activity where a gain can be made through superior market knowledge or by bridging the gap between one person's perspective and another's.
3. Arbitrage can also be a verb, used either technically or loosely, meaning to act as a middle-man or go-between.

Arbitrage Pricing Theory (APT)
Conforms to the assumption at the basis of the Capital Asset Pricing Model which states that investors are rewarded for systematic risk, i.e. market risk which cannot be diversified away. Unlike CAPM, however, which gauges risk solely by the sensitivity of a security's return to movements in a broad equity market index, APT identifies sources of systematic risk as sensitivity to particular economic factors, for example, inflation.

Ask
The price at which a security is offered for sale. In the UK, it is referred to as the offer price, the opposite of the bid price.

Asset-backed securities
Debt securities which have value because of the physical or financial assets, the income from which is dedicated to their repayment. Often these underlying assets are placed in a special purpose vehicle or trust for this purpose.

Asymmetric information
Refers to any situation in which the different parties, e.g. buyers and sellers have unequal information as to value.

Auction
There are two main types of security market auctions:
1. Discriminative price, sealed-bid auction. Bidders place multiple price and quantity bids and winners pay what they bid.
2. Uniform price, sealed bid auction. Winners pay only the lowest bid price to clear the auction.

Auto-correlation
The idea that the size and direction of today's price changes are not independent of yesterday's price changes. This idea underlies technical analysis of price patterns. By contrast, much market theory assumes the opposite – that today's price changes are independent of what happened yesterday. Many market participants are happy to believe

both at once. Thus, they simultaneously use both charts and valuation models dependent on random price change models.

Backwardation
When a product's price for immediate or imminent delivery is higher than for later delivery.

Bank capital requirements
The capital, mainly equity capital, estimated by banks or regulators is necessary to cover unexpected losses.

Basis risk
The possibility that price changes in two related but not identical markets or instruments may differ.

Beta
The degree of sensitivity of the return on any asset to that on the equity market. It is a measured systematic risk.

Bid
A motion to buy a security, such as an option or futures contract, at a specified price.

Bid-ask spread
The difference between the offer price and the bid price which is the dealers' spread.

Black-Scholes model
The standard option pricing model, in which the main determinants of the price of an option, given the exercise price, are the time to exercise, the interest rate and the expected volatility of the price of the underlying asset.

Block trading
Trading involving large transactions in which at least 10,000 shares of stock are bought or sold.

Bonds
A debt security.

Bond ratings
Bonds are rated by many different rating agencies including Standard & Poors, Moody's Investor Services, Duff & Phelps, Fitch Investor's Service and IBCA. Although rating agencies act on behalf of investors, they are paid by borrowers. There is, therefore, a potential conflict of interest. Most ratings are 'solicited'. That is to say the borrower approaches the rating agency expecting that an explicit rating will improve that borrower's access to the financial markets. Some ratings are 'unsolicited'. That is to say that the ratings agency assigns a rating to a borrower's debt, where the agency sees investor need for such a rating, without having the detailed discussions with financial management which would be part of a typical solicited rating process.

Book-to-market value
Book value is the value of an asset as recorded in a company's books. This often differs from market value and the ratio of one to the other may be significant.

Call
The right of an issuer to redeem a bond before its specified maturity date.

Call option
Right to buy a share or other asset at a fixed price at some time in the future.

Capital Asset Pricing Model (CAPM)
Theoretical framework comparing risk and return on shares. The expected rate of return on a share is said to have two components: first, the required return from a risk free asset; second, the beta risk associated with the investment. The expected return on a specific asset equals the risk free return plus a risk premium depending on its beta.

Capital structure
The relative proportions of a company's funding provided by short-term debt, long-term debt and owners' equity. It is the composition of corporation's securities used to finance its investment activities. Also known as financial structure.

Capitalization
The market value of a company traded on the stock exchange, that is, the share/stock price multiplied by the number of shares/stocks in issue.

Chapter 11
US arrangements allowing a financial

reconstruction to be put together when a firm cannot meet its debt obligations. Similar to the UK practice of administration, which is not quite as satisfactory and is not used as much.

Chinese Walls
Inter-departmental security procedures and barriers to prevent one part of a financial institution from knowing privileged information held by another department.

Clearing house
Company which registers, monitors, matches, settles and often guarantees trades on a futures or options exchange.

Closed end fund
A fund holding securities financed by a given capital.

Collaterized Mortgage Obligation (CMOs)
Securities backed by a pool of mortgages owned by the issuer and guaranteed by a federal agency such as the Federal National Mortgage Association. See also **Asset backed securities.**

Commercial paper
Normally tradeable short-term instrument issued by a company.

Commodity futures
Contracts to buy or sell commodities on a futures exchange at some future date at a price now specified.

Control premium
The excess over market price that is paid by a bidder in order to acquire control of a company.

Convertibles
Bonds or preference shares that can be exchanged for equities on predetermined terms. They pay a fixed rate of interest and normally have a fixed maturity date.

Corporate governance
The rules and procedures to ensure that a company is properly run, that the right directors are in place with their rules defined, and that directors behave appropriately and in accordance with both the law and best practice. How companies are governed varies widely from country to country and even within countries, and there is no simple, universal model that can be followed.

Costs of bankruptcy
The potential loss of value due to the possibility of insolvency, arising from the legal costs etc. associated with insolvency, the possible diversion of management time and other problems as a firm approaches insolvency.

Counterparty
A party to an agreement or contract.

Counterparty risk
The probability of a counterparty failing to make payment when the obligation is due. A significant consideration in over-the-counter transactions. See also **OTC markets**.

Country risk
The risk of investing in unstable countries or those that may default on obligations to shareholders, bond holders or joint venture partners. Agencies rate individual countries on their perceived political risk.

Currency risk
The risk of an investment's value changing because of currency exchange rates. Also referred to as exchange rate risk.

Currency swap
A swap which commits two counterparties to exchange interest payments denominated in different currencies and, at the end of the agreed period, the principal amounts. The final exchange is at an exchange rate set at the outset of the swap at or close to the spot rate, not at the forward rate for the final maturity date. This is so because the interest differential between the two currencies is paid over the life of the swap.

Dealer
1. A person or firm which acts as a principal in buying and selling securities and derivatives, commodities or foreign exchange in contrast to a broker who acts as an agent for others.
2. A financial institution dealing in or placing a borrower's debt under a debt issuance program, particularly used in relation to Eurocommercial paper programs.

Delta hedging
The number of shares/stocks required to hedge

against the price risk of holding an option. In general terms, it is the number of units of an asset required to hedge a single unit of liability. Also known as option's delta.

Derivatives
Securities whose value depends on the value of an underlying asset. The principal forms of derivatives are futures, options, forward contracts and swaps.

Disclosure requirements
What must by law be revealed to shareholders or other interested parties (such as trade unions) by companies.

Discount
1. In a management or marketing context, reduction given from list price.
The word also has a number of narrowly financial meanings:
2. The amount by which an invoice or bill of exchange is valued below its face value, or the action of buying or selling such a claim at a discount.
3. The amount by which the future value of a currency is less than its current, spot, value.
4. The amount by which a share is valued below its issue price.
5. The amount by which an option is valued below its intrinsic value.

Discounted cash flow
The present value of a future cash flow. Calculation used in valuation and investment appraisal which involves listing all the cashflows from a particular business or investment, applies a discount rate to each of them to arrive at their effective value today (on the grounds that £100 cash this year is worth more than £100 cash next year), and then adds them up to provide a total present value.

Discounted value
The value of investment obtained after applying a suitable discount rate.

Disintermediation
Having fewer 'middle men'. Originated and most often used in banking, disintermediation occurs, for example, when firms raise finance in securities markets rather than via banks, which in turn borrow from depositors.

Diversifiable risk
Firm-specific; a risk that specifically affects a single asset or a small group of assets. Also known as unique or unsystematic risk.

Diversification
Reducing risk by holding a range of different securities.

Dividend growth model
A model wherein dividends are assumed to be at a constant rate in perpetuity.

Dividend yield
Gross (pre-tax) dividend per share/stock divided by the market price of the share/stock.

Earnings yield
After tax earnings which is expressed as a percentage of the share price.

Economic value added (EVA)
Method of cost and profit analysis that can be used to calculate the Return on Net Assets (RONA) of any product line, by imputing a capital cost to it. EVA is calculated as the normal operating profit on a product minus the imputed cost or capital. In other words, it is the price minus all operating costs and raw materials minus the cost of capital.

Efficient markets hypothesis (EMH)
Theory developed by Fama and others, which states that the process in financial markets reflect all publicly available information. One of the consequences is that, provided the conditions of an efficient market are met, individual investors will not achieve risk-adjusted returns above the market average in the long run.

Equity
Also known as 'capital and reserves', 'shareholders' equity' and 'shareholders' funds'. Funding by shareholders in the form of shares (in contrast to funding by bankers in the form of debt), in return for which shareholders are entitled to part of the company's assets: the latter is the technical meaning of equity.

Eurobonds
Bonds issued in a currency that is different from

the currency of the market in which the bond is issued.

European Monetary Union (EMU)
Under the Maastricht Treaty members of the European Union are planning to lock their exchange rates in 1999 and introduce a single European currency by 2002, subject to certain criteria as to member qualification.

Event risk
The risk of an investor suffering a loss due to unforeseen events such as a merger, or takeover. This risk is distinct from credit risk, market risk or political risk.

Excess return
The excess of return over the relevant risk-free rate.

Externality
A negative or positive by-product that is not paid for by an individual, a firm, or society. For example, if a firm sets up alongside a restaurant and the restaurant's lunch trade increases, that is an externality for the restaurant. Similarly manufacturers' pollution is a negative externality for society.

F

Federal Deposit Insurance Corporation (FDIC)
A US federal agency which manages the bank insurance fund and the savings association insurance fund which guarantees to depositors, in banks and in savings and loans associations respectively, up to US$100,000 per account.

Financial Accounting Standards Board (FASB)
US institution whose seven board members set accounting rules for certified public accountants which are the basis for what are known in the US as 'Generally Accepted Accounting Principles' (GAAP).

'First-dollar loss' cover
A provision in securitization by which the issuer undertakes to meet some first tranche of any future loss.

Fisher effect
Named after Fisher (1896) who provided a systematic analysis of the effect of expected inflation on interest rates. Increase in the former should generally result in higher nominal rates of interest.

Float
1. The amount of an issue in the hands of traders or other ready sellers.
2. The balance of cash in the hands of a bank which occurs in the course of making and receiving payments for customers.

Floating charge
1. Correctly, a charge that 'floats' above named assets and that can descend on them (that is, the lender can gain access to the assets) only when a predefined event occurs, such as receivership.
2. In the UK, it is used to mean a charge over all the assets of a firm, rather than over any specific asset.

Floating rate
Same as variable rate; varies according to current benchmark rate.

Forward contract
A forward contract obliges the forward buyer to purchase a specified financial instrument or commodity at a specified price on a specified future date, the settlement date. The seller of a forward contract is also obliged to deliver a specified financial instrument or commodity in settlement of his obligation. Generally no payments are made under a forward contract until the settlement date.

Forward exchange rate/spot exchange rate
An exchange rate that is fixed today for exchanging currency at a future date.

Forward Rate Agreement (FRA)
An agreement to borrow or lend at a future date at an interest rate fixed today.

Free cash flow
Cash in excess of that required to fund all of a company's profitable projects – those with a positive net present value of cash flow calculated at the relevant cost of capital.

Free-rider problem
The problem, arising in many situations, that no individual is willing to contribute towards the cost

of something when he hopes that someone else will bear the cost instead. It normally arises in the case of public goods meant for the community at large.

Front running
When a trader deals for his own account in advance of known customer orders to take advantage of privileged information about the order flow. Usually considered illegal.

Futures
Futures are contracts to buy or sell a fixed quantity of an asset – goods or securities – at a fixed price and a fixed date, regardless of any intervening change in price or circumstances. Futures fall into two main groups – financial and commodities – and cover foreign currencies and interest rates as well as stock indices, potatoes or even orange juice. A future has three important advantages over a forward contract. First, being exchange-traded, the price is readily ascertainable. Second, futures are a robust mechanism for controlling and reducing credit risk. Third, futures are, for the most part, very liquid, traded instruments, so that the owner of a future can always sell it. They are guaranteed by the futures exchange.

Gearing
Gearing or net debt, measures a company's debt as a proportion of its total assets. Calculated by dividing the net borrowings of the company by its shareholders' funds, including minority interests and preference share capital. Use of debt to increase return for equity shareholders (although at added risk). The equivalent American term is 'Leverage'.

Generally Accepted Accounting Principles (GAAP)
A common set of accounting concepts, standards and procedures by which financial statements are prepared. See also **Financial Accounting Standards Board (FASB)**.

Gilts
Bonds issued by the UK government.

Glass Steagall Act
US Act of 1933 which separated the functions of banks and securities firms.

Green shoe
An option granted to the lead underwriter by an issuer allowing the underwriter to purchase more shares to cover the short position created by over-allotting the offering. This was first done in an issue for the Green Shoe Manufacturing Company.

Herding
A phenomenon where people follow the crowd instead of purely using their own information. Observed in stock markets when an informed agent discards his own information and instead makes an investment decision based on the observed decisions of other traders.

Index fund
An investment fund that invests in all stocks in a stock market index and whose performance will therefore approximate that of the index.

Initial public offering (IPO)
The first offering to the general public of a company's equity on the stock market.

Insolvency
Another word for bankruptcy; when a person or firm cannot meet its liabilities.

Institutional investors
Financial investment firms that take money from the public and manage it by investing in shares, bonds, or other assets. This includes mutual funds, insurance companies, pension funds, unit trusts, investment trusts, and venture capitalists.

Insurance principle
Based on the law of averages. It simply states that the average outcome of several independent trials of an experiment would approach the expected value of the experiment.

Interest rate risk
The change in capital values of the investment introduces a serious risk into what may be a safe investment.

Intermediation
A process of investing through a financial institution.

Internal rate of return (IRR)
A discount rate at which the net present value of an investment is zero. Used for capital expenditure proposals.

Jensen's Alpha
A measure that uses the Capital Asset Pricing Model to determine whether a money manager has outperformed a market index or not.

Jobbers
Dealers on the London Stock Exchange before the 1986 reforms.

Junk bond
A speculative grade bond, i.e. below the investment grade. Usually carrying a high coupon, hence also known as high-yield bond.

Legal, jurisdiction, litigation and documentation risk
Also known as legal and regulatory risk, it is one of the greatest obstacles to the effective functioning of the market for risk management instruments. The solution is to clarify the legal and regulatory frameworks of the parties to risk management agreements so they need not fear endangerment of the financial structure.

Lemons problem
First pointed out by Akerlof in 1970. Refers to the inability of one trader to assess the quality of the other making it likely that poor-quality traders would dominate. Also referred to as adverse selection. An example is the second-hand car market, where sellers know whether or not the car is a lemon, i.e. performs badly, but the buyers cannot make that judgement without running the car. In such a situation, all the cars of the same type will sell at the same price, regardless of whether they are lemons or not. The risk of purchasing a lemon will lower the price buyers are prepared to pay for the car and as the second-hand prices are low, people with good cars would be less inclined to put them in the market.

Leverage
See **Gearing**.

Leveraged buy-out
Relates to the acquisitions involving a major part of the purchase price financed through debt and the balance equity privately held by a small group of investors.

Limit order
Order to buy or sell at, or better than, a particular price.

Liquid assets
Those assets which can be cheaply and easily converted into cash, like cash itself and short-term securities.

Local
A dealer who trades for his own account on a derivatives exchange.

Margin calls
A demand by a futures exchange or by an individual broker for clients to increase their margin payments in response to a change in the value or their positions.

Mark-to-market
When an investment or a liability is revalued to the current market price.

Market capitalization
Price per share of a stock multiplied by the total number of shares outstanding.

Market portfolio
In concept, a value weighted index of all securities. In practice, it is an index like the FTSE 100 or S&P 500 that proxies the return of the entire value of the stock market through the returns on the stocks composing the index.

Market risk
Also known as non-diversifiable risk, price risk and position risk. Risk in holding shares that is not specific to the particular company or

companies' share price performance, but that is sensitive to fluctuations in the stock market as a whole.

Market value
1. Generally a synonym for market capitalization, that is, the value of 100% of a firm's shares on the stock market.
2. The break-up value of a firm, often thought to be higher than its current market capitalization.
3. The liquidation value of a firm, that is, what you would be left with for the shareholders after selling all assets and paying off all liabilities.
Market value is most often used in the first sense.

Mean-reversion
The tendency of a random variable to incline towards its average. It has been found that the stock prices in the long run approach to their intrinsic value, referred to as the mean-reverting behavior. Corresponds to negative serial correlation.

Momentum effect
Relates to positive serial correlation, e.g. positive stock returns would be followed by positive returns.

Money market
Wholesale market for funds and marketable securities, dominated by banks, large corporations' liquid funds, and those of rich individuals.

Moral hazard
The risk emerging from a contract provoking perverse change in behaviour of one or both the parties to the contract, e.g. an insured firm may take fewer fire precautions.

Mutual funds
A firm pooling and managing funds of investors. Known as unit trusts in the UK.

N

Net asset value (NAV)
The company's shareholders' funds divided by the number of shares/stocks in issue.

Net present value (NPV)
The discounted sum of all future cash flows from an investment, minus all out-flows.

Non-diversifiable risk
Market risk that cannot be diversified away by investors holding a portfolio of assets.

Off-balance sheet financing
Using financial engineering to avoid having to put assets on the balance sheet; any form of finance that does not require a liability to appear on a firm's balance sheet.

Open outcry
Trading method on the floor of an exchange in which buyers and sellers call out their bids and offers face to face, often using hand signals because of the noise.

Operating cash flow
Cash brought in to a company during a particular accounting period as a result of a company's activities, not including cash-flows of a non-operational nature (e.g. payments of interest or dividends). Earnings before interest and depreciation minus taxes. It measures the cash generated from operations, not counting capital spending or working capital requirements.

Operational risk
Risk related to the sequence of events and decisions that create the firm's cash inflows and outflows. These activities may include manufacturing and selling a product, buying and paying for raw materials, and collecting cash.

Opportunity cost
The cost of not doing something else (generally, a non-quantifiable alternative); time and effort which could achieve higher returns devoted to another task.

Options
An option gives the right, but not the obligation, to buy or sell something at a given price and time. There are two types – traditional and traded. A call option gives the right to buy something at a fixed price. A put option gives the right to sell something at a fixed price.

Option pricing theory
Relates to the valuation of options or various other contingent contracts whose value depends on the

underlying securities or assets. See also **Options** and **Black-Scholes model**.

OTC markets (Over-the-counter)
Lightly regulated trading separate from established exchanges. Contracts so traded can be tailored to a counterparty's needs.

Pass-through security
Certificate representing an ownership interest in a pool of mortgages.

P/E ratio
Price/Earnings ratio; share price divided by the earnings per share. Stock market analysts' basic tool for comparison of shares by measuring a company's earnings against its price. A high P/E means that a company is rated more highly, relative to its earnings, than a low P/E company.

Private placement
Issue of securities that is offered to one or more large or sophisticated investors as opposed to being publicly offered. Private placements by virtue of their large denomination and private nature are generally exempt from those securities laws intended to protect retail investors.

Put, Put option
The right, but not an obligation, to sell shares or other financial instruments at a fixed price at some future time, thus giving protection against a fall in the value of the instruments.

Random-walk
The contention that in efficient markets, successive price changes are random. This implies that shares move regardless of historic patterns, and therefore that chartism is nonsense.

Rating
1. Independent assessment of the quality of a company's debt.
2. Credit rating.

R-squared statistic
It measures the explanatory power of a linear statistical model. Technically, defined as the square of the correlation coefficient; it gives the proportion of the variability explained by the linear model.

Real rate of return
Approximately, the nominal rate of return, less the rate of inflation.

Receiver
Someone who takes charge of a liquidation (the process of winding up a company).

Reserve
Accounting term meaning an account giving shareholders a claim over some assets of a firm. Examples of reserves are 'retained profit' and 'revaluation reserve'.

Retained earnings
Profit after tax in any year which is retained by the business rather than distributed amongst shareholders as dividends.

Return
Increases and decreases in returns are governed by two factors or laws:
1. variations in the proportions in which the factors of production are combined;
2. a change in the scale of production.

Return on capital
Operating profit divided by some measure of capital employed.

Rights issue
An issue of shares to existing shareholders in proportion to their holdings in exchange for payment (and therefore unlike a scrip issue of free shares).

Risk
In investment, risk is referred to as the uncertainity of return from any asset.

Risk-free asset
An asset providing a certain return over some holding period.

Savings and Loan Association (S&L)
US institution which takes local deposits and

lends primarily for residential mortgages. S&Ls now operate under a tight regulatory environment created by the Financial Institutions Reform, Recovery and Enforcement Act (FIRREA) of 1989.

Seasoned issue
A security which, under US Securities and Exchange Commission rules, is non-exempt, but may be sold to US residents, because it has been outstanding for a period of time.

Self Regulating Organization (SRO)
A professional association or body which has responsibilities for overseeing the conduct of its members.

Semi-strong form efficiency
A form of pricing efficiency in which the price of a security fully reflects all public information including but not limited to, historical price and trading patterns.

Settlement risk
This is the risk of the transaction failing at the time of settlement (when documents are exchanged). Settlement is normally carried out via a bank and clearing house mechanism. The main types of settlement risk are: evidence of ownership, cash settling and periodic evaluations of the instruments.

Shares
Companies divide their capital into equal units called shares. Buying the shares brings rights – a share in the business – and risks – the possibility of losing your investment. Shareholders are last in the queue when the assets are shared out if a company goes out of business.

Sharpe ratio
A measure of a portfolio's excess return divided by the total variability of the portfolio.

Sovereign risk
A special kind of risk attached to a security, deposit or a loan because of borrower's country of residence being different from that of the investor. Also referred to as country risk.

Specialist
An exchange member who makes a market in a particular listed security and to whom orders in that security are directed.

Specific risk
Risk attaching to a particular company's security rather than to any relationship with a market movement.

Spin-offs
1. To take a subsidiary and make a separate company, usually a publicly quoted one, out of it. This is a frequent practice in the USA, where the original owner usually retains a stake but sells a majority of the equity to a third party. Management often obtains a small stake in the business. If ownership does not change at all, a spin-off is more correctly called a demerger.
2. Used rather more loosely to indicate a splinter group that leaves one firm and sets up its own business, usually without the original firm having a stake in the new one, and in competition with the first firm. Most often used in professional services, especially in consulting and investment banking.
3. Also describes incidental benefits from a project, development or technology, as in 'the project achieved its goals, but also had unforeseen spin-off benefits'.

Spread
The difference between buy (bid) and sell (offer) prices for a financial security. Spreads can be quite large on shares with low liquidity, such as penny shares or emerging market shares, making it expensive to deal.

Spot market
The here-and-now market for immediate delivery, as opposed to the futures market.

Standard deviation
A statistical measure of the degree to which observations within a group vary. Measured by formula: square root of the mean of the squared deviations of members of a group from their mean. In a group of numbers, it is the square root or the average of the squared deviations of the numbers from their average. To take a simple example, the standard deviation of 1,2,3 is the square root of (1–2) squared, (2–2) squared and (3–2) squared, that is, the square root of (1 x 1) plus (0 x 0) plus (1 x 1) = 1.

Stockpicking
An active portfolio management technique that focuses on advantageous selection of particular

stocks rather than on broad asset allocation choices.

Stocks/Inventory
Raw material, work-in-progress and finished goods, ready for sale. American word for shares.

Strip
1. An interest in all elements of a security's financial structure, hence a strip including some risk equity, some mezzanine, some senior debt and some subordinated debt, or whatever the relevant entities are.
2. Almost the opposite meaning, when a bond is split into its capital element (the zero coupon bond) and an interest-only instrument. The process of detaching the interest coupons from a fixed-rate security so that they may be traded as a set of zero-coupon securities.

Subordinated debt
A low ranking long-term loan; in liquidation, all other creditors take priority over holders of subordinated debt.

Sunk cost
A cost that has already occurred in the past and cannot be recovered. It cannot be changed by the decision to accept or reject the project, hence irrelevant for capital budgeting and other decisions.

Swap
1. To barter.
2. An exchange of debt. Some swaps are highly complex pieces of financial engineering.

Systematic risk
Not to be confused with systemic risk, it is the risk of the stock market as whole, as opposed to the risk of attaching to a particular company ('un-systematic', or 'a specific', or 'diversifiable risk').

Systemic risk
The risk that the failure of any financial institution, especially a large bank, may cause severe strains in the financial system as a whole.

T

Takeover premium
The amount paid for acquiring a company over and above its market capitalization to secure acceptance.

Tender offer
US term where a company offers to buy the shares of another at a fixed price, usually above the previously prevailing price.

Tobin's Q
The ratio of a quoted company's market value to the replacement cost of its assets.

Translation risk
Mainly affects multinational corporations which have trading operations in different jurisdictions, and need to report consolidated earnings in one currency.

Unbundling
1. When a firm (especially a takeover) decides to sell off non-core businesses and focus on just one or two core businesses. Sometimes less politely called asset stripping.
2. Process of segmentation whereby customers are offered the chance to buy individual parts or modules of a product, rather than having to buy everything together.

Unit trusts
See **Mutual funds.**

Value at Risk (VAR)
A single number that identifies a statistically probable minimum return or maximum loss within a given time interval and a stated confidence interval.

Warrants
Issued as an add-on to bonds or ordinary shares, warrants are a type of call option which give the right, without obligation, to buy new shares in a company at a fixed price and on a fixed date.

Weighted average cost of capital
The weighted average of the cost of equity and the cost of debt.

When issued or 'gray market'
Trading in securities which have been announced, but not yet issued. Such securities are said to trade on an 'if, as and when-issued' basis. Also called the gray market in the Euromarkets.

Window dressing
Making use of laxity in accounting rules to make the P&L and balance sheet look better than they really are, without actually breaking the law.

Writedown
Decrease the value of an asset on the balance sheet.

Yield
Yield measures the annual income from an investment against its current market price. Yields fall when prices rise, reflecting the fact that investors have to pay more for the same level of income.

Yield curve
Graph showing the return on fixed-interest securities according to the length of their maturity; normally slopes gently up to reflect a risk premium required on long-term funds. If it slopes down at some point, this indicates the expectation that medium- or short-term interest rates will fall.

Zero-beta CAPM
A model developed by Fischer Black similar to the conventional Capital Asset Pricing Model when there are restrictions on risk-free investments and the market is no longer a common optimal portfolio.

Subject index

Figures and tables are shown in bold

D

K

L

M

V

W

Y

Z

Name index

Organization index

Have you Mastered Finance?

We hope that you have found this book useful. If so, why let your pursuit of management excellence end here?

We have recently developed a series of opportunities for executives to stay in touch with the latest management thinking (see overleaf). These will enable you constantly to upgrade your management skills as part of an international community of those who are **Mastering Management**. Membership of this select community will give you privileged access to a range of learning opportunities, tailored to meet your needs as the world of management evolves.

To find out more about the Masters of Management Club, fill in the application form below and return it to:

Masters of Management Club,
FT Mastering,
28 Long Acre,
London WC2E 9AN.
Fax: +44 (0) 171 240 8018

✂ --

Mr/Mrs/Miss/Ms Initial ______________ Last name ______________

Department ______________

Job title ______________

Company ______________

Address ______________

____

Telephone no. ______________ Fax no. ______________

Areas of special interest: ______________

1. ______________
2. ______________
3. ______________
4. ______________
5. ______________

Preferred newspaper ______________

Preferred business magazine ______________

Any comments on *Mastering Finance* or proposals for future projects:

____

____

Financial Times
Mastering Management Service

Edited by Tim Dickson, George Bickerstaffe and James Pickford

Business School Partners include:

IMD Switzerland • Wharton School at the University of Pennsylvania • London Business School • INSEAD • Chicago Graduate School of Business • Manchester Federal School of Business Management

Improve your strategic management skills

The new *Financial Times* Mastering Management Service introduces the three Rs of management: **The Reader, The Review** and **The Resource**. Ideas you can use, issues that matter, practices that are already working for others.

Every month, **The Reader** and **The Review** combine to bring you the thoughts, opinions and advice of the very best management minds from across the spectrum. Leading business schools, top managers and management experts bring you in-depth insight and information on the issues confronting today's corporate manager.

The Resource gives you unlimited access to a unique on-line information center for managers. Here, you can find further reading, hold discussions in our newsgroups, or browse through our case studies, conference and book summaries.

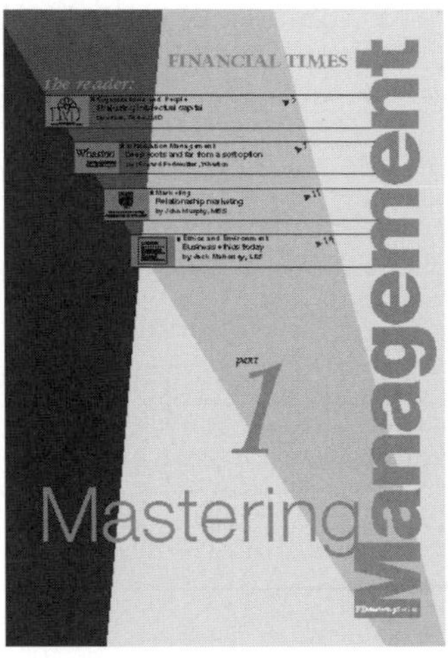

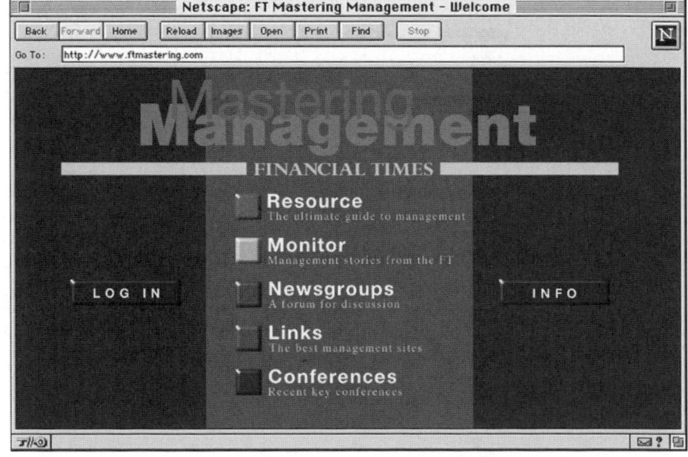

How much?

12 issues each of The Reader and The Review plus unlimited on-line access for one year for £190.00 plus postage and packing: £20 Continental Europe; £48 North America/Africa; £60 Asia Pacific

How to subscribe?

To subscribe and/or request a trial copy call on +44 (0) 1483 733 899 or e-mail subscribe@ftmastering.com

Please quote ref code: 7911MF

Payment can be made by credit card, cheque or proforma invoice.